LYON COLLEGE, 1872–2002

LYON COLLEGE

1872–2002

ARKANSAS MALE AND FEMALE COLLEGE, BATESVILLE.

The Perseverance and Promise of an Arkansas College

BROOKS BLEVINS

The University of Arkansas Press
Fayetteville
2003

Manufactured in Canada

07 06 05 04 03 5 4 3 2 1

Designed by Liz Lester

∞ The paper used in this publication meets the minimum requirements of the American National Standard for Permanence of Paper for Printed Library Materials Z39.48–1984.

LIBRARY OF CONGRESS CATALOGING-IN-PUBLICATION DATA

Blevins, Brooks, 1969–
Lyon College, 1872–2002 : the perseverance and promise of an Arkansas college / Brooks Blevins.
p. cm.
Includes bibliographical references and index.
ISBN 1-55728-742-2 (cloth : alk. paper)
1. Lyon College (Batesville, Ark.)—History. I. Title.

LD3141.L98 B54 2003
378.767'26—dc21 2002153532

FRONTISPIECE: An artist's rendering of the Arkansas College campus, c. 1880s. From Fay Hempstead, A *Pictorial History of Arkansas* (St. Louis: N. D. Thompson, 1890), 908.

For Jane and Betsy

CONTENTS

PREFACE		ix
PROLOGUE	"The destitute and more isolated portions of the Master's vineyard"	xiii

PART I: 1872–1916

CHAPTER 1	Isaac Long on One End of a Log	5
CHAPTER 2	A Reluctant President in an Age of Change	35

PART II: 1917–1937

CHAPTER 3	"Heroic and Pathetic in the Extreme"	77
CHAPTER 4	"Muddling through Somehow"	125

PART III: 1937–1969

CHAPTER 5	Little Haverford or Maryville of the West: The College Seeks a Purpose	155
CHAPTER 6	Bricks and Mortar: Paul McCain Builds a Campus	205

PART IV: 1969–1997

CHAPTER 7	Arkansas College in the Wild West Years	259
CHAPTER 8	Tossing Our Hats over the Wall: The Griffith Years	313
EPILOGUE		353
APPENDIX I	Life after Lyon: Post-Presidential Careers	365
APPENDIX II	Lists of Leaders and Honors	369
APPENDIX III	Brief Historical Sketches of Selected Arkansas Institutions, Past and Present	389
Notes		395
Bibliography		431
Index		437

PREFACE

About thirty miles to the northwest of Batesville, Arkansas, lies the hamlet of Lacrosse. Today there is practically nothing to the place, a handful of houses scattered around an abandoned general store and post office that sits at the southwestern corner of an old crossroads. For a time, however, generations ago, Lacrosse was a bustling little village, a college town. In 1868 Michael Shelby Kennard, a thirty-five-year-old Confederate veteran and graduate of the University of Alabama, left a teaching post in Batesville to move to this farming community in the center of Izard County, where he established the Lacrosse Collegiate Institute. For fifteen years Professor Kennard and occasional assistants drilled students of all ages, from primary school to lower college level, in the finer points of Latin, Greek, mathematics, and modern languages. Lacrosse Collegiate Institute's brief life was extinguished, however, in 1883 when a raging tornado leveled the college's building and most of the town. Kennard's little school, never anything more than a hand-to-mouth operation, did not reopen.[1]

Michael Shelby Kennard's college-building experience was not unique in nineteenth-century America, and neither was his failure. Even in a state as remote and off the beaten path of higher education as Arkansas was, "colleges" such as the one at Lacrosse seemed to rise like dandelions in the springtime, only to wither away after a season or two. In the half century between Reconstruction and World War I, colleges of various degrees of legitimacy sprang up in such unlikely locales as Quitman, Jamestown (Independence County), Searcy, Judsonia, Altus, Eureka Springs, Bentonville, Sheridan, Helena, Princeton (Dallas County), Vilonia, Witcherville, and Subiaco. In the 1890s Kennard even served as president of another of these upstarts, Mountain Home Baptist College. As historian Frederick Rudolph has observed: "College-founding in the nineteenth century was undertaken in the same spirit as canal-building, cotton-ginning, farming, and gold-mining."[2] In other words, for a time, at least, it seemed that any young man with a college diploma and a relative mastery of Latin, Greek, and mathematics could hang out his shingle and found an academy, even a "college." It was within this educational and cultural milieu that Arkansas College made its inauspicious debut in the little White River town of Batesville, perhaps only slightly less unlikely a college town than a Reconstruction-era Quitman or Lacrosse. For at least a generation Arkansas College would remain mostly indistinguishable from what esteemed southern historian C. Vann Woodward has described as the "multitude of superfluous institutions that hung on in a dying condition from the Old Order or sprouted up thickly in the New."[3]

There would have been scant reason in the nineteenth century to predict that Arkansas College would somehow survive, that it would greet the twenty-first century (as Lyon College) while most of its contemporaries would never see the twentieth. There was little about Isaac J. Long, founder of Arkansas College, that differentiated him from his fellow academic entrepreneurs. In fact, few people in Reconstruction

Arkansas could have matched the academic credentials of Kennard, and both of the institutions he shepherded eventually failed. Unlike Lacrosse Collegiate Institute, Arkansas College did have the denominational support, albeit relatively weak support, of the Presbyterians. Nevertheless, church affiliation was no guarantee that an institution would be able to keep its doors open, a fact underscored by the failed colleges at Quitman and Mountain Home.

Like the small independent colleges that did not survive, as well as the many that did, Arkansas/Lyon College has experienced triumphs and faced challenges. The frontier of the old Confederacy was not a particularly hospitable environment for the liberal arts in the 1870s. Even as we begin the twenty-first century, that situation has not changed appreciably. Like many institutions of its kind, Lyon College has throughout its history struggled with the twin challenges of enrollment and finances. Together with the democratic spirit that tended to render obsolete the East's rigid dedication to the liberal arts ideal, the challenges of slim enrollments and institutional poverty—challenges that were seemingly endemic to the educational experience in Arkansas—bred a willingness among the school's leaders to alter the curriculum and mission in pragmatic ways. In other words, the mere fight for survival undermined any strict adherence to the classical course of study almost from the start and engendered a spirit of experimentation that has been an integral part of the college for more than 130 years. In spite of the different missions and approaches in this heritage of experimentation, more often than not the college has fallen short of its recruiting goals, which has in turn placed undue pressure on finances. Nevertheless, as Isaac Long must have known it would when he chose the motto, *Perseverantia Omnia Vincet Deo Volente* (Perseverance conquers all, God willing), the college has survived. God must have been willing.

In many respects, then, the story of Arkansas/Lyon College is the story of the American small college in microcosm, especially the denominational liberal arts school that has long been a fixture in the more isolated sections of the South and Midwest. Like her sister institutions, Lyon College has become increasingly marginalized as American higher education has fallen more firmly into the grip of the public sector and a handful of elite private institutions with international reputations and billion-dollar endowments. The story of Arkansas/Lyon College is also representative of the challenges of educational idealism in the egalitarian heartland and in an impoverished state. Like dozens of other small institutions whose financial frailties have bred pragmatism and compromise, Lyon's history is marked by wide-ranging fits of experimentation that often obscured the thoroughness and excellence found in the classroom.

From the standpoint of the present, historical developments often assume the cloak of inevitability. Whether or not the Lyon College that exists today is the product of some unseen, relentless force of history, and whether or not there is such a thing as inevitability, is the arena of the metaphysician, not the historian. What we can reasonably be sure of is that the modern Lyon College is in essence the sum total of myriad deeds, decisions, and experiences and that these usually involved human interaction. Although there is no simple explanation as to why Batesville's little school survived and thrived while so many others did not, as we shall see there are any number of key moments, of forgotten decisions, of watershed events in which the actions of one or more individuals ultimately made the difference: between extinction and survival, between mediocrity and excellence, between one path and the other. Above all, then, the story of Arkansas/Lyon College is one of persistence—of the human spirit, of the educational ideal, of the communal will to survive, and of the idea of the promise of a better day to come.

Persistence is also a key to writing a book, although it is a persistence that often requires the assistance and leadership of dozens of individuals. This book is a better work due to the help and guidance provided by many people within and outside the Lyon College community. First mention should be given to President Walter B. Roettger, whose vision and foresight brought this project to life, and to Chairman Robert A. Young III and the Lyon College Board of Trustees, whose generous funding allowed me to devote fourteen months almost exclusively to researching and writing the fascinating history of Arkansas's oldest independent college. I thank them also for showing enough faith in me and in the integrity of the historian's process to grant me creative freedom and in turn eschew the filiopietism that too often pervades institutional histories.

I have received invaluable assistance from several archivists, librarians, and other suppliers of information, including Kris Toma at Austin Presbyterian Theological Seminary, Robert E. Glass at Centre College, Jan Blodgett at Davidson College, Catherine Pollari at Hampden-Sydney College, Stacy B. Gould at the College of William and Mary, Edith M. Brawley at Erskine College, Lea Ann Alexander at Henderson State University, Randall Watts at the University of Arkansas at Monticello, Renee LeBeau-Ford and Larry Smith at Arkansas Tech University, Donna McCloy at Southern Arkansas University, Mary Helen Thomas at Hendrix College, Henry Terrill at Harding University, Wendy Richter at Ouachita Baptist University, Kenneth J. Ross at the Presbyterian Historical Society in Philadelphia, and the whole staff at the Presbyterian Historical Society in Montreat, North Carolina, Stuart Stelzer at the University of the Ozarks, Gwen Simmons at the College of the Ozarks, Elaine Berg at Austin Peay State University, and Ethel Simpson at the University of Arkansas Special Collections. Among historians and others to whom I owe a debt of gratitude are Trudy Baker, Lynn Morrow, Ben Johnson III, Light Townsend Cummings, Bill Parrish, Betty Jean Moore, Patrick Williams, and Margie McKenzie.

I deeply appreciate the alumni, trustees, and current and former faculty and staff of Lyon College who shared with me their memories of life at the institution, memories that together spanned more than three-quarters of a century. The names of those with whom I conducted formal interviews appear in the bibliography; there are many more whose casual conversations enhanced my understanding of different eras of the college's past.

My year at Lyon College was made eminently more enjoyable by the entire staff at the Mabee-Simpson Library: Dean Covington, Kathy Whittenton, Camille Beary, Marjorie Seasholtz, and my good friend and former collaborator Gene Hyde. I thank Kathy for her prompt replies to my interlibrary loan requests and Gene for his help in introducing me to the college archives, for tracking down valuable materials, and for the countless other things he did to make the project easier. Others at Lyon College during the 2000–2001 session whose assistance contributed to the project or to my well being were Lucy Yeager and Donald Taylor in the alumni office, Tracy Branson, Terrell Tebbetts, David Stricklin, Lynn Rose, Karen Austin, and my five student research assistants—Kathy Cater, Zeda Paysinger, Kelly Callahan, Greg Manry, and Judy Blackwell.

I owe perhaps my greatest debt of gratitude to a group of people whose previous efforts made my work easier and much more manageable. I am indebted to everyone, past and present, who has written bits and pieces of the story of Arkansas/Lyon College. Isaac J. Long was not only the college's first president; he was also its first historian. His son Eugene Long recorded a good bit of the college's history, as did longtime board chairman James P. Coffin and former president John D. Spragins. I have an especial appreciation for the historical writings of alumnus and one-time faculty member John Quincy Wolf Jr., whose devotion to his alma mater remained unshakable during his three decades on the faculty of Southwestern at Memphis. This book has also benefited from more recent works on the institution's history by Virginia Fitzhugh Jeffery, A. C. McGinnis, George Lankford, Barbara Lindsey-Allen, and Diane Tebbetts. Undoubtedly, the person in this category to whom I owe the greatest thanks is former college archivist Nancy S. Griffith, who in eight and one-half years organized the college's scattered and diverse records and collected a wealth of historical resources without which this history would have been much poorer. It is unfortunate that only a handful of historians ever come to appreciate the unseen labors of such archival efforts.

Finally, I wish to express my gratitude to a trio of women who exercised a tremendous impact on my own days at Lyon College. As always, I thank my wife, Sharon, for her unwavering support and, this time, for helping make my experience as a student enjoyable and memorable. My final acknowledgment goes to my two Lyon College mentors to whom this book is dedicated. I admire Jane Fagg for her perseverance—thirty-four years at Lyon College, the last eleven without the companionship of her beloved Dan—for her dedication to her profession and her students, and for her high expectations inside and outside the classroom. I thank her for her steadfast support over the years and for her guidance in this project. Serendipity, perhaps, introduced me to Betsy Jacoway, and I am thankful for it. While Jane and Dan Fagg had already herded me into the field of history, it was Betsy—serving a one-year sabbatical replacement for the Faggs—who introduced me to southern history, which has been my passion since. No briefer academic acquaintance ever produced such a lasting and mutual admiration. The process of writing this history began years ago in those engaging history courses in the Alphin Building, and no two professors were more influential than Jane Fagg and Betsy Jacoway.

PROLOGUE

"The destitute and more isolated portions of the Master's vineyard"

It was a sultry July afternoon that greeted young Isaac J. Long upon his arrival in the Arkansas capital. Having never ventured west of the Bluegrass, he must have found Little Rock a raw, coarse little town, too small perhaps for a place claiming to govern an entire state, even one as sparsely settled and peripheral as Arkansas. The Civil War had ended scarcely more than a year earlier, and this southwestern town and Confederate border state still bore the physical scars of bombardments and occupations, raids and sieges. As the weary traveler made his way up Markham Street toward the Anthony House he must have been struck by the familiarity of scurrying freedmen and drawling greetings. He must also have sensed beyond doubt that he was in his native South Carolina no longer. In fact it was easterners' unfamiliarity with Arkansas that had brought the young minister to the western edge of the cotton kingdom.[1]

The war had rendered every element of southern society a shambles, organized religion included. Concerned about the "condition of (their) scattered and feebled churches" in Arkansas, leaders of the newly rechristened Presbyterian Church in the United States (colloquially known as the Southern Presbyterian Church) had dispatched Long to observe firsthand the destitution and potential for growth among their small band of churchmen in the west.[2] The Rev. Isaac Long would find a vast field in dire need of cultivation, a place particularly suited to his own personal endeavors. But on this July day in 1866 the stifling humidity turned his thoughts to his young family and his state.

Isaac Jasper Long was born 23 February 1834 in South Carolina—not the South Carolina of James Henry Hammond or William Gilmore Simms but the Carolina of John C. Calhoun and Andrew Jackson, the upcountry whose terrain and society bore little resemblance to the vaunted plantation districts and Charleston society downstate.[3] Like so many southern Presbyterians, Long was descended from the Scotch-Irish settlers who fled Ulster for the freedom and challenges of the American backcountry. Droves of these hearty settlers, the "Irish" as their descendants would often somewhat erroneously refer to them, poured into the Pennsylvania backcountry and from there down the Great Wagon Road hugging the mountains or fanning out into the Piedmont or the trans-Appalachian foothills. Long's father, also named Isaac, had entered the South's most belligerent state not with the Huguenots or Barbadians via the Cooper and Ashley but through the back door across the mountains from eastern Tennessee. Long's maternal grandfather, Luke Hamilton, like thousands of fellow immigrants from Northern Ireland, had plied the length of the southern backcountry, eventually settling in Anderson County, South Carolina. It was here that Long was born and raised. When

Isaac Jasper Long was only ten years old his father received a lethal bite from a spider. Four years later his mother died, leaving him to labor on an older brother's farm until he reached the age of sixteen, at which time he struck out on his own.[4]

Long's journey into the Presbyterian ministry and the antebellum southern academic world was an arduous one. The orphaned teenager enjoyed few of the privileges bestowed upon many of those with whom he would come to study and for whom he would serve as mentor. His personal struggles and physical labors would shape his philosophy of education and suit him to the more practical pursuits and frontier demands of a largely rural, impoverished postwar Arkansas. In 1850 Long departed his brother's farm with only two suits of clothes and a single-barrel shotgun and found work as a laborer on a cotton plantation, earning five dollars a month and board. He managed to save enough money to complete his "English education" and enrolled in Thalian Academy, operated by Presbyterian minister Rev. J. Leland Kennedy, a former Oglethorpe University professor who would become Long's father-in-law in 1859, when Long married Callie Penelope Kennedy.[5] After working his way through Thalian by tutoring younger students, Long received from another minister the financial and moral assistance necessary to attend Centre College, a Presbyterian institution in Danville, Kentucky. Older than his adolescent fellow students, he thrived at Centre and graduated second out of twenty-seven in the class of 1858. In the fall of 1860, after a year at Danville Theological Seminary and another as a teacher in Centre's preparatory department, Long returned to the Palmetto State to study under James Henley Thornwell at Columbia Theological Seminary.[6] The outbreak of war cut short his studies. Isaac Long served out the war years as pastor of Concord Church in Sumter, South Carolina, just east of Columbia. He was still Concord's pastor when commissioned by the General Assembly's Committee on Domestic Missions to journey to Arkansas.

It was thus a brief but active history that the tall, angular, lightly bearded minister carried with him into the Anthony House to rest after a difficult journey. He knew no one in Arkansas; nevertheless, his arrival did not go unnoticed. No sooner had Long begun to recuperate when a servant knocked to inform him of a visitor. Thomas R. Welch, pastor of Little Rock's Presbyterian Church and probably the state's most prominent representative for the denomination, had been informed of the young South Carolinian's impending arrival and was eager to share his knowledge of the state of the church in Arkansas. This would be the first of many conversations between Long and Welch. The two would become intimate friends and would do more for the cause of higher education than any other religious leaders in Reconstruction-era Arkansas. Arkansas College would be in large measure the fruit of their labors.

Thomas Rice Welch, like Long, was a graduate of Centre College. A native of Jessamine County, in the Kentucky Bluegrass and adjacent to Danville's Madison County, Welch also shared Long's Scotch-Irish heritage. His grandfather, John Welch, had arrived in America just in time to join the Revolutionary Army and eventually settled in central Kentucky. The Presbyterian roots on his mother's side were quite strong, his grandfather, Samuel Rice, having served as a ruling elder and a collateral

Isaac Jasper Long, founder of Arkansas College and president of the institution until his death in 1891.

ancestor having founded Union Theological Seminary in Virginia.[7] Thomas R. Welch grew up on his father's farm, attended Bethel Academy in nearby Nicholasville, and received his A.B. from Centre in 1846. A year later Welch forsook the study of law to attend Princeton Theological Seminary for two years. In 1851 he graduated from New Albany Theological Seminary in Indiana and within the week departed for "the destitute and more isolated portions of the Master's vineyard," arriving by boat at Helena, Arkansas, on the tenth of May. At the time he was the only Presbyterian minister with a college degree in the state.[8]

By the time Long and Welch met, the latter had been in Arkansas more than fifteen years and at Little Rock almost seven. The elder minister probably knew more than anyone else about the Presbyterian Church in the state. But Long would soon learn for himself. He spent the next few months traveling from congregation to congregation, preaching, attending presbytery meetings, and generally observing. As his friends back east had anticipated, Long found church rolls depleted by the war and buildings and pastorates suffering from empty coffers. In August he paid his first visit to the tiny church at Batesville. Though fewer than two dozen communicants greeted

Thomas Rice Welch, president of the board of trustees of Arkansas College from 1872 until 1886. Courtesy of Betty Jean Moore, Little Rock, Arkansas.

him there, Long stayed on at the little church at First and Main to assist in a week-long service. So impressed were the small band of Batesville Presbyterians that they soon invited him to pull up roots in South Carolina and return as a stated supply.[9]

From a financial standpoint the offer could not have been appealing. The small congregation could promise not to let Long and his family starve, but it could not hope to match his respectable salary back in Sumter. And Batesville was certainly no metropolis, even by Arkansas standards. The little White River town that Isaac Long visited in 1866 had a population of slightly less than 900 people, about three-quarters of whom were white. Like most western towns, Batesville was home to an assortment of small merchants, physicians, lawyers, skilled artisans, and laborers. What little manufacturing took place was small scale, and the town's economy depended primarily on the seasonal river trade and the retail patronage of local farmers. Surrounding Independence County, which had attracted thousands of late antebellum settlers, contained an additional 13,500 residents, the vast majority of them small farmers, tenants, and their families. Among Arkansas's oldest settlements, Batesville had nonetheless experienced little growth since midcentury so that by the late 1860s almost a dozen other Arkansas towns boasted larger populations. There was still no telegraph office, and it would be two decades before the railroad would arrive. Batesville would greet the twentieth century as one of the last real steamboat towns.[10]

In many respects Batesville was and would remain to be identified by its special geographical location. The earliest settlers, who made their livings from the river trade, had settled this escarpment area because of its location at the edge of the Ozark plateau. The lifeblood of northern Arkansas, the White River originated in the Boston Mountains and zigzagged a crooked course through southern Missouri and northern Arkansas before spilling out of the rugged White River Hills onto the vast and barely undulating Mississippi Alluvial Plain. The rolling waters cast a backward glance at Eagle Mountain before relaxing into the wide, creeping expanse that was the lower White. It was this abrupt change that lent Batesville its dual nature, highlander on the one side and lowlander on the other, the meeting place of the upland and lowland Souths. The country below Batesville stretched into one broad, fertile bottom that, when cleared and drained, invited large-scale plantation agriculture. The valleys above Batesville, when cultivatable at all, were narrow and small, the inland fields rocky and steep. The Ozarks would remain the domain of the small, semi-subsistence farmer and thus a

Main Street in Batesville as it would have appeared around the time of the founding of Arkansas College.

limited market for Batesville; Ozark residents would long occupy a place of mystery, revulsion, or amazement within the collective consciousness of townsfolk. As a result, the dominant commercial and social interests of postwar Batesville would increasingly come to identify with the cotton planter and river towns downstream, and Batesville itself would grow more consciously southern because of it.

A vocal contingent within Batesville's small middle class had for several years also been interested in improving the area's educational opportunities, and the cessation of war allowed for the reappearance of such domestic concerns. Thus it is likely that Isaac Long's erudition and teaching experience invited as much interest among local Presbyterians as did his pulpit prowess. This would also explain the existence of non-Presbyterian names on the petition and pledge presented to the minister to induce his removal to Arkansas. By 1866 Batesville could recount a long, if spotty, record in educational endeavors dating back to the incorporation of Batesville Academy in 1836, the first such school chartered by the new state legislature and an outgrowth of the Presbyterian academy tradition stretching back to seventeenth-century northern Ireland. The school lasted less than a decade, but in 1849 local Methodists established Soulesbury Institute. By the eve of war Batesville was home to two such academies, the Presbyterians having established Batesville Male and Female Academy in 1854. At the time of Long's visit, both schools were defunct and had been replaced by Batesville Male Academy, an independent institution under the guidance of former Whig editor and Baptist layman M. Shelby Kennard. Girls could attend the Batesville Academy for Young Ladies directed by Carra Lyon, wife of prominent Presbyterian and principal of the original Batesville Academy, Aaron W. Lyon.[11]

Whether inspired by educational motives or ministerial needs, the entreaties of the Batesville Presbyterians and their neighbors fell on responsive ears. Isaac J. Long accepted the meager but earnest offer. After settling his affairs in Sumter and saying his farewells to family and brethren, Long arrived in Batesville the following April accompanied by his wife, Callie, a small son and daughter, and an unmarried sister-in-law, Sallie J. Kennedy. He would serve the next four years as stated supply for the Batesville church, which included delivering periodic sermons downriver at Jacksonport, until being installed as pastor in 1871. As expected the new family took an active role in the town's educational enterprises. Sallie Kennedy almost immediately assumed the principalship of the renamed Batesville Female Academy. At his first meeting of the Arkansas Presbytery in May 1867, Long was appointed, along with A. W. Lyon, to the presbytery's executive committee on education. When M. Shelby Kennard left Batesville in early 1868 to establish his academy in neighboring Izard County, Long began tutoring a select group of boys from prominent local families, including the sons of future governors Elisha Baxter and William Miller. Eventually his boys' class was merged with Kennedy's academy to form Batesville Male and Female Academy, and Long took control of its operation. Soon, from his seat as educational as well as moral leader, Isaac Long would, like many another pious and ambitious churchman of the nineteenth century, attempt to turn a tiny, private high school into a tiny, private college and, surprisingly, would succeed.[12]

PART I: 1872–1916

Throughout the nineteenth century the Presbyterians were pioneers in higher education on the American frontier. The descendants of the Ulster Irish—whom one historian has labeled "the best educated peasantry in Europe" in the eighteenth century—were inheritors of a strong tradition of educational attainment, a heritage that included book clubs, reading societies, and the ever-present academy.[1] The American backcountry wilderness of the eighteenth and nineteenth centuries provided every bit the challenge that the Catholic wilderness of Northern Ireland had in the early seventeenth. Alone among the great "people's churches" of the post-Revolutionary era, the Presbyterians maintained their insistence on a college-educated clergy even as they crossed the Appalachians and headed into the vast interior of the Mississippi Valley. Consequently, the American offspring of the Scotch-Irish founded academy after academy and college after college as the waves of the great western migration swept through mountain gaps, down wide valleys, across the undulating expanses of trans-Appalachia, and into the swamps and narrow hollows of the midcontinent's most isolated areas. The Presbyterians founded Lafayette College, Western Reserve University, Hanover, Wabash, Muskingum, Knox, Carroll, Lake Forest, Monmouth, and others in the Ohio Valley and the Old Northwest. In the slave states they established Tusculum, Centre, Maryville, Oglethorpe, Davidson, Austin, Erskine, Westminster, and more. By the outbreak of the Civil War, Presbyterians had founded, or helped to found, more than four dozen colleges and universities, almost one out of four institutions of higher learning in the United States.[2] The war proved but a temporary impediment to college founding, and the process was reinvigorated after 1865, following the westward movement of Americans toward the closing of the frontier.

The little state of Arkansas provided perhaps the ultimate challenge to the Presbyterian tradition of college building. With the exception of Roman Catholic-dominated Louisiana, of the trans-Mississippi states before the Civil War only Arkansas claimed no Presbyterian institution of higher learning. Even California and Oregon boasted Presbyterian colleges by the time of Abraham Lincoln's election in 1860. More than any other state, the characteristics of Arkansas's denominational settlement patterns were largely dictated by the frontier religious and social ferment known as the Great Revival. The Methodists and Baptists emerged from this early nineteenth-century commotion as the dominant southern and western sects, with Alexander Campbell's and Barton Stone's Disciples of Christ running a distant third. It was the adherents of these three groups who reigned on the Arkansas frontier. Presbyterians made up the fourth largest segment in the state's denominational makeup, though perhaps as many as half of all Presbyterians who came to Arkansas were members of the new Cumberland Presbyterian Church, a rural and evangelical wing that had splintered from the old church in opposition to, among other things, the strict education requirements for clergy. Even with such a small constituency—there were fewer than three thousand communicants in Arkansas by the Civil War—the Presbyterians' zeal for education resulted in a failed attempt to found an institution known as Makemie College. Like other western denominational schools, Makemie College, named for Francis Makemie, father of American Presbyterianism, was to be used to supply the state's congregations "with an educated ministry of the Gospel."[3]

By the early 1870s, when Isaac Long and others began discussing the possibility of establishing a college, there were barely three thousand Southern Presbyterian church members in the state. Methodists and Baptists outnumbered Southern Presbyterians eight to one; Disciples of Christ outnumbered them perhaps four to one. Only half a dozen congregations numbered at least one hundred members, and only one of those lay north of the Arkansas River. The Batesville church, one of only a handful of Southern Presbyterian congregations in the Cumberland-settled northern part of the state, had barely received one hundred members *total* in its thirty-year existence.[4] Of all the Arkansas towns and communities with Presbyterian congregations, it would have been difficult to find a more unlikely candidate for a denominational college, had it not been for Isaac Long and the town's tradition of educational endeavors. The unlikely establishment of a Presbyterian college in the most un-Presbyterian section of a decidedly non-Presbyterian state would shape not only

Arkansas College's first four decades, but its entire history as well. The minuscule Presbyterian population in and around Batesville bred a reliance on interdenominational support and genuine nonsectarian education. The same fact also positioned Long's little college to come under attack from the state's Presbyterian leaders who sought to move the school to a more suitable and marketable location. And the relative paucity of Southern Presbyterians in northern Arkansas and in the state in general challenged recruitment and fund-raising efforts from the beginning. But the conquerors of Ulster and of the American frontier were not ones to back down from a challenge, even one partly of their own making.

Chapter 1

Isaac Long on One End of a Log

The evening of Friday, 15 December 1876, was a heady time in Batesville and for friends of higher education in Arkansas. The gathering of parents, trustees, and townspeople in the Presbyterian Church at First and Main would witness the first commencement of Arkansas College and bid farewell to the largest class of college graduates yet produced by an Arkansas institution. The ceremony capped off a three-day affair involving faculty, students, and trustees. On Wednesday and Thursday inside the school's one building, eight prospective graduates had undergone intensive examinations in Latin, Greek, French, geometry, integral calculus, biblical and secular history, physiology, and moral science. The faculty, consisting only of President Long and Professor T. J. Stubbs, administered the examinations orally and received their charges' rote responses in kind. All the trustees but one were on hand to observe, as well as a special examination committee appointed by the presbytery and any other interested persons. The mood was lighter and more celebratory at the Friday commencement exercises. The bulk of the service consisted of orations delivered by the five young men—it being considered improper for ladies to declaim in public—interspersed with music provided by the town band. After the final speech, board president Thomas R. Welch called out the names of the eight graduates, and Long presented each a diploma conferring the degree of A.B. Arkansas College's first graduating class consisted of five Batesville residents, a Virginian, a Tennessean, and a young man from the lower White River town of Des Arc. Among their number were Susie Butler, Mary Maxfield, and Cynthia Scherer, the first three women to receive bachelor of arts degrees in Arkansas.[1]

This little ceremony during the waning days of the Grant administration was a cause for celebration in Batesville and among the small circle of college friends. It had been almost four and a half years since the school's inauspicious beginning. The production of eight graduates heralded a coming of age for Arkansas College, though certainly not a maturation, and lent the institution an air of credibility. Tiny by almost any standard of the day, young Arkansas College stood as a testament to the perseverance of its founders, especially Isaac Long, and to the generosity of a group of concerned townspeople. The school already faced financial problems—indeed, persistent poverty and perpetual indebtedness would plague the college for decades to come—and by late 1876 the excitement and novelty of its founding had begun to wear. When Isaac Long considered Arkansas College's brief past and uncertain future, he must have felt both pride and trepidation.

The birth and childhood of Arkansas College was not unlike the early experiences of scores of other American colleges, especially those of the nineteenth-century South and West. Presidents and board members in small towns and cities throughout the nation at the time would have found much in Long's experience quite familiar. The half century or so ending in 1890 was, after all, the great era of the American college, an epoch that witnessed an almost constant replaying of the drama still unfolding in Batesville in the late autumn of 1876. As historian Frederick Rudolph has observed: "College-founding in the nineteenth century was undertaken in the same spirit as canal-building, cotton-ginning, farming, and gold-mining."[2] Unfortunately for college builders, the products of their labors were often too intangible to attract the investors who sank funds into canals and gins. This was particularly true in impoverished Arkansas. Isaac Long was cognizant of the economic obstacles his college faced when he later remarked: "It would have been . . . a more hopeful undertaking at the time . . . to have started to build a railroad from White River to the Pacific ocean with a pick and shovel and fifty dollars to start on, for there would have been hopes of enlisting the interests of capitalists in such an undertaking as that."[3]

It was in large measure economic shortcomings, combined with the underdeveloped and sparsely settled nature of most parts of the state, that allowed Arkansas College to assume the role of pioneer almost four decades after Arkansas entered the union. By the 1870s Arkansas's experience with higher education was still nothing to brag about. The outbreak of war had found only three small colleges in the state—Arkansas College, a Disciples of Christ institution in Fayetteville; Cane Hill College, a Cumberland Presbyterian school not far from Fayetteville; and St. John's College, founded by Masons in Little Rock. Fayetteville's Arkansas College did not survive the war, and the latter two, though functioning at the time of the emergence of Arkansas College in Batesville, would not live to see the twentieth century. Like most western and southern colleges, all three remained small and underfunded. Severe poverty, war-induced disillusionment, and political instability delayed the establishment of any new institutions of higher learning for half a dozen years after Appomattox. In 1871 the Reconstruction Republican legislature enacted legislation that paved the way for the chartering of new colleges. The first to emerge under the new law was the Arkansas Industrial University (now the University of Arkansas.)[4]

In 1862 Congress, devoid of southern members, passed the Morrill Act, which provided federal funds for the support of state mechanical and agricultural colleges or universities. Nine years later the Arkansas state assembly invited bids from interested counties and municipalities for the purpose of choosing the state land grant university's location. Several localities around the state submitted bids backed by bond issues, tax dollars, and citizen donations of money and land. The two most competitive bids came from two extremes of the Arkansas Ozarks, Batesville and Fayetteville, and warranted personal visits to each area by the committee responsible for choosing the location. The citizens of Batesville voted unanimously in July 1871 to subscribe $50,000; in addition prominent citizens promised $19,000 in subscriptions of land and money. Independence Countians outside Batesville were less enthusiastic, however, and voted down a $100,000 countywide subscription 428 to 162. In the end a concerted effort on the part of Fayetteville and Washington County produced promises of about twice as much money, and Batesville lost her bid for the university. The committee voted in October 1871 to locate Arkansas Industrial University (AIU) in the most inaccessible corner of the state.[5]

Because of the timing of the university's establishment and because of Batesville's role in the process, it has long been assumed that Arkansas College originated as an outgrowth of north central Arkansas's failure to secure the university for herself. In fact, as we shall see, the circumstances that inspired Arkansas College's founders were more complex, involving religion and ego as well as provincial competition and a desire to bring culture and learning to the far reaches of southern society.

As Isaac Long would himself recall years later, it was an event completely unrelated to Arkansas's university that actually sparked the earliest conversation about a Presbyterian college in the state. The idea of Arkansas College may, in fact, have emanated from a case of hurt feelings. At the same time that Batesville and Fayetteville were dueling for AIU, Southern Presbyterians west of the Appalachians were making plans for a new university. (The Presbyterian penchant for college founding had survived the Civil War.)[6] Presbyterian leaders in central Tennessee invited representatives from western Tennessee, Alabama, Mississippi, Texas, and Louisiana to discuss the founding of Southwestern Presbyterian University on the site of Stewart College in Clarksville, Tennessee. Perhaps by accident, perhaps not, no one from Arkansas was invited to participate, although it was assumed that the Synod of Arkansas would eventually contribute financially to the institution. Long and a few other Presbyterian ministers in the state "impudently made a little fuss" to remind the Tennesseans of Arkansas's existence. More importantly the slight led to "some conference and correspondence" between and among Long, Welch, and two other Presbyterian ministers with eastern backgrounds: Samuel W. Davies, a graduate of Hampden-Sydney College and Danville Theological Seminary who had been at Cotton Plant since 1861, and David C. Boggs, a South Carolinian who had arrived in Jacksonport in 1868.[7] It appears that the rallying of the forgotten Presbyterian ministers coincided with the failure of Batesville's leading citizens to secure the university. The result was six months of frenzied activity that would transform a high school into a college almost overnight and that would bring Batesville an institution of higher learning at a price substantially lower than the $69,000 put up for the university.

In early 1872, shortly after Arkansas Industrial University opened its doors to 101 students (none of whom were enrolled in college courses), Isaac Long informed a group of Batesville citizens gathered at the courthouse that a movement was under way within the Arkansas Presbytery to establish a college somewhere within its bounds.[8] These citizens, many of whom had promised funds and land for the university, agreed to raise half the money necessary for erecting a college building on two conditions: that the college, though denominational in control, remain nonsectarian, and that the college be permanently located in Batesville. At the April presbytery meeting in Searcy, Long, on behalf of the Batesville church, offered the presbytery control of the Batesville Male and Female Academy for the purpose of rapidly developing it into a "literary institution of high order." The presbytery accepted and proceeded to appoint a provisional board for the "Presbyterial High School"; the board was to collect financial contributions, oversee the erection of needed buildings, procure faculty, and take care of any other business until the presbytery's fall meeting. Ministers Long and Boggs were joined on this board by seven prominent Presbyterian laymen from Batesville, Jacksonport, and Powhatan.[9]

The most pressing needs for the new college, or Presbyterial High School, were a faculty and facilities. The board of trustees of the old Batesville Male and Female Academy had recently been deeded a full city block on the eastern edge of town, one block from the old academy site, on which Isaac Long had hastily erected a twenty-feet-by-forty-feet frame building in late 1871.[10] This, of course, was grossly insufficient, even for a respectable academy. Consequently, the provisional board agreed to the construction of a two-story brick building, seventy by twenty-four feet, and promptly secured the services of Batesville resident William J. Joblin as architect and contractor at a cost of $6,000. It was also resolved that half of that amount would be raised in Batesville, $1,000 in Jacksonport, and the remaining one-third in other parts of the presbytery. The building committee, chaired by Long with the assistance of three prominent members of the Batesville Presbyterian Church, worked quickly "in the face of difficulties" and watched construction begin during the summer. In the meantime, the board sent out letters to the churches in the presbytery asking for individual and congregational subscriptions to match the needed funds. As opening day neared it was becoming obvious that Batesville would surpass its goal of $3,000 but the rest of the presbytery would fall far short, a pattern that would be repeated from time to time in the college's financial travails.

To make matters worse, only a few weeks before classes were to begin Long received word that the husband and wife he had hired as faculty had suddenly decided to stay in Iowa. E. C. Ebersole, a graduate of Amherst College in Massachusetts, was to assist Long with preparatory and college-level instruction, while his wife was to take charge of the primary department. Fortunately, Long found suitable last-minute replacements for the respective positions: Thomas Jefferson Stubbs, a young Virginian who had been teaching in Woodruff County, and Fannie Davis, a Batesville resident who had attended a female college in Alabama.[11]

The frenetic pace of the summer continued into the fall and beyond the school's opening day in September. At the October meeting of the presbytery in Dardanelle, final steps were taken to turn Presbyterial High School into a full-fledged college. The presbytery approved the name Arkansas College, which in a moment of creative inspiration had been suggested by provisional board member John F. Allen. In lieu of the difficulties experienced in raising funds outside of Batesville, the delegates at Dardanelle voted to tack $500 onto Batesville's subscription goal, thereby reducing the amount to be collected elsewhere in the presbytery to $2,500. The presbytery also appointed Long, Welch, and Vincent H. Henderson of Cotton Plant to apply to the state legislature for a charter. A few weeks later the legislature passed a succinct and "very liberal" charter, which was signed by acting governor O. A. Hadley on 24 October 1872. Arkansas College was now a legal entity, though, as we shall see, perhaps not yet an actual college.[12]

The charter of Arkansas College established the institution's first permanent board of trustees, whose members had been selected by the presbytery at Dardanelle. With the exception of Rev. Thomas R. Welch of Little Rock, the board consisted entirely of representatives of Batesville and the lower White River valley. Interestingly, the board contained three times as many laymen as ministers, unusual for a denominational college at the time. Though it appears that all the trustees were Presbyterian, this would change in a couple of years. By and large the dozen men on the original board represented the moral, educational, and in some cases commercial, leadership of their respective communities. As might be expected in this time of challenging travel and slow communication, the six Batesville trustees, along with Welch, became the dominant and most active wing of the board. Of the four Jacksonport representatives, only one, Col. William K. Patterson, ever attended a single meeting. Rev. David C. Boggs, who had participated in the ministerial brainstorming that hatched the idea of a college, soon moved across state to Bentonville and out of Arkansas College's restricted orbit. William W. Kerr had served the provisional board as treasurer but soon bowed off the permanent board. Dr. William J. Burt, a Jacksonport physician and another holdover from the provisional board, also declined to take an active part in the new college's life. Colonel Patterson, whose son would graduate with Arkansas College's inaugural class, soon returned to his native Tennessee. The lone representative of Cotton Plant, Vincent H. Henderson enrolled his son in the Presbyterial High School in 1872 but never attended a meeting of the board.[13]

With the exception of Isaac Long, the Batesville board members were all Presbyterian laymen, representing varying degrees of local educational and financial prominence. A relatively diverse lot, they included merchants, a physician, and a farmer, college graduates and the barely formally educated, southerners, a northerner, and a border state native. The eldest of the group and perhaps the most biographically remarkable was A. W. Lyon. Aaron Woodruff Lyon, seventy-five years old in October 1872, was a native of New Jersey and veteran of the War of 1812. Lyon was almost twenty-seven when he received his A.B. from Eliphalet Nott's Union College in Schenectady, New York; he later spent three years studying in the Princeton Theological Seminary before making his way to territorial Arkansas where he established an academy at the former Dwight Mission in 1829. By 1872 Lyon had been a Batesville resident for almost forty years. He had served as first principal of the original Batesville Academy and had been a founding member of the Presbyterian Church. Finding little prospect and remuneration in the teaching profession, Lyon had entered the mercantile and drug business during the antebellum era. Batesville's oldest and truest friend of education, he was elected vice-president of the board, a position that he would hold until his departure for California more than ten years later.[14]

Lyon had immediate connections to two other board trustees, Eugene R. Goodwin and Dr. John F. Allen. Goodwin, only twenty-six at the time of his appointment to the board and subsequent election as secretary and assistant treasurer, was a Mississippi-born, Memphis-raised druggist who had moved with his merchant father and siblings to Batesville on the eve of the Civil War. A Confederate veteran, Goodwin had boarded with the Lyon family before marrying a fellow boarder and eventually entering into a partnership with A. W. Lyon. Though Goodwin's service to the board would last only two years, his relationship with the college would continue into the twentieth century as three of his four daughters would receive Arkansas College diplomas.[15]

Lyon's connection with trustee John F. Allen was both commercial and familial. John Farrell Allen was a native of southeastern Missouri. Descended maternally from a prominent French Canadian family, Allen was raised a Roman Catholic and received his A.B. from St. Mary's of the Barrens Seminary, a small Catholic college in Perry County, Missouri. In 1847 he received a degree in medicine from the University of Pennsylvania and soon thereafter settled in Batesville to begin his practice. After marrying the niece of A. W. Lyon's first wife, Allen entered into a drugstore partnership with Lyon. By 1872 the forty-eight-year-old Allen was one of Independence County's wealthiest citizens, with extensive real estate holdings and several tenant farms. Dr. Allen had also joined the Presbyterian Church and in 1867 had been elected a ruling elder. His fellow board members trusted his business acumen and honesty enough to elect him treasurer, a post he would hold until his death almost thirty years later.[16]

Like Goodwin, the final two members of the Batesville group were not college educated. Like Allen, they would both give many years of service to the board and the college. Marion Adolphus "Dolph" Wycough was the only Batesville native on the board, having been born in the territory of Arkansas in 1835 to North Carolinian parents. Wycough followed his father into the carpentry trade before serving alongside Goodwin in the Confederate 28th Arkansas Infantry. Since the war he had been engaged in the mercantile business. Despite his lack of education, Wycough was recognized as one of Independence County's "most scholarly men" and enrolled his son Ralph during the college's initial year. In 1874 he would succeed Goodwin as secretary of the board and hold that post until his departure from the board in 1893. The lone farmer of the original twelve trustees, William Lewis McGuire was born near St. Louis, Missouri, also to parents from North Carolina, but grew up in Independence County. His parents, Elam and Catherine, had been charter members of the Presbyterian Church in Batesville. Will's father's death and the war cut short his formal education back in St. Louis, and after service for the Confederacy he returned to the family farm northeast of town. Only thirty-two in the fall of 1872, McGuire would remain a lifelong bachelor and a faithful member of the board for almost two decades.[17]

Only forty-one students arrived for classes on Monday, 2 September 1872; eight more enrolled before the end of the second week.[18] Of the forty-nine students who entered week three, thirty-seven hailed from Batesville, eight from Cotton Plant, and one each from Des Arc and Jacksonport. Two students came from other states, including Isaac Long's brother-in-law from South Carolina, D. H. Kennedy. As was common among small western colleges at the time, Arkansas College also contained primary, intermediate, and preparatory departments. Surviving records suggest that the Presbyterial High School, as it was still known in September 1872, may not have offered any college-level education for at least a year after its founding. Of the first forty-nine students, thirty were classified "academic" (roughly equivalent to what would later be referred to as preparatory) and the remaining nineteen fell into either the primary or intermediate category.[19]

Tuition costs during Arkansas College's inaugural year amounted to five dollars per month for "academic" students, four for intermediate, and three dollars for primary students. As was the practice of most denominational colleges, children of Presbyterian ministers could attend school tuition-free. Young men who planned to enter the ministry of any evangelical, Protestant denomination were admitted at one-half tuition, provided they could produce a letter of recommendation from a pastor or some other church authority. Each student was expected to pay a twenty-cent incidental fee in advance, a fee that was gradually increased to fifty cents per quarter. The college year was divided into two five-month sessions, the first ending in late January and the second in June. One-half of a session's tuition, or $12.50, was due by the end of the first month of classes, and the remainder was to be paid before the end of the session. Books and supplies, purchased through local merchants, cost five to ten dollars a session. Students from outside Batesville boarded with the Longs or another local family for fifteen dollars per month. Arkansas College's various fees and costs would change remarkably little throughout the remainder of the century.[20]

Although not costly by eastern standards, board, tuition, and fees could add up over the course of a year; consequently, most of the out-of-town students came from financially comfortable, Presbyterian homes or received support from wealthy, interested patrons. Although Long, reflecting on his hardscrabble rise to genteel respectability, vowed not to turn away any boy or girl on account of the inability to pay, the poor student would have been in the minority at Arkansas College and other colleges in the 1870s. Isaac Long's account book provides an intimate view of the expenses for education in the school's first year. By the end of December 1872, trustee V. H. Henderson already owed more than one hundred dollars for the education of his son Robert. In addition to tuition and boarding charges, Henderson purchased books of Latin and Greek and other works totaling about eight dollars. Laundry costs were a dollar and a half a month, and purchases of socks, a coat, stamps, pencils, and quinine pills required another seven dollars. One full term for Robert Henderson at Arkansas College finally cost his father almost two hundred dollars, an expense far beyond the reach of the great majority of Arkansans of the late nineteenth century.[21]

The campus and grounds that greeted students that fall were nothing to write home about, at least not in any positive manner. The little twenty-by-forty frame building stood in the northeastern corner of the barren lot. This building would serve as classroom for the primary and intermediate departments. A few yards to the west, construction had just begun on the two-story brick building, which would not be completed until the waning days of the academic session in June 1873. In the meantime, President Long and Professor Stubbs moved here and yon around town in Socratic fashion looking for empty rooms in town sufficient for a couple of dozen students. Long's ancient languages and moral science classes were especially nomadic, bivouacking in about a dozen different places at one time or another, including the old Soulesbury Institute building and the kitchen of a friendly neighbor.[22]

As if his trials were insufficient, Long, as chairman of the building committee, also oversaw construction of the college building and had the even more difficult chore of ensuring the steady collection of pledges made by townspeople and others in the presbytery. Not surprisingly, the subscription drive in Batesville proved a success. More than fifty citizens pledged a total of almost $4,000, of which over $3,200 was eventually collected. Trustee Dr. John F. Allen contributed $500, easily the largest sum, and seven other Batesville residents pledged at least $200 each. Reflecting the nonsectarian purposes of the institution, several of the contributors were not Presbyterian, including Jewish merchant Simon Adler. For years Isaac Long delighted in recalling the fact that the very first man to donate money for the college building was a Baptist, William W. McDearmon. Outside of Batesville, however, the fund drive had far different and potentially disastrous results. Only four individuals and five churches pledged money to meet the $6,000 building cost. Slightly more than $900 in subscriptions came in from these sources, over half of which was contributed by trustees Welch and Patterson. As a result of the poor return outside of Batesville the trustees were forced to borrow money to pay the contractor in the spring of 1873.[23]

Long and his fellow teachers relied almost exclusively on tuition revenues for the pittances that qualified as salaries. Although advertisements and publications listed a faculty of four for the new institution, in reality only two teachers, Long and Stubbs, handled all instruction above the intermediate level. Fannie Davis taught primary and intermediate students, and Mollie McKee served as music teacher for the female students. Long, in a time when most college administrators still frequented the classroom, taught Latin, Greek, moral science (Christian ethics), and the Bible. (Moral science was generally reserved for upper-level college students and thus was probably not a key feature of Arkansas College's first-year curriculum.) Long's partner in what would soon become the college curriculum was Thomas Jefferson Stubbs, whose breadth and range of teaching duties would intimidate the most erudite scholar of modern academe. His official title at the genesis of Arkansas College was associate principal and teacher of mathematics, higher English, sciences, German, and French. Within a few years Stubbs would simply be listed as professor of mathematics, sciences, and modern languages.[24]

For more than a decade Long and Stubbs would constitute the only full-time faculty members at the college and preparatory level. Stubbs was thirty years old when school commenced in September 1872. Born into an old Tidewater family in Gloucester County, Virginia, he had crossed the York River to attend the College of

Thomas Jefferson Stubbs, an original member of the Arkansas College faculty, left in 1888 to join the faculty of his alma mater, the College of William and Mary. Photograph P1980.75, University Archives, Earl Gregg Swem Library, College of William and Mary, Williamsburg, Virginia.

William and Mary, graduating in 1860. He joined a Confederate artillery unit shortly after Virginia's secession and served in the army until his capture at Petersburg a week before Lee's surrender. After the war Stubbs attended graduate school at his namesake's University of Virginia for a year before moving to Woodruff County, Arkansas. He returned to Williamsburg and received his A.M. (master of arts) in 1869 before coming back to Woodruff County. He was teaching in the little White River town of Augusta when Long invited him to join the staff of the Presbyterial High School.[25] When the young boys heard that their distinguished instructor had ably served the Lost Cause, they attempted to soften his resolve and endear themselves by addressing the former Private Stubbs as "Captain." Nevertheless, the Virginian declined the promotion and failed to give ground, so the students soon returned to calling him professor. Undoubtedly, this Tidewater Confederate would affect the atmosphere of the college over the next decade and a half in a much different, a more southern, way than would have the New Englander Ebersole, who had backed out of coming to Arkansas at the last moment.

From the outside the little college that emerged in Batesville looked like any other of the dozens of struggling southern log colleges that had preceded it. Typical of these trans-Appalachian institutions, labeled "hilltop" colleges by historians John S. Brubacher and Willis Rudy, Arkansas College's faculty was made up of clergymen—Stubbs was a licensed minister—and funded by tuition payments and modest donations. The typical two-story brick building was taking shape, and the rigid, classical curriculum was in place. But in some important ways Arkansas College was atypical. One departure from tradition was a sincere and open nonsectarianism, a not uncommon trait among rural, western colleges that we have seen evidenced in the taking of Jewish and Baptist dollars, though, obviously, financial donations have a way of battering down the doors of dogmatism. The nonsectarian pledge taken by Arkansas College's Presbyterian founders was the result of matters both practical and theoretical, and the college's ability to follow the mandates of nonsectarianism reflected small-town dynamics and the uncrowded field of Arkansas higher education. In theory most Presbyterian institutions of the nineteenth century were nonsectarian in character, due in part to the influence of Scottish Common Sense philosophy on Presbyterian thought and the effects of the Revolution and the Second Great Awakening on the spirit of evangelical commonality. Nevertheless, some Presbyterian colleges of the day maintained limits on the number of non-Presbyterian students enrolled, and Presbyterian church membership was generally a requirement for faculty or board membership. At Arkansas College this was never the case. The most obvious explanation concerns the Batesville citizenry and the strength, or lack thereof, of Presbyterianism in Arkansas. We have already seen that many, perhaps a majority, of Arkansas College's earliest financial contributors and supporters were not Presbyterians. Furthermore, the size of the Presbyterian community in northern and central Arkansas (barely more than one thousand communicants) was not sufficient to support a college on its own. In fact, Batesville's congregation consisted of only about thirty members at the time.[26]

One other explanation for Arkansas College's nonsectarianism is that the small college was not founded in a spirit of pious defensiveness. According to historian Frederick Rudolph, almost all western colleges were formed in some degree out of the fear of an illiterate, barbarian society, and the sentiments of the educated fathers of Arkansas College tended to reflect such thoughts. But the founders of the college were not reacting to actual or perceived secularism in the state's higher education system, primarily because there barely was a higher education system in Arkansas in 1872. Whereas colleges such as Centre, Davidson, and Central of Kentucky, among others, had emerged in part as pious, conservative reactions to the decline of orthodoxy or Christian control in older denominational or state colleges, Arkansas College was not born in the spirit of denominational fear. Arkansas College had a different raison d'être. The college's only real competitor in 1872 lay 175 miles to the west across the treacherous Ozark highlands, and, besides, the president of Arkansas Industrial University, Gen. Daniel H. Hill, was a staunch Presbyterian and former Davidson faculty member. Within the first decade of its existence board members representing three different, non-Presbyterian denominations and faculty members belonging to Methodist and Episcopal churches would serve Arkansas College.[27]

But nonsectarianism at Arkansas College in no way denoted a lessening of Christian enthusiasm. As at most small denominational colleges in the South, the liberal arts at Arkansas College meant "liberal Christian education." According to one historian of southern higher education: "Truth was ultimately defined by the scriptures and it was generally accepted by advocates of Christian education that religious truth was ultimate truth." One obvious and conscious goal of Arkansas College's founders was to provide a forum for the education of future ministers for Arkansas and the Southwest. In fact, one would have been hard pressed to find an American college more consciously pious. One writer in a Batesville newspaper noted in 1890 that the Bible's "doctrine, its morality, and its authority are inculcated daily." This was nowhere more evident than in Arkansas College's proudest curricular innovation, the Bible history course. By the mid-nineteenth century the rise of separate theological seminaries had largely effected the formal removal of Bible study from the curriculum at most denominational colleges. An element within the Southern Presbyterian Church had come to deplore this development by the postbellum era. Among this element was Isaac Long, who lamented that during his student days at Centre the Bible had "never in any way . . . constituted the theme of attention in the class room, on a level with Homer, Tacitus, or Trigonometry." According to Long, Welch, and their cohorts, the Presbyterian colleges, although enlightening minds, were endangering the souls of students by leaving spiritual training to ministers and Sunday School teachers. "The devil has but little to fear from an occasional sermon or a smattering of the catechism, hastily imparted on the Sabbath, while all scriptural knowledge is practically ignored and carefully excluded in the great work of daily education."[28]

Shortly before Arkansas College's establishment, Rev. J. B. Shearer had begun teaching a Bible course at Stewart College in Tennessee, precursor to Southwestern Presbyterian University. Isaac Long, who enjoyed almost complete autonomy in establishing the original curriculum, decided to go a step further and make the study of the "English Bible" (and not only the Greek New Testament or Hebrew passages) a mandatory and foundational component of Arkansas College's preparatory and college course. Students were required to take courses in Bible study (in effect, biblical history) every year from the primary grades through college graduation. Furthermore, ecclesiastical, or church, history was required for all degree-seeking students. For many years Long, who published a text on the subject, boasted that Arkansas College was the only college in the land with such a requirement.[29]

With such a morally conservative distinction, it is perhaps surprising that Arkansas College was also a pioneer in higher coeducation in the state and region.

From the very first day of classes at the college, females were admitted on an equal basis with males and were expected to complete the same prescribed course of study. Although a handful of colleges, beginning with Oberlin in 1837, had sought to equalize men's and women's curricula in the preceding decades, Arkansas College's decision to institute a truly coeducational system was nonetheless significant, especially for the South. Admittedly, Long and the trustees approached the experiment with some hesitation, coeducation being undertaken, it seems, with less gusto than either nonsectarianism or biblical instruction. Ultimately, the decision was probably a practical one. Half of the Batesville Male and Female Academy's spring 1872 enrollment had been female, and the enrollment prospects for a male college with no military component in a small town in rural Arkansas were bleak. As it turned out more than half the student body at Arkansas College for the 1872–73 term was female.[30]

Many coeducational colleges provided special 'ladies' classes in nontraditional areas considered feminine: music, art, belles lettres. Long criticized this practice as "an insult to the sex, as though it were useless to expect a girl to study such subjects as require any close thought, or protracted attention, but something comparatively easy must be selected." Arkansas College did, however, make two minor concessions to its female students. The board of trustees agreed to allow students to substitute two years of French for senior mathematics (analytical geometry and calculus.) This option was open to both sexes but was consciously directed toward young ladies and most often exercised by them. Furthermore, the board from the beginning made arrangements for instruction in music, both vocal and instrumental, though it would not become an official department of the college until the twentieth century. Within a few years Long and the trustees could declare their experiment a success and assure prospective students and their parents that "it has been found to be a mutual restraint and stimulus to *both* [sexes] to recite in the same classes."[31]

And what the boys and girls were reciting in the early days of Arkansas College were in most cases the subjects their teachers had recited a generation earlier, the classical and mathematical curriculum. This curriculum traced its roots back to the seven liberal arts, the trivium and quadrivium, of the Middle Ages, but had undergone subtle transformation at the hands of Renaissance, Calvinist, and Enlightenment scholars in the ensuing centuries. Long, Welch, and Stubbs were inheritors of the classical notion that knowledge was a fixed body of truth; the role of higher education was to inculcate through rote memorization and strict discipline this body of truth. Their methods of inculcation relied on the old faculty psychology, the idea that the mind is comprised of faculties such as memory, reason, judgment, and imagination that require disciplined exercise. Long summed up the basic ideas of this educational approach at his inauguration. "Education means the leading out, strengthening, expand(ing) and developing the physical, intellectual and moral powers or faculties bestowed upon us by the Creator. There can be no true Education which does not have for its objects all of these ends united in due proportion." According to classicists, the best apparatus for mental exercise were Latin and Greek classics and mathematics. By the mid-nineteenth century this formula had been supplemented with elementary instruction in natural sciences, ethics, and, at Arkansas College anyway, studies of the English Bible.[32]

Although Arkansas College emerged at a time when the classical curriculum was coming under increasingly harsh attacks at the hands of such administrators as Charles W. Eliot at Harvard and Andrew White at Cornell, classical graduates of previous generations would not have felt out of place in Batesville's little college. Students matriculating at Arkansas College in the 1870s, and for many years thereafter, were expected to have begun the study of Latin and Greek and could expect three years of intensive reading and memorization of the classics. According to the earliest record of the college's curriculum, Latin was the clear focus, with readings of Sallust, Virgil, Tacitus, Eusebius, Horace, Juvenal, and Cicero, traditional hero of the humanists. Readings in Greek were limited to Xenophon's *Anabasis* and three years of the New Testament. Students who opted for the mathematical tract over all three years scaled the ladder from algebra and geometry through plane and spherical trigonometry to a senior year of analytical geometry and differential and integral calculus. Natural philosophy, or science, included chemistry, mineralogy, geology, and physiology. In addition studies in history, geography, English grammar, rhetoric, logic, and political economy appeared along with three years of biblical history. Typical of most colleges of the day, the course in moral science (basically Christian ethics taught by Long) capped off each senior's college education. Each student completed every part of the prescribed course of study—except in the aforementioned cases of substituting French for higher mathematics; the elective lay far in Arkansas College's future.[33]

The curriculum, though in most ways quite indistinguishable from myriad others at small colleges across the South and West, bore the unmistakable stamp of Isaac Long. Given almost free rein to design his college's course of study, he selected what he felt to be the most valuable components of his Centre curriculum (his limited faculty preventing him from following it thoroughly) but tempered the curriculum by elevating the study of biblical and ecclesiastical history to a position on par with the classics and mathematics. Long also reduced the college course from four years to three, again probably due to faculty and financial constraints. Long was also perhaps more understanding of the poor, working student than many other college presidents. Consequently, he discarded the old rigid class system in which each student was expected to complete each subject with his classmates within a given year. Instead, Arkansas College awarded degrees based on "the satisfactory completion of a prescribed course of study," regardless of the brevity or longevity of one's time on campus.[34]

For almost two decades Isaac Long and Arkansas College would be synonymous. Long possessed the stern but compassionate countenance that was the hallmark of the nineteenth-century minister-scholar-president. His long white beard and prematurely gray hair lent him the physical requisites for patriarchy and college founderhood. But Long enjoyed little time for reflection. By his own account, he served Arkansas College in those earliest years as president, "ex-officio professor of whatever no one else wanted, . . . Chairman of the Building Committee, General Manager,

Solicitor, Collector and disburser of funds, Organizer, etc., etc., on a prospective salary of $300 per annum." As might be expected from such a load, "sixteen to eighteen out of every twenty-four hours were filled to overflowing seven days of each week, for months in succession." In addition to his college duties, Long also maintained his busy pastorate for several years after 1872. Although this proved burdensome, his pastoral salary permitted him to turn most of his would-be presidential salary back into the college's operational fund.[35]

Long's tenure of more than nineteen years as president still ranks as the longest consecutive term of presidential service in the college's history. Despite the staid, traditional nature of the original curriculum and the perpetual poverty of tiny Arkansas College, the 1870s and 1880s were not decades of stagnation for the young institution. On the contrary, the first two decades of Arkansas College's existence marked a relatively dynamic period of maturation in which many of the forces and elements affecting American higher education in general came also to bear on life and learning in Batesville. Long's years as president were marked by modest expansions of physical facilities and faculty and staff and more notable expansion in enrollment. The curriculum underwent subtle changes, and extracurricular activities slowly emerged to enhance the college experience. The social milieu of the post–Civil War South also permeated student life. But perhaps the most conspicuous and persistent theme in Arkansas College's development reflected a continuation, the continuous and fruitless search for elusive dollars.

By any standard Arkansas College was a poor college. It operated without an endowment throughout the nineteenth century. This perennial poverty helped account for the relatively stagnant curriculum and engendered a Spartan lifestyle among faculty and students. Even when compared to the typical western college, Arkansas College received a weak financial sendoff. The process of college founding took place so rapidly in a depressed era and state and Batesville was such an out-of-the-way place, that insufficient funds plagued the school immediately. The first problem faced by the trustees was paying for the original building. Not surprisingly, many of the pledges never materialized, forcing the board to borrow money to pay the contractor in the spring of 1873. By the time the trustees reassembled, more than a year and a half later, the young college's debt had surpassed $2,000. The board placed the burden of collecting unpaid subscriptions and raising additional funds on the backs of Long and treasurer Allen and requested that the presbytery collect one dollar per member from each Presbyterian church. Less than $170 flowed into the board's coffers through the latter method; nevertheless, by the spring of 1878 the college was free from debt, due in no small measure to the personal generosity of John F. Allen.[36]

The building fund deficit probably played a key role in the Arkansas Presbytery's decision to approach Arkansas's other presbytery, Ouachita, concerning control of Arkansas College. As early as 1874, Arkansas Presbytery officials had broached the topic, but it was not until 1877 that Ouachita Presbytery officially agreed to support the college and take part in its administration. Ouachita's sponsorship worked better on paper than in reality. The most tangible result was the addition of three southern

Arkansas representatives to the board: Henry Merrill of Camden, Rev. F. M. Howell of Arkadelphia, and W. S. McCain of Drew County. From a financial standpoint, the change made little difference; Arkansas College never received more than $800 from the churches in any given year during the 1880s, and most of this continued to come from churches in the Arkansas Presbytery. The one positive result for the college was the relationship with Merrill, a native New Yorker and longtime southern Arkansas entrepreneur and industrialist who in 1878 donated a couple hundred volumes to the library and established a scholarship fund that would generate $50 per year. Nevertheless, Ouachita trustees rarely attended meetings in distant Batesville, and most ultimately resigned their positions before their terms were completed.[37]

In 1883 the Arkansas Synod split the two presbyteries in half to form two new ones, Washburn in the northwest and Pine Bluff in the southeast. Four years later, at the request of the synod, the Arkansas College Board of Trustees agreed to reduce its number to a dozen and reapportion the seats. The Arkansas Presbytery maintained majority control with seven positions, Pine Bluff and Ouachita received two each, and Washburn one seat. In 1889 the board agreed to have the college placed under synod control. The synod reduced the number of trustees to nine, six from Arkansas Presbytery (all Batesville residents) and one each from the other three presbyteries.[38]

The Isaac Long administration also witnessed a succession of well-meaning but ultimately unsuccessful fund-raising drives. As early as November 1875, in the midst of the first financial crisis, the board had called on Long to lead a campaign to raise an endowment of $12,000; the endowment would be used to fund Long's and Stubbs's $600 per year salaries. Of course, the endowment drive was just one more burden the overworked president did not need. Long may even have been morally and ideologically opposed to the idea; at least he suggested as much later in life. Long felt that the principal financial burden for "*true Christian education*" should fall on the Church, which "was never organized to handle stocks and bonds, or manage investment funds." So it may be no surprise that this initial drive bore little fruit. By 1880 twenty-seven individuals had pledged subscriptions ranging from $25 to $500, but more than one-third of the almost $5,000 endowment subscriptions had been rendered null due to death or failure to pay.[39]

Despite this poor showing, in the fall of 1883 the Arkansas Presbytery advised the board to raise an endowment of $50,000, part of which was to be used for establishing a theological department. When nothing came of this request, the Arkansas Synod in 1886 urged that the board honor its recently deceased president (later chairman) by raising a more modest $10,000 Welch Memorial Fund. The synod even appointed Long's brother-in-law, Rev. A. R. Kennedy, then pastor of Little Rock's Second Presbyterian Church, as financial agent. But Kennedy's busy pastorate and a lack of financial support doomed the campaign from the start. By June 1887 Kennedy had raised only about $650, and few more contributions were forthcoming. Subsequent synod-appointed financial agents would have no more success.[40]

Though the Welch Memorial Fund attracted few donors, the late minister continued to contribute to the school even after his death. The childless Welch became

Arkansas College's first significant benefactor, willing the college money, real estate, and enough books to substantially enlarge the tiny library. In the two years after Welch's death, the board received over $7,000 from sales of Welch's deeded lands, money that proved vital to continued operation. The college would receive another timely financial boost from Welch's widow's death five years later.[41]

At the time of Welch's death, 25 March 1886, Arkansas College had already reached a relatively comfortable level of stability.[42] Much of that was due to the influence of a stable corps of trustees. Though only three original trustees (Allen, McGuire, and Wycough) would outlast President Long, Arkansas College benefited from the emergence of a handful of trustees whose interest and benevolence would carry the college through the rocky years ahead. Among the more influential were Thomas B. Padgett of Batesville, a druggist, longtime county official, and Confederate veteran who served as trustee from 1882 to 1890 and watched two daughters graduate from Arkansas College; Col. W. A. Bevens, a Batesville lawyer who served as trustee from 1881 to 1890; Capt. Charles A. Bridewell of Hope, an attorney and politician whose son Charles P. graduated from Arkansas College in 1888; and Dr. T. D. Chunn, a Searcy physician who served seven years on the board.[43]

By far the most important quintet of trustees joined the board at the same time. In the fall of 1875 the presbytery elected as trustees three Batesville residents and a representative from Powhatan. These four men would devote a combined 150 years to the affairs of Arkansas College, often playing key roles in the life of the institution. The oldest of the four, and the only one whose service to the board would not reach twenty-five years, was Dr. J. B. Crane. Forty-nine years old when he joined the board in November 1875, Crane had just moved to Batesville the previous year. A native of South Carolina and graduate of South Carolina College, Crane became a lay leader in the Presbyterian Church and, though he never held office, he was a respected member of Arkansas College's board of trustees, serving for several years on the executive committee. By the time he resigned from the board in 1893, J. B. Crane had watched three of his children take diplomas from the small college.[44]

Judge James W. Butler joined Crane on the board in 1875. A prominent jurist and judge of Arkansas's Third Judicial District, Butler was a native of Tennessee and graduate of the University of Nashville. One year after he joined the Arkansas College Board of Trustees, Butler's daughter, Susie, became the first woman in Arkansas to receive a diploma for the degree of A.B. Judge Butler succeeded Aaron W. Lyon as vice-president of the board in 1883 and in 1890 was elected president. Three years later he resigned the presidency and resumed his post as vice-president, an office that he would hold until his separation from the board in 1903.[45]

The other two trustees, Theodore Maxfield and James P. Coffin, would each serve more than half a century on the board. In his own way each would become an integral part of the college. Maxfield, as a Methodist the most prominent non-Presbyterian of the early trustees, was born in Batesville in 1844 to parents who had migrated westward from Maryland. A Confederate veteran (like most of the early trustees) Maxfield had begun work in the family mercantile by the time Arkansas College was founded and thus never received a formal higher education. One year after joining the board, however, Theo Maxfield had the pleasure of watching a younger brother and sister join six others in Arkansas College's first graduation ceremony. By the early twentieth century, Maxfield would rank among the town's wealthiest citizens. For many years Maxfield served on the executive committee of the board; in the twentieth century he would hold the office of vice-president for several years until his death in 1926. Maxfield played an active role in student life and, through appearances on campus and student gatherings hosted at his home, was probably the most recognizable trustee among the student body. All six children of Theo Maxfield graduated from Arkansas College.[46]

By far the most active and influential trustee in the development of Arkansas College over the first half century of its existence was James Park Coffin. Coffin also boasted the best academic pedigree of Arkansas College's early leaders. His grandfather, Charles Coffin, was a Presbyterian minister and Harvard graduate who served as president of Greeneville (now Tusculum) College in Tennessee for more than twenty years and of East Tennessee University (now the University of Tennessee) for another decade. James Park Coffin was born in the eastern Tennessee town of Rogersville, where his father was president of the local bank, and grew up in Knoxville. After graduating from the Presbyterian-dominated University of North Carolina in 1859, Coffin served four years in the Confederate Army of Tennessee. After the war Coffin brought his young family west, eventually settling in Powhatan, the little Lawrence County seat perched atop a bluff overlooking the Black River. Here he served as a county officer and entered the banking profession, which would become his lifelong pursuit.[47]

A devout Presbyterian, Coffin was thirty-seven years old and living in Powhatan at the time of his election to the Arkansas College Board of Trustees. During the administration of Isaac Long, James P. Coffin proved the most faithful and energetic of the non-Batesville trustees. His sons, Charles and Maxwell, graduated from Arkansas College in the mid-1880s, and in 1891 the widower left Powhatan and moved to Batesville to be near his daughter. At the previous year's board meeting Coffin had been elected vice-president, initiating a span of almost forty years as an officer. He would later serve as secretary and for many years as president of the board.[48]

Without the presence on the board of such men as Coffin, Maxfield, Allen, and Wycough, the death of Thomas R. Welch could have proved an even more serious blow to the young institution. But by 1886 the board's decision-making power was firmly rooted in the Batesville contingent. Following precedent perhaps, the Batesville-centered board went back to Welch's Little Rock to find the old minister's successor. In June 1887, after more than a year without an official trustee president, the Arkansas College board elected to the post newcomer Rev. A. R. Kennedy. Brother-in-law to Isaac Long and to future president Woodrow Wilson, forty-four-year-old Anderson Ross Kennedy was a Confederate veteran and graduate of Davidson College in North Carolina and Columbia Theological Seminary. He had come to Batesville a dozen years earlier as joint supply of the Presbyterian Church, but left a couple years later to serve churches at Augusta and in Kentucky. At the time of his election as president of the board, Kennedy had been pastor of Little Rock's Second Presbyterian Church for four years. But Kennedy's service to Arkansas College proved to be too brief. Bothered by the frailties of health that seemed to plague the Kennedy and Long families, A. R. Kennedy died in Batesville less than three years later.[49] His successor, Judge James W. Butler, appears to have been a temporary replacement; nevertheless, Butler's temporary duty would turn into a three-year term during a tumultuous period in the college's history.

Arkansas College's small faculty also remained unusually consistent throughout Isaac Long's years as president. As mentioned earlier, Long and Stubbs for many years constituted the entire college faculty. One can only imagine the tremendous workloads involved in teaching all preparatory and collegiate subjects. And this was done on a salary that would not have satisfied most urban artisans of the day. We have seen that Long's pastorate, which he held until 1883, helped the president make ends meet. Stubbs, however, found other sources of outside income. The Virginian periodically filled Protestant pulpits in the area and edited a local newspaper, the *North Arkansas Pilot*, for three years. Stubbs also occasionally taught independent, business-related classes during the summer break and served two terms as an Independence County delegate to the Arkansas house of representatives.[50]

Long and Stubbs lightened their pedagogical burdens somewhat by employing tutors from the student body, generally seniors with exceptional academic records, who instructed preparatory pupils in selected subjects. But this system could be stretched only so far. As the enrollment grew so too did the need for additional faculty. As early as 1875 the board of trustees established a third professorship, natural science and belles lettres, which was filled in 1875–1876 by A. Ross Kennedy. But it appears that financial constraints prevented the college from replacing Kennedy when he reentered the ministry the following year. Long tried to get around the faculty shortage by securing Batesville-area trustees to offer classes in their fields of expertise, such as Judge Butler for constitutional law and Dr. Crane for physiology and hygiene. It is unclear, however, to what extent this early adjunct system was employed. By 1880 increasing enrollments led Long to petition the board for a third professorate.[51]

The board's failure to address the problem of faculty shortage likely sparked Long's sudden resignation from the presidency in the fall of 1880. The board initially accepted Long's resignation and reappointment as chairman of the faculty, but after Thomas R. Welch declined the board's offer to assume control of the institution, Long returned to his post in June 1881. In the spirit of placation, the board of trustees scheduled an official inauguration ceremony for Isaac Long and agreed to appoint a third full-time faculty member. Their choice was Long's choice, young ministerial candidate and alumnus of the class of 1880, John E. McMillan. Long obviously saw himself a generation earlier when he looked at his student and former boarder McMillan. Like Long, McMillan had faced an uphill battle to secure his education. A native of rural Boone County deep inside the Ozarks, he had walked over one hundred miles in wintertime to reach Batesville and Arkansas College. And like his mentor, McMillan had received his A.B. at the ripe old age of twenty-four. But Long would have a yet longer wait for faculty assistance. Tragically, young John McMillan took suddenly ill and died in August 1881, just weeks before the beginning of classes.[52]

It was not until the fall of 1883, eleven years into the college's life, that a third full-time faculty member was permanently added. Long and the board of trustees reorganized the three professorships. Isaac Long became professor of ancient languages and biblical literature (in addition to his duties as president); Stubbs took the title of professor of mathematics, history, and modern languages; and Long's son, Eugene, an 1878 graduate of Arkansas College, became professor of natural sciences and political economy. Amazingly, Eugene Long was only twenty years old when he first entered the classroom as a professor. At the same time the presbytery suggested appending a theological department to the college and adding a fourth faculty member. The board of trustees, apparently not sold on either idea, declined the fourth faculty suggestion and instead secured the services of Rev. George R. Waddell, new stated supply at the Batesville Presbyterian Church, as instructor of Hebrew. As we have seen, the projected endowment for the theological department never materialized, and the only lasting results of the presbytery's suggestion were Long's theology course and a Hebrew course taught for a few years after 1883 by local Presbyterian ministers.[53]

Arkansas College's faculty remained stable for the next five years, but in the spring of 1888 Thomas Jefferson Stubbs resigned to return to Virginia and help resurrect his alma mater, William and Mary. He had served side by side with Isaac Long for sixteen years and would not easily be replaced. The board hired as his replacement Maj. John F. Green, whose wife, R. K., taught French and algebra and thus may have been the first woman to officially teach on the collegiate level for Arkansas College.[54] When Major Green resigned due to poor health after the 1889–1890 academic year, the board hired twenty-two-year-old Evander D. "Van" Brown, a native of Drew County and member of the most recent graduating class. Brown became the college's second youngest faculty member to date when he took over as professor of mathematics. The board also agreed to add a fourth faculty member in 1890 and continued a budding tradition by hiring an alumnus of Arkansas College and son of Isaac Long to occupy this new position. Ross Kennedy Long was an 1887 graduate of the college and had spent the last half year as professor of ancient languages at Presbyterian College in Clinton, South Carolina. But tragedy again struck the Long family and Arkansas College when Ross died of typhoid fever during the first week of classes in September 1890. He was only nineteen. Although R. K. Long was apparently not replaced, Arkansas College expanded its adjunct faculty (and continued its nonsectarian tradition) that year by hiring local Baptist minister W. A. Giboney as the school's first instructor in elocution, a subject aimed toward pre-ministerial students.[55]

The youthful inexperience of Eugene Long and Van Brown—both barely beyond their teens when they became regular faculty members—appears quite shocking today. But such cases of college-aged "professors" were not terribly rare in the small colleges of the late-nineteenth-century South and West. It is quite possible that historian Richard Hofstadter's denunciation of the provincial small college as "little more than a high-grade academy with an intensive program of classical studies learned by rote" could have been leveled at tiny Arkansas College.[56] After all, the majority of graduates from the Batesville institution were teenagers and even in the 1890s the course of study still covered only three years in an era when four years had become the norm. Isaac Long and other college leaders were well aware that they were open for criticism and took pains to deflect any ridicule that might come their way. Early Arkansas College catalogs listed the institutions from which the trustees had graduated, and newspaper articles consciously and favorably compared the quality of education to that bestowed by eastern colleges. Thomas R. Welch wrote to the *Arkansas Gazette* shortly after Arkansas College's first graduation: "There is now no need for any parent to send his children out of state to get a thorough collegiate education. Such an education can be obtained at Arkansas College, a home institution and one that should be patronized by our people."[57]

The result of this defensive posture combined with the practical necessities of higher education in rural Arkansas was a somewhat schizophrenic curriculum that was in part stridently, conservatively traditional, in part pragmatic and experimental. In the college's first catalog, Isaac Long set forth a description and defense of the traditional small college and in the process took a shot at the elective system then coming into vogue in the East and North. "We do not claim to be a University; neither do we claim to have taken any stock in the modern patent system, by which we can impart to students, in a few months, an extensive knowledge of a great many things, of which we know nothing ourselves, but we do profess to afford opportunities to acquiring a sound and thorough Classical, Mathematical and Scientific course, equivalent to an old fashioned college curriculum." A decade and a half later Long still evinced a traditionalist's reaction to trends in American higher education. "When an institution calling itself a college proposes to bestow a so-called A.B. without even a knowledge of the Greek alphabet, or a B.S. without knowing a Latin declension, it is certainly time to call a halt, to take a reckoning and determine whither, in an educational point of view, the profuse list of *optionals* are drifting us . . . (B)y all means make a *degree* mean something."[58]

Again, Long could have been paraphrasing the Yale Report of 1828, the classic defense of the old faculty psychology and liberal arts education, when he penned the following: "I am thoroughly persuaded that for the attainment of the chief end of education, the Latin and Greek languages and the ordinary branches of mathematics form the basis for which there is no substitute, all the plausible declarations of flippant empirics to the contrary notwithstanding." Tellingly, Arkansas College's founder followed that strong statement with the practical reassurance that "ample opportunities . . . will be afforded by the Institution for those who cannot take anything more than an irregular course."[59] Although the classics and mathematics would remain at the core of the curriculum throughout the Isaac Long years and into the twentieth century, Arkansas College frequently altered and expanded the basic course of study to appeal to a wide range of students and interests during what has been called the "heyday of curricular laissez faire."[60]

The first compromise with the original curriculum occurred in December 1876, when the board of trustees authorized the faculty to grant certificates of proficiency for courses completed satisfactorily by students who were not pursuing a degree. By the early 1880s, as the acquisitive New South movement began to infuse even the most staid southern institutions with a spirit of utilitarianism, more substantial changes had been made. The catalog published after the 1881–1882 year lists four separate courses of study, the "parallel course scheme" that remained an option for liberal arts colleges well into the twentieth century. Two of the courses of study offered students a certificate of proficiency while the other two promised bachelor's degrees. Arkansas College offered a Common School Course "with the special view of fitting those who complete it to be teachers in the common schools of Arkansas." The Literary Course allowed students to earn a certificate by avoiding higher mathematics and ancient languages, among other subjects. Following the lead of most other small colleges, Arkansas College also adopted the bachelor of science degree. The course of study for the B.S. was almost identical with that for the A.B. except that the former, which Arkansas College originally named the Commercial or Practical Business Course, allowed students to avoid either Greek or Latin and substituted bookkeeping and business courses for some higher mathematics. By the mid-1880s, however, the business element had been dropped and the B.S. was basically the A.B. without Latin.[61]

In the nineteenth century, at least, it was clear that the institution viewed the B.S. as an inferior degree. By 1886 the college catalog even referred to the A.B. degree as "the highest conferred on graduation." Nevertheless, Minatree M. Carter of Pocahontas proudly took home the first B.S. diploma presented by Arkansas College in 1885. A.B.'s continued to outnumber B.S.'s at Arkansas College graduations until the mid-1890s.[62]

Although college catalogs made no mention of the practice, Arkansas College also awarded master of arts (A.M.) degrees in the nineteenth century. There was no official policy for the granting of such degrees during Isaac Long's lifetime, and no graduate school or graduate classes either. Nevertheless, Arkansas College bestowed seventeen A.M. degrees "in course" during the elder Long's tenure and four more after his death. Again, though it appears strange to modern eyes, this was not an unusual practice at the time. Arkansas College awarded its first A.M. in 1881 to T. J. Horne, a member of the inaugural graduating class. Eventually, all five male graduates in the class of 1876 received A.M.'s. Three women also took the degree from Arkansas College. As was the practice at most small colleges, Arkansas College granted master's degrees only to alumni and only upon their request. Most often recipients were ministers, lawyers, or members of some other "learned" profession who had graduated at least five years earlier.[63]

Another popular practice of the era that Arkansas College's board of trustees eagerly took part in was the granting of honorary degrees. This practice has obviously had a longer life than the granting of master's degrees. Scarcely a commencement passed during the nineteenth century without the board bestowing an honorary D.D. or LL.D. The board honored three men with D.D. degrees at the 1876 commencement exercises, including Isaac Long. The vast majority of recipients of honorary degrees were Presbyterian ministers from Arkansas and around the South. The board gave out three LL.D. degrees during Isaac Long's presidency, all to prominent Little Rock lawyers. Even honorary Ph.D.'s and A.M.'s were on occasion awarded. The board rewarded Thomas Jefferson Stubbs for his many years of service with an honorary Ph.D. in 1889 and granted Eugene Long the same degree two years later.[64]

The granting of honorary degrees was, and remains, the domain of the board of trustees and thus had little effect on everyday life on the college campus. Unfortunately, the activities of students and faculty on a daily basis, the most basic function of any college, is perhaps the murkiest area of Arkansas College's history. We can, however, achieve some understanding of student life and common activities with the help of a student diary and a few other reminiscences. The student body slowly increased during Isaac Long's tenure; the combined total of primary, preparatory, and collegiate students had surpassed 100 by the early 1880s and never fell below that mark before Long's death. As the years went by the percentage of non-Independence County students grew steadily so that by 1890–1891, Isaac Long's last full year as president, more than 40 percent of the 149 students came from outside the county. The trip to Batesville also became easier as time passed. In 1873, on a day with good weather, the trip from Little Rock to Batesville took at least twelve hours. The easy part was the train ride on the Cairo and Fulton from Little Rock to Newport. From there a prospective student could take a slow steamboat or more likely would travel by coach to Jacksonport and there catch a hack for the seven-hour overland journey to the Independence County seat. The entire trip cost about eight dollars. Within a few years daily stage service had been improved between Newport and Batesville, but rail service did not connect the two towns until 1883, when the thirty-mile White River Branch of the St. Louis, Iron Mountain and Southern Railway opened for business.[65]

Once in Batesville students faced hours upon hours of reading, writing, and memorization. Students were expected to memorize their Greek and Latin lessons each night, until they could "spin it off coming and going, backwards and forwards"; mornings and afternoons were spent in the recitation, or classroom, sessions in which the teachers supervised memorized regurgitations. Eugene Long later recalled his first experience with the classical curriculum: "There was pleading, mixed with sobbing and copious tears, to be allowed to stop Latin." He was not alone. In that timeless fashion of students, there was also an occasional reason for rejoicing—such as when Isaac Long left town on church business. One student recorded in her diary in 1880: "Mr. Long will be gone this week to Presbytery, so there might as well not be any school. There will be no studying." And one day the following fall she exclaimed, "Mr. Long is gone—goodie."[66] Teachers were also expected to have complete mastery of their subjects. "No teacher has a right to use a book in recitation unless he grants his students the same privilege." In the early years of the college all examinations were taken orally; by the end of Isaac Long's life, however, the faculty had begun to use occasional midterm written examinations. All final examinations were oral

One-half of the first graduating class of Arkansas College. *Standing:* Charles Maxfield. *Seated:* Susie Butler (Lawrence), Will Patterson, and Mary Maxfield (Fitzhugh).

until the mid-1890s. As we have seen, these examinations were semipublic affairs observed by faculty, trustees, and other interested persons.[67]

Unquestionably, the course of study at Isaac Long's Arkansas College was demanding. Through the 1890–1891 session, only seventy-nine young men and women received bachelor's degrees from Arkansas College. After the initial graduation of eight students in 1876, it took a dozen years for the college to produce a larger class on commencement night. Even the 1891 graduating class, the largest of the nineteenth century, contained only a dozen students. And Isaac Long appeared to be quite satisfied with the slim alumni list of a rigorous institution. Speaking for the faculty he posted this warning for slackers: "We are not unduly ambitious to multiply the number of so-called graduates."[68]

Isaac Long and the faculty also practiced the traditional *in loco parentis* system of discipline. "Going off to college" in the 1870s and 1880s lacked the sense of freedom and exploration implicit in the phrase today. Instead, students left home only to fall under the parental discipline of Christian men and women on the college campus and at boardinghouses. One Little Rock parent praised Isaac Long for having "the singular and valuable faculty of enforcing rigid discipline, and yet winning the affections of his scholars." He continued: "If, as I do, you wish your boy to knuckle down to good behavior and hard patient study, Batesville is at least one of the places to send him . . ."[69] Like many postwar southern colleges, Arkansas College tried to instill a sense of honor and integrity in its matriculates, but a student who dared to defy authority could expect swift judgment. After suspending a young man for playing billiards in a Batesville gambling hall, Long addressed readers of a local newspaper:

> The public may be fully assured that so long as Arkansas College is under its present control, whether it be a popular measure or not, . . . when a student neglects his business, and it becomes next to a useless expense for his parents to keep him here (and I claim to be the judge of that), a constant source of annoyance to those that have charge of him and a bad example to others—after being timely admonished and failing to receive benefit therefrom, as a final resort *he will be expelled*, after which no Institution of any well founded pretensions to respectability will ever knowingly admit him as a student in regular study.[70]

Because a majority of the students were Presbyterians, they probably thought little of the spiritual demands of college life. An original student of the college recalled years later, "The Ten Commandments were just as binding in Arkansas College as they were during the time of Moses." Students were expected to attend Sunday School and Sunday church services in the Protestant church of their parents' choice, and if no preference was given they were required to attend the Presbyterian Church. In addition to mandatory classes in biblical and ecclesiastical history, students and faculty were required to gather each school morning for prayers in the little wooden-frame chapel, which the students derisively referred to as the "Bach Hotel." With burgeoning enrollments, at least by rural Arkansas standards, packing the tiny chapel, the board of trustees began discussions with the newly formed Alumni Association in 1885 concerning the building of a new chapel. Thirty-two of the thirty-seven living alumni agreed to donate money—twelve dollars for men and seven dollars for women—as did a dozen more from the next three graduating classes. Members of the board pledged several hundred dollars as well. The result of this fund-raising was the erection of a thirty-five-by-ninety-feet stone building just south of the college building. The new chapel, Alumni Hall, was a little box of a building that one alumnus described as "two shotgun houses put end to end." Alumni Hall was completed in 1888 and would be the last physical addition to the college in the lifetime of Isaac Long.[71]

Despite the *in loco parentis* atmosphere and the stringent demands of the traditional classroom, students were never wholly without extracurricular activities, although those activities sanctioned by the faculty generally possessed some sort of academic value. As was the case at most small colleges, a student-controlled extracurriculum did not spring

A group of Arkansas College students posed before the college's original building (Morrow Hall), 1885.

up immediately but evolved gradually. Throughout the college's first decade there arose a succession of short-lived literary clubs and societies. One of the first recorded examples of students' extracurricular activity was a public program presented by the Phylogian Society in the little frame chapel in December 1873. The program of events resembled performances typical of later literary societies: Bible readings, music, orations, declamations, and the evening's highlight, a somewhat humorous debate over the question, "Which has the most influence over society—women or wine?"[72]

The college students would continue to provide entertainment for townspeople over the next few years. In June 1875 the cessation of public examinations provided the occasion for a Friday night student exhibition at the courthouse. An opening chorus of "My Native Hills" was followed by a lengthy succession of declamations, readings, orations, instrumental and vocal musical performances, and a spelling match that eventually involved all the collegiate students and many of the younger ones as well. Future graduate William H. Wycough capped off the speeches with a valedictory address, followed by a closing chorus performed by the primary school children. The evening dragged on so long that Jacksonport politician and trustee W. K. Patterson declined an offer to address the crowd at the cessation of events.[73]

There was mention of an Arkansas Literary and Debating Society as early as 1879, and in November 1880 a group of students formed a reading club. Their choices for discussion were quite typical, relatively recent works of English and American literature that rarely cracked the traditional curriculum. In this way, according to historian Frederick Rudolph, the literary societies offered a sense of educational completeness to students and served as "advance agents of secularization." During the year the club read Longfellow, Milton, Washington Irving, and *Hamlet* among others, but by the end of the academic term flagging interest had brought an end to the club.[74]

Arkansas College's extracurriculum assumed a new vibrancy and a sense of permanency and purpose after the organization of the Philomathean Society in June 1883. The college's first permanent literary society, the Philomathean Society was originally founded by a group of young men as a debate society, though it eventually branched out into other literary pursuits. In the fall of 1884 six young women established the first female literary society, L'Etoile. The Philomathean and L'Etoile societies dominated extracurricular life at Arkansas College in the 1880s, a common development in American colleges of the era. The Philomatheans' "Intermediate Celebration," held each February on George Washington's birthday, became a high point of the academic year. The Philomatheans also held annual commencement exercises, featuring orations by members and perhaps a speech delivered by a prominent adult guest, as did the L'Etoile Society. L'Etoile was especially significant for providing a forum in which young women could speak in public, something the college for many years forbade in official mixed company functions.[75]

For the most part the topics of orations, declamations, and essays presented at society functions were typical of student efforts at other American colleges, consisting of a mix of history, politics and government, literature, and moralistic inspiration. For instance, presentations at the Philomatheans' 1887 intermediate celebration included

Members of Arkansas College's original literary society, the Philomathean Society, 1885.

the following titles: "Power of Trifles," "LaFayette and Robert Raikes," "The Achievements of the Thirteen Colonies," "James A. Garfield," "Mother, Home and Heaven," "Obligations of the American Youth," and "History of a Party Government." As the 1880s gave way to the 1890s—and especially after the death of Jefferson Davis in 1889—Philomathean presentation topics tended to grow more "southern." For example, oration topics in the late 1880s included "Historic Richmond," "The Old South," and "Chivalry." In 1891 and 1892 the Philomathean Society went so far as to rename its midyear program the "Lee-Jackson Intermediate Celebration" and to move it to 20 January, Robert E. Lee's birthday. By this time, however, the Philomatheans had competition, for in early 1891 a dozen members of the old society broke away to form a new one, the Erosophic Society. The early 1890s witnessed the establishment of a third male debating society called Delta Sigma, but it apparently had only a brief existence. The Erosophic and Philomathean societies would survive deep into the twentieth century as sometime friends and rivals.[76]

It is difficult to overestimate the importance of the literary societies in broadening the scope of education and student experience. In addition to the emergence and solidification of the literary society system, college students also benefited from and participated in the Rude Mechanicals, a literary society formed by Batesville citizens that, according to the student magazine in 1890, maintained the best library in town. The college literary societies maintained their own libraries as well, which proved a valuable source and perhaps necessity since the college library contained only about one thousand volumes. In addition to the small library, which was personally maintained by Isaac Long for years before Eugene Long took over its management, students also had access by 1890 to a reading room containing current secular and religious magazines and newspapers as well as reference works kept in the classrooms.[77]

Another product of the growing popularity and prominence of literary societies at Arkansas College was the emergence of student awards. The literary societies helped elevate public speaking to an exalted position. And it was oratorical skill that was first officially rewarded at the college when in 1885 John Stayton, a lawyer from Newport whose son had graduated three years earlier, established the Stayton Medal of Oratory. The gold medal was awarded to the graduate (male, of course) whose commencement night oration was judged superior to the others. Ben Shive of Lonoke County won the first Stayton Medal in 1885, and the award was presented annually for several years thereafter. In 1887 the first Greek Medal was awarded to Ross K. Long; the Greek Medal, however, seems to have disappeared rather quickly. By the early 1890s two additional medals were presented in the spring: the Bridewell Medal for biblical and ecclesiastical history, presented by trustee C. A. Bridewell of Hope, and the William and Mary mathematics medal given by former professor T. J. Stubbs.[78]

In addition to the proliferation of student awards, the final years of Isaac Long's presidency witnessed an explosion of extracurricular activity at Arkansas College as enrollments approached 150 in 1889–1890 and 1890–1891. By 1890 Arkansas College could boast a Young Men's Christian Association with a membership of forty. The YMCA, a popular group on most college campuses, held meetings each Sunday afternoon in the Philomathean Hall of the college building. The YMCA was open for membership to all evangelical Protestants, a requirement that almost every young man at Arkansas College in the 1890s could meet. Students in the early 1890s also participated in a short-lived glee club and a sort of future businessman's club, the Fun and Profit Society, organized by trustee Theo Maxfield.[79]

In March 1890 a group of young men and women from the Philomathean and L'Etoile societies collaborated in the establishment of Arkansas College's first student publication. Published monthly, the *Arkansas College Magazine* was largely the pet project of its first editor-in-chief, W. A. Ramsey from Mississippi. Most issues contained between twenty-five and thirty-five pages and sold for fifteen cents; a year's subscription cost a dollar. But most of the money for production of the magazine came from the sale of advertisements to local merchants. The format was typical of other college publications: articles and essays by students, editorial notes, a department for women headed by a female associate editor, exchanges from other college newspapers and magazines, and a local campus gossip section. Readers perusing the first issue found poems, including "A Tribute to Jefferson Davis," an essay entitled "Young America," a short story called "Two Graduates," a detailed description of the Philomatheans' intermediate celebration, and brief pieces on "Woman's Power," "Home," and "Shakespeare's Will." In the spring of 1891 an alumni section, "Among the Old Students," was added to the *Magazine*.[80]

Within a year or so of the founding of the *Arkansas College Magazine*, readers began to catch frequent glimpses of athletics and sporting life on campus. Sporting events, and especially football, were just beginning to transform student extracurricular life on American college campuses in the 1880s and 1890s. The aging Isaac Long must have found the growing hysteria over athletics on his small campus a strange phenomenon. Although he would not live to see the development of organized athletics or intercollegiate competition at Arkansas College, Long did watch increasing numbers of his students participate in local athletics during their free time. In the early 1890s Isaac Long added a brief note on "Physical Culture" in the back of the catalog. But the "remarkable caves, cliffs and springs near town" that he mentioned were the destinations of active students of the 1880s.[81] The students of the early 1890s were more interested in baseball, football, tennis, and boxing. Nevertheless, the maturation of college athletics awaited future presidents.

When Arkansas College's twentieth academic year got under way in September 1891, Isaac Long was ill, forcing Eugene Long to take over his father's classroom and administrative duties. By November, however, the "venerable sage" seemed to be recovering nicely, prompting the *Arkansas College Magazine* to rejoice, "Dr. Long is rapidly improving." In early December President Long felt spry enough to return to campus and address the student body in Alumni Hall. But it was to be his last march across the little stage. He died a few days later on the tenth day of December. He was fifty-seven.[82]

Long had served as president of his little college for just over nineteen years, had watched its student body more than double, had watched its curriculum and focus evolve but remain traditional, had witnessed the dawning of the age of the extracurriculum. To the people of Batesville and the friends of the institution, Isaac Jasper Long *was* Arkansas College; the college had become Isaac Long. In a photographic portrait taken late in life—the one most often seen on campus by generations of students to come—Long appeared much older than his fifty-odd years. Gray hair, a stern countenance, and a long, thin white beard shrouded an almost youthful, even delicate face. Similarly, a traditional curriculum and Presbyterian tradition of higher education rendered Arkansas College deceptively older and more mature than its nineteen years.

Meeting just a few days after Isaac Long's death, the board of trustees appointed the old president's youthful son to lead young Arkansas College. The days and years ahead held unfathomable challenges for twenty-nine-year-old Eugene R. Long. He would come to miss his father most of all.

Chapter 2

A Reluctant President in an Age of Change

Basketball was barely five years old in February 1897, but it was the rage at tiny Arkansas College. Although created to serve as a winter diversion for athletes between football and baseball seasons, it was perfect for a small college that had no football team and struggled to scrape up nine boys for a baseball team. It was a basketball game that provided the arena for one of Arkansas College's most exciting events of the 1890s. On Friday night, 5 February 1897, students and townspeople crammed themselves into small Alumni Hall to witness a caged "contest for the championship of the state of Arkansas." The ten Arkansas College players, ranging in age from sixteen to twenty-three, entered the cramped quarters wearing football-style uniforms of crimson and cream; the other students cheered them on with the school yell: "Ark-an-saw; Hiss boom bah; boom-a-lang, boom-a-lang; Rah, rah, rah." Their opponents were the state's most feared team, the Little Rock YMCA. What followed the 8:45 tip-off was "the most exciting [event] that has been witnessed in a long time." The college boys took an 8 to 4 lead into halftime and, perhaps with the help of some home cooking, held on for the victory, 17 to 12. Center Alva Miller, a sophomore ministerial student from Russellville, led the college team with seven points, all scored on foul shots. Juniors Eugene Bracy from Camden and Art Coombs from Batesville both nailed two field goals; their young Latin professor, Eugene Blandford, refereed the game.[1] The basketball craze died down after the celebration of the great victory. It proved to be the final game of the year and the last at Arkansas College for some years. The fleeting interests of the students were quickly diverted to other things.

The events of February 1897 are representative of a good deal of Arkansas College's experience during the quarter century following the death of Isaac Long. At the very moment that students were caught up in the frenzy of a new sport and the budding passions of school spirit, the college was in the midst of one of its darkest times: enrollments plunging, controversies swirling, debts mounting. But among the small band of students, life at Arkansas College went on as usual. There were Latin declensions to memorize and exciting new adventures to be experienced. Such dual experiences—the dynamism and growth of the student experience versus the innumerable challenges of administrators and trustees—characterized the two and a half decades preceding World War I, an era that witnessed four presidential changes, lows and highs in fund-raising, and no fewer than three challenges to Arkansas College's future in Batesville. It is no wonder Eugene R. Long was a reluctant president.

In one of those tragic coincidences that occasionally occur in life and seem to compound the grief that is our inheritance by right of our humanity, Isaac J. Long died on his eldest son's birthday. Eugene Rufus Long's birthday present was thus the presidency, *ad interim,* of his alma mater. He was the most logical choice to replace his father at the head of Arkansas College. Though only twenty-nine, he was now the senior statesman on the small faculty; he had joined his father and Thomas Jefferson Stubbs in the fall of 1883, less than five years after his graduation. Like most of Arkansas College's faculty members in its first two decades, the South Carolina-born E. R. Long had very little formal higher education beyond his three years or so in Batesville. After graduation he had worked as a tutor and as a store clerk before spending a year at Southwestern Presbyterian University. Those ten months in Tennessee rounded out his formal schooling, though he was granted the A.M. in course by Arkansas College in the spring of 1884. Half a year before his father's death, the board of trustees had granted him an honorary Ph.D.[2]

A baptism by fire awaited the young interim president. A general financial depression, especially among farmers, coupled with the loss of confidence in the young school generated by Isaac Long's death resulted in falling enrollments in the 1890s. The 1891–1892 student body represented a 25 percent decrease from the previous year's all-time high, and within two years of the elder Long's death total enrollment (primary through college) would fall below one hundred for the first time since the early 1880s.[3] To compound matters Eugene Long and the board of trustees also faced the synod's threat to relocate the struggling institution.

The first year of the Eugene R. Long era at Arkansas College would be an eventful one, packing as much drama and activity into twelve months as Isaac Long had experienced in perhaps his entire presidency. Supporters of the college would be faced with the possibility of repeal of the controversial Three Mile Act by the state legislature. The physical appearance of the little campus would undergo a major alteration as the largest construction project in the college's history sprouted from the spring soil. And the faculty would undergo a nearly complete overhaul before September of 1892. But before all this could happen there was that little matter of the synod considering moving the college elsewhere.

The question of moving the college first arose in a synod meeting at Batesville in November 1890, just one year after the college's charter had been amended to give the synod power to nominate members of the board of trustees. "The subject was not pressed vigorously at that time," according to Eugene Long, writing almost two decades later, "due largely to the reply made" by Isaac Long. Apparently, the president's unwillingness to move should the synod relocate the college squelched any immediate plans for action. Nevertheless, the synod appointed a committee to consider the move and

Eugene R. Long, son of Isaac Long and second president of Arkansas College, was associated with Arkansas College as a student, teacher, or administrator for almost half a century.

to accept bids from other towns and cities. By the fall of 1891 the movement had lost its urgency, but the death of Isaac Long in December rekindled the smoldering embers of discontent, and by the spring of 1892 Eugene Long and the Arkansas College board members were beginning to feel the heat. With the elder Long and statewide respect for his erudition gone from the scene, it seemed the perfect opportunity for a couple of towns to make a push for the institution that Presbyterians outside of Batesville had begun to refer to generically as the "Synodical college." Furthermore, though Eugene Long was in many respects "a chip off of the old block," he was nonetheless only twenty-nine, relatively inexperienced in the synod's affairs, and a layman, an oddity for denominational college presidents of the late nineteenth century.[4]

On 26 March 1892, four days before the synod's special meeting to consider the permanent location of the college, concerned citizens and friends of Arkansas College gathered at the courthouse in Batesville to decide on a plan of action. Board treasurer John F. Allen produced the old subscription list and pledge of support that had originated in Batesville almost twenty years earlier, pointing out that more than half of the money raised for the original building had come from non-Presbyterian citizens who had pledged their support only with the agreement that Arkansas College would never leave Batesville. A besieged defensiveness enveloped the college community and Batesville citizens. The editor of the college magazine observed: "The citizens of Batesville seem very much aroused on the subject and no doubt will make a hard and brave struggle to save her [Arkansas College] from the grasp of the enemy." A local newspaper editor blamed the threatened relocation on intrigue "worked up from Little Rock" and noted that "Batesville people are both surprised and pained to find persons engaged in [the relocation effort] whose friendship and good will they had every reason to expect."[5]

The 30 March meeting failed to solve the question when a group of Searcy citizens blocked an effort to transfer control of the "Searcy College" property and facilities to the synod. But Batesville defenders were faced with yet another challenge when the synod scheduled a meeting in Little Rock for late April at which delegations from competing towns would be given the opportunity to present their bids and a final decision would be rendered. Arkansas College sent trustee James P. Coffin, who had recently moved to Batesville and had emerged as the college's most vocal champion, and interim president Eugene Long to Little Rock to present the case for leaving the school alone. Coffin and Long faced stiff competition from much larger delegations representing Arkadelphia and Malvern. Twenty-four men made the trip from Arkadelphia to Little Rock to plead their town's case; Malvern, perhaps on paper the strongest competitor, sported a delegation of more than a dozen carrying a pledge of $25,000 from local citizens. James P. Coffin presented a written guarantee—signed by John F. Allen, Theo Maxfield, Joseph Rutherford, and Simon Adler—to raise $10,000 for physical improvements should the synod see fit to keep Arkansas College in Batesville. More persuasively, however, Coffin produced the original 1872 pledge of Batesville citizens and instructed the synod committee that the Independence County seat would take whatever legal measures necessary to keep Arkansas College. This last tactic caught the committee off guard and must have been enough for victory, for by a near unanimous vote the committee found in Batesville's favor. The only administrative result of the wrangle between Batesville and the synod was a June 1892 amendment to the college charter giving the synod veto power over all faculty appointments made by the board of trustees.[6]

Though one might have caught wind of an audible, collective sigh of relief in the Batesville air around 23 April 1892, the most tangible result of the moving controversy was the erection of a new building. The $10,000 promised by citizens of Batesville proved enough for the construction of a three-story brick building with native stone trimming. Completed at an approximate cost of $8,500 by local firm Hoffman and Ryan, the new building, christened the Isaac J. Long Memorial Building, was ready for use in January 1893. Although only the first two floors were originally designed for classroom use, the new building proved large enough to allow Eugene Long to move all preparatory and collegiate classes into it, leaving the old college building to the primary school. Furthermore, the new facility contained rooms designated for a library and a chemical laboratory, two long overdue additions; the library room had recently become a necessity with the addition of more than a thousand volumes from the collection of the late Rev. Thomas R. Welch.[7]

The synod's threat to move Arkansas College and the maddening activity surrounding the planning of a new building was perhaps more than Eugene Long wanted to deal with; more likely he had never had any desire to undertake the strain of administration. At the June 1892 meeting of the board, he submitted his resignation as interim president. The board accepted the resignation and appointed him chairman of the faculty and professor of ancient languages and political science. Furthermore, the death of Isaac Long and the departure of professor E. D. "Van" Brown at the end of the tumultuous year demanded a serious reorganization of the college faculty. Counting on the synod's recent promise to launch a new endowment drive and hoping to allay further Presbyterian fears that Batesville was unfit for a college, the board voted to permanently expand the full-time faculty to four persons. This required the hiring of three new teachers. To fill the chair of modern languages and natural science the board recruited J. Ray Morton, a graduate of Hampden-Sydney College in Virginia who had for several years been teaching at an academy in Nashville, Tennessee. The other two newcomers were Arkansas College alumni James H. Townsend and T. J. Horne. Townsend, who took the chair of mathematics and English, was a twenty-two-year-old Lawrence County native who had briefly attended West Point and the Lacrosse Collegiate Institute (Izard County) before earning his A.B. in 1891. At forty-one, Rev. Tillman Josiah Horne, a member of the first graduating class, became the oldest faculty member and the only minister among his comrades when he was appointed professor of biblical literature, moral science, and history, subjects usually reserved for minister/presidents during the era. Horne had most recently served as evangelist for the Arkansas Presbytery after a twelve-year pastorate in the eastern Arkansas town of Marianna. In addition to the four full-time instructors, the college maintained the services of alumnus and local Presbyterian minister Arthur G. Jones as teacher of Hebrew.[8]

Friends of Arkansas College looked on anxiously in September 1892 as the institution's twenty-first year got under way. As most expected, enrollment was down slightly during the first quarter, but gradually picked up throughout the remainder of the session as the business-as-usual approach of Long and his faculty began to restore confidence among parents and patrons. The scare of the previous spring and the faculty overhaul resulted in minor and peripheral curricular changes designed to provide "additional flexibility in the degree courses, without lowering . . . the previous standard." Among the additions were a series of oral lessons on practical business matters—which by the 1893–1894 year had expanded into a "Business Course" offering a certificate of proficiency—and a series of lectures on various topics presented by guest speakers such as editor John Temple Graves and Congregationalist ministers J. H. Boggess and Samuel P. Leland. The first post–Isaac Long catalog also offered students opportunities for taking lessons in vocal and instrumental music, crayon work, stenography, and typewriting, but these subjects were not official curricular offerings and required additional fees.[9]

Despite such modern fare, the foundation of the degree-earning courses of study did not change. Neither did the college's financial standing. The local outpouring of love for Arkansas College was quickly swallowed up by the Isaac J. Long Memorial Building. When the dust from the construction cleared, things looked remarkably familiar; the college found itself once again on hard times. In the wake of the debate over moving the college, the synod pledged to raise an endowment of $50,000 and recruited five prominent Presbyterian laymen, but none from Batesville, to oversee the campaign. By the following fall, however, nothing had been done to initiate this drive, resulting in a critical financial strain and prompting the college board of trustees to "demand active, renewed and persistent effort on the part of Synod to provide an adequate endowment." Nevertheless, the synod failed to take any steps beyond requesting an annual church collection of $1,500 to help defray Arkansas College's operating costs. The first collection in the fall of 1893, in the midst of a terrible, national financial panic, produced barely half the requested amount; almost no financial support came from the churches in the western and southwestern parts of the state. Furthermore, collections on the old Welch Memorial Fund fell by more than half in the years after Isaac Long's death. The tightening financial constraints led the board to separate the primary school from the college's budget in the fall of 1893, making the primary school self-sustaining and thus not a burden on the college's severely taxed resources.[10]

In the midst of the college's financial struggles, a different crisis threatened to tear the Batesville community apart and perhaps endanger the future of the small school. In 1887, at the behest of Isaac Long and several Batesville-area trustees, the state legislature had passed a bill prohibiting the sale of liquor within three miles of the Arkansas College campus. By the early 1890s, the "Three Mile Act," as it was colloquially known, was at the center of a divisive debate in town. In a series of referendums, townsfolk repeatedly voted in favor of repealing the law. The opposition to the law, led by such prominent merchants as H. L. Miniken, A. C. Yancey, Simon Adler, and M. A. R. Wycough, brother of college trustee Dolph Wycough, argued that the law was no longer effective and that "blind tigers" and other illegal liquor sources were more harmful to the community than were legally licensed saloons. The bitter dispute came to a head in January 1893 when an opposition delegation submitted their grievances, along with a petition bearing more than three hundred signatures, to the Temperance Committee of the state assembly. Trustee Theo Maxfield of Batesville and former trustee C. A. Bridewell of Hope spoke for the college in defense of the Three Mile Act. Although the committee ultimately voted unanimously not to recommend repeal of the act, the aftermath of the January debate proved more problematic than the prohibition act around which it centered. During his emotional remarks, Bridewell singled out Jewish merchant Adler with disparaging remarks that the Batesville merchants interpreted as antisemitic. The town of

Batesville quickly rallied around Adler and demanded a public apology from Bridewell, who steadfastly refused to apologize but remained on the board. Arkansas College emerged from the fracas with a black eye and facing an uphill climb to reclaim the good graces of its neighbors. The college and the legislature had not heard the last from the Three Mile Act's opposition.[11]

When Judge J. W. Butler resigned the board's presidency in December 1893, the college trustees, perhaps in an attempt to bring their own efforts into closer cooperation with the inactive synod trustees, elected Judge Harry Gaston Bunn of Little Rock as Arkansas College's fourth president of the board. Bunn, a native of Rocky Mount, North Carolina, was raised on a Tennessee farm and matriculated at Davidson College before the Civil War cut short his education. The fifty-five-year-old former Confederate colonel had just recently been appointed Chief Justice of the Arkansas Supreme Court by Governor William Fishback, and was one of the five laymen appointed by the synod to oversee the endowment campaign. His son was a recent matriculate at Arkansas College. The struggling college board hoped Bunn's prestige among Arkansas Presbyterians and influence within the synod would energize the moribund endowment campaign. But, in the face of a budding general depression, the college received little benefit from the new board president beyond perhaps a higher profile among the state's political elite.[12]

By the fall of 1894 the situation had deteriorated to the point where tuition income, church donations, and the paltry amount from the Welch Memorial Fund were not sufficient to cover bare living expenses for the four faculty members. The enrollment was still small, and, according to Eugene Long, one out of three Arkansas College students attended classes for free or at reduced rates. The general financial panic gripping the country, generated in Arkansas primarily by low cotton prices, left usual contributors unable to meet pledges. Long even began accepting payment in kind from local merchants in lieu of their financial commitments to the college. In October 1894, tired of his role as unofficial president and determined to escape the Spartan life of thanklessness that had been his father's lot, Eugene Long declined the board's offer to formally assume the presidency and submitted his resignation as chair of the faculty, to take effect at the end of the 1894–1895 session. At the board of trustees' annual meeting the following June, James P. Coffin, chair of the committee appointed to hire a new president, reported that it was impossible for Arkansas College to provide a salary adequate to attract a presidential candidate and asked Long to return for one more year as chairman of the faculty. Long agreed, largely on the understanding that Rev. R. B. Willis of Searcy, whom the synod had recently hired to revive and direct the endowment campaign, would actively and immediately canvass the state. At the time Long had received only $316.15 for the entire year.[13]

A month and a half after the June board meeting, Eugene Long abruptly and immediately resigned and announced that he had taken a position as professor of English at Southwestern Presbyterian University (SPU) at Clarksville, Tennessee. The board expressed its "gratitude for his noble self-denial in behalf of Arkansas College" and immediately fired off an official letter to the board at SPU damning their "unfriendly act," a letter that Long would years later recall as "exceedingly distasteful." The board's animosity toward Southwestern Presbyterian University carried over into the fall when the Arkansas Synod voted to sever its ties with the Tennessee institution, the school whose formation had indirectly spurred the founding of Arkansas College. Despite Coffin's earlier claim of the board's inability to pay a president, the trustees now had no choice. After convincing the synod to cover presidential costs through a subscription among the churches, the board promised the future president a fixed salary of $1,200 (far more than Long had ever received) and dispatched Reverend Willis, he of the stalled endowment drive, to head up the search for the new president.[14] The Long era at Arkansas College had come to an end—or so it seemed.

The man who replaced Long was surprisingly able, considering that $1,200, though significantly more than either of the Longs' earnings, was not a terribly attractive financial offer for one qualified to lead a college. At a special August 1895 meeting, the board announced the hiring of John Irvine Cleland as Arkansas College's third president (though, as we have seen, Eugene Long never held that title except on an ad interim basis) and second consecutive layman president. Although only thirty-one years old at the time, Cleland could claim nine years' experience in higher education. A native of western Kentucky, Cleland matriculated at Centre College and graduated from Central University in Richmond, Kentucky, in 1886. Cleland took the presidency of Presbyterian College in South Carolina at the age of twenty-seven and held the position three years before resigning in 1894 to pursue graduate studies at the Johns Hopkins University in Baltimore. When Cleland came to Batesville he had just finished a year at Johns Hopkins, making him the first member of Arkansas College's faculty with training in a graduate school founded on the German university model. Cleland remains a somewhat enigmatic figure, at least in his relationship to Arkansas College. A dashing young man (his middle-parted hair and burly mustache suggest a young Theodore Roosevelt), Cleland's experience in Baltimore, as well as his knowledge of curricula and methods at other small, southern colleges, would prove integral to his plans for Arkansas College. The traits that had accounted for past difficulties—cryptically—would also accompany him to northern Arkansas.[15]

Cleland would not be the only unfamiliar face on campus in the fall of 1895. Whether related to Long's resignation or not, James H. Townsend and Rev. T. J. Horne resigned their respective positions, leaving only professor of Latin and German W. S. Morton, who had succeeded his brother, J. R. Morton, when the latter returned to Virginia due to illness in the early spring of 1894. Pressed for time, the busy trustees found Townsend's and Horne's replacements through the most accessible channel, the alumni pool. As professor of English and history and provisional professor of biblical literature, the board appointed Charles F. Bizzell, a member of the class of 1888 who had the previous spring been granted the A.M. in course by his alma mater. Bizzell had for several years successfully operated an academy in his hometown of Austin in Lonoke County, and over the next decade and a half would endear himself to a generation of students in Batesville. His new colleague for the 1895–1896 session was John Samuel Nisbet, a twenty-six-year-old from Clark County who had earned the A.B. in 1894. Nisbet replaced fellow alumnus Townsend as professor of mathematics. During the session, Cleland also secured the services of new Batesville Presbyterian minister James E. Latham, a Tennessean and graduate of King College in Bristol, to teach a Bible studies course once per week.[16]

The brief Cleland administration grew into one of the most eventful and controversial in the college's history. Not one to ease himself into a position, Irvine Cleland barely made it to Batesville in time for the opening of classes and immediately made his presence felt. The young Kentuckian, fresh from the intellectual stimulation and international atmosphere of Johns Hopkins, disapproved of much that he saw, and "many changes were deemed advisable from the outset." Cleland attempted, apparently without complete success, to separate the preparatory department from the college, "resulting in dissatisfaction among patrons" of the former.[17] He criticized the college's lack of a laboratory for chemistry and physics and made plans to remedy the shortcoming. Cleland attempted to streamline the college's degree-granting system by abolishing the master's degree as well as all honorary degrees except the popular D.D. and by adding the fashionable B.Litt. (bachelor of literature) degree. Cleland also took steps to bring the college curriculum more into line with the traditional four-year course of studies. In place of the old system of sub-junior, junior, intermediate, and senior—which Cleland found to offer little more than three years of college education—the new president instituted the familiar freshman-sophomore-junior-senior classification system. He also stiffened admission requirements, which hitherto had gone unwritten. The admission requirements for incoming freshmen were specified in the 1895–1896 catalog: "a thorough knowledge of the principles of Latin grammar, Prose Composition, and Roman history," a knowledge of algebra through quadratic equations, and complete familiarity with the principles of the English language. To test each incoming student's mastery of his native tongue, Cleland required a two-page essay "on some work of some standard English author."[18]

The new president left the core of the classical curriculum in place but attempted to strengthen it and offer peripheral classes of interest. The most obvious changes involved an increased emphasis on the sciences, including requirements of a year and a half of chemistry, one year of physics, and astronomy and geology for seniors. Perhaps more significant, though, was his decision to discontinue the traditional, senior moral science class and to substitute in its place classes in psychology and a more modern, less Bible-centered study of ethics, both of which Cleland personally taught. The young president also elevated the study of Greek, another course that he taught, to a level almost equal with the favored Latin. Replacing the Longs' focus on the New Testament with studies of dialects, epics, drama, and Greek history, Cleland hoped to "impart as much as possible of that peculiar mental discipline and culture which appear at their best in Greek, which means so much for true scholarship and high culture." Furthermore, Cleland secularized the junior logic course and did away with biblical history for seniors. All of this curricular tinkering, the sum total of which was a not insignificant secularization of learning, must have raised some eyebrows among Arkansas's conservative Presbyterians and possibly played some role in the brevity of Cleland's tenure.[19]

In addition to the alterations of the classical curriculum, Cleland also introduced several semi-academic devices, some of which had been used at Arkansas College in the past. Professor Bizzell taught a bookkeeping class that, though not a regular part of the prescribed curriculum, Cleland strongly urged all students to take. Bizzell's class instructed students in the methods of letter writing, business computation, and basic bookkeeping. Cleland, like his predecessors, arranged musical instruction for interested students and in November 1895 recruited an elocution instructor, Augusta Malone from Tennessee. He also continued the practice of recruiting guest lecturers, including Judge U. M. Rose of Little Rock and Independence County physician R. C. Dorr. Among Cleland's innovations at Arkansas College were the introduction of written examinations at the mid-point and conclusion of each session, the establishment of a gymnasium in Alumni Hall, and in the fall of 1896 an experiment with military drilling for young men, a common practice on southern college and university campuses but one quite foreign to small Arkansas College.[20]

But much of life at Arkansas College was still familiar. The literary societies, the YMCA, and athletics dominated extracurricular affairs. The library was still pitifully small. Discipline remained strict. Cleland, like the Longs before him, continued to send home quarterly progress and deportment reports. Tuition still cost fifty dollars per year, and most out-of-town students boarded with local families. All students were required to attend Sunday School and Sunday morning worship as well as morning prayers each day of the school week. Enrollment was still slight, and the college continued to suffer financial problems.

The latter two problems began to reach emergency status not long into Cleland's administration. By the June 1896 annual meeting of the board of trustees, the flow of funds into the small college had dwindled to a trickle. Rev. R. B. Willis's canvass for an endowment fund had been a failure; he actually managed to spend seventy-five dollars more than he collected. The Welch Memorial Fund was quickly drying up due to disinterest, death, and financial hardship among its patrons; and the synod's subscription to cover Cleland's $1,200 salary came up almost one-third short of its goal. To add insult to injury, tuition receipts had fallen to a disturbingly low point of less than $1,800, including the primary school. Cleland, with perhaps little appreciation for the history of poverty at Arkansas College and perhaps blindly intent on rapidly turning it into a first-rate school, seems to have viewed the institution's financial straits as only a temporary impediment and asked the board to borrow $1,000 for the purpose of transforming the unused third floor of the Isaac J. Long Memorial Building into a boys' dormitory. Incredibly the board agreed, plunging itself further into debt. The board also accepted Cleland's recommendations to set all three faculty salaries at $800—though this figure was later reduced when the synod expressed disapproval of fixed faculty salaries—for the upcoming session and to complete the separation of college and preparatory departments by hiring a new instructor to take charge of preparatory teaching.[21]

Although a student writing in the newly revived *Arkansas College Magazine* in May

1896 trumpeted: "The prospects for next session are flattering," all was not well in Batesville. Enrollment had fallen to its lowest point in years; attendance during the 1895–1896 session included only thirty-seven college-level students and thirty-five preparatory students. Alumni participation was on the wane, likely due to the departure of the revered Eugene Long; the June 1896 alumni banquet attracted the poorest turnout to date. Arkansas's oldest private college was also facing increasing competition for patronage within the state. It seemed that a new college sprang out of a little academy or out of the bare soil on a weekly basis; and Batesville's relative inaccessibility began to take its toll as other more conveniently located colleges attracted more press and more matriculates. Old Professor Thomas Jefferson Stubbs, longtime friend and colleague of both Longs, informed the board that he was discontinuing the William and Mary mathematics medal. And, probably due to Cleland's dissatisfaction with their academic credentials, W. S. Morton and J. S. Nisbet turned in their resignations at the end of the session in June 1896, forcing the board to replace half its faculty just one year after replacing three-quarters of it. Bizzell maintained his position by agreeing to attend the University of Chicago during the summer.[22]

As the twenty-fifth session got under way in September 1896, several obvious alterations at Arkansas College cloaked the school's declining financial prospects with an aura of progress, growth, and modernization. The most obvious physical change was the new dormitory on the third floor of the Isaac J. Long Memorial Building. Designed and largely completed over the summer by President Cleland, the dormitory could accommodate up to thirty boys living two each in the tiny partitioned rooms. Each room contained two narrow wooden beds with no springs and a thin cotton mattress; each was hinged to the wall so that it could be stood erect when not in use. Because the college buildings did not yet have electricity or water, students relied on outdoor lavatories, bed and wash pans, firewood, and other such rustic amenities. Although meals were provided at a cost of about six dollars per month, one resident of Arkansas College's first dormitory recalled walking "several blocks for every meal."[23]

Although Cleland had planned for his two new, single faculty members to live in the dormitory with the preparatory and college boys, they balked, forcing him to employ the new preparatory instructor, J. Garnett Wood, as the dormitory's resident adult. Despite being "accused of noncooperation," the two new professors suffered no long-term ill effects from their insubordination. D. M. Frierson and Eugene C. Blandford would become fixtures on the Arkansas College campus for a generation and more. The two appear to have been handpicked by Cleland. Daniel Manton Frierson, professor of mathematics and natural science, was a former colleague of the president at Presbyterian College. An 1890 graduate of Davidson College and native of Isaac Long's Anderson, South Carolina, Frierson, like Cleland, had left Presbyterian College to pursue graduate studies at the Johns Hopkins University, where he had spent the previous academic year. Eugene C. Blandford lacked Frierson's graduate school experience but also shared a connection with Cleland. Blandford was a Kentuckian and a fellow alumnus of Central University, having earned the B.Litt. degree in 1895. He was teaching at a high school in Kentucky when Cleland invited him to Batesville.[24]

Interestingly, the athletic accomplishments of both young men appear to have been somewhat critical to their hiring. As we have seen, Cleland was a champion of physical fitness and athletic activities, and he may have sought out Frierson and Blandford as much for their accomplishments in the field of sports as in the field of education. The announcement of their hiring carried by the *Batesville Bee* in the summer of 1896 is suggestive: "Mr. Frierson has the reputation of being the best amateur base ball pitcher in northwestern South Carolina. He is a keen sportsman, being especially skillful with the gun. He has devoted much time to athletic [*sic*], and at Hopkins took the full course in gymnastics." Eugene Blandford's athletic achievements received even more profuse praise. According to the article, Blandford was considered the best all-around athlete in his native state, having established records with the hammer and shot, in pole vaulting, and in the high jump. A multimedal winner in statewide contests, he was reported to have run the second fastest one-hundred-yard dash in the South. All of this was certainly atypical praise for a new professor of Latin and modern languages.[25]

The two young bachelors, Frierson only twenty-six and Blandford one year younger, must have cut an interesting figure for the college students that fall. Frierson, who soon became "Little Dan" to friends and students, was a short, slim fellow with a narrow, taut face, a beak nose, and large, mournful eyes. His friend Blandford was quite the opposite. The "Gentle Giant," as he was known in athletic circles back home, was a tall, muscular man with a full face and cheery countenance. Frierson and Blandford immediately became fast friends and would remain so throughout their lives. Together with Charles Bizzell, they would constitute the core of the college's faculty for the next fifteen years.

The main problem for Arkansas College in the fall of 1896 was that there were not many students to greet the new professors. During the 1896–1897 session college-level enrollment dropped to thirty-three and preparatory attendance fell to sixteen, the lowest levels since the earliest days of the college's life. By comparison, all-female Galloway College in nearby Searcy boasted more than 300 preparatory and collegiate students at the time, Hendrix College approximately 150, and Arkadelphia Methodist College over 200. In addition Arkansas College faced competition for students from two new junior colleges in northern Arkansas, Mountain Home Baptist College and Arkansas Normal College. Arkansas Normal College, located less than ten miles from Batesville in the small Independence County village of Jamestown, proved especially threatening in the years following its establishment in 1895. Boasting a graduate of Yale on its faculty and a larger building than the Isaac J. Long Memorial Building, Arkansas Normal offered five different kinds of degrees for students of pedagogy and business until it lost its charter in 1904. Erratic attendance due to illness made matters worse for Cleland and the trustees. By midterm it was clear that the situation at Arkansas College, both in terms of income and enrollment, had reached the level of emergency. In January the synod's fund-raising committee promised that any individual or church donating at least twenty-five dollars could select a student to attend classes free of tuition for the remainder of the session. In February Cleland attempted to lure a few additional students by announcing that combined costs for tuition, room, and board for the final five and half months of the session would be reduced to eighty dollars. The same notice observed with satisfaction that Arkansas College's "curriculum is high and the courses of instruction are complete," but added the distress call, "TIMES ARE HARD."[26] They would get harder.

At the very moment that students and alumni were reading the above plea, Cleland and the college were embroiled in an ugly controversy. Four years after the first imbroglio over the Three Mile Act, the state legislature decided to reopen the dispute, sparking another heated debate in Batesville. But whereas Eugene Long and most of the college community had served as the law's staunchest defenders in 1893, Cleland took the opposite stance and argued that the law had actually harmed the college's prospects by antagonizing a large segment of the Batesville business community, a segment that in Cleland's opinion might otherwise have come to the financial support of the struggling institution. Although a local newspaper editor and others in the community came to Cleland's defense, most within the college's family disapproved of his public stance with the "wets."[27] Without a strong defense from the college, support for the Three Mile Act dwindled and the legislature repealed the law in January 1897. During the debate on the floor of the senate, one friend of the act referred to Cleland as a "red hot whiskey man." The president's reply to this accusation and subsequent defense of his stance in a letter to the *Arkansas Gazette* in late January may have sealed his fate with the conservative board of trustees, many of whom still supported the Three Mile Act.[28]

Less than a month after his letter appeared in the *Gazette* and only weeks after the big basketball game versus the Little Rock YMCA, Cleland submitted his resignation to the board, to take effect at the end of the session. The trustees, meeting in special session in Little Rock, accepted his resignation and expressed its "unqualified appreciation of the very high degree of Prof. Cleland's ability as a scholar and teacher, and of his skill in organizing and systematizing the scholastic work of the college." Little else in the way of praise could be offered for the past session and a half. When trying to explain Cleland's abrupt resignation one can pick his poison. Meager enrollments and rapidly mounting debts (about a $2,400 deficit by February 1897) certainly worked against the young president. The significant secularization of the curriculum must have been unpopular among many Presbyterians, among them some trustees, and Cleland's failure to defend the college and Batesville from the wet minions could only have lessened his stature in the eyes of his detractors. Ultimately, however, Cleland's personal indiscretions, rather than professional ones, may have been his hemlock. On 10 April 1897, two months before the end of the session, he resigned immediately and left town with his new bride, a young woman from a prominent Batesville Presbyterian family who had a couple months earlier gone to Texas "for [her] health."[29] The Cleland interregnum, once so promising and vigorous, had come to an inglorious end.

The board of trustees, jolted into action by the mounting and possibly scandalous events of the previous months, acted unusually swiftly. Old reliables Theo Maxfield and James P. Coffin presided over an assembly of students and faculty to inform them of Cleland's hasty departure and to announce the appointment of Rev. James E. Latham, pastor of the Batesville Presbyterian Church and college Bible instructor, as interim president. The treasurer quickly scraped up the back salary due Cleland, and the board removed from the payroll the young preparatory teacher Cleland had hired for the session. Most importantly for the college community and for the future of the institution, the trustees convinced prodigal son Eugene Long to return to his alma mater as president at an annual salary of $1,000, which was $200 less than Cleland had received.[30]

What the trustees faced in the spring and summer of 1897 was in many respects more than a search for a new president and a serious financial struggle. Arkansas College, now almost a quarter of a century old, faced an identity crisis. John I. Cleland had introduced the institution, in at least a small way, to the modern world of higher education then in development around the country. Had Cleland stayed and had the college been able to recruit enough students to stay afloat, Arkansas College would likely have taken additional steps toward bringing its liberal arts curriculum into line with national norms and toward further, though not drastic, secularization of mission and practice. Had the Johns Hopkins-trained Cleland remained at his post, it is quite possible that Arkansas College would have kept pace with Hendrix College during its march to academic respectability under innovative president A. C. Millar.[31] But the union of Cleland and Arkansas College was not to be. The many problems of his year and a half in Batesville, some of them beyond Cleland's control, ultimately forced the trustees into a defensive and conservative position. Restricted by financial limitations and yearning for the happier and simpler days associated with the Longs, the trustees, by offering the presidency to Eugene Long, agreed to take a step back and reevaluate the developments of the past two sessions. Implicit in Long's hiring was a desire to return to normality and a rejection of at least part of Cleland's progressive program. Explicit in the board's decision was the conscious recruitment of the man who could save the floundering college.

As was so often the case in the history of the institution, the most pressing demand was the financial situation. To meet mounting debts resulting from back salaries, taxes, attorney fees, and other demands, the trustees were forced to completely drain the already shrinking Welch Memorial Fund and use most of the Merrill Scholarship fund. An $800 fund from the synod and a handful of personal gifts from Batesville residents and Little Rock banker Charles F. Penzel provided enough money to cover the remaining deficit. Eugene Long was already quite familiar with the hand-to-mouth existence that Arkansas College would face in the coming years.[32]

Long finished the session at Southwestern Presbyterian University and returned home to Batesville in June 1897. He was about to embark on a journey of more than sixteen years at the head of his alma mater, the third-longest consecutive tenure in the college's history. As we shall see, it was probably not his intention to serve as president for such an extended period. As the college opened to the second Eugene Long era in the fall of 1897, the atmosphere offered a mixture of the old and new. Long's faculty was the same as Cleland's the year before. The third-floor dormitory was still in use. The gymnastics and athletic equipment collected at Cleland's urging was still on campus. Cleland's more strenuous admission requirements remained in place, as did most of his curricular changes. But the return of Long also meant the return of some things common to the pre-Cleland era. The catalog reverted, in both style and content, to the one Long had used in the early 1890s. Long's popular political science class, which to the students' delight concentrated heavily on current events, returned to the classroom. The B.Litt. degree disappeared (actually no such degree had ever been conferred) and the A.M. resurfaced at least one more time. The focus of Greek studies changed from prose composition and the inherent cultural value of Greek literature to an emphasis on comparison and contrast with English and a revival of the Greek New Testament. And though the catalog continued to list logic, ethics, and psychology, the old moral science course returned intact under the tutelage of Reverend Latham.[33]

During the years sandwiching the turn of the century, the college began to acquire much of the mental makeup and personal philosophy of Eugene Long. Long, still a young man at thirty-four when he returned to Arkansas College, was among that small group of classically educated men who were watching the American higher educational system abandon them in the late nineteenth and early twentieth century. In the university world he would already have been labeled a dinosaur. But in the society of small, poorly funded, denominational colleges in the South and West, Long and his kind would toil on for another generation, defending Latin, Greek, and Bible studies against the growing horde of gate rattlers and among a generation of youth suddenly wise to the anachronism that was the decrepit classical curriculum. Lacking the endowment to attract and keep superior teachers and the funds and facilities necessary to provide a superior scientific education, Long, like many other leaders at small colleges, resigned himself and his school to a precarious middle ground between the burgeoning university culture and the traditional liberal arts college. This middle ground in many ways represented Batesville's physical environment and development —somewhere between frontier and modernity; it also reflected the western tradition of experimentation and practicality that had always played a part in the development of Arkansas College.

Eugene Long expressed his philosophy for Arkansas College in the first post-Cleland catalog when he informed readers that the school's "watchwords shall be *solid, progressive and practical*." "The Institution aims to excel in substantial work rather than showy pretensions," promised the president. As had always been the case since the days of Isaac Long's presidency, "true character-building (was) sought as the highest end." The curriculum, from an insistence on a practical use for Greek and Latin to his appreciation for current events classroom discussions, eventually bore Long's stamp.[34]

Despite the focus on practicality and substance, Eugene Long's second administration was not a stagnant one. During his time as president, the college would undertake its first somewhat successful endowment campaign and would undergo a significant "female-friendly" alteration of the curriculum and degree programs. Extracurricular life would continue to expand and occupy the attention of students as enrollment increased. Buttressing these developments were an increasingly seasoned and stable faculty and a core of interested local trustees.

The frequent turnover of officers that contributed to institutional instability in the 1890s gave way to extraordinary stability and solidity on the board in the early twentieth century. Chief Justice H. G. Bunn vacated his position on the board and the office of president in 1899 and was replaced with fellow Little Rock layman, Charles F. Penzel, a Bohemian immigrant, Confederate veteran, and founder of Little Rock's German National Bank. During his two-year tenure, Penzel's chief contribution was financial; on different occasions he made personal donations to cover lapsed salaries and other debts. In 1901 Batesville banker James P. Coffin was elected to succeed Penzel. Coffin would serve more than twenty-five years as president of the board, still the longest tenure in the history of the college, often providing stability and a voice of reason and tradition in trying times. The college lost a valuable member of its family in September 1901 when Dr. John F. Allen, last of the original trustees, died in Batesville. Allen had been among the most generous supporters of the institution, coming to her aid more than once during his three decades as treasurer. His replacement was Allen N. Johnson, a Little Rock businessman and scion of the "Arkansas Dynasty" who had graduated from Arkansas College with Eugene Long in December 1878. Upon his death four years later, the board appointed as treasurer another Little Rock resident, Charles McKee. The day-to-day operation of the board continued to rest with the important executive committee, which during the first two decades of the new century was anchored by the two senior trustees, Coffin and Theo Maxfield.[35]

Eugene Long's faculty was equally stable throughout most of his administration. Daniel M. Frierson and Eugene Blandford both outlasted Long's second presidency at Arkansas College, and Charles F. Bizzell taught history and English until his resignation in 1911. In June 1899 Long, always the reluctant president, once again submitted his resignation. The trustees placated their overworked and underpaid president by sending Blandford on the annual summer canvass for students and by agreeing to hire a fifth faculty member. Don K. Brown, an 1898 alumnus and native of Fordyce, joined the faculty in the fall of 1899 as professor of Greek, a limited position that paid considerably less than the other teaching positions. When Brown resigned in 1902, Arkansas College reverted to a four-man faculty for a year before the board hired yet another alumnus, William S. Lacy. Lacy, a twenty-seven-year-old prospective minister, was a native of southern Arkansas and the lone graduate of the class of 1900. As we shall see, Lacy's value to Arkansas College lay not so much in his teaching ability as in his unparalleled effectiveness as a fund-raiser. Lacy taught Greek and philosophy for four years, now at a salary equal the other professors', and served a fifth year as financial agent for the college before leaving to enter a seminary in 1908. His successor was William Arthur Cook, a Westminster College (Missouri) graduate with a master's degree from Princeton who had taught at Park College in Missouri and Berea College in Kentucky. Cook's most valuable service during his brief time in Batesville may have been reviving the moribund library.[36]

The most significant alteration of the faculty during the early 1900s took place in 1908. In what was becoming a predictable ritual, Eugene Long once again submitted his resignation to the board in June 1908, asking to be relieved of his presidential, though not teaching, duties. Long agreed to rescind his resignation, however, when the trustees offered to appoint Frierson vice-president and business manager of the college, a first step toward hierarchy and modern bureaucracy. For an extra one hundred dollars a year, Frierson was given Long's previous responsibilities of collecting and disbursing fees and overseeing all advertising, catalog production, and canvassing. The extra burdens proved to be more than Frierson could handle—while continuing to teach all mathematics and science classes—and when Cook left in 1910 the board left the professorship of philosophy and Greek vacant in favor of hiring a mathematics professor to lighten Frierson's load. The new professor of math was middle-aged Nathaniel Smylie, an ordained Presbyterian minister who held bachelor's and master's degrees from Southwestern Presbyterian University and had most recently held the presidency of a small college in Mississippi. Students benefited from the division of mathematics and science because Frierson was able to devote more time and energy to laboratory buildup and instruction. The last new faculty member to join the Long administration was Andrew Lucas Whitfield, a former Cumberland Presbyterian minister who succeeded Charles Bizzell as professor of English and history in 1911. A graduate of Trinity College in Texas, Whitfield brought with him a bachelor's in divinity from Cumberland University in Tennessee and an honorary Ph.D. from Central University in Indiana.[37]

The modest expansion of the faculty during the new century's first decade was accompanied by a fiscal expansion for Arkansas College. The institution began to claw its way out of debt around the turn of the century due to the assistance of an unlikely source, former board president Thomas R. Welch. Although the minister had been dead since 1886 and his wife since 1891, the land and other gifts they bequeathed the college remained tied up in court for several years. Between 1899 and 1903 the board of trustees divested itself of a ten-acre orange grove in southern California and several lots in Little Rock that had belonged to the Welches for about $10,000. But such a relatively small sum of money was easily swallowed up in a struggling institution.[38]

Consequently, the synod kicked off yet another endowment campaign in the fall of 1900, this one in conjunction with the Southern Presbyterian Church's one-million-dollar Twentieth Century Fund drive. In an effort to generate $50,000 for Arkansas College, the synod hired alumnus J. Franklin Lawson, pastor of the church at Warren, to canvass the state soliciting funds. He was soon replaced in the field by the synod's evangelist, Rev. Xenophon Ryland. By June 1901, Ryland had raised more than $12,000, but much of it was in the form of scholarships that required donors to give only a percentage of a pledged amount on a yearly basis. The Twentieth Century Fund established three different kinds of scholarships. The first was actually a loan, which the student had to repay after graduation or separation from the college. The two regular scholarships included a "limited, non-transferable" one that covered only a relative of the donor or a student handpicked by the donor and a $1,000 "unlimited transferable" scholarship that could be applied to any student's expenses. By 1905 the college offered one loan and eight scholarships based on the fund's stipulations. Nevertheless, after the drive of 1900 and 1901 there appears to have been no more effort on behalf of Arkansas College's portion of the Twentieth Century Fund.[39]

With momentum from the synod's Twentieth Century Fund campaign sapped, the college trustees again faced the prospect of securing an endowment by their own initiative. In the summer of 1904 the board appointed new faculty member William S. Lacy to conduct the annual canvass for funds. The intense but effective Lacy proved to be a persuasive speaker and valuable college representative. In just about two months of work, consisting mainly of speeches to Presbyterian congregations around the state, he secured almost $850 in pledges and congregational offerings. Though typically several pledges were never honored, the canvass did produce funds sufficient for the modest remodeling and furnishing of the new students' home. Perhaps most promising for the college was Lacy's success in his native southern Arkansas, a region of relative Presbyterian strength but a source that Arkansas College had never successfully tapped. The following summer Lacy was again placed in charge of the state canvass, with the incentive that he could keep a percentage of the money raised. A second successful campaign produced approximately $775, which was used for dormitory repairs and for the purchase of badly needed equipment for the chemistry and physics laboratory.[40]

It did not take long for the board of trustees and the synod to realize what an asset they had in young Lacy. After another successful campaign in 1906, the trustees agreed to place Lacy in the field as full-time financial agent, the first in the college's history. Lacy embarked on his new mission in June 1907 at a salary of $125 per month plus expenses, considerably more than the current faculty salaries of about $1,000 a year. In the heady days surrounding his appointment, the trustees also dropped efforts to collect past-due Twentieth Century Fund notes and voted to expand the endowment goal to $75,000, an increase of almost fourfold. Lacy's campaign got off to a fast start and clicked along before it was derailed by a widespread financial panic in November 1907. The flow of dollars quickly dried up during the ensuing winter and spring. Nevertheless, in the five months before the panic Lacy managed to drum up endowment notes worth $13,700. By the time he left Arkansas College to enter Union Theological Seminary in Richmond in the late summer of 1908, Lacy's herculean efforts—at least when compared to past college fund-raising campaigns—had generated more than $17,000 in endowment notes and ten-year pledges and another $4,000 from Batesville citizens, which was earmarked for physical improvements. So impressed was a student writer in the *Index* that he suggested granting Lacy an honorary degree as "Getter of the Almighty Dollar for Religious Purposes." In their report to the synod in October 1908, the trustees estimated, perhaps optimistically, that more than three-quarters of the endowment notes and possibly half the ten-year pledges would be honored. Again, Lacy's effectiveness in southern Arkansas was evident. Almost three-quarters of the potential endowment came from areas south of Little Rock; the small town of Fordyce, with five notes valued at $2,550, even generated more money than Little Rock. College supporters in Texarkana, Junction City, Hope, and Stamps also contributed a thousand dollars or more to the endowment fund.[41]

Although Lacy had conducted the college's most successful fund-raising campaign, the results proved discouragingly familiar. A few years later Eugene Long observed that fully half the pledges secured by Lacy had either never been paid or had disappeared after only one payment. According to the president, less than a quarter of all endowment and ten-year pledges were paid promptly every year. To make matters worse the board had invested almost every penny, both in hand and on paper, generated by the campaign; most of the investments were loans to Little Rock businessmen or struggling Presbyterian congregations. Within a few years the returns from both the loans and the endowment notes began to dwindle. Furthermore, Lacy's departure in 1908 in effect brought an end to successful fund-raising efforts for several years. In the fall of 1909, at the insistence of Long and board president Coffin, the trustees hired former teacher and minister J. E. Latham as financial agent. But Latham's personal entreaties went largely unheeded, and Arkansas College's subsequent attempts to secure matching funds from the General Education Board amounted to nothing. By the time Woodrow Wilson, an old Southern Presbyterian himself and former brother-in-law of past board president A. Ross Kennedy, emerged as the Democratic candidate for president in 1912, disappearing endowment notes and ill-advised loans had forced the board of trustees into a familiar posture—on its knees begging for money.

The excitement surrounding the early days of Lacy's endowment drive and the steadily growing portion of the student body demanding boarding arrangements required the college to meet new standards of housing and modernization in order to stay competitive. Enrollment climbed steadily in the early twentieth century. In the 1907–1908 session, buoyed by Lacy's summer canvass, combined college and preparatory attendance reached a then record level of 115. Growing numbers of students from out of town, and especially from southern Arkansas, required Arkansas College to consider dormitory expansion. Since 1896 the college had maintained the third-floor boys' dorm, but girls and some boys had continued to board with local families. In the fall of 1903 Arkansas College purchased a spacious two-story home on Harrison Street a few blocks from campus to use as a dormitory. It first housed college students during the 1904–1905 session. In the spring of 1910, with more than half the 118 college and preparatory students coming from outside of Independence County, the board decided to build the college's first structure designed as a dormitory. The two-story native white sandstone building measured 107 feet by 41 feet and stood less than a block away from campus. Consisting of twenty-six double-occupancy rooms, a kitchen and pantry, and a bathroom on both floors, the new dormitory was designated for young women and opened during the 1911–1912 session.[42]

By the time the girls' dormitory was completed the college's other buildings had already experienced an infusion of modernization. In the spring of 1908 Batesville's City Board of Trade had begun working with college authorities on a plan to raise $5,000 for physical updates and improvements. Although the drive came up about a thousand dollars short, the funds covered the costs of connecting the campus with city water and sewer facilities and of installing a steam heating plant (complete with a boiler room, coal bins, and a forty-foot smokestack) in the basement of Alumni Hall. The steam heating system was connected to the Isaac J. Long Memorial Building as well as to the old college building. Furthermore, the locally raised funds also allowed the college to meet the city's mandate to lay sidewalks on the north and south sides

Arkansas College's male boarding students, 1898. The bearded man is Charles Bizzell, alumnus and longtime faculty member.

of campus along South (College) and Boswell streets. The year 1908 also witnessed the college's first large land acquisition when the Maxfield Bank and Trust Company, of which trustee Theo Maxfield was president, donated two and a half blocks east of campus for use as an athletic field.[43]

Physical expansion and modernization helped attract students, and, fortunately for the college, the persistent financial woes did not distract the student body from their studies or their extracurricular activities. One of the remarkable characteristics of college students, at Arkansas College and elsewhere and in all eras, has been their ability, whether by naivete or youthful vigor, to carry on with the collegiate life in the face of institutional and financial hardship. Throughout the turmoil of the post–Isaac Long era and in spite of the fiscal ups and downs, Arkansas College students forged a vibrant extracurriculum, one that complemented the primarily traditional and prescribed curriculum in ways intellectually, socially, and physically stimulating.

The oldest symbol of the extracurriculum, of course, was the literary society. Throughout the 1890s and early 1900s Arkansas College students maintained three societies: Erosophic and Philomathean for men and L'Etoile for women. Each society had its own hall; the Erosophic, because of its status as the youngest, used a room on the second floor of the Isaac J. Long Memorial Building while the older groups continued to hold meetings and programs in the old college building. A description of the Philomathean hall written in the spring of 1907 noted impressive furnishings: a five-light chandelier, three drop lights and a wall light, new opera chairs, and a Brussels carpet. In the absence of fraternities, literary societies tended to take on the characteristics of secrecy and comradery and, for the young men at least, competition. Societies adopted official colors and concocted competitive yells. But the societies also continued to serve their traditional purpose of intellectual and social gratification on a small college campus. Professor Eugene Blandford found the literary societies essential for their "practical application of much that was not secured in the classroom."[44]

Although literary societies gradually lost their position of prominence in the extracurriculum to athletics in the years surrounding the turn of the century, their programs and presentations honed members' speaking, writing, and debating skills and added an integral element to college life. Each society held periodic programs and participated with other societies in the presentation of joint programs. Each program was organized and carried out completely by students. A typical program was the one sponsored by the Erosophic Society on 6 December 1897. E. C. Lynch opened the night's events with an oration entitled "What's Next?" D. K. Brown's essay, "The Influence of the Bible on Modern Civilization," followed and preceded the program's highlight, a debate between W. S. Lacy and T. E. Radford over the resolution: "That free institutions in the United States are now in danger." W. C. Norment then read "The Death of Julius Caesar," followed by A. E. Miller's declamation on "Man's Immortality." After R. J. Morrow's discussion of current events, Guy Powell concluded the program with an oration, "The Hero of the Future."[45] By the early 1900s joint sessions or celebrations involving all three societies were common, often taking place on George Washington's birthday, the traditional date of the Philomathean intermediate celebration. Joint programs generally featured musical performances in addition to the orations and recitations.

By the early twentieth century, both male literary societies annually awarded gold medals for speaking excellence to a new member. The societies also inaugurated intersocietal contests. Beginning in the spring of 1906, the Philomathean and Erosophic societies held an annual contest, usually a "double debate," the winner of which was rewarded with a banner to be displayed in their hall during the ensuing year. The Philomathean boys won the first year's contest, but within a few years the rivalry grew so ugly that the college canceled the competition. It was reinstated, however, in the spring of 1915. Although the Stayton Medal, the William and Mary mathematics medal, and other nineteenth-century awards were gone by the early twentieth century, various alumni continued to sponsor student medals. Beginning in 1914 an

Members of the L'Etoile Literary Society, c. 1899.

"Orator's Medal," sponsored by an alumnus, was awarded to the winner of the annual Inter-Society Oratorical Contest; one year later another college graduate established the "Essay Medal," to be awarded each spring for the best essay submitted by a female student. The early twentieth century also marked the establishment of what was to become the college's longest-running student award. In 1906, Charles Coffin, son of board president James P. Coffin and a member of the class of 1884, anonymously established the "Alumni Medal." The Alumni Medal, which Coffin paid for, was to be awarded annually by the faculty to both a male and female graduate whose "average standing during the last three years of the College course has been the highest, provided that standing reaches an absolute grade." The first Alumni Medal was awarded to George McKee, the lone member of the class of 1907. After Coffin's death

Members of the Erosophic Society, 1912–1913.

in 1916, one of his classmates permanently endowed the award, which was renamed the Charles H. Coffin Alumni Medal. Eventually limited to only one senior regardless of sex, the Coffin Medal remains the highest honor bestowed upon a graduate of the college.[46]

Although the activities of the literary societies often contributed elements of secularism to the extracurriculum, many of the Philomathean and Erosophic boys also held membership in one of the various organizations focusing on the Christian tradition at Arkansas College. The most successful and longest lasting of these was the Young Men's Christian Association. YMCA activity on the Arkansas College campus dates back to the 1880s, but the twentieth-century incarnation of the group stemmed from an official reorganization effort during the 1893–1894 session. The YMCA held weekly Sunday afternoon Bible study meetings in its hall in the old college building. By the early 1900s the YMCA boys also gathered for a midweek prayer meeting. For several years the organization also maintained a mission Sunday School on the outskirts of town. In the spring of 1914 female students organized a chapter of the Young Women's Christian Association. A directory of college organizations compiled in the fall of 1896 also listed a Missionary Study Class and a Workers' Training Class. In the early twentieth century, ministerial candidates formed their own organization as well.[47]

There were other extracurricular diversions also. In the spring of 1896 female members of Augusta Malone's elocution class presented a dramatic reading of the Greek play "Sappho." The first play staged by college students may have occurred more than a decade later when in April 1909 the wife of Eugene Blandford directed a student presentation of "Mrs. Wiggs of the Cabbage Patch." Praised as "the best amateur play ever seen in Batesville" by the *Index*, it was encored a few nights later; the student thespians even took their show on the road to play before a Newport audience later in the month. Such was its impact that a writer for the *Index* began clamoring for an annual student play, a call unheeded in the years before the First World War.[48]

Music also played an increasingly prominent role in campus productions. Vocal and instrumental performances had been included in commencement exercises and society programs since the earliest days of the college, but in the early twentieth century a college orchestra was formed and recitals began to appear as programs in their own right. One of the earliest surviving records of such an event documents a piano recital that took place in Alumni Hall on 6 May 1907. The program featured thirteen solos and three duets, all performed by the female students of a Miss Burton. Selections ranged from such light fare as Merkel's "In the Green Meadow" to more challenging works such as Chopin's "Prelude, Opus Twenty-Eight." After music became a regular part of the curriculum in 1911, students organized a glee club, an orchestra, and a musical group called the Gamut Club, and recitals and performances became regular features of college life.[49]

For those more inclined to literary endeavors there were student publications. The original *Arkansas College Magazine*, whose rise was chronicled in the previous chapter, ceased publication after April 1893. Three years later student editor C. P. Radford and

Members of the Philomathean Society gather in their hall located in the original college building.

members of the three literary societies revived the *Arkansas College Magazine*, maintaining a format and style similar to that of the earlier one. The new *Arkansas College Magazine*, like most college papers of the day, featured student articles and essays, excerpts from national news publications, local gossip, correspondence from other college newspapers, alumni news, and coverage of literary society events. The most notable difference from the old magazine was the new *Arkansas College Magazine's* heavier emphasis on athletics. The June 1896 edition was the first to feature an "Athletic Department," and the various accomplishments of basketball and baseball teams received a steadily increasing amount of attention in the pages of the magazine.[50]

After this version of the *Arkansas College Magazine* disappeared in the spring of 1898, the college went without a student publication until November 1906 when the first issue of the *Index* made its appearance. The oldest surviving issue of the *Index* (from December 1906), edited by junior Horace Sloan of Lawrence County, featured five student essays on such topics as "Good Roads" and "The Evolution of Government," several editorial musings, an exchange section with news from other colleges, and sections entitled "Local," "Athletic," "Alumnal," and "Query." Like the *Arkansas College Magazine* before it, the *Index* relied primarily on advertisement revenue, and the last few pages were devoted to Batesville's merchants. Each issue cost ten cents, but an entire session's worth could be purchased for seventy-five cents. The spring of 1907 marked a historic occasion in student publishing at Arkansas College; the eighty-eight-page double issue of the *Index* was the first publication resembling a modern yearbook. Dedicated to the memory of Isaac Long, the large issue contained photographs of faculty, societies, students, and athletic teams in addition to the normal fare contained in the *Index*. The lone senior pictured in this first yearbook represented the emergence of a new breed of college go-getter. Little Rock native George Taylor McKee was president of the Philomathean Society, business manager of the *Index*, manager of the baseball team, a member of YMCA, and golden voice of the college quartet. Remarkably he had also found time to study, enough time to complete the curriculum in only three years. Despite the popularity of this yearbook-style issue and its reported boon to enrollment the following fall, it would be more than a decade before the *Index* transformed itself into an annual yearbook-style publication.[51]

By the time the *Index* arrived on the campus of Arkansas College, athletics had claimed a position of prominence above all other elements in the extracurriculum. Organized and team athletics first arrived at Arkansas College around 1890 and the importance of sporting events grew throughout the subsequent decades. In the 1890s and early 1900s student publications made reference to a number of activities: fencing, fishing, hunting, boxing, gymnastics, rowing, and others. Arkansas College students were not unique in their growing obsession with athletic events. The era in question marked the rise of football, the most popular sport on most American campuses, and the emergence of the culture of college athletics. At Arkansas College, as at many denominational institutions, the emphasis on athleticism blended nicely with current views of Christianity and with perceptions of antiquity. This was also the era of Dwight Moody's "masculine Christianity"; Billy Sunday, baseball player turned evangelist, was becoming the ideal role model for young Christian men around the country. This spirit of the age reached Arkansas College by way of John I. Cleland, Eugene Blandford, and Daniel Frierson. Cleland established the college's first gymnasium class in the spring of 1896. The athletic Blandford, in an article published in the *Arkansas College Magazine*, praised the character-building element of sports and deemed athletics necessary for producing a young "man in all the strength, power, and beauty of true manhood."[52]

Throughout most of the period covered in this chapter athletics remained an unofficial, student-organized component of college life, much like literary societies or the early literary magazines. Track and field, basketball, and other sports began to take on a quasi-official, faculty-sanctioned air during the brief Cleland administration, but the return of traditionalist Eugene Long meant several more years of peripheral existence for sports teams and events. As early as the fall of 1896 individual student athletes formed an athletic association and contributed money to a fund used for the purchase of athletic equipment, but it was only around 1900 that an official Athletic Association was formed. The Athletic Association was open to any male student who was willing to pay the fifty-cent fee. Despite the presence of faculty authority, students maintained complete control of their association, electing their own coach and manager. In the early years the coach was generally an older student himself or a faculty member such as Frierson or Blandford, though by the latter years of Long's administration roving athletes were often brought in for a month or more to serve this purpose. The college did not hire a full-time director of athletics until 1914 when V. A. Wilber, former coach at Hendrix and a noted athlete, joined the faculty as a preparatory teacher and coach.[53]

In 1907 the Arkansas College Athletic Association joined the newly formed Arkansas State Athletic Association in order to bring some sense of regularity and order to intercollegiate competition. Within a few years college athletics in Batesville began to assume some of the characteristics of the modern system. The college Athletic Association developed into a committee composed of two faculty members and several students, and student athletes were required to meet certain eligibility standards regarding class loads and academic performance. The growing influence of athletics also affected the curriculum; beginning in 1914 all students were required to participate in a varsity or intramural athletic club at least two hours per week.[54]

It appears that America's pastime was the first semi-organized sport to interest college students in Batesville. The first issue of the *Arkansas College Magazine* in March 1890 mentioned baseball playing among college students. In light of Thomas J. Stubbs's role in championing baseball at William and Mary in the 1890s, it is probable that the sport was played even earlier at Arkansas College. The first mention of competition between a college team and an outside squad appeared over two years later when the *Magazine* reported in October 1892: "Base ball seems to be at fever heat." The article noted with enthusiasm the recent 27 to 12 victory of the "College Nine" over a club at Greenbrier, an Independence County community across the river from Batesville. The student reporter praised the hitting of Leland Kennedy, E. F. Matheny, Harry Bunn, and Joe Kennedy and the hustling of Miller Joblin. According to the article, the defense of second baseman Octave Williamson was above reproach, and the glovework of shortstop Joe Bevens was "out of sight." Three weeks later on 29 October, Arkansas College's team defeated the boys from the "free school," or public high school, in Batesville by the score of 24 to 22.[55]

Due to gaps in student publications and in Batesville newspapers from the era, little is known about Arkansas College's baseball team during the decade and a half after 1892. In the critical years of the 1890s it is likely that college enrollment fell to the point that organizing a team became impossible. But Cleland's emphasis on athletics and the arrival of athletes Blandford and Frierson kept sports at the forefront of student activity. By 1900 an open section of the campus had been set aside as a baseball field; according to the college bulletin published that spring, this was done so that the faculty could supervise the players. The same bulletin also featured a photograph of the college team, the first picture of an athletic club in an Arkansas College publication. By the spring of 1907 baseball still ranked as Arkansas College's most consistently popular sport, though basketball was gaining ground and the emergence of football lay just around the corner.[56]

In the first years of the new century a baseball game challenged the old intermediate celebration of the literary societies as the college's most notable spring event. By 1907 the annual game against the town team of Sulphur Rock, "reported to have the best amateur team in the Northern part of the State," had become an occasion for studied excess on the part of the student body. Each year the baseball team and a gathering of fans from the college piled into carriages for the ten-mile ride to Sulphur Rock. "The fluttering pennants, the inspiring yells and the encouraging faces of the College maids could have no other effect upon our team than to cause them to win." And win the college team did in 1907, 23 to 5, behind the expert battery of Edgar Rogers on the mound and Asa Drew behind the plate. By 1908 the game had become an afterthought, just a sublime prelude to the much-awaited moonlight picnic afterward.[57]

The spring of 1908 also marked Arkansas College's first season in the Arkansas State Athletic Association and the school's first regularly scheduled matchups with other colleges. The baseball team bought new uniforms, a catcher's mitt and chest protector, and new bats and balls, but lost their star player when Edgar Rogers left school to join a semiprofessional team at Helena. Playing their home games on a rented field, the college team won only two of eight games against Ouachita, Henderson, and Hendrix; in addition they lost both games to Newport's town team. The following season got off to a bad start when a new railroad line through the old ball field forced the boys to put up a backstop on campus. Again, Arkansas College proved no match for its three rivals. The 1912 season brought Arkansas College its first intercollegiate athletic championship when the baseball team, coached by former star Rogers, bested the four other schools in the association: College of the Ozarks at Clarksville, Normal at Conway, Hendrix at Conway, and Ouachita at Arkadelphia. Inspired by the championship season, an enthusiastic student sports editor urged each Arkansas College student "to make an effort to secure new recruits for next year's team and especially pitchers." His readers must have obeyed for Arkansas College repeated as champs in 1913 under new coach V. A. Wilber. The college's key players in the 9–3 season, according to the *Index*, were pitcher and shortstop David Shepperson, second baseman Edward "Pig" Bridgers, and diminutive T. R. "Doc" Brown, the best catcher in the state, all three from southern Arkansas. Two years later the baseball team withdrew from the State Athletic Association, apparently in protest over the "professionalism" of other teams, but continued to play Hendrix, Ouachita, and Henderson.[58]

Varsity basketball at Arkansas College was permanently established during the 1913–1914 session. But, as we saw at the beginning of the chapter, students had participated in the caged sport intermittently since the late 1890s. During Cleland's administration students transformed the campus chapel, Alumni Hall, into a gymnasium by stacking movable chairs on the stage at the front of the small building. The hall was home to the college's first basketball game in December 1896 when a team of college boys, organized by former Little Rock YMCA captain and current student Eugene Bracy, beat a Batesville team 28 to 15; President Cleland served as referee in that game. Two months later the college boys played a practice game against a makeshift opposition consisting of Charles Bizzell, Eugene Blandford, and preparatory instructor J. Garnett

Wood along with a few players from the town team. The college team followed this easy victory with triumphs over the Little Rock YMCA and Hendrix College, the first recorded intercollegiate athletic contest for Arkansas College.[59]

Inexplicably, enthusiasm for the new sport died rapidly. The major obstacle to establishing a successful basketball team at Arkansas College was the lack of a gymnasium. Soon after Eugene Long's return, Alumni Hall ceased to serve as a makeshift gym, forcing interested students to erect a goal behind the chapel. The sport survived in the early twentieth century as an intramural activity. In January 1912 the *Index* mentioned a Philomathean team; it is likely that the Erosophic Society, not to be outdone, formed a squad of their own. By the following fall it appears that the college once again sported a team; in November 1912 the college boys, now directed by a Coach Buchanan, lost to Batesville High 16 to 18. Arkansas College's first intercollegiate basketball competition of the twentieth century actually grew out of intramural activities on campus following the construction of the college's first gymnasium, Erwin Gymnasium. In the fall of 1914, Coach Wilber, with the assistance of English and history professor W. F. Rogers, organized the young men into class teams for the purpose of stimulating intramural competition. From these class teams Professor Rogers selected a varsity team of six players. The first varsity basketball team, led by J. Richard Brown and Max Brown, won all three of its home games in the new gymnasium (two over Hendrix and one against Cabot High) and won three of six games on a four-day road trip through Conway, Arkadelphia, Stamps, and Hope. The stop in Conway included a night game with Hendrix on an outdoor court lit by "small electric lights . . . scattered promiscuously around in the tops of the trees." Although the team did not officially participate in the State Athletic Association, the confident sports editor of the *Index* assured readers that "in a few years [Arkansas College] will probably have one of the best teams in the South."[60]

Basketball also afforded young ladies the opportunity for athletic competition. Again, Cleland's influence was prominent in introducing female sports. In January 1897 the *Arkansas College Magazine* mentioned the formation of a girls' basketball club. The boys and girls used Alumni Hall on alternate days, and the girls shut the blinds to prevent the boys from catching glimpses of such unladylike activity. By 1908 the young women had formed intramural teams, the Reds and the Blues. It appears that as early as 1911 a girls' college team competed against a basketball squad from Batesville High, and the May–June 1912 issue of the *Index* featured a photograph of the women's basketball team.[61] Of course, organized intercollegiate competition for women lay far in the future.

Football, the sport most associated with the rise of modern college athletics and the collegiate age, was a late arrival on the campus of Arkansas College. The tiny student body likely provides the best explanation for the college's lack of a team in the late nineteenth and early twentieth centuries. Football made a brief appearance, in an unofficial capacity, in the early 1890s before disappearing for almost two decades. By 1896 the *Arkansas College Magazine* was pleading, "We can and must make foot-ball and basket-ball features of our sports." But the declining enrollment

Arkansas College's first basketball team, 1897. The young men wearing suits are professors Eugene Blandford (*left*) and Little Dan Frierson (*right*).

of the Cleland years rendered such a statement hopeless. Even after the Maxfield Bank and Trust's donation of a large plot of land in 1908, the college Athletic Association continued to fail in its efforts to organize a football team.[62]

The first serious effort to establish varsity football took place in the fall of 1911. Professor Blandford agreed to train the team, and the Athletic Association secured a temporary coach. But Coach Stein left after only one game against Batesville High. After failing to field a squad the next year, Arkansas College played its first varsity football game in the fall of 1913. New president J. P. Robertson recruited coach John Adamson from Sherman, Texas, and his team lost both games that fall. On the first day of October the college team fell 12 to 0 to the Aggies from the First District State Agricultural School in Jonesboro in what was most likely Arkansas College's first intercollegiate football game. The first real season, however, came the following autumn under the direction of new coach V. A. Wilber. Thirty boys, more than half the number enrolled in college, went out for the team. The play of the Arkansas College Lambs apparently befitted the ill-chosen moniker. In an all-or-nothing season, the Lambs defeated weak Little Rock College twice but lost to Hendrix, Christian Brothers College, Henderson-Brown, and State Agricultural School by a combined score of 146 to 0. The only close match was the college's 6 to 0 loss to the Aggies from Jonesboro. The preparatory team, the Midgets, had better luck and defeated Batesville High 48 to 0.[63]

Just as it had done on countless other campuses across the country, football conquered the extracurriculum at Arkansas College. There must have just been something about the crisp fall air and the thuds and cracks of body-to-body contact. Whatever the reason football was seen as the glory sport, and at Arkansas College it hastened the march toward a modern conception of collegiate athletics. The dormitory girls, chaperoned by the president's wife and the dorm matron, threw a party in late November 1914 to celebrate the Lambs' less-than-stellar season. The 1914–1915 session also witnessed the establishment of the college's first letterman's club, the "'A' Association." Among the athletes awarded letters for the year were twenty football players, ten basketball players, and nine baseball players. Three students, J. Richard Brown, Thomas Rush Brown, and Hamilton Patton, earned letters for all three sports.[64]

The big three sports certainly maintained center stage, but Arkansas College students participated in other athletic activities and competitions around the turn of the century. The first sport to gain widespread popularity among both sexes was tennis. The issues of the *Arkansas College Magazine* from the late 1890s contain numerous references suggesting the appeal of tennis. By the early 1900s college students had access to three tennis courts, two on campus and one at the students' home. Track and field also attracted a few followers in the early days. Likely due to the influence of new faculty member Eugene Blandford, Arkansas College sent representatives to the state Inter-Collegiate Athletic Contest in the spring of 1897, probably the college's first participation in intercollegiate athletics. Commencement week in 1897 also featured a new highlight when faculty and students showcased a field day for visitors. The fall of 1897 witnessed a gymnastics exhibition for the public in Alumni Hall. Although there is no evidence of success in the endeavor, a group of students in the fall of 1909 tried to organize a rowing team to take advantage of the placid White River waters in the eight-mile stretch between locks one and two. Cross-country racing also experienced a brief surge of popularity. On 30 March 1908, the college Athletic Association sponsored what it claimed was the first five-mile cross-country race held in Arkansas. B. B. Conine, a student from the little village of Moorefield east of Batesville, took the silver cup for first place. Two years later he repeated his victory in another cross-country race in Batesville and anchored the college's state record-setting two-mile relay team at the state track meet in Little Rock. The rise of organized intercollegiate competition a few years later, however, tended to quash such peripheral fare.[65]

Although Eugene Long understood the allure of athletics for twentieth-century teenagers and realized that Arkansas College must keep extracurricular pace with other schools to stay competitive in the recruiting field, he seems never to have reconciled the demands of a new age with his disdain for its curricular effects. In his 1908 faculty report to the board of trustees, Long reacted with caustic sarcasm to the challenges facing traditional education: "(S)hould balloon ascensions, air-ship maneuvers, etc., soon become as common in our communities as moving picture shows, skating rinks, theatricals, peripatetic base ball teams, etc., some method should be devised to attach these as leading parts in the curriculum of schools and colleges, which, of course, should continue to carry some scholastic studies as a side line!"[66]

The final years of Eugene Long's presidency marked a time of change and conflict as Arkansas College experimented with curricular changes and struggled against financial constraints. Most of the time the increased emphasis on athletics was simply a mild diversion compared with other developments. The students matriculating at Arkansas College and other American institutions in the 1890s and early 1900s represented a new generation. The Collegiate Age was in full swing, and the motives and expectations of college students differed significantly from those of an earlier age. Most often the mindset of the new student, who was more likely than ever before to view college as a means to securing a comfortable job or as an avenue of socialization, struck traditionalists as abhorrent. In his 1904 faculty report to the board of trustees, Long, though barely past forty, had already begun to strike the pose of his late father, that of the disenchanted, cynical old classicist. "While many students evince gratifying interest in their work, we are impressed with a growing on the part of an increasing proportion to avoid laborious application to studies that require serious application. It is not a sign of promise in the educational world that such an increasing number are encouraged by parents to avoid those subjects which require the greatest mental effort."[67]

Five years after the president's pained observation, the board of trustees agreed to institute significant curricular changes. The first change undertaken involved a general loosening of the traditional, prescribed course of study. Beginning in 1910 all courses of study at Arkansas College led to the bachelor of arts degree. The decision to discontinue the B.S. degree did not represent a conscious effort to elevate the curriculum to a more traditional liberal arts standard. Rather, according to the new curricular guidelines, the A.B. at Arkansas College would come to resemble the old B.S. Following the example set by other colleges and universities as early as the 1860s and 1870s, the new Arkansas College curriculum included rigidly prescribed freshman and sophomore years followed by a limited system of electives in the final two years. The most notable casualties under the new curriculum were the ancient languages. Greek received a lethal blow, albeit one that would kill the subject gradually over several years. The curriculum adopted in 1910 made Greek totally elective by allowing students to substitute French or German. Latin, though still prescribed for all freshmen and sophomores, was reduced to elective status after the second year. Only the traditional Bible class maintained its three-year requirement.[68]

Under the new curriculum a freshman at Arkansas College in the 1910–1911 session took classes in five areas within a mostly prescribed course of study. Long's Bible class covered biblical history up to the reign of David. Nathaniel Smylie taught the newcomers plane and solid geometry. English consisted of advanced rhetoric and composition under Professor Bizzell, and Eugene Blandford grilled students on Cicero's orations and Livy. Each freshman also chose among Greek, German, and French and was expected to study the same language for two more years. Sophomores faced five prescribed classes in addition to their chosen language. Bizzell's medieval and modern history, which required three essays from each student, was similar to later western civilization courses. Little Dan Frierson taught beginning physics, a required course for anyone seeking a degree. Sophomore mathematics consisted of trigonometry and analytic geometry. Eugene Long's students finished the historical study of the Old Testament, while Latin class featured readings from Horace, Plautus, and Terence.[69]

Although juniors and seniors did not exactly enter the cafeteria of freedom, they did have choices within the limited range of subjects. Required upper-level courses included psychology, logic, ethics, the history and problems of philosophy, New Testament history (using the textbook written by Isaac Long), government, political economy, English literature and language, American and English literature in the nineteenth century, chemistry, astronomy, and geology. The handful of electives from which interested students could choose included modern constitutions, history and philosophy of education, history and philosophy of religion, junior and senior Latin and Greek, differential and integral calculus, plane surveying, advanced physics with emphasis on laboratory work, and organic chemistry.[70]

It was during this era that the college began to further regularize admission standards and procedures. For several years all entering freshman had been expected to display a mastery of the subjects taught in the college's preparatory division; a student showing any deficiency was expected to complete the particular subject or subjects in Arkansas College's preparatory school before advancing into college work. Beginning in 1909 the college began to narrow its choices of topics for entrance essays. Freshman enrolling in the college that fall were required to complete a satisfactory essay on one of four works: Edmund Burke's essay, "Moving His Resolutions for Conciliation With America," George Eliot's *Silas Marner*, Shakespeare's *Julius Caesar*, or James Russell Lowell's poem, "Vision of Sir Launfal." Three years later the choices were narrowed to three: Shakespeare's *Macbeth*, George Washington's "Farewell Address," and Carlyle's "Essay on Burns."[71]

The second curricular change was a more obvious one and grew out of the synod's desire for true "co-education." As we saw in the first chapter, Arkansas College, quite by accident, had embarked on a rather modern coeducational program, one in which young women were expected and required (with a few noted exceptions) to meet the same standards and take the same classes as their male counterparts. This, of course, was not the norm in Arkansas. The Baptists and Methodists of the state maintained separate institutions for men and women into the twentieth century, and where coeducation did occur, young women were provided with musical and artistic alternatives to mathematics, Latin, and other studies considered at odds with the workings of the female mind. Female students at Arkansas College had always had access to music classes and lessons, but such studies had never been absorbed into the official curriculum and had always required additional fees.

By the early twentieth century there was a movement afoot within the synod to establish a separate female college. In the fall of 1908 the synod gave its official approval to the female college plan, and leaders in Little Rock immediately secured pledges amounting to $25,000 if the proposed college could be located in the capital city. Though the separate college idea apparently had the support of a majority of Arkansas College's faculty and trustees, the $40,000 the synod attempted to raise outside of Little Rock may as well have been $40 million. Anyone who had ever tried to raise funds for Arkansas College could probably have sensed the futility of the effort. By the fall of 1910 it was clear that the synod's plan for a female college in Little Rock would never materialize. Consequently, the synod appointed a committee headed by Rev. J. L. Caldwell of Pine Bluff to discuss the needs of coeducation with the trustees of Arkansas College. As a result of these talks, the college trustees agreed to build a girls' dormitory and to modify the curriculum and degree courses by incorporating "feminine" subjects such as music and art on an equal footing with traditional subjects.[72]

As classes got under way in the fall of 1911, there was a different look and sound to the small Batesville campus. For one thing, the small children were gone. At the board's meeting the previous June, the trustees had voted to eliminate the primary department and all other precollegiate instruction with the exception of three years of preparatory school. Charles Bizzell, after sixteen years teaching history and English, had resigned after the last session to enter the insurance business. His successor was A. L. Whitfield, a forty-five-year-old minister and veteran educator who, along with his wife, was placed in charge of the new girls' dormitory. The new Young Ladies' Home, as the dormitory was named in the absence of one large donor, also housed the music and art departments. Three young single women joined the faculty to handle the new offerings: Genevieve Rutherford for piano instruction, Nell Jordan for voice, and Floy Nesbitt in art.[73]

The purpose of the new course in music (piano), according to the college catalog, was to "lay a foundation for musical knowledge, to develop a love for the beautiful, and to promote intellectual growth." The college also attempted to integrate the study of music into the wider curriculum by stressing the "relation of music to the general literary studies." Piano instruction followed a six-grade format beginning with rudimentary studies and building up to instruction in selections from Beethoven, Schumann, Chopin, and Liszt. Miss Rutherford also offered two years of harmony and a class entitled "History of Music." Students completing the first five grades as well as one year of harmony and History of Music were awarded teaching certificates; those completing the entire course were eligible for a music diploma. Although the college catalog did not specify the certificates or diplomas available to voice students, Nell Jordan utilized the "Italian method" through a four-year course that built from basic breathing and sight singing exercises to advanced performances of German, French, and Italian operas. In 1914 the board of trustees approved the degree of B.M., bachelor of music. Students who completed the first two years of the A.B. course and the full slate of musical offerings qualified for this new degree. Art offerings appear to have been more limited. Nesbitt offered two general courses: object drawing in pencil, charcoal, crayon, pen and ink and oil, water color, pastel and China painting. Only advanced studio work beyond these elementary classes, however, could be counted toward the A.B.[74]

The expanded curriculum and faculty brought on by Arkansas College's coeducational efforts demanded increased funding, most of which was not met by expanding tuition receipts. Furthermore, by the spring of 1912 the college was more than $5,000 in debt on the new Young Ladies' Home. Eugene Long, who had been the largest individual donor to the dormitory fund and had spent two months during the summer of 1911 helping prepare the building, was particularly disappointed that only $1,500 was forthcoming for the dorm fund from the Batesville community. Part of the problem may have been poor timing, for simultaneously the Presbyterian Church in Batesville was attempting to raise more than $10,000 for a new church building. Almost all the money generated by the earlier endowment drive was by this time tied up in loans, thus putting the college in a poor position to meet immediate demands for cash. The synod attempted to help alleviate the debt by scheduling a day in February 1912 and another the following December to collect congregational offerings for the college, but the underpublicized events failed to produce the desired results.[75]

Caught in the middle of this all-too-familiar situation was President Long. In an inexplicable and unprecedented move, Long had been appointed to the board of trustees in the fall of 1911, and in December of that year was elected chairman of the executive committee, the most demanding job on the board. Long suddenly found himself in a situation similar to that faced by his father almost forty years earlier. In addition to his classroom and administrative duties, to say nothing of the various other civic and church-related responsibilities of the overextended man, Long faced the daunting prospect of getting the college out from under the weight of the dormitory debt, all at a salary of $1,500 per year. By December of 1912 Long was complaining to his good friend and former brother-in-law, Arthur G. Jones, that he could "never see a place for a let up" from the sixteen-hour days he had been burdened with since the session began. In early January 1913 Long wrote to Jones, who lived in San Antonio, Texas, requesting a private meeting later that month to discuss something that Jones had mentioned before. It is likely that that something was a new job. On 22 February 1913, Eugene Long submitted his resignation to the board, to take effect at the end of the session. By now Long had resigned at one time or another about half a dozen times, but this one was no threat or implicit request for relief of some sort. Near the end of his letter Long announced that he had already agreed to take a new faculty position at Austin College in Sherman, Texas, which Arthur G. Jones served as trustee.[76]

Once again the Long era at Arkansas College came to an end. Counting the three and a half years he served as acting president after Isaac Long's death, Eugene Long had served roughly nineteen and a half years as college president, besting his father's tenure by just a couple months. He had overseen the recovery from the Cleland interregnum and had watched the little college grow steadily throughout the first dozen years of the new century. Although the curriculum, extracurriculum, and physical campus had undergone obvious alterations in recent years, Arkansas College still resembled, at least in spirit, that tiny school of fewer than fifty students in which Eugene Long had enrolled in 1872. But Long, recently turned fifty and still grieving the death of a beloved nephew a year earlier, had had enough of fiscal deficits, bickering Calvinists, and unconcerned townsfolk. Referring to the presidency as "this intolerable situation," Long informed the board that he "realized fully that I was between the upper and the nether millstones—that of pronounced apathy on the part of the great majority of the synod on the one hand, and even greater local apathy on the other hand." He also warned that he saw little hope for increasing enrollment as long as the college suffered from pitiful student housing and no athletic facilities.[77] In the summer of 1913 Eugene Long said good-bye to his aging mother, the only family he had left in Batesville, and took his wife, Sallie, and niece Margaret to Texas to begin anew.

The board of trustees reacted to this "most serious crisis" by appointing four of their number as a "look out committee" charged with finding a suitable replacement. Organized searches still lay in the college's future in 1913, which meant the search for a new president was quite informal. According to the board's instructions, the committee was to correspond with "men mentioned as desirable, and any others . . . deemed eligible." In an unintentional mud-in-the-eye move, the board repeated its actions following Long's resignation eighteen years earlier and voted to increase the president's salary by 20 percent to $1,800. This was obviously an unintentional slight, for at their next meeting, in an attempt to retain Eugene Long on the faculty, the trustees voted to create the I. J. Long Memorial Chair of Bible and called on the synod to raise $30,000 for its endowment. At a special meeting in March, trustee Rev. Joseph I. Norris of Pine Bluff nominated fellow minister Fred Graves of Helena, a middle-aged Georgian with a degree from Southwestern Presbyterian University. The board offered the presidency to Graves, only to have him decline the position in late April. When the board reconvened the following month, Theo Maxfield nominated Arkansas College alumnus J. P. Robertson, and Robertson accepted.[78]

Rev. Jerome Pillow Robertson was the second alumnus to be named president of Arkansas College and the first native Arkansan to hold the title. A native of the Mississippi River Delta town of Marianna, Robertson had received his A.B. degree from Arkansas College in 1886 and his A.M. in course three years later. With the exception of three years in Virginia, he had spent the previous quarter century pastoring various Presbyterian congregations in Texas and establishing a reputation as a friend of higher education. Austin College had rewarded his efforts in the latter field by bestowing upon him an honorary D.D. degree in 1910. At the time of his election to Arkansas College's presidency, Robertson was fifty years old and pastor of the church at Paris, Texas, a position he had held for six years.[79]

The transition from Long's administration to the era of J. P. Robertson also occasioned a drastic overhaul of the faculty. Long's resignation was immediately followed by the resignations of the two junior faculty members, math professor Nathaniel Smylie and English and history professor A. L. Whitfield, both of whom reentered the ministerial field. Though he did not resign, Eugene Blandford became ill over the summer holiday and was unable to resume his duties as professor of Latin and modern languages when classes opened in September 1913. He sat out Robertson's first session on leave of absence before leaving Batesville in 1914 to recover his health. Students in the fall of 1913 may have suspected they had returned to the wrong campus until they saw Dan Frierson, the lone remaining faculty member from the previous year. Robertson was given near complete autonomy in recruiting new faculty. The new president imported Austin College graduate Earl R. Parker as professor of physical science and placed Vice-President Frierson in charge of mathematics. Eugene Stuart Gregg assumed the professorship of philosophy and Greek, a position that had gone unfilled for the previous three sessions, and took charge of the library. Robertson also hired A. Deane Johns, the first woman to hold a full-time academic faculty position at Arkansas College. Johns, who had been a high school teacher and acquaintance of Robertson in Texas, had also studied English in graduate school at the University of Virginia. Blandford's unexpected absence left the faculty one member short during the 1913–1914 session. His duties were parceled out to other faculty and student instructors until January 1914 when Robertson hired recent graduate Victor Wade to teach Blandford's courses for the rest of the year.[80]

Robertson's second year witnessed another infusion of new blood in the faculty. Lewis D. Amis, son of a Presbyterian minister, replaced the ailing Blandford as professor of Latin and German. V. A. Wilber joined the school as preparatory teacher and director of athletics; his wife joined the staff as matron of the Young Ladies' Home. Thomas Dawes, a graduate of London's Trinity College of Music, replaced Genevieve Rutherford as piano instructor, and Lucy Fitzhugh assumed the vacant voice teacher position. Arkansas College also replaced its first instructor in expression with Lillian Elizabeth Owens, as well as increased the number of faculty members with master's degrees from legitimate graduate schools. W. F. Rogers, a graduate of Ouachita College with a master's degree from Princeton, replaced Earl Parker as professor of physical science, and Ida M. Hillerman, a graduate of the Mississippi College for Women who had earned a master's degree at Columbia University, took Johns's place as professor of English and history.[81]

Although his tenure would ultimately be almost as brief as Cleland's, Robertson did not face many of the problems that John I. Cleland had in replacing Eugene Long. In some ways the outpouring of regret and grief over Long's unexpected departure actually helped Robertson's administration get off to a positive start. Long's accusation of widespread apathy and his dire predictions for the college's future apparently had an effect both in Batesville and throughout the state. In the four months following his resignation, various churches and individuals in Arkansas contributed a total of about $2,500 to the college, about three times the previous session's collection. The largest donations ($500) came from new trustees A. H. Whitmarsh of Texarkana and W. C. Brown Sr. of Stamps. While this unexpected windfall helped chip away at the dormitory debt and lapsed salaries, Batesville citizens rallied to remedy Arkansas College's lack of athletic facilities. Spurred by Long's remarks and perhaps also by the competition from the newly established Batesville Business College, a group of prominent merchants and professionals, the Citizens' Committee on College Improvement, held a meeting in downtown Batesville in May 1913 to discuss the possibility of raising up to $8,000 to be used for new construction and improvement of existing buildings. This meeting generated about $1,000 from those in attendance and promises for more. One month later the Citizens' Committee announced the college's largest cash gift to date, a donation of $3,500 by local bank president Maj. W. J. Erwin. Citizens' Committee representatives Dr. R. C. Dorr and Paxton Thomas presented the gift to the college trustees on the condition that the money could only be used for the construction of a gymnasium. Erwin Gymnasium, which eventually cost the college about $700 more than the original gift had supplied, opened for student use in January 1914 with athletic equipment, a bowling alley, and showers. Under the supervision of Coach Wilber, boys and girls used the gymnasium on alternate days.[82]

Robertson's administration, buoyed by the frantic construction and physical improvement of the summer, jumped out to a positive start. The new president and first lady hosted a reception for students on the first Friday night of classes, a gala highlighted with songs and dramatic readings by the new voice and expression teachers and ice cream for all. The massive defection of students predicted shortly after Long's resignation the previous winter failed to materialize, and college enrollment actually increased by almost 25 percent to 119. By January Arkansas College had its first gymnasium (albeit one with a smaller-than-regulation basketball court), and an additional $4,000 worth of repairs and upgrades improved the overall appearance of the campus and its buildings.[83]

Encouraged by a successful first year, Robertson undertook several administrative and curricular changes. It was he who suggested the board adopt the bachelor of music degree in the spring of 1914, and the following year Robertson convinced the board to introduce a pedagogy course. Robertson adopted a detailed list of entrance requirements for freshmen; primarily following the guidelines established by the newly founded Southern States Association of Colleges and Secondary Schools, the new requirements consisted of fourteen units in mathematics, English, Latin, science, and ancient history. The new president managed to reinstate the old inter-societal contest that had been abandoned a few years earlier, and organized the first permanent student body organization. He also established the college's first demerit system for behavior. Though the new disciplinary system was not a traditional honor system in that the faculty and administration oversaw its operation, each student was required to sign a pledge to "observe all regulations . . . [and] exert themselves towards the preserving of order." The demerit system penalized students for certain infractions (for instance, an unexcused absence from class earned five demerits and a missed examination ten) and expelled any student collecting at least sixty demerits. Under Robertson's direction the college opened its first on-campus bookstore; managed by faculty members, the store offered for sale textbooks and supplies as well as school pennants, pins, banners, and other signs of growing college pride. Robertson also introduced the mandatory senior thesis as a requirement for graduation, and assembled what may have been the college's strongest faculty to date for the 1914–1915 session. When science professor W. F. Rogers resigned at the close of that session, Robertson recruited Elmer R. Sims, a young man who was just completing a master's degree through the University of Chicago. Sims, who spent seven years as director of a Cuban mission college, also offered Arkansas College's first classes in Spanish in the fall of 1915. The success of the first year influenced a quite significant hike in tuition and fees. At their June 1914 board meeting the trustees accepted Robertson's recommendation of raising tuition from fifty to sixty dollars per year and of instituting thirteen dollars' worth of new fees to help cover library, gymnasium, and science laboratory costs.[84]

But the halcyon days seemed always to be few in Batesville. The depression created by the onset of the First World War and the increase in tuition and fees took their toll on enrollment for the 1914–1915 session, resulting in a decrease of more than 25 percent from the previous year's total. In December 1914, while the students were back home for Christmas break, the boys' dormitory (the old Rutherford home the college had acquired almost a decade earlier) burned to the ground, forcing college authorities to scramble to acquire living arrangements for out-of-town boys. Robertson and the trustees decided to house the boys in the Young Ladies' Home, a move that eventually became permanent, and sent the homeless girls to board with President Robertson or the wife of an alumnus in town. And by the spring of 1915 financial problems had begun to resurface. The costs of the physical improvements of the previous year had not been completely met by local donations, and several old debts had never been retired. By May 1915 the board owed more than $2,000 in back salary and had begun borrowing money to pay debts using college property as collateral.[85]

But ultimately it was another familiar threat to the college's integrity that ended the Robertson era. At their fall meeting in 1914 the synod once again broached the topic of moving the college, and rumors circulated widely that Robertson himself had proposed relocating the institution to Arkadelphia. In the past the threat of moving the college had usually been followed by a flurry of activity and spending on the part of Batesville supporters. Oddly, this time the subject of a possible relocation arose after just such a flurry of activity. Just as Cleland had done when faced with the Three Mile controversy eighteen years earlier, Robertson, who had no familial ties to Batesville, stood by while others came forward to defend Batesville's right to the school. Robertson informed the board of trustees that his position as chairman of the synod's committee on schools and colleges prevented him from actively lobbying against any proposed move. However, the mere fact that Robertson had been placed in this position was proof enough for many of the college's supporters that their president was not opposed to relocation. Although there is no surviving evidence indicating that Robertson was pressured to leave, in late June, just a couple weeks after the board's spring meeting, he submitted his resignation to take effect 1 July 1915. Robertson reentered the ministry and would never again hold intimate affiliation with an institution of higher learning. Another brief but eventful post–Eugene Long presidency had drawn to a close.[86]

At a special meeting to accept Robertson's resignation and consider the future, the trustees agreed to divert the endowment income to pay off outstanding bank loans and to cut their on-campus losses by closing the short-lived bookstore. The trustees announced the hiring of alumnus and former faculty member E. D. "Van" Brown as financial agent for the summer. (Rev. James H. Morrison of Holly Grove took over fund-raising efforts in early 1916, but with the same poor results.) To replace Robertson the board appointed Little Dan Frierson, easily the college's senior faculty member, as acting president and chairman of the faculty.[87]

Frierson's charge was simply to keep the college afloat until (it was hoped) a dynamic new president could be recruited to rescue the faltering school. Frierson's job was not as simple as it sounded. Although the college benefited from the return of all its faculty members for the 1915–1916 session (except, of course, Robertson), the lack of a president and the uncertainty of Arkansas College's long-term stability combined with the terrible flood of 1915 to reduce college enrollment by more than 40 percent to the lowest level since the immediate post-Cleland era. More pressing were the ever-present financial problems. The severe operating deficit of the previous session had forced the board to take out an additional $3,500 in loans from Batesville banks. Each year brought additional cancellations of endowment notes and pledges as donors went bankrupt or lost confidence in the college's ability to survive; by early 1916 this dwindling source of income failed to match the college's loan payment requirements.[88]

By the time the trustees convened for their midterm meeting in late February 1916, it was obvious that Reverend Morrison's campaign for funds was meeting with little success and that drastic action was necessary if Arkansas College was to be saved and maintained in Batesville. Whereas the fiscal catastrophe of the Cleland administration had influenced the board to retrench and look to the past in the person of Eugene Long, the financial crisis of the World War I era spurred the trustees toward administrative modernization. Realizing that "in modern education, a strictly teaching President is out of date," the trustees agreed to seek "a man whose business it is to represent [the college], not in the class room, but before the people—a man who can go out and present the cause of the College, and lay everything before the people of the synod, show its needs and its possibilities for the future."[89] What the college needed now was a business-minded, charismatic leader who could convince Batesville residents and the Presbyterians of Arkansas that little Arkansas College was worth saving and best kept in Independence County. What Arkansas College needed was a master fund-raiser. What the college needed was a man like William S. Lacy.

PART II: 1917–1937

On 15 April 1927, White River reached 42.8 feet at Batesville. Beyond mere flood level, this rise signaled a natural disaster unmatched in twentieth-century Arkansas. The flooding of the White River bottoms represented one small appendage of the great flood of 1927, which threatened lives, homes, and livelihoods throughout the expanse drained by the Mississippi and its tributaries. Unbridled torrents and rising backwaters engulfed communities, swept away houses, and kept farmers from their fields during the crucial planting season. Few Arkansans, either directly or indirectly, escaped the wrath of rising waters in the spring of 1927, a spring of torrential rains coming on the heels of an unusually snowy winter on the Plains and in the Ozarks. Few institutions escaped immediate danger or the economic and social aftershocks of devastation.[1]

If the flood of 1927 did not usher in the Great Depression for Arkansans, it was certainly a harbinger of things to come. It was a particularly ominous and crucial event—what under any other circumstance a historian might refer to as a watershed—in the development of Arkansas College. Just one month to the day before the river's crest at Batesville, a group of college and Presbyterian leaders had launched a $750,000 expansion campaign for Arkansas College, the most ambitious undertaking in the school's fifty-five-year history. In the coming months and years it would seem as if the college's lofty dreams had somehow been washed away amid the mud and driftwood in that terrible spring.[2]

Although the flood had little effect on the normal operation of the college in the spring of 1927 (beyond being an obvious source of curiosity for students and posing a potential health threat should the dank waters dally in receding) it serves as a useful symbol for the two decades beginning in 1917. Taking place in the exact middle of the era now in question, the flood illustrates the polarities of experience at Arkansas College in the 1920s and 1930s. The post–World War I era ushered in an unprecedented period of optimism, expansion, and prosperity. But the spirit of progress and promise soon vanished in the face of almost insurmountable barriers, both of the natural variety and of the man-made kind. Consequently, the late 1920s and 1930s marked an era of extreme uncertainty, the most treacherous in the college's history, and a time of poverty and trepidation more strident than the prosperity and confidence of the previous decade. In this way the experience of Arkansas College during the interwar years mirrored that of most American institutions. More specifically the story of Arkansas College represented in microcosm the triumphs and defeats of tens of thousands of Arkansans in the two decades after World War I.

Chapter 3

"Heroic and Pathetic in the Extreme"

The tiny campus of Arkansas College was abuzz on Tuesday, 6 June 1922. The grounds and buildings had not witnessed such excited and boisterous crowds since local farmers had invaded campus a dozen years earlier to hear the spellbinding oratory of William Jennings Bryan. The throng that snooped and chatted on this late spring day was likely more subdued than the agrarians had been, though perhaps equally intent on merry making. The occasion was Arkansas College's semicentennial celebration. Among those in attendance were three members of the first graduating class—Charles Maxfield, Mary Maxfield Fitzhugh, and T. J. Horne—and many more current students whose parents were only children when Isaac Long died thirty-one years earlier. Eugene Long was there, as were trustees James P. Coffin and Theo Maxfield. Although the four buildings on campus were familiar to almost everyone, most took the opportunity to walk the six blocks up the hill to view construction progress on the new boys' dormitory, a magnificent structure that rivaled any modern college building in Arkansas. In the shadow of this dormitory lay the college's new football field. On the heels of the most lucrative fund drive in school history, the physical changes had come fast and furious in the last few years, permeating the college community with a sense of destiny and triumph. Times, it seemed, had never been better. The semicentennial celebration provided a symbolic bridge between the college's past and future. Men like Long and Coffin were physical links with the beginning. Within a few years they would pass from the scene just as their institution was undergoing its greatest changes. Arkansas College was entering the modern era.

In many respects Arkansas College students and faculty received their first tastes of twentieth-century collegiate life only after World War I. Spurred by blossoming enrollments and an infusion of much-needed money, the decade following the war witnessed unprecedented dormitory construction, the purchase of a new campus, curricular experimentation, and extracurricular developments, such as a new football field, an honor code, and the introduction of fraternities and sororities. All these developments promised to bring Arkansas College into line with the modern world of the college campus and its burgeoning youth culture. Unfortunately, once the economic tide began to turn, the setbacks to college advancement materialized just as furiously. Consequently, the depression decade brought economic retrenchment, narrowing of the curriculum and extracurriculum, and recurring threats to the very existence of Arkansas College.

The man most associated with all this excitement, both the heady days of the early 1920s and the lowest days of the Great Depression, was William Stokes Lacy, whose two separate presidencies provided bookends to the twenty-year period in question. Although "white knight" is not an epithet his contemporaries would likely have used when describing the stern, laconic Lacy, he seemed always to be riding to the rescue of his alma mater, scooping her up into the security of his strong will, and simultaneously resuscitating and defending her in the face of formidable foes. His three separate stints of employment at Arkansas College attest to his effective leadership and tireless effort as well as to his grating self-righteousness and peculiar ability to grow irksome even in the company of friends.

But a teetering little Presbyterian college can scarcely afford to reject a cross personality when it accompanies a successful money-raiser. And so it was when Arkansas College began the search for a president in early 1916. Extenuating circumstances had rendered the decision more critical than usual. In addition to the uncertainty occasioned by the escalating war in Europe, a rare late summer, White River flood in 1915 decimated blooming cotton fields in much of eastern Arkansas, and the flood's economic repercussions compounded recruiting problems caused by the recent departure of president Jerome P. Robertson. College enrollment for the 1915–1916 session dropped to fifty, and the preparatory branch counted only twenty-four students. With Little Dan Frierson overseeing the school's operation for the year, the board of trustees in February 1916 unanimously elected William S. Lacy president. They also nominated prodigal son Eugene Long, then in his third year on the faculty of Texas's Austin College, to the chair of Bible and political science. Long's decision to turn down his alma mater's offer for a more promising position at Hampden-Sydney College in Virginia in the spring threatened to derail the board's plans, for Lacy had agreed to accept the presidency only if his mentor Long would be at his side in Batesville. Apparently the board was able to assuage Lacy by promising to continue recruiting Long and by hiring alumnus and former faculty member Rev. Evander D. "Van" Brown as vice-president and dean of the faculty. Brown, a former president of Daniel Baker College in Texas who had spent the preceding decade as a minister in southern Arkansas, assumed his position in the summer of 1916 and served as interim president until Lacy's arrival.[1]

Brown's tenure as interim president turned out to be longer than he expected. In the fall of 1915 Lacy had accepted a position as Bible instructor and field secretary (fund-raiser) at Peace Institute, a Presbyterian-controlled female college and academy in Raleigh, North Carolina. Having just launched a fund-raising campaign at the time of his election to Arkansas College's presidency, Lacy asked that he be allowed to complete his work at Peace before moving to Batesville. As a result he did not physically assume his new position until January 1917.[2] Nevertheless, absence from the state did not prevent Lacy from making his presence known to his Presbyterian brethren in Arkansas.

Lacy's delayed arrival in Batesville seems to have contributed to a latent movement to restructure Presbyterian higher education in Arkansas. As we have seen Arkansas College had faced periodic challenges from leaders in areas with more substantial Presbyterian constituencies. After all there was no denying that, as far as Arkansas Presbyterianism was concerned, Batesville was on the Calvinist frontier if not altogether beyond the pale. At the October meeting of the Synod of Arkansas, several ministers and laymen began discussing the possibility of raising money for the establishment of a new Presbyterian college in Little Rock. Under this plan Arkansas College would be downgraded to junior college status, in essence a feeder school for the larger Little Rock institution.[3]

If the goal of this whispering campaign was actually to found a new college then it ultimately failed. If, however, the purpose of this threatened revolution was to light a fire under the leadership of Arkansas College (and this is very unlikely) then it succeeded beautifully. Upon hearing of this potential Presbyterian mutiny, Lacy rushed back to Little Rock for a special December meeting of the board of trustees. He sought assurances from the board and synod that the rumors had no basis in fact. Lacy warned his listeners that he would not come back to Arkansas College if it were to be made a junior college. More importantly, the new president came armed with a plan for expansion that dwarfed all previous campaigns and that, if carried out properly, would forever squelch the naysayers who continually undermined the church's confidence in the little college. Because one of the most common criticisms of Arkansas College concerned the inadequate condition and size of the campus and buildings, Lacy proposed to raise $100,000, including a $50,000 matching grant from the General Education Board (which never materialized), to be used for the immediate renovation of current buildings, the construction of a new boys' dormitory, and the purchase of a new campus on the heights east of town. In addition, Lacy called on the board to sponsor a campaign to raise an endowment of $300,000. The new president's strategy of facing criticism head on worked. The board heartily approved his ambitious plans and authorized the executive committee, working in conjunction with a Batesville banker, to immediately set about purchasing land for the new campus. As an incentive to ensure Lacy's diligence, the trustees promised him a $600 raise after $50,000 had been added to the endowment. Lacy's bold vision especially impressed the non-Batesville trustees, who quickly took the initiative in carrying out his plans.[4]

Such boldness in the face of potential opposition would have been unthinkable for most people, especially first-time presidents. But, as the people of Arkansas College and of Arkansas were about to find out, William S. Lacy was not like most people. Forty-two years old when he arrived in Batesville in late January 1917, the sixth president of Arkansas College was a short, narrow, ramrod-straight man with a demeanor to match. A straight-talker with a zealot's belief in the cause of Christian higher education, Lacy could also effect a certain charm in social situations, though his ability to summon this lighter side seemed to diminish with age. With his wide puritanical streak and penchant for penury, he was well suited to the demands of the presidency of a small southern Presbyterian college. While Lacy's "dour incivility" may have rendered him a perfect foil for the wild college crowd of a Fitzgerald novel, he was a perfect fit for his cash-strapped alma mater.[5] In many ways his life's experience and work had prepared him for the job.

Lacy was born near El Dorado in Union County on Halloween 1876 into a prominent Presbyterian family. His grandfather, also named William S. Lacy, was a pioneer minister in southern Arkansas who helped organize several congregations before the Civil War. His uncle, Beverly Tucker Lacy, had served as Stonewall Jackson's chaplain, and a great uncle had labored as president of Davidson College in the late antebellum period. After earning his A.B. at Arkansas College in 1900—he was the only member of the graduating class—Lacy spent three years as principal of a Presbyterian academy in Indian Territory and was ordained to the ministry. Following his five years on the faculty of Arkansas College, including his successful endowment drive in 1907, he moved to Richmond to attend Union Theological Seminary, from which he received the bachelor of divinity degree in 1911. Lacy lent his considerable fund-raising talents to the seminary, serving as an assistant field secretary and later as head of the endowment drive. He left Richmond in 1911 to become pastor of a church in Belmont, North Carolina, the only pastorate he would ever hold, and from there went to work for Peace Institute in Raleigh.[6]

Lacy's fund-raising skills and experience were already in demand when he physically assumed his duties as president. By late January 1917 the executive committee, chaired by local physician R. C. Dorr, had already purchased approximately fifty acres in the East End Heights Addition worth about $7,000. All transactions were to be paid in full, at 6 percent interest, within the year. In addition, due to recent operating deficits and building demands, the college owed $3,500 to local banks and $8,500 to the endowment fund of the board of trustees. Lacy immediately set about erasing the college's debts and raising funds for promised physical expansion and improvements. In fact, the raising of money and recruiting of students seemed to be his only real mandates. William S. Lacy was Arkansas College's first modern president; unlike his predecessors, he was not burdened with classroom duties and not confined to campus during times when class was in session. The blossoming hierarchical faculty structure, with Van Brown as vice-president and dean and Dan Frierson as second vice-president (essentially bursar and treasurer), even freed him from most administrative duties. Lacy's campaign led to further modernization and stratification of the college's administration. Responding to the increased flow of funds, both incoming and outgoing, in 1921 Arkansas College hired board secretary and Batesville resident J. L. Boggs as college treasurer (a part-time position with a salary of $600), and by the fall of 1922 Boggs had his own office in the Long Memorial Building. In essence then, for the time being at least, Lacy was president turned field agent.[7]

Not surprisingly, Lacy first delivered his vision for the college's expansion and his entreaties for money to the people with whom he was most familiar—the Presbyterians of southern Arkansas. The congregations south of Little Rock had proved fertile ground ten years earlier, and Lacy hoped to repeat his success, but on a much larger scale. Within a month of his arrival, Lacy had received pledges from Presbyterians in southern Arkansas totaling $24,000, including a $5,000 promise from Texarkana lumberman and college trustee A. H. Whitmarsh. The tireless president rarely spent a Sunday in Batesville; instead, he traveled from one Presbyterian congregation to the next delivering sermons and extolling the virtues of Arkansas College. He continued to dedicate a significant amount of time to cultivating friendships and interest south of Little Rock, but Lacy was also careful to maintain positive relations with Batesville citizens. At a June 1917 meeting various Batesville businessmen endorsed Lacy's goal of $300,000 and organized a local campaign to raise $50,000. In words that could have come from Lacy's mouth, the business representatives warned readers of the *Batesville Guard:* "Let there be no slackers or shirkers in the movement."[8]

By the end of the 1916–1917 academic session there was reason for cautious optimism in Batesville. Still, Lacy and the trustees had plenty to worry about. College enrollment for the session was the lowest in twenty years, and the spring commencement showcased but two graduates. An operating deficit for the third consecutive year forced the board to borrow an additional $3,500 to cover faculty salaries. Furthermore, the American declaration of war in the spring of 1917 led several male students to leave school and enlist in the military, a trend that would continue into the following session. Mindful of the increasing difficulties of recruiting young men to the college classroom during wartime, Lacy hired a female canvasser for the summer of 1917. But there were also triumphs for Lacy. Pledges continued to amass, though not at a pace necessary to raise $300,000 in five years, and the trustees granted Lacy and the executive committee the authority to start construction on a new dormitory once the college had received three-quarters of the building's projected cost. More importantly for Lacy the college succeeded in bringing Eugene Long home to Batesville. Dissatisfied with the "so called Christian education" at Hampden-Sydney, Long gladly returned to the more conservative and familiar confines of Arkansas College to teach Bible and to replace his former student, Van Brown, as dean. The college had once again established a direct link with its founder and founding, and Long's third and final tenure with his alma mater would prove to be longer than his first.[9]

Although the next couple of years brought setbacks, the endowment drive began to produce results unrivaled in Arkansas College's poor history. The first windfall came in November 1917 when aged Henry Moore of Texarkana, Texas, presented the school with a gift ten times larger than any single benevolence ever before received by the college. Moore's gift of $40,000 in gold coupon bonds of the Louisiana and Arkansas Railway Company established the first endowed faculty position at Arkansas College. The James Wilson Moore Chair of Biblical Instruction, named in honor of Henry Moore's father, the titular father of Presbyterianism in Arkansas, would be funded by the $2,000 generated annually by the railway bonds. The James Wilson Moore Chair was promptly awarded to Eugene Long, and he would maintain this position for the rest of his life. The college's second substantial World War I–era gift came barely more than a year later when in December 1918 the four children of late board member W. C. Brown Sr. donated $15,000 in liberty bonds. Unlike Moore, the Browns did not earmark the approximately $700 per year produced by the bonds, which allowed Lacy and the board to put the funds toward salaries, physical improvements, or other pressing demands. Fortunately, Arkansas College's fruitful relationship with the Brown family was just beginning.[10]

Lacy was certainly not about to turn away such significant gifts, but the college also needed immediate inflows of cash that were not available in endowment donations. By March 1918 Arkansas College still faced a $9,000 debt. To make matters worse, on 13 December 1917 the college's only dormitory, a native stone structure on Boswell Street southeast of campus, burned to the ground and with it most of the school's winter supply of coal. The $2,500 insurance policy would provide only a fraction of the money needed to build a spacious new dormitory of high quality. Consequently, the trustees decided to sell six lots on Harrison Street, site of a boys' dormitory a few years earlier, and the tract of land that trustee Theo Maxfield had donated for use as an athletic field. The money generated by the land sales and insurance settlement paid off most of the standing debt, which left the pressing matter of building not one but two dormitories.[11]

It was at this point that the war actually became an asset to the college. The increased demand for American goods as a result of war in Europe sent agricultural prices skyrocketing between 1917 and 1920. Cotton, which fueled Arkansas's economy and by extension affected the well-being of all the state's institutions, reached 23.5 cents per pound in 1917, an increase of 50 percent over 1910, and peaked in 1920 at almost 34 cents. The results of this agricultural prosperity for Arkansas College were a significant rise in enrollment, despite the absence of many young men in military service, and a noticeable quickening of pledges and endowment payments. During the 1917–1918 session, the treasurer of the board took in more than $22,000 in endowment payments, many of them on previously unproductive notes. The sudden prosperity also rendered audiences more receptive to Lacy's requests for money.[12]

Arkansas College experienced the effects of wartime via the increased flow of money, but an event in 1918 brought the war effort directly to campus and introduced the federal government to the tiny denominational college for the first time. In August 1918 Congress approved a bill establishing the Student Army Training Corps (SATC), a cooperative program through which the federal government would pay colleges and universities to provide both collegiate and vocational training to prospective officers. According to the bill, in order to qualify for an SATC unit a college had to have had a male enrollment of at least one hundred students during the 1917–1918 session. Although Arkansas College's male enrollment barely exceeded one-quarter of that, President Lacy decided to make a bid for a unit. Just as classes were getting under way in early September, Lacy and Batesville insurance agent E. C. Parsons traveled to Washington, D.C., to plead the college's case. Inexplicably, the college was awarded a small unit of fifty students. Lacy hurried back to Batesville to oversee the hasty erection of a wooden barracks on the site of the burned dormitory and the recruitment of

Cadets of the Student Army Training Corps (SATC) holding maneuvers on the college grounds, 1918.

young men for the Arkansas College SATC. The Batesville Chamber of Commerce raised $5,000 in thirty minutes to help defray the estimated $8,000 cost of the barracks, a miraculous show of charity that some intimates of the college must have greeted with raised eyebrows.[13]

There was a financial motive behind Lacy's effort to obtain an SATC unit. Under the government's plan, colleges would receive about $100 a month per student soldier during the life of the program. Arkansas College had been fortunate to earn $100 a year from its civilian students. Working under the watchful eye of army inspectors, construction crews completed the two-story barracks, with a partially submerged basement, in about a month's time, and in October fifty young men moved into the barracks to begin their training. The army provided a unit commander, Capt. W. L. Barry, and a uniform curriculum that was taught mostly by current preparatory faculty and other community members recruited for their excellence in a needed field. Most of the young SATC cadets hailed from within a fifty-mile radius of Batesville, though some came from as far away as Yellville and Camden and three from out of state. The heavy representation from the counties north and west of Batesville injected an element of rural upland culture hitherto quite rare on the college campus, a promise of things to come. But the SATC provided only a brief excitement for Arkansas College.

The unit had been in operation a month when the warring nations signed an armistice on 11 November. The army demobilized the college's SATC unit on 20 December 1918. Arkansas College received an enrollment boost when several SATC men decided to return after Christmas. Four SATC students eventually earned degrees.[14]

By January 1919 the only reminders of Arkansas College's brief flirtation with the military were updated science laboratories, as mandated by army inspectors, and the barracks on Boswell Street. The latter surreptitious bequest turned out to be the first of three dormitories built during Lacy's administration. The college had been without a dormitory since the December 1917 fire, and the necessity of procuring rooms in boardinghouses and with college friends and faculty threatened to curtail enrollment at a time when peace and prosperity promised to fill college classrooms. When new students arrived in Batesville in September 1919 they found two dormitories on the block southeast of campus. At a cost of about $10,000, Lacy and the board's executive committee had overseen the remodeling of the SATC barracks into a twenty-nine-room boys' dormitory. The boys' dormitory, later christened Willis Hall after Newport benefactor Dr. Lemuel Edwin Willis, featured a sink with hot water in each of the rooms, community showers, and a kitchen and dining room in the basement. The busy summer had also produced a girls' dormitory on the west side of Willis Hall. Standing diagonally across Boswell Street from the Isaac J. Long Memorial Building, the two-story Welch Hall, named in honor of Arkansas College's first board president, provided rooms for unmarried female faculty members in addition to out-of-town female students. Welch Hall cost about $11,000 and sported a distinctive look with brown-stained weatherboards on the ground floor and a stuccoed upper level topped by gray-green shingles. Each room contained a sink with running water, white enameled bed frames, a dresser with mirror, and a table and chairs. Ida Hillerman, professor of history and English, was placed in charge of the girls in Welch while President and Mrs. Lacy moved into Willis Hall to monitor the young men. Because residents of Welch Hall took their meals in the dining area located in the Willis Hall basement, college officials soon constructed a covered walkway between the two dormitories that a generation of students would refer to as the Dixie Highway.[15]

Arkansas College experienced little trouble filling the dormitories in the following years. Like institutions across Arkansas and around the nation, the college watched as enrollment climbed quickly in the post–World War I era. Academic enrollment (excluding music and speech) at Arkansas College grew 40 percent between the 1919–1920 session and the 1920–1921 term, prompting Lacy to boast: "(T)he past year has been one of decided progress and probably the best in the history of the College." By the fall of 1922, enrollment (preparatory and college) had reached a record level of 173, including a freshman class of 60 students. Despite this significant growth, Arkansas College continued to lag behind other Arkansas institutions in terms of size. By comparison, Hendrix College in Conway and Henderson-Brown College in Arkadelphia enrolled about twice as many students, and the student body at the University of Arkansas was about eight times as large in the early 1920s. Even

Mountain Home College, a Baptist junior college that had reopened during the war, enrolled as many students as Arkansas College.[16]

But for Batesville's college this was unprecedented growth. By the early 1920s the increasing number of boarding students and the changing demographics of college campuses had convinced Lacy that two small dorms were grossly insufficient for a modernizing college. Luckily for him and for the board of trustees wartime prosperity had begun to fill the long empty coffers of Arkansas College. In the spring of 1920 Lacy's endowment drive topped the $100,000 mark. In spite of the ominous fact that less than $9,000 of this total had been in the form of traditional endowment notes, the trustees in June 1920 noted "with great satisfaction the large amount of money collected for the College during the past year, the prosperous condition of the College and the wholesome condition of its finances."[17] Two major reasons for such optimism were the receipt of more than $18,000 from the will of Dr. L. E. Willis, most of which was used to erase the college's debts, and recent synod actions that greatly increased the college's share of congregational benevolence offerings. Although prices for cotton and other crucial agricultural commodities dropped drastically after 1920, Arkansas College continued to prosper. The June 1921 meeting of the trustees found the college in the black for the first time in years, and the following academic session produced an operating surplus of more than $6,000.[18]

This sudden financial success and security inspired the most ambitious construction project in the first half century of the college's existence. In October 1921 workers began clearing ground on the new East End Heights campus for the erection of a massive (at least by Arkansas College's standards) boys' dormitory estimated to cost $80,000. The architect's plans called for a V-shaped, Lombard Romanesque style, two- or three-story brick and native stone structure with rooms for one hundred students and a kitchen and boiler room in the basement. Built between the new football field and South Street (now College Street), Independence Hall, as it was later named, was completed in the spring of 1923 and first opened to students the following fall. In addition to the furious construction of dormitories and the completion of the college's first football field, Lacy oversaw other physical improvements during his administration. The older campus buildings underwent extensive renovations in the postwar era, and cash expenditures significantly strengthened the science laboratories and music department. In 1921 Erwin Gymnasium was transformed into a library. The lack of a replacement gymnasium took its toll on indoor athletics in the 1920s, but the transformation permitted Arkansas College to claim the only building used exclusively as a library on any college campus in the state.[19]

The need for a separate building and the hiring of a full-time librarian reflected the steady expansion of library holdings; nevertheless, by 1923 Arkansas College's 7,500-volume collection remained insufficient for an effective college library. The curriculum also branched out in the immediate postwar years, but not in any radical directions. For the most part Lacy's presidency was one of brick-and-mortar expansion and money raising, not of curricular innovation. In the nine years that Lacy had been

Groundbreaking ceremony for Independence Hall, 1921. Standing on the platform with open Bible is President W. S. Lacy; directly beneath him, leaning on the platform, is Eugene Long. The man holding the shovel is James P. Coffin, president of the board of trustees from 1901 until 1926.

absent from the college, music and expression had been absorbed into the regular curriculum—the result of the synod's decision to bring "co-education" to Arkansas College—and the ancient languages had been pushed to the periphery by the growing importance of science. In addition the college had begun experimenting with a limited system of electives. Despite these changes the curriculum in 1917 did not represent a significant departure from that of a decade earlier; it certainly shared more in common with the plan of study of Isaac Long's day than with the modern system.[20]

Due to the demands of Lacy's modern presidency, most curricular adjustments and changes that occurred during his presidency were the result of faculty initiative or a desire to tap into subjects currently in vogue at other institutions. An example of the former was the two-year premedical program established by young science professor John B. Daffin in the fall of 1922. Examples of the latter included the establishment of a commercial department and a course of study in domestic science. The commercial department, first taught during the 1919–1920 session by Kittie Sanderson, was in essence a course of study for secretaries (shorthand, typing, and spelling) and as such was limited to young women and classified under preparatory instruction. Women also provided the clientele for domestic science, or home economics. Begun during the war under the tutelage of Mrs. Leland Bunch, home economics consisted of a series of food preparation classes until 1922 when new instructor Ruth Merrick introduced additional classes in sewing. Commercial classes, however, were never accepted as credit toward the A.B. degree, and home economics became an accepted and regular part of the curriculum only in 1924. Due to lack of interest and budgetary concerns the commercial department was discontinued in 1925, and as a result of financial straits and the proliferation of similar high school courses Arkansas College dropped home economics in 1929. Neither of these two new departments fit into the traditional liberal arts curriculum and both attracted students from among the college population and the town at large. The existence of both, as well as the premedical program, reflected a tradition of minor experimentation at Arkansas College as well as the efforts of a small denominational college to meet the demands of its surrounding region and a fickle constituency.[21]

By far the most significant curricular change of Lacy's administration was a restructuring of the degree program in 1921. Since the introduction of electives a decade earlier, students seeking the A.B. had continued to face a mostly prescribed course of study with freedom to choose a foreign language and with most electives relegated to the senior year. Beginning with the 1921–1922 session, the Arkansas College faculty directed students into one of four courses of study: classical, science, modern language, or English and history. This marked a first step in the direction of the modern system of majors and minors. The classical course, which quickly proved the least popular among students, was the only one of the four to require Latin (three years of it) and placed a heavy emphasis on traditional subjects such as English and mathematics. The science course was geared heavily toward the study of chemistry, but even science majors faced two years each of German and French. The modern language course was for the most part indistinguishable from the English and history course except for the former's concentration on languages beyond the sophomore year. Within each course of study the curriculum was mostly prescribed, and all students were required to take three years of Bible, at least two years of mathematics and English, and one year each of physics and chemistry.[22]

Influenced by the unwieldy and confusing nature of the four-course program and perhaps even more so by the general education movement sweeping the nation's institutions of higher learning in the early 1920s, Arkansas College made further adjustments to the curriculum and degree program before the 1922–1923 session. Influenced by the SATC's "War Aims" courses, which were in effect early examples of western civilization surveys, and academic reactions to perceived negative effects of the elective system, the general education movement argued that there existed a core set of studies or courses (thus the term *core curriculum*) that should serve as a foundation for any student's college education. The result of this movement at Arkansas College was the reinstatement of the prescribed courses for freshmen and sophomores, and an altered "major" system in which students chose between three areas of concentration resembling the language, science, and English and history courses of study from the previous year. The curriculum underwent further cosmetic modernization in the fall of 1922 when the faculty adopted the modern semester hour system for tabulating student credits.[23]

A major reason for Arkansas College's attempts at curricular modernization in the early 1920s was an infusion of new blood into the faculty after World War I. Although the size of the faculty failed to keep pace with the burgeoning student body in the postwar years—only one new position was added to the regular faculty during Lacy's tenure—Arkansas College benefited from the addition of a group of talented and experienced young professors and instructors during Lacy's administration.[24] Veterans such as Eugene Long and Dan Frierson welcomed the first of these postwar newcomers in the fall of 1919 when R. C. Sommerville, a handsome Hampden-Sydney graduate, came to Batesville to teach mental philosophy, ethics, and French. Sommerville was appealing to Arkansas College as a Presbyterian (though the college never officially barred teachers of other denominations from the faculty) and as a representative of a disappearing breed of southern Christian academicians trained in a mostly classical curriculum. Although he held no university graduate degree, he was a devout Christian in the mold of Lacy and had spent seven years running small female Presbyterian colleges in West Virginia and Texas. Two other similar men arrived the following year, and both would leave an indelible imprint on Arkansas College students of the 1920s. Redden Kirby Timmons was middle-aged when he left his position as president of Stillman Institute, a seminary and preparatory school for young black men in Tuscaloosa, Alabama, to become dean and professor of history and Spanish at Arkansas College. A graduate of Davidson College and Union Presbyterian Theological Seminary in Richmond, Timmons had served three years as a missionary in Cuba and had spent most of his career in the ministry. He was joined in the fall of 1920 by a young man barely half his age, John Baker Daffin. Facing the tall order of teaching chemistry, physics, and biology, Daffin had graduated from Davidson just two years earlier and had just begun work on a master's degree at the University of Chicago.[25]

Interestingly, the women faculty members at Arkansas College in this era tended to be more highly educated than their male counterparts, though their salaries rarely reflected such standing. Annie W. Stevens brought a master's degree when she joined the faculty in 1921 as professor of English and the college's first dean of women. She was succeeded two years later by Jane Brookfield Brown, a graduate of George Washington University with a master's degree from Columbia. Brown remained on the faculty for the remainder of the decade.[26] The rapid faculty turnover of the post–World War I era was primarily the result of low salaries. Between 1917 and 1923 the average professor's salary at Arkansas College increased by about 90 percent as Lacy and the trustees tried to recruit and maintain qualified and effective teachers. In 1916–1917, when Lacy first arrived in Batesville, the three faculty members with no administrative duties each earned $1,200. Salaries for faculty-administrators ranged from $1,500 to $2,000. By 1920–1921, all nonadministrative faculty earned $2,000 for the session (still below par for college teachers in the region), and President Lacy's salary was $3,000. Faculty in special subjects such as music, expression, and home economics earned less, their salaries often commensurate with the popularity of their programs. Although female professors generally earned the equivalent of male professors, the addition of dean responsibilities for Annie Stevens in 1921 did not noticeably increase her salary.[27]

In the spring of 1923 the board of trustees approved a 10 percent raise for all faculty members and an even larger $500 raise for Lacy.[28] This action seemed justified in light of the various reasons for optimism. Enrollment had steadily risen. The new dormitory had just been completed and would be ready for students in the fall. And most promising of all was a recently launched new campaign for funds. Lacy's whirlwind campaign of the war years had by 1923 run its course. In fact, after the gift of the Brown family in late 1918, the flow of new gifts (except for congregational offerings and the residuals from court-delayed bequests) had dried up. Endowment note payments had also begun to shrink as a result of waning fervor on the part of donors and quickening economic constraints caused by postwar price collapses. Thus, when college and synod leaders got word of a region-wide Southern Presbyterian campaign for educational funds, the financial clouds that had begun to darken the Batesville horizon seemed to dissipate.

In early 1923 Henry H. Sweets, Secretary of Christian Education and Ministerial Relief for the Presbyterian Church in the United States, dispatched a group of workers to Arkansas to organize and direct that state's portion of the Presbyterian Educational Movement, known in the college community as the Greater Arkansas College Movement. The goal, as established by the General Assembly of the PCUS, was to raise a minimum of $406,000 for the benefit of educational institutions supported by the Synod of Arkansas. As the only college directed by the synod, Arkansas College was appointed the major beneficiary of this money; the college would receive 80 percent of funds generated by the campaign, with most of the remainder earmarked for Austin Presbyterian Theological Seminary in Texas. Working through the pulpits of Presbyterian churches, the movement swept the state in the spring and summer of 1923. Pledges, payable annually over a five-year period, exceeded the goal by about $50,000.[29] For many associated with the college it appeared that times had never been better.

But William S. Lacy was not to share the excitement of the campaign. Nor would he be on campus in the fall of 1923 to welcome the freshman class of ninety-five, easily the largest in the school's history, many of them lured to Batesville by the promises and recruiters of the Presbyterian Education Movement. At the annual trustees' meeting on 5 June 1923, the board discussed "rumors of widespread dissatisfaction with, and antagonism to the Rev. W. S. Lacy, D.D., personally and as President of Arkansas College." Although no action was taken, the trustees resolved that "in some cases [Lacy] may have been indiscreet." Two days later at a special session of the board, Lacy announced his resignation "after a great deal of explaining and restatement of things that had already been questioned in the regular meeting of the Board." After expressing "deep and sincere regret [over] conditions which Dr. Lacy nor this Committee seem able to control," the trustees accepted his resignation but asked that he submit it in writing at a later date.[30] According to a letter written by Eugene Long later in the summer, Lacy may have expected the board to reject his resignation. (Remember, Long was a master at threatened resignations.) But Lacy's belligerent attitude in the weeks after 8 June probably sealed his fate.[31] Although it is unclear what series of events prompted this sudden parting of the ways between Lacy and his alma mater, it is likely that the president's sometimes prickly and tactless personality played some role in the affair. Given the fact that he would be asked to return less than a decade later, it is improbable that Lacy's indiscretions amounted to anything more than offending some prominent person or persons. Lacy was certainly not above rebuking wealthy Presbyterians when he believed they failed to take an adequate interest in the cause of higher education.

Lacy's presidency had spanned six and a half dizzying years. Since January 1917 Arkansas College had branched out to a new campus and had begun the process of modernization. The value of the physical plant had increased sixfold, operating income for Lacy's final year had been five times that of his first year, receipts from tuition and fees had increased from just over $2,000 per year to more than $16,000, and the student body had more than doubled. Lacy had recruited a stronger faculty and had funded substantial improvements in the areas of science and music. And the college had celebrated its golden anniversary with a week of festivities in June 1922. Despite the school's financial shortcomings, an inspector for the state department of education in the spring of 1923 rated Arkansas College as one of the two best colleges in Arkansas. But the construction of Independence Hall, whose price tag ballooned to more than $100,000, plunged the college back into debt.[32] The dormitory would remain a monument to Lacy's hard work, but it would prove a burden for his successor.

The board of trustees wasted no time in finding that successor. Unburdened by modern search committee requirements, individual trustees put out informal feelers within the educational and religious communities with which they were familiar. No sooner had the ink dried on Lacy's resignation letter than Arkansas College had a new president. On 26 June 1923, the trustees met to officially accept Lacy's written resignation and to choose his replacement. Upon the recommendation of new trustee Governor Thomas C. McRae, the board unanimously elected E. B. Tucker of Little Rock as the seventh president of Arkansas College. The trustees also appointed Eugene Long chairman of the faculty and interim president, but his third time in the president's office would be extremely abbreviated. The board immediately wired Tucker the news of his election and requested that he take the train for Batesville that night. By the first day of July E. B. Tucker's administration was in place.[33]

Tucker was perhaps an odd choice for president. Although he had spent his career as an educator, he had no experience in the field of higher education beyond his days as an undergraduate and a brief stint as a graduate student. Everett Brackin Tucker was a Tennessean, born in 1881 near Smyrna, a small town southeast of Nashville. Raised on the farm by devout Presbyterian parents, Tucker earned his A.B. from Vanderbilt in 1905 and spent the next five years as a teacher and administrator in private academies in central Tennessee. In 1913, after three years convalescing on his family's farm, he moved to Arkansas to become superintendent of schools in Searcy, and later became superintendent at Helena. In 1921 Tucker helped organize the Forward Education Movement, in essence a lobby for more stringent educational standards in Arkansas, and left his job in Helena to direct the movement and to serve as executive secretary of the Arkansas Education Association in Little Rock. As director of the Forward Education Movement, Tucker endorsed the reelection campaign of Thomas C. McRae in 1922, a move that the governor had not forgotten in June 1923.[34]

What Tucker may have lacked in college-level experience, he made up for in boundless energy and zeal, traits he shared with his predecessor. But in many regards he was Lacy's complete opposite. Tucker was a short but solidly built fellow; the first issue of the college newspaper in the fall of 1923 called him a "small man full of pep."[35] E. B. Tucker was also a kind-hearted, nonconfrontational man, soft-spoken but given to loquacity in his writings and speeches on the college. As an experimenter and relatively open-minded leader, he may have been the perfect president for such a crucial time in the college's history and such a dynamic era in the development of collegiate life and the American youth culture. As it turned out, unfortunately, he was less than the perfect candidate for a decade that also brought financial strictures and increased demands for fund-raising.

It is hard to imagine student life at Arkansas College undergoing the dramatic changes that took place in the 1920s without the 1923 change in administration. It is important to note that Tucker was the first president of Arkansas College who had not been trained in the Presbyterian, liberal arts tradition. This fact was probably a two-edged sword. As the recipient of a relatively progressive, southern education at Vanderbilt and as a longtime administrator in the public sector, E. B. Tucker was not as restricted by the conservative, narrow confines of Christian education and its traditional views of discipline and student-teacher relationships. Likewise, Tucker's prior experiences may also have dampened his devotion to an unfettered liberal arts curriculum; yet, as we have seen, Arkansas College's curriculum had rarely reflected any ideological loyalty to the pure liberal arts.

The story of Arkansas College in the 1920s, as it was in American higher education in general, was the maturation of a modern student culture. Extracurricular activities expanded in all directions as the postwar generation struggled to establish its own identity.[36] The decade following World War I at Arkansas College witnessed the introduction of fraternities and sororities and the concomitant decline of literary societies, the establishment of an honor code, the arrival of modern college athletics, the emergence of music, drama, and debate as integral components of the curriculum and extracurriculum, and a transformation in student publications. Students of the 1920s displayed a spirit of independence and subtle rebellion that frequently caught the faculty off guard. All of these developments were fueled in part

Everett Brackin Tucker, president of Arkansas College from 1923 until 1931.

by an increasingly able and talented body of students that drew from the best of Independence County and a growing number of high-school-educated young men and women from around the state.

Wartime financial stringency and declining enrollment proved terrible blows to extracurricular life. Inflated paper costs forced students to cease publishing the *Index* after the 1914–1915 session; the college remained without a student publication until after the armistice.[37] The paucity of male students after the United States's entry into the war wiped out the athletic program for the duration of hostilities. Even the literary societies and well-established organizations such as the YMCA struggled to stay afloat and maintain student interest during the war. As more and more young men left school to enlist in the armed forces, female organizations took a leading role in student life. In the fall of 1918 the L'Etoile Literary Society sponsored a "Win the War" program of music and speech, and the girls of L'Etoile raised money to support a French war orphan. Mrs. Leland Bunch, who began teaching cooking classes in 1918, organized a Domestic Science Club. Enough young men remained at Arkansas College to keep the Philomathean and Erosophic societies alive and to participate in new musical groups such as Sophia Mount's glee club and the male quartet, Lost Chord Four.[38]

The rebirth of student life after the war proved far more spectacular than anything Arkansas College had yet witnessed. The literary societies stepped forward to reclaim their position of prominence, apparently oblivious to the fact that they were a dying breed on American campuses by this time. L'Etoile resumed its series of dramatic and musical presentations, and the Philomathean and Erosophic boys reinstituted their midsession programs as well as debate and oratory contests. The Philomatheans even inaugurated an annual minstrel show after the war and formed a short-lived band called the Philo Syncopaters.[39] At times in the early 1920s it seemed as if the literary societies had secured a new lease on life. In February 1923 Arkansas College junior Catherine "Kitty" Robertson (Barnett) described the annual intermediate debating contest between the "Philos" and the "Sophs." Dressed in white skirts and sweaters and wearing white caps emblazoned with a purple "Philo '23," the Philomathean Society's female supporters (one of whom was Robertson) marched to the steps of Alumni Hall bearing a cane wrapped in purple and white, the society's official colors. The young ladies conducted several society yells to inspire their beaus and friends before marching into the chapel singing the Philomathean song. One must assume that the Erosophic boys enjoyed the support of an equally enthusiastic throng of young women dressed in crimson and gold. But the Philos were ultimately victorious in this debate, and it is their side of the story that survives.[40]

The literary societies continued to thrive in the administration of William S. Lacy and into the early years of Tucker's tenure. By October 1923 the membership of L'Etoile, still the only female literary society, had grown so large that the girls decided to split their organization into two chapters—Alpha Epsilon and Alpha Phi. In January 1926 a third male literary society was formed when former "Philos" and "Sophs" led by Archie Smith and J. B. Woods organized Delta Rho. There were also signs, however, that indicated a growing dissatisfaction with literary societies. As early as the fall of 1922 a half dozen male and female students had organized a literary coterie for the purpose of studying contemporary literature, which had been one of the reasons for the rise of the societies in the nineteenth century. In subsequent years concerned students and faculty began to decry the "decadence of Literary Societies" until a full-fledged movement to abolish literary societies erupted in the fall of 1927. Disgruntled students charged the societies with shunning literary endeavors in favor of fraternity-like activities and with covert attempts to dominate campus politics. Although the literary societies did not suffer execution at the hands of an angry student mob, their days were numbered in the late 1920s. They would die a natural death, but one quickened by the rise of fraternities and sororities and by the curricular co-optation of traditional society activities such as debate and oratory.[41]

One of the earliest threats to the health of literary societies was the rise of debating and oratory as college-sponsored activities. In the fall of 1919 new professor Richard Clarke Sommerville oversaw the formation of a debating league featuring affirmative and negative teams from Henderson-Brown College and Arkansas Cumberland College (soon to be renamed College of the Ozarks) as well as Arkansas College. Because debating had traditionally been an activity associated with literary societies, Sommerville initially utilized society participation in organizing the college's teams. The Philomatheans' best debating squad served as Arkansas College's negative team, while the Erosophic Society provided the positive team. In subsequent years Sommerville continued to rely on the experience of and natural competition between the societies to prepare students for debates and oratorical contests with other colleges. Although Arkansas College's team efforts were not particularly successful, Erosophic member Warren Scott captured first place in the oratorical contest at the first statewide debate and speech meet sponsored by the Arkansas Association of Christian Colleges in the spring of 1922. Don Lawson, a member of the Philomathean Society, brought home a second-place trophy the following year. The societies continued to play an important role in this arena when President Tucker and two faculty members sponsored the establishment of the Forensic Council in the fall of 1923. The council, whose purpose was to arrange and carry out debates with other colleges, was comprised of three faculty members and two representatives from each of the three literary societies. But it appears that a relaxation of standards within the societies threatened to weaken the college's standing in state debating and oratorical contests. In January 1925 Eugene Long chided the Philos and Sophs for their "(h)asty meetings with little mental effort expended."[42]

Within a few years the Forensic Council had slipped out of society hands, and intercollegiate debating was in full swing at Arkansas College. The college held frequent matches with Henderson-Brown, Ozarks, Hendrix, and other Arkansas schools in which one team (either the negative or affirmative) would host the opposition in Batesville on the same night that the other Arkansas College team would travel to face their rivals on a competing campus. By the late 1920s the Forensic Council was scheduling a more diverse array of opponents than was the football team. In 1927 Arkansas College's debaters faced teams from as far away as the University of Wyoming and McMurray College, and the 1928 schedule featured matches with Wisconsin State Teachers College, Texas A & M, and St. Edward's University.[43]

Forensics received a further boost in the fall of 1928 when Ury McKenzie, superintendent of Batesville's schools, joined the college faculty as part-time education professor. McKenzie developed a course in argumentation and debate (known officially as public speaking) and took over duties as coach of the debate team. Under his leadership Arkansas College joined the new Arkansas Forensic League and began a rise to prominence in state and regional debate contests. By the dark days of the early 1930s the debate squad was one of the few bright spots at Arkansas College. During the 1931–1932 year Arkansas College's Forensic Council applied for a chapter of the national forensic honor society Pi Kappa Delta. Apparently this ended in failure, but by the spring of 1934 seven students had joined the local chapter of a new national forensic fraternity, Kappa Gamma. In the spring of 1932 the duo of Bill Rogers and Therrill Heasley won first place in the statewide debate of the Arkansas Forensic League and later took first honors among forty-five teams at the Southwestern Interstate College Tournament. Rogers and Heasley finished eighth in the national Pi Kappa Delta meet. Arkansas College's women's team won second place at the 1932 state meet, and the following year Ella Myrl Dobson and Sophia Norment swept both the Arkansas debate and the Inter-State Debate Tournament held at Conway. Although records for most of the depression era are incomplete, surviving trophies indicate that the men's team won state titles in 1933 and 1935 and the women's team in 1936. In addition to the success in debate, Chester Crawford won at least two state oratorical tournaments in the early 1930s.[44]

Just as the college's co-optation of debate and oratory claimed a traditional practice of the literary societies, the introduction of fraternity life threatened the existence of the societies by usurping their long-held social functions. Before the mid-1920s membership in one of the literary societies was a necessity for a complete extracurricular experience. Although literary societies had been in retreat at most colleges and universities before World War I, it was only in the 1920s that L'Etoile, the Philos, and the Sophs began to feel the pressure of Greek societies. Even before the organization of fraternities and sororities, literary societies had begun to lose their original focus and had begun to metamorphose into social clubs. But for the student in the Jazz Age, the very phrase "literary society" was passé; there was no alternative but the creation of brand-new organizations to bring a modern feel to campus.

The development of fraternity and sorority life at Arkansas College was an informal process, for several years unsanctioned by the administration or board of trustees. Among the earliest mentioned social groups were the A. O. O. Club (also known as the Oscars), the C. O. B. Club (the Oscarinas), and a young ladies' club known variously as K. K. K.'s, the K's, or the Kays. In the next two years half a dozen more small women's clubs sprang to life: the F. D. Q. G. Club, the P. A. T. Club, K. D. B., J-A-M, the Seven 'Levens, and Theta Chi. Little is known concerning the origins or purposes of these groups. One of the most intriguing and best publicized in the school newspaper was the K. K. K. club, which the school newspaper first mentioned in early 1920. The Kays held frequent social functions at members' houses in town and occasionally put on plays for the student body. It appears that the Kays' mission, along with the acronym they shared with an increasingly active and controversial organization of the era, may even have elicited curiosity among their peers. Speaking of Thelma Pickens, daughter of education professor Sidney Pickens, in the fall of 1921, a writer for the *Panther* observed: "She is one of the guiding spirits of the 'K.K.K.' bunch, and whether it means Ku Klux Klan or not, we don't know, but don't think so, for Thelma's ready smile and never-failing cheeriness is not at all connected with weird 'doings' of a mystic clan."[45]

The demise of the Kays remains unchronicled, but at least during the administration of William S. Lacy there appear to have been no imitators. The existence of local fraternities and sororities at Arkansas College was made public only in the middle of E. B. Tucker's presidency, though at least a couple of the organizations had been in operation for some time before. The 1927 *Index* lists a number of social organizations, some with Greek letter names and others with catchy club monikers. Young women's organizations included Beta Beta Beta, K. A. T., B. E. L. L., and Alpha Mu Alpha, while various groups of young men had founded H. B. K. and Delta Kappa Sigma. By the 1927–1928 academic year there were five mostly new "social groups" on the Arkansas College campus, three fraternities and two women's organizations. In addition to Delta Kappa Sigma, local fraternities included Zeta Chi, whose membership included several top athletes, and Eta Beta Kappa, which traced its roots back to 1925. The 1928 *Index* lists two women's clubs whose origins and purposes were unspecified: the L.U.C.K. Club and Gamma Epsilon Theta, though neither appeared in the following year's annual. At the March 1928 board meeting, Tucker reported that Delta Kappa Sigma had asked permission to join a national fraternity. The trustees promptly appointed a faculty-trustee committee to research the matter and report back at the June meeting. The committee's report, prepared primarily by Tucker, recommended allowing national fraternities on campus but cautioned patience and further deliberation on the matter of fraternity houses.[46]

Several factors accounted for the board's and the administration's ready acceptance of fraternity and sorority life at Arkansas College. First of all, as the young men of Delta Kappa Sigma pointed out, almost all larger Presbyterian colleges and universities had already accepted such social organizations. Consequently, Arkansas College's leap of faith was a relatively small one. Recent changes in leadership in the Batesville institution also paved the way for a more modern conception of extracurricular life. Tucker had proven himself more amenable to student-inspired change than his predecessor, and longtime board chairman James P. Coffin, both a physical and spiritual link with the college's earliest days, had stepped down a year and a half earlier. Tucker himself attempted to head off a major concern—that fraternities and sororities would ruin the moral climate of campus—by reminding the trustees that Arkansas College already suffered the problems associated with Greek organizations: poor scholarship, dancing, drinking, and gambling. Besides, insisted the president, fraternities and sororities brought to campus positive attributes such as the inculcation of social values and the cooperative spirit and a tendency to promote school spirit and alumni loyalty.[47]

Perhaps the most important reason for the success of the Greek movement at Arkansas College was the clientele of the new organizations. Fraternities and sororities generally claimed the most socially active students from the most well-placed families. Among Delta Kappa Sigma's members were Shuford Nichols, scion of a prominent landholding Presbyterian family and future chairman of the board of trustees, and Carleton McRae, grandson of former governor Thomas C. McRae. Denying these students the freedom to dabble in the developing Greek system would have meant alienating Arkansas College's core constituency. And this core constituency of Presbyterians seemed to rally around their college during the 1920s more so than in the past. Many Presbyterian families continued to send their children, especially sons, to more prestigious schools out of state, but more and more decided to try Arkansas College. Whether due to the influence of Governor McRae, the state's most prominent Presbyterian layman, or the residual effect of the goodwill and publicity generated by the Presbyterian Educational Movement, Tucker's Arkansas College began to draw an increasing number of students from outside of Independence County, most of them from middle-class Presbyterian families of the plantation belt south and east of Little Rock. Although Batesville and Independence County had historically provided half or more of Arkansas College's students, by the fall of 1926, when pre-depression enrollment peaked at 207, more than 60 percent of matriculates hailed from outside Independence County. Less than 30 percent of the following year's freshmen lived in Independence County.[48] One of the results of this sudden growth in boarding students was an outstanding student body perhaps unrivaled in the college's history, a student body whose collective energy and experimentation fueled the rise of Greek life and other postwar developments.

Eventually only two Greek organizations at Arkansas College secured charters from national groups. Declining enrollments and financial stringency caused by the depression prevented a fuller development of Greek life. Delta Kappa Sigma, whose petition had signaled the arrival of Greek life at Arkansas College, was not one of the two nationally affiliated chapters. The first social club to gain national affiliation was actually a sorority. In the summer of 1928 the members of a local sorority (most likely Alpha Mu Alpha) applied to forty-year-old Beta Sigma Omicron for a charter, and a chapter was installed in Batesville in September 1928. Five months later local fraternity Eta Beta Kappa received a charter as Nu chapter of Alpha Lambda Tau, a young national fraternity founded during World War I at Oglethorpe University in Georgia. The leadership of James Johnson Jr., a recent transfer from the University of Arkansas who had joined Alpha Lambda Tau's chapter at Fayetteville, apparently proved a key to the successful affiliation of Eta Beta Kappa, which was a smaller fraternity than Delta Kappa Sigma.[49]

Eta Beta Kappa was also the first and only Greek organization at Arkansas College to establish its own house. In April 1928 both Eta Beta Kappa and Delta Kappa Sigma had rented houses near campus to use as meeting places, but no members moved into these residences. Although Tucker had not wholeheartedly endorsed the Greek house concept in his report to the board in June 1928, the trustees left the door open by referring fraternity building requests to the executive committee. During the summer the executive committee approved both fraternities' plans for constructing houses, demanding only that the houses be built on college property and at no cost to the college. By the time classes resumed in September 1928, Eta Beta Kappa had erected a house just east of Independence Hall on the new campus. Crafted in the Old English style using brown sandstone gathered from the undeveloped fields of the new campus, the college's new fraternity house contained five rooms and a stone fireplace. Eta Beta Kappa immediately ran into problems, however, when, forced to recruit students to fill their rented rooms, President James Ferrill and his fraters invited three freshmen

The brothers of Alpha Lambda Tau in their fraternity house, c. 1930.

to live in the house, a move that elicited protest from the administration and faculty. Although the freshmen were allowed to live out the year with the fraternity boys, the episode convinced the faculty that the college required a standard set of rules dealing with Greek organizations.[50]

By February 1929 President Tucker regarded "the coming of fraternities under strict faculty regulation and cooperation as being of a decided benefit to the College." They proved anything but a benefit to the health of the old literary societies. Delta Rho, the youngest of Arkansas College's four literary societies, disbanded in the spring of 1928, and Philomathean, the oldest, called it quits the following fall after forty-five years of service. By the date of Tucker's statement, the Erosophic Society had dwindled to insignificance, and L'Etoile was engaged in a heated rearguard action against the sororities. Both disappeared in the early 1930s. Fraternity and sorority life peaked in the final years before the Great Depression and massive debts threatened to close Arkansas College. Although no new fraternities sprang up to challenge Delta Kappa Sigma and Alpha Lambda Tau, two additional sororities were founded before the end of the decade. A group of Batesville and Independence County girls gathered in the Terry-Casey Drug Store in October 1928 to form Kappa Kappa Alpha, the only Greek organization that would survive the depression. A little over a year later seven young women founded Arkansas College's last sorority, Delta Theta. Declining enrollments, especially among boarding students, took its toll in the early 1930s. By 1934 only Delta Kappa Sigma, Beta Sigma Omicron, and Kappa Kappa Alpha remained. Three years later Kappa Kappa Alpha was the only Greek organization on campus.[51]

The literary societies were not the only organizations to suffer during the rise of fraternity and sorority life at Arkansas College. Religious organizations also experienced declining memberships and prominence in the 1920s. Before World War I the YMCA and YWCA were synonymous with student Christianity on campus. The postwar era found these groups still in existence but in decline as more and more students focused their extracurricular attentions elsewhere. In fact, the YMCA disappeared from the Batesville campus in the early 1920s before being resuscitated in the fall of 1925. In the 1920s religious organizations attracted fewer and fewer nonministerial students; consequently, the YMCA and YWCA were supplemented by groups advertising a more narrowly defined mission. The first of these organizations to appear at Arkansas College was the Life Service Band. Founded during the 1921–1922 session, the Life Service Band was comprised of preministerial students as well as others who planned careers in some branch of church service. By the mid-1920s Arkansas College also contained a Christian Endeavor Society, a group whose membership was more inclusive than that of the Ministerial Association (later known as the Preachers' Club) formed in the fall of 1927. The spirit and composition of Christian organizations at Arkansas College reflected the institution's nonsectarian traditions as well as the diversity of evangelical Protestant denominations represented in the student body. Statistics gathered during the 1928–1929 session revealed that Presbyterians accounted for only 41 percent of the student body. The total number of Methodist students almost equaled the number of Presbyterians. The Ministerial Association included future clergymen in the Methodist and Disciples of Christ denominations, and as early as 1922 Methodist students established a branch of the Epworth League on campus. By the mid-1930s all of these Christian organizations were inactive.[52]

But the Christian quest for perfection was far from the minds of many students in the 1920s, a fact that distressed administrators and faculty. Even a small college campus in Batesville, Arkansas, could not escape the reverberations of the Jazz Age. Hair-bobbing and mustache-growing were simply subtle physical manifestations of a new era and a vibrant, revolutionary youth culture. The decade of prohibition brought to the college campus a growing number of students for whom automobiles, consumerism, cigarettes, and an increasingly open affinity for the opposite sex were staples of life. These students encountered rules and regulations that had gone unchanged since before the war. The stage was set for generational conflict, and the college's expectations of students' religious and social duties often provided the backdrop.

Like other small denominational colleges of the era, Arkansas College entered the 1920s with a catalog of restrictions and regulations for students, especially boarding students and more so young women. Warnings against the usual sins—drinking, smoking, dancing, gambling—were accompanied by restrictions on dormitory leave, visitation with the opposite sex, and riding in automobiles. These restrictions differed slightly depending on sex, class standing, and classroom performance. For instance, seniors enjoyed more privileges than freshmen, and students maintaining excellent grades were rewarded with more leave nights than underachieving students. Violations of college rules, from the petty to the severe, were regularly considered by the faculty as a whole. The minutes of faculty assembly meetings from the 1920s contain endless synopses of these hearings and the various punishments meted out. Students faced the faculty for any number of crimes: academic dishonesty, "indiscreet conduct" with a member of the opposite sex, excessive absences, dormitory untidiness, drinking, and a "persistently defiant attitude toward the Faculty and its regulations." Most trials ended with the student suffering a temporary loss of privileges, though expulsion was not unusual.[53]

By the mid-1920s the number of serious infractions was on the rise. In his March 1926 report to the board of trustees, Tucker lamented: "For the first time during my administration there has been a small group of students of the revolutionary or bolshevistic type, whose influence was perceptible but not by any means controlling." There is no evidence of Communist activity on Arkansas College's campus in 1925–1926, but the faculty assembly minutes report a rise in probations and expulsions due to alcohol use and automobile-related incidents. The particularly poor student deportment of that session was in part overcome, according to Tucker, by an unusually effective series of on-campus religious services during the college's annual revival week in February. "Seldom in our experience have faculty, students and friends been so profoundly moved to thought and quiet resolve toward the higher planes of Christian living."[54] Tucker's description of a revival sparking "thought and quiet resolve" did not exactly inspire images of Cane Ridge–style spontaneity. Bolshevism would return and once again lay siege to the bastions of Arkansas College's Christian traditions.

In succeeding years a bolder, empowered student body began to lob significant challenges at two of the college's most hallowed Christian traditions, daily chapel service and Sunday School. Since the days of Isaac Long and T. J. Stubbs, Arkansas College had commenced each day with morning chapel or prayer service, and since 1888 this service had been held in Alumni Hall. A tradition at most denominational colleges, morning chapel gave the administration and faculty an opportunity to remind students on a daily basis of the higher things in life and also served a practical purpose as a forum for important announcements and bulletins. In the fall of 1926, faced with several years of declining chapel attendance and with rising student dissatisfaction with this tradition, the faculty agreed to allow each student three unexcused absences, or cuts, from morning chapel. A year and a half later, again in response to student protests, faculty members voted to establish a graded system of chapel cuts whereby unexcused absences increased with class standing, from four per semester for freshmen to ten for seniors. In March 1929 the Student Government Association (SGA) petitioned the faculty unsuccessfully to make chapel attendance completely optional. Nevertheless, the SGA won an important battle the following fall when the faculty approved its abolition of Thursday morning chapel, the one day in the week given to student control. Students also challenged another tradition dating to the days of Isaac Long, mandatory Sunday School attendance. By the late 1920s each student was required to record his Sunday School and morning worship service attendance on a card prepared and inspected by the dean. Faced with rampant cheating on these cards, the inability to monitor the Sunday activities of a growing student body, and more student protests, the faculty in the fall of 1928 agreed to suspend the mandatory Sunday School attendance rule for the fall semester as an experiment. (Students were still required to attend morning worship services at the church of their parents' choice.) Apparently, the experiment produced satisfactory results, for the faculty voted to continue the policy indefinitely thereafter.[55]

As student protests of one sort or another intensified in the 1920s, the student newspaper took on a more prominent role as the unofficial voice of protest and the sounding board of the dissatisfied. Student publications underwent a transformation in the years after World War I, and the process of that transformation reveals a great deal about changes in student life at Arkansas College and around the nation. The *Index,* Arkansas College's prewar literary magazine whose spotty publication record stretched back more than a decade, was rejuvenated in January 1919 after almost four years of dormancy. The new student editors temporarily revived the familiar prewar literary magazine format before Henry W. Sanderson transformed the *Index* into a newspaper-style publication in the fall of 1919. Gone from the new version were the essays, poems, and short stories contributed by students; the postwar *Index* featured brief reports on campus and club activities, athletics, and alumni. An editor of the college newspaper in 1924 praised Sanderson and his fellow student reporters for abandoning the old-style "more or less pretentious magazine." The new college newspaper, he wrote, attempted only to reflect and record life at Arkansas College, "a much more attainable and not less worthy ideal."[56]

It was also during the 1919–1920 academic session that the publishers of the *Index* decided to put together the college's first yearbook. John D. Spragins Jr., a senior from Hope and future Arkansas College president, was given the difficult task as editor of this annual. In the spring of 1920, once the college had voted on a new mascot, the editors of the *Index* agreed to use the title *Index* for the yearbook only. Consequently, in October 1920 Arkansas College students picked up the first edition of the new college paper, the *Panther.* Students continued to publish the *Panther* once a month until the fall of 1922 when the *Panther* staff introduced a semimonthly schedule. Under the watchful and frequently censorious eye of faculty advisor Eugene Long, the *Panther* gradually assumed a prominent voice in student and campus affairs. By the mid-1920s activist editors had begun to take the lead in movements to abolish literary societies, to protest mandatory chapel and Sunday School attendance, and to establish a greater degree of student autonomy through such developments as an honor code and student government. The paper had become sufficiently outspoken and risqué by the early days of the Great Depression that editor Blake Downie had to deflect criticism from those who felt the *Panther* was not suitable for a general Presbyterian readership. Less than a year after Downie's defensive editorial, a new staff of students complained to the faculty of Long's censorship.[57]

Student resistance to faculty censorship reflected a growing sense of independence and campus participation among the youth of the 1920s. The two most prominent manifestations of this spirit of independence on the Arkansas College campus were the honor system and the student government. Although it is unclear who, or what group, provided the impetus for Arkansas College's honor system, it was first mentioned and adopted during E. B. Tucker's initial year as president. On 10 January 1924, Tucker appointed Eugene Long and new faculty member Lincoln Barker to consult with a group of students in the organization of an "honor committee." One week later the faculty assembly approved the new constitution of this committee, thereby establishing the college's first honor code. By early February students had elected the first Honor Committee (eventually referred to as Council), composed of two representatives from each class as well as two preparatory students. Beginning in the fall of 1924 all freshmen were required to sign an honor code pledge, promising not only to maintain personal standards of academic integrity but also to assist in enforcing the code by reporting any infractions they might witness. Concerning itself only with student conduct on examinations and term papers, the Honor Council left matters of student deportment to the faculty and reserved the right to request two faculty members at any hearing on potential violations of the code.[58]

By the 1920s the honor system was a hallowed tradition on many American campuses, especially those of small southern colleges. But the honor system never took root in Batesville. Almost from its inception, the honor system drew verbal challenges from student detractors and subtle challenges from many more who simply ignored its mandates. Consequently, just two years after the establishment of the code and committee, the *Panther* reported that the honor system faced a crisis as the result of widespread student dissatisfaction with recent Honor Council actions. It appears that the Honor Council ceased to exist for a year or more before a group of students once again lobbied for more self-disciplinary control during the 1927–1928 session. After reworking the honor system, students and faculty reestablished it for the 1928–1929 session, but the results were equally disappointing. According to President Tucker the system failed because of a general unwillingness on the part of Arkansas College students to actively enforce the code on their peers. In the fall of 1929 Tucker issued a proclamation informing the student body that the faculty would resume full responsibility for maintaining academic honesty.[59]

The students' second push for an honor system during the 1927–1928 session was accompanied by a movement to establish Arkansas College's first student government. By late November 1927 plans were under way to form a student senate and to draft a constitution for a student government association. Chaired by junior Harvey Booth of Batesville, a committee of students, including vocal *Panther* editor Shuford Nichols, presented the new constitution to the faculty in December. The constitution established a Student Government Association consisting of two parts, a senate and a slate of officers elected by campus-wide vote. The backbone of the SGA was the senate, which consisted of two members from each of the three upper classes and one freshman. Each class elected its own senators, and all students voted for the SGA's president, vice-president, secretary, and treasurer. After the faculty approved the SGA's constitution in January 1928, Arkansas College students elected junior John Benish of Batesville president and Laman Gray, a senior from Batesville, vice-president.[60]

Composed of some of the college's most outspoken and innovative students, the

SGA and senate immediately assumed an activist stance on campus. Within two months of its founding, the senate petitioned the faculty to repeal the compulsory Sunday School attendance rule, which the faculty initially denied but eventually approved the following fall. In the spring of 1929 senior SGA members led the successful push to have the senior thesis requirement discontinued, but calls for optional chapel attendance fell on deaf ears.[61]

The Student Government Association was also responsible for introducing one of the more heinous facets of post–World War I student life to Arkansas College: hazing. One of the first acts of the new SGA was the appointment of vigilance committees, male and female committees whose purpose was to draft a set of rules to be followed by all freshmen. Hazing had taken place at Arkansas College throughout the post–World War I decade (especially among athletes), but it was not until the fall of 1929 that freshman hazing achieved official status. The freshmen rules adopted by the vigilance committees reflected a systematic and none too subtle attempt by upperclassmen to intimidate and initiate newcomers. All freshmen were required to address upperclassmen as Mister or Miss, to remain standing in the dining hall until all upperclassmen had been seated, to wear green caps during the first quarter and touch their caps when meeting or addressing upperclassmen, and to remain seated in the chapel until the last upperclassman had left the building. The new rules demanded that freshmen attend all pep rallies and ballgames and forbade them from gathering in the halls and talking during times when class was in session. In addition, male freshmen were required to carry matches for upperclassmen and to weather the secret initiation rites of R.O.S.A., the Royal Order of Sanguine Asininity. Freshmen could win relief from the rules only if a frosh football squad defeated the upperclassmen in an autumn intramural game. Despite the rather benign nature of the vigilance committees' rules, by the early 1930s the hazing of freshmen had become severe enough to earn a rebuke and warning from the administration and faculty.[62]

Fortunately, the rise in student initiative and extracurricular participation after World War I frequently ended in positive results. The postwar years witnessed impressive growth in music and athletics as well as phenomenal expansion of speech and theater at Arkansas College. At the end of World War I the music department, housed on the bottom floor of the original college building, consisted of only two faculty members whose salaries depended on enrollment in their respective classes. Bess Maxfield, an alumna of the class of 1909, taught piano, and Sophia Mount instructed fewer than a dozen students in voice. Their clientele was overwhelmingly female, and the music department remained separated from the regular college curriculum. Mount directed a small glee club and a male quartet known as the Lost Chord Four. The addition in the spring of 1919 of a new Steinway Grand Piano in Alumni Hall kicked off a period of steady growth in the music department and in extracurricular musical activities.[63]

In April 1920 the music instructors directed students in the operetta, "Yanki San," to help raise money for the college's first yearbook, and by the fall of 1920 Arkansas College had its first orchestra, directed by Maxfield, and a choral club under Sophia Mount. In spite of frequent turnover of the music faculty, the department

The Arkansas College Orchestra, 1922–1923.

continued to expand during Lacy's administration, and by 1922 the college had begun referring to the department as the Conservatory of Music. But the progress of the department during Lacy's tenure paled in comparison with developments during his successor's administration. Music was one of several areas on which E. B. Tucker concentrated his tireless energy. One of Tucker's first actions as president was the hiring of a new director of the music department, Edward H. Scherubel, a former pupil in the Royal Conservatory in Leipzig, Germany. Scherubel's hiring was important not only because his salary equaled that of regular, literary faculty members but also because the presence of a man in a department generally dominated by women in small southern colleges lent Arkansas College's school of music an air of legitimacy that, fairly or not, it had lacked under his predecessors. As it turned out Scherubel lasted only one year at Arkansas College before being replaced by Mrs. Samuel Deener, but the spirit of progress that Tucker had invoked continued unabated.[64]

Under the direction of Mrs. Otice C. Dooley, the Arkansas College Orchestra conducted its first statewide tour in February and March 1924, performing in Newark, Newport, Pine Bluff, Hope, Gurdon, and Little Rock. The orchestra was also accompanied by the Philo Syncopaters, a band formed by the literary society, and the Alpha Epsilon Quartet. The 1924–1925 session brought the organization of men's and women's glee clubs and a Thanksgiving Day dedication of the college's new Kimball Pipe Organ in Alumni Hall. The latter event made Arkansas College one of only two institutions in the state (the other being the University of Arkansas) to offer instruction on the pipe organ.[65]

The quantity and quality of musical productions at Arkansas College improved throughout the decade. In the spring of 1926 the college orchestra was invited to play on a Memphis radio station, and in the summer the Philo Syncopaters, led by star pupil Glenn Metcalf, performed for passengers on an Atlantic cruise ship. By the late 1920s the music faculty had increased to four, and students could take courses in theory, piano, voice, violin, and organ; diplomas were available for students of the last four. And though the college did not establish a music major within the bachelor of arts program, regular college matriculates were eventually allowed to count up to twenty-four hours from the special departments of music and speech toward an A.B. Graduates of the music department were expected to perform a graduation recital; piano graduates regularly performed their recitals as part of a music/expression program with a graduate from the speech department.[66]

Even more significant at Arkansas College in the 1920s was the development of a school of speech and a first-rate theater program. Both owe their existence to one of the college's most colorful personalities and faithful faculty members of the interwar years, Lois Ball. A graduate of Virginia Intermont College who had studied expression and drama from New York to Chicago, Ball arrived at Arkansas College during World War I as instructor of expression, a position that carried no fixed salary but relied on student fees of twenty-five dollars per semester. As was the case at the vast majority of colleges and universities around the country, expression was not a regular part of the Arkansas College curriculum. The idea of formal academic theatrical training was even more far-fetched. For the most part Ball's teaching duties consisted of two classes—a public speaking course for young men and "training in the technique and art of natural expression" for young women. With ideas of a greater role for herself and the expression department, Lois Ball began door-to-door solicitation of students in Batesville.[67]

By early 1922 Ball had organized a Dramatic Club. Made up completely of female students, the Dramatic Club presented two one-act plays—"Joint Owners in Spain" and "Enter the Hero"—on 20 February 1922, marking the arrival of what would become Arkansas College's most consistently successful extracurricular activity of the next two decades. Two years later Ball directed her students in three one-act plays—"Suppressed Desire," "The Slave with Two Faces," and "Neighbors." After the departure of William S. Lacy in 1923, the faculty approved a recommendation to upgrade the expression department to the "School of Speech" and to allow regularly enrolled students to count up to twelve hours of speech toward a bachelor's degree. With E. B. Tucker's moral support, if very little monetary support, Ball quickly expanded her school into perhaps the most successful and popular division of the college. By Tucker's second year in office, 1924–1925, enrollment in the School of Speech had jumped to almost sixty, and in the winter of 1925 Ball and her students, using money donated by local businesses and generated by play ticket sales, remodeled Alumni Hall with new stage furniture and a blue velvet curtain.[68]

In the fall of 1925 Lois Ball changed the name of the Dramatic Art Club (formerly Dramatic Club) to the Harlequin Little Theatre and established the Mask and Dagger Club, an honorary society open only to the best actors in Harlequin Little Theatre. On 30 November 1925, the Harlequin Little Theatre performed its first play, "Moon Magic." In early 1928 the Mask and Dagger Club, or Alpha Xi, received the state's first charter from the national dramatic fraternity, Alpha Psi Omega. In April of that year Harlequin Little Theatre received an invitation to compete against eight other colleges and universities for the Cumnock Cup at the National Little Theatre Tournament at Northwestern University in Evanston, Illinois. With the college in financial straits and local businessmen suffering from Arkansas's early depression, Ball and her five-member cast were unable to raise enough money to buy train tickets and were forced to squeeze themselves, their luggage, and their props into a Pontiac for the long and treacherous ride to Evanston. The valiant troupe—Hugh Shick, Stuart Salmon, Laman Gray, Iris Dobson, and Miriam Carlton—overcame their fatigue and took second-place honors for their performance of the last act of "Sun-Up." Dobson, a Batesville native and Harlequin's beautiful leading lady, brought home the cup for outstanding player.[69]

Buoyed by their success, Ball and Harlequin Little Theatre conducted their first tour of the state in March 1929, performing the comedy "Express Yourself" in Fayetteville, Russellville, Morrilton, and Malvern. Later that spring they headed back to Northwestern University to compete for the Cumnock Cup but received only an honorable mention. Although this proved to be Harlequin's last venture into national competition, Arkansas College and Lois Ball took the lead in promoting the little theatre movement in Arkansas. In late April 1929, Ball organized the first high school play contest in Arkansas, advertising a silver cup for the winning school and a $100 scholarship for the outstanding player. The following spring Ball helped organize the Arkansas Little Theatre Tournament, and her Harlequin Little Theatre immediately became a dominant cast in the annual event. Harlequin took home several first-place awards during the 1930s, as well as many personal awards, such as best individual honors for Doris Hammett in 1930 and Ella Myrl Dobson and Chester Crawford in 1932. By 1932 Arkansas College had won more cast and individual awards than any other school in the Southwest. Topping off more than a decade of excellence, the newly formed Arkansas Association of Teachers of Speech Festival honored Harlequin's sustained success by awarding Arkansas College the Lawrence Burrow Cup in 1936.[70]

The Harlequin Little Theatre proved a valuable ambassador for Arkansas College in the 1920s and 1930s. Nevertheless, theater could not supplant the era's dominant extracurricular activity—athletics and specifically football. Arkansas College had boasted some form of organized sport since the 1890s, but it was only in the last few years before the assassination of Archduke Franz Ferdinand that college athletics in Batesville began to assume the look of modernity. The war presented a temporary obstacle to further development of athletics, but peacetime ushered in an era of unprecedented expansion and popularity as students, administrators, and alumni sought the notoriety and respect that could come only with success on the playing field.

From the moment it was first introduced to Arkansas College in 1913, football had claimed the most exalted position in the extracurriculum. After two years of old, rugby-style play, the Lambs began to enter the modern era in 1915 when Coach L. J. Quigley introduced the forward pass to aid his "light but fairly fast" team of eighteen players. The cantankerous Quigley left to coach Little Rock College the next year, leaving the Lambs under the direction of Galloway Harrison. The lone bright spot for Arkansas College gridiron players in the 1916 season was a 62 to 0 victory over their old coach and his new team. Coach Harrison also helped organize the Athletic Association of Arkansas Colleges, consisting of Arkansas College, Arkansas Cumberland College, Henderson-Brown, and Ouachita. By the following year the war had depleted Arkansas College's male population to the point that no football team could be organized. The only football action the students would see during the war was a game between the SATC units of Arkansas College and Little Rock College in November 1918. Arkansas College's boys once again suffered defeat.[71]

With the return to normalcy in 1919 football reemerged under the leadership of young Coach W. C. Munn, a former Ouachita College star. But it was another young newcomer who would shepherd Arkansas College's football program, as well as other athletic programs, into the 1920s. After a limited schedule in 1919—one that included games against two high schools and a Batesville town team—new science professor John B. Daffin took charge of athletics in the fall of 1920. Daffin, a former Davidson letterman, shared President Lacy's desire for clean athletics that did not rely on recruited ringers and did not threaten academic integrity. Daffin's leadership in the early 1920s set the tone for the college's athletic program. In the fall of 1921 he led a committee of four faculty members charged with drafting regulations for athletes. These regulations—including requirements for minimum hours passed and restrictions against athletic scholarships and extended sports-related absences from campus—would remain relatively unaltered for years to come. The result was a program that *usually* avoided any hint of scandal but one that also frequently found itself at a disadvantage when playing schools that did not share the Presbyterians' stated ideals. Students and administrators were always quick to point this out when defeats piled up. Despite changing the school's mascot from the lamb to the more ferocious panther, Daffin's teams managed only one win in nine games in 1920 and 1921.[72]

In spite of his poor record as coach, the affable Daffin retained his popularity in the classroom and laboratory and with the administration. With hearty student and administrative support, the college named its new athletic field (completed on the heights of the new campus in the spring of 1921) Daffin Field. But even in the 1920s the self-satisfaction of honor and integrity provided little salve to the wounds of failure. By the fall of 1922 Arkansas College had a new coach. The decision to hire a full-time athletic director benefited the college because it allowed John B. Daffin, a master teacher by most accounts, to devote his full energy to the classroom and laboratory. But such thinking was not the primary impetus for the change. By the spring of 1922 there was a growing spirit of dissatisfaction among alumni with the college's lack of athletic success, especially on the football field. At the June 1922 board meeting, Rev.

C. P. Bridewell, an alumnus and prominent Presbyterian minister from Malvern, delivered a lengthy address to the trustees concerning the need for a better athletic program. After a brainstorming session among a group of alumni and trustees, Sam Y. T. Knox, an alumnus from Pine Bluff, offered $1,500 toward the salary of a bona fide coach. Unwilling to pass up such a generous opportunity, the board appointed Knox, Bridewell, and trustee Rev. J. V. Johnson of Arkadelphia as a committee to locate and hire the new coach. The search produced Kent V. Morrison, a former football and baseball star at Vanderbilt who had been teaching at a military preparatory school in Tennessee. Morrison looked the part. A muscular, square-jawed man with a high-perched crew cut, the intimidating Morrison arrived in Batesville in the late summer of 1922 to prepare for his position as athletic director and teacher of Latin and history in the preparatory department. Daffin Field had been whipped into good condition over the summer, and grandstands were scheduled for construction some time in the fall. Morrison also enjoyed the advantage of the college's most talented group of players to date, the result of a statewide recruiting campaign by Arkansas College's new number-one booster, Sam Knox.[73]

The campaign for a new coach and a stronger athletic program paid immediate dividends in the fall of 1922 when the Panthers reeled off three straight victories to begin the season, more than in the previous three seasons combined. Morrison's first season ended on a sour note when Arkansas College suffered a 40-point defeat at the hands of their arch rival, Hendrix, in the final game; nevertheless, the 4–2–1 record signaled the first winning football team in the school's history. Yet the college's relationship with Knox endangered the future and the reputation of the football program when in the spring of 1923 it was discovered that the eager booster had paid tuition and boarding costs for two of the Panthers' best players, Jack Fowler and Ewin Grisham. Both had been recruited from out of state for their athletic abilities. Knox soon moved away from Arkansas and out of the college's affairs, and the new administration of E. B. Tucker attempted to maintain previous standards of clean play.[74]

Although Morrison was able to coax consistent competitiveness out of his players, Arkansas College remained at best a mediocre team, dominating weaker foes such as Mountain Home College but falling year after year to stronger squads from Hendrix and Ouachita. After winning four of seven games in 1923, a season that witnessed a campus-wide celebration after the Panthers lost by only one touchdown to powerhouse Hendrix, Coach Morrison's squads experienced fewer successes in his last three seasons at Arkansas College, winning just six of nineteen contests during that span. But the Morrison years also produced local heroes, college boys whose weekly exploits were dutifully praised in the *Panther* and whose glories and foibles were shared by an admiring student body and a faithful alumni. In a special "Football Edition" of the *Panther* printed in October 1926, a student writer praised Jack Fowler, Harold Phillips, Ewin "Pigiron" Grisham, and J. C. White as Arkansas College's best football players since World War I. Two Panther players, guard J. C. White in 1922 and halfback Lowell Manning in 1925, were selected to first-team all-state status.[75]

By the mid-1920s Morrison could claim at least part of the credit for football's

The Arkansas College Panthers football team, 1922.

dominance of extracurricular life at Arkansas College. By 1923 football games on the Batesville campus featured yell leaders from the student body, and students received "Panther Pep" pamphlets containing the words to yells and songs. "Rickety, Rackety, Russ/ We're not allowed to cuss/ But never-the-less, we must confess/ There's nothing wrong with us" was one of nineteen yells featured in "Panther Pep." Songs included those written for specific foes as well as others to be sung to such tunes as "Turkey in the Straw" and "Old Gray Mare." In the fall of 1926 a student editor of the *Panther* gushed, "There is nothing like football—nothing remotely like it." Of particular delight to the Arkansas College student body was the annual match with Hendrix, even though the Bulldogs defeated the Panthers year after year. In the relative isolation of postwar Batesville another student could state with sincerity: "The [W]orld [S]eries, student activities and certainly study pales into insignificance besides [*sic*] the bitterly contested Bulldog-Panther game."[76]

By the time Kent V. Morrison resigned in the spring of 1927, Arkansas College had discontinued its preparatory department, thus requiring the administration to find a replacement who could also complement the college curriculum. Within a couple weeks of Morrison's announcement of his impending resignation, President E. B. Tucker secured as his successor Samuel Jasper Patterson Jr. Jap Patterson, son of a Presbyterian minister, had grown up in Arkansas and Colorado before attending Tarkio College in northwestern Missouri, where he received his A.B. and earned thirteen letters in four sports. For the last few years he had put together a succession of outstanding football and basketball teams as a high school teacher in Fort Morgan, Colorado. In addition to his duties as all-purpose coach, the tall, blond Patterson was expected to teach physiology and hygiene as well as the school's first coaching class.[77]

Under Patterson's direction the Panther football schedule expanded to nine games, but the results were less than stellar. During his five years as coach, Patterson's teams averaged just three wins per season; the 1929 campaign produced the best record at 4–4–1. The larger schedule presented Arkansas College the opportunity to establish new rivalries, which it did with recently established Harding College in Morrilton as well as such out-of-state institutions as Southwest Missouri Teachers College (now State University) in Springfield, Union College in Jackson, Tennessee, and Southwestern at Memphis. Patterson inherited two all-state players from Morrison's old squad—Earl Stokes and Lowell Manning—and recruited eight more players who eventually earned all-state accolades. Among Patterson's top players were two-time all-state nominees Paul Fiser, Mac Trimble, and Hugh Patterson (Jap's younger brother) as well as Myron "Butch" Schlater, the most decorated football player in Arkansas College history. Schlater, a Coloradan who had followed Coach Patterson to Batesville, received third-team all-state honors as a freshman halfback and for the next three seasons was honored as the state's second-best fullback.[78]

Butch Schlater also emerged as the focal point in a scandal that provided considerable negative publicity for Arkansas College and possibly influenced the departure of Coach Patterson. In the fall of 1931, after Schlater had already completed his four years of eligibility with the Panthers, Patterson decided to suit up his star fullback for a fifth season. The football season—the first at Arkansas College to feature lights on Daffin Field and a ten-piece student band at games—got off to a bad start with a lopsided loss to Arkansas Tech, but the Panthers and their fifth-year star rallied for victories over Arkansas State Teachers College and First District A & M in Jonesboro. Perhaps smarting from a 65 to 6 drubbing at the hands of the Panthers, A & M's president publicly accused Arkansas College and the College of the Ozarks of using ineligible players and sent letters to the member schools of the Arkansas Intercollegiate Athletic Conference requesting that they boycott all athletic contests with the two Presbyterian colleges for the remainder of the academic year. Coach Patterson and his counterpart at Ozarks did not deny playing ineligible players; both coaches as well as their administrators responded to criticisms by accusing other state schools of also indulging in the illegal practice. Patterson, who estimated that there were perhaps as many as twenty ineligible players suiting up each Friday for college squads, claimed that by inserting Schlater into the Panther lineup he was simply "meeting fire with fire."[79]

Patterson promptly removed Schlater from the team. The Panthers won only two of their final six games that season, but for the most part the college was successful in mending the strained relationships with other schools. Although there is no surviving evidence to link his departure with the football scandal, Jap Patterson resigned in the spring of 1932 to become director of religious education for the Synod of Arkansas. Patterson would be Arkansas College's last full-time coach until after World War II. Amidst the college's severe financial problems, the board agreed to leave the hiring and paying of a coach up to a group of Batesville boosters headed by Pat Hogan, owner of the local livestock auction. In the fall of 1932 this group brought in a new coach, J. Courtney White, an alumnus and Panther star of the early 1920s who also happened to be the son-in-law of new president William S. Lacy. Under White's guidance the Panthers suffered through two more difficult seasons, including a school-worst 0–9 record in 1933. Public outcry among alumni and the college's Batesville supporters led White to resign in the spring of 1934. As fate would have it, the gridiron Panthers saved their best effort for their dying days. In 1934 Coach Henry Hudson, a former Hendrix star, led Arkansas College to its best football season in history. Behind the play of all-state sophomore Lloyd Berry of Hope, the Panthers posted a record of 5–1–2, including a scoreless tie with arch nemesis Hendrix.[80] But as always, athletic success proved a fleeting thing in Batesville. In 1935, under the direction of Lucien Abraham, local high school coach and commander of Batesville's National Guard unit, the Panthers returned to their losing ways. The gridiron Panthers were so overmatched, recalled their scorekeeper and chaperone John P. Morrow Jr., that in a game against Southeast Missouri State Teachers College everyone on the Arkansas College side came away injured, except the coach, the bus driver, and "a boy from Warren who was so fast they couldn't catch him." Plagued by serious financial problems and beset with declining grades among football players, President Lacy and the board of trustees decided to drop the football program after the 1935 campaign, a season of "pure manslaughter." For years afterward Abraham would boast, only partially in jest: "If [I] didn't do anything else for Arkansas College, [I] did stop football."[81]

The organization that came to characterize Arkansas College's football program in the decade and a half after World War I often escaped the baseball team. Baseball was so strongly identified with summertime that it failed to fit neatly into the college calendar. Furthermore, a plethora of minor league, semiprofessional, and amateur town teams tended to drain both fans and players away from the college ranks. Arkansas College's 1919 baseball schedule reflects the variety of opponents even for a college team. Of seven games played by the Lambs that spring, only three were against another college squad. The college also played the traditional game against Sulphur Rock's town team as well as a three-game series with an independent club from Little Rock. In subsequent years the baseball Panthers faced such foes as an army team from Little Rock's Camp Pike, a town team from Cave City, and the local minor

The Panthers baseball team, 1925.

leaguers of the Batesville White Sox. Despite the odd schedule and the fact that baseball had lost its once-hallowed position of prominence to football, the diamond continued to produce local feats of heroism. One of the more notable occurred in May 1921 when Lester "Stogie" Evans, whom the *Panther* referred to as the best pitcher in the state, beat Little Rock College twice in three days, including a seven-inning no-hitter in the series' rubber game.[82]

The arrival of Coach Kent V. Morrison, a former Vanderbilt baseball star, in the fall of 1922 brought a sense of structure to the baseball team that had heretofore been lacking. Beginning with the 1923 season the baseball Panthers played a schedule made up almost exclusively of other college squads. Morrison's first team posted a 5–4 record behind the strong play of catcher Alfred Kelly. The 1924 season featured the longest road trip to date for an Arkansas College baseball team. The Panthers played eight games in four different locales, including two matches against Bethel College in Morrison's hometown of McKenzie, Tennessee. During Morrison's five years as coach, the baseball team tended to play teams in northern Arkansas and western Tennessee. First District A & M, West Tennessee State Teachers College, and Southwestern at Memphis were the Panthers' most common opponents.[83]

After Jap Patterson took over coaching duties in 1928, the baseball schedule gradually came to resemble the football schedule. By the late 1920s and early 1930s the strong gridiron rivalries with Ouachita Baptist, College of the Ozarks, Hendrix, Arkansas State Teachers College, and other in-state institutions had found their way to Daffin Field's baseball diamond. Like his football squads, Coach Patterson's baseball teams were generally competitive though not outstanding, except for the 1930 lineup. Although there was no season-ending tournament to decide the best team, the *Index* staff rightly declared the Panthers the 1930 state champions after the baseballers posted a perfect 15–0 record against six in-state opponents. Stars on "the best team in Arkansas College history" included pitchers Doc Williams and Red Fiser, who between them hurled five shutouts, and outfielder Lonnie Ethridge, "the Babe Ruth of Arkansas collegiate circles."[84] After Patterson's departure two years later, declining enrollment and increasingly scarce financial resources placed athletics on the back burner once again, and, though baseball did not receive the administrative death sentence handed down to football, most springs in the 1930s found Arkansas College with no varsity baseball team.

The one varsity sport that survived the era intact, though not without struggle and hardship, was basketball. Arkansas College's first post–World War I basketball team participated in the state's first college basketball tournament at Arkadelphia in late February 1920. Playing without center Joel Spragins, the Lambs finished fourth in the five-team field. After a winless season the following year, the college sported no basketball team again until the 1925–1926 session. Shortly before Christmas 1925, Kent Morrison selected a varsity in the same manner that V. A. Wilber had used more than a decade earlier. After an intensive intramural tournament featuring squads from each class, Morrison selected the top twelve to play rival college teams. The highlight of the 1925–1926 season was a 34 to 28 victory in Conway over Hendrix, the first loss in two years for the state's most dominant team. Over the next few seasons the mediocre Panthers consistently defeated weaker junior college opponents such as First District A & M and Mountain Home College, but struggled against tougher teams like Hendrix and Arkansas State Teachers College.[85]

The college's most obvious drawback throughout most of the 1920s was the lack of a gymnasium. At the end of World War I Erwin Gymnasium had been transformed into a library, and subsequent efforts to build a new gym failed. A basketball goal was erected at Daffin Field, but inclement winter weather rendered this a poor substitute. As a result, Arkansas College was forced to rent the local high school gymnasium for home games. In the fall of 1927 a proposal to build a combination gymnasium/national guard armory using state funds fell through. When Batesville High School increased its rental charges and limited the college's use of its facility the following year, President Tucker took the initiative and, with the help of student labor and $1,200 raised among local boosters, oversaw the erection of a "temporary gymnasium" east of Independence Hall. The "Barn," as students came to refer to the new structure, could hold five hundred spectators but its seventy-six-by-thirty-eight-feet court was far below regulation size. Nevertheless, the temporary gymnasium, cold and rustic as it may have been, had an immediate impact on the basketball program. The convenience of a home court allowed Coach Jap Patterson to expand his schedule to fifteen games in 1928–1929. The following season produced a winning record of 8–6 for the Panthers; four of the six losses came at the hands of powerful Hendrix. Three of Coach Patterson's players garnered all-state honors. Lonnie Ethridge, the "Babe Ruth" of the baseball team, made second-team all-state, while two players performed well enough during the season to earn first-team berths: James "Slim" Carvell and Travis "Pete" Creed, whose twenty-eight-point effort against Ouachita Baptist in Arkadelphia tied a state record for most points in a game. Although Ethridge returned to all-state form again the next two years, the Panthers won few games against a tough college schedule. Coach Patterson's departure in 1932, combined with the college's financial inability to hire a full-time athletic coach as a replacement, left the basketball team in the hands of student coaches throughout the remainder of the decade. The most successful of these student-coached teams during the mid-1930s was Wesley Carpenter's 1934–1935 squad, which posted a then school best record of eleven wins in seventeen contests.[86]

Football, baseball, and basketball tended to eclipse Arkansas College's other varsity sports during the 1920s and 1930s. Nevertheless, coaches and students in various years put together track and tennis teams for competition with other schools. The Panthers entered their first post–World War I state track meet in May 1922 and brought home four ribbons, including two for long-distance running won by freshman Charley Robinson. With the arrival of Coach Morrison, track became a regular part of the athletic program at the college. Morrison's teams never challenged for a state title, but a few Panthers usually managed to bring home second- or third-place ribbons each spring. In the spring of 1924 alumnus Harry Ponder of Walnut Ridge donated the materials for the construction of a cinder track around Daffin Field. In the annual statewide meet that year—featuring teams from Hendrix, Henderson-Brown, Ouachita, and Ozarks as well as Arkansas College—Tillar Conner, also of Walnut Ridge, took first-place in the 800-yard run. In 1925 Morrison scheduled the college's first head-to-head track meet against First District A & M, which the Panthers won; the 1926 schedule included track meets with A & M and Mountain Home College. At the annual state meet that spring, Cecil "Red" Justus of Black Rock won the two-mile race and finished second in the mile to lead Arkansas College to its best finish in third place. The expanded baseball schedule under Coach Jap Patterson erased track at Arkansas College until 1930, when the Panthers lost head-to-head meets to First District A & M and College of the Ozarks. Arkansas College hosted the state meet in 1931, but that year's track team proved to be the last at the college until the latter part of the decade.[87]

The only other sports to achieve varsity status during the inter-war years were tennis and golf. As early as the spring of 1921 students had established a tennis club, but it would be several more years before the sport rose above the level of intramural competition. Throughout the 1920s Arkansas College featured an annual interclass tennis tournament, but it was only in 1930 that Patterson organized a squad for intercollegiate competition. In 1931 the tennis team held individual matches with

Hendrix, Harding, and College of the Ozarks. But the sport appears to have fallen victim to the depression; the 1932 team was the last for the Panthers until just before World War II. Golf's claim to varsity status was even more brief and tenuous than that of tennis. Although the various volumes of the *Index* for the 1920s and 1930s never mentioned a golf team, a story from the student newspaper, the *Panther*, reported that in the spring of 1929 the duo of Mac Albright and William "Spider" Irving represented Arkansas College in the state golf tournament and brought home a third-place finish. Irving, from Morrilton, was perhaps the busiest athlete in college history. A letterman in the four primary varsity sports, he also partnered with his brother James to form the Panthers' most effective tennis doubles team. Irving must have also found the time for academics for in 1931 he earned his A.B. after the standard four years of study.[88]

Along with varsity sports in the post–World War I era came the typical contingency of related organizations and events: cheerleaders, lettermen's clubs, homecomings, and other phenomena fueled by unbridled student energy. As early as 1923 Panther football games featured student cheerleaders, or yell leaders. Four years later students organized the college's first pep club. Arkansas College held its first homecoming celebration on Saturday, 9 November 1928. The day of festivities featured an intramural girls' field hockey contest, music, speeches, a luncheon, and a parade to Daffin Field. At halftime of the game against First District A & M, which eventually ended in a 6 to 6 tie, Eugene Long crowned Iris Dobson homecoming queen.[89]

Even more synonymous with the maturation of varsity athletics in the inter-war period was the lettermen's club. The tumultuous war years ended the brief life of Arkansas College's first such organization. In the fall of 1920 John B. Daffin helped students organize the "A" Association, whose purpose was to "promote clean and successful athletics." The following spring the twenty lettermen of the "A" Association held their first annual banquet in the Masonic Hall room of First National Bank in Batesville. In January 1923 the association changed its name to the more contemporary sounding "A" Club, but within a couple of years the administration abolished the club due to misconduct on the part of some of its members. Coach Patterson reorganized the "A" Club upon his arrival in the fall of 1927. The upper-class lettermen celebrated the rebirth of their organization by organizing a massive public hazing campaign just a few weeks later. Freshmen initiates were forced to attend classes in blackface or dressed as women, in pajamas, or in tuxedos. One student in a tuxedo was required to ride a donkey to and from classes, while others begged for meals in town and directed Main Street traffic. Fortunately, the "A" Club's stated purposes did not include year-round hazing of freshmen. According to a description in the 1928 *Index*, the "A" Club's responsibilities included promoting clean athletics in northern Arkansas, recruiting high school athletes for the Panthers, and maintaining interest among the alumni.[90]

In some cases the quality of varsity play in the 1920s and 1930s was little different than that of intramural athletics, and in rare instances intramural athletics actually generated more student interest and participation. Informal athletic competition had existed on the college campus since its founding, but it was only after World War I that

Women's basketball team, 1921.

it began to take the recognizable form of organized intramural athletics. Tennis remained a popular intramural sport throughout the era, and informal track contests, such as the first Arkansas College pentathlon in 1925, were not uncommon. During the 1924–1925 session men's basketball assumed the intramural spotlight when Coach Morrison organized a tournament between class teams. The freshmen, behind the play of captain Lowell Manning, swept undefeated through their six games and convinced Morrison that the student body contained enough talent for a varsity squad. At various times male students even competed in intramural football games and boxing.[91]

The real pioneers of intramural competition at Arkansas College, however, were the women. Like other colleges in the nation, Arkansas College sponsored no organized intercollegiate athletic competition for women. The one exception appears to have been a women's basketball game staged between the college and Hendrix on 17 December 1920. Coached by voice and piano teacher Sophia Mount, the Arkansas College girls lost by the score of 12 to 37. Aside from this one aberration, women's sports would remain a local affair. The gradual formation of a women's intramural program began during World War I when the college mandated at least two hours per week of physical training for all students, male and female. In the fall of 1921 female students founded the Women's Athletic Association, which organized basketball and field hockey games between teams representing each class. Women's athletics received another boost in the fall of 1922 when Arkansas College hired a director of physical education for girls. Despite the rapid turnover in this low-paying position, the Women's Athletic Association survived, and the field hockey matches between the Danes and Vikings or Blues and Maroons grew more intense each year. By the 1925–1926 session the women's intramural schedule of activities included field hockey, basketball, volleyball, baseball, tennis, track, and hiking.[92]

It was only after the demise of Panther football that an organized intramural program was extended to young men. In the spring of 1936 Arkansas College faced the prospect of having only one varsity sport, basketball, the following session. Consequently, Lucien Abraham, who had taken over as director of athletics in the fall of 1935, drafted a detailed plan for implementing a thorough program of men's and women's intramural sporting events, which the faculty and board of trustees approved. Beginning in the fall of 1936, Arkansas College offered tennis, volleyball, field hockey, softball, archery, and physical education classes to young women. Young men had access to coaching classes as well as competition in softball, tennis, soccer, cross country, volleyball, basketball, track, baseball, archery, and even horseshoe pitching. Much of this intramural program remained intact even with the reintroduction of varsity athletics after World War II.[93]

Although the pace of curricular change did not match that of athletics and the rest of the extracurriculum in the 1920s, the Tucker era displayed a certain dynamism within the faculty and its course of study. Arkansas College's faculty experienced the frequent turnover common among low-paying denominational colleges of the era, but this almost constant infusion of new blood and talent into classrooms and laboratories resulted in a diversity of specialities, interests, and courses that often enhanced a student's education. During the eight academic sessions of the Tucker era, almost sixty different individuals served at one time or another on a faculty that generally consisted of twenty to twenty-five full- and part-time educators each year. Especially prone to revolving-door positions were the special, semi-academic fields such as home economics, music, and speech, fields most likely to be populated by underpaid young, single women. No fewer than twenty-two teachers served in one of these areas during Tucker's administration. Aside from Lois Ball in speech and alumna Bess Maxfield in music, most stayed no more than a year or two. Even the more traditional literary and scientific faculty positions experienced frequent turnover. Twenty-nine different professors filled the approximately dozen spots on the literary faculty. Only two—Eugene Long and Lincoln Barker—served throughout Tucker's tenure.[94]

Sometimes new professors cooperated with students to create new organizations and programs in this age of student activity. Ernest F. Haden helped his upper-level French students organize the college's first French club, Le Circle Français, in the fall of 1925. New history professor A. L. Bramlett, the first Arkansas College professor with an earned doctorate, introduced the first course in Arkansas history and founded a history museum in the library in the fall of 1928; students and townspeople contributed artifacts from the Civil War and World War I, and former student Harry Ponder of Walnut Ridge loaned the museum his collection of Native American relics. Nevertheless, the museum disappeared when Bramlett, like so many others, moved on after only one year in Batesville.[95]

Fortunately, Tucker also enjoyed the benefit of a small core of professors whose tenures extended throughout or through much of his administration. Chief among this latter group was the venerable Eugene Long. Had he exchanged his burly white mustache for a beard of the same shade, Long would have borne a striking resemblance to his father. As it was, the increasingly dour and stern former president represented a direct physical and spiritual link with Arkansas College's earliest days. Many students of the post–World War I era must have thought their strict and old-fashioned Bible professor a refugee from a bygone era of Latin recitations and oral examinations. And in many ways he was. At the least he frequently found himself at odds with the new breed of student who populated the Batesville campus during the Jazz Age.[96]

Tucker's faculty featured a blend of old and young, alumni and newcomers. In the fall of 1924 Eugene Blandford, who had been forced off the faculty a decade earlier by poor health, rejoined Arkansas College as professor of Latin and rekindled his old friendship with Dan Frierson. Their time as colleagues proved brief, however, when Little Dan, who had for several years conducted his classes from a wheelchair, retired in early 1925. At the time of his retirement Frierson's twenty-eight and a half years of continuous service were the most in the college's history. At their midsemester meeting in March, the board of trustees named him Arkansas College's first emeritus professor and voted to grant Frierson a lifetime pension of $1,800 per year. (Sadly, faced with growing financial problems, the board gradually reduced Frierson's pension to $300 before discontinuing it completely in 1930.)[97] Frierson's successor as professor of mathematics, Samuel W. Williams, would compile an even more impressive record of service to Arkansas College.

Long and Blandford embodied a sense of tradition and heritage, but it was the young professors whose innovations and methods melded more easily with the spirit of the student body in the 1920s. Several newcomers stayed long enough to leave lasting impressions, including Jane Brookfield Brown in education and William T. Garrett in biology. Tucker was also responsible for recruiting Samuel W. Williams, who left his post at the Peebles-Tucker School in Springfield, Tennessee, a school that Arkansas College's president had helped found, to come to Batesville in 1924. A fellow Vanderbilt graduate, Williams would devote almost four decades to the college as professor of mathematics and several years as dean of the faculty.[98]

Two young men who joined the faculty in the fall of 1923 became student favorites. Lincoln Barker, a mild-mannered and proper Westminster College graduate who had undertaken graduate studies at Princeton, first introduced the study of modern psychology at Arkansas College. Students were equally taken with Barker's erudite wife, Catherine, whose New Deal experiences in the hill country around Batesville she translated into a book after the Barkers left the college in the mid-1930s. Even more familiar with the hill culture of the Ozarks was John Quincy Wolf Jr., a 1922 alumnus and Batesville native who returned to his alma mater after earning a master's degree at Vanderbilt. In a development not uncommon on small college campuses of the era, Wolf spent three years teaching history before becoming a professor of English, the field in which he had actually pursued graduate studies. Arkansas College suffered one of its greatest losses when, due to severe financial problems, it could no longer support Wolf's efforts toward a Johns Hopkins doctorate and let him get away. John Quincy Wolf Jr. went on to a distinguished career as an English professor and folklorist at Southwestern at Memphis.[99]

On Wolf's first leave of absence (1928–1929) to pursue his doctorate in Baltimore, he was joined by fellow faculty member John Baker Daffin. (On their return to Arkansas College in the fall of 1929 the two directed students in the formation of one of the school's more unusual organizations, the Arts and Sciences Club, made up of English and chemistry majors.) More than any other individual, young Professor Daffin left his stamp on Arkansas College in the 1920s. Although by the end of the depression his name would be associated with the athletic field in the minds of most students, Daffin's contributions in the classroom and laboratory had far more lasting results. Daffin came to Arkansas College in the fall of 1920 as a scientific jack of all trades. After teaching subjects throughout the scientific spectrum in his first few years in Batesville, faculty enlargement and specialization eventually allowed him to concentrate on chemistry, his specialty and the subject of his University of Chicago master's degree. Daffin developed the college's first two-year premedical course and, with the help of unusually generous administrative funds, expanded and modernized the college's three chemistry laboratories in the attic of the Isaac J. Long Memorial Building. The young teacher's appealing classroom demeanor and ability to perform practical demonstrations of theoretical concepts endeared him and his classes to students, so much so that by the late 1920s chemistry was Arkansas College's third most popular major. As one student noted years after Daffin's departure from Batesville, the chemistry professor had "a breadth of vision, a kindly interest and gentlemanly enthusiasm that surpass(ed) all of the other teachers."[100] Arkansas College also produced an unusually large number of students bound for medical school or graduate school in the sciences during the decade. Daffin's decision to take a position at Mary Baldwin College in Virginia in 1930 left the science department in disarray for years to come.

Daffin, Wolf, and the other teachers participated in the Tucker administration's most significant curricular change when in the spring of 1926 the faculty approved a plan to abandon the old "group system" and adopt the more modern major-minor system. In the fall of that year all underclassmen were required to choose among fourteen major fields of study and sixteen minor ones. Reflecting the continuing popularity of the humanities, English and history quickly developed into the two most popular majors, with chemistry and mathematics as distant runners-up. Students could also choose such traditional fields as Latin, Greek, and philosophy or more modern fare like biology, education, and psychology. Although regular matriculates could earn a limited number of hours for courses in music and speech, these departments were not yet fully integrated into the curriculum and continued to offer their own diplomas. One could, however, take a minor in home economics until that department was discontinued in 1928. Under the new system, most freshmen and sophomore courses continued to be prescribed; a major required eighteen semester hours beyond freshman-level courses, the minor twelve hours. (Within a couple of years the requirements for majors and minors were raised to twenty-four and eighteen hours, respectively.) Of the 124 hours needed for graduation, half were required and half elective. Latin had already been removed from required status, but all Arkansas College students continued to face twelve hours of Bible, twelve hours of English, and fourteen hours of a foreign language, along with smaller requirements in history and science. Students were allowed to substitute a third year of their foreign language for freshman mathematics (college algebra and plane trigonometry), and all freshmen were required to attend year-long orientation and hygiene classes.[101]

By the spring of 1930 a statistical analysis of student major preferences influenced Tucker and the faculty to make alterations to the system. Tucker's spring report to the board of trustees revealed that two-thirds of Arkansas College's students claimed either English or history as a major (though, incredibly, the faculty contained only one professor in each of these fields) and that half the major fields contained no more than five students. There were no Greek majors and only one German major. With the hiring of additional professors a financial impossibility, the faculty and board approved a plan implementing five new "combination" majors: science, social science, foreign language, philosophy and psychology, and psychology and education. Combination majors required thirty hours instead of the standard twenty-four hours, and all students retained the right to select one of the older major fields. In addition to adopting combination majors, the faculty also developed the college's first "readings" course in the spring of 1930. Boasting no classes or exams, this two-hour course extended over two years and required a student to read and report on twenty-four novels selected from a list of fifty compiled by the faculty.[102]

Although there is little to suggest that E. B. Tucker came to Batesville with a mandate to "purify" Arkansas College's liberal arts curriculum, most of his suggestions and the results of his administration tended to streamline the liberal arts nature of the institution. Suggesting the brief presidency of John I. Cleland more than a quarter century earlier, two of Tucker's first suggestions were to tighten entrance requirements and to get rid of the college's preparatory wing. For many years the preparatory school had been an integral component of Arkansas College's mission. The paucity of quality high schools in the state, especially in northern Arkansas, demanded the existence of a prep school, not only for preparing potential college students but also for covering the remedial work of students who came to Batesville unprepared for the rigors of the liberal arts curriculum. But in the years immediately preceding and following World War I, Arkansas's public education system had undergone significant improvement, resulting in a growing number of Class A high school graduates. Consequently, by the mid-1920s the college-operated preparatory school had begun to look antiquated. At Tucker's request, in the spring of 1924 the faculty voted to close the preparatory school after the 1924–1925 session and further agreed that all incoming freshmen must have completed all fifteen units defined by the National Conference Committee on Standards of Colleges and Secondary Schools. The board of trustees approved both actions at their June 1924 meeting, and the college preparatory school graduated its last class one year later.[103]

The utilitarian subjects introduced during the Lacy years also gradually disappeared during Tucker's administration. The courses in shorthand and typewriting, which had been offered through the preparatory school, were erased from the college's catalog along with the prep school. Faced with declining interest and a tightening budget, Arkansas College abandoned its brief flirtation with home economics in 1928. But the fact that these changes were not motivated by a desire for a pure liberal arts curriculum was reflected in the tremendous growth of the education department during Tucker's administration. Tucker himself had come to Arkansas College from the arena of public school education, and under his influence the education curriculum expanded its role in the college and in north central Arkansas. By the fall of 1926 Arkansas College boasted one full-time professor of education, Jane B. Brown, and one part-time professor, Sidney Pickens, who also served as superintendent of Batesville's schools. In addition to nine courses offered by Brown and Pickens, students found offerings in the philosophy of education, athletic coaching, and teaching music in public schools. In the fall of 1928 a poll conducted during registration revealed that half of the college's 203 students were preparing themselves for careers as teachers, though the vast majority continued to claim another field as a major. Another one of the innovations of the Tucker era, summer school, was quickly dominated by the demands of potential and actual teachers. First conducted by Lincoln Barker and other professors in June and July of 1926, the six-week session was designed specifically with the area's public schoolteachers in mind. In addition to a variety of education courses required of those hoping to upgrade their teacher's licenses, the summer term ordinarily offered freshman-level classes for those who had failed and were trying to stay on schedule for graduation.[104]

The introduction of the major-minor system and the limited tinkering with the curriculum during the Tucker administration were undertaken with an eye toward accreditation. The process of accreditation, whereby some sort of governing body or association develops a set of standards that colleges and universities must meet before they can attain membership in the association, was a product of the standardizing and professionalizing forces at work in the Progressive Era. The various accrediting agencies that sprang up in the late nineteenth and early twentieth centuries, or, as historian Hugh Hawkins refers to it, the "age of standards," had little influence on higher education in Arkansas before World War I, but in the 1920s, as Arkansans attempted to catch up with neighboring states, accreditation became a key word in higher education circles.[105] The state of Arkansas maintained no governing body to oversee institutions of higher education, and the state department of education had never drafted procedures for ranking public or private colleges. In the early 1920s, however, the state department of education announced that beginning in 1926 it would begin accepting the rankings handed down by the various national accrediting agencies (such as the Southern Association of Colleges and Secondary Schools and the North Central Association) as its own classifications. W. S. Lacy's only nod in this direction was his somewhat unsuccessful attempt to hire only faculty members who possessed a legitimate graduate degree.

When Tucker assumed the presidency in 1923, he set about immediately to ready Arkansas College for accreditation. In addition to abolishing the preparatory school, Tucker installed a formal, hierarchical structure more extensive and detailed than anything that the little Batesville college had yet seen. In the spring of 1924 the board of trustees accepted Tucker's proposal for a seven-tiered faculty ranking system that assigned qualifications and proposed salary ranges for a hierarchy of educators extending from undergraduate assistants at the bottom to full professors at the top. Under this new system, rank and salary would be commensurate with educational attainment and experience. Nevertheless, Tucker's plan allowed the college to continue hiring low-level professors who had not yet completed a master's degree, a practice frowned upon by accrediting agencies. Tucker also urged the board to raise all faculty salaries, which he characterized as "entirely too low." Furthermore, an administrative bureaucracy began to take shape under Tucker's guidance. To his amazement, the new president discovered that the college had never developed a standardized record-keeping system for registering, transferring, and certifying students. In 1924 the board agreed to hire a registrar (Annie Frierson, daughter of Little Dan) as well as the college's first full-time treasurer, J. L. Boggs. (By 1926 the title of treasurer had been changed to bursar.) In 1925 the new position of vice-president was created, and two years later the old version of the dean was replaced by two modern positions: dean of the faculty and dean of students. By the late 1920s the administrative and nonteaching staff—which included two nurses, a superintendent of buildings and grounds, and five secretaries—had grown larger than the faculty.[106]

During Tucker's first year at Arkansas College, the state department of education hired a professor from the University of Missouri to visit denominational colleges and grade them according to the criteria used by the North Central Association of Colleges and Secondary Schools. Tucker used this report card to develop a strategy for accreditation. Only one denominational college in Arkansas, Hendrix, met all NCA standards. Arkansas College, though ranked the second-best denominational school in the state, came up short in at least three categories: size and quality of the library, the existence of a preparatory school, and the size of the endowment. Tucker put librarian Irene Ferrill to work reclassifying the college's 8,000 volumes according to the Dewey Decimal system, but the expansion of holdings would take a significant increase in funds. The preparatory school was in the process of being phased out. The major obstacle for accreditation proved to be the NCA's minimum endowment requirement of $350,000, more than three times as much as the college currently held. But with the more than $400,000 recently pledged by Arkansans in the Presbyterian Educational Movement campaign, this too looked like an obstacle that would soon be overcome. When Hendrix and the University of Arkansas became the state's first two institutions to gain admittance to the North Central Association in 1924, Tucker held out hope that Arkansas College would join them in a couple of years. But by March 1927, when Ouachita Baptist College received accreditation, Tucker and Arkansas College were in fact further away from achieving their goal than they had been three years earlier. By 1927 Arkansas College had joined a growing body of small, poorly funded denominational colleges who had no real hope of building the endowment necessary for full accreditation. The NCA created the classification of "equivalent college" for these colleges whose standard of work approximated that of accredited colleges, but Tucker would be an old man and long gone from Batesville by the time Arkansas College joined the ranks of the accredited.[107]

Tucker's struggle for accreditation continued, however, as did his upbeat reports to the faculty and the board. With a favorite Uncle Remus story or an impassioned defense of national fraternities, the energetic president may have been able to convince naive students that there was no better or safer place on earth than Arkansas College. He may even have found occasional solace in the oblivious rush of the burgeoning youth culture on his tiny campus and in the unbounded hopes and ambitions of his young charges. But from the very moment he arrived in Batesville in July 1923, Everett Brackin Tucker knew in his bones that it was all about the money, that not only the growth and success but also the very survival of this isolated little school depended on raising cash, and lots of it. The years ahead brought this truth to light more brilliantly than he had ever imagined.

Chapter 4

"Muddling through Somehow"

In the fall of 1927 Eugene Blandford introduced a course in mythology to the Arkansas College curriculum. Not a required course for any student, mythology nonetheless instantly became one of the most popular electives in the college schedule.[1] Blandford's mild classroom demeanor—he was somewhat like a favorite old uncle when compared to the stern, fatherly figure of Eugene Long—and the seeming whimsy and lightness of the subject appealed to a generation of students who were experiencing, and often driving, the college's gradual move into modernity. Although his class notes have not survived, it is almost a certainty that at one time or another Blandford and his students discussed one of mythology's most unforgettable and tragic characters, Sisyphus. It would have been tragic indeed had the fate of Sisyphus not been discussed on the campus that by World War II could have adopted him as a mascot.

According to Greek mythology, Sisyphus, king of Corinth, watched as Zeus carried the beautiful maiden Aegina off to Mount Olympus. Despite being warned not to divulge the secret of Aegina's disappearance, shrewd Sisyphus defied the gods and informed Aegina's father in exchange for the latter's pledge to supply Corinth with water. When word of this betrayal reached Olympus, an incensed Zeus condemned Sisyphus to Tartarus, the lowest level of the underworld. As punishment Sisyphus was subjected to an eternity of rolling a large stone to the top of a hill, only to have it roll down again as he neared the pinnacle each time. A more discouraging and hopeless fate the ancient Greeks could not imagine.

In some ways the financial experiences of Arkansas College in the decades preceding World War II resembled the fate of Sisyphus. Presidents and trustees must have wondered on occasion if some terrible sin of the past had condemned them to a lifetime of incessant struggle and constant failure. Each time the money began to flow and the college appeared to be on its way to achieving economic security, some cruel twist—perhaps a recession or a flood—emerged to dash nascent dreams. More than once the financial boulder slipped through the tired grip of a William S. Lacy or an E. B. Tucker and cascaded back down the slope to the level ground below. If the 1920s at Arkansas College was synonymous with the birth of a modern student culture, it was equally synonymous with the constant compounding of financial woes.

Most students remained oblivious to the mounting debt—at least until the college's very life was threatened in the early 1930s—but administrators and concerned trustees felt this thorn in their sides at all times. And, despite repeated efforts to manage the debt throughout the depression decade, the various men who willingly hurled themselves into Batesville's Tartarus faced still more years of stone rolling.

If we search for the origin of Arkansas College's post–World War I financial disaster—and the finiteness of human nature almost demands that we do—we are invariably led back to the crowning achievement of the administration of William S. Lacy, the magnificent dormitory that eventually came to be known as Independence Hall. In 1921, when Lacy and the board began planning the new dormitory, the boom economy of the war years was just beginning to settle into peacetime doldrums, and the flow of cash generated by Lacy's earlier fund-raising campaign had already begun to abate. By the spring of 1922, when it became apparent that completion of the first two floors of the dormitory would exceed the $80,000 estimate by almost 25 percent and that all available funds had already been turned over to the construction firm, college officials faced a daunting choice. They could either halt construction until sufficient funds had come in (and thereby risk losing matriculates over the next few years due to lack of boarding space) or they could put college property up for collateral on loans that were by local standards massive. At their June 1922 meeting the trustees opted for the latter course of action and authorized Lacy and secretary of the board J. L. Boggs to obtain loans of up to $80,000 to cover construction expenses. Between Independence Day and Christmas, 1922, the college borrowed from local citizens and Batesville banks $50,000, the bulk of the money to be paid back in five years at 8 percent interest. Nevertheless, by early 1923 Arkansas College still owed more than $21,000 on the new dormitory. The trustees were confident enough in their ability to repay the loans that they voted a faculty-wide 10 percent raise in April 1923, but soon after Lacy's departure in the summer the board obtained additional loans totaling almost $13,000.[2]

Thus, before E. B. Tucker could settle into his office in the Isaac J. Long Memorial Building, Arkansas College was burdened by a debt more than half the size of its endowment. The new president faced several immediate challenges, in addition to the demands arising from recent loans. In a letter written one month after Tucker took over the presidency, Eugene Long assured a friend that "Mr. Tucker, of course, has had his hands full since he accepted." In the two months before classes resumed, Tucker had to replace a handful of former teachers, and the promise of the largest freshman class in history forced him to create two new faculty positions. In addition the president had to find new dormitory matrons and purchase equipment and furniture for the newly finished Independence Hall. Even with the larger enrollment, the increase in receipts from tuition and fees failed to offset mounting operation costs. In his spring 1924 report to the trustees, Tucker noted that Arkansas College's combination of fees and tuition, which amounted to about $375 a year for a full-time boarding student who took no music or speech classes, was lower than that at other denominational colleges in the state.[3]

Although Tucker already recognized that the college's chief problem was its financial situation, there was little reason for panic at the end of his first year. The Arkansas Synod's new policy of donating 22 percent of congregational benevolence offerings to the college had resulted in a significant increase in cash funds; these offerings produced $14,000 for Arkansas College during the 1923–1924 session. More important, by the spring of 1924 Tucker and others were lauding the success of the recent Presbyterian Educational Movement (PEM) in Arkansas. Chaired by trustee and governor Thomas C. McRae, the statewide campaign had exceeded the goal of $406,000 in pledges during 1923. By the time all pledges were calculated, Arkansas College stood to receive $325,000, which would come in through annual payments over a five-year period. If all who pledged money to the PEM carried through on their promises, announced Tucker, the college would not only reach its goal of a $300,000 endowment but would also be able to retire the debt from the new dormitory.[4] But William S. Lacy could have told Tucker a thing or two about not counting his chickens.

In fact, the college's existing endowment fund reflected the problems inherent in relying on pledge payments and the income from investments. By the 1923–1924 session endowment income had dwindled to a mere $6,000, slightly more than 10 percent of the college's gross receipts. To make matters worse, the paltry, poorly performing endowment and the standing debt prevented Arkansas College from tapping into other sources of financial assistance available to denominational schools. Both Ouachita and Hendrix, and many other small, private colleges around the nation, received substantial grants from Rockefeller's philanthropic General Education Board, a source that remained off limits to Arkansas College as long as its finances were in disarray.[5]

Many PEM pledges were earmarked for scholarship funds or other endowment concerns and were thus unavailable for immediate needs. Nevertheless, the college received enough unfettered cash payments to reduce the dormitory debt to about $35,000 by June 1924. In a show of goodwill Governor McRae, who in addition to his gubernatorial duties was a successful banker and lawyer from Prescott, agreed to loan Arkansas College $40,000 (at 7 percent interest) in order to retire the mortgage and other small debts. Still, the rapid increase in enrollment during the mid-1920s left the administration and board little choice but to spend money to keep up. In the summer of 1924 construction began on the third floor of Independence Hall, a project that would cost the college more than $15,000 and would contribute to growing deficits in succeeding years.[6]

By the spring of 1925 Tucker had begun to grasp the gravity of the college's financial problems. Payments from the college's endowment fund were $50,000 in arrears, and PEM pledges had produced only $66,000, less than half the amount projected for the campaign's third year of collections. Lamenting the "disappointingly slow" rate of collections from PEM pledges, the president suggested that the board address the "serious but not hopeless" situation by turning to the wealthy Presbyterians of the state. Tucker urged pastors and lay leaders to put C. T. McCully, PEM campaign director, in touch with "men of means" and suggested that the college might find a friend to donate the money for the building of a new gymnasium. Turning to the rich was a time-honored practice of America's private colleges and universities, though the strategy had produced few results for Arkansas College. Perhaps Tucker hoped to emulate the success stories of other small liberal arts colleges. Davidson College in North Carolina received a boost toward financial security in this same era from the Duke family. Fund drives conducted by Hendrix College had produced an endowment of $300,000 by 1920, and that amount would almost double before the end of the decade. And by the time that Arkansas College's old Presbyterian competitor, Southwestern, moved to Memphis in 1924, the previously poor institution boasted an endowment of almost $1.5 million.[7] But Arkansas College was not destined to find one friend, nor a group of supporters, who could place the school on solid financial ground.

The wealthy bankers, lawyers, and businessmen to whom Tucker hoped to turn for support were not immune to the general rural economic malaise that threatened Arkansas College at the very moment that so many in the country were prospering like never before. And the source of much of this financial distress underscored the college's awkward dependence on the health of the Arkansas economy and the fundamental weakness of a one-crop state. Even the wealthy Presbyterians of the state's small towns and cities prospered and suffered, to some degree or another, as the returns of the cotton market rose and fell. Arkansas was in many ways a vastly different and more modern place in the 1920s than it had been in the 1870s or even in the early 1900s. But when it came right down to it, Everett Brackin Tucker's Arkansas College continued to weather the same vicissitudes of a rural state and its monocultural economy that had rendered the business of higher education such a precarious undertaking for Isaac Long half a century earlier. Among the chief reasons for the failure of so many Arkansans to honor their pledges were the declining cotton market and the poor crop and boll weevil infestation of 1924, which, according to Tucker, decreased enrollment by at least forty-five students. Tucker was cautiously optimistic about the enrollment for the fall of 1925: "There is every indication of a Freshman class of 75 to 100 students, if crops do not fail. But it should never be forgotten that we are subject to all the hazards of businesses in a one-crop state, with the necessity of maintaining and raising standards all the time." The president would soon realize just how true this was.[8]

Tucker and the board did not have the luxury of waiting until Arkansas's economy improved. The college needed money, and it needed it now. In hopes that the tide would turn, at its June 1925 meeting the board of trustees approved a set of goals that if achieved would produce more than $600,000 for endowment and building purposes over the next seven years. But the plan went nowhere. The college, facing mounting operational deficits, could not afford to hire full-time field workers to carry out this campaign. (Some argued that Arkansas College could scarcely afford *not* to hire such workers.) In addition, the very people whom the college would ask for money were the same ones who were still trying to meet their PEM pledges from 1923. This fund-raising logjam ultimately forced Arkansas College to wait until the PEM had run its course.[9]

In the meantime, Tucker had a growing college to run. Although the board had placed a moratorium on further new construction, the college's physical plant was in obvious decline. The construction of new sidewalks, the installation of new water and sewer connections, and the remodeling of the Isaac J. Long Memorial Building cost the college another $15,000 in 1926. Arkansas College once again faced the prospect of turning female students away due to lack of dormitory space. The expanding student body also demanded the addition of new faculty members. In the spring of 1926 the board approved Tucker's recommendation to raise tuition from $80 per year to $100; the extra income would provide enough money to pay one professor's salary. But these were only stop-gap solutions. Tucker knew something more had to be done and questioned his ability to do it. In his report to the board of trustees in March 1926, E. B. Tucker expressed his reservations over the future well-being of Arkansas College and threw out what amounted to a feeler for a vote of confidence:

> I am beginning to doubt if the great future which I believe possible can be accomplished under my direction of affairs at Arkansas College. So far, I have not been successful as a money-getter, and from now on Arkansas College needs a money-getter . . . I have devoted myself unstintedly and whole-heartedly to my tasks, neglecting practically every private interest in the belief that friends would rally to our financial needs when they became convinced that we were worthy. They have not so rallied. Henceforth, the College can not go forward without money.[10]

But go forward it did. The board's response to Tucker's plea was to decline the president's offer of resignation and to embark on an ill-timed expansion program. Just days after the March meeting of the board, the college hired an architectural firm to develop plans for a new college plant on the East End Heights campus. Within a few months construction had begun on a president's home across the street from Independence Hall.[11] It was hoped that this native stone dwelling would lend a bit more dignity to the office than had Tucker's rented house or Lacy's dormitory suite. The board seemed to think that such a bold and aggressive move as planning for elaborate physical expansion would inspire confidence in Arkansas's Presbyterian community and especially among the wealthy. If that indeed was the logic behind the trustees' actions, the gamble failed.

By the summer of 1926 Tucker found himself throttled at every turn by catch-22's. The "men of means" expressed interest in giving to Arkansas College only after the debt had been retired, yet there seemed no hope of retiring this debt without their help. With the accreditation of Hendrix and the University of Arkansas, Arkansas College faced a crisis of reputation, but accreditation was nothing more than a distant dream as long as the college groaned under a growing debt. The expansion of the student body required a concomitant expansion of facilities, but the presence of more students did not translate into more income for the college. Besides, the mere planning for physical expansion cost money with which the college could ill afford to part.

Complicating matters was the board of trustees' lack of consistent leadership. On Easter Sunday in 1926 the board's octogenarian vice-president, Theo Maxfield, died at his home in Batesville. He had served continuously on the board since November 1875 and had held the post of vice-president for almost twelve years. Seven months later Maxfield's close friend James P. Coffin, plagued by ill health and grieved by the loss of his one-time confidante, relinquished his spot on the board. The eighty-eight-year-old had also joined the board back in November 1875 when he was a resident of the Black River town, Powhatan. Coffin had served the college for all but three years of its fifty-four-year existence, and his twenty-five years as president of the board is unrivaled to this day.[12] Between them, Maxfield and Coffin dedicated more than a century of service to the little Batesville institution. It would be two decades before Arkansas College regained the stability of trustee leadership that Coffin and Maxfield had provided throughout the first quarter of the twentieth century. The indecision and inability to commit to long-term plans that would characterize the college's depression years were in part attributable to this crisis of leadership.

The trustees voted to replace the retiring Coffin with Thomas C. McRae. Almost two years removed from the governor's mansion, McRae was no spring chicken himself. Seventy-four years old at the time of his election to the board's presidency, he would not survive the decade.[13] McRae's death in 1929 created a vacuum that the board struggled to fill for more than ten years. Between the stock market crash of 1929 and the bombing of Pearl Harbor in 1941, five different men served as president—the title was changed to chairman in the early 1930s—of the board, not one of them for more than three years. The vice-presidency/vice-chairmanship was equally unstable until a Batesville judge, S. Marcus Bone, took office in 1934. As we shall see, Arkansas College's only consistent leadership during the late 1920s and 1930s came from a core of Batesville residents on the executive committee, which was chaired throughout the era by John P. Morrow Sr.

By the fall of 1926 it was obvious that PEM funds were drying up and that the college's proposed campaign was going nowhere. At the November board meeting that resulted in McRae's election to the presidency, the trustees authorized their executive committee to take out loans to cover the college's operating deficits and to meet upcoming debt payments.[14] The college had already borrowed more than $60,000 by this time—most of it from McRae—and the annual deficit had risen steadily throughout Tucker's three and a half years in office. In fact, it was the college's inability to meet basic operating expenses that threatened its future. The residual effect of the Independence Hall debt could have been chipped away at if only Arkansas College could have covered current expenses. But all sources of income began to shrink. Returns from the old Lacy-era endowment fund gradually decreased throughout the 1920s. By the fall of 1926 the flow of PEM monies had become little more than a trickle, and dwindling synod benevolence offerings had begun to reflect the faltering economy. According to Tucker, it would take an annual emergency fund of $15,000 to replace the lost funds needed for the everyday operation of the college.

In late 1926 and early 1927 the executive committee, on behalf of the entire board of trustees, borrowed $25,000 from Worthen Bank in Little Rock. By the time the trustees met for their annual March conference, the total college debt had surpassed $87,000, and Tucker had resorted to financing the new president's house out of his own pocket. The college president delivered the trustees some sobering facts. Tucker reported tuition and fee receipts at an all-time high, but, as with every bit of good news for the college, there was a distressing side to this development. The expanded student body, the college's largest until the late 1930s, left the tiny campus bursting at the seams. To accommodate this influx Tucker had been forced to rent a two-story house to catch dormitory overflow and had ordered the building of a temporary structure for extra classroom and laboratory space. As a result of such unexpected expenses the annual deficit ballooned to about $18,000 for the 1926–1927 session. There was also one other distressing bit of news related to student fees. Arkansas College, according to Tucker, received almost 70 percent of its total income from student fees and tuition, or about twice the percentage of the average American college. On most campuses in the 1920s, endowment income covered roughly half of all expenditures; it paid for only 10 percent of Arkansas College's expenses.[15]

Tucker's defensive explanations may have pinpointed the structural problems behind the college's financial deterioration, but they did nothing to solve those problems. The board of trustees did, however, take the first steps toward alleviating the debt in the spring of 1927. The executive committee combed the budget for the upcoming year and recommended several cuts. Upon the advice of McRae, the board agreed to consolidate its debts by offering the college's property as collateral for a $100,000 loan from the Bank of Prescott, of which McRae was president. Under this plan, Arkansas College would begin paying off the loan in April 1929 and continue making annual payments until the debt was erased in 1937.[16]

McRae also took the initiative in the college's long-range plan to raise money. He and A. B. Banks, a Little Rock businessman and prominent layman, called Presbyterian leaders to a special meeting at the Marion Hotel in Little Rock on 15 March 1927. Much of the discussion at this meeting revolved around the same issues that the board had dealt with over the past few years. Attendees urged those who had not met their PEM pledges to do so and encouraged the college to seek the cooperation of "men of means." The most ambitious result of this meeting was a hearty approval of the Arkansas College Expansion Program, sometimes referred to as the Greater Arkansas College Program. The Arkansas College Expansion Program was in essence an expanded version of the campaign that the board of trustees had approved a year earlier. Of the $750,000 goal, $350,000 was to be used for the erection of new buildings with the rest going into the endowment fund. By the summer of 1927 the board had spent about $1,000 on a promotional campaign featuring a twenty-page booklet that included an artist's representation of the Expansion Program's proposed buildings—an administration building, gymnasium, a chapel and a conservatory, and a girls' dormitory. President Tucker attempted to rouse the college's slumbering supporters: "Presbyterians! Churchmen! Citizens! Patriots! the call is to you. Will you respond, or will you hesitate and let the opportunity pass?"[17]

By the time Arkansas College began circulating these booklets the following summer, the Arkansas College Expansion Program had already washed away on the muddy waters of the great Mississippi Flood. Just days after the Little Rock meeting reinvigorated the slumping Tucker, the rains began to fall. Exactly one month after the meeting the flood waters peaked, and the college's hopes for financial success began to recede right along with the rivers and streams. By Christmas 1927 the executive committee had borrowed another $18,000, a figure that would have been considerably higher if not for a timely $14,000 bequest from the late Baxter B. Cannon. Despite the tireless efforts of Tucker and C. T. McCully, by March 1928 the Arkansas College Expansion Program had produced barely enough money to cover expenses and pay McCully's salary. Responding to this sorry state of affairs, Tucker warned "that the Presbyterians of the state must soon decide whether they are going to support Arkansas College or let it deteriorate until it dies."[18]

In the spring of 1928 the board once again approved a bevy of budget cuts and another consolidation of debts. This time the college took out a $150,000 (6 percent) bond issue from Merchants and Planters Bank and Trust in Pine Bluff. Two-thirds of this amount was dedicated to paying off the previous bond issue with the Bank of Prescott; the remainder was quickly absorbed by old debts and the current operating deficit. Under the new bond issue the college would be required to pay $11,000 each April beginning in 1930 and ending in 1944. But the flow of incoming funds continued to slacken and the debts continued to pile up in this avalanche of financial futility. By the time the trustees gathered for their annual commencement week meeting in June, Arkansas College had amassed another $30,000 in debts, and the school's liabilities totaled $233,000, far more than the amount of money in the endowment.[19] The following academic year brought no better news. Another disastrous flood hit the White River valley in June 1928, which in some ways was worse than the previous year's catastrophe because farmers were unable to replant their crops. Despite the synod's stamp of approval on the Expansion Program, Tucker received chilly receptions at a number of churches whose members were growing tired of incessant fund-raising efforts from the college and other institutions; in a few cases congregations refused to give him the floor. Such rude treatment led the president to conclude that "the church does not want a college enough to pay for it." By early 1929 the executive committee had resorted to using endowment funds for collateral on loans, and the committee's members had begun considering such drastic budgetary cuts as dissolving entire departments and dropping varsity athletics, although neither took place.[20]

The E. B. Tucker who faced the trustees in March 1929 was not the cheerful dynamo who had arrived in Batesville almost six years earlier. The failures of the last two years had drained his optimism and sapped his energy. In a twenty-seven-page letter to the board, Tucker outlined the history of Arkansas College's debt problem, restated his failure as a "money-getter," and surveyed the college's dim prospects. "The disappointments have been many and the results meager so that now the situation is very embarrassing. The College can not continue longer without a drastic cut in its program or perhaps an entire change of policy and direction." It must have seemed to Tucker that the walls were tumbling down from every direction on the little college. Accreditation was no longer an option, though Tucker realized that the longer Arkansas College persisted without meeting the NCA's standards the more tarnished its reputation would become. Every day that the college remained open cost more money that the college did not have, but each additional campaign for funds further antagonized supporters. Tucker informed the board that the college needed $35,000 in cash immediately in order to satisfy overdue debts, but a recent emergency fund drive had raised less than 10 percent of this total. The only bright spot in the college's financial picture, as far as Tucker was concerned, was the continued loyalty of a small corps of Batesville supporters, some of whom had helped pay for a recently constructed temporary gymnasium. The president was "persuaded that the community would make heroic efforts to meet any conditions which our Board should ask of them because locally we have never had finer support and better feeling toward the College."[21]

Complicating matters for the president and the board were simultaneous movements within the field of higher education in Arkansas as well as pessimistic announcements from Southern Presbyterian authorities. A recent report from the Presbyterian Church in the U.S.'s Special Survey Committee stated that there were perhaps three or four times as many denominational colleges in the South as there were churches and funds to support them. And many people had long questioned the ability of Arkansas's small Presbyterian community to support a four-year college. A minority within the synod had even suggested reducing Arkansas College to junior college status. Tucker quickly dismissed such a move—arguing that it would have no bearing on the college's financial woes—but left open the possibility of merger, a word that would for years haunt the proponents of keeping Arkansas College in Batesville. The merger option was beginning to look like a viable alternative in the late 1920s. At this very moment Arkansas Methodists were in the process of combining their three schools—Hendrix, Henderson-Brown, and Galloway—on the Conway campus of Hendrix, and Texas Presbyterians were preparing to merge their colleges. Had Arkansas contained two Southern Presbyterian institutions it is almost a given that a merger would have taken place. But the nearest Presbyterian schools were Southwestern and College of the Ozarks. Southwestern's recent move to Memphis had reinvigorated the small college and set it on the path to distinction; thus a merger held little allure for its leaders. College of the Ozarks was not only supported by a different denomination, the Northern Presbyterians or PCUSA, but its finances were in equally pitiful shape; a merger with this institution would have resulted in an even larger fiasco.[22]

The irony of the college's situation must have been apparent to Tucker. At the very moment that student extracurricular life had achieved a vibrancy unknown a few years earlier and in the very era when the college had begun to send out more and more capable young men and women to graduate and professional schools and to a variety of careers, the school was about to collapse under the weight of its financial burdens. Tucker was ready to throw up his hands in defeat. But as it had done since the 1870s, the community of Batesville rallied around its college. At the request of local trustees, the board called for a special April meeting of the Arkansas Synod in Little Rock. On 16 April 1929, one week before the special synod meeting, the Batesville Chamber of Commerce met and adopted a set of resolutions to be presented to the synod. The members of the Batesville chamber pledged their community's response to the Expansion Program and promised to raise 10 percent of whatever goal the synod would choose to adopt. More important for immediate needs, the chamber promised to raise an emergency fund of $15,000 by the first day of August.[23]

Members of the synod gathered in Little Rock on 23 April and immediately appointed a committee of eight, chaired by alumnus John F. Lawson, to study the reports supplied by the board of trustees and Tucker as well as the Batesville Chamber of Commerce resolutions. After a brief discussion of the possibilities for merger with Southwestern, the full synod adopted all three of the committee's resolutions. Arkansas College would remain in Batesville as a four-year institution. Most important, the synod would recognize the college's debts as its own, and it would appoint a committee of five to cooperate with the board of trustees in retiring this debt. Although the synod's action was far from universally popular within the Presbyterian community, the decision to tie the synod's reputation to the success of the college introduced an element of stability and promise heretofore lacking in efforts to retire the debt. According to Tucker, the synod's action was enough to replace the air of gloom and dread with a spirit of confidence and hope.[24] Subsequent developments would prove the president's statement more than a little premature.

A renewed Tucker and the board's executive committee went to work following the synod meeting. After a close inspection of the budget, the executive committee once again suggested a wide range of cuts, especially among nonfaculty personnel. The board and the synod's committee of five oversaw the dissolution of the old Presbyterian Educational Movement in the summer of 1929; the college received about $1,500 in the liquidation of the PEM's assets in addition to an automobile and office furniture. But the Batesville Chamber of Commerce was unable to raise the promised $15,000 emergency fund. Reports of just how much money the chamber raised are conflicting, but the board's October report to the synod stated that barely more than half the amount had come in. Soon after the beginning of classes in the fall, the synod's committee of five hired a full-time field worker to collect unpaid pledges; he experienced no more success than had the great majority of his predecessors.[25]

The synod's committee of five launched a fund-raising campaign of its own. At a gathering of ministers and laymen in June, the committee announced plans to raise $75,000 and assigned quotas to thirty churches. By November only $42,000 of this amount had been pledged—more than a third by Batesville Presbyterians—and most pledges were contingent on the committee's ability to secure pledges for the entire $75,000. The committee also reported its first breakthrough with the "men of means" in late autumn 1929. In November the synod's committee of five brokered a deal with one of the state's wealthiest Presbyterian families, the Browns of Hot Springs. Allan Brown, an old friend of the college and former student, agreed to place $50,000 worth of Federal Farm Loan Bonds in a five-year trust for Arkansas College. The college would receive only the annual interest from the bonds, but, promised Brown, if at the end of the five-year period Arkansas College was still Presbyterian and still in Batesville and if the endowment had reached half a million dollars, he would donate the bonds to the permanent endowment fund. This provisional gift was obviously more effective as a publicity tool than as a direct assault on the college's debt.

Arkansas College would receive only a couple thousand dollars each year from the bonds, but Tucker and the board hoped that Allan Brown's tentative vote of confidence would inspire other wealthy Presbyterians to follow suit.[26]

The uncertainty surrounding the college's future took its toll on enrollment in 1929. The freshman class of sixty-six was only two-thirds the size of the freshman class four years earlier. By November Tucker noted that the college continued to live a "hand to mouth" existence, and he forecast doom if the committee of five's $75,000 campaign failed. The outlook was no better five months later at the March 1930 board meeting. Only about one-quarter of the $75,000 had been raised. Most discouraging to the synod's committee and the board of trustees was the near refusal of Little Rock's Presbyterians to cooperate. Arkansas College faced the daunting task of paying $25,000 in bond payments and interest by the first day of April. The complete lack of cash on hand and the inability to liquidate assets forced the administration and board to consider the unthinkable, selling endowment securities to pay off debts. Tucker first broached the subject in a letter to trustee Vann Howell in early February. "But," the president cautioned, "these [endowment securities] should be marketed only as a last resort. The bonds constitute a prior claim on practically all our real estate, buildings, and equipment in Batesville and a moral claim upon whatever else we possess."[27]

The March 1930 meeting took place in room 227 of Little Rock's Marion Hotel. It turned out to be a meeting that would long haunt the board, taint the college's reputation for trustworthiness, and divide the college community. Arkansas College's longtime endowment treasurer, Little Rock banker F. J. Schmutz, informed the trustees that most of the securities in the school's endowment fund could be liquidated. Consequently, the synod's committee of five requested that up to $65,000 of this endowment fund be sold to cover the upcoming bond payment, current expenses, and old debts to various banks and individuals. The committee hoped that a significant reduction of the college debt using endowment monies would "have a stimulating effect upon the constituency of our Church." The motion passed the board, in large measure due to an unwritten understanding that the synod would replenish the endowment fund when the money became available. Although the minutes recorded no protests, it was just a matter of time before the board's action came under attack. By the time of the June meeting of trustees in Batesville, $15,000 of the endowment had been liquidated. When the trustees authorized the liquidation of the rest of the $65,000, secretary John P. Morrow Sr. objected. By early October the executive committee had ordered the sale of about three-quarters of available endowment securities. The meeting of the board that month exposed deep divisions among the trustees. Many, like Morrow, felt betrayed and misled by the synod committee's insinuated promises and opposed any further liquidation of the endowment. Most of those who continued to support endowment liquidation did so out of loyalty to the synod and a desire to protect the good name of Arkansas Presbyterians.[28]

The quagmire of debt and divisiveness threatened to sink Arkansas College. The threat was more real and immediate than ever before. Another natural disaster, the drought of 1930, had compounded the economic woes of the early depression era, and the college's fund-raising efforts over the scorched summer had produced nothing. To make matters worse, instability in leadership positions resulted in a wavering, indecisive board, which proved a poor partner for the equally irresolute Tucker. The death of Thomas C. McRae in the spring of 1929 had left the board without a prominent, widely respected voice of authority. In fact, the summer of 1930 actually found the college without an active board president. McRae's replacement, Presbyterian minister and college alumnus Stuart R. Oglesby, had recently left the state, and the board had deferred electing a successor until the fall. When the trustees finally chose a new president (now called chairman) in October, it was Little Rock businessman Vann Howell, former chairman of the synod's committee of five who had served on the college's board for less than two years. A thirty-six-year-old native of Fordyce, Howell had attended Arkansas College for a year before going to work for millionaire A. B. Banks. By 1930 he was one of Banks's most trusted associates and his business interests extended from insurance and banking to lumber and lime production. Despite the unanimous approval of his election, Howell did not exactly inspire confidence among the college's oldest supporters nor among the opponents of endowment liquidation.[29]

Just a week before Howell's election, yet another entity entered the picture. At the request of Tucker and a group of trustees who sought closer cooperation between the college's board and the synod, the latter body created the Educational Commission of the Synod of Arkansas, a fifteen-member committee made up of both clergy and laymen. The synod empowered the Educational Commission to help the board of trustees solve the college's financial problems, thereby injecting a greater degree of synod influence into the affairs of Arkansas College. At a Little Rock meeting two weeks before Christmas, the Educational Commission recommended discontinuing Arkansas College as a four-year institution at the end of the current academic year. The commission then proposed two options for the future: keeping the school open as a junior college or Tucker's favored plan, merging with Southwestern at Memphis.[30] For the remainder of the month rumors circulated wildly throughout the state that the demise of the college was imminent. There seemed no reason to believe otherwise.

Tucker found a life raft and abandoned ship. At a special meeting of the board five days after Christmas, E. B. Tucker handed in his resignation, announcing that on 1 February 1931 he would leave to become president of Austin College in Texas. Although it is unclear what had transpired in the three weeks since the Educational Commission's meeting, it is evident that Tucker had given up hope that the little college would survive, at least in its present form. Just two days after the October board meeting, the executive committee had disposed of the final available endowment funds, and the administration had struggled during the fall to supply faculty members with at least half their salaries. The resigning president suggested that the trustees appoint two committees—one to confer with Batesville residents concerning the feasibility of keeping the college afloat and the other to meet with representatives of Southwestern and the College of the Ozarks to discuss the possibility of merger. The flummoxed Tucker, who had in recent months waffled from one stance to another on the college question before finally coming out in favor of merger, apparently had no faith that either committee would meet with success. The board's other actions were equally ominous. Allan Brown gave the trustees authority to dispose of $15,000 out of the Brown Family trust fund for the purpose of paying teacher salaries and other current expenses; the Browns were to receive a synod note guaranteeing repayment of the fund. Finally, the board voted to contact all living donors to discuss potential uses of their money should the college close its doors. One month later, on the day before Tucker left for Texas, the board named education professor Uriah "Ury" McKenzie as acting president for the remainder of the year.[31]

The succeeding years would not be kind to Tucker's legacy. Although Tucker received the obligatory honorable send-off from the board of trustees, his seven-and-a-half-year administration would be remembered by most as the era of debt and overspending, not the era of student innovation and academic expansion. Some in the college community would even come to blame him for the college's financial failure. Most damning to his legacy was the fatal decision to liquidate much of the permanent endowment fund, even though the board of trustees had endorsed this action on at least two occasions. Tucker obviously struggled to meet budgetary constraints and curtail expenses he deemed necessary to the college's growth. According to one observer, E. B. Tucker suffered from a lack of the "fear of indebtedness." As far as the president was concerned, a loan extension was almost as good as a loan payment.[32] It would be a gross oversimplification, however, to pin the blame for all the college's problems on Tucker. When he arrived in Batesville in 1923 the new dormitory had already placed the college in debt, and the Presbyterian Educational Movement had instilled false promises of a grand and prosperous future. By the time Tucker and others realized that the flow of funds would be nowhere near as plentiful as projected, the college's financial difficulties had already begun to snowball. And a succession of uncontrollable and unforeseeable natural disasters simply compounded these difficulties. Tucker's most critical mistake was his, and the board's, reluctance to come to grips with the gravity of the situation until it was practically too late.

By 1931 it was also too late to dwell on "what ifs." The supporters of Arkansas College found themselves faced with deciding between letting the college wither away or rallying in hopes of some miracle plan of salvation. There were at least a few who were unprepared to say good-bye to their alma mater. Foremost among these vehement supporters were a circle of Batesville residents and alumni led by trustee John P. Morrow Sr. and Nels and Kitty Barnett. Morrow was an 1896 graduate of the college who had been elected to the board in 1926. By 1931 he was secretary of the board as well as chairman of the crucial executive committee. Ira Nelson Barnett III had graduated from Arkansas College in 1921 at the age of eighteen and had received the Coffin Medal for academic excellence. After earning a second degree at Emory University in Atlanta, he had returned home to Batesville to join his father and older brother in the family's large mercantile business. Barnett's wife, the former Catherine Robertson, or Kitty as she was called, was a 1924 Arkansas College alumna and niece of former president J. P. Robertson who hailed from a prominent Presbyterian family in eastern Arkansas. When the synod announced plans to hold a meeting on

10 February 1931 to consider the college's future, the Barnetts and other concerned Batesville residents started to work.[33]

On the evening of 6 February, a group calling itself the Batesville Citizens' Committee held a public meeting attended by college representatives as well as prominent members of the town's business and professional classes. The result of the meeting was a set of resolutions the committee called the "Proposal for Arkansas College." The centerpiece of the proposal was the Citizens' Committee's promise to raise $10,000 annually for college operating expenses for the next five years—if the synod agreed to keep Arkansas College afloat by assuming its debts. On the chilly morning of 10 February, more than a dozen college supporters made the long drive from Batesville to Little Rock, where the synod convened in the old brick building of the Second Presbyterian Church. After the report by the synod's Educational Commission, the floor was handed over to the contingent of Batesville citizens. Following the reading of a brief telegram from the college's Christian Endeavor Society, Nels Barnett presented the Citizens' Committee's proposal. The life or death of Arkansas College had perhaps come down to the performance of a nervous, twenty-eight-year-old Methodist who had never before attended so much as a Presbyterian session meeting, much less a gathering of the synod. The ministers and laymen listened closely as Barnett, with factual assistance from acting president McKenzie and bursar Malcolm Evans, spelled out Batesville's case for keeping the college open. Whether it was scripted or spontaneous we may never know, but when Nels Barnett's proposal elicited little reaction from the men of the synod, Kitty Barnett rose to deliver her own defense of her alma mater. Displaying none of the nervousness of her husband, the confident young woman presented a brief but impassioned defense of Arkansas College and explanation of its importance to the town.[34]

Although many of the synod's representatives were noticeably moved by Kitty Barnett's heartfelt address, after a lengthy discussion a majority of those in attendance voted to close Arkansas College. No sooner had the spirits of the Batesville citizens deflated than the finality and severity of this action began to breed doubt and reconsideration. At the request of Rev. John Van Lear, pastor of Little Rock's First Presbyterian Church and a staunch supporter of the college, the members agreed to appoint a special committee of three to confer with the Batesville citizens over lunch hour in an attempt to draft a more acceptable proposal. The committee, consisting of the moderator J. P. Snipes along with Arkansas College alumni J. C. Williams and H. L. Paisley, brought back a more detailed and far-reaching proposal. The synod remained deeply divided, but balance of power shifted in the direction of Arkansas College; the vote on the amended proposal showed twenty-seven for keeping Arkansas College open and twenty-two against. Only two, University of Arkansas professor A. W. Jamison and Fort Smith minister Frank Anderson, disapproved of the action vehemently enough to place their opposition on record. The college had a new lease on life, but a lease that in no way guaranteed permanent security.[35]

Under the plan adopted, the synod agreed to assume the full indebtedness of Arkansas College, which by the end of the current academic session was estimated to be about $200,000. At the request of Vann Howell, chairman of the college's board, the synod agreed to undergo incorporation so that it could issue its own bonds in the amount of $200,000. The bonds would bear 5 percent interest, and the synod would begin paying off the notes in 1934. The report demanded that no additional endowment principal be liquidated for the next five years and that Arkansas College maintain a balanced budget during that period. In addition, the synod promised to continue its annual payments of no less than $10,000 to the college and required the Batesville Citizens' Committee to do the same. The synod's action also extended the life of the Educational Commission and instructed the commission to cooperate with the board of trustees of the college.[36]

Just fifteen years earlier the Synod of Arkansas had provided practically no dependable financial support for Arkansas College. The new plan suddenly increased the synod's financial responsibility to the college to an unprecedented level. Once the notes from the synod's bond issue began to come due, the synod would have to spend a minimum of $30,000 per year on the college, or about three times its average annual payment during the preceding decade. This amounted to roughly two dollars from each Southern Presbyterian Church member in the state, a level of denominational support probably unmatched in the nation at the time and one sure to engender resentment within the growing community of Arkansas College's detractors. But greater denominational support would prove of little benefit to the college if the administration was unable to maintain a balanced budget. Working with the board's executive committee and representatives from the Batesville Citizens' Committee, Ury McKenzie and bursar Malcolm Evans drafted a new streamlined budget for the 1931–1932 session. Estimating a gross income for the year of $41,500, the group slashed salaries, positions, and incidental costs to lower projected expenses to $40,000, less than 60 percent of annual expenses during the Tucker administration. Again, the new budget would work only if the synod and the Citizens' Committee met their pledges.[37]

In the heart of the Great Depression there was no guarantee that the synod would even be able to find buyers for the full $200,000 in bonds. Nels Barnett warned the executive committee of such a scenario a month before the Texarkana National Bank issued the bonds on April Fool's Day. As security for the bond issue, Arkansas College deeded title to all its property to the synod. In a show of good faith, the synod agreed to substitute its own notes for almost all the liquidated endowment securities, including $30,000 of the Brown Trust Fund. For all practical purposes, the synod's Educational Commission (and specifically the commission's subcommittee on the college) now possessed as much as or more authority in the affairs of Arkansas College than did the board of trustees. In March the Educational Commission suggested that the board elect its chairman, Vann Howell, as president of the college. Howell balked at the request, and the committee appointed to track down a permanent successor to E. B. Tucker decided it was a bad time for a search. Consequently, it appears that the board's decision to name McKenzie the eighth president of Arkansas College was a move of convenience.[38]

Ury McKenzie was in most regards a strange choice for president. The son of a Yell County farmer, McKenzie had earned his teaching certificate and an A.B. at George

The original campus of Arkansas College. *From left to right:* the Music Building (Morrow Hall), Alumni Hall, and the Isaac J. Long Memorial Building.

Peabody College in Nashville, Tennessee, before returning to his native state. Middle-aged by 1931, like Tucker before him he had spent most of his career as a public school administrator. Just two and a half years earlier he had left Hot Springs to join Arkansas College's faculty as professor of education. Popular with the students—the amiable McKenzie received a standing ovation in Alumni Hall when the student body received word of his election—he had also become increasingly active in efforts to remedy the college's financial problems, including an exhaustive but unrewarding canvassing campaign in the summer of 1930. It was also during that summer that the college had worked out an agreement with the Batesville school system whereby McKenzie would continue to teach half time and would serve as superintendent of the cash-strapped local school district. When the board named him president in the spring of 1931, he did not relinquish his duties as superintendent; it appears that no one expected him to. Thus, throughout his brief administration, Ury McKenzie would be burdened with both jobs and unable to devote adequate time and attention to either.

Before McKenzie could settle into his new position, the college community suffered another tragedy. On 29 June 1931, Eugene Long passed away at the age of sixty-eight. The founder's son had been associated with Arkansas College as a student, teacher, or administrator for forty-eight of the school's fifty-nine years. He taught right up until the end and had just been appointed vice-president of the college. Eugene Long had never received the respect and admiration that the college community and Arkansas Presbyterians had bestowed upon his father; those who follow trailblazers rarely do. He had even experienced the awkwardness of outliving his era and facing a generation of students whose ornery experimentation and disregard for authority he struggled to come to grips with. Nevertheless, Long's length of service as college president remains unmatched, as does his tenure on the faculty. In a brighter time the college community could have afforded their longtime friend the period of mourning and send-off he deserved. It was the old president's last misfortune to exit the stage when all eyes were focused elsewhere.

Ury McKenzie, the one man in Batesville who could sympathize with the travails of Long's past, had little time to dwell on the death of a colleague. By summertime Arkansas's economy was in worse shape than ever, and the sale of the synod's bonds was progressing more slowly than had been hoped. A major reason for the drastic economic downturn was widespread bank collapse. Ironically, for the college at least, the most notable string of bank failures could be traced to a prominent Presbyterian layman and Arkansas College donor. At the time of the stock market crash, A. B. Banks's American Southern Trust Company in Little Rock was the largest bank in Arkansas. Its collapse in late 1930 "set off a domino effect that brought down sixty-six other banks around the state."[39] Not only did the college lose several thousands of dollars personally pledged by Banks, it also saw its already meager endowment returns dwindle as donors went bankrupt and canceled pledges.

Realizing that it would be equivalent to suicide to sit back and wait for the synod's plan to unfold, McKenzie, Barnett, and others sprang to action. Nels Barnett and various trustees began discussing the necessity of approaching the college's wealthy friends in southwestern Arkansas, especially the Browns and Duncan L. McRae, son of the late governor. In the meantime, McKenzie recruited four women—Kitty Barnett, music and voice instructor Katherine Brooks, theater instructor Lois Ball, and 1930 alumna Bess Millen—to tour the state in an effort to attract students and raise money. The Arkansas College Flying Squadron, as the four were known, visited Presbyterian churches in sixteen cities and towns from Wynne to Texarkana in hopes of generating sufficient local interest to start a local alumni association known as an Arkansas College Club. At each stop the Flying Squadron performed a program of music and dramatic reading, followed by a rousing call to action by Kitty Barnett.[40] From the standpoint of fund-raising, the Flying Squadron experienced little success.

Yet, the college's ability to stave off massive student defection in the fall was almost wholly attributable to the efforts of the four young women.

With benevolent offerings at their lowest point in years, in October the synod agreed to increase the college's allotment of this fund to 34.5 percent in order to meet the pledge of $10,000. From the very beginning of the term, however, the college was plagued by rumors predicting its inevitable death. As the new year approached, the atmosphere seemed eerily familiar to McKenzie and the college's supporters. Although the first payment of principal lay a couple years down the road, the synod faced a $6,000 interest payment on the bond issue, with no visible means of meeting that payment.[41] Consequently, the movement within the synod to close or merge Arkansas College reignited and gained momentum. Once again, the synod convened a special meeting in Little Rock to consider the future of the college.

On 23 January 1932, the student newspaper, the *Panther,* reported that the campus was filled with constant talk of Arkansas College's doom. Three days later the synod met at Little Rock's First Presbyterian Church to discuss the feasibility of meeting the upcoming bond interest payment. Despite the frequent discussion of negative rumors, there is no evidence to suggest that the college community approached this meeting with the same sense of anxiety that had accompanied the February 1931 synod gathering. Nevertheless, this second special meeting turned out to be equally harrowing. Late in the afternoon, after a full day of debate and discussion of mergers, a motion to close the college at the end of the current session passed twenty-five to twenty-one. In a replay of the previous year's events, the delegates agreed to hold a re-vote after further discussion. After a second round of talks the synod voted twenty-six to fifteen to keep Arkansas College alive at least until June 1933. Newspaper accounts at the time attributed the turnaround to two causes. First, McKenzie and his scaled-down administration had thus far been able to run the school within the budget mandated the previous spring. Second, a majority of the synod's voting members reacted favorably to McKenzie's promise that he would be able to assume the presidency full-time—meaning he would relinquish his duties as Batesville school superintendent—in June 1933.[42]

The second issue turned out to be a hollow promise when in April the Batesville school district required McKenzie to choose one of his two positions and give up the other. Opting for the job that best suited his talents and personality and the one that promised a greater degree of security, McKenzie decided to resign the college presidency. The board of trustees asked McKenzie and the Batesville school district to reconsider but appointed Charles W. Barnett and Duncan L. McRae to find a replacement in case a compromise could not be reached. Two weeks later at a special meeting of the board in Little Rock, McKenzie handed in his official resignation, to take effect on the first of June.[43] The president's resignation turned out to be but a secondary concern of the meeting. An old familiar face was back—though many current board members may not have recognized it—and the man behind the face was ready as always to take center stage. Ury McKenzie had not enjoyed a minute's rest in his brief tenure as president. Many credited him with saving the college in January, but the trustees were looking into the bleak future when they asked William S. Lacy to join them on this first Saturday in May.

Since leaving Arkansas College almost nine years earlier, Lacy had experienced both the good and bad, the rich and poor, of Presbyterian higher education. Soon after his resignation in 1923, he had gone to work for Southwestern as executive secretary and had participated in that school's move to Memphis and rise to financial and academic notoriety. For the past two years Lacy had been serving the Synod of Mississippi as superintendent for schools and colleges.[44] After listening to his speech on the college's financial situation, the desperate trustees voted to offer him another go-round in the president's chair. Lacy, on the other hand, perhaps bemused that the board was now begging him to return after it had happily bade him farewell those years ago, seems to have been in no hurry to jump into the new position. And who could blame him. The college had narrowly avoided death on two different occasions within the last fifteen months, and the prospects for meeting upcoming bond payments were grim indeed. Lacy's long and sometimes contentious relationship with Arkansas's Presbyterian community had taught him never to count on eager and sustained support, financial or moral. There appeared to be little reason for anyone to seek a job like the presidency of Arkansas College, unless out of loyalty to an alma mater or out of the desire for a supreme challenge.

Lacy's answer to the board was "no," but not a firm "no." Much like he had done in 1916, Lacy agreed to assume the presidency only if certain demands were met in advance. His demand in the spring of 1932 was that actions be taken immediately to reduce the size of the college's (or synod's) debt. Lacy realized that Arkansas College could not go on under the current debt structure and within the depressed economy. Once again, Nels Barnett and John P. Morrow Sr. came forward to rescue their alma mater. When members of the executive committee failed to drum up financial support in Little Rock, Barnett and Morrow took to the road in June and July and held personal meetings with Duncan L. McRae and Allan Brown, who between them controlled almost three-quarters of the synod's $200,000 bond issue. By late July the four men, with occasional assistance from Lacy, had crafted a complex agreement that could potentially reduce the college's debt by more than half. In essence, the Brown family would donate its $50,000 trust fund to the college, and the children of the late Horace E. Bemis, acting through their uncle, Duncan McRae, would cancel at least $45,000 worth of bonds. The plan threatened to fall apart, however, when the wealthy families grew understandably reticent. The key to the deal turned out to be a personal, written guarantee of $20,000 from Lacy, Barnett, Morrow, and other Batesville members of the executive committee.[45]

But by late August, just days before classes were scheduled to begin, Arkansas College still did not have a president. On 26 August 1932, Lacy announced that he would not accept the presidency unless the college's supporters could raise $10,000 in cash immediately. Though there is no surviving record indicating the community's success or failure in meeting this challenge, two days later the *Batesville Guard* announced that the immediate payment of cash had successfully induced the Brown, Bemis, and

McRae families to carry through with their bond-canceling plans. One week later the college sponsored a rally on campus to announce the hiring of William S. Lacy as president.[46]

Even with the significant reduction of the synod's debt, Lacy faced an unenviable task. By the fall of 1932 the depression was reaching its nadir; by mid-September there was not so much as a penny in the college's treasury. The synod's promise of $10,000 from the benevolent offerings had come up almost $4,000 short the previous year and would fall to below $5,000 for the current session. The Batesville Citizens' Committee had successfully met its $10,000 pledge during the previous academic session, but a rash of bankruptcies and canceled pledges forced Nels Barnett to initiate a fresh campaign for donors in November. One solution was the practice of paying faculty members in produce and other goods from local merchants who could then credit these transactions toward their pledges. The college faced additional, unexpected liabilities that years later would seem almost farcical, though Lacy probably found little humor in them at the time. During the summer a student canvasser had struck a pedestrian while driving the college automobile, and the college found itself paying medical expenses in the fall. To make matters worse, in November the Giant Manufacturing Company, from which McKenzie had purchased lights for the football field in 1931, brought suit against Arkansas College for the unpaid balance of the bill. And student fees and tuition failed to produce the amount that had been projected into the budget a year and a half earlier. In spite of the board's decision to reduce tuition from $100 per year to $80 and room and board from $270 to $200, only 133 degree-seeking students greeted Lacy in September, and the freshman class of 38 was the smallest in eleven years. Compounding economic constraints was the college's tradition of waiving tuition to all children of Presbyterian ministers as well as to all students studying for the ministry in any evangelical Protestant denomination.[47]

Lacy, who had shown an ability to pare expenses to a minimum during World War I, took several steps in an effort to maintain a balanced budget. In fact, it was in large part Lacy's legendary tightfistedness that endeared him to the board at this crucial time in the college's history. Within a month of the opening of classes, he announced that the *Panther* would be discontinued and that there would be no yearbook for 1932–1933. The paucity of out-of-town students also allowed the president to cut costs. In December Lacy decided to move all boarding girls into Welch Hall and all boys into Willis Hall. This allowed the college to close cavernous Independence Hall for the second semester, though it would be reoccupied the following fall. At the beginning of the second semester the president informed students that no one would be allowed to graduate or transfer credits to another institution until all bills had been paid. In addition, Lacy continued to assign the Bible classes formerly taught by Eugene Long to other faculty members, thereby avoiding the necessity of hiring a full-time professor for the old James Wilson Moore Chair. On at least one occasion, the president's cost-cutting measures resulted in an unexpected benefit to the college. In order to save money, Lacy forbade college canvassers to stay in hotels when traveling around the state; instead, he personally arranged for them to board with Presbyterian constituents in each town visited.

On a canvassing trip in southwestern Arkansas, Bess Millen Wolf had been invited to spend a night at the Brown family's palatial estate in Hot Springs. When Wolf pulled into the Browns' driveway, the dustpan fell off the rickety college automobile, resulting in quite a commotion and a pitiful scene. The following day Allan Brown wired Lacy enough money to purchase a new car for the college.[48]

Lacy was relatively successful in overcoming the college's dearth of funds during his first year, but his greatest challenges lay ahead. The collapse of Little Rock's Union Trust Company in March 1933 cost Arkansas College about $30,000 of its dwindling endowment. Interest on the remaining synod bonds continued to pile up while returns from the Batesville Citizens' Committee and the synod's benevolent offerings slowed. In August 1933 Lacy announced that all faculty salaries would be based on the amount of money raised by the college, which translated to severe pay cuts and led to the resignation of philosophy and psychology professor Lincoln Barker in May 1934. History professor Margaret Berry Pruden received only $450 plus room and board in Willis Hall for the entire year. Nels Barnett continued his heroic efforts to the point of personally pledging several thousand dollars in late 1933. Had it not been for a timely infusion of Federal Emergency Relief Administration dollars for work-study students in the spring of 1934, Arkansas College would have faced an even more troubling year.[49]

Despite a decade of finagling and restructuring, the financial morass seemed more inescapable than ever. By the fall of 1934 the number of full-time, literary faculty had been reduced to seven (not counting Lacy), the music and speech departments had been switched to self-supporting status, and the president had turned over financing and control of the football program to a group of Batesville boosters. In October 1934 it was revealed that the synod was $27,900 in default on its bond payments. After months of negotiations between bondholders and the synod's Educational Commission, in April 1935 the bondholders agreed to yet another complex refinancing of all bonds maturing over the next four years.[50] As with so many of the college's and the synod's plans, this one was threatened with failure as well. By the November 1935 annual session the synod had yet to approve the debt restructuring plan; meanwhile, the debt had ballooned to more than $200,000, most of it attributable to Arkansas College and almost 20 percent of it due to unpaid interest charges.[51]

At the fall meeting of the synod, Educational Commission chairman W. H. Williams announced that a majority of his commission favored closing Arkansas College, but that they would not now recommend such a move. The moderator of the convention, Rev. S. J. Patterson, father of the former Panther coach, even suggested closing the college or merging it with another institution. By this time, however, it seemed that the college was impervious to such talk; once again, the synod agreed to keep the college open but voted to direct all its benevolent funds toward debt reduction instead of to the school. The synod also approved the debt restructuring plan presented by the Educational Commission, which sparked a massive visitation and fund-raising campaign during the final weeks of 1935 that generated enough money to retire the past-due interest. This was sufficient to stave off death for the time being. Nevertheless, Lacy's revelation that only about one in five

Independence Hall, outside and inside, c. 1927.

churches in the synod participated in this last-minute campaign highlighted the college's precarious position within an increasingly unsupportive denominational community.[52]

Although financial concerns troubled the college throughout the 1930s, administrators and faculty attempted to maintain some semblance of normality on campus. William S. Lacy, in particular, attempted to reclaim what he viewed as Arkansas College's lost focus on its mission of "character building." As we have seen, the Tucker administration accompanied, and in many ways encouraged, the growth of the modern youth culture and collegiate spirit on the Batesville campus. Lacy found many facets of this culture and spirit disturbing and worked diligently to resurrect defunct religious organizations on campus and to reinstate the spirit of Christian commitment that had slowly dissipated in the rush of the Jazz Age. Claiming that "[w]eak and compromising attitudes on moral and ethical issues and an effort to adopt the standards of worldly institutions is the bane of so-called Christian institutions," the president reestablished mandatory Sunday School attendance and waged war on students who habitually skipped morning chapel. Lacy's first year was especially trying. Cases involving drinking and dancing kept the faculty committee busy, and the decision to house boys and girls in adjacent dorms produced problems. The destructive habits of some of the boys—including setting off fireworks in the dormitory and tossing furniture—led Lacy to contemplate hiring a night watchman for Willis Hall. In the fall of 1933 the faculty committee held a special meeting to discuss the spiritual welfare of students, and in early 1934 Lacy ordered faculty members to compile a list of all students who were not members of a church. The unwavering president gradually regained control of the little college—thanks in part to the small enrollment—and by the spring of 1937 he could boast about the "fine attitude" of the student body.[53]

Lacy's second administration also combined practices from the college's past with suggestions of its future. Lacy's background in the tiny Arkansas College of the pre-Tucker era was reflected in the adoption of practices that encouraged attention to the needs of individual students and student-teacher cooperation. In what must have been an incredible scene, and one unthinkable today even at a small college, in January 1933 Lacy and the faculty met to discuss and consider the performance of each student one by one. They would repeat the process the following year. In the spring of 1934, due to the "distressingly low level of scholarship," Lacy and the faculty instituted a tutoring program whereby any student making a "D" or lower in any class was required to meet in private session with the professor at least two hours per week. Because it occurred simultaneously with severe cutbacks in pay, this may have been as unpopular with the faculty as it most likely was with students. In 1935 Lacy started a semiannual program in which faculty members met to hear one of their colleagues read an original paper. The faculty also took measures to stiffen the requirements for awarding the Coffin Medal, requirements that had been lowered during the Tucker administration.[54]

Ironically, it was during Lacy's tumultuous and impoverished second administration that the college faculty began to assume a more modern look as well. During the administrations of Tucker and McKenzie, the college had hired only two teachers with university Ph.D.'s, history professors A. L. Bramlett in 1928 and Anne King Gregorie in 1929.[55] By the 1936–1937 session, however, the Arkansas College faculty contained no fewer than four Ph.D.'s. Several developments accounted for this sudden influx of university-educated personnel. Having worked for Southwestern for seven years and having followed its development after that time, Lacy was well aware of that college's preference for Ph.D.'s and especially for former Rhodes Scholars. Furthermore, the declining number of teaching positions available in American colleges and universities during the depression made it easier for a small, low-paying institution like Arkansas College to attract professors with doctorates.[56]

Most important, however, were developments that took place within the Arkansas College community. Although the massive debt blocked any chance of accreditation, Arkansas College continued to rely on rankings from other institutions. As the state's representative for the North Central Association of Colleges and Secondary Schools, the University of Arkansas periodically inspected the state's unaccredited colleges. By the early 1930s Arkansas College regularly received a "Number One" rating for its freshman and sophomore instruction, meaning that students who transferred from Batesville to the university or another accredited institution received full credit for underclass work. The university would grant Arkansas College only a "Number Two" rating for junior-and senior-level instruction, however, which meant that Arkansas College graduates looking to attend graduate school at the university could receive credit for a course only if they had made at least a "B." One of the reasons for the lower rating of upper-level instruction, according to the university's registrar, was the scarcity of Ph.D.'s on the college campus. In his visits to Batesville in 1933 and 1934 the registrar of the University of Arkansas warned Lacy that Arkansas College was in danger of seeing its ratings drop even farther if Ph.D.'s were not added to the faculty. But Lacy was not the type to go looking for any old Ph.D. The college still had no written rule requiring the administration to hire Presbyterian faculty members, but the old minister tried to find candidates who fit both descriptions, not an easy task. In the fall of 1934 Arkansas College welcomed Presbyterian layman Stanley Walker Rockwood, an Ivy League undergraduate with a Ph.D. from the University of Wisconsin, as professor of Spanish and French. In addition, Lacy hired two other Presbyterian faculty members with the understanding that they would complete their Ph.D.'s shortly. When one Ph.D. and two others nearing their degrees failed to placate the university's registrar in 1936, Lacy immediately hired three more doctors, all "men of fine Christian character": psychology and education professor Walter Scott McNutt, professor of physical sciences Leo B. Roberts, and English professor Roger Penn Cuff.[57]

Not only did the addition of Ph.D.'s alter the makeup of the faculty on paper, it introduced Arkansas College students to the eccentricities, perceived and real, long associated with the university-trained scholar. Leo Roberts proved an especial delight for students. Whether he consciously cultivated an air of absent-mindedness or not, the science professor satisfied student preconceptions. Franklin Williams, a member of the class of 1938, recalled Roberts's penchant for wearing "high-water britches" and coming to class with his tie on backwards. Students were also amused by his habit of staring into the sky whenever walking around campus or town. Another result of the university's demand that the college hire more Ph.D.'s was a threatened resignation by Lacy. Soon after commencement in 1936 the president submitted his resignation, citing both his opposition to the necessity of replacing current faculty members who did not hold the Ph.D. and the trustees' failure to provide him moral support for this egregious task. Although Lacy eventually agreed to rescind his resignation, the board came to no firm agreement on the subject of academic hiring, a lack of focus that would plague the college for years to come.[58]

Declining enrollment and incessant rumors of the college's demise took their toll on student life during the depression era. After surpassing the 200 plateau in the late 1920s, annual enrollment during the five years of Lacy's second administration averaged only 127 students. By 1936–1937 the number of full-time students had dropped to 118, the lowest level since the immediate post–World War I era. One of the most obvious effects of the depression on enrollment was an alteration of student body demographics. More and more families found it too difficult to send a child away to school. Consequently, by the mid-1930s more than half of Arkansas College's students were from Independence County, and administrators scrambled to fill empty dormitory rooms. Fortunately for Lacy and the college, New Deal programs provided the funds that kept some students in school. After a year of funneling federal money into the pockets of needy students through the Federal Emergency Relief Administration, President Franklin Roosevelt created the National Youth Administration (NYA) in the spring of 1935. NYA students received monthly stipends in exchange for labor on campus and around town. Lacy utilized NYA student workers and lumber donated by the Southern Lumber Company of Warren to make badly needed repairs during the 1935–1936 session. The following year the college's NYA students received a total of $3,900.[59]

The decrease in enrollment, combined with the financial constraints and general spirit of disaffection during the depression, exercised a negative effect on extracurricular activities. All the Greek organizations founded in the 1920s, with the exception of local sorority Kappa Kappa Alpha, disappeared in the 1930s, as did most other clubs and social organizations. The honor system and the Student Government Association were both dissolved in the early 1930s, though a movement began after mid-decade to revive student government. Football was discontinued after the 1935 season, and organizing a baseball team remained a year-to-year proposition throughout the decade. Rare bright spots in the extracurriculum were the theater and debate programs, which, under the direction of Lois Ball, continued to garner positive publicity for the struggling college. The small student body and rumors of the college's closing appear to have precluded the rise of protests, which were quite common on many university and college campuses during the era. The "sense of betrayal [that] permeated many a college campus" was perhaps better reflected in Batesville by the numerous examples of personal misconduct and rebellion.[60]

As one might expect, the depleted student body also challenged curricular offerings. In general, however, the curriculum at the end of Lacy's second administration was little changed. In April 1933 the faculty approved a plan reducing the number of majors to eight: chemistry, English, French, history, mathematics, philosophy and psychology, sciences, and foreign languages. Although Eugene Long's death was followed by a succession of short-term Bible and religion teachers, Bible continued to be a required course for all freshmen and sophomores. The education department gradually assumed a more prominent position in the curriculum due to the growing percentage of students studying to become teachers, and the old bachelor's of music degree was reinstated.[61]

But Lacy's second administration was no more about curricular issues than had been his first. The overriding concern of his depression-era presidency was money and survival. By the end of the 1935–1936 year, after the eleventh-hour campaign for funds the previous December, Lacy could breathe a cautionary sigh of relief. Shortly before commencement, the president announced that "[f]inancially, we are in better shape than we have been for many years, in that all old accounts have been paid and the Synod of Arkansas is out of default in respect to its bonds." But the college and the synod were a long way from solving their fundamental financial problems. The spring of 1936 also marked the end of the five-year plan worked out by the Batesville Citizens' Committee and the Educational Commission in February 1931. Most of the plan's resolutions had not come to fruition. The synod's promise to funnel $10,000 per year from benevolent offerings into college coffers failed miserably, producing less than half the projected amount. The Citizens' Committee had experienced more success—raising about three-quarters of their $10,000 per year pledge—but had watched as proceeds diminished each year. The synod had managed to delay further bond payments until 1940, but interest continued to build on the debt of more than $100,000.[62]

As Lacy looked to the future, he realized that Arkansas College was no closer to financial security than it had been four years earlier, or even ten years earlier. The synod still had no workable plan to pay off the standing debt. There was no guarantee that the college would be able to avoid massive operating deficits any longer. The synod had voted to redirect benevolent monies formerly earmarked for the college toward paying off the bonded indebtedness. Endowment proceeds were unreliable and unexceptional. Presbyterian support for the college within the state had sunk to a dangerous low. And the end of the five-year plan threatened to cut off the dwindling supply of funds from the Batesville Citizens' Committee. Nels Barnett and Lucien Abraham, a local high school teacher who had recently joined Arkansas College as physical education instructor, went to work to maintain a flow of funds from the community. Barnett and Abraham hoped to drum up local pledges sufficient to produce at least $6,000 per year until 1939. The tireless Barnett and the Batesville Chamber of Commerce launched an additional campaign to raise another $3,000 per year locally.[63]

When the Presbyterian Church in the United States determined to devote the year 1937 to a campaign for the Ministers' Annuity Fund, the Synod of Arkansas decided to place the debt issue on the back burner until the following year. But Arkansas College did not have the luxury of taking a year off from its financial troubles. At a special Little Rock meeting of the board in April 1937, Lacy challenged the apathy of the trustees and openly criticized the synod's lack of financial and moral support for Arkansas College. He also denounced a recent letter from Henry Sweets, in which the Secretary of the General Assembly's Committee on Christian Education had advised the college to seek a merger with another institution. The trustees responded by reaffirming their commitment to the college, by appointing a committee to study ways to repay the bond issue, and by selecting representatives to campaign for the college in churches throughout the state. At the spring meeting of the board the following month, Lacy revealed that, despite the shoestring budget, the college had amassed an operating deficit of about $6,000 over the past two years, a third of which was back salary due the president.[64]

This mounting debt played a key role in Lacy's decision to resign the presidency. There is no surviving record of the immediate events leading up to this development, but on 19 August 1937, just weeks before the beginning of classes, the president submitted his resignation to the chairman of the board, Rev. H. L. Paisley, and the chairman of the executive committee, John P. Morrow Sr. Citing the failure of Batesville citizens to meet their pledge of $6,000 for the year, Lacy, who prided himself on his ability to run a taut ship, vowed to lead the struggling institution no longer.[65] In fact, he had attempted to resign the previous summer but had agreed to stay when Barnett and Morrow convinced him to give the town another year to meet its promises. In retrospect, it seems odd that he would single out the Batesville community for condemnation, especially since it was the town's citizenship who had offered the most consistent support for the college throughout the economic ordeal. There were likely other bees in the volatile Lacy's bonnet. Nevertheless, one can certainly understand the sense of desperation that the sixty-two-year-old president must have felt after five years of sacrifice and constant labor for his alma mater. Most in the college community respected Lacy's yeoman labor during the darkest days of the depression, but almost no one was sad to see the rancorous fellow go.

Perhaps all that was needed was a bit of serenity. In September 1937 the board of trustees elected John Crockett president of Arkansas College. Crockett, a mild-mannered, middle-aged minister with practically no administrative background, was not a business-minded man by any means. Like Arkansas College, he had spent most of his days living a simple, God-fearing life. He would not be remembered as the president who brought an end to more than a decade of constant struggles with debt and deficits because, for the most part, he chose to step aside and leave the financial dealing to people better qualified. Luckily for Crockett, then, the economy had begun to rebound slightly by the late 1930s, enough anyway to inspire a sense of hope among businessmen and investors. Furthermore, the college's and the synod's ordeal had dragged on so long that many bondholders had probably begun to doubt that they would ever receive a penny for their investment.

On 2 August 1938, in another special meeting at the First Presbyterian Church in Little Rock, the synod voted to adopt the lengthy report of its debt committee, which had been appointed almost two years earlier to work out a repayment plan. The debt committee—primarily chair W. H. Williams of Little Rock, John P. Morrow Sr., and former Arkansas College faculty member and Presbyterian minister Alexander Henry—had traveled the state during the preceding year to convince bondholders to accept 40 percent of the value of their bonds and in some cases to cancel their bonds completely. The result was a drastic reduction of bonded indebtedness from more than $150,000 to only $50,000. The debt committee arranged to cover this indebtedness with a new $50,000 bond issue that would be paid off over a ten-year period ending in 1948. The committee also agreed to deed all property of Arkansas College back to the college, this property once again to be used as collateral for the new bond issue.[66]

After years of uncertainty and numerous brushes with death, it appeared that Arkansas College and the synod had finally reduced the debt to a manageable level. Sisyphus had finally rolled his stone to the summit of the hill; one more firm push could send it tumbling into the valley beyond and bring an end to his redundant labors. From an operating standpoint, the college would be no better off; actually, one byproduct of the bondholder negotiations was a reduction of the college's projected annual income. But the administration and board of trustees had already begun plans to expand the student body and erase the deficits of previous years. Although, as we shall see, Arkansas College was not completely clear of economic hardships, the anxiety of previous administrations had already begun to subside. Pervasive financial problems had masked a developing crisis of identity since World War I. Now it was time for Arkansas College to declare its mission. John Crockett offered one alternative.

PART III: 1937–1969

The thirty-two years that encompass this era in the history of Arkansas College were among the most eventful, dramatic, and transformative in American history. The period between 1937 and 1969 witnessed the end of the worst economic depression the country had ever known and the beginning of the greatest and most terrible war the world had ever seen. In the years between 1937 and 1969 scientists in the United States developed the atomic bomb; the world's two greatest powers, one democratic and one communist, squared off against one another in a struggle of words and waiting known as the cold war; the American people achieved an unparalleled level of financial and material comfort; popular entertainment and the new youth culture became inextricably linked with the rise of rock and roll; the civil rights movement brought the issues of race and justice to the forefront of American social and political life; and the United States's escalating involvement in Vietnam mobilized an entire generation in one way or another.

Yet, in a very fundamental way these changes had only a minimal effect on life at Arkansas College. Certainly, even a small, isolated institution like Arkansas College experienced some of the most obvious pangs of the era's development: a dearth of boys during World War II, a flood of G.I.'s afterward, bobby socks and duck tails in the 1950s, and the beginnings of student discontent and hippie culture in the late 1960s. For the most part, however, it was business as usual during most of the three decades in question. Like most small, independent colleges, Arkansas College missed out on the post–World War II boom in scientific research—and the millions of federal dollars that accompanied it. Likewise, cold war witch hunts, civil rights showdowns at the schoolhouse door, and student sit-ins and marches remained things that happened elsewhere, not on Batesville's little campus.

Although the reasons for the absence of such seminal events of the era are numerous, Arkansas College was not alone in largely avoiding the more colorful aspects of that age in higher education. Most small colleges, and especially those in the South, remained at best on the periphery of the educational world in the years between the Great Depression and the Nixon administration. Even in the 1960s, when Arkansas College experienced dramatic demographic change with the enrollment of African Americans and large numbers of students from the urban Northeast, most institutions of Arkansas College's class maintained a conservatism and orthodoxy that seemed especially alien when compared with the currents dominating the national consciousness.

Perhaps the most important reason for the insularity of Arkansas College—besides the obvious conservatism of the school's region and sponsoring denomination—was the ongoing internal struggle first to survive and second to identify and embrace a mission. For most of the period between 1937 and 1969 Arkansas College administrators and trustees were so preoccupied with keeping the doors open while simultaneously debating what the college was, or what it should become, that external forces affecting the nation's universities and even its elite liberal arts colleges went largely unnoticed in Batesville. When Isaac J. Long greeted the first matriculates in the fall of 1872, any debate over mission and purpose would have been a moot point. Any college-educated Presbyterian—or Methodist or Baptist for that matter—understood higher education's function to be both religious and cultural: to train ministers and to produce adults who possessed a body of knowledge widely regarded as both fitting and necessary for the learned. By the latter days of the Great Depression most of the nation had discarded such a notion as outdated, and even on a campus as isolated and provincial as Arkansas College, Long's original unspoken but understood purpose was no longer sufficient. Arkansas College's quest for survival demanded the search for an identity.

Little Haverford or Maryville of the West: The College Seeks a Purpose

Mack Long was the last surviving child of Isaac and Callie P. Long. After earning his degree from Arkansas College in 1891, just six months before his father's death, Mack Long rejected the career of his father and brothers and spent years scaling, sliding down, and re-scaling the rungs of Arkansas's financial ladder before finally achieving a measure of prosperity and security as a banker and businessman in Little Rock. In the process he drifted in and out of the college's orbit during good years and lean years, never doing much beyond contributing a few dollars here and there and gaining tidbits of college news from his brother, Eugene. Mack Long remained a devoted Presbyterian, however, and in the years after Eugene's death he and his family began to take a more active role in college affairs. In 1936 Mrs. Long, the former Mary Louise Jones, joined the board of trustees, and in 1946 Mack was appointed treasurer of the Synod of Arkansas's campaign to raise more than half a million dollars for his alma mater.

Mack Long's last official activity at Arkansas College took place only three months before his death. On Saturday, 25 October 1947, during the second day of the college's diamond jubilee celebration, Long joined a crowd of alumni, students, and faculty in a procession from the campus to Oaklawn Cemetery. Led by Eugene Blandford, the old Latin and German professor who had arrived in Batesville more than half a century earlier, the procession was in fact a pilgrimage to the grave of the founder of Arkansas College. The throng snaked its way out of the college's neighborhood, toward the outskirts of town, and then to the center of the cemetery, where Hugh Shell, president of the student body, ceremoniously placed a wreath over the weathered gravestone marking Isaac Long's final resting place. College president John D. Spragins Jr. decorated the grave of his old professor, Eugene Long, with a similar wreath, and Mack Long honored his mother's marker in like fashion. After a fourth wreath was placed on the grave of Blandford's longtime friend and colleague, Little Dan Frierson, the Arkansas College faithful prayed and dispersed, leaving the freshly decorated graves silent beneath a canopy of green leaves whose yellow and gold borders reflected a coolness in the air and suggested the changing of the seasons, the inexorable march of time. Mack Long would die in the heart of the coming winter, only one year younger than his father's college.[1]

The mood on the Batesville campus in the fall of 1947 was hardly as somber as a cemetery pilgrimage, though. It had been more than two years since the end of history's greatest war. The return of the G.I.'s and the federal government's program to send them to school had inflated college enrollments around the nation; the number of full-time matriculates at Arkansas College had almost quadrupled since the end of war. And the country's and the college's newfound prosperity had quashed the incessant discussion of the college's imminent demise, often public discussion that had plagued Arkansas College throughout the years of the depression. Yet, there was little reason for blind optimism. In a couple of years the G.I.'s would be gone, and with them the government money currently funding college expansion. The reckless curriculum, whose fly-by-night variety reflected an attempt to meet the demands of the G.I.'s, undermined the college's liberal arts stance and clouded its mission. Furthermore, the pilgrimage to Isaac Long's grave was not the only evidence that Arkansas College was never far from its past. A glance at the school's financial records revealed a pitifully small endowment and a yearly budget too dependent on student tuition and fees. An inspection of Arkansas College's physical plant revealed buildings rich in history and folklore but in dire need of repair. And, though lying dormant in the face of record enrollments and ballooning budgets, the old spirit of disaffection with the college had never completely disappeared. It would soon resurface in a different form, with consequences both revolutionary and long-lasting.

By the post–World War II era, criticism of Arkansas College often focused on the school's mission, or lack of one. In many ways the college was in a holding pattern during the decade and a half covered by this chapter. Persistent financial struggles translated into an inability to bring the college's future and its long-term goals into clear focus. The fifteen years surrounding World War II marked a prolonged crisis of identity for Arkansas College. As the Synod of Arkansas struggled to repay the debts accumulated by the college during the 1920s and 1930s, Arkansas College flailed about in an attempt to discover a purpose within a rapidly changing society and a culture of higher education undergoing transformation. It was a tough ordeal, one affected by economics, religion, and other variables. Arkansas College was only one of dozens, even hundreds, of similar small denominational colleges faced with a climate of change during the crucial World War II era.

The late 1920s and 1930s had brought the most trying times in Arkansas College's history. The immediacy of the bottom line had forced William S. Lacy to focus so intensely on keeping the college from going under that he had by necessity neglected all other matters. Consequently, by the time he resigned in the summer of 1937, the college in almost every way bore a striking resemblance to the one he had taken charge of two decades earlier—tiny enrollment, small but strained budget, narrow and limited curriculum, a student body made up largely of Batesville kids and resi-

President John D. Spragins walks away after placing flowers on the grave of Eugene Long during the Diamond Jubilee, 1947.

dents within a twenty-five-mile radius of campus, a limited extracurriculum, underpaid and in some cases underqualified faculty, a library and science laboratories described as "deplorable" by an inspector from the University of Arkansas, and a focus on Christian character development over intellectual attainment manifested in an emphasis on mandatory chapel, Sunday School, and worship service attendance.[2] Perhaps most ominous was the strained relationship between the college and the synod and the concomitant sagging support for the college within the state's Presbyterian community.

Into this breach stepped John Crockett, a soft-spoken Presbyterian minister whose labors in southwestern Missouri had earned him the moniker (misnomer actually) "Bishop of the Ozarks." No records survive to indicate the motives of the board of trustees in selecting Crockett to succeed Lacy. Perhaps Crockett's success in the field of evangelism suggested his potential for winning converts to the cause of Arkansas College. Perhaps Lacy's last-minute resignation produced an equally last-minute search for a successor. Perhaps the trustees, weary from five years of constant tussling with the fiery Lacy, simply sought a man with whom they could live in peace. Whatever the motivation, Crockett, like various predecessors, seemed an odd choice for president of a college.

"Born to the manse" in Laclede County, Missouri, John Crockett earned his bachelor's degree at Westminster College in Missouri in 1906 and received his bachelor of divinity from Louisville Presbyterian Theological Seminary four years later. For the next quarter century he served in various facets of the ministry, including a brief stint as superintendent of the School of the Ozarks in Forsythe, Missouri. For many years afterward, Crockett served as either official or unofficial field secretary for the school after its removal to a Taney County site near Hollister. For the six years before accepting the call to Arkansas College's presidency, Crockett had served as the Synod of Missouri's evangelist in southwestern Missouri. It was there that his labors earned him the nickname that would remain with him for life.[3]

If the trustees had indeed sought Lacy's opposite, they came very near to succeeding with Crockett. Slight of stature, John Crockett was a kind-hearted, talkative bachelor whose pleasant wit and ability to spin a yarn endeared him to the hill folks of southern Missouri as well as the students of Arkansas College. He was also no stranger to the campus at Batesville. In the spring of 1937 he had been the featured guest speaker for the college's annual religious emphasis week. Furthermore, for years Crockett had made a practice of taking under his wing poor Ozark boys, especially those who displayed an interest in entering the ministry, and of shepherding them through the School of the Ozarks and on to college. Some of these boys he had led to Arkansas College in the years before his arrival. In addition to moral support, Crockett often provided financial support for his needy mentees, a practice that strained his personal resources but earned him the permanent gratitude of many a student who otherwise would never have made it off a hillside farm. In fact, by the time he assumed the presidency of Arkansas College, Crockett believed his primary mission was the work of providing Ozark youth with a Christian education. His decision to come to Arkansas College must be viewed in this light. There is no question that part of the allure of the job was the promise it held for extending his educational and missionary efforts. Shortly after making the decision to come to Batesville, he informed a reporter in southwestern Missouri that Arkansas College would "give me a greater opportunity to carry on the work I have started."[4]

The move to Batesville represented a fresh start for the fifty-three-year-old Crockett, whose house had burned the previous winter leaving him with little more than the clothes on his back and a few hundred dollars. But it is quite likely that he did not fully comprehend the mess he was getting into. By the fall of 1937 the synod's bonded indebtedness was rapidly approaching the $200,000 mark, and even Lacy's belt-tightening had failed to balance the budget during the previous two terms. As a gesture of good will toward the new president, a committee of the Batesville Chamber of Commerce promised to raise $2,500 to put toward immediate expenses and pledged to provide the college with at least $6,000 each year for the next three years. Lacy's budget cutting had also reduced faculty salaries to perilous lows. Crockett's $3,000 per year salary was more than double the average professor's pay, a situation that boded ill for Arkansas College's ability to maintain its relatively highly trained teaching force. By the time Crockett arrived on campus in late October, the interim administration had already been faced with a challenge to its authority. In an uncharacteristically brazen example of freshman hazing, a group of upperclassmen gathered freshman boys in Willis Hall and buzzed strips through their hair. Acting president Samuel W. Williams promptly suspended all further hazing on campus and expelled the upperclassmen's ringleader. Ultimately, Crockett's biggest shock may have come when he finally grasped the level of Presbyterian animosity toward the little college. This was a problem he could do something about.[5]

Although John Crockett's tenure as president would ultimately last less than twenty-four months, he oversaw significant changes and accomplishments. Under his direction students revived the moribund Honor Council in the fall of 1938. Lois Ball's Harlequin Little Theatre continued to give superior performances, and junior Eugene Bartlett of Siloam Springs reorganized and directed the student band in 1938–1939. Crockett personally oversaw the expansion of activities of the Ministerial Club and Gospel Team, whose members taught Sunday Schools and filled pulpits in the Batesville area. Crockett's two years at Arkansas College also witnessed a modest expansion of extracurricular activities, including the establishment of new clubs for out-of-state students (several of them Missouri Ozark boys) and students from southern Arkansas. The Bishop's primary contribution to student life was his cheerful and friendly presence. In contrast to the dour Lacy, who seemed a distant and often threatening figure to students, Crockett's became a familiar visage around campus. On any given morning a visitor might find the president cooking breakfast for students in his home, the stone cottage near Independence Hall that had originally served as a fraternity house but upon Crockett's arrival soon became known as "Dr. Johnnie's Waffle House." The most common guests at the waffle house (the Ozark natives whom the president had personally guided to Arkansas College) earned a nickname of their own, "Dr. Crockett's boys."[6]

Beyond the daily affairs of campus life, Crockett's presidency would be remembered for three events and two overarching themes. All three events took place within a six-month span in 1938—the Panthers won their first state basketball championship, the Synod of Arkansas refinanced its staggering debt, and the National Youth Administration established a girls' training program in Independence Hall. The two themes were in effect Crockett's long-term, personal contributions to Arkansas College and are thus more difficult to quantify. In essence, his brief presidency helped bridge the chasm that had developed between the college and a significant portion of Arkansas's Presbyterians and presented the college a reasonable option in its search for a mission.

Despite the apparent incompatibility of the first two events mentioned above, the basketball championship and the refinancing of the debt were not unrelated. The decision to drop the Panther football program after the 1935 season had been accompanied by a resolve to build the basketball team into a championship-caliber club. The effort paid immediate dividends. The Arkansas College basketball team overcame numerous obstacles—reliance on a student coach, dependence on mainly nonscholarship players, and a dilapidated, nonregulation gymnasium—during the 1936–1937 season to put together the school's best record to date. Under the tutelage of student coach Enid Barron, the Panthers rode the strong play of local boys

Carl Garner of Sulphur Rock and Charles Taylor of Cave City to a season record of 16–2, their final loss coming in the state Amateur Athletic Union (AAU) tournament to the powerful Bears of Arkansas State Teachers College.[7]

With the starting five returning for another year, boasted the 1937 yearbook, the Panthers would "have little trouble annexing the state title next season." The 1937–1938 season took its time in developing into a storybook year, however. Under a new student coach, Robert Lee Calaway of Bethesda, the Panthers finished a disappointing regular season schedule with a record of nine wins and eight losses. Considering Arkansas College's obvious disadvantages, it is a wonder that the boys performed as well as they did. The Panther gymnasium was easily the poorest facility found at any college in the state. The Barn, as it was known among the student body, had been built a decade earlier using scrap lumber and student labor ostensibly as a temporary structure until a better gymnasium could be built. By the late 1930s the tiny clapboard building—the gym was so small that the walls stood just a step from the out-of-bounds lines on each end of the court—was a sweatbox during the warm months and a freezer during the winter basketball season. Weathered and warped boards let in sunshine and cold alike, and winter mornings occasionally found players sweeping a fresh dusting of snow off the hardwood court.[8]

Compared with the Barn, Arkansas State Teachers College's new, spacious gymnasium must have looked like Madison Square Garden. And it was here that the 1938 state AAU tournament was held, on the home court of the three-time defending champion Bears. The AAU featured business teams and other organizational squads in addition to the state's small colleges; consequently, the Panthers defeated a team of boys from a Civilian Conservation Corps camp in the first round. In the second round of play, Arkansas College faced Arkansas Tech. The two schools had split a pair of games during the regular season, and it took an overtime period for the Panthers to advance to the semifinals. The semifinal game proved another heart stopper, with Kohn Bray, another Cave City boy and midyear addition to the roster, providing the heroics with a last-minute shot to propel the Batesville squad over Little Rock-based independent club Staf-O-Life by the score of 43 to 42.[9]

The tournament final was a classic David versus Goliath matchup. Arkansas State Teachers College was heavily favored to win its fourth consecutive championship, even though the Panthers had managed to capture one of the three regular season duels between the two. In the championship game on the night of 2 March, the Panthers jumped out to a quick lead but found themselves trailing 25 to 27 at the halfway point. Things looked especially grim for Arkansas College after center and co-captain Carl Garner, faced with the daunting task of containing State Teachers's big man Cecil Mathis, fouled out shortly before the half. Furthermore, the Bears attempted to quell the Panthers' offensive game by keying on all-state point guard Charles "Squirt" Taylor, who, according to a reporter for the *Batesville Guard,* was "watched closer than a chorus girl at a prayer meeting." But Arkansas College received brilliant second-half play from Garner's replacement, Arlis Glover of Batesville, and from all-state forward Bray, who scored fifteen of his game-high twenty-three points

The 1938 Panthers basketball team, champions of the state Amateur Athletic Union tournament. The man in the three-piece suit is President John Crockett.

in the final half. When the horn sounded, the Panthers had pulled off the improbable upset, defeating the Bears 57 to 51 on their own court.[10]

The victorious Panthers returned to Batesville with Arkansas College's first state basketball crown. Crockett declared the next school day after the game a holiday, and the cagers were treated to a pep rally, parade, and picnic on the grounds. The celebration rendered the ultimate trip to the AAU national tournament in Denver a rather anticlimactic affair. Local boosters raised enough money to finance the trip out and back, though the tight budget allowed for only two cars and eleven people to make the journey. Eight players joined Coach Calaway and two chaperones, Thomas M. Lowry Jr. and a local booster. The national tournament featured a hodgepodge of college, city, and corporate teams, many of the latter basically professional squads. At Crockett's request, tournament officials agreed to reschedule Arkansas College's first-round game so that the Panthers would not have to play on a Sunday. When the Panthers finally did play they raced to a halftime lead over Montana State College. But the altitude and Montana State's size proved too much to overcome, and Arkansas College fell 46 to 59. Despite their quick exit from the field of fifty-five teams, the squad of country boys from tiny Arkansas College turned out to be one of the tournament's most intriguing stories, and newspapers from Denver to Memphis ran features on the scrappy Panthers.[11]

The basketball championship was just the kind of shot in the arm Arkansas College had been needing for years. The fact that the Panther players were legitimate student athletes and campus leaders and that the squad was the first (and last) to ever win an Arkansas championship under a student coach added to the mystique of the college's Cinderella story. High hopes for a repeat in 1939 ended when the Bears of Arkansas State Teachers College got their revenge with a thirty-point whipping in the semifinals of the AAU tournament. Behind the prodigious scoring of Kohn Bray and his successor, Vic Stewart of McHue, the Panthers continued to rank among the state's top teams in the years leading up to World War II, including a runner-up finish in the 1940 state tournament. The 1938 championship would live on in Arkansas College lore for years to come. More important, the Panthers' unlikely championship run generated more positive statewide publicity than the college had enjoyed in years, a timely antidote to a decade of stories charting the institution's near-death experiences. It would, of course, be a gross overstatement to attribute the synod's successful debt restructuring program to the fortuitous outcome of a basketball game some six months earlier. At the same time it would be folly to completely dismiss the almost irrational devotion conjured up by athletic success.

In some ways the efforts to refinance the synod's debts featured the drama and suspense of a tightly contested championship game, only the drama took place out of the public's view and the suspense dragged out for weeks and months instead of seconds and minutes. It was only a month or two after the Panther championship that John P. Morrow Sr., longtime secretary of the board of trustees, contacted Alexander Henry of the synod's debt committee to discuss plans to reduce the stifling financial burden. By early summer, when "the prospects of bankruptcy for the Synod and the closing of Arkansas College seemed imminent," Morrow, Henry, and W. H. "Bill" Williams, chairman of the debt committee, had developed a plan to rid the synod of thousands of dollars of debt. Henry and Williams were not averse to seeing the college close—Williams was even labeled an enemy of the school from time to time—but both were determined to save the synod and Arkansas's Presbyterians from embarrassment. Morrow, on the other hand, sought to keep Arkansas College open and realized that the only way to give the college a fighting chance was by reducing the synod's debt to a manageable level. During the heat of the summer, Henry, an Arkansas College alumnus and pastor of the church at Newport, traveled from the Gulf of Mexico to the Great Lakes to meet face to face with each bondholder in an attempt to work out an equitable settlement. Morrow and Williams canvassed Arkansas attempting to raise $50,000 within the Presbyterian community. By late July the three men had worked out an intricate plan whereby a combination of cancellations and bond reductions would shrink the synod's bonded indebtedness by more than two-thirds to $50,000. Meeting at Little Rock's First Presbyterian Church on the second of August, the synod approved the debt restructuring plan and agreed to a new $50,000 bond issue, which was promptly purchased by Morrow, Williams, a few Batesville citizens, and a handful of Presbyterians from half a dozen Arkansas congregations. The bonds were to be canceled at the rate of $5,000 per year plus interest.[12]

From the college's standpoint the synod's decision was bittersweet and foreboding. On the positive side was the fact that the debt, most of which had been generated by the college, had finally been reduced to a level within the synod's ability to pay. The debt restructuring also promised to ease some of the latent tension between the state's Southern Presbyterians and their college. But in order to ensure the prompt, annual payment of the bonds the members of the synod had taken the drastic step of diverting all benevolence funds that had previously been earmarked for Arkansas College toward the retirement of the bonds. In short, until the $50,000 bond issue was retired, and possibly even longer, Arkansas College would receive no money from the synod. Although the synod's benevolence funds had declined sharply since the mid-1920s, the sudden loss of this valuable revenue (usually a few thousand dollars a year) threatened the very survival of the cash-strapped institution. Some friends of the college suspected that this caveat was simply a ploy on the part of members of the synod's debt committee to finally close the doors of Arkansas College and rid the state's Presbyterians of the burdensome school. It may not have been a ploy, but for some the prospect of the college's demise was certainly a welcome byproduct of the debt restructuring plan.

By the time the new academic year got under way in early September, the college's prospects seemed a little brighter. Due in no small part to publicity over the Panther state championship and Crockett's recruiting efforts in the hill country around Batesville, a region that up until the 1930s had provided very few matriculates at Arkansas College, freshman enrollment doubled and overall enrollment experienced an increase of almost 50 percent. Two weeks into the semester the president made an announcement that the student body would shortly undergo another increase. Crockett and the trustees' executive committee had just signed a contract turning over use of vacant Independence Hall to the National Youth Administration. By early October Independence Hall was the site of an NYA girls' training center. One of several such NYA projects around the country in the latter years of the depression, the Batesville facility housed about sixty young women from low-income families across a twenty-county area of north central and northeastern Arkansas. The NYA girls were required to work five hours per day, or one hundred hours per month, at a variety of public labor-type activities. They were also expected to take from six to eleven hours of course work at the college. The young women received twenty-five dollars each month, fifteen of which they owed to the college for room and board with the remaining ten dollars used for covering tuition and personal expenses.[13]

The National Youth Administration (NYA) girls of Arkansas College pose before Independence Hall, c. 1940.

As one might expect, this sudden and rather unexpected influx of freshmen taxed an already overworked and underpaid faculty, and without the benefit of a salary increase. The majority of Arkansas College's NYA girls sought only the state's minimum elementary teaching certificate and thus planned to attend college no more than a year. Under Arkansas state law at the time, a person could obtain one of these certificates—designed especially for one-room and other small rural schools—by completing thirty hours of college credit accompanied with minimal classroom observation. Consequently, most of the NYA students gravitated to the classes offered in this program, which in the initial semester consisted of freshman English, educational psychology, drawing and arts, and classroom observation.[14]

Both the increase in freshmen from Batesville's rural hinterland and the introduction of the NYA program at Independence Hall were in keeping with Crockett's mission of providing higher education to children of rural, underprivileged families. The college's decision to throw open its doors to a class of students not traditionally recruited to Batesville also had unforeseen academic consequences. Many of the newcomers, both NYA girls and regular freshmen, came from small, underfunded high schools in poor areas of the state and had obviously not enjoyed access to the quality of education reserved for students from Batesville and other larger and richer high schools. By early October it was evident that, on the average, the college's largest freshman class in history did not measure up to Arkansas College's established standards, especially in freshman English. As a result the faculty established noncredit classes in spelling, diction, and sentence recognition, and any student deemed deficient in one or more of these areas was required to devote extra time to remedial studies. The remedial classes would survive into the World War II years.[15]

The depression decade witnessed a significant transformation in student origins and goals as well. Arkansas College attracted fewer and fewer students from southern and eastern Arkansas, and higher percentages of Batesville-area students stayed at home to save money and enrolled at Arkansas College. By the time Crockett arrived in Batesville a significant majority of the college's students were commuters living within a twenty-mile radius of campus. The decline in students from middle-class Presbyterian households around the state, the group that had played such a key role in the flourishing of collegiate life in the 1920s, was accompanied by a rise in the number of students from the rural region north and west of Batesville. One result was an increasing number of matriculates studying to become teachers; and the college had no trouble placing all its graduates and recipients of teacher certificates in any number of rapidly expanding teaching jobs in north central Arkansas. Another factor in the massive concentration of college students in teacher training courses was the depression's debilitating effect on white-collar jobs and the declining appeal of professional and graduate study in an age of cash shortages. The depression combined with constant rumors of Arkansas College's demise to create an atmosphere of gloom. But Crockett's optimism and cheerfulness went a long way toward offsetting the pessimism so prevalent on American campuses. Students, like most Americans by the latter part of the decade, often used humor to try to make the best of a bad situation. The Arkansas College senior class of 1939 reflected this spirit with its motto: "Goodbye N. Y. A., Hello W. P. A."[16]

From a financial standpoint the dramatic increase in student enrollment was not enough to offset the loss of revenue from the synod's benevolence fund. Consequently, by the end of Crockett's second session as president, the college's standing debt had risen to $7,500 with little hope of balancing the budget in the near future. Furthermore, Arkansas College, now a dozen years removed from the loss of former stalwarts James P. Coffin and Theo Maxfield, continued to suffer from a lack of consistent and committed trustee leadership. The Rev. H. L. Paisley had ended his brief term as chairman of the board when he moved out of state in the summer of 1938, and his replacement, fellow minister and alumnus David Shepperson, had failed to display a firm resolve to battle the naysayers in the synod who waited for the opportunity to close the college. Too many of the board's seats remained revolving-door positions occupied by prominent Presbyterians with little interest in college affairs. As in the past, the most consistent leadership continued to come from a few Batesville

The Presbyterian Students Club, c. 1941. This small group reflected the declining percentage of Presbyterian students in the Arkansas College student body after 1930.

trustees and friends, including Judge S. Marcus Bone, vice-chairman of the board, and Nels Barnett. By the late 1930s the mantle of leadership had come to rest on the considerable shoulders of trustee secretary John P. Morrow Sr. Morrow, whose extensive landholdings in the Oil Trough bottom of southeastern Independence County made him one of a dying breed of town-dwelling planters with the money and time to devote to numerous civic affairs, had been on the front lines of the battle to save his alma mater since the threatened closing in 1931. It was Morrow who had managed to rally sufficient Batesville support for the locally unpopular 1938 debt restructuring. He was one of the few who could operate with equal ease within the complex political mazes of the synod and among the loyal, local supporters of the college.[17]

As fate would have it, Morrow's leadership came into demand once again in the summer of 1939 as the survival of Arkansas College was thrown into question. On 26 June, John Crockett submitted his resignation to the board of trustees. Citing his "unhealthy financial situation" and his desire to return to the field of evangelism, Crockett announced that he would leave Batesville at the end of July to assume an evangelistic post in Texas.[18] For those familiar with the career of the Bishop of the Ozarks, the announcement came as no surprise. John Crockett possessed a wanderer's soul and had rarely tarried more than a couple of years in any one position or place. He also realized that he was not cut out for higher education administration. Crockett was always more comfortable behind the pulpit or on the back roads of the evangelist's trail. The neophyte president had overcome his inexperience well enough to hold Arkansas College together for two more depression years, no mean task. And he also managed to leave town before he had worn out his welcome, an accomplishment rarely achieved by his predecessors. Crockett's presidency had obviously produced little in the way of innovation or revolution. Instead, the Bishop's legacy at Arkansas College was a cheerier image of the school in the minds of many Presbyterians—"where before," according to trustee John D. Spragins Jr., "there was distinct hostility"—and a brief flirtation with a philosophy of outreach to poor students of the Ozarks, a mission that would find another champion in just a few years.[19]

When the board finally reconvened in early July, the trustees reluctantly accepted Crockett's resignation and elected Tom Lowry acting president. Lowry, thirty-seven years old at the time, had just completed his fifth year on Arkansas College's faculty and had recently married Margaret Goodwin, an alumna and niece of Sallie (Mrs. Eugene) Long. Like his predecessor, Thomas McCall Lowry Jr. was also the son of a Presbyterian minister. Born in Knoxville, Tennessee, and raised in Memphis, he graduated from Davidson College in 1922 and earned an M.A. in history five years later at Princeton. After a year on the faculty of Haverford College near Philadelphia, Lowry returned to the Southeast where he farmed and taught for a few years before reentering graduate school to pursue a Ph.D. He was living in his father's native York, South Carolina, in the summer of 1934 when, through an old college friend, he learned that William S. Lacy was looking for a new dean for Arkansas College. After a hastily scheduled interview in Shelby, North Carolina, Lowry was offered the position of professor of social sciences and dean of the faculty; he arrived in Batesville a few weeks later eager to tackle his new responsibilities.[20]

By 1939 Lowry had become a faculty favorite among the Arkansas College student body. A dapper gentleman, tall and thin, "Sourpuss," as he was affectionately called by students, used his keen intellect and professional but compassionate manner to earn the loyalty and respect of depression-era students, much the way John Daffin had during the previous decade. To the students of Arkansas College, T. M. Lowry Jr. embodied Ivy League, academic sophistication; to the board of trustees the young professor possessed the force of personality necessary to assume the burden of the presidency as well as the denominational heritage to match the expectations of the synod. To the synod's debt committee and a number of trustees, Crockett's resignation was as good as a death knell for Arkansas College, and the subsequent plugging of Lowry into the president's chair was, in their minds at least, a formal move that would provide the college with leadership until it could be dismantled by the synod. Lowry was at best an unwilling administrator. Known for his love of teaching and his skill in the classroom, the young professor practically had his new duties thrust upon him, noting in a letter to the chairman of the board that he had taken the job "under protest." The situation looked even darker for Lowry when the board of trustees tabled the duty of appointing a search committee.[21]

The latter decision served as a red flag for the new chief executive, and for good reason. In the late summer of 1939, shortly before the beginning of the fall session, Lowry received a visit from the members of the synod's debt committee. The visitors informed Lowry that if the college ended the coming academic year with another deficit, which would be the fifth consecutive year in the red, the debt committee would recommend that the synod close Arkansas College. By this late date such threats were not idle. With the loss of the synod's benevolence funds and with the prospect of fund-raising no more hopeful than usual, all signs pointed to another money-losing year in Batesville. In spite of the debt restructuring and Crockett's two-year good will ambassadorship, the synod was still divided over the issue of maintaining the college. Furthermore, by 1939 several trustees had resigned themselves to accept the college's demise. Most troubling to Lowry and others dedicated to keeping the doors open was the apparent apathy of new board chairman David Shepperson, alumnus of the class of 1913 and minister of the El Dorado church. Much to the acting president's chagrin, Shepperson seemed willing to watch Arkansas College die a slow, peaceful death during the 1939–1940 year. According to one board member, Shepperson and fellow trustee Bruce Boney, minister of the Warren church, crimped fund-raising efforts in southern Arkansas by trumpeting the college's hopelessness. By the end of 1939 several trustees feared that their chairman had "handicapped the college by not taking any steps to help [it]."[22]

Lowry got his first taste of an Arkansas College near-death experience just three days after Christmas in 1939. For longtime trustees and members of the synod, such affairs had become commonplace by the end of the decade. On 28 December 1939, Arkansas College's trustees held a special meeting in Little Rock to discuss the current conditions of the college as well as the prospects for its future. President Lowry warned that a sizable deficit was imminent unless the flow of gifts picked up dramatically. In a move that caught Lowry off guard, trustee Edwin Williams of Little Rock, a vocal supporter of the college, made a motion to close Arkansas College at the end of the academic year, a move that Williams used to "feel out" the weak members by forcing an open vote. A majority of those present opposed the motion, and the trustees proceeded to request that Chairman Shepperson appoint two investigatory committees, one to study the college's financial conditions and another to study academic policies. A second special meeting on Leap Year 1940 found the college's prospects unchanged. By early April Shepperson had failed to appoint members to either committee, and his inaction had begun to breed resentment on the board and in the president's office. Lowry chastised Shepperson and other inert trustees for their lack of leadership, declaring that secretary John P. Morrow Sr. had "borne the brunt of the College for many years." The acting president also threatened to resign if Shepperson did not make a public statement concerning the board's decision to continue the life of Arkansas College or terminate it.[23]

When the board gathered in Batesville on 4 April, the trustees most adamant about maintaining the college predicted they would have "a fight on [their] hands" in order to save it. But this time the fight was unnecessary. Lowry played a hand full of wildcards when he announced to the stunned trustees that Arkansas College was on pace to balance its budget for the first time in five years. And a perusal of the books revealed that Lowry's statement did not depend on creative bookkeeping by bursar June Hall. Incredibly, the numbers were all there and in the right columns, all of them supporting the president's claim. After trustee Edwin Williams delivered a brief defense of the college, W. H. Williams, representing the synod's debt committee, informed the trustees that he would not call a special meeting of the synod to consider closing Arkansas College and suggested that the life of the institution be extended for another year.[24] With that the trustees returned to discussion of normal items of business, and Tom Lowry joined the growing list of individuals who could make the claim of saving Arkansas College.

Few people expected Lowry to succeed in balancing the budget. The fact of his ultimate success is all the more incredible considering he maintained a full load of classes, seventeen hours to be exact, while serving as president. Like most of his predecessors in the president's office, Lowry was forced to devote most of his official duties to monitoring the bottom line. He tightened the belt more firmly than any of his forerunners had ever considered, even William S. Lacy. Lowry eliminated any expense bordering on superfluous and some that were closer to necessity. The college spent only eight dollars for library books for the entire academic year. The president maintained his heavy class load to prevent hiring another faculty member. Perhaps most important, Lowry cracked the whip on delinquent student accounts. Throughout the institution's history, Arkansas College had absorbed thousands of dollars in losses from unpaid student accounts, the result of a lenient policy on student loans and payment plans and a tradition of lax follow-up on delinquent accounts. Lowry changed all that by declaring that students could not graduate or transfer hours to another institution without first settling all old accounts with Arkansas College. Eventually, the acting president took more drastic action by proclaiming that any professor who administered a final examination to a student with a delinquent account must then pay that student's account.[25]

Lowry's various financial machinations proved the doubters wrong and extended the college's lease on life. In the aftermath of the dark 1939–1940 year, both Lowry and board chairman David Shepperson resigned their respective positions. Shepperson, who according to one trustee "had left the board confused and disheartened," was replaced by a well-known supporter of the college, J. Herndon McCain, pastor of the church at Arkadelphia and a 1927 graduate of Arkansas College. The trustees refused to accept

Lowry's resignation, however, and appeased the unwilling administrator by appointing a presidential search committee composed of Batesville trustees John P. Morrow Sr. and Nels Barnett and Pine Bluff minister John D. Spragins Jr.[26]

Things would get no easier for Lowry and Arkansas College. By the end of the summer it was evident that the search for a new president was proceeding at a snail's pace and with no success in sight. In August the committee narrowed a small list of candidates to Louis C. LaMotte, a young junior college president in North Carolina. When rumors surfaced that John Crockett was considering a return to the presidency (unsubstantiated rumors, as it would turn out) the search lost its legs, and there is no evidence that the search committee ever contacted LaMotte. Simultaneously, dissension within the board continued to hamper Lowry's attempts to operate the college. By the fall of 1940 a group of trustees devoted to keeping Arkansas College afloat had begun discussing ways of ridding the board of its uncommitted members. Search committee chair Spragins informed Lowry that "we are going to see that the board is weeded of its members who are either indifferent or antagonistic as fast and as tactfully as we can." (In fact, within a couple of years the chief culprits cited by Spragins were gone from the board.)[27]

But Spragins also had another reason for promising a purge. Once the 1940–1941 term got under way, the search committee practically abandoned any efforts at finding a permanent replacement for Lowry. This development was in part due to the continuing uncertainty of the college's future, but it was also attributable to the trustees' faith in Lowry's abilities. The acting president had not only proven his fiscal mettle in the face of adversity; he had also displayed an excellent combination of firm resolution and tactfulness that fit well his position. Secretary of the board Morrow even considered him the best president that the college had ever had. In early December 1940, trustee chairman J. Herndon McCain, after months of persuasion, insisted that Lowry assume the presidency on a permanent basis. Lowry, who less than a year earlier had declared that "under no conditions would I take the presidency of Arkansas College," had apparently experienced no change of heart and once again refused the appointment. Still, the board would leave the college in his hands for another year and a half.[28]

Tom Lowry had proven an effective administrator, but he continued to yearn for his old duties as a full-time classroom professor. Furthermore, his months in the president's office had led to his own doubts about the college's future. In his October 1940 report to the trustees, Lowry argued that "unless the Board takes steps to stimulate the Presbyterians of the Synod of Arkansas and unless the Presbyterians of Arkansas indicate that they want to see Arkansas College go forward, it is the reasoned opinion of this Acting Administration that it would be wise to consolidate with some Christian college in the state or . . . outside of the state." Several conditions prompted his warning. Physically, the campus was in the worst condition of its life. Before the end of the session the clapboard gymnasium would be condemned. The Isaac J. Long Memorial Building was approaching its fiftieth birthday, and the music building (the original college structure) and Alumni Hall were even older. All were in decline from a lack of upkeep and care due to budget constraints. Independence Hall, still home to the NYA's girls' facility, was under attack from termites, and rats were a problem in several college buildings. Upon a visit to the campus, the chairman of the board was shocked to find a puddle of water surrounding the drinking fountain near Lowry's office and a makeshift men's urinal made out of an old tin gutter. More than ever before the college's physical appearance had begun to reflect its financial poverty.[29]

Arkansas College also experienced a gradual decline in enrollment during Lowry's temporary administration. In addition to a 30 percent decrease in the number of NYA girls living in Independence Hall, regular enrollment fell significantly in the fall of 1940, due in part to the paucity of financial aid available. Nevertheless, the majority of Arkansas College's students continued to receive some sort of financial aid, including forty-four regular matriculates who earned differing amounts of NYA funds through on-campus work. More than one-quarter of all students, almost half of them ministerial candidates or children of Presbyterian ministers, paid no tuition at all. Under Lowry's new system, students unable to pay tuition up front were required to sign loan notes carrying 3 percent interest. By the spring of 1941 a shrinking base of student revenues forced college officials to raise tuition by ten dollars to $90 per year and room and board for the less than three dozen boarding students to $225 a year, an increase of twenty-five dollars.[30]

Declining enrollments did little to allay faculty alarm over the influx of poorly prepared freshmen. Reflecting a business-as-usual approach on campus, the faculty instituted a mandatory English proficiency examination for all prospective graduates. Lowry developed a study clinic along with a six-week "How to Study" course required of all freshmen. The Lowry years also saw a minor resurgence of the old utilitarian spirit that had periodically drifted across campus. In an attempt to attract more students and meet the growing demand for vocational education, the faculty in the spring of 1941 recommended adding courses in business law, accounting, and shorthand and stenography, most to be offered at night for accessibility to working people in town.[31]

The demand for vocational courses was the direct result of an awakening American economy. And the economic rejuvenation was a direct product of the growing war in Europe. Tom Lowry's introduction to Arkansas College's presidency coincided with the onset of global war. On the first day of September 1939, exactly one week before classes got under way on the Batesville campus, Adolf Hitler's armies rumbled across Poland's western border, providing the spark for half a dozen years of bloodshed and destruction. The uncertainty of the world's future over the next few years did little to advance Arkansas College's fortunes, but by directing the anxieties and energies of Arkansas's Presbyterian community elsewhere the war also allowed the college to hunker down and wait out the storm. During the twenty-seven months between the German invasion of Poland and the United States's entry into the war, the college, much like Americans and American institutions in general, attempted to carry on life as usual, in varying degrees of success. All that changed on 7 December 1941, when the Japanese attacked Pearl Harbor. The students who sat on the floor of matron Brownie "Miss B" Davidson's dormitory room and listened to crackling radio broadcasts that Sunday could not have grasped the full significance of the event, but almost all knew their lives would never again be the same.[32]

By December 1941 Lowry had served almost two and a half years as acting president of Arkansas College, already a longer term than four of the institution's previous presidents. He had successfully balanced the school's budget in each of the previous two years, but all signs pointed to a deficit for the 1941–1942 session. The United States's declaration of war would all but assure it. Lowry must have pondered on several occasions what a relief it would be to escape the pressures of the president's office in this poor little college in this poor little town. The federal government would soon grant him a leave from his academic duties. Since his days at Davidson College in the early 1920s, Lowry had served in the National Guard, and with American belligerence he realized his days in Batesville were numbered. Uncle Sam would soon come calling, and Arkansas College would once more be thrown into disarray.

President Lowry was called to active duty on 20 April 1942. The day before leaving Batesville he made a farewell speech to the tearful student body gathered in Alumni Hall. At his request the board granted the exiting president an indefinite leave of absence for the duration of the war. As he had done when William S. Lacy left in 1937, Dean Samuel W. Williams assumed the role of acting president until the two-year-old search committee could locate a replacement. But Lowry would not return to Arkansas College; instead, upon his discharge from the Army Air Corps he would choose to join the faculty of Southwestern at Memphis. The little college that Lowry left behind faced a bleak future, and the students sensed it. A spirit of demoralization had descended upon the campus in the months since Pearl Harbor. Enlistments and the draft had taken their tolls on male enrollment, and the war's demand for bodies would decimate the college's male population in the years to come. Regular enrollment had dropped below the one hundred mark for the first time in years, and the NYA in its last year of operation in Independence Hall had cut its student workforce to forty. Fund-raising efforts in southern and eastern Arkansas continued to produce few results. Less than two weeks after Pearl Harbor, the college came perilously close to tragedy when the rotting rafters gave way in the gymnasium, bringing down the ceiling and injuring a professor and five boys who had been attempting to rebuild the roof. All six victims escaped death, though student Maurice Speed suffered a skull fracture and a broken arm.[33]

As if conditions on campus were not depressing enough, the uncertainty surrounding Lowry's exit was compounded by a sobering evaluation of the college. The general assembly of the Southern Presbyterian Church had set aside the 1941–1942 academic year as a time for inspecting and studying its educational institutions. The evaluator's "Survey Report," which arrived on campus just days before Lowry's departure, presents us with a stark view of the tiny college as seen through the eyes of an outsider. When Norman Burns of Chicago visited the campus in the early spring of 1942, he found only 117 full-time students; among colleges of the Southern Presbyterian Church only King College in Bristol, Tennessee, could rival Arkansas College in paucity of students. Of the students at Arkansas College, fully one-half lived in Independence

County and only one in five had traveled farther than seventy-five miles to reach Batesville. Consequently, the boys' dormitory, Willis Hall, was only at half capacity, and Welch Hall, though it had room for only eighteen girls, was plenty large enough for the female boarding population. The survey also revealed that the overall quality of incoming freshmen had declined during the past decade. For the past few years a majority of Arkansas College's freshmen had scored below the national average on the American Council on Education's psychological examination, an intelligence test administered during freshman orientation week.[34]

The decline in student enrollment had apparently not lessened the workload on the faculty. The six nonadministrative faculty members spent on average sixteen hours per week in the classroom. The evaluator warned that two professors were burdened with serious overloads. Henry Jinske, professor of education, philosophy, and psychology, taught twenty hours each week, while his colleague William Luther, the college's jack-of-all-trades scientist, labored twenty-one hours in the laboratory or classroom. Not surprisingly, the faculty's heavy workloads were not accompanied by increased salaries. The average salary of the six, three of whom held university Ph.D.'s, was $1,520, and that after a $200 raise granted by the board the previous spring. Those faculty members who volunteered for Dean Williams's summer school did so at their own risk. Faculty received no guaranteed pay for summer teaching, relying instead on the distribution of surplus funds at the end of each term. Budgetary constraints had even led the administration to give preference to unmarried candidates when filling faculty vacancies. Due to a shortage of affordable housing in Batesville and the college's inability to supply anything more than a living wage, administrators found it more convenient and cost-effective to provide dormitory suites for professors at the expense of a lower salary. Consequently, in the spring of 1942 five unmarried faculty and staff lived in dormitories at a cost of $25 a month. In spite of the obvious shortcomings, the quality of teaching at Arkansas College remained remarkably consistent. When the dean of the education department at the University of Chicago arrived on campus in May 1942, he was most surprised by the excellence of the impoverished faculty and assured the weary souls: "You are doing a million dollar work on very little money."[35]

The shortage of operating funds had other negative effects as well. The survey revealed that during the past four years only thirty-four new books had been purchased for the library. June Hall, perhaps the campus's most overworked person as bursar, registrar, and secretary to the president and dean, labored year round for only $1,400 plus room and board. The college's endowment had shrunk to about $70,000 by 1942, and even this figure was misleading because much of the endowment was nonproductive. During the 1940–1941 year the endowment had provided only 7 percent of Arkansas College's income, or a paltry $2,500. Almost one-third of the school's income came from tuition and student fees, an unhealthy ratio by any measure. This situation was even more incredible when considering the fact that Arkansas College's total annual expense of $375 (for boarding students) was $55 cheaper than it had been a decade earlier and ranked as the lowest sum among all Southern Presbyterian colleges.[36]

Perhaps the low cost was fitting. Depression-era declining enrollments had curtailed the number of extracurricular activities available to students and had restricted the curriculum. Men's basketball was the only intercollegiate sport played on a consistent basis. The Honor Council and Student Government Association had been reduced to relative insignificance. By 1942 no men's fraternities or social organizations existed, and despite the recent administration-prodded organization of two new sororities (Delta Sigma Chi and Sigma Alpha Sigma) female club life was only slightly more active. In the classroom most students continued to crowd into traditional majors such as English, mathematics, and history, while constant faculty turnover and faculty shortages in science relegated the formerly popular study of chemistry to inconsequential status. The survey also revealed that Arkansas College was plagued by a low rate of student retention, largely due to the dozens of students who matriculated only to obtain a minimum, thirty-hour teaching certificate.[37]

Holding all this together, at least for a few more weeks, was Tom Lowry. By the spring of 1942 he had experienced a taste of the life of Isaac Long. At a salary of $3,000, which was below the average for a common professor in many places, Lowry ran the school's affairs, spent six hours each week in the classroom, supervised study clinics in his office, and oversaw the publication of the *Index* and the *Panther*. The acting president had even made a few no-cost attempts to improve academic life at Arkansas College. Emulating a practice he had observed during his days at Davidson, Lowry urged faculty members to hold Sunday evening open houses at their respective residences in order to stimulate teacher-student interaction and intellectual conversation outside the classroom. He also designed an interdisciplinary seminar in which a select group of superior students gathered periodically with several professors to discuss assigned readings. Lowry did all this with the synod's debt committee looming over him like the "sword of Damocles," ready to kill the college should financial insolvency return.[38]

Lowry's successor would inherit the precariousness of the office. When it became apparent that Lowry's days at Arkansas College were numbered, the search committee of Spragins, Morrow, and Barnett began to discuss names for a new president. By late March the committee was considering two candidates: George McKee, an alumnus of the college who had spent three decades as a missionary in the Congo, and Malcolm Lockhart, assistant to the president at Westminster College in Missouri and a noted fund-raiser. Once again, it appears that Spragins, chairman of the committee, had been unsuccessful in convincing either man to take the job by the time Lowry left a month later. Instead, by early May a number of trustees and Batesville college supporters, perhaps doubtful that a highly qualified candidate could ever be lured to Batesville on a $3,000 salary, were clamoring for Spragins himself to assume the presidency. Within days Spragins, whose lack of confidence in his ability to run the school filled him with "much fear and trepidation," assured his supporters that he was ready to take the position; at the next meeting of the board on 25 May 1942, the trustees unanimously elected him Arkansas College's eleventh president, and Spragins agreed to assume his duties as quickly as he could conclude his affairs as pastor of Pine Bluff's Central Presbyterian Church.[39]

The staff of the student newspaper, the *Panther,* 1939.

In retrospect, it would seem that Spragins was somewhat of an emergency choice as president. In an age when even many denominational colleges were abandoning the old minister/president in favor of an administrator with higher education credentials and experience, Spragins's election represented not only Arkansas College's unwillingness to part with tradition but also its financial inability to embrace the changing culture of an increasingly standardized American higher education system. Yet, Spragins could claim educational credentials superior to those of many of his predecessors. And his personal and familial credentials were enough to sway any good Arkansas Presbyterian. Born in the little Hempstead County town of Hope, John Diggs Spragins Jr. was raised in Arkadelphia, where his father moved the family in the early twentieth century for business purposes. Spragins grew up in a devoutly Presbyterian home; in fact, he could trace his ancestry to the Union County community of Mount Holly, one of Arkansas's earliest Presbyterian settlements and boyhood home of former governor and Arkansas College board chairman Thomas C. McRae. Kinship ties connected him to several prominent Presbyterians in southwestern Arkansas, including trustee John T. Barr, a minister and home missionary in the Ouachita Mountains. The new president also had a personal connection to Batesville. His wife, the former Mary Fitzhugh, was an alumna, a native of Batesville, and the niece of Charles Maxfield, one of the members of Arkansas College's first graduating class. As a result of this connection, the Spraginses did not move into the old fraternity house-turned-president's residence recently vacated by the Lowrys. Instead the new first family occupied the old Uriah Maxfield home on Harrison Street that Mrs. Spragins had recently inherited.[40]

Spragins had spent the First World War as a student at Arkansas College, where he edited the school's first modern yearbook and graduated in 1920. After graduation he made his way to Davidson College and earned a master's degree in history, one of the few awarded in that institution's short-lived graduate program of the 1920s, before preparing for the ministry at Louisville Presbyterian Theological Seminary. This was to be Spragins's last brush with higher education until his election to Arkansas College's board of trustees in 1939. In the seventeen years between his graduation from seminary and his decision to assume the presidency of his alma mater, Spragins devoted himself to the ministry, serving pastorates in rural Union County and Mena before going to Pine Bluff in 1928.[41]

Fortunately for Spragins, Lowry's untimely departure did not spark a mass exodus among the college's staff and faculty. Most important, the new president inherited registrar-bursar-secretary June Hall, and she knew as much as anyone about the functioning of the college. The man who arrived to take over as Hall's new boss in the summer of 1942 probably did not appear as "presidential" as his predecessor. In many ways John D. Spragins Jr., in terms of appearance and personality, bore a stronger resemblance to John Crockett. Of nondescript heighth or girth, Spragins's most notable feature was his round, youthful face, a countenance which may have belied his forty-four years if not for his thick, tinted spectacles. The president was a kind-hearted, gentle fellow, a deeply spiritual and soft-spoken man with the patience of Job. The latter quality would serve him well in the coming years, even in the coming months.[42]

Spragins found his patience as well as his resilience tested immediately. In late June 1942 a former parishioner wrote the new president offering "my congratulations or my condolences, I don't know which would be proper." Spragins would soon ponder that debate himself, for two days later, while preparing to leave Pine Bluff, he received a letter from trustee secretary John P. Morrow Sr. informing him that the executive committee of the board was trying to raise $1,845 in a week in order to prevent a deficit for the year. Surprisingly, Morrow asked Spragins if he would contribute $100 to this drive. The stunned president, who was being forced to pay his family's moving expenses out of his own pocket and had been informed a month earlier that there would be no deficit, was getting his first taste of presidential life in a poor denominational college. Spragins diplomatically declined to contribute, but he did help solicit money and the deficit was finally erased by the end of summer.[43]

The deficit confusion was a harbinger of things to come in what Spragins would call the "year of crisis." Facing a war-depleted enrollment and a bleak financial future, Spragins attended his first synod meeting as president in October 1942, a gathering in

El Dorado he described to a friend as a "baptism by fire." On the third day of the meeting C. A. VerBeck, a prominent Fayetteville layman and longtime champion of eliminating Arkansas College, read the report of the Christian Education Movement committee, which concluded by recommending closing the school on account of financial shortcomings and Batesville's poor location for a college. The attack had a broken record quality to it, as did the rebuttal. A group of loyal friends rallied to stave off such a move by striking a compromise with the opposition. The synod appointed a committee of three members—Spragins, board chairman J. Herndon McCain, and noted college detractor W. H. Williams—to act as a watchdog on all financial matters. The synod then granted this watchdog committee the authority to call a special meeting of the synod to consider closing Arkansas College should a mounting deficit demand such action. In effect this development simply placed another "sword of Damocles" over the college's head, though the watchdog trio was much less likely to recommend closure due to the presence of Spragins and McCain. In addition to the longtime opposition of certain synod members to the college, Spragins came away from the October meeting convinced that there was a second, and perhaps more sinister, front in the battle for the college's safety. Claiming that "the opposition to Arkansas College is aided and abetted in an undercover way from Memphis," the president criticized Southwestern's constant and successful canvassing efforts in eastern and southern Arkansas and the institution's "sly criticisms of our work." In Spragins's mind, Southwestern's recent administrative hiring of Roy Davis, former leader in the Arkansas Synod and outspoken critic of Arkansas College, simply confirmed his suspicions that the Memphis school sought to drive Batesville's little college out of the business.[44]

Spragins emerged from the 1942 synod meeting with a new appreciation for the perseverance of individuals like Nels Barnett, Ury McKenzie, John P. Morrow Sr., and Tom Lowry. He also realized that he was faced with the same sort of do-or-die ultimatum from the synod. Just two days after the meeting, Spragins wrote to a friend: "I am in the fight of my life. This year is our decisive year. Arkansas College hangs in the balance."[45] Although Spragins possessed a minor flair for drama that had been conspicuously absent in his stoical predecessor, his fears were legitimate. Arkansas College was entering a second decade of year-by-year, hand-to-mouth existence. This precariousness was the result of poverty and in turn it bred poverty. The products of this cycle of decline were a growing sense of both apathy and disaffection on the part of Presbyterians around the state and a dangerous and unhealthy stagnation of collegiate life in Batesville.

John D. Spragins Jr. could scarcely have chosen a more inopportune time to take the reins of his alma mater. By the spring of 1943 the gradual disappearance of young men from class rolls had reduced full-time enrollment to fewer than seventy students, the lowest level since World War I. The 1944 graduating class of two was the smallest since 1919. Efforts to secure some sort of military training unit for the college, something like World War I's Student Army Training Corps, came to naught. Rampant, war-fueled inflation compounded the difficulties of balancing the budget and reduced the purchasing power of already meager faculty and staff salaries. The

NYA had packed up and left town after the 1941–1942 session. Independence Hall stood abandoned on the heights east of campus, a stark reminder of the dreams of the past and the vibrant youth culture of an earlier generation.[46]

But the new president was not one to back away from a challenge. Spragins came to Batesville intent on spending the rest of his working life as president of Arkansas College, and he had a definite vision in mind for the future of the institution. Spragins would ultimately spend ten years at the helm of the college, a decade that can best be described as a roller coaster ride. He would see the grim days of the war when the campus seemed deserted and lifeless as well as the boom years after 1945 when the G.I.'s crowded hallways and classrooms. Then Spragins and his school would once again come face to face with hard times and the threat of closure. Spragins's tenure witnessed considerable curricular change and expansion of the extracurriculum. He also introduced budgetary innovations and developed a more modern and efficient blueprint for the board of trustees.

Like all his predecessors, Spragins, regardless of his long-term goals for the institution, was forced to deal with the fiscal bottom line before handling any other business. When it became apparent in the fall of 1942 that drastic actions would be required to prevent an operating deficit for the year, the president developed a strategy that he would utilize throughout the war years. Eschewing his predecessors' focus on potentially large gifts from wealthy friends, Spragins inaugurated the "Budget Balancers" drive just before Christmas. Spurred by the promise of Batesville citizens to raise $5,000, the president solicited one thousand gifts of ten dollars each from Presbyterians and alumni. Although the Budget Balancers movement fell far short of its goal of $10,000, it generated about $3,300 and helped keep Arkansas College in the black. In addition, Spragins persuaded most congregations in the Synod of Arkansas to hold a spring "Arkansas College Day" in conjunction with the synod's annual Christian Education Day. The Sunday event featured special presentations on the work of the college, after which church officials passed the plate on the school's behalf. Arkansas College Day became an annual event throughout the synod during Spragins's administration. Using the Budget Balancers drive and the good will created by Arkansas College Day, Spragins was able to balance the budget again the following year.[47]

The tireless president also found time to devote to campus matters. After a dismal winter of 1942–1943 in which nearly vacant dormitories and anxiety over the war brought extracurricular activity to a halt, the campus and student body began to show signs of life. At Spragins's request, Roberta Dorr of Batesville and other students formed the 250 Club, a student organization devoted to increasing Arkansas College's enrollment. In the spring of 1943 the 250 Club sponsored the first Hi-Day, a campus program for high school seniors from schools in the Batesville area. The club never succeeded in raising enrollment above one hundred until after the war, but its efforts may have been instrumental in stabilizing the number of students in the final two wartime sessions. Spragins also oversaw the resurrection of campus publications. The *Highlander*, successor to the old *Panther* student newspaper, made its first appearance in the spring of 1944 under the editorship of John T. Barr Jr., and the 1944 yearbook, the *Index*, was the first published by the college since the beginning of the war. One extracurricular activity that persisted throughout the war was theater. The Harlequin Little Theatre, under the direction of Lois Ball and, after 1943, former Ball student and alumna Ella Myrl Dobson Shanks, continued to perform at least two plays per year throughout the war. Despite the dearth of young men, students continued to hold the autumn Sadie Hawkins Day race that had been adopted from Al Capp's "Dogpatch" comic strip in the late 1930s as an annual event. When they were not being chased by coeds dressed like Daisy Mae, some of the male students underwent military drilling in the college's contingent of the local National Guard company. Others continued to play basketball, though there were no intercollegiate games of any kind during the final three years of the war.[48]

Spragins's influence was also evident in the significant growth of religious organizations on campus during the war years. By the spring of 1945 three denominational organizations were in existence on the Arkansas College campus: the Westminster Fellowship for Presbyterian students, the Methodist Student Union (later Wesley Foundation), and the Baptist Student Union. More than half the student body belonged to one of the three groups. The president, who had always shown an interest in home missions, continued the depression-era practice of teaching rural Sunday Schools and conducting Presbyterian services in area "mission chapels" using college students who were preparing for careers in church service. Spragins also supplied pulpits himself, a practice that he would maintain throughout his time at Arkansas College.[49]

Wartime demands affected other functions of the college as well. Curricular alterations and additions included an increased emphasis on science and mathematics courses (ostensibly to prepare young men for military service) and the establishment of a business administration department consisting of mostly lower-level course offerings in office practices, typing, accounting, and other rudimentary business skills. In an attempt to provide a more efficient and less time-consuming degree track, the faculty approved the expansion of the length and offerings of summer school. Furthermore, Arkansas College opened selected freshman-level courses to superior high school seniors, who received college-level and high school credit for their work. The faculty also drafted regulations designed to handle the special cases of students who were drafted in midsemester. One of Spragins's proudest accomplishments injected a dose of modern efficiency into the board of trustees. Hoping to avoid the indecision and unpredictability of the old ad hoc committee system, in 1944 Spragins recommended, and the trustees approved, the creation of four new permanent committees: finance, buildings and grounds, policy, and curriculum and personnel. The new committee structure of the board would do much to help streamline and focus the trustees' activities.[50]

The peculiar exigencies of World War II demanded much of Spragins's attention during his first three years as president, but the demands did not deter him from attempting to implement programs and practices that were part of a larger vision for the future of Arkansas College. In retrospect, the college's curriculum and objectives during Spragins's ten-year presidency appear to have been racked by chaos and aimlessness. The war and the subsequent flood of G.I.'s made messes of many a college curriculum. But dismissing the Spragins years for a lack of direction and a decline of standards, as some of his detractors would later, was a judgment that failed to consider the president's overall educational philosophy.

Almost without exception the developments, programs, and innovations of the Spragins administration can be traced to his original vision for his alma mater. Spragins approached his duties at Arkansas College with what might be called a missionary's philosophy of education and the role of the college in its physical and spiritual environment. A clergyman first and foremost, he never claimed an intense loyalty to the traditional liberal arts as had his predecessor Tom Lowry. Instead, Spragins's primary vision for Arkansas College involved its potential as a tool for outreach and Christian education. Although he believed that the college should continue to develop the independence of thought and the fullness of character traditionally championed by the liberal arts institution, Spragins also looked to expand Arkansas College's mission. Much of this mission would be determined by Batesville's geographical location. As the only college in north central Arkansas (and more specifically within the eastern Ozark region), Arkansas College, Spragins thought, had a duty to reach out to the underprivileged students of the hill country in Batesville's hinterland. Furthermore, according to the president, such a mission, when combined with Christian missionary work, was in full accord with the avowed aims of the Presbyterian Church.[51]

Spragins's goal for Arkansas College, then, was to continue offering a mostly traditional course of study for the Presbyterian students who chose to come to Batesville (an ever-decreasing minority of the student body) while providing the financial aid and curricular flexibility necessary to serve a steadily increasing number of high school graduates from the small towns and hillside farms of north central Arkansas. Ultimately, in this vision the college would come to resemble a higher education version of Crockett's old School of the Ozarks in southwestern Missouri—a self-supporting, inexpensive campus with students engaged in work-study pursuits ranging from agriculture to small industry. In later years Spragins would speak of his desire to transform Arkansas College into a "Maryville of the west."[52]

Just how John D. Spragins Jr. developed this vision for Arkansas College is not entirely clear. From a religion and church standpoint, Spragins had always shown an interest in home mission work. He had also for many years possessed a fondness and reverence for Arkansas's hill people, though he was certainly not an inheritor of this heritage himself. His love of the hills and their inhabitants may have been cultivated by his four years as a student in Batesville and his pastorate in the Ouachita Mountain town of Mena. It is also quite likely that Spragins's philosophy had been shaped by two friends and fellow ministers, John Crockett and John T. Barr Sr. By the time he came to Arkansas College in 1942, Spragins had long been an admirer of the work of the Bishop of the Ozarks. Barr's influence was probably even more significant. A relative and lifelong friend, Barr was the founder and longtime superintendent of one of the Arkansas Synod's two mountain mission schools, Caddo Valley Academy in the Ouachitas of southwestern Arkansas. Spragins was quite familiar with the work of Caddo Valley Academy, and Barr remained one of the president's most loyal supporters throughout his administration. The president's appreciation for the hill country, many of whose inhabitants were descended from the irrepressible Scotch-Irish of the southern frontier, also became intertwined with his intense interest in Scottish history.[53]

Emanating out of this new vision for Arkansas College were a number of developments that promised to alter the college's appearance and reputation. Among the most notable were a conspicuous focus within college publications on Batesville's location in the Ozarks, an intensification of college-directed home mission work in north central Arkansas, a new focus on recruiting students from rural areas and small towns in the hills and bottom lands surrounding Batesville, and the establishment of a "Self-Help" program. Spragins was the first president of the college to openly embrace the culture and people of the Ozark region and to direct the college's attention toward the north and west of Batesville. John Crockett had obviously helped pave the way for this change by actively recruiting more Ozark students during his two years at the school. But it was Spragins who advertised Arkansas College as the "only college of the beautiful White River Country" and who praised the "sturdy, hard-working, law-abiding, industrious people [who] live in the towns and villages and on the farms." Despite the school's location at the southeastern edge of the region, Arkansas College had never associated itself with the hills and hill people of the Ozarks. The Southern Presbyterian Church was practically nonexistent in the region, and the concentration of old school Presbyterians in central and southern Arkansas had always caused the college to fix its gaze to the south. Furthermore, most middle-class supporters of Arkansas College within Batesville did not particularly identify with the people and communities of the hills. Even Mrs. Spragins, a native of the town, did not share her husband's fascination with the Ozarks. Perhaps most important in the historical divide between the college and its region was the paucity of high schools and academies in the Ozark counties, a challenge that had largely been overcome by World War II.[54]

Spragins took advantage of the proliferation of rural high schools in north central Arkansas by focusing recruiting efforts in this region. The administration utilized several methods in its attempt to draw more local students to campus. The 250 Club, and later its successor, the Piper Club, sponsored annual visits to almost all the high schools in Independence and neighboring counties, even the smallest and most remote schools. In the spring of 1943 Spragins recommended offering full tuition scholarships to all valedictorians and salutatorians in the White River country; the board adopted the plan after extending the scholarships' geographical boundaries to the entire state. Budgetary restraints resulted in a gradual decline in canvassing within the Presbyterian communities of southern and eastern Arkansas. Furthermore, the expansion of junior colleges in Monticello and Magnolia into four-year institutions provided other alternatives for students from the southern part of the state. Consequently, the student body at Arkansas College underwent a noticeable transformation during the Spragins years, a transformation that had its origins in the depression and the influence of John Crockett. In the 1927–1928 session, for example, during the height of Arkansas

College's 1920s enrollment boom, more than half of the 202 full-time students had to travel more than fifty miles to reach Batesville. Due to the rarity of high schools in the region, the hill country to the north and west of Batesville was sorely underrepresented in the student body, with the border counties of Lawrence, Sharp, Izard, and Stone providing less than 5 percent of total enrollment. Twenty years later fully two-thirds of Arkansas College students hailed from Independence or one of these four counties. Simultaneously, the number of students from southern Arkansas had dropped precipitously, especially in terms of their percentage of enrollment. Between 1928 and 1948, the number of students from Little Rock and the areas to the south and east of the capital fell by almost 50 percent; their percentage of the total student body declined from about thirty in 1928 to less than 10 percent in 1948.[55]

One result of this demographic shift within the student body was a continuing decline in the percentage of Presbyterian students. The bulk of the young men and women from Batesville's hinterland tended to come from Baptist, Methodist, or Church of Christ backgrounds. Within a couple of years after the end of World War II, the Westminster Fellowship was the smallest of the college's three denominational organizations, and its membership was less than half that of the Baptist Student Union. But Spragins remained a devout Presbyterian and used his position at the college to further the cause of denominational home mission work in northern and eastern Arkansas. During the war years he filled pulpits at small congregations in towns such as Searcy and Augusta, and other college officials and preministerial students served congregations at Cotter, Walnut Ridge, and Black Rock. Throughout his ten-year administration, Spragins served on home missions committees in the presbyteries of Arkansas and East Arkansas. Utilizing the labor and youthful vigor of the students in the Life Service Alliance, a coeducational organization founded after World War II, the president helped establish Sunday Schools and Presbyterian churches at Bull Shoals, Hardy, Heber Springs, and other locations in northern Arkansas.[56]

The centerpiece of Spragins's vision for Arkansas College, however, was the Self-Help Division. One of the president's first official acts upon arriving in Batesville was the establishment of this program, which in the beginning was little more than a work-study program. In October 1942 Spragins hired Harvey McKinley Bevel, the fifty-seven-year-old pastor of Pine Bluff's Second Presbyterian Church, as the first director of the Self-Help Division. The president patterned his Self-Help Division (or at least his vision for it) after the labor and learning programs on such small, rural institutions as Maryville College in eastern Tennessee, Berry College in northwestern Georgia, and School of the Ozarks in southwestern Missouri. The purpose of the program was to provide needy students with a means by which to work their way through college by performing one or more tasks on campus. Spragins's ultimate goal was to "broaden the scope of the Division to include dairy farming, stock raising, fruit growing, bee keeping, and the construction of new buildings." But the exigencies of war and the college's lack of a tradition in such affairs, as well as the absence of any available farmland, forced the president to start humbly in 1942. Under Bevel's direction, several male students repaired buildings and equipment and built a small coop for laying hens in the vacant lot behind the old dormitories. Bevel then purchased 250 baby chicks to raise to maturity. The poultry flock would not only provide eggs and meat for student meals, but it would also, Spragins and Bevel hoped, produce a profit through the sale of surplus production. And this it did. During Spragins's second year as president, the Self-Help Division's poultry flock netted the college almost $300. In the spring the Self-Help crew raised a truck garden adjacent to the chicken coop to supply fresh vegetables for the meals of boarding students.[57]

Accompanying Spragins's Self-Help Division was a decision to significantly reduce student costs at Arkansas College. In the spring of 1943, at the behest of the president, the board of trustees voted to reduce annual tuition from ninety to eighty dollars and room and board from $225 to $202.50 per year. After decreases in various student fees were taken into account, total costs for a boarding student at the college decreased almost 14 percent after 1943, allowing Arkansas College to boast of being the most inexpensive private institution in the state. Nevertheless, Spragins continued to publicly champion his vision of a "church college that can reach the masses" through the Self-Help Division. With male enrollment adversely affected by war, Bevel used female Self-Help workers as library assistants, office workers, and kitchen and dining hall aides. Spragins sent out a challenge for someone in the community to donate the college a farm so that Bevel's boys could expand their range of activities. But no farm was forthcoming.[58]

Although the president never explicitly tied his Self-Help Division to his mission of bringing higher education to the poor youth of the hills, the implication was quite obvious. The first donation to the work scholarship fund at Arkansas College, given by Spragins and his siblings in memory of their mother, was earmarked for graduates of Caddo Valley Academy. When the Synod of Arkansas disposed of its property from the defunct Mountain Crest Academy in northern Franklin County, the money from the sale was donated to the college to be used for scholarships for students from the Ozarks.[59] Most of the students who participated in the Self-Help program did in fact come from the hill country around Batesville.

Spragins's interest in the people of the Ozarks and Ouachitas exercised at least an indirect bearing on his most lasting legacy—the adoption of the trappings of Scottish history and heritage. A passionate student of Scottish and Presbyterian history, Spragins first suggested changing the school's mascot in January 1944. Reasoning that the adoption of the trappings of highland Scotland would celebrate Arkansas College's Presbyterianism as well as the determination and independence of the Ozark highlanders, Spragins convinced the faculty that it was time to borrow the Highlander as the college's official mascot, a move that would have the added benefit of creating much-needed publicity for the little school. The trustees left the decision to the administration, and after several weeks of faculty and student discussions in the late winter of 1944 the student body voted by a two-thirds majority to drop the Panther in favor of the Highlander. The mascot change had only a limited effect at first because in 1944 Arkansas College had no varsity athletic teams. The student newspaper, which resumed publication that same spring, was now the *Highlander,* however, and its weekly feature sections reflected the influence of the new mascot: "The Bagpipe Blows," "The Piper," and "Plaid and Gab." Another immediate result was the 250 Club's adoption of the name Piper Club. The president was surprised to find that many of the G.I.'s who returned to campus after the war objected to the mascot change, and a second student referendum in the fall of 1946 produced only a slim majority in favor of the Highlander. The movement to reinstate the Panther quickly subsided, and Arkansas College continued to develop Presbyterianism's Scottish heritage.[60]

Although Arkansas College's Scottish mascot and adopted traditions have survived, Spragins's Self-Help Division was not so fortunate. Ultimately, the Self-Help Division was a victim not only of the financial and enrollment challenges of wartime but also of the postwar boom created by the federal government's G.I. Bill. The sudden rush of ex-servicemen into colleges and universities around the nation forced administrators everywhere to scramble to keep pace. In the process, Spragins's vision became lost in the shuffle of things, or at least obscured in the light of the prosperity and promise of the postwar world.

The Servicemen's Readjustment Act of 1944, or G.I. Bill as it was popularly known, was one of the most important pieces of social legislation of the twentieth century and perhaps the most important higher education-related congressional act in American history. During the latter stages of World War II the Roosevelt administration grew concerned over the dire economic possibilities of millions of ex-servicemen reentering the workplace after the cessation of hostilities. One alternative, the one embodied by the G.I. Bill, was to provide federal financial assistance for those who opted to return to college or enroll in college for the first time. Qualified G.I.'s were eligible for up to $500 per year in tuition, room and board, and other costs plus a monthly stipend of $50 for single students and $75 for married ones. These amounts rose steadily in the years after 1944.[61]

Despite warnings from such idealistic luminaries of higher education as University of Chicago president Robert M. Hutchins that the G.I. Bill would reduce campuses to "hobo jungles," the bill was a godsend for struggling little institutions like Arkansas College. Every small denominational school, no matter how poor and remote, had access to dozens of returning servicemen looking to take advantage of the federal government's offer. In January 1945 Arkansas College received its first G.I. Bill enrollee in Lowell Southerland from the little Independence County community of Floral. A few days later Charles A. McCombs, a freshman from Darlington, Pennsylvania, joined the student body as the second G.I. Despite the Japanese surrender on 2 September 1945, the beginning of classes in Batesville later that month found most G.I.'s still in uniform. Only six of the college's 122 matriculates that fall came in on the G.I. Bill. In the six months after the end of the war the floodgates were opened and hundreds of thousands of G.I.'s poured into college and university classrooms. By February 1946 the number of ex-servicemen at Arkansas College had increased to two dozen. The haphazard manner by which G.I.'s received their discharges and the young men's haste to take advantage of federal education dollars led the faculty to accept new enrollees up until the midpoint of each semester. The steady growth of the G.I. population throughout the first postwar session was largely responsible for a two-thirds' increase in the size of the student body between May 1945 and May 1946. The following academic year witnessed an even more dramatic increase as enrollment almost doubled to more than 300 full-time students. Arkansas College's postwar G.I.-fueled boom peaked during the 1947–1948 session when the number of full-time students surpassed 400.[62]

The enrollment of so many discharged servicemen proved to be a mixed blessing for Arkansas College. The G.I. Bill provided a boon to the college's revenues. In the fall of 1946 Arkansas College received $14,000 from G.I.'s alone, and G.I. revenues rose over the next couple of years. During the years of heaviest enrollment the college's annual budget, which had hovered around $35,000 during the war years, ballooned to more than $125,000. Revenues from tuition and student fees surpassed $100,000. The 1947–1948 session produced a budget surplus in excess of $11,000, an unheard of sum for those who had ridden out the tough depression years in Batesville.[63]

But the college's sudden prosperity did not come without a cost. The most daunting challenge for the administration was overcrowding, both in the classroom and in the dormitory. Just a few years earlier the scarcity of young men on campus had inspired one student to refer to Arkansas College as a "female dungeon," while a former student, upon finding the dormitories almost empty, wrote: "It seems lonesome to me when I go back." The rush of G.I.'s and other postwar students filled all available dormitories to overflowing. Independence Hall was reopened as a girls' dormitory in the fall of 1945, and its large dining hall replaced the one in the basement of Willis Hall as the dining area for all boarding students. Welch Hall was converted to a men's dormitory. The population explosion on campus the following year demanded immediate action. Unable to afford a new dormitory, Spragins found relief for his overcrowded college through an arrangement with a nearby orphans' home. Since 1909 the Grand Lodge of F & A Masons of Arkansas had operated a home for orphans on a one-hundred-acre farm just east of the college's East End Heights campus. By 1946 the dwindling number of children housed at the Masonic home did not justify the continued use of the property's three two-story brick buildings. The spacious buildings looked like the answer to Arkansas College's problems.[64]

Before the opening of classes in the fall of 1946, the Masons agreed to lease their three buildings to Arkansas College for use as boys' dormitories in exchange for the use of Welch Hall as an orphans' home. Spragins gladly agreed, and the nine orphans remaining in the Masonic home were moved into Welch Hall. The new dormitory arrangement did provide a logistical challenge, however, because the Masonic buildings stood more than a mile from the downtown campus. The administration solved this problem by purchasing two surplus army buses from the War Assets Administration and by hiring students, brothers Charles and Rogers Edmondson from nearby Locust Grove, to drive shuttle routes to and from campus and the dining room at Independence Hall. The replacement of one of these old Studebaker buses with a newer Chevrolet model a year and a half later was cause for celebration among those who rode to class and back on a daily basis.[65]

In the meantime, old Willis Hall, originally built as an army barracks during World War I, was remodeled for the purpose of housing married G.I.'s and their families. Before World War II it had been rare to find married students enrolled at the college, at least on a full-time basis. Thus, the need to provide boarding facilities for married students was something that had never crossed the minds of administrators until after the war. Before the fall session of 1946, Willis Hall was converted into something of a G.I. family apartment building, offering kitchenettes as well as traditional dormitory rooms for those who preferred to take their meals in Independence Hall.[66]

The sudden influx of students also caused overcrowding in the classrooms. With the exception of the small building housing the biology laboratory, another one of the "temporary" structures from the Tucker era, the campus and buildings that greeted the G.I.'s in 1945 and 1946 were the same facilities that had been in use for the past half century. The music and speech departments were housed in the college's original building, and almost all other classes were held in the Long Memorial Building. As enrollment pushed beyond three hundred and approached four hundred, it became obvious to Spragins and the faculty that the college's facilities were not only antiquated but inadequate. With all building gifts earmarked for the construction of a gymnasium and another dormitory, Spragins once again turned to the federal government for supplies. In the spring of 1947 Arkansas College purchased two prefabricated metal buildings (the ubiquitous Quonset huts of the era) and hastily erected them on the open yard of the downtown campus. The Quonset huts housed the physics and biology laboratories and the business department for several years afterward.[67]

Arkansas College's postwar enrollment boom strained the faculty to the breaking point and demanded a significant addition of teachers. The final year of the war found the college with eleven full-time faculty members. One professor continued to teach all natural science classes (chemistry, biology, and physics), while another was responsible for everything under the umbrella of psychology, philosophy, and education. Only the music department boasted more than one teacher. Within two years after the war the size of the faculty had doubled. During the height of the postwar boom, the college maintained three professors in the area of history and social science and one English professor with two assistant instructors. Another result of the faculty increase was a greater degree of disciplinary specialization. By 1947 Arkansas College had separate professorships for chemistry, physics, and biology and a history professor whose duties did not also include such subjects as political science and economics.[68]

The postwar years were also characterized by a high rate of turnover as some positions resembled the revolving-door professorships of the dynamic 1920s. Only two faculty members—Spanish and French professor Stanley Rockwood and mathematics professor and dean Samuel W. Williams—remained on the faculty throughout Spragins's ten-year administration. Nevertheless, the president was successful in bringing to Batesville three men in 1943 who would outlast him at Arkansas College: chemistry professor B. Elwood Fahl, psychology and education professor Frank H. Harrin, and Harry King. King, an ordained Methodist minister who taught history and social science and was appointed dean in 1947, was destined to be one of the last

Arkansas College faculty members with no graduate degree. Spragins also recruited his good friend Ellis G. Mosley to the faculty after the war. Mosley, an ordained Presbyterian minister from Mayflower, would teach Bible and social studies at Arkansas College for a quarter century. It is instructive to note that of the six professors listed above only Rockwood held a university-earned Ph.D. This observation underscores another faculty-related challenge of the post–World War II era. Since the mid-1930s Arkansas College had generally maintained three or four Ph.D.'s on its faculty, and this in spite of the pitifully low salaries. When the return of the G.I.'s sparked an enrollment explosion after 1945, the job market for college professors improved dramatically. Professors with Ph.D.'s could now find positions offering more money, better security, and lighter teaching loads than Arkansas College could promise. Consequently, the average education attainment level of the college's faculty dropped after 1945 as Arkansas College struggled to attract and keep Ph.D.'s on board. By 1947 Rockwood was the sole Ph.D. on the faculty at Batesville. By the early 1950s the number of Ph.D.'s at Arkansas College had increased to three, still unimpressive by accreditation standards.[69]

The growing postwar faculty also reflected an expanding curriculum. As we have seen, the poverty created by the debt crisis and the depression had the effect of streamlining Arkansas College's curriculum into a no frills, traditional liberal arts course combined with a strong emphasis on teacher training. The only wartime alterations to the curriculum were the addition of a major in Bible (Spragins's suggestion) and the establishment of a department of business administration with classes ranging from typewriting to commercial law. The college reacted eagerly to the demands of the G.I.'s and expanded course offerings at such a rate that by the spring of 1947 Spragins could boast that the selection of classes at Arkansas College "approximat[ed] those offered by the majority of colleges." At Spragins's behest the college once again established a home economics department; by the end of the decade the college catalog listed two instructors and more than a dozen different courses in home economics. The business administration department also underwent significant expansion, and in 1947 the faculty voted to establish a business major. That same year marked the emergence of a separate physical education department. Responding to the interest of a good number of G.I.'s, Arkansas College also established a short-lived aviation course after the war and contracted with a local pilot instructor to provide flying lessons.[70]

Among the most significant curricular developments during this era was the resurrection of the B.S. degree, which Arkansas College had scrapped early in the century, and the introduction of the B.S.E. Beginning with the 1946–1947 session, students could earn one of three degrees: bachelor of arts, bachelor of science, or bachelor of science in education. The college added biology and political science to its growing list of majors the following year. In 1949 the faculty voted to reinstate the defunct bachelor of music degree, but it was dropped in favor of the music major after 1953. By the early 1950s the number of B.S.E. recipients easily outpaced the number of graduates earning the B.A. or B.S. This fact reflected, among other things, the growing importance of Arkansas College's summer school and its program of extension classes, both of which were designed primarily for teachers. By the late 1940s the numbers of students enrolled in summer school and extension classes catapulted the total count of individual students affiliated with Arkansas College to more than six hundred each year. The demand for summer courses grew so intense that the college inaugurated a brief pre-summer term that started in April and continued until commencement.[71]

The same forces that spurred curricular expansion and experimentation—burgeoning enrollments and postwar prosperity in general—affected the college's administration as well. In the spring of 1945 the board of trustees created the position of business manager to take charge of the financial operation of the college, a task that had been shared in the past by the president and the bursar. After a succession of short-term business managers, H. T. MacDonough, a former hotel manager and public relations executive, brought a measure of stability to the post in 1948. Nevertheless, the trustees' failure to thoroughly outline the duties of the business manager and his position within the growing administrative hierarchy resulted in a series of misunderstandings and ultimately to a thinly concealed enmity between the president's office and the business office. Throughout the Spragins administration the business manager reported directly to the board, creating a tense situation in which the business office often acted without the president's approval or foreknowledge.[72]

While the creation of the business manager position may have created a bit of bureaucratic confusion, other administrative developments infused the college with a modern efficiency. The college's all-purpose dean (combining the duties of an academic dean with those of a dean of students) was made obsolete by the growing student body. Consequently, Spragins revived the positions of dean of men and dean of women to assume student counseling and disciplinary duties. In 1946 the registrar's office was separated from the duties of the bursar, leaving Bitha Vanemburg as Arkansas College's first full-time bursar and promoting fellow alumna Roberta T. Dorr from her job as the president's secretary to a new position as registrar. One year later the college hired its first full-time alumni secretary in recent alumna Ruby Barr, daughter of Spragins's friend John T. Barr Sr. of Caddo Valley Academy. The small library, as well as the college's accreditation rating, received a boost when Dorothy Sydenstricker joined the staff as librarian in 1948, marking the first time that the college had employed someone with university training in library science. Both Dorr and Sydenstricker were destined to become beloved fixtures in the Arkansas College community for years to come. Spragins also hired a full-time bookstore manager for the first time in 1946.[73]

The effects of the G.I. era on Arkansas College's curriculum, faculty, and administrative bureaucracy were noteworthy. Still, the effects on the extracurriculum may even have been more profound. Although there were always exceptions, on the whole the veterans approached the college experience with a maturity and grasp of purpose rarely witnessed in such a large group. This maturity was a result of age (many were well into their twenties by the time they were discharged) and the sobering experiences of war. Educational experts were surprised when G.I.'s began outperforming traditional students in the classroom; these experts were equally unprepared for veterans' wholehearted participation in extracurricular life. The postwar years introduced a bevy of new and revived extracurricular organizations: Art Club, Shakespearean Society, a home economics club, Interdenominational Council, International Relations Club, Pan-Hellenic Council, and pre-professional clubs in law and medicine. Other postwar extracurricular developments had only a peripheral connection to the G.I. boom. Although beloved Lois Ball had exited the Arkansas College stage during World War II, her Harlequin Theatre continued to thrill crowds in Alumni Hall under the direction of Ball protégés and alumnae Ella Myrl Dobson Shanks and Doris Hammett. The role of the music department in campus and community affairs received a boost from the arrival of Dorothy Hope Landis in 1946. A recent graduate of Princeton's Westminster Choir College, the young Pennsylvanian and her effervescent personality had an immediate impact on the college community. Landis, as she was popularly known even after her marriage to Batesville physician Paul Gray a few years later, reestablished the college choir and inaugurated an annual spring tour of the state. Landis also revived the college band, whose direction was soon taken over by another member of the music faculty, and arranged a yearly Christmas concert.[74]

The G.I.'s also affected extracurricular life by challenging traditions. Veterans objected to the hazing of freshmen, especially when they were the victims of such hazing, and the practice ceased soon after the war. The fall of the honor system was also in no small part due to G.I. protest. Believing that the honor code was in essence an affront to their hard-earned integrity and honesty, many veterans refused to participate in the system, which by the spring of 1949 was defunct at Arkansas College. Veterans also joined the growing chorus of voices decrying mandatory Sunday School attendance. Reacting to widespread protest, in the spring of 1948 the faculty voted to make Sunday School and worship service attendance voluntary, though all students were required to keep a weekly report on church attendance that would become a part of their permanent record. Dean Harry King's decision to abandon Saturday classes in late 1947 was also due in part to veteran influence.[75]

The slight loosening of traditional rules in the late 1940s reflected a spirit of tolerance influenced by changing societal norms in the postwar era as well as an unexpected infusion of foreigners into the student population. Although Arkansas College remained closed to African Americans, the expanded student body of the G.I. era included a handful of Americans from areas of the United States never before represented on campus as well as a larger number of international students. Improvements in transportation routes and the G.I.'s familiarity with travel resulted in enrollees from New Jersey, Pennsylvania, Chicago, and other areas far beyond Arkansas College's traditional sphere. More significant was the sudden influx of internationals. One of the most popular of the foreign students was H. G. M. "Gary" Jones, a Welshman who had served in the British Merchant Marine during World War II. But Jones was an ethnic minority among Arkansas College's foreign students because almost all other foreigners on the Batesville campus were Asian. Kenneth Au-Young, a Chinese student from Hong Kong who had heard about the college from an American G.I. during the war, enrolled in the fall of 1947 along with fellow Hong

The cast of Harlequin Theatre's production of Shakespeare's *Twelfth Night* on the stage of Alumni Hall, 1950.

Kong natives Hing Yan Kwok and Chun Wai Chow. By the spring of 1949 sixteen additional Asian students (all males) had enrolled at Arkansas College, including young men from Bangkok and Singapore. At least one, Fook Kong Li of Hong Kong, spoke no English upon his arrival. The number of Asian students peaked during the 1948–1949 session, a year that featured an intramural basketball team called the Chinese and the college's first intramural ping-pong tournament. Their numbers declined significantly afterward—possibly due to the unrest caused by Mao Zedong's Communist takeover of China and the succeeding Korean conflict—so that by the spring of 1952 only two foreign students remained.[76]

One of the few lasting contributions of the Asian students may have been the game of ping-pong. Ping-pong joined a growing list of sporting activities in the G.I.

era as intramural and varsity sports underwent a terrific rejuvenation after 1945. During the war years intramural athletics had taken center stage. The return of varsity competition took the spotlight off intramurals; nevertheless, intramural competition in volleyball, baseball, softball, and track and field continued to involve almost all male students after the war. After the completion of the field house the highlight of the intramural season was basketball, and during the height of the G.I. era there were often as many as ten different teams sporting such colorful names as Buzzards, Mules, Schmoos, Goons, and Geeks.[77]

The flood of G.I.'s returning to the classrooms occurred too late to salvage the 1945–1946 varsity season; only the tennis team participated in intercollegiate competition that year. Tennis reappeared as a varsity sport intermittently over the next few years, as did track and field and golf. Only the Highlander tennis team, which won the 1950 AIC doubles championship behind the play of Peckham Broadwater and Bob Lotridge, managed to hold its own in intercollegiate competition. Baseball also made a comeback after the war, though it turned out to be a short-lived one. After a poor showing in 1947 under Coach N. H. McDaniel, the Highlanders disappeared from baseball competition until 1950, and a losing conference campaign that season did little to convince fans and foes that they had in fact reappeared. The Highlanders posted a respectable 7–6 record the following season under the tutelage of former Panther star Pryor Evans, a local insurance agent who agreed to coach the team without pay. The 1951 squad, which proved to be the last Arkansas College baseball team for several years, produced two all-conference performers: shortstop Sonny Conine, a Batesville native who won the AIC batting title, and catcher Frankie Shell, a sophomore from Izard County.[78]

As it had been before the war, basketball remained the only varsity sport that students and townspeople could expect to watch year after year. The primary drawback for the basketball program was the lack of a gymnasium. The former gymnasium, the Barn, was razed during the Panthers last varsity season (1941–1942), and Batesville's high school gymnasium burned during the war, leaving the town with no indoor athletic facility. When Coach N. H. McDaniel resurrected basketball after the war, the re-christened Highlanders used the Desha High School gymnasium for practice and home games. The 1946–1947 season, in which the weak Highlanders posted a record of six wins and twelve losses, was to be Arkansas College's last without a home court. Since the war years Spragins had made it clear that a new gymnasium was the top building priority. In March of 1946 ground was broken adjacent to Daffin Field and east of Independence Hall for the erection of a field house. On 9 December 1947 the Highlanders hosted Morgan Insurance of Little Rock in the first game played in the new $100,000 building; the 41 to 74 loss was a sign of things to come. Despite the packed crowds of close to one thousand spectators and the excitement generated by the new field house, the Highlanders won only three games in the tough Arkansas Intercollegiate Conference (AIC) and finished eighth in the nine-team field. One of the few bright spots for Arkansas College in the late 1940s was all-conference center and Batesville native Bobby Rutherford, a former B-24 pilot who had lettered for the

Panthers in 1942 before entering the Army Air Corps. Harry Neff of Mountain View, a left-handed shooter and outstanding rebounder, took Rutherford's place in the early 1950s, but the basketball program would achieve stability and success only after the arrival of Dick Winningham in 1951.[79]

Arkansas College's weak basketball teams of the G.I. era were for the most part attributable to a lack of focus on the sport. And this was directly attributable to the rebirth of football. In the fall of 1946 a group of G.I.'s organized a football club and began lobbying for the reinstatement of varsity football at Arkansas College. Backed by the administration, student body, and a group of prominent Batesville boosters, including trustee W. B. "Chubby" Menard, representatives of this club along with athletic director McDaniel argued their case before a special meeting of the board of trustees in January 1947. After a motion by trustee Frank Lyon Sr. of Little Rock, the board voted to reinstate football for the coming season.[80]

As it had done a quarter century earlier during the heyday of the gridiron Panthers, Highlander football quickly overshadowed all other sporting and extracurricular events. Reacting to a recent AIC ruling that allowed outside groups to fund athletic scholarships, the members of the Booster Club in Batesville busied themselves raising money and recruiting players. Student volunteers set to work transforming tattered Daffin Field into a gridiron for the first time in a dozen years. The administration hired Paul McFerran, a successful high school coach from Wynne, as the first Highlander football coach. More than two thousand fans arrived at Daffin Field on 3 October 1947 to watch the first post–World War II Arkansas College football game, a one-point loss to Lambuth College of Jackson, Tennessee. It was all down hill from there on. The Highlanders slogged through a winless campaign highlighted only by a scoreless tie with old rival Hendrix. Arkansas College's footballers, inexperienced and undersized, were outscored 191 to 20 on the season. Despite the predictably poor showing for a first-time team, the Scots (as they were often referred to) found themselves showered with praise and attention. The 1948 *Index*, for example, devoted twenty-one pages to the football team compared with only one pictureless page to the basketball Highlanders. Although the yearbook staff evened things out a bit the following year (ten pages for football and four for basketball), football maintained its position atop the extracurriculum.[81]

The 1948 football season brought a new coach and a new style of play to Daffin Field, but the results changed little. Marcus "Bruno" Kaufman, a former Ouachita Baptist College standout, replaced McFerran and introduced a new offense called the Notre Dame box. Kaufman's first Highlander team suited up only twenty-three players and failed to score in the first six games of the season. Arkansas College's first football victory in fourteen years finally came in game seven of 1948. Fueled by two Bob Lotridge touchdown passes and a key fumble recovery by defensive lineman Ray Brown, the Highlanders defeated Bethel College of McKenzie, Tennessee, 19 to 14 at Daffin Field. The 1949 season proved to be the best on the Highlander gridiron. Although Arkansas College did not claim a conference victory, the Highlanders defeated two junior college squads and continued their dominance over weak Bethel with an impressive 33 to 6 thrashing. The season also produced two tie games with conference foes, including a 7 to 7 stalemate with powerful Arkansas State Teachers College, a game that would eventually live on as the pinnacle of the Highlanders' unsuccessful stab at football greatness.[82]

By 1950 Daffin Field finally had the look of a real college football facility, even if the Highlanders remained unimpressive. New steel bleachers had increased seating capacity by almost 300 percent, and a new sprinkler system installed the previous spring had produced a lush green turf where only dirt and stubble had been before. But this was to be the last season of intercollegiate football at Arkansas College. Once again, the Highlanders overcame only one four-year foe; Coach Kaufman must have been very thankful for Bethel College. Although fans and players were unaware of it at the time, the embarrassing 47 to 0 loss to Magnolia A & M to close out the season would be the last game at Daffin Field. In the spring of 1951, with the Korean War drawing young men out of the classrooms and with athletic budget deficits on the increase, the board of trustees voted to abandon football. Even before the official announcement, scouts from Arkansas Tech and other schools were on campus to recruit the best Highlander underclassmen. Arkansas College's four-year, post–World War II experiment with football brought few moments of success to the little school. It did, however, generate excitement on campus and in the community. And it did produce a few stars about whom another generation of students could boast and debate. By far the greatest Highlander gridiron performer was Ray Brown. A three-time all-conference defensive end despite his relatively small frame, Brown followed Paul McFerran, his high school coach at Wynne, to Batesville and was the only student to play all four years of Highlander football.[83]

While football and other extracurricular pastimes dominated the daily lives of many students during the postwar era, President Spragins and the trustees faced more crucial considerations. For almost two decades Arkansas College had survived a hand-to-mouth existence, and the endowment at the end of World War II was smaller than it had been twenty years earlier. But that was all about to change. It had to change if the college were to survive, much less prosper. An event during the waning months of the war promised a new era for the college. On 21 May 1945, just minutes after the conclusion of the commencement ceremony, an eager throng of college supporters crowded around the steps of Alumni Hall to watch John P. Morrow Sr. and Alexander Henry burn the synod's bond notes. The Synod of Arkansas had succeeded in paying off the $50,000 bond issue three years ahead of schedule, an incredible feat considering the synod's and college's past struggles with finances. The rapid repayment had come about as the result of the synod's decision in 1943 to appoint a committee to raise sufficient money to pay the remaining bond notes by the spring of 1945, and through the tireless efforts of men like Morrow and Henry this had been accomplished. A friend of Arkansas College noted Morrow's leading role in the entire debt repayment saga by exclaiming: "But for you there would be no Arkansas College today."[84]

Arkansas College entered the postwar era with a clean slate. Even more important for the school's health was the synod's decision to restore the college to the list

John P. Morrow and Alexander Henry burn the notes of indebtedness following the 1945 commencement.

of institutions receiving portions of the benevolence fund. The 16.5 percent of the synod's annual benevolences would help shore up the college's wobbly operating budget. No sooner had the slate been cleaned when the flood of G.I.'s and the subsequent student population explosion forced college officials to consider launching a major fund-raising drive, the first since President Tucker's ill-fated campaign of 1927. At the request of Frank Lyon and other new, business-minded trustees, in the spring of 1946 the board agreed to launch an "Expansion Campaign" and hired a Chicago-based fund-raising agency to oversee the project. By the end of the summer the firm, Beaver and Associates, had drawn up detailed plans for the $750,000 campaign, a goal that was reduced to $543,500 in October. About half the projected funds would be used to erect a gymnasium and a new main building. The campaign plans called for the addition of $200,000 to the tiny endowment, with the remainder of funds slated to cover current and campaign expenses and incidental costs.[85]

By almost any standard the Expansion Campaign was a modest undertaking. The goal of just over half a million dollars was considerably less than the campaign goal of the 1920s, and compared with other college and university fund drives of the era Arkansas College's was downright cheap. But those who had been associated with the college for any length of time had learned above all else never to underestimate the reluctance of Arkansas's Southern Presbyterians to give to their school. Besides, Arkansas still claimed the smallest number of Southern Presbyterians of any state in the old Confederacy, and no other denominational college in Arkansas held a smaller constituency. As Spragins's predecessors had learned, there was no such thing as a sure bet when dealing with money.

The campaign got under way in November 1946, just weeks after the announcement that Arkansas College had received a $50,000 bequest from the late Josephine Brown of Hot Springs. Beaver and Associates provided the strategy but left most of the actual work up to college treasurer Bruce C. Boney and a small group of regional chairmen spread throughout the state. For its part the synod appointed a central committee to direct the campaign within the state's churches. Headquartered in Little Rock's Donaghey Building, the central committee was chaired by trustee Van Weathersby; Mack Long served as treasurer. At the synod's urging, several churches set quotas, and a few met their quotas before the end of 1947. As with past money-raising efforts, the Expansion Campaign proceeded slowly. When the end of the 1946–1947 academic year rolled around (the time when the campaign was supposed to be finished), less than half the goal had been pledged and only a fraction of the money had actually been collected. In the summer of 1947 the campaign's headquarters was transferred to Batesville so that Boney could run things from his office at the college. Pledges and payments dwindled, however, and Boney resigned in October, leaving the campaign without a full-time director for six months. By the fall of 1948 the campaign had almost ground to a halt with less than half the projected amount raised. H. T. MacDonough assumed the position as college treasurer and campaign director during 1948–1949 and injected new life into the program. By the time MacDonough left in the spring of 1951, more than $400,000 had been collected and all but $50,000 of the goal had been pledged.[86]

Even with a growing endowment in the late 1940s and early 1950s, Arkansas College faced an uphill battle for accreditation. Spragins and the board realized that the college's nonaccredited status would continue to impede development and tarnish the school's image within the state. By the late 1940s Arkansas College's main competitors within the state had all been accredited by the North Central Association, but constant financial shortcomings had prevented the Batesville school from joining this group. With the debt issue resolved and enrollment increasing, the administration and faculty turned their attention to the issue of accreditation during the 1947–1948 academic year. Part of the reason for the timing was a recent announcement by the University of Arkansas's medical school that in the future it would accept only those applicants who had completed at least three years of undergraduate work at an accredited institution. Such mandates became increasingly common at professional and graduate schools after World War II. Furthermore, the administration had long observed the trend of students completing their first two years at Arkansas College only to transfer to the University of Arkansas or some other accredited school to complete their degrees.[87]

In the fall of 1947 Spragins appointed psychology and education professor Frank H. Harrin to study the NCA's guidelines and analyze Arkansas College's degree of compatibility with those requirements. Shortly before Christmas, Harrin reported his findings to the faculty committee; his sobering observation that the college was deficient in at least ten areas ignited a frenzied discussion among the faculty and administration that lasted throughout the following spring and into the next academic year. In a series of meetings during the spring of 1948, faculty members discussed almost all aspects of the college's shortcomings, from the deficiencies of the library to the small endowment. Because most shortcomings could be traced to the lack of money, these faculty sessions produced little of a tangible nature. A committee appointed by Spragins reduced the college's old statement of objectives—an unwieldy and rambling two-page essay—to a succinct paragraph promising "a general education according to the best tradition of the liberal arts college." The faculty also agreed to alter the freshman orientation program to comply with NCA recommendations. Little else could be accomplished on such a limited budget. In the spring of 1949 Spragins sought an outside opinion and invited Theodore Stephens, president of Aurora College in Illinois, to spend a couple of days in Batesville as an unofficial NCA observer. Stephens's conclusions were for the most part the obvious issues that the faculty had spent the previous year discussing, though he advised the college to devote most of its efforts to improving the library, the financial situation, and the faculty, which consisted of too few Ph.D.'s and too many individuals with very little graduate training and no record of scholarship.[88]

Stephens further suggested leaving the congested downtown campus behind and relocating to the spacious and attractive new site (the old Masonic property) on the bluff east of Independence Hall and the new field house. This option had only recently been made available. As we have seen, the college began leasing the Masonic Home buildings in the fall of 1946 for use as men's dormitories. A year and a half later college officials began bargaining to purchase the entire Masonic property in Batesville, which in addition to the three brick buildings consisted of roughly one hundred acres. On 1 August 1948 the Grand Lodge of Arkansas deeded the land and buildings to Arkansas College in exchange for $35,000 and a total of forty full-tuition scholarships to be spread out over the following twenty years. The college paid the Masons $20,000 up front and financed the remainder over a fifteen-year period.[89]

The purchase gave Arkansas College its third separate campus and represented the last leg of the school's leapfrogging from downtown to the eastern edge of the city. Considering Spragins's personal philosophy and vision, it is likely that the president viewed the new property as a future farm site for his languishing Self-Help Division. At the very least he realized that the college was facing a physical crisis, and the new campus would serve as a safety valve to relieve overcrowding. Spragins would long consider the acquisition of this property as one of the chief contributions of his presidency.

Although few people were aware of it at the time, the Masonic property also had a historical connection to Arkansas College. The one hundred acres on the bluff overlooking the Miller Creek valley had once belonged to Judge J. W. Butler, a former trustee who had served briefly as president of the board in the 1890s. In 1909, a few years after the death of his wife and his subsequent relocation to St. Louis, Judge Butler had sold "Oak Hill" to the Masons. The trustees must have agreed with Theodore Stephens's recommendation to adopt the Masonic land as the primary campus, for in May 1950 the board voted to limit all future expansion to the new property and to begin selling off the unused portions of the East End Heights, or middle, campus.[90]

The trustees' decision to begin selling off the middle campus property only thinly veiled another developing financial crisis of sorts. The Expansion Campaign was not proceeding as smoothly or quickly as had been hoped. Furthermore, national education experts predicted that, with the disappearance of G.I.'s from college classrooms, enrollments would plummet in the early 1950s. The 1949–1950 session proved to be Arkansas College's last with a G.I.-bloated enrollment. Just weeks after the 1950 commencement, North Korean communists invaded South Korea, setting off a two-year struggle that would once again draw thousands of young men into military service. In a meeting of the board held one week after the beginning of classes in September 1950, Spragins sounded the first alarms of the postwar era. Due to a bad crop year, the gradual reduction of G.I. students, and the uncertainty engendered by the Korean War, enrollment was down about 25 percent. Making matters worse was the discouragement caused by the college's delay in building the women's dormitory that had been on the drawing table for several years. The size of Arkansas College's student body steadily decreased throughout 1950–1951—twenty-five young men left for military service before the end of the first semester—and full-time enrollment fell below two hundred the following year, the lowest level in half a dozen years.[91]

Retrenchment became the theme for Spragins's final years as president. The college's growing but tiny endowment failed to compensate for the loss of thousands of dollars from the G.I. Bill, and declining enrollments threatened the institution with insolvency once again. In the fall of 1950 the board approved a resolution calling on the administration to suspend any students who failed to pay tuition and fees; a second act demanded that the bookstore be operated on a cash-only basis. More drastic measures came in the spring. When venerable Eugene Blandford announced his retirement in February 1951 (after a career at Arkansas College that spanned a remarkable fifty-five years), the trustees decided not to hire a replacement. This was the first action in what became a massive downsizing campaign. Through voluntary resignations, retirements, and layoffs, Arkansas College's faculty was reduced from twenty-six positions to sixteen. The board also voted to discontinue the offices of business manager and bookstore manager and combine the duties of the bursar and accounting instructor. And in a move that signaled a changing of the guard within the power structures of the board, the trustees voted to limit preministerial scholarships to Presbyterian students only and to discontinue the tradition of waiving tuition charges for the children of Presbyterian ministers.[92]

The trustees' decision to begin collecting tuition payments from non-Presbyterian preministerial students, as well as the children of Presbyterian ministers, served as an alarm for Spragins and the small group of ministers on the board. As they would soon come to realize, it was only the first volley in a power struggle that would engulf the college for a year and a half and whose outcome would decide the future of Batesville's little college. The struggle was between cliques of trustees and other interested persons with markedly different visions for the future and mission of Arkansas College. The euphoria and prosperity of the G.I. years had buried any serious discussion of the college's educational mission just as surely as had the two decades of debt and struggle. The economic crisis of the early 1950s suddenly brought the college's future and its mission, or lack thereof, into focus. The prosperity and swelling classrooms of the immediate postwar era had certainly been a welcomed contrast to the years of precarious and anxious existence, but such a boom would probably never occur again. It was time, many believed, for a serious appraisal of the college's long-term prospects and a reconsideration of its place and purpose within the world of higher education in general and within Arkansas specifically.

Spragins, of course, had already fashioned a vision for his alma mater. The president's desire to transform Arkansas College into a work-centered campus for poor students from the Ozarks and other rural Arkansas areas had never vanished. Spragins's natural reaction to the declining enrollments and sagging finances of the 1950–1951 session was to turn once again to his Self-Help plan. In September 1950 the president convinced the board to study other colleges' work-study programs for the purpose of crafting such a plan for Arkansas College. In December J. Leighton Scott, a West Memphis minister and longtime friend and former classmate of Spragins, spent a week at Maryville College in Tennessee observing that school's student work program. When Scott made his report at the February 1951 meeting of the board, Spragins promptly suggested implementing a broad Self-Help program at Arkansas College and suggested hiring Stafford Beck, a 1941 alumnus with several years experience at the School of the Ozarks, as director of the program. Furthermore, Spragins suggested that the college appeal to needy students by reducing tuition and room and board costs, both of which had ballooned in the late 1940s, and by redoubling efforts to increase scholarship funds. The trustees tabled the matter until the next meeting in early April. The April board meeting proved the beginning of the end for John D. Spragins's presidency and his vision for a little college in the Ozarks, though the ending would take a year to exhaust its twists and turns. Not only did the trustees not implement Spragins's Self-Help program but the board also found itself discussing the potential demise of Arkansas College.[93]

In early 1951 the president of the College of the Ozarks in Clarksville approached Arkansas College trustees Frank Lyon Sr. and H. W. "Bill" McMillan to discuss the possibility of merging the two institutions. This was not the first mention of such a development. A 1946 study conducted by representatives from the George Peabody College had recommended combining the two institutions on the site of the Clarksville campus. The Arkansas College board had responded by appointing a committee to meet with a similar committee from Ozarks to discuss possible consolidation. Talks fell through, however, during the summer of 1946, and the subsequent G.I. rush helped both schools forget about the matter for a time. By the spring of 1950 merger talks were evidently circulating once again, for Spragins used the threat of consolidation to encourage donors to contribute to the Expansion Campaign. Therefore, it is quite likely that Spragins's haste to implement a Self-Help program was in effect a preemptive measure to forestall or prevent a merger.[94]

But the forces supporting the merger were gathering steam by the spring of 1951. The primary movers in the Arkansas College camp were McMillan and Lyon, both of whom had served on the college's first merger committee in the summer of 1946. McMillan, especially, adopted the merger of the two schools as his personal mission. Bill McMillan, who had joined the board of trustees as a young man in his thirties during World War II, was a fiery attorney and real estate developer from Arkadelphia. Although educated at Ouachita Baptist College, he was a dedicated Presbyterian layman, and it was his church affiliation that led him into Arkansas College's sphere. A boisterous and confrontational man, McMillan was elected vice-chairman after just a few months' service on the board and quickly established himself as the vocal leader of a growing contingent of young professionals and businessmen who did not hesitate to challenge the status quo or the Presbyterian ministers sometimes associated with it.

In recent years McMillan had grown increasingly dissatisfied with what he viewed as a decline in the quality of education at Arkansas College and with Spragins's direction of the institution. The two men cherished divergent visions of the future of Arkansas College, and McMillan openly criticized the administration and Spragins's missionary/Self-Help concept of higher education. For McMillan, Lyon, and their supporters, a merger with the College of the Ozarks held the promise of a single, elite Presbyterian institution in Arkansas, one that could rival Southwestern at Memphis, Westminster College in Missouri, and possibly even the premier denominational colleges back east. Neither the College of the Ozarks nor Arkansas College could lay claim to any reputation of academic excellence—though Ozarks had recently been accredited by the NCA—but a consolidation of their resources and a subsequent substantial fund drive might, McMillan and Lyon believed, set a new institution on the path to greatness. So McMillan threw himself wholeheartedly into the effort to effect a merger.

At the April 1951 meeting of the board, McMillan, Lyon, and their fellow trustees requested that the Synod of Arkansas appoint a committee to study the merger issue. At a special meeting in Little Rock on the first of May, the synod's moderator appointed a committee of seven, three clergymen and four laymen, to confer with a similar committee established by the Synod of Oklahoma (U.S.A.), the denominational overseer of the College of the Ozarks. McMillan was appointed chairman; among those on the committee with him were trustees Lyon and John P. Morrow Sr. and prominent ministers Roy L. Davis and Marion A. Boggs of Little Rock and W. L. McColgan of Pine Bluff. By the time Arkansas College's trustees gathered for their annual commencement week meeting in late May, the two synod merger committees (now a joint committee chaired by Boggs) had already held discussions in Batesville and Clarksville and had decided to appoint an advisory committee of educational experts to study the situation and serve as a consulting body. At McMillan's behest, Arkansas College's board formed yet another committee to "survey and develop enthusiasm in the churches toward the study of a merger."[95]

The three men appointed to the advisory committee to study the merger were all well known within Presbyterian higher education circles. E. Fay Campbell, who became the de facto leader and spokesman for the trio, was the Secretary of Higher Education for the Northern Presbyterian Church. His counterpart in the southern church, Hunter Blakely, joined him on the committee. The third member was Raymond McLain, president of Kentucky's Transylvania University. In July 1951 the three men visited the campuses at Batesville and Clarksville, interviewed administrators and faculty, and studied the various records at each institution. On 20–21 July 1951 the advisory committee met with the joint merger committee in Little Rock to disclose its findings and present its report. The "Campbell Report" recommended immediate consolidation of the two institutions. The new college, which the advisory committee recommended naming the College of the Ozarks in Batesville, would be located on the one-hundred-acre, former Masonic Home site on the bluff overlooking Miller Creek valley. The Campbell Report suggested using the Clarksville campus as a temporary home until contractors could erect a chapel, a library, a science building, and a women's dormitory on the new Batesville location.[96]

The advisory committee's report came as a shock to no one. For years educational leaders in both the Southern and Northern Presbyterian churches had urged Arkansas College and the College of the Ozarks to consolidate, if not with each other then with another small institution of similar principles. The champions of consolidation had attempted to pave the way for the advisory committee's announcement by publicly criticizing both colleges during the early weeks of the summer. The Campbell Report's statement that "we can not ask our young people to accept an inferior product of education under the guise of spurious piety" echoed a familiar refrain among the friends of merger. John Quincy Wolf Jr., an alumnus and former Arkansas College faculty member, expressed his dissatisfaction with the detractors who complained "'let's have a first-class college or none'" but had made little effort in the past to ensure progress for the Batesville school. Trustee Charley Robinson, superintendent of home missions for the Pine Bluff presbytery, complained to Spragins that too many of the college's critics wanted to "'have the best,' yet would not try to build our own institution."[97]

Activities in Batesville in the weeks preceding the announcement of the Campbell Report suggest that most residents of the area considered consolidation imminent and that the primary concern was keeping the new school in Batesville. On 31 May 1951 the Batesville Chamber of Commerce sponsored an open forum meeting at Kelley's Shamrock Room to discuss a campaign to prevent the merged institution from locating in Clarksville or some other location. As he had done twenty years earlier during the debt crisis, trustee Nels Barnett stepped forward to lead the movement to convince the merger committee that Batesville was the best site. In early July the *Batesville Guard* sponsored an essay contest and promised a fifty-dollar prize for the student who crafted the most convincing argument for keeping a college in Batesville. In another maneuver, students, faculty, and friends circulated a petition among the students who commuted to summer school from an eight-county region. The petition argued that due to its strategic location in an area with no other college, Batesville should retain the consolidated school. In addition, the chamber of commerce and interested citizens promised that the city of Batesville would purchase the old downtown campus for $100,000 should the college remain in town. The fact that the merger plan did not elicit as much anxiety and community action in Clarksville was probably due to the fact that most people assumed the advisory committee would recommend locating the new college in Clarksville, just as the Peabody Report had suggested five years earlier. But Arkansas College's recent acquisition of the Masonic property had altered the situation, and the one-hundred-acre, mostly vacant Batesville site appeared to Campbell and his cohorts as a tabula rasa full of opportunities for a fresh start.[98]

On 22 July 1951 the *Arkansas Gazette* featured a front-page article concerning the Campbell Report and the proposed merger. Built largely around an interview with E. Fay Campbell, the piece revealed just how radical a transformation the advisory committee and champions of merger were contemplating. In a statement reflecting both an ignorance of the institutions' differing backgrounds and an unfortunate lack of tact when dealing with such an emotional issue, Campbell quickly dismissed Spragins's vision in favor of the goals of McMillan, Lyon, and their supporters. "Both these colleges have been primarily missionary colleges, that is, they have existed principally just to serve the young people of the Ozark region. Well, we aren't interested in the merged institution's being of that sort—we want it to attract students from all over Arkansas and, for that matter, all over the nation." Whether Campbell served as a mouthpiece for McMillan and Lyon—as Spragins and others suspected—or was simply in accord with their way of thinking—the more plausible explanation—Spragins began to realize he was being pushed aside along with his lost vision. Campbell informed the *Gazette*'s reporter that the new college would require a new leader, a "great president [and] fine administrator." He called for higher entrance requirements and an improved, highly educated faculty. Interestingly, Campbell even offered his ideas on the architectural style for the new campus. Ideally, according to Campbell, the institution that resulted from the merger would come to resemble an Arkansas version of a college like Haverford or Swarthmore, two eastern Pennsylvania schools with which the Philadelphian Campbell was familiar.[99]

The joint merger committee decided to meet again shortly before the beginning of classes in September to work out a detailed plan of consolidation that would then be presented to the Synod of Arkansas, U.S., and the Synod of Oklahoma, U.S.A. For McMillan and the supporters of merger the month and a half leading up to this meeting was a time of frenetic activity and planning. For Batesville residents, relieved that the advisory committee had recommended their town for the consolidated college, it was a period of anxiety and even excitement, though many like Nels Barnett vehemently opposed the plan to temporarily move operations to Clarksville. With the exception of Barnett, Batesville was almost strangely silent during the long summer. Conspicuously absent from most of the public rhetoric was John P. Morrow Sr. and elderly board chairman Judge S. Marcus Bone. Their silence may have been the result of acquiescence in the merger or of a general disinclination to challenge the young, aggressive trustees who seemed full of ideas for the college. For President Spragins, whose own public silence cloaked his opposition to the merger plans, the weeks between the July and September merger committee meetings brought trepidation and agony. Distressed by Campbell's comments in the *Gazette* piece, in August Spragins wrote to Roy Davis, secretary of the joint merger committee, to inquire about those comments and about his own future at Arkansas College. Incredibly, Davis, who like McMillan had never seen eye to eye with Spragins, assured the president that the advisory committee actually favored the old "Maryville of the West" Self-Help idea, though Campbell's statements clearly suggested the opposite. But a letter that Davis wrote to a Georgia minister three days later, in which Davis noted that the merger would free Spragins to devote himself to home mission work, indicated that those who favored the consolidation did not view John D. Spragins as an integral part of the new institution.[100]

At the September meeting the joint merger committee drafted a resolution recommending consolidation of Arkansas College and the College of the Ozarks, based on the Campbell Report. On 26 September 1951 the Synod of Arkansas approved the merger plan and authorized a November meeting to work out the details of consolidation with representatives from the Synod of Oklahoma. Two weeks later the Synod of Oklahoma balked over the proposed Batesville location and tabled the resolution indefinitely, an action that surprised some members of the Synod of Arkansas and the Arkansas College family. In response the Synod of Arkansas's merger committee canceled the proposed November meeting, effectively ending the merger talks. Although it is unclear how the merger process could have advanced as far as it did only to be shot down at the last moment, it is obvious that a significant group within the Synod of Oklahoma did not agree with the Campbell Report's conclusion that Batesville was the best location. The Synod of Oklahoma's role in shutting down merger talks also suggests that the prime movers within the whole consolidation movement were McMillan, Lyon, and their supporters and that they were able to exercise considerable influence on the advisory committee.[101]

The failure of the merger movement left Arkansas College in a precarious position. Even before merger talks fell through, Nels Barnett observed that "the Arkansas College outlook has been changed for the worse very definitely . . . since April 1." McMillan's public statement in late September that "the only possible solution to gaining a school of outstanding caliber in the state is completion of the merger," left him in an uncomfortable position and trapped the college in a defensive posture. The previous summer's rhetoric concerning the "'utter failure'" of the college and the weakness of its administration had dampened morale and, according to Spragins, was largely responsible for the 25 percent decline in enrollment for the fall of 1951. The Expansion Campaign, which was nearing completion when the merger push commenced the previous spring, had ground to a complete halt, and construction of the women's dormitory had been put on hold. Even without the expensive football program, the college was facing a possible operating deficit larger than any since the 1920s. To compound matters, the publicity surrounding the Campbell Report had set forth a new vision for the college, one that was not going to go away just because the proposed merger failed to materialize. Reacting to this atmosphere of uncertainty, Spragins pressured the board of trustees to come to some sort of decision on the college's future and purpose and asked for a clarification of his role in future developments.[102]

McMillan and his supporters reacted to the merger's failure by "exploring plans to achieve through Arkansas College at Batesville the same objectives of Christian education that would have been accomplished by the proposed merger." On 1 November 1951 the synod's merger committee met in Little Rock to make recommendations for Arkansas College's future. The committee recommended drafting long-range goals in accordance with the Campbell Report and keeping the advisory committee for guidance. The committee requested that Arkansas College aim for quick accreditation and explore the possibilities of securing financial aid from various educational foundations, something that the college had never successfully accomplished. The members of the committee also voted to keep the door open for a possible merger in the future should the Synod of Oklahoma experience a change of heart. In a meeting of the college board later that day the trustees adopted the merger committee's recommendations. The gravity of this brief but monumental meeting did not immediately set in for Spragins and several of the trustees. But a subsequent meeting of the merger committee with E. Fay Campbell's advisory committee, in which the attendees discussed at length the mission of an elite liberal arts college and the possibility of garnering foundation funds, convinced Spragins that his days at Arkansas College might be numbered.[103]

The winter months of late 1951 and early 1952 were a tense and crucial episode in the college's history. Relations between the two sides—Spragins and his supporters and McMillan and his followers—soured in the chilly air. McMillan, Lyon, Davis, and probably even Morrow were determined that Arkansas College would not become a "missionary college" or, as McMillan derisively referred to Spragins's vision, a "Caddo Gap school." Spragins and his coterie of ministers such as Charley Robinson, John T. Barr Sr., and J. Herndon McCain were equally convinced that the Campbell Report's vision of an elite liberal arts college in the foothills of the Ozarks was not only unrealistic but irresponsible. Furthermore, Spragins feared that the group of relative newcomers such as McMillan and Lyon had "no deep-seated loyalty" to Arkansas College and would abandon the school when "their visionary plans do not materialize." By early January 1952 Spragins had decided to force a showdown by submitting his resignation, which would serve as a sort of parliamentary vote of confidence. Although the president informed a friend that he believed the board would reject his resignation, Spragins actually suspected that McMillan had gained the upper hand; therefore, he delayed his official resignation until he had secured a job to fall back on. By the time the president submitted his resignation letter to the board in March and announced he was assuming the superintendency of home missions for the East

Arkansas Presbytery, Spragins had become increasingly pessimistic over the college's immediate and long-term prospects.[104]

Spragins's letter of resignation set forth for the final time his doomed vision of a Self-Help college and encapsulated the antithetical views concerning the future of Arkansas College. Describing his position at the college as "untenable," the president criticized policies recently adopted by the board: the elimination of scholarships for non-Presbyterian ministerial students and the children of ministers, the rejection of his Self-Help program, and the decision to take a hard line on collecting student fees. These actions, Spragins argued, were "in direct violation of the historic position of Arkansas College . . . , i.e., assisting worthy students to obtain an education under Christian influences." Spragins's chief concern continued to be the worthy but underprivileged to whom he had been reaching out over the past decade. He warned the trustees that "church colleges are rapidly becoming 'class Colleges.' They are ministering only to the middle and upper classes. There is a crying need for a church college maintaining a low student expense and a strong work program along with high scholarship and Christian idealism." But Spragins's suspicion that his vision represented the minority opinion of the board was confirmed when the trustees voted ten to seven to accept his resignation.[105] A decade earlier the message of his letter would have received almost universal agreement among the trustees, but times had changed. So would the college, it seemed.

Chapter 6

Bricks and Mortar: Paul McCain Builds a Campus

Moving a college is not a casual undertaking, not even at a tiny institution like Arkansas College. So it is little wonder that the administration and local trustees began planning months in advance for the operation of M-Day, 18 May 1954. Moving day at Arkansas College, though lacking the drama, danger, and gravity of an earlier era's D-Day, was by all accounts a logistical success, a model of efficiency and organization. It was also a model of town and gown cooperation. Local physician Wesley Ketz headed up a $20,000 campaign to fund moving expenses and renovation of the three Masonic Home buildings on the new site. Stanley Wood, local trustee and automobile dealer, coordinated the move itself by rounding up more than thirty trucks from local businessmen as well as a crew of more than one hundred students and Batesville residents. In less than three hours Wood's troops hauled two safes, eight pianos, thirty desks, thirty-five typewriters, fifty tables, sixty cabinets, six hundred chairs, and fifteen thousand books from Arkansas College's downtown campus—the institution's home for eighty-two years—to the Masonic buildings perched on the bluff overlooking Miller Creek valley. The movers were so expeditious that they had to loiter for an hour anticipating the picnic barbeque dinner at noon.[1]

The new campus, consisting of three large brick buildings and a sandstone dormitory sitting in the northwestern corner of a one-hundred-acre pasture, was not terribly impressive in the spring of 1954. To be certain these buildings were in a much better state of repair than the vacated ones downtown, but it would have been difficult to fully appreciate the grand visions then being developed for this plot by the administration and trustees. Although the downtown campus's deteriorating structures and lack of room for expansion were the obvious motivations behind the college's relocation, the move to Butler Hill (as only a select few old-timers referred to the new site) carried a symbolic weight. The new campus, with its views of expansive valleys to the north and south, offered a fresh start, a clean slate. Nothing was more valuable for such an embattled institution. This was a new era. Americans were shedding the memories of depression and war; they were looking to the future. Arkansas College was leaving the ghosts of its past to tread the green before old

Alumni Hall. The trustees and friends of the college hoped the new campus would reinvigorate the aging school with a youthful spirit. And they looked to their youthful president to lead the way into the promised land.

The young man tabbed by the trustees to build Arkansas College into an elite institution left an indelible mark on Batesville's little school. Paul McCain's seventeen years at the helm of Arkansas College still constitute the second-longest consecutive presidential tenure in school history, second only to Isaac Long's nineteen-and-a-half-year administration. No president before or after McCain could match his record of physical expansion and construction. No other president, however, has ever been faced with the necessity of such brick and mortar activity. Paul McCain's presidency ushered Arkansas College into the modern era of post–World War II higher education. The move to the new campus in 1954 was followed by an almost constant procession of events and developments crucial to the college's survival and progress—self-studies and accreditation, faculty improvement, curricular development, millions of dollars' worth of building construction, and the adoption of modern fund-raising techniques. This seventeen-year tenure witnessed an almost threefold increase in enrollment and, in the 1960s, a dramatic demographic alteration of Arkansas College's traditional student body. All of this took place against the backdrop of American life and Arkansas society in the 1950s and 1960s, an era marked by cold war anxieties, racial integration and the civil rights movement, the rise of rock-n-roll and the subsequent flowering of a vibrant sixties youth culture, and emotional debates over the United States's involvement in Vietnam. By the time McCain left Batesville in 1969 Arkansas College had a modern campus and an annual budget that had ballooned from less than $150,000 to more than a million dollars. Despite the progress and sense of accomplishment, some things remained unchanged. Arkansas College continued to live a hand-to-mouth existence, the product of a meager endowment and declining church support, and the administration as before struggled against the odds to build and sustain enrollment.

Considering his lasting imprint on Arkansas College, it is more than a little surprising that Paul McCain found his way to Batesville quite by accident. After the collapse of merger talks with the College of the Ozarks in the fall of 1951, a majority of the trustees had embraced the goal of developing Arkansas College into a first-rate liberal arts institution to rival such regional, Presbyterian colleges as Westminster and Southwestern. But the search committee appointed to find a replacement for John D. Spragins in the spring of 1952 conducted its business much like its predecessors, through the old boys' network of clergymen and Southern Presbyterian educators. After a couple of fruitless months, the chairman of the committee, Little Rock minister Roy L. Davis, contacted Charles McCain, a young minister in Canton, Mississippi. Although McCain was uninterested in the job, he had a brother, a young college history professor, who was more qualified for a post in higher education. Upon learning of Paul McCain's interest, Davis directed the young scholar to Montgomery, Alabama, where Davis's friend Charles Diehl, retired president of Southwestern at Memphis, interviewed McCain for the Arkansas College board. With Diehl's stamp of approval, Paul McCain made his first trip to Arkansas in late August to lay out his terms before Davis, Bill McMillan, Frank Lyon Sr., and the other members of the search committee. He was hired on the spot.[2]

Despite their new president's youth—he was only thirty-two at the time of his election—and complete lack of administrative experience, the trustees felt fortunate to secure the services of Paul Moffatt McCain. Foremost among their reasons for optimism was their young leader's pedigree. Within the world of Southern Presbyterian higher education few names carried more clout than the Scotch-Irish McCain. Paul's father, James Ross McCain, had retired a year earlier after twenty-eight years as president of Agnes Scott College, a women's school in Decatur, Georgia, and his grandfather, James I., had devoted almost half a century as an English professor at Erskine College in South Carolina. Raised on the campus of Agnes Scott, Paul McCain knew the life of small college academe inside and out. He also possessed an instinctive understanding of the Southern Presbyterian mindset. McCain followed his father and grandfather to Erskine. A tall, broad-shouldered young man, he lettered in football before earning a degree in history in 1940. After two years teaching at a private boys' school in northern Georgia, McCain received an army commission that eventually landed him at West Point as an instructor of military history. When a postwar stint at his father-in-law's North Carolina garment factory proved unsatisfying, McCain returned to the classroom, earning his master's degree at Duke in 1948 and a Ph.D. in history in 1951. At the time he was elected Arkansas College's twelfth president, McCain had just completed his second year on the faculty of Brenau College, a women's institution in Gainesville, Georgia.[3]

Hundreds of college presidents and other leaders throughout history have been lauded as the right person at the right time. Paul McCain's presidency can certainly be regarded in like fashion. In light of the trustees' recent resolution to build a superior academic program in the Ozark foothills, McCain appeared to be a godsend to the little college. As the first Arkansas College president with an earned Ph.D.—in fact, he was the first inaugurated president with any kind of advanced university degree—McCain lent the struggling institution an air of academic credibility that had been lacking since the departure of Tom Lowry more than a decade earlier. McMillan, Lyon, and the other trustees hoped that McCain's academic credentials would open doors and checkbooks at educational foundations that had heretofore ignored the college's pleas for funds. The trustees' decision to hire the young scholar, who was more than twenty-two years his predecessor's junior, indicated a conscious attempt to inject new life into the staid and floundering college. Yet McCain's youthful vigor blended nicely with his solid denominational heritage to produce a leader with the energy and ability to get things done as well as an innate knowledge of the requirements for leadership within the conservative community of Southern Presbyterians.

Paul McCain looked the part of a mid-twentieth-century small college president when he arrived on campus in September 1952 with his wife, Eleanor, and two small children. "Tall Paul," as he quickly became known to students, sported wire-rimmed glasses, starched white shirts, dark suits, and a dome of slightly receding but neatly combed short brown hair. This look of impeccability changed remarkably little over the course of his seventeen years in Batesville. As far as most students and faculty could tell, McCain possessed a personality to match his conservative, bland look. Although kind and empathetic, the young president displayed little of the warmth and friendliness that had been a trademark of his predecessor. Throughout his administration McCain made a conscious effort to avoid losing touch with students by periodically teaching upper-level history courses; nevertheless, an inability or unwillingness to communicate personally with employees and students earned him a reputation for aloofness and an unwavering professional demeanor.

Despite his shortcomings in interpersonal communication, McCain quickly proved himself a decisive administrator and an able fund-raiser. The president's unflappable professionalism, a characteristic that often intimidated students, worked as an advantage when dealing with trustees, educational bureaucrats, and foundation representatives. Within a few short months, McCain had mastered the college's somewhat convoluted financial situation, and a historian's memory for detail allowed him to manage almost every facet of the school's operation from high-level fund-raising and curricular alterations down to maintenance and cafeteria concerns. In fact, by the time McCain left in 1969 his dictatorial style was a relic of the past on most small college campuses. This take-charge, micromanaging style was much more amenable to Arkansas College's dire situation in 1952, however. It was probably even necessary.

One thing that McCain did have in common with almost all of his predecessors was that he inherited a grim situation. Although the trustees had offered McCain a salary that was 65 percent greater than Spragins's had been, they had also glossed over some of the college's financial shortcomings. An operating deficit of almost $10,000 for the 1951–1952 session had been buried in accounting, and more than a third of the paltry $320,000 endowment was completely unproductive. Arkansas College had received only $8,600 from the endowment during Spragins's final year. The college did not own a president's home, so the McCains spent their first year in a small apartment suite on the first floor of Independence Hall. The new first family did not find themselves crowded by students, however; in spite of a significant increase in the freshman class for the fall of 1952, full-time enrollment was only 158 and would drop to 138 by the beginning of the spring semester. Construction on the new dormitory, located on the Masonic Home campus, had come to a halt due to lack of money; it would take more than $75,000 to complete the building.[4] The college also continued to suffer the aftershocks of the failed merger movement and its negative publicity, and accreditation seemed as unobtainable now as it had been during the depression. Beyond the small world of the downtown Batesville campus hostilities in Korea were almost two years old, and Americans eagerly anticipated the upcoming presidential election.

These were certainly unpleasant conditions under which to start a presidency. By now such a baptism had become tradition for Arkansas College administrators. Fortunately for McCain, though, the drumbeat for closing the college had subsided by 1952, and trustee support and interest was far better than it had been at the beginning of the Spragins administration. More important, McCain, despite the indirect avenues of communication in the summer of 1952, had the approval and backing of Bill McMillan, Frank Lyon Sr., John P. Morrow Sr., and the board's other most prominent and active trustees, and this would prove invaluable to the young president in the rocky days ahead.

When McCain moved into his office on the first floor of the old Isaac J. Long Memorial Building, a room first occupied sixty years earlier by a young Eugene Long, there was scarcely a facet of the college's operation that did not demand improvement. Consequently, McCain's first couple of years in office were a whirlwind of activity. Most obvious to visitors was the physical condition of the downtown campus. McCain and the trustees realized the need to relocate to the new expansive campus as soon as possible, but they also understood that this could not be accomplished until the new dormitory was standing and enough money could be raised to renovate the three Masonic buildings. In the meantime, McCain went to work on immediate problems. Because chief among these was the need for money, for operating expenses and completion of the dormitory, McCain borrowed an idea from his predecessor and instituted the Loyalty Fund, a fund-raising campaign similar to Spragins's Budget Balancers except that it did not limit gifts to ten dollars. At the president's behest, the trustees in January 1953 approved reducing the grant money offered to preministerial students (of whom there were only five) and raising tuition and room and board by thirty-five dollars per year. McCain also sought a small grant from the General Education Board and a low-interest government loan to complete the dormitory; Arkansas College's unaccredited status was largely responsible for the failure of both requests. The college eventually resorted to floating another ten-year bond issue in the summer of 1953 to ensure the dormitory's completion by the fall semester. McCain's Loyalty Fund was more successful and enabled him to finish his first year as president without an operating deficit.[5]

In academic matters the new president convinced the board to reinstitute a system of faculty rank, in which only faculty with an earned Ph.D. or some other terminal degree could qualify for full professor status. Each of the four levels of faculty rank also carried a different salary, and McCain requested across-the-board raises for the underpaid faculty. In addition the board accepted the president's plan for a mandatory faculty retirement age of sixty-five, with a loophole that allowed the trustees to retain elderly teachers whose services were deemed valuable to the college. McCain did not hesitate to use the sixty-five rule to rid the faculty of persons he viewed detrimental or unfit for service, a practice that resulted in hurt feelings and at least one lawsuit. The president also convinced the trustees to cease granting B.S. and B.S.E. degrees and to boost the annual library budget from a meager $350 to $2,500. Furthermore, McCain appointed a faculty committee to draft a new and more succinct statement of purpose to be included in the college catalog published in 1953.[6]

The motivation behind these steps was the necessity for accreditation. The administration of Paul McCain can be divided into two major phases—the push for accreditation and the building of a campus. Upon arriving in Batesville in 1952, McCain's primary goal was getting the college accredited. It was a significant hurdle, but one that had to be jumped if Arkansas College hoped to progress and expand, even to survive. So it was around this bull's-eye that all other things revolved during the early years of McCain's presidency.

Arkansas College had made little effort to secure accreditation since the issue was first brought up during the presidency of E. B. Tucker in the 1920s. The major stumbling block had always been money; in the 1920s the college had lacked the minimum endowment required for accreditation, and even though the North Central Association relaxed its requirements in the 1930s Arkansas College remained hopelessly mired in debt until the end of World War II. The boom-and-bust conditions of the postwar G.I. invasion waylayed the Spragins administration's timid efforts, so that by the early 1950s almost every facet of the college's operation demanded significant improvement. Put matter of factly by an educator who visited the campus in the fall of 1953 on behalf of the NCA, "Arkansas College (could) only be described as being in dire straits." The faculty contained too few Ph.D.'s, too many instructors who were considered underqualified by modern educational standards, and "all too many [who were] well beyond their productive period." Dean Harry King was "too old," and the deans of men and women were "unsatisfactory." According to the NCA representative, the student body was "apparently well below the national average in ability [and] very probably below that of many other Arkansas colleges." The college's physical plant was obviously deteriorating, and the endowment had stagnated after the merger crisis. The curriculum was disjointed and appeared to lack a well-articulated overall purpose. And the president, though well qualified and effective, was, like so many small college leaders, burdened with too many mundane chores that should have been delegated to faculty and staff.[7]

The various NCA representatives who visited the Arkansas College campus during McCain's second year in Batesville offered the young president several recommendations for improvement, including reorganizing the curriculum into divisions, hiring a new academic dean as well as directors of student personnel, alumni, and fund-raising, developing a core of general education courses required of all matriculates, and moving the college to the new Masonic campus. Most of McCain's actions in the early years of his administration directly addressed one or more of the weaknesses pointed out in NCA reports. During his first year in Batesville, McCain and the faculty organized the curriculum into five divisions: Arts and Skills, Education and Religion, Language and Literature, Sciences, and Social Studies. By the fall of 1955 the faculty had developed a four-division setting that would remain in place throughout McCain's presidency. With the retirement of Harry King in the spring of 1954, McCain recruited Lorne Kerr McAdam, a professor of psychology and education at Westminster College in Missouri, as academic dean and counselor of students. McAdam's Ph.D. and his extensive experience in higher education immediately improved Arkansas College's standing with NCA investigators. The board also approved McCain's request to hire an assistant to the president, whose duties included recruiting, fund-raising, and alumni relations. After a few years this position was dissolved, and by the early 1960s the assistant to the president's duties had been separated into individual jobs.[8]

One of the most common sources of criticism from NCA visitors was the faculty. When McCain arrived in Batesville in September 1952, one-quarter of the full-time faculty members held no graduate degree, including Dean King, and of the three Ph.D.'s, excluding McCain, two had surpassed the soon-to-be-instated retirement age of sixty-five. The president attempted to improve the faculty through the use of the mandatory

The Arkansas College administration and faculty, 1954–1955. *Seated from left to right:* Ben Jordan, Lorne McAdam, Bertram Hughes, George Hollis, Margaret Pruden Lester, Roberta Dorr Brown, Doris Hammett, Dorothy Sydenstricker, Henry Schwartz, Orville Jones, James Vernon Balch, Lyndell Watkins, Ellis Mosley, Sam Williams, and Paul McCain.

retirement policy and by recruiting Ph.D.'s. Three of the five new faculty members in the fall of 1953 held the Ph.D., and all four new professors in the fall of 1954 boasted that terminal degree. McCain successfully purged the faculty of all instructors not holding a graduate degree; nevertheless, by the fall of 1957 Arkansas College's campus contained only three Ph.D.'s, including the president. Low salaries were to blame for the college's high faculty turnover rate. Although frequent raises (a priority for McCain) increased professor salaries at Arkansas College by two-thirds between 1952 and 1958, the salary of $6,000 for a Ph.D. in 1958–1959 represented only about 70 percent of the national average. By the early 1960s the college's average faculty salary had dropped to below two-thirds of the national norm. Arkansas College's faculty salaries were much closer to regional standards, but the steady rise in academic remuneration during the cold war era proved a constant hardship for small, independent institutions. The demand for Ph.D.'s in the sciences was particularly high, which translated into a succession of one- and two-year appointments in biology and chemistry until Charles C. Smith and Virginia Kirk joined the faculty in 1957.[9]

By the late 1950s McCain had abandoned the practice of recruiting young Ph.D.'s, most of whom stayed only until a better-paying job offer came along, and had reverted to hiring teachers with master's degrees who were then given the opportunity to pursue further graduate training. Faculty members in the 1950s who sought advanced graduate education benefited from several sources of money. The Board of Christian Higher Education of the PCUS offered $1,500 grants (matched by the institution) to those pursuing doctorates, and in the early and mid-1950s various foundations offered matching grants for the same purpose. Several Arkansas College teachers of the 1950s and early 1960s took advantage of these programs, but of the four who eventually earned doctorates only business and education professor Roberta Dorr Brown stayed in Batesville. The early McCain era witnessed other advances for faculty members as well. In May 1955 the board of trustees took steps to make life more palatable for teachers, and to move Arkansas College closer to accreditation, by adopting an academic freedom policy, by instituting a system of tenure and promotion, and by developing a retirement system in conjunction with the Carnegie Foundation's Teachers Insurance and Annuity Association College Retirement Equities Fund.[10]

While the issue of faculty improvement was a long-term problem made complex by issues of salary and small-town life, the suggestion that the college relocate to the new campus seemed to the president both urgent and almost immediately attainable. By Christmas 1953 McCain had made the decision to move the college at the end of the academic year. Although the expansive Masonic campus contained only four buildings, it proved large enough to accommodate the small student body and represented a significant structural and aesthetic improvement over the original downtown campus. The new sandstone dormitory had just opened in the fall of 1953 as a men's residence hall; Independence Hall on the middle campus became the women's dormitory. The three sturdy old Masonic buildings, each a two-story, red brick structure with a basement, supplanted the Isaac J. Long Memorial Building as the focus of activity for Arkansas College. Renovations in the spring and summer of 1954 prepared them for use as modern facilities of higher education, while the dark interior woodwork and canopy of massive oaks outside lent the new campus an atmosphere of history and tradition that would have been missing on a campus of new buildings. The center and largest of the Masonic buildings was converted into a library and chapel, with the student post office, bookstore, and Scot Shop in the basement. To the east of the library was the administration building, which contained meeting rooms for the trustees and seminar classes. The science building flanked the library to the west and contained additional rooms for the music department and student publications. Each of the three buildings housed classrooms and faculty offices.[11] As with any monumental move, there were those who regretted the loss of the old campus, but the town and college community had been gearing up for such a step for several years. The new campus offered amenities that the old one never could have, not least of which was the ability to expand.

The move to the new campus in May 1954 represented a physical break with Arkansas College's past. McCain hoped that it would also signal a separation from the struggles and failures of the past. With the move behind them, McCain and the faculty could concentrate on the primary goal, accreditation. Arkansas College's drive toward academic respectability became intertwined with the nation's most significant higher education development of the immediate post–World War II era, the general education movement. Fortunately, the preoccupation of American colleges and universities with this movement generated millions of foundation dollars, and Arkansas College took advantage of its share of the money to conform to NCA ideals.

Actually, by the spring of 1954, the faculty and administration had been working toward accreditation for more than two years. In May 1952, a consortium of fifteen institutions led by the University of Arkansas launched the Arkansas Experiment in Teacher Education (AETE). Funded by grants from the Fund for the Advancement of Education, a division of the Ford Foundation, the AETE was designed to modernize and standardize the college training of prospective teachers. Students who entered the AETE at one of the participating institutions faced four years of college work followed by a year of professional study, or student teaching. The foundation for the four years of college study was to be a strong general education program. It was this general education component that demanded most of the time and grant money of Arkansas College, as well as of many other participating institutions.[12]

General education, or core curriculum, was not a new concept in the early 1950s. In the 1930s Columbia University and the University of Chicago had headed up efforts to combat the negative effects of the elective system. At Chicago, President Robert Hutchins had developed the "Great Books" curriculum, a two-year mandatory core that stressed the western intellectual tradition. Hutchins and his "conservative" followers also challenged what they viewed as the intellectual fragmentation caused by John Dewey and his "progressive" educational philosophies, which championed a mixture of experimentation and theory and refused to make value distinctions between utilitarianism and the traditional liberal arts. In 1945 a report generated by Harvard University, an institution that had been one of the leading culprits in the late nineteenth century takeover of the elective system, lauded the general education curriculum as a remedy to the division and specialization of modern higher education. Harvard's championing of general education reverberated throughout the nation after World War II, and its effects were obvious even on campuses as remote as Arkansas College's.[13]

By combining a general education core with modern methods of student teaching, the curriculum favored by the AETE reflected elements of Dewey's progressivism and Hutchins's conservatism. In fact, the development of general education courses at Arkansas College did not mark a radical restructuring of the B.A. curriculum; Arkansas College and most small denominational colleges had never abandoned a core of required courses as had many large universities. The new general education core did, however, represent a significant change for the institution's teachers in training and business majors, who made up a majority of the student body at the time of McCain's arrival and whose curricula had gradually been shorn of some of the traditional liberal arts requirements after World War II. The faculty's simultaneous decision to discontinue the B.S.E. and B.S. degrees meant that even students majoring in business or the sciences and those planning to teach would be required to complete the standard core. The goal at small colleges such as Arkansas College was to craft traditional courses (western civilization, introductions to sociology, philosophy, and psychology, foreign languages, and others) into a unified and interrelated curriculum, a foundation upon which every student would build his or her upper-level, specialized education. Arkansas College offered its first general education course, basic mathematics, during McCain's first year as president. By the fall of 1953 a faculty committee had instituted a core of general education courses consisting of fifty-five mandatory hours. Most of the general education curriculum, such as courses in Bible, social studies, English, and foreign languages, had already been required of all B.A. students. The most serious changes involved reinstating math and science requirements, consciously attempting to integrate ideas and goals among the various core subjects, and applying general education requirements to all students. With the exception of occasional tweaks and touch ups, including the establishment of an Introduction to Fine Arts course in the fall of 1954 and retraction of the foreign language requirement three years later, the general education curriculum established in 1953 remained in place when McCain left sixteen years later.[14]

From a practical standpoint the most valuable aspect of the AETE was the money it generated. During McCain's first five years in Batesville, Arkansas College received $66,500 in Ford Foundation grants through the AETE. Some of the money went toward hiring new faculty members; much of it, however, was funneled into self-study assessments, through which the faculty first determined areas for improvement and later analyzed the gains made through the AETE. The self-studies were especially important because they were also required for the accreditation process. The faculty and administration undertook its first exhaustive self-examination during the first three years of McCain's presidency. In the fall of 1953, after a year of studying other institutions and of working on the general education program, the faculty was divided into ten committees to analyze every facet of the college's life. For two academic years the various committees studied Arkansas College and compared each phase of the institution's operation (faculty, administration, curriculum, library, finances, and others) with operations at accredited colleges with similar missions. In the meantime, McCain and the faculty hosted a succession of NCA representatives who reported their findings in written assessments, to faculty assemblies, and at board meetings. By the summer of 1955 Arkansas College's first self-study was complete, and McCain forwarded the report to NCA headquarters in Chicago in anticipation of applying for membership. To the dismay of McCain and the faculty, the NCA's Board of Review declined to allow Arkansas College to proceed any further with the application process and specifically cited the institution's weak financial standing as a major obstacle to accreditation.[15]

As it had always done in the past, the lack of money negatively affected everything at Arkansas College: the endowment, the library, faculty salaries, the physical plant, even the curriculum and extracurriculum. Fortunately for Paul McCain and Arkansas College, the 1950s did not witness a continuation of the tradition of financial futility. Although the little college could not find the one magnificent donor that all struggling liberal arts institutions prayed for, the prosperity of the Eisenhower years did not completely pass Batesville by, either. In the quest for accreditation, Arkansas College benefited from a more active and giving constituency in the 1950s, much of it due to the efforts of McCain, as well as an improving climate for foundational giving to higher education.[16] By the time McCain received the bad news regarding Arkansas College's accreditation application in the fall of 1955, efforts were already under way to improve the school's financial situation.

Arkansas College's first attempt to generate new sources of income during the McCain administration was actually a cooperative effort. In March 1954 Arkansas College and six other independent denominational institutions in the state formed the Arkansas Foundation of Associated Colleges (AFAC). Following a trend that had swept through most of the nation in the post–World War II era, the member institutions of the AFAC hoped to pool their limited resources in an attempt to attract gifts and donations from corporations and foundations. Headquartered in Little Rock and directed by retired army general Hugh Cort, the AFAC's mission was to raise money and distribute it among the seven colleges according to enrollment and other formulas. Arkansas College's participation in the AFAC served as a further impetus to speed the accreditation process because the articles of incorporation stipulated that any college not accredited within five years would be removed from the foundation. Since Arkansas College and Southern (now Williams) Baptist College in Walnut Ridge were the only nonaccredited schools among the seven, it was obvious to whom this injunction was directed. On occasion, donors stipulated that their gifts be distributed only to accredited institutions, which provided yet another incentive for rapid accreditation.[17]

Despite its nonaccredited status and its tiny enrollment, which by the late 1950s had been surpassed even by two-year Southern Baptist College, Arkansas College benefited from membership in the AFAC. During the 1955–1956 academic year the AFAC's efforts generated $10,000 for Batesville's college, and the following session produced almost twice that amount. It was the AFAC that also first brought Winthrop Rockefeller into the orbit of Arkansas's independent colleges. In 1955, shortly after making Arkansas his adopted home state, Rockefeller summoned Robert Bates, secretary of the recently established Rockefeller Brothers Fund in New York, to assess the needs of the seven colleges in the AFAC. As a result of the interaction of the AFAC with the Rockefeller Brothers Fund, Arkansas College and her sister institutions received several thousand dollars for faculty development, such as attendance at professional conferences and work toward advanced degrees. In the fall of 1956 the AFAC, using grant money from the Rockefeller Brothers Fund, established a Fine Arts Series, whereby distinguished artists and lecturers gave presentations on each of the seven campuses. Most impressive, however, was the collaboration's effect on libraries. Between 1956 and 1963, Arkansas College's library holdings increased from fewer than 20,000 volumes to more than 30,000, with perhaps 25 percent of the additions purchased with the $3,000 given annually by the Rockefeller Brothers Fund. Furthermore, the members of the AFAC developed an interlibrary loan system consisting of only the books purchased with Rockefeller funds. Under the direction of Dorothy Sydenstricker, Arkansas College's library expanded rapidly during McCain's first decade, in spite of the general stagnation in enrollment. By the early 1960s Arkansas College students had access to almost 50,000 books either on campus or through the AFAC's cooperative agreement, all of them newly catalogued under the Dewey Decimal System.[18]

Even with the obvious benefits to the library and faculty, the AFAC's most valuable contribution to Arkansas College in the 1950s was its service as a goad to achieve accreditation. The mid-1950s also witnessed an increasing interest in accreditation on the part of the college's board and constituency. After the move to the new campus in the spring of 1954, this interest in accreditation became entwined with the movement to erect a new chapel and fine arts building. Such a structure would serve several purposes. The new campus offered only the makeshift chapel in the library building, and a Presbyterian college campus just did not look or feel like a Presbyterian college campus without a free-standing chapel. A new chapel and fine arts building would also impress NCA visitors. Amazingly, it had been more than six decades since Arkansas College had constructed a new building to be used for academic purposes; such a poor record of physical expansion was unlikely to impress skeptical investigators. Finally, a new chapel would serve as the focal point of campus and would be more likely to interest the state's wealthy Presbyterian laymen than would some generic academic structure.

After almost a year of discussion and deliberation, in March 1955 a group of the synod's leaders meeting in Little Rock suggested that the college conduct a campaign for half a million dollars, most to be used for the construction of a chapel and fine arts building with the remainder earmarked for the endowment and for the purchase of laboratory and office equipment and supplies. In October 1955 the ADVANCE Arkansas College Campaign kicked off in Little Rock under the direction of trustee and businessman Frank Lyon Sr. The first major fund-raising effort since the Expansion Campaign of the late 1940s, the ADVANCE Arkansas College Campaign received an immediate boost when an anonymous donor promised to give $100,000 when the rest of the half a million goal had been reached. Consequently, in less than two months the campaign, coordinated by the firm of Ward, Wells, Dreshman & Reinhardt, had pledges exceeding the goal of $500,000, including a gift of $125,000 from Jean Brown and W. C. Brown Jr. of Hot Springs, members of one of Arkansas College's most loyal and generous families. A second anonymous pledge to match dollar for dollar all donations over the half-million mark generated almost $100,000 more in pledges. Less than a week after a celebration dinner held in Batesville on 9 December 1955, the board's executive committee secured the services of Fred Arnold, an architect with the firm of Wittenberg, Delony & Davidson in Little Rock. Arnold's design for a red brick, colonial-style chapel and fine arts building, an understated yet classical and sturdy structure containing a five-hundred-seat auditorium, classrooms, offices, music rooms, and a small chapel, met the approval of the understated and sturdy Presbyterians. With slightly less than three-quarters of the more than $400,000 needed to complete the chapel in hand, the college held groundbreaking ceremonies in April 1957. The new chapel and fine arts building, which would remain nameless until the mid-1960s, was completed just in time to host the 1958 spring commencement services. Although payment of pledges continued to trickle in throughout the late 1950s, in true Arkansas College tradition unforeseen campaign expenses and canceled pledges, as well as gifts earmarked for other purposes, prevented the college from retiring the chapel debt for several years after 1958.[19]

The new chapel and fine arts building was worth the expense. Erected south of the Masonic buildings at the bottom of the small hill, the chapel faced west toward the old campus and downtown Batesville. It was an imposing sight for those first visiting the new campus, and the white steeple could be seen from the northern end of the Miller Creek valley. Nevertheless, the building of the chapel provided a financial hardship at a time when the college could scarcely afford one. When construction got under way in the spring of 1957, Arkansas College found itself once again in a precarious and momentous situation. Only two years remained on the grace period before the college would be banned from the AFAC for nonaccreditation. As a result of this time limit, the college was in the midst of another self-study, one designed to eventually serve as an application for acceptance into the NCA. Just a year earlier the college's NCA consultant, Donald M. Mackenzie, academic dean at Blackburn College in Illinois, had warned McCain to address the college's two primary setbacks, low enrollment and financial instability, before applying to the NCA. But time was running out, and the longer Arkansas College remained among the shrinking ranks of the unaccredited the more difficult it would be to escape those ranks.[20]

McCain realized that the enrollment problem was a long-term issue, a challenge that had plagued his predecessors and would likely continue to puzzle administrators for years to come. The president's efforts to attract more Presbyterian students had met with little success, mainly due to the college's nonaccredited status, and the rigid general education core and limited offerings hampered efforts to attract large numbers of regional students. By the late 1950s Arkansas College's student body remained the smallest among the state's four-year institutions, and the senior class of fifteen in 1957 was the smallest since the World War II era. NCA representatives recommended raising full-time enrollment to at least two hundred before applying for accreditation; this meant an increase of 25 percent in just two years. In August 1957 McCain hired recent graduate Yvonna Wilson as the college's first full-time admissions counselor; Wilson's intensive recruiting paid off in the fall of 1958 when more than two hundred full-time students registered for classes, the largest enrollment to date during the McCain administration.[21] With its student body seemingly on the increase, Arkansas College had a chance of achieving accreditation if it could only shore up its finances.

Achieving financial stability was much easier discussed than accomplished in 1957. When placed beside each other and in the context of the history of Arkansas College, the words financial and stability had a sort of oxymoronic quality. Furthermore, the state's Presbyterians winced each time an Arkansas College president started talking about things like "physical expansion" and "financial stability," for such phrases were always followed by requests for money. Imminent banishment from the AFAC demanded immediate action, however. In the spring of 1957 Arkansas College still owed more than $30,000 on the men's dormitory that had been completed almost four years earlier. The rooms, kitchen, and dining area in Independence Hall were in need of renovation, and the grounds of the new campus had never been landscaped. Salaries for professors with Ph.D.'s were more than 25 percent below the national average of $7,000 per year and needed to be raised to at least within striking distance of the norm. And without an immediate influx of cash, McCain warned, the college faced an operating deficit of several thousands of dollars. These remaining weaknesses at Arkansas College, as well as the achievements of the past five years, were highlighted in February 1957 when a group of five educational consultants gathered in Batesville to conduct a survey sponsored by the Synod of Arkansas's Council for Christian Higher Education. Although the results of this survey would not be made public for another year, the college community was aware of the findings as well as the consultants' recommendations. In the summer of 1957 Judge James H. Pilkinton of Hope, chairman of the synod's Council for Christian Higher Education, called a special meeting in Batesville to discuss the future of Arkansas College and the feasibility of gaining accreditation by the spring of 1959. Unlike similar meetings of years past there were no votes on whether or not to close the doors of the college, though there were still a few negative voices to be heard around the state. The meeting's representatives (among them trustees, Presbyterian laymen, alumni, and others interested in the college) resolved that rapid accreditation must become the institution's overriding goal and that physical repairs, debt payments, and other upgrades would require at least $86,000 during the coming academic term, a goal that was eventually raised to $96,000.[22]

The most lasting result of this meeting was a transformation of the college's money-raising strategy. McCain's annual campaign, known as the Loyalty Fund, as well as Spragins's Budget Balancers program, had been carried out largely within the network of the state's Presbyterian churches. The summer meeting in Batesville, and a couple of subsequent trustee sessions, changed the name of the Loyalty Fund to the Progress Fund and appointed Shuford Nichols, former Arkansas College student and prominent lay and business leader from Des Arc, to direct the new annual campaign. Unlike the old Loyalty Fund, the Progress Fund was not tied to the Presbyterian establishment; the Progress Fund also benefited from a greater degree of publicity. Nichols kicked off the 1957–1958 Progress Fund with a November luncheon in Little Rock, complete with guest speakers and an explanation of the accreditation process. After the success of the Little Rock program, Nichols sponsored similar events in cities and towns throughout the state. By the time the chapel and fine arts building was completed in the spring of 1958, pledges for the Progress Fund exceeded $100,000; the college eventually received $90,000 of this, more than a quarter of which came directly from the trustees. The successful campaign allowed the college to pay off the dormitory debt, to make other needed physical improvements, and to increase the scholarship endowment, something that the board and administration hoped would help enlarge enrollment. The following year's Progress Fund drive was even more successful. Directed by G. E. Wilson, a trustee and businessman from El Dorado, the 1958–1959 Fund received more than $100,000 in both pledges and actual payments.[23]

The success of the Progress Fund turned the tide in Arkansas College's quest for accreditation. Although he warned McCain that the college could use another year or two to strengthen its case for accreditation, Donald M. Mackenzie, Arkansas College's consultant since the early 1950s and now an executive with the NCA, understood the young president's urgency in the spring of 1958. Only a year remained before Arkansas College lost its membership in the AFAC, an organization that by the late 1950s was funneling close to $20,000 into the college's coffers each year. In early 1958 McCain and the faculty received the report prepared by Mackenzie and other educators at the behest of the synod's Council for Christian Higher Education and used the report to put the finishing touches on the latest self-study. McCain submitted this latest self-study as Arkansas College's application to the NCA in the summer of 1958. In December 1958 two NCA representatives conducted a two-day official examination of the college. In Chicago four months later, on 24 April 1959, Paul McCain and new dean Roland Dickison received the report formally accrediting Arkansas College. The following day a throng of Arkansas College students, faculty, staff, and friends cheered the president and dean as they stepped off the train in Newport. A makeshift band played as jubilant students hoisted the victorious president to their shoulders and carried him through the station.[24] The long-awaited goal of accreditation had been accomplished. The first phase of McCain's presidency was complete. Much more remained to be done.

Accreditation is a watershed event in the history of any institution. It was no different at Arkansas College. The last four-year, white college or university in the state to be admitted into the North Central Association, Arkansas College found itself free of the restraints imposed by nonaccreditation as the decade of the sixties dawned.[25] The lack of accreditation had for years affected everything at Arkansas College from fund-raising to enrollment to physical expansion. The 1960s would bring gains in each of these areas. One other result of the accreditation process was that Arkansas College had, via the NCA's carrot-and-stick methods, come to resemble most other small, independent colleges in the region, if not in the number of students or buildings then certainly in terms of curriculum, faculty composition, and administrative organization. Since the early twentieth century, educational foundations and accrediting agencies had served as homogenizing forces in higher education, as great levelers of institutional distinctiveness. Much of what had long made Arkansas College appear somewhat distinct within the state had disappeared in the 1950s with the move to the new campus and the mad push to satisfy the NCA. What made the small college distinct from the university in general, however, remained in the form of the family atmosphere and close interaction between teachers and students that had always been evident at Arkansas College. If McCain and the board were to have their way, this small college intimacy would remain, but with about twice as many students and many more buildings to house and educate them.

The Arkansas College campus during the McCain era, beginning and end. These two photos reflect the physical expansion of the McCain years, 1952–1969.

When it became apparent that accreditation was imminent, the first action of the trustees and administration was to discuss long-range planning. It had been more than three decades since the Mississippi Flood of 1927 and the subsequent depression had throttled the college's first ambitious long-range goals. As early as the spring of 1954 Paul McCain had presented the board with his vision for the future of Arkansas College. Although vague as to a target date, McCain's goals were specific when it came to expansion: 400 students (325 of whom would live on campus), a faculty of thirty-one (half of whom would hold the Ph.D. or an equivalent terminal degree), an endowment of $5.5 million with an annual budget of $575,000, and a physical campus with three new dormitories, a chapel, a library, a dining hall/student union, a science building, and a new gymnasium. The president's vision informed the long-range talks that accompa-

nied the self-study and NCA evaluation in 1958, and the faculty established a target date of 1972, the college's centennial. The new long-range goals mirrored McCain's earlier vision, with only minor alterations: thirty-eight faculty instead of thirty-one, 500 students instead of 400, and an extra half a million dollars in the endowment. In February 1958 the trustees once again retained the services of Fred Arnold, the Wittenberg, Delony & Davidson architect who had designed the chapel and fine arts building, and instructed him to draft a master plan of the projected 1972 campus based on the college's long-range goals. One year later, just two months after the promising visit of the NCA evaluators, the trustees convened on campus to consider the architect's proposals as well as to discuss the college's long-range goals and the strategy for achieving those goals. The two-day conference featured speeches and presentations by three noted Presbyterian educators: McCain's father, the president emeritus of Agnes Scott College; John Moseley, president of Austin College; and vice-president R. P. Richardson of Southwestern at Memphis.[26]

The long-range plans adopted in 1958–1959 served as a blueprint for the furious expansion of the ensuing decade. As Arkansas College entered the 1960s, the two campuses consisted of only seven buildings: the Masonic structures, a sandstone dormitory, and a chapel on the new campus and Independence Hall and the gymnasium on the old middle campus. By the end of the decade the institution's appearance had been radically altered by the construction of nine new buildings and the beginning of a tenth. The decade of the 1960s, then, easily represents the most intensive phase of physical expansion, of brick-and-mortar work, in the history of Arkansas College. Orchestrating this steady stream of construction projects was Paul McCain with the consistent guidance and assistance of an increasingly dedicated and active board of trustees. In fact, the strength and stability of the board during the McCain years contrasted with the directionless and often lethargic boards of the frequent eras of struggle and division in the college's past. Unlike many of his predecessors, McCain always enjoyed the support of a loyal and generous core of trustees, and the president, with his talents for fundraising and diplomacy, was in no small part responsible for his favorable situation.

By the early 1960s McCain had gathered around him, either by inheritance or by his own assembling, a collection of trustees whose dedication to and interest in the development of the college was unmistakable. Throughout the history of the institution, the local contingent of the board had always provided loyal leadership, and the tradition continued during McCain's administration. Among the college's local trustees were businessman Nels Barnett, who had remained dedicated to his alma mater through good times and bad, attorney W. D. "Pete" Murphy Jr., businessman H. Carter Jeffery, who replaced John P. Morrow Sr. as secretary of the board in 1956, automobile dealer Stanley Wood, and banker John W. Edwards. Foremost among the Batesville trustees was Morrow, who by the 1950s had earned the nickname Mr. Arkansas College. By the time he replaced Judge S. Marcus Bone as chairman in 1956, Morrow had already dedicated more than three decades as a trustee to his alma mater. A devout Presbyterian and a successful planter and businessman, he had helped save the college during the depression, and he remained a voice of authority until his health began to fail in the early 1960s. The 1965 commencement, which took place just three months after Morrow's death, was the first that Arkansas College had held without his presence in seventy-five years.[27]

Although clergymen would never regain the influence they had held on the board in years past, McCain benefited from the advice of some of the state's leading ministers, such as W. L. McColgan and alumni Kenneth F. Snipes and Basil Hicks. For much of the college's past, the lack of interest and participation of non-Independence County trustees and laymen in general had hampered development. The McCain presidency, on the other hand, witnessed a gradual and permanent shift of influence and power away from the Batesville trustees and clergy and toward Presbyterian laymen in other sections of the state. Several of these trustees were already on the board when McCain was elected president, including Little Rock insurance executive and noted patron of the arts Van Weathersby, Camden banker and alumnus H. T. "Ham" Patton, and W. W. "Whit" Shaver Jr., a Wynne banker who raised the money for a new college bus in 1954, a forty-seat Chevrolet that the students referred to for years as "Ole Whit." A few of the trustees who greeted McCain in 1952 remained active members of the board throughout his seventeen-year administration. W. C. Brown Jr., a businessman and one of the two surviving members of the generous Hot Springs family, had joined the board on the eve of World War II. Brown and his sister Jean were most notable for their unflagging financial support for sixty years. Arkadelphia attorney H. W. "Bill" McMillan, the orchestrator of the failed merger plan of 1951, remained a vocal force on the board and an unflinching proponent of the college's liberal arts program, as did Pine Bluff businessman and accountant Glen Railsback.[28]

McCain was also responsible for recruiting some of the era's most active and effective trustees, including W. W. Campbell, R. C. and Willie Bryan, and Gordon Love. A banker and businessman from Forrest City, Campbell joined the board during McCain's first year in Batesville and served for many years as chairman of the important finance committee. R. C. Bryan, owner of extensive farmlands in Mississippi County and a member of the board during the latter days of the Spragins administration, maintained an active and benevolent interest in the affairs of Arkansas College until his untimely death in 1955. Three years later Willie Bryan assumed her husband's old trusteeship. Another trustee from eastern Arkansas was Gordon Love, a Presbyterian layman who owned an automobile dealership in Hughes. One of several McCain-era trustees who were not college graduates, Love's major contribution during his ten years on the board was assisting the college in tapping into the wealth of a few aging rural Presbyterians in the Hughes area, including H. M. Brinkley and Wooten Anderson, whose bequest of the bulk of his estate almost doubled Arkansas College's small endowment.[29]

McCain's most impressive recruit, however, was Shuford Nichols. An active and popular student and campus agitator who never avoided voicing his opinions during two years at Arkansas College, Nichols was among a group of young men who received suspensions in the spring of 1928 for violation of the school's alcohol policy, as well as violation of federal law. (This was the prohibition age, remember.) Although the college later reduced his penalty to probation, Nichols left Batesville behind and finished his degree in Virginia at Washington and Lee. After a year at the Harvard Business School in the early 1930s, he returned to his home town of Des Arc and proceeded to amass a fortune through banking and the cotton business. Not one to hold grudges, he drifted back into the college's orbit during the 1950s when he suggested, and helped establish, a revolving loan pool for promising male students who planned to enter the ministry or the business world in Arkansas. By the time he formally joined the board in 1960, Nichols had already directed the first Progress Fund drive and had assumed a leading role in college affairs. In 1961 he was appointed chairman of the newly established development committee. When Morrow died in 1965, the trustees unanimously elected Nichols to replace him as chairman of the board, a position that Nichols would hold for ten years.[30]

By the time Nichols became the chairman of the trustees in 1965, another member had already established himself as the backbone of the board. Frank Lyon Sr., a self-made multimillionaire, emerged as one of the board's most thoughtful and loyal members during the McCain years and would eventually serve as counsel to five different Arkansas College presidents. Born to a humble Camden family in 1910, Lyon had begun working at age eleven and at age fourteen, after the death of his father, moved to Little Rock with his mother. After two years at the University of Alabama, he returned to Little Rock to wed Marion Bradley and find a job. When a bout with tuberculosis cut short a budding managerial career, Lyon went into business on his own as a wholesale appliance and furniture distributor during World War II. The successful Frank Lyon Company eventually branched out from Little Rock into other regional cities, and Lyon himself branched out into other business ventures, including realty, banking, and ownership of the Coca-Cola Bottling Company of Arkansas. When the young Presbyterian layman joined the Arkansas College board in 1946—having been introduced to the school by his wife and her family—he was just beginning to reap the financial fruits of his labors. As his wealth and influence expanded in the 1950s and 1960s so did his interest in the college. In addition to his own generosity, Lyon successfully directed the $500,000 ADVANCE Arkansas College Campaign in 1956 and later directed the institution's first $1 million drive in the 1960s. Frank Lyon was in no small part responsible for helping to restore the college to the good graces of Little Rock's Presbyterian community. He also lent his financial acumen to the board, helping to strengthen the limited endowment through shrewd investments and the abandonment of the tradition of making risky loans to churches, a practice that had rendered much of the endowment worthless by the early 1950s.[31]

Lyon helped kick off Arkansas College's postaccreditation expansion when he accepted the chairmanship of the Synod of Arkansas's United for Christ Campaign and launched a $1 million drive on 1 March 1960.[32] Although the majority of the campaign's proceeds were to be used for other synod activities, $200,000 had been designated for use in the construction of a new dining hall and student union, a project given first priority by the administration and board. The current dining facilities in Independence Hall were outdated, and Arkansas College had no student union. The basement of Independence Hall contained a small but poorly equipped recreation room; other student services such as the post office, bookstore, and Scot Shop were located on the main campus in the basement of the library building, or the central Masonic building. When it became obvious that the college would be fortunate to receive half the promised amount from the synod's campaign, McCain went looking for other sources of income. Fortunately for Arkansas College, the Kennedy and Johnson administrations oversaw a rapid expansion of federal programs available to small, independent colleges. With a $150,000 low-interest loan from the Community Facilities Agency of the Home Finance Administration, the college broke ground for the new dining hall—a student union addition was planned for a later date but never completed—in May 1962. The federal government would become a popular source of money during the college's expansion era. Abiding by the campus master plan developed by architect Fred Arnold, the new dining hall was a red brick, colonial-style structure erected immediately northeast of the chapel and fine arts building. Construction crews put the finishing touches on the dining hall, later named for Hazel Alphin of El Dorado, in the waning days of the summer of 1963, and students ate their first meals in the building on 9 September 1963, the first day of freshman orientation.[33]

Although the dining hall was first on the drawing board in the 1960s, the first building to materialize was actually the new president's home. Since 1953 the college had rented a brick house on east Main Street (now Highland Road) for the McCains, about the same distance from the new campus and the middle campus. As more activities moved to the bluff and with significant building planned for the near future on the new campus, the president requested a new home on campus. The president's home, a brick, ranch-style house whose design the McCains had discovered in an issue of *American Home* magazine, was completed in February 1962 on the bluff at the entrance to campus. Part of the $35,000 it cost to build the home was supplied by the sale of the college's first president's home, the native stone cottage constructed during the E. B. Tucker administration which for many years had served as the home of Arkansas College's deans. With occasional remodeling and redecoration, the new house would serve as the president's home for more than thirty years.[34]

When the new dining hall opened in the fall of 1963, the resident population was at an all-time high of more than 160 students; the college had no more available dormitory rooms, or so McCain thought. Independence Hall, which had been converted to a men's dormitory a year earlier due to a sudden influx of male students, held 94 young men, and the dormitory on the main campus had reached capacity with 59 young women; in addition, ten basketball players resided in the gymnasium, which had been remodeled to house the entire team in 1960. When enrollment topped the 300 mark in the fall of 1964 for the first time since the post–World War II G.I. boom, the college found itself stretched beyond the limit of its resources. For the first time in its more than forty years of existence, Independence Hall reached a capacity of 130 residents; the administration even converted the old fraternity house (known as Highland Cottage) next to Independence Hall into a makeshift apartment building and squeezed ten young men into the small house.[35]

The steady rise in enrollment, from 177 full-time students in the fall of 1960 to 316 in the fall of 1964, was the result of several factors. Accreditation had lifted a major burden on which McCain had blamed the college's enrollment problems throughout the 1950s. By 1963 colleges and universities across the United States were beginning to attract the first wave of the baby boom generation, and more and more young men sought the sanctity of the college campus to ward off draft boards and service in Vietnam. But the sudden increase in enrollment at Arkansas College was also the product of a recruitment strategy developed in the early 1960s. In the fall of 1961 the board of trustees created a development committee to oversee long-range planning and growth. The following spring the college hired development consultant Gonser and Gerber, a Chicago firm that had pioneered in higher education development at Northwestern University, to institute and direct a plan for development and expansion. Following the advice of Gonser and Gerber representative Robert Tinker, Arkansas College began recruiting heavily out of state, especially in the urban Northeast. Using this "cotton patch method" (the thicker the cotton the quicker one fills his sack), beginning in 1962 admissions counselors Yvonna Wilson and Jim Mitchum recruited dozens of northeastern students to Batesville, Arkansas. This sudden growth in the on-campus population demanded immediate action.[36]

Like most colleges and universities around the nation, Arkansas College had expected this sudden increase in enrollment in the early 1960s—in fact, the actual increase never reached the level predicted by consultants—and had already begun to plan for the baby boomers. After more than a year of planning, in the summer of 1964 the college undertook its most ambitious building project to date, a quadrangle consisting of three small dormitories and a fourth building to be used as a student lounge and apartment for a resident director. The architects borrowed the quadrangle concept from a recent, innovative study conducted by Knox College in Illinois and designed for the small campus. Under Arkansas College's quadrangle plan, the three, red-brick dormitories (two of them consisting of two floors and another of three stories) would house a total of 112 young women, or 16 per floor. Each dormitory floor was to contain its own little community with eight rooms, common bathrooms, and a lounge area. Once again, McCain turned to the federal government for financial assistance and secured a low-interest loan of half a million dollars, which covered all but about $35,000 of the eventual cost of the four buildings as well as the elevated common area that students came to refer to as the quad.[37]

When the first female students moved into the new dormitories in the fall of 1965, full-time enrollment was at 320, the highest of McCain's seventeen-year presidency. Nevertheless, resident enrollment remained the same as the previous fall. As a result male upperclassmen moved into the former women's dormitory (recently named Spragins Hall in honor of the former president) on the main campus, leaving Independence Hall at half capacity and used only for freshman boys. Arkansas College's on-campus population reached a peak of 224 in the fall of 1966, the vast majority of whom were young men and most of those from out of state. As a result of the institution's inability to attract larger numbers of resident female students, Bryan Hall, the largest of the new dormitories, was converted to a men's residence hall, leaving Blandford Hall and Love Hall for the few young women who lived on campus. Independence Hall continued to house male freshmen residents until it was closed after the 1969–1970 session.[38]

The expanded population of resident students, many of them out-of-state students with no automobile, also created a demand for better recreation facilities on campus. Since the G.I. boom days of the late 1940s the college had maintained a small rumpus room in the basement of Independence Hall. By the fall of 1965, however, the bulk of the resident students lived on the main campus, and the sheer number of young men rendered the old Independence Hall facility inadequate. Consequently, in the summer of 1965 the board's executive committee oversaw the construction of a sixty-by-one-hundred-feet metal building on the bluff east of Spragins Hall. The recreation building, which was completed shortly before Christmas 1965, was given a brick facade to blend in with the other new buildings on campus. Featuring two bowling lanes and two pool tables as well as vending and pinball machines, the recreation building represented a significant improvement in campus life at Arkansas College. In the fall of 1967 the Scot Shop and bookstore were relocated to the recreation building from their old home in the basement of the central Masonic building, recently dubbed the Long Memorial Building.[39]

With basic student housing and recreation facilities taken care of, McCain and the board turned their attention to completion of the physical expansion called for in the long-range plans. In early 1965, even before completion of the Morrow Quadrangle, the administration and trustees began planning the construction of a science building and a library. The college's construction timetable proved advantageous, for in 1963 Congress had passed the Higher Education Facilities Act, a bill that provided not only more low-interest loans for independent colleges but grant money as well. By early 1966 Arkansas College had secured $475,000 in grants from the federal government in addition to another long-term, low-interest loan. This left the college with the responsibility of raising almost $800,000 to complete the science building and library, estimated to cost about $1.6 million. On 12 March 1966, Frank Lyon Sr., now chairman of the trustees' development committee, launched the Forward Arkansas College Expansion (FACE) Campaign at the Hotel Lafayette in Little Rock. The FACE Campaign got off to a promising start thanks to a $50,000 matching pledge from Republican gubernatorial candidate Winthrop Rockefeller; nevertheless, it took almost two years to reach the goal of $795,000 in pledges. A second wave of challenge pledges catapulted the campaign across the $1 million mark in March 1968, although another year would pass before actual cash payments reached a level sufficient to pay for the two buildings.[40]

In the midst of the largest inflow of money the college had ever witnessed, construction crews began work on the new science building in the spring of 1966. Located just to the southeast of the chapel and on the lowest elevation of the western part of campus, the science building proved a challenge to Fred Arnold and the architects. They responded by designing a long, split-level, skylighted structure with a modern appearance unique from the rest of the buildings on campus. The upper, or northern, side of the building contained classrooms, faculty offices, and a spacious lecture hall, while the lower side housed laboratories designed with movable interior walls. The science building, sporting at least the familiar look of red brick, opened for use in the fall of 1967 as the first Arkansas College facility designed with air conditioning; in the spring of 1970 it was named in honor of J. Paul Smith, a Jonesboro landowner and businessman and Presbyterian layman who had bequeathed a significant portion of his estate to Arkansas College. The library, erected to the northeast of the science building, was a three-story structure built on a slope so that, like the science building, it

Commencement, 1961.

featured ground-level entrances on the first and second floors. Designed for a capacity of 100,000 volumes (almost twice the amount that the college owned at the time), the library also featured a language laboratory with modern audio equipment on the ground floor. The library opened in the fall of 1968, freeing the Long Memorial Building (or main Masonic building) for other uses. The 1967–1968 academic year also witnessed extensive landscaping, including improvements on the new quadrangle (eventually Couch Gardens) created by the construction of the science building and library. In December 1968 the college officially dedicated both new buildings with a ceremony featuring a speech by Dr. William G. Pollard, a former physicist with the Manhattan Project and director of the Oak Ridge nuclear facility in Tennessee.[41]

Pollard's dedication speech took place during Paul McCain's final year at Arkansas College; thus the president would not remain long enough to see the completion of the final piece of the long-range plan, the gymnasium. In the spring of 1968 McCain received word that the college had been awarded a $300,000 federal grant and a federal loan of $382,000 for the construction of a new "physical education building."

Because the federal government would not grant funds for the construction of buildings that would be used for events for which the general public paid admission fees to attend, McCain and the administration ceased referring to this project as a gymnasium. In fact, the facility's lack of a ticket booth or permanent gymnasium seating stems from this caveat. Once the college had secured enough money to complete construction of the $900,000 building, contractors started work in the fall of 1968. Students used the regulation basketball court and Olympic-sized swimming pool for the first time when the James C. Becknell Physical Education Building opened in the fall of 1970.[42]

The completion of the Becknell Building fulfilled the long-range plan adopted more than a decade earlier. Only two quadrangles of men's dormitories, rendered superfluous by enrollment stagnation in the late 1960s, failed to materialize. With the exception of a few brief lapses of no more than a few months at a time, the Arkansas College campus had been the site of continuous construction since work began on the president's home in 1961. The extensive building campaign between 1956 and 1970, McCain's most obvious and lasting legacy, cost $4 million. Almost one-fifth of this amount came from federal grants for the final three buildings, and another $1.7 million was in the form of federal loans bearing an average annual interest rate of just 3.25 percent. At the time of McCain's arrival in Batesville in September 1952, Arkansas College's activities had been unwieldily scattered across three campuses; by the fall of 1970, one year after his departure, all the college's activities were consolidated on the new campus.[43]

The brick-and-mortar facet of the long-range blueprints developed almost exactly according to plan during the decade following the college's accreditation. McCain and the trustees were less successful when it came to the other components of the long-range plans adopted during the 1958–1959 session, endowment and enrollment. In the fall of 1962 the faculty and staff prepared a ten-year budget that revised the goals to be achieved by the time of the centennial in 1972. Under this new budget, adopted by the board in February 1963, the target endowment was raised to $10 million and the enrollment goal was increased from five hundred to six hundred full-time students. Both goals were long shots and, in retrospect, unrealistic. At the time of Arkansas College's accreditation in April 1959, the endowment fund was slightly less than $375,000, more than a third of which languished in nonproductive or barely productive church mortgages. A little more than a year earlier the board had hired a Little Rock investment firm to manage the endowment; within two years this professional assistance had generated a 10 percent increase in endowment earnings. Nevertheless, these earnings remained meager and accounted for only about 6 percent of the annual budget. In the fall of 1960, however, the trustees voted to transfer the endowment funds to the Presbyterian Foundation of Arkansas, Inc., which eventually resulted in increased maintenance costs and a lower rate of return.[44]

By the late 1950s it had been a decade since the endowment had grown by an appreciable amount. The Progress Fund of the late 1950s and 1960s simply sought to cover annual operating expenses, and the college's two major fund-raising campaigns during the McCain years, the ADVANCE Arkansas College Campaign and the

FACE Campaign, were both designated for physical expansion. Instead of holding separate campaigns to build the endowment fund, McCain's and the trustees' strategy was to sow the seeds that would be reaped in a later season. In the late 1950s McCain and board chairman John P. Morrow Sr. began to concentrate on wills, a popular subject among struggling institutions looking to pad their endowments. Morrow challenged all the trustees to write the college into their wills and to promote the practice within their constituencies. The college also worked with the Synod of Arkansas to influence prominent laypersons to bequeath at least a portion of their estates to the cause of higher education. This strategy paid its first substantial dividends in 1962 when Arkansas College received more than $350,000 from the estate of the late Wooten Anderson, a self-made St. Francis County planter who had died six years earlier. Largely through the influence of trustee Gordon Love, Anderson had left the college five-sixths of his estate to be used for a student scholarship fund. At the time, the bequest represented the largest single gift to the college in its ninety-year history, and it almost doubled the endowment to more than $725,000. Unfortunately, the endowment would not experience any significant growth throughout the remainder of the decade, although the seeds sown by McCain and his board would produce unimaginable results years after his departure.[45]

The drive to expand the endowment to $10 million by 1972 fell far short. The goal of six hundred full-time students by the centennial year ultimately proved just as unattainable. Nevertheless, the college's strident efforts to more than double its enrollment after 1959 produced an unparalleled demographic shift within the student body that changed the face of the institution. To compound matters, this alteration in the makeup of the student population at Arkansas College took place against the backdrop of the turbulent 1960s and in the context of the burgeoning youth culture that would define an entire generation and an era of American history. Not only did the 1960s mark the most intensive phase of physical expansion in the college's history, the decade also witnessed a blooming religious, cultural, and ethnic diversity within the student body that had been unimaginable and unforeseeable only a few years earlier. Furthermore, the 1960s ushered in an era of student activism unlike any the college had seen since the 1920s.

With the exception of a couple years in the 1920s and the G.I. boom following World War II, there had never been a time in the history of Arkansas College when enrollment had not posed a major concern. From the moment Arkansas College was founded in 1872, Isaac Long and his successors had struggled to overcome the various obstacles that prevented the college from attracting large numbers of students. Batesville's relative isolation from the larger population centers of the state and region proved a constant problem, as did the fact that the little town lay in an area whose ruralness and poverty limited the appeal and accessibility of higher education. For years the college's detractors had argued that the state's Presbyterian population was simply too small and poor to support a college. And they were right. By the late 1950s Arkansas's Southern Presbyterians (PCUS) numbered fewer than 22,000, or about one-third the denominational constituency considered necessary to adequately sustain an institution of higher education. No state in the old Confederacy contained fewer Southern Presbyterians than did Arkansas. Furthermore, with the existence of the College of the Ozarks in Clarksville, operated by the Northern Presbyterians (PCUSA), it was unlikely that the two branches of Presbyterianism would ever come together to support one or both institutions, as had happened in Missouri with Westminster College.[46]

As always, Batesville remained far removed from the state's concentrations of Presbyterian population, a fact that influenced most Presbyterian students to attend college elsewhere. For years the percentage of Presbyterians in Arkansas College's student body had been declining. By the late 1940s fewer than 20 percent of Arkansas College students were Presbyterian, compared with 64 percent at Davidson College and 63 percent at South Carolina's Presbyterian College. Within the state large numbers of Baptists and Methodists contributed to the success of Ouachita Baptist College and Hendrix College, whose student body during the same era was more than two-thirds Methodist. By the 1950s Arkansas College's nonaccredited status and the expansion of several former two-year, state-supported colleges into four-year institutions further exacerbated recruiting challenges. A study conducted during the 1956–1957 academic year revealed that the Presbyterian population at the University of Arkansas was more than four times as large as Arkansas College's entire student body.[47]

This report sparked a fresh wave of grumbling within the Presbyterian community, and even on the eve of Arkansas College's accreditation victory McCain continued to fight off suggestions that the Synod of Arkansas could more cheaply educate its congregants' children by funneling its benevolence funds into Westminster Fellowships at state colleges and universities. But by the late 1950s things were beginning to look up for McCain and Arkansas College. His first few years at the helm had been a different story, however. McCain came to Batesville just as the last of the G.I.'s were leaving town. During Spragins's last year as president full-time enrollment had dropped below two hundred for the first time in six years, and the downward spiral continued into the mid-1950s. Enrollment bottomed out during the spring of 1955, the first year on the new campus, when barely more than one hundred full-time students finished the semester. Statistics gathered by the Arkansas Experiment in Teacher Education in the fall of 1955 revealed that Arkansas College was easily the smallest of the state's four-year institutions; the state's second smallest college, John Brown University in Siloam Springs, boasted an enrollment 72 percent greater than that at Arkansas College. Enrollment rebounded in the latter half of the 1950s and, with the help of the college's first full-time admissions counselor, exceeded two hundred by the fall of 1958, still lowest in the state.[48]

One of the major drawbacks of Arkansas College's recruiting challenges was that by the time the institution received accreditation it had practically no selective admissions standards. Without the luxury of an ample pool of applicants, the college had never instituted any specific standards for admission, such as minimum scores on standardized entrance exams or minimum high school grade point averages. Furthermore, many of the students who made their way to Batesville came from small, poorly funded high schools in Independence and surrounding counties. As a result, the quality of the student body declined sharply in the postwar era. Although 56 percent of freshmen scored above the state average on a standardized I.Q. test (the American Council on Education Psychological Exam) administered in the fall of 1956, only 12 percent ranked above the national average. And almost half of all freshmen entering Arkansas College scored in the lowest 10 percent when compared with students across the nation. Of the nine Arkansas institutions that administered the Graduate Record Examination to sophomores, Arkansas College ranked next to last. Two years later, in the fall of 1958, almost three out of four freshmen at Arkansas College scored below the national average on an I.Q. test, and almost four in five scored below the American norm on a standardized English examination. That at least part of this deficiency was attributable to the poor state of public education in Arkansas is attested to by the fact that 70 percent of Arkansas College freshmen scored above the *state average* on the same I.Q. test and 60 percent did so on the English exam.[49]

The transformation of policies dealing with scholarship money served as the college's only unofficial selective admissions tool during McCain's early years. One of the young president's first actions was to abolish the practice of granting academic scholarships to unqualified students. McCain also instituted Arkansas College's first merit scholarships for freshmen matriculating in the fall of 1953. Faced with limited financial resources, the president created a $500 scholarship, which was awarded to Fitzhugh Spragins, son of the former president, and two $250 scholarships. The following year Arkansas College offered fifteen merit scholarships, including one of $1,200 and another of $800. These merit scholarships were awarded on the basis of the students' high school grades as well as scores on standardized aptitude tests. By the mid-1950s NCA evaluators accepted the college's limited scholarship program as at least a step toward more selective admissions policies.[50]

When Arkansas College was accredited in the spring of 1959, the administration and board immediately began discussing the possibility of adopting selective admissions policies. McCain worried that such policies would reduce the number of local students, who had sustained the college throughout his administration, and could possibly even turn away Presbyterian students, a situation that would prove a detriment to the college's relationship with its denominational constituency. Although the board adopted no policy instituting a minimum test score or high school grade point average, it appears that the administration did turn away a few students in the fall of 1959 for poor aptitude scores. McCain's report to the trustees in September 1959 attributed the reduction in enrollment to "stricter admissions"; fall enrollment fell more drastically in 1960, representing an 18 percent decline in two years. This unexpected, postaccreditation enrollment downturn erased further discussions of selective admissions. Arkansas College would maintain an open admissions policy throughout the remainder of the McCain era.[51]

It is just as likely, perhaps more so, that the sudden decrease in enrollment was the result of rising student costs. Along with the discussion of selective admissions, the administration and trustees reacted to accreditation by raising tuition and room and board, reasoning that students would be willing to pay more money for an accredited education. Like the consideration of selective admissions policies, the decision to increase student costs also harkened back to the failed merger of 1951 and the subsequent discussions of establishing a little Haverford College in north central Arkansas. Since the late 1940s, Arkansas College had claimed the distinction of offering the cheapest tuition fees of any independent college in the state. But whereas John D. Spragins had donned the college's low costs as a badge of honor, McCain and his trustees viewed these bargain prices as a sign of Arkansas College's second-rate status. Tuition charges at Arkansas College, $300 during the 1958–1959 year, were $50 lower than those at Ouachita Baptist College and $100 cheaper than tuition at Hendrix, College of the Ozarks, and John Brown University. Furthermore, Batesville's little school was by far the least expensive of all the Southern Presbyterian colleges. Of all Southern Presbyterian institutions in 1958–1959, only Arkansas College and Belhaven College in Mississippi featured total costs (tuition, room and board) of less than $1,000 per year. Arkansas College's annual costs of $750 was $150 cheaper than Belhaven's; within Arkansas only Ouachita Baptist College offered lower total costs.[52]

In the spring of 1959 the trustees approved McCain's proposal to raise tuition to $400 per year and room and board and all other fees to $500. This $150 increase represented a 20 percent hike in total costs, one of the two most drastic alterations of student fees in the college's history. A second $100 increase two years later lifted total costs for resident students to just over $1,000 during the 1961–1962 session. Although it was obvious that the college's low costs had never attracted large numbers of students, steadily rising fees in the 1960s widened the disparity between the price of an education at Arkansas College and other independent institutions and the price at state-supported colleges and universities. This was not likely to bolster the college's poor recruiting record within the state. As an alternative source of enrollment, as early as 1958 educational consultants had mentioned the possibility of looking outside of Arkansas for students, and an increasing number of out-of-state students began to trickle into Batesville in the late 1950s and early 1960s. In fact, 20 percent of the freshman matriculates in the fall of 1960 came from beyond Arkansas's borders, from as far away as California, Michigan, and New York. But it was only in 1962, on the advice of Robert Tinker of the firm of Gonser and Gerber, that Arkansas College began to actively recruit non-Arkansans. The logic was simple. The baby boom generation was reaching college age, and growing American involvement in Vietnam was influencing more and more young men to pursue a career in college. Furthermore, states and municipalities in the nation's most populous areas were slow in reacting to the demand for more seats at the table of higher education; consequently university expansion and community college founding failed to keep pace with the burgeoning college-age population in urban areas. Some states, especially in the Northeast, attempted to make up for their shortcomings by offering grants to students who traveled to other states for their education. Arkansas College was not the first or only struggling, independent institution to look to take advantage of this ripe situation.[53]

In the summer of 1962 admissions counselors Yvonna Wilson and Jim Mitchum made the first of many trips to New York City and other points along the northeastern coast in an attempt to round up students, none of whom had ever heard of Arkansas College or Batesville. Despite the heavy competition for these urban and suburban students and despite Arkansas College's lack of name recognition and the negative images associated with the state, admissions counselors managed to lure several students to the Ozarks. The fall 1962 enrollment of 120 full-time matriculates was the largest freshman class since the days of the G.I. boom. Most of the increase was due to the new recruiting strategy. More than one-third of these freshmen were non-Arkansans, with New York and New Jersey supplying more newcomers than any other state. Although Arkansas College failed to experience the enrollment boom that consultants had forecast, full-time enrollment surpassed 300 in the fall of 1964, for the first time since the G.I. boom, and peaked at 320 a year later before leveling off and then falling sharply in 1967 after the college temporarily eased recruitment efforts in the Northeast. The expansion of the student body in the early and mid-1960s was attributable almost exclusively to recruiting efforts in the Northeast.[54]

In just a matter of a few years this strategy completely altered the demographics of the Arkansas College student body. As recently as the late 1950s, almost three-quarters of the student population hailed from within a fifty-mile radius of Batesville. By the mid-1960s what had been a largely small-town and rural Arkansan student body had become a diverse mix featuring a large percentage of urban and suburban kids from New York, New Jersey, Pennsylvania, and elsewhere back east. By the fall of 1964 barely one-third of the freshmen at Arkansas College were natives of Arkansas, and for three years, 1965–1968, Arkansans accounted for fewer than half of all full-time students. New Jersey consistently supplied the largest number of out-of-state students at Arkansas College; the representation from the Garden State reached a high of forty during the 1964–1965 session and again in 1966–1967. New York, Pennsylvania, Virginia, and Connecticut sent large contingents to Batesville as well. At the peak of out-of-state enrollment during the 1966–1967 academic year, the combined population from these five states accounted for more than 40 percent of the student body. The vast majority of these students were young men, reflecting the influence of Vietnam among other things. And the fact that these students required campus housing quickly transformed Arkansas College into a residential institution. The high dropout and failure rate among the northeastern students suggests that Arkansas College did indeed often serve as a relief valve for students unable to get into universities closer to home.[55] It also perhaps reveals another, less quantifiable aspect of this rapid demographic shift—the difficulty of adapting to what was in effect a different culture.

At its best the college's efforts to grow its enrollment in the 1960s produced a vibrant environment in which a Baptist kid from Charlotte, Arkansas, could interact with a Jewish kid from Brooklyn, New York, the experience enriching the education of both. At its worst the experiment produced culture clash, with "damn Yankees" ridiculing a southern drawl or "redneck townies" driving by Independence Hall to holler "go back home" to anyone within earshot. At its best hard-working northeastern students overcame their unfamiliar surroundings, forged lasting friendships with both local students and non-Arkansans, and finished degrees more than a thousand miles from home. At its worst suburban kids from New Jersey and New York found the staid college and its tiny campus stifling and oppressive, rebelled, and were sent home for the draft board to consider. At its best college professors used the students' diverse backgrounds and experiences to their advantages in the classrooms, helping to overcome suspicion and misunderstanding in the process. At its worst local merchants resented the irreverence of these "foreign" students and the college for bringing them to Batesville.[56]

Cultural conflict was perhaps inescapable. Most students raised in the suburban Northeast brought their cultural baggage with them to Arkansas College. Faculty members, local merchants, and Arkansas students frequently found the northeastern students irreverent and obnoxious, traits that any good southerner always avoided. For their part, the newcomers to Arkansas often thought they had stepped off the edge of the world when they left the airport in Memphis, and the bus ride to Batesville rarely persuaded them otherwise. To make matters worse, these young men found themselves trapped on a campus in a town with none of the amenities of city life and with a shortage of female companionship. It is no wonder that freshman attrition reached an all-time high in the mid-1960s.

In addition to bringing students from New York City together with those from rural Arkansas, the influx of northeastern students in the 1960s also introduced a level of religious and ethnic diversity heretofore only imagined. By the fall of 1965 a list of students' religious or denominational preferences enumerated seventeen different categories, whereas a few years earlier the big four of Presbyterian, Baptist, Methodist, and Church of Christ generally encompassed the student body. By the mid-1960s the Presbyterian campus was home to Roman Catholics, Lutherans, Jews, Congregationalists, and at least one Albanian Orthodox Christian. By the 1964–1965 academic year the Roman Catholic population had grown large enough to spark the formation of a Newman Club; since the college had no Catholic faculty member, Ellis Mosley, an ordained Presbyterian minister, served as sponsor of the new organization. The diversity of religious persuasions reflected the diversity of ethnic backgrounds among these newcomers to Arkansas: Jewish, Irish, Polish, Italian. Nothing better represents the change at the old Scotch-Irish institution than the students' selections for Mr. and Miss Arkansas College in 1970—Elizabeth Orsi of Gladwyne, Pennsylvania, and John Coccaro of Brooklyn, New York.[57]

From an economic standpoint, the influx of urban and suburban students was a godsend for struggling Arkansas College. For years the McCain administration had been trying to reduce students' reliance on scholarship money; Progress Fund goals bloated in the 1960s in an attempt to cover basic operating expenses that normally would have been met by student payments. Most of the students recruited by Jim Mitchum and his successors on their trips to the Northeast and other urban centers came from families who had no trouble paying the full costs of an education at Arkansas College. In spite of a steady rise in tuition costs and room and board fees throughout the 1960s, the level of financial aid had reached an all-time low by mid-decade. During the 1965–1966 session, the college covered less than one-quarter of students' costs with scholarship and work-grant money, down from almost half during the early 1950s. Another development that improved the institution's ability to collect a higher percentage of student fees was the National Defense Education Act of 1958, through which Congress established the National Defense Student Loan Fund. Although originally designed to serve mathematics and science majors as well as prospective teachers, additional federal laws made the delayed-payment, low-interest loans available to almost any college student. By the late 1960s Arkansas College students were annually obtaining more than $170,000 from this federal source. The combination of more affluent students and federal student assistance allowed Arkansas College to increase costs. By the 1968–1969 academic year, tuition had risen to $1,100 and room and board cost another $950, making Arkansas College the most expensive institution in the state.[58]

Students from outside the state made up the majority of the resident population throughout most of the 1960s. One result of this was a strange dichotomy in which the culture of the dormitory and on-campus life differed sharply from that of the commuter population, whose relative strength shrunk significantly. Because resident students tended to take a more active role in extracurricular life, non-Arkansans quickly assumed important campus offices and positions. By the fall of 1965 three of the four Student Government Association officers came from states outside of Arkansas, including president Clarence Whichard (Frederick, Maryland) and vice-president Cary Worthington (Cairo, New York). Three years later none of the SGA's officers was a native of Arkansas. It was during that year, 1968–1969, that tensions between eastern students and Arkansans reached a peak. In the spring of 1969 editorials in the student newspaper, the *Highlander*, commented on an ongoing "Civil War" between the students on campus and those from the local area, or between the "long-haired Yankees" and the "rednecks, rebels, and townies." This first mention of a culture clash at Arkansas College may have been due to a new editorial perspective supplied by Herman Hammerschmidt, a New Jersey native who was the first of the eastern students to be selected editor of the *Highlander*.[59]

The collision of cultures on the small Batesville campus was such an omnipresent and monumental event that it tended to overshadow an equally momentous development in the college's history, the desegregation of the student body. For more than ninety years Arkansas College closed its doors to black students, not through any written policy but through accepted southern social custom. Almost from the beginning of its existence Arkansas College had enrolled a smattering of students from various ethnic and religious minority groups: Jews and Choctaw Indians in the late nineteenth century, a young Persian man during World War I, a Mexican student in the 1920s, and several Asians in the post–World War II boom era. But the admission of African Americans posed a unique cultural problem, even on the fringes of the old Confederacy. President John D. Spragins had first broached the subject in 1949, just two years after Jackie Robinson had broken major league baseball's color line, when he informed the trustees that some members of the local black community had asked to take classes at

Arkansas College. The board took no official action, and the student body would remain free of African Americans for another decade and a half.[60]

By the time Arkansas College received accreditation in 1959, at least five Arkansas institutions had admitted black students. The University of Arkansas had enrolled African Americans in its medical and law schools as early as 1948 and had admitted the first black undergraduate students in 1955, shortly after the U.S. Supreme Court issued its second ruling in the *Brown v. Board of Education of Topeka, Kansas* case. Within two years four other colleges had joined the University's desegregation efforts: Arkansas State College (now University) in Jonesboro, Arkansas Tech in Russellville, Arkansas State Teachers College (now the University of Central Arkansas) in Conway, and the College of the Ozarks in Clarksville, the state's first independent college to admit African Americans. Although it remains unclear what motivated the timing of Arkansas College's decision to integrate its student body, in the spring of 1964 Dick Kinser, dean of students, visited Batesville's black high school, the E. O. Miller School, in an effort to recruit students for the college. Although the dean was unsuccessful in convincing any of his listeners to attend Arkansas College, a former E. O. Miller graduate, Mitcheal Brown, heard about Kinser's visit. Brown was just finishing his second year at Arkansas A, M & N in Pine Bluff, the state's historically black land-grant college, and decided he would rather live at home while pursuing his degree.[61]

Following the high-profile and violent integration proceedings at the University of Alabama and the University of Mississippi, Brown's enrollment at Arkansas College in the fall of 1964 turned out to be a quiet and anticlimactic affair. This is not surprising considering the state's relatively solid record on higher education integration, in spite of the infamy of the Little Rock Central High crisis of 1957. By the time Mitcheal Brown enrolled at Arkansas College, only three four-year institutions in the state remained all-white: Hendrix College, Southern State (now Southern Arkansas University) in Magnolia, and Arkansas A & M (now the University of Arkansas) at Monticello. A model student, Brown went about the tasks of student life in a matter-of-fact fashion, made friends, won election as vice-president of the SGA in 1966, and persevered through the rare moments when the ugliness of reaction to the civil rights movement reared its head on campus, such as the day when he and the few Jewish students at Arkansas College found fliers denouncing their presence. For two years Mitcheal Brown remained the only black student on the Arkansas College campus. By 1967, the year of his graduation, the number of African Americans had increased to three, and by the time President McCain left Batesville in 1969 there were seven black students. Significant integration would wait until the 1970s.[62]

The admission of black students and the rapid demographic transformation of the student body provided clear proof that this was no longer the same old Arkansas College that generations had known. Change defined the decade. Around the nation the civil rights movement, protest over America's involvement in Vietnam, and the flowering of a new youth culture challenged tradition and authority. This spirit of irreverence and experimentation was nowhere more obvious than on college and university campuses, where the younger generation most often converged to forge their own identity. Even at Presbyterian Arkansas College, professors of a bygone generation read the *Highlander* as editor Drew Ponder barked tersely: "Arkansas College, it's time you caught up. Times are changing."[63] In many ways the student body at Arkansas College in the mid- and latter 1960s resembled that of the late 1920s, albeit with more New York and New Jersey accents. Both contained a vocal minority of active, interested, and often disaffected young men and women who emerged as spokespersons for a generation, while most remained somewhere in the background almost oblivious to the goings on or mildly fascinated by the excitement generated by a tumultuous age. And, despite the large numbers of bystanders, both eras produced a level and intensity of student involvement rarely matched on the college campus.

Much of the student activity in the decade of the 1960s reflected the nation's youth culture and its concerns. Under the editorship of Clarence Cash Jr. of Batesville, the *Highlander* during the 1964–1965 year featured the newspaper's first candid discussions of the civil rights movement. During the same session, the Student Christian Association (SCA) inaugurated a tutorial program at Batesville's black E. O. Miller School. In the spring of 1965 three white Arkansas College students, two of them native Arkansans, joined a host of others from colleges and universities around the country on a trip to the Mississippi Delta to rebuild African American churches that had been burned in the struggle for civil rights. A year and a half later the SCA sponsored a public discussion on the "Black Power" movement and invited speaker Elijah Coleman to occupy the "hot seat" and field student questions.[64] Events on campus also paralleled trends in popular culture. The fall of 1960 featured a beatnik party with poetry readings, sponsored by the Kappa Kappa Alpha sorority. Three years later two eastern students formed a folk song duo and eventually joined five others in the formation of the Brandywine Singers, Arkansas College's first folk music group. By the late 1960s Kappa Kappa Alpha had left the beatnik generation behind for a Psychedelic Luv-In dance in the recreation building, complete with go-go dancers in cages.[65]

By far the hottest topic of student discussion and protest in the latter half of the decade was Vietnam. One of the earliest Vietnam-themed student articles to appear in the *Highlander*, in the fall of 1965, approved U.S. involvement in southeastern Asia, reflecting a general conservatism that characterized much of the student body. When the SCA invited an anti-Vietnam speaker to take the "hot seat" in the spring of 1967, the activist was met by a hearty group of sign-toting conservatives who voiced their desire for escalation of American military involvement. The following fall former Governor Sid McMath received a gentler reception when he defended the policies of Lyndon Johnson's administration, just weeks after young religion professor Fitzhugh Spragins had taken the faculty's first public stance in opposition to the war. As the decade wore on and as the Johnson administration did in fact escalate American activity in Vietnam, student opinion began to change. A January 1968 poll conducted by the *Highlander* revealed that more than 75 percent of the student body opposed President Johnson's policy on Vietnam. The announcement two months later that college graduates would no longer receive deferments from the draft further antagonized male students. Student protest of the war in Vietnam reached a pinnacle as the 1960s gave way to the 1970s. In December 1968 students applauded an assembly speaker who presented "The Case Against Vietnam"; a year later concerned students organized a Vietnam Moratorium day and decorated the quad behind Brown Chapel (now Couch Gardens) with dozens of small black crosses to commemorate the senseless deaths of Americans in southeastern Asia.[66]

While the Vietnam debate elicited emotional outbursts from both sides, and especially from the young men who faced an uncertain future at the hands of local draft boards, the majority of student protests concentrated on matters of little global import, mundane things like speed bumps, hair, and Salisbury steak. Whether because of Batesville's relative isolation from the more dynamic currents of American social development or due to the youthful proclivity for capturing the stormy emotions of a wider cultural consciousness and unleashing them mercilessly and jubilantly on the quotidian affairs of everyday existence, protest at Arkansas College remained relatively tame and reached its most fevered pitch when directed toward local issues. During the 1960s students directed their anger toward everything from a speed bump installed on campus in 1964 by dean of students Dick Kinser to the administration's refusal to grant the full allotment of basketball scholarships approved by the Arkansas Intercollegiate Conference. One of the first such issues involved student dress. Faculty and trustees disapproved of the Bermuda shorts, cut-off jeans, and ripped t-shirts that the eastern students introduced to campus in the early 1960s. As a result in the fall of 1965 the Arkansas College administration instituted a new, stricter dress code that prohibited such attire in classrooms and around campus during class hours. The Student Court of the SGA responded by drafting a more lenient dress code, which the administration agreed to implement during the 1966–1967 year. When male students celebrated their greater sartorial freedom in the fall of 1966 with a beard-growing contest and a fresh set of sweatshirts and shorts, the stricter dress code was reapplied for the remainder of the year, and a version of the dress code remained in place for the rest of the McCain era.[67]

Students also chafed under the burden of strict alcohol policies, and Batesville's location in a dry county proved especially bothersome to eastern students who had not inherited the Presbyterian's devotion to abstinence. By the mid-1960s the road to Newport, and its dealers of spirits, was a well-traveled one for many Arkansas College students, and the administration and faculty were well aware of the high regard in which the youth of campus held Batesville's sister city. In January 1967 a majority of the faculty responded to months of student lobbying by amending the old alcohol-free policy to allow students of legal age to drink as long as they did so outside the boundaries of Independence County. Some out-of-state students then turned their anger toward what they viewed as Arkansas's antiquated liquor laws, but with no success.[68] Independence County remained a dry one in 2002.

Another source of student unrest was cafeteria food. Even with the new Alphin Dining Hall, students complained about the quality of food and service and the administration of the cafeteria until longtime dietician Irene Parse retired after the fall

The library under construction, c. 1968. During the 1960s the campus often seemed like one big construction zone, especially to students.

semester of 1965. The administration replaced Parse by contracting with Professional Food-Service Management Company to operate the dining hall. This contract brought to the Arkansas College campus Mark Smith, a trained chef who would remain in the kitchen for more than three decades; nevertheless, two years later the dining hall was the scene of the most flagrant display of discontent at Arkansas College when a "food riot" broke out in October 1967. Although there were rumors of a planned protest over the quality of the food, the *Highlander* editor Tom Arnold chalked the incident up to general disillusionment. This general disillusionment reached its height during the 1967–1968 session not so much because of escalation in Vietnam, the strict dress code, or lousy food as from the physical state of campus. That academic year, McCain's second-to-last in Batesville, marked the high point in campus chaos created by construction. Not only was the library under construction, but extensive landscaping between the Masonic buildings and the Brown Chapel and in the quad behind the chapel created a muddy maze of trenches and ditches that made the campus resemble a World War I battle zone. Wooden planks provided poor excuses for sidewalks and bridges over trenches, and students frequently found themselves without electricity or water due to construction demands. To make matters worse, the administration's decision to level the ground in front of the dining hall so that the building could be seen from the front of campus led to the removal of several large oak trees, including an ancient one near the chapel whose destruction elicited howls of protest from students. The administration rewarded the students who remained at Arkansas College through the entire year with "Mud Scholarships" of $100 for the following session.[69]

Not even endangered trees and Bermuda shorts bred as much discontent as did mandatory chapel. Ever since the boom years following World War II, the college's chapel policy had faced increasingly harsh attacks from students who resented the practice, a relic of an earlier day in the nation's halls of learning. By the time McCain arrived on campus in the fall of 1952, the G.I.'s had already convinced the faculty and administration to abandon the policy of required Sunday School and church service attendance, but attendance at morning chapel services remained mandatory. The chapel program at Arkansas College underwent a significant transformation in the early years of McCain's administration. In the fall of 1954 mandatory chapel attendance was reduced to three days per week, although the Student Christian Association, the organization formed to coordinate all religious activities on campus, continued to sponsor a "meditation period" five mornings per week. Furthermore, the inauguration of the Introduction to Fine Arts course, which occupied two of the three required chapel sessions, meant that only one morning each week was devoted to religious observance. In spite of the more liberal chapel policy, students continued to protest, their objections directed as much toward the musical and artistic presentations of the fine arts course as toward the weekly religious service. On surveys conducted in the mid- and late 1950s, students consistently identified chapel attendance as the school policy most in need of change.[70]

With the influx of eastern students in the 1960s resentment of the thrice-weekly chapels (renamed assemblies in 1962) reached a crescendo of complaints in mid-decade. Facing difficulties in securing speakers and presentations three times a week and enduring catcalls and open hostility from an unappreciative student audience, in the fall of 1964 dean of students Dick Kinser tried without success to convince the faculty to limit mandatory chapel to two days per week. Ultimately, mandatory chapel at Arkansas College suffered a quiet demise. After the mud and muck of the 1967–1968 session generated a fresh wave of protests and after the *Highlander* conducted a poll in which two out of three students admitted to sleeping through chapel period, in the fall of 1968 the faculty and administration instituted a new policy that reserved Tuesday and Thursday mornings for optional chapel services and required students to attend at least 75 percent of these services. By the mid-1970s mandatory chapel attendance had drifted into memory.[71]

The gradual chipping away of the college's traditional morning chapel services reflected a loosening of the reins of authority, especially during the 1960s. Although this youthful spirit of freedom was part and parcel of the American campus experience during the era, it was perhaps confronted more quickly and drastically on the Batesville campus than at other colleges in Arkansas and in the region due to the influx of a large number of students whose urbanity and unfamiliarity with the mores of southern evangelical Protestantism rendered many of them strangers in a strange land. Of course, students from New York and New Jersey were not the only ones testing the limits of authority in the 1960s. One of the most striking signs of a newfound freedom of student expression was the evolution of the yearbook, known as the *Index* until renamed the *Scot* in 1965, from a traditional, buttoned-down publication in the early 1960s to a racier, even rebellious one by the latter part of the decade. The inclusion of photographs featuring young men drinking beer and ogling *Playboy* magazine, of young women in bathtubs, and of students engaged in amorous embrace on the quad would hardly have been thinkable just a few years earlier. The brashness of this new youth culture repelled some, including a number of trustees. Whether or not the spirit of disillusionment that defined the decade had arrived in suitcases from faraway places like Brooklyn, West Orange, or Pittsburgh, a few vocal trustees suspected it had, and by the middle of the decade the admissions staff was receiving pressure to recruit more southern students. When board sentiment led the college to temporarily discontinue its northeastern recruiting efforts in 1967, fall enrollment declined by 15 percent, which in turn led to an emergency midsession recruiting trip back east. Nevertheless, this proved to be one of the college's final attempts to attract students from the urban Northeast. By the mid-1970s the student body at Arkansas College had largely been purged of non-Arkansans.[72]

Although many student protests in the 1960s were directed toward things that they did not want to do, others concerned the lack of things to do on campus. In 1967 one student captured the general disaffection of the time when he wrote: "It is very simple, as students, we pay more, do less, receive less, and are forced into more than any other student body in the state." The sudden growth of the resident population in the early and mid-1960s left the administration and faculty searching for things to keep town-bound students entertained and contented. The town of Batesville offered little in the way of activities. Many students frequented the popular hangouts such as Ray's Sandwich Shop downtown, Tommy's Kingburger, the Spur coffee shop, and the Rainbow Drive-In on the highway beneath the campus bluff; by the mid-1960s students flocked to the late-night "owl shows" at the Melba Theater. Nearby Newport, of course, offered attractions and refreshments not found in Batesville.[73]

When McCain first arrived at Arkansas College, the recent decline in enrollment had also affected extracurricular activities. Only a handful of clubs and organizations existed, and most did little beyond hold occasional meetings and elect officers. Two sororities, Kappa Kappa Alpha and Sigma Alpha Sigma, contributed to social life for young women. Varsity basketball provided a welcome relief in the winter months. Otherwise, most student organizations were religious in nature (Westminster Fellowship, Wesley Foundation, and the Baptist Student Union) or were affiliated with some facet of the curriculum (the Art Club, the Home Economics Club, and the English Club). The student newspaper had even gone defunct in the early 1950s and would not be revived until 1954. By the early 1960s Arkansas College's extracurricular offerings had expanded little.

Theater and music provided the most consistent avenues of extracurricular participation during much of the McCain era. Alumna Doris Hammett took over direction of the Harlequin Theatre in the fall of 1952 and remained at the head of the speech department throughout McCain's seventeen-year administration. Despite the fact that Hammett's primary training and interest was in the field of speech instead of drama, she directed students in at least two plays each year and occasionally took her troupe on the road or to festivals. It was during Hammett's tour as director of the Harlequin Theatre that operations were moved from old Alumni Hall to the chapel and fine arts building (Brown Chapel) on the main campus and that the speech major became a speech and theater major in 1966. Drama at Arkansas College received a much-needed boost in the fall of 1966 with the addition of Johnny Homesley to the faculty. A native of Independence County and member of the class of 1963, Homesley had been a star member of Harlequin Theatre before going off to earn a master's degree at Louisiana State University. His arrival allowed Hammett to concentrate on teaching speech, and Homesley passionately threw himself into both the technical and artistic elements of the theater department. By the spring of 1967 the *Highlander* was praising Homesley for reviving drama at Arkansas College; his innovative Tartan Troupers, a small drama team, performed in six different states the ensuing summer. During his second year at Arkansas College, Homesley's productions drew crowds of unprecedented size, and Harlequin's production of Thornton Wilder's "The Skin of Our Teeth" was the best-received play in years. McCain's final year at Arkansas College witnessed what was perhaps the institution's most ambitious extracurricular undertaking when Dorothy Gray's choir and the Harlequin Theatre collaborated on a production of *Lil' Abner* and then took the show on the road for performances in El Dorado and Little Rock.[74]

Even more dynamic than Harlequin Theatre during the McCain years was the music department; and no extracurricular activity gained the college as much publicity. Under the direction of Dorothy Landis Gray, a young Pennsylvanian who had made her way to Batesville shortly after World War II, the college choir had already begun the practice of touring the state in the late 1940s, presenting programs of sacred music in Presbyterian churches and singing secular songs in various high schools. In the mid-1950s Gray's choir appeared on radio programs in Little Rock and Batesville, and in 1959 the choir cut its first records when it recorded four Christmas carols in Little Rock. The highlight of the decade came in the fall of 1956, however, when the choir was featured on the NBC television program *Wide, Wide World* singing "The Catfish Song," a tune Gray had written for her students to perform at Batesville's Catfish Derby.[75]

The 1960s witnessed the emergence of a musical coterie that would become synonymous with Arkansas College for several years, the Lassies. Formed in 1947 to provide musical enrichment for local church services conducted by preministerial

The Lassies, 1965–1966. *Top row, left to right:* Annette Jobe, Kay Evans, and Charlene Prickett. *Middle row:* Carole Frizzel, Myrl Griffin, and Lucy Jeffery. *Bottom row:* Dianne Cargill, Mayola Satterfield, Dorothy Landis Gray, Paula Melton, and Beverly McCullough.

students, the Lassies, known through the 1950s as the sextette, burst onto the international scene after a rousing performance at the Rotary International convention in St. Louis in the summer of 1963. Featuring nine female voices and an accompanist at the piano, the Lassies performed Broadway hits, popular songs, classics, and an occasional sacred tune. Their successful outing in St. Louis led to numerous engagements during the following academic year capped by an invitation from the United Service

Organizations (USO) to conduct a five-week, expenses-paid tour of U.S. military installations along the Arctic circle in the summer of 1964. The USO tour turned out to be the first of four such excursions for the Lassies during the latter years of the McCain administration. Two years later a new group of Lassies visited American bases in the Far East, followed by tours of the Caribbean Command and western Europe in 1967 and 1969, respectively. For the latter tour, Gray's girls abandoned their traditional plaid skirts and white blouses for a collection of five different folk costumes. By the late 1960s the Lassies faced a grueling schedule of approximately forty different events per year. In the process they became the most recognizable student ambassadors in the history of Arkansas College.[76]

The emergence of the Lassies as busy emissaries for Arkansas College paralleled the rebirth of a dynamic extracurriculum in the 1960s. Most new organizations were the same ones found on any college campus—Circle K, the Alpha Chi honorary society, the student branch of the National Education Association, the Library Club, the French Club, and the Science Club. Some of the new organizations of the decade, such as the Roman Catholic Newman Club, simply reflected the changing demographic composition of the student body. Others mirrored the spirit of the times. By the 1966–1967 academic year there was a Young Republicans club on campus, and the following session featured a debate between the Young Republicans and the Young Democrats over the issue of Vietnam and the presidential election of 1968. As we have already seen, student publications and their editors grew more outspoken and brash during the decade. Likewise, the Student Government Association, which for years had occupied only an insignificant role on campus, began to assert itself as the voice and arm of the student body. The SGA's Student Senate drafted drinking and dress code policies during the 1966–1967 year. The SGA enjoyed its most active campaign in 1967–1968. Under the leadership of president Cliff Jackson, who had been elected on a fifteen-point platform, the SGA published its own weekly newspaper, *Pravada*, maintained office hours, and held periodic assemblies to update students on the progress of ongoing struggles over drinking and dress code policies and discussions concerning mandatory chapel.[77]

One phase of 1960s-era extracurricular life that was directly affected by the influx of non-Arkansans was the rebirth of fraternities. The paucity of social activities available for the largely captive resident population in 1964–1965 spurred two groups of students to organize fraternities. In the fall of that year John Mernone, a freshman from Amityville, New York, and more than a dozen other freshmen founded Chi Beta Phi. A few months later an even larger group of underclassmen, led by Dennis Banker of Chicago, Illinois, established Sigma Phi Omega. The two fraternities, originally comprised entirely of resident students from outside Arkansas, maintained a hold on male social life for two years until the creation of Gamma Delta Iota, whose first president was Bob Kasper of New York City. Describing itself as a "service fraternity," as opposed to a social fraternity, Gamma Delta Iota (the Greek code name for "God damn independents" on many campuses) sought to "combat apathy on the campus" and published its own critical newsletter for a time. Sigma Phi Omega suffered a quick demise, but Chi Beta Phi and Gamma Delta Iota thrived in the late 1960s and survived into the post-McCain era to eventually become Tau Kappa Epsilon and Kappa Sigma, respectively. The meager female population at Arkansas College precluded a similar expansion of Greek life; consequently, Kappa Kappa Alpha and Sigma Alpha Sigma remained the only two sororities throughout the McCain era.[78]

Until the mid-1960s young men suffered the claustrophobia of on-campus life without the benefit of the physical release offered by an intramural athletic program. (The intramural program would not be extended to female students until the 1970s.) A once-vibrant intramural program had fallen victim to the financial woes and rapid downsizing of the early 1950s, so that by the time McCain took over as president the only organized athletic activities at Arkansas College involved varsity athletes. The administration responded to growing student protests by hiring Fred Wann as director of intramurals and resident of Independence Hall in the fall of 1965. (It was probably no coincidence that the 1965–1966 year also brought the construction of the recreation hall.) To the delight of dozens of campus-bound students, the energetic Wann, a Batesville native and 1959 alumnus, instituted a full program of intramural athletics, kicking off with touch football in the fall and wrapping up with softball in the spring. In between, students competed in, among other things, basketball, volleyball, table tennis, bowling, billiards, and badminton.[79]

The 1965–1966 academic year also brought about the formation of Arkansas College's first bowling team, an official Arkansas Intercollegiate Conference (AIC) varsity sport that allowed the college to take advantage of the new bowling lanes in the recreation hall. The late 1960s witnessed a rapid expansion in the development of varsity athletics at Arkansas College due to a 1966 AIC ruling that required all member institutions to sponsor at least four sports. The college had dropped baseball after a weak attempt to revive the sport in the late 1950s, which meant that basketball was the only show in town before bowling arrived in 1966. In response to the conference's ruling, the administration founded a golf team and cross-country team during the 1967–1968 session and began making plans for the reintroduction of baseball, which would not take place until 1971. In addition, Wann formed a soccer team; after an abbreviated season consisting of two matches with the College of the Ozarks in the spring of 1968, Arkansas College joined the fledgling, and short-lived, Arkansas Collegiate Soccer League the following fall.[80]

At best, bowling, golf, and soccer served only as brief diversions from the college's primary varsity sport, basketball. For most of the McCain era varsity athletics meant basketball, and in the 1950s and 1960s Arkansas College basketball was synonymous with Coach R. C. "Dick" Winningham. A native of the little central Arkansas community of Formosa and a graduate of Arkansas State Teachers College in Conway, Winningham joined the Arkansas College faculty in the fall of 1951 as director of athletics. At the time the college had just dropped its football program, and Winningham became the institution's first professional coach dedicated exclusively to basketball. Cut from that mythical coach's mold, he was a strict disciplinarian but practical joker who earned the steadfast loyalty and lifelong affection of his players, most of whom were smaller and slower than the competition in the AIC. Winningham did have a knack, however, for taking one or two outstanding players, usually sharp-shooting guards, and building a competitive team around them using hard-working role players. Only five times during his twenty-year career as head coach did the Scots fail to place at least one player on the all-AIC first team, a remarkable accomplishment considering that Arkansas College rarely offered the maximum number of athletic scholarships allowed by conference rules. Winningham was also one of the earliest coaches in the state to utilize the fast-paced, high-scoring, run-and-gun offense in the 1950s, a system he adapted to fit his players' size and ability.[81]

Dick Winningham brought Arkansas College its first winning athletic teams since before World War II. Despite a mediocre conference season in 1951–1952, the Scots won their second AAU tournament in the spring of 1952 and repeated the feat in 1953 with a season record of twenty-one wins and seven losses. Winningham's 1953 club, led by all-conference players Harry Neff of Mountain View and Bobby Smith of Batesville, narrowly missed a trip to the National Association of Intercollegiate Athletics (NAIA) national tournament when it lost to Arkansas Tech in the district finals in Little Rock but went on to a second-place finish in the national AAU tournament. Nevertheless, by the early 1950s Arkansas's stronger college teams had ceased competing in the AAU, and Winningham's efforts to move the Scots toward a tougher schedule and into the ranks of the state's elite basketball programs met with mixed results throughout the remainder of the decade. In spite of the strong play of all-conference players such as Jim Harris of Bryant and Corbett Passmore of Oxley, the Scots struggled to post winning records against colleges with much larger enrollments and athletic budgets.[82]

The decade of the 1960s brought Winningham's teams more success. The administration's decision to increase scholarship funds for the 1959–1960 season produced the school's best squad in years. Behind the strong play of three all-conference performers, including first-team selection Francis "Birdie" Rogers of Mammoth Spring, the Scots scored a last-second victory over powerful Arkansas Tech on homecoming night and advanced to the championship game of the 1960 NAIA district tournament before falling to Arkansas A & M. Just at the point when it appeared that Arkansas College was ready to cement its position among the elite AIC basketball teams, the administration's disciplinary suspension of four Scots in the spring of 1960, including two all-conference players, dashed Winningham's hopes and sparked a campus protest in which hooded students burned an effigy of McCain on the president's front lawn. The Scots suffered through their worst season of the McCain era the following year before returning to old form as "contenders [who] often filled the role of classic spoilers."[83]

By the fall of 1960, Winningham had convinced McCain to convert the old stage at one end of the basketball court into dormitory rooms, and for the rest of the decade Scots players would live in the gymnasium, which they cleaned to help pay for their room and board. Winningham also avoided the college's recruiting trends in the 1960s and continued to gather his players from the small towns and rural schools of northern Arkansas. The result of these factors was a string of scrappy teams that earned the respect of opposing players and coaches as well as referees, to which Arkansas College's five consecutive sportsmanship trophies attest. Among these northern Arkansas boys were two of the most decorated players in the history of Scot basketball, Lavaughn Robertson and Jim Haney. Robertson, a pure-shooting guard from Rector, scored more than 2,100 career points, an average of more than eighteen per game, and became Arkansas College's first athlete to be named to the all-conference first team three times, 1962–1964. Haney, a guard from Salem, repeated the latter feat when he was named to the all-conference team for the third consecutive time in 1968. The 1968 season turned out to be the peak of success for the Scots during the McCain era, as well as the Winningham era. Relying on the scoring of Haney and fellow all-conference player Bill Cossey of Rector, the Scots posted a record of twenty-three wins and only ten losses during the 1967–1968 campaign, despite the fact that no one on the team stood taller than 6'4". The Scots followed a strong regular season by winning the AIC tournament championship in Pine Bluff, which was attended by more than half the student body in a convoy of chartered buses. Once again Arkansas College's bid to advance to the NAIA national tournament fell short when the Scots lost a three-game playoff series with Henderson State College. For his efforts, Winningham received area and district coach of the year awards; the euphoria over the Scots' great season also spurred local boosters to raise money to pay the expense of room and board for basketball players, a fee not covered by Arkansas College's athletic scholarships. The 1967–1968 season proved to be the last winning year for Coach Winningham, who resigned in 1971 after twenty seasons, still the longest tenure for a coach in the history of the institution.[84]

Like most coaches at small liberal arts institutions, Dick Winningham realized that basketball was of secondary importance at Arkansas College. Consequently, he demanded steady class attendance and academic effort from all his players. Most players recruited into the Scots circle eventually earned degrees. Some excelled just as much in the classroom as on the court, such as Ronnie Brogdon, who in 1970 became the first varsity athlete to win the prestigious Coffin Medal. By the final years of McCain's administration, competition for the Coffin Medal and other student awards had intensified due to the larger student body as well as the college's efforts to attract a larger pool of highly qualified students. Although the McCain administration never adopted official admissions policies requiring minimum entrance examination scores or high school grades, administrators and faculty tried to improve the quality of the student body through other means, such as scholarships and testing programs. Since the early 1950s Arkansas College had granted a limited number of merit scholarships to each incoming freshman class, but the scholarship endowment remained pitifully small until 1962 when Wooten Anderson's bequest gave the college more than $350,000 to be used exclusively for student aid. The board moved quickly to establish five new Trustee Scholarships, soon renamed Wooten Anderson Scholarships, to be awarded to members of the 1962 freshman class. By the fall of 1964 the Anderson Scholarships provided students $3,000 over the course of four years at Arkansas College, which covered the bulk of tuition and room and board fees. During the decade the Anderson Scholarships, awarded primarily to Arkansas natives, brought several outstanding stu-

Three-time All-AIC performer Jim Haney accepts the 1968 AIC tournament championship trophy as Coach R. C. "Dick" Winningham and teammates look on.

dents to Batesville, including Cliff Jackson of Donaldson, the 1968 Coffin Medal recipient who was the first Arkansas College graduate to receive a Fulbright Fellowship and a Woodrow Wilson Scholarship.[85]

Students who found their way to Arkansas College in the 1960s were greeted by a stable faculty and a limited but relatively focused curriculum. Although the faculty experienced frequent turnover in certain areas, such as the sciences and languages, the McCain administration benefited from a corps of experienced and dedicated professors. Seven faculty members, including Coach Winningham and librarian Dorothy Sydenstricker, greeted McCain in 1952 and were still around to say farewell seventeen years later. In addition, ten others served for more than half of the McCain era.[86] Throughout the 1950s and 1960s the strength of the faculty was its dedication to the classroom and its personal interaction with the small student body, characteristics common to most small colleges of the era. During the early years of his administration, McCain, himself a Ph.D. and published scholar, repeatedly stressed such modern concerns as faculty publication, attendance at professional conferences, and pursuit of terminal degrees. The young president was successful in some regards but gradually came to realize that university-style scholarship, the kind appreciated by accrediting bodies, was not easily attainable in the cash-starved and teaching-intensive atmosphere of the independent liberal arts college. With the exception of the various studies of salamanders conducted by biology professor Charles C. Smith, a University of Oklahoma Ph.D. who served on the Arkansas College faculty from 1957 to 1964, academic research and writing rarely emanated from the Batesville campus. Even with the adoption of academic freedom and tenure policies and with the relatively early institution of a faculty retirement program, low salaries, cultural isolation, and lack of resources plagued McCain in his quest to recruit more professors with doctorates. More often than not, when the college patiently assisted current faculty members in their pursuits of terminal degrees, the newly minted Ph.D.'s left Batesville for higher-paying jobs elsewhere. After fighting this system for a decade, by the early 1960s McCain's administration had stopped pursuing Ph.D.'s and had settled on the humble, but still unattainable, goal of one faculty doctorate for each major area of study.[87]

By the time of Arkansas College's accreditation in 1959, the foundation of the McCain-era faculty had already been established. Although not particularly scholarly, most were dedicated to the college and to their profession. Among the alumni who had returned to their alma mater were English instructor Thelma Pickens, an active poet who began publishing students' verses in *Heather from the Hill* in 1959, James Vernon Balch, whose charm and classroom demeanor made business and economics the McCain era's most popular major, and speech teacher Doris Hammett. Balch and Hammett were among the handful to serve under President Spragins and throughout the McCain administration. Roberta Dorr Brown joined the college staff before either Balch or Hammett and would outlast them both. A 1944 graduate and Batesville native, Brown had started work during World War II as Spragins's secretary. Attending graduate school in the summers, she ascended to the faculty in the late 1940s and during the McCain years rose through the ranks from registrar to professor of business skills to assistant academic dean and professor of education. In 1961, a few years before receiving her Ed.D. from the University of Arkansas, Brown was appointed to the post of academic dean and became the first woman to hold that position at an Arkansas institution. Her appointment as dean also brought some stability to the position of academic dean, which changed hands no fewer than six times during McCain's first dozen years in Batesville. The McCain years also witnessed the retirements of several beloved professors. Harry King, Frank Harrin, and Stanley Rockwood all exited the scene in the 1950s. In 1963 longtime mathematics and Greek professor, and former dean, Sam Williams "wasted his sweetness on the desert air" of the classroom for the last time. Williams, born during the administration of President Rutherford B. Hayes and only half a dozen years after the founding of

Arkansas College, had served on the faculty for thirty-nine years. Only Roberta Dorr Brown and Dorothy Landis Gray would serve the college for longer consecutive terms. Williams's retirement also quietly marked the end of an era; although Thelma Pickens would occasionally offer courses in Latin for the remainder of the decade, the regular study of Greek left the campus with the eighty-four-year-old professor. By the mid-1970s Arkansas College's century-long relationship with the classical languages, the heart of the original curriculum, had come to an end. Four years after Williams's departure, longtime history professor Margaret Pruden Lester, whose extensive summer travels had given life to her lectures for two decades, retired and returned to her hometown of Rome, Georgia.[88]

The final years of McCain's administration saw the beginnings of a faculty overhaul that would help shape the college's future. In 1965 McCain hired Fitzhugh Spragins, son of the former president, as professor of religion; Spragins became the first alumnus with an earned doctorate to serve on the faculty. In 1966 Arkansas College was one of 158 institutions nationwide to receive "Developing Institutions" grants from the federal government to fund three National Teaching Fellowships. Using money from this program to pay salaries, the college hired chemist (and alumna) Roberta Bustin and biologist Veryl Board, both of whom would dedicate long careers to Arkansas College, as well as the aforementioned Johnny Homesley. The college received enough "Developing Institutions" money to hire five new faculty members the next year. By the time McCain left in 1969, the faculty had been expanded to include several young professors who would exercise an impact at Arkansas College into the 1980s and 1990s, including Charles Oliver, Fred Wann, Ann Rhodes, Herman Hess, Stanley Reed, and Dan and Jane Fagg.[89]

Once the general education core was put in place in 1954, the curriculum taught by the faculty at Arkansas College remained relatively stable throughout the balance of the McCain administration. By design, the curriculum in the 1950s and 1960s steadily moved away from the experimentation that had defined the late 1940s and toward a more traditional liberal arts focus. At McCain's request, the trustees agreed to drop all home economics courses in 1954; six years later the faculty voted to discontinue the commerce, or business skills, major. By the mid-1960s the catalog had been purged of all business skills offerings, which consisted of shorthand, typing, and other practical courses designed for secretarial training. Nevertheless, in 1968 Arkansas College added its first course in computer programming, reflecting the institution's long history of responding to popular demands no matter how utilitarian in nature. Although most curricular alteration involved streamlining existing academic programs or eliminating those that were deemed too far removed from the college's mission, the one significant addition to the curriculum during McCain's years in Batesville was a major in religious (later Christian) education in 1954. The new major, whose purpose was to train young men and women for nonministerial careers in the church, reflected the Synod of Arkansas's growing interest and financial investment in Arkansas College during the 1950s. In 1958 the college received $10,000 in grant money from the synod and the general assembly of the Southern Presbyterian

Church and used the funds to expand its Christian education offerings and recruit a husband and wife team, Dick and Mary Kinser, to oversee the program's direction. In 1964 the faculty voted to replace the Christian education major with a more general major in religion.[90]

Most other curricular changes mirrored current developments in American higher education or the influence of specific faculty members. Arguing that the antiquated foreign language requirement caused many students to abandon Arkansas College for state institutions with no such demand, in 1957 the faculty approved a recommendation to drop this traditional rite of passage for the B.A. In the early 1960s the faculty reinstated the practice of administering senior examinations, and by mid-decade most students had access to at least one seminar-style class in their major area of study. The federal largesse of the latter half of the 1960s that resulted in a rapid expansion of the faculty also led to a fresh round of curricular experimentation. A 1967 federal grant allowed the college to establish divisional seminars that were taught jointly by Arkansas College professors and faculty members from the University of Arkansas. The grant also led to meetings and workshops in which representatives from both institutions discussed other ways to enrich the small college curriculum. Within specific disciplines, curricula tended to mirror the strengths and interests of faculty members and experienced only slight changes during the 1950s and 1960s. The one exception was in mathematics where the retirement of aged Sam Williams and the efforts of young professor Glen Haddock led to significant modernization and a change in focus from the practical to the theoretical.[91]

By the time Arkansas College began to reevaluate its curriculum in the late 1960s, it was in many ways a vastly different institution than the one that had greeted a young Paul McCain in 1952. Most important of all, McCain would leave behind an accredited institution in the place of what had been a teetering, struggling little school. Physically, the college had undergone a complete change. A modern red-brick campus sat on what had been a sage grass field. The original campus now belonged to the First Presbyterian Church, and only the original college building (renamed Morrow Hall) and the old gymnasium/library remained. Daffin Field, Independence Hall, and Williams Gymnasium stood on the old East End Heights, or middle, campus, but all three were in the twilight of their usefulness to Arkansas College. The number of full-time faculty members had increased by 50 percent in McCain's seventeen-year presidency, and their average salary had more than doubled, although it remained among the lowest in the state. Like most institutions during the post–World War II decades, Arkansas College had experienced bureaucratic expansion and modernization. In the fall of 1952 the administration's offices in the Isaac J. Long Memorial Building had been sparsely occupied; joining the president were the academic dean, the registrar, the bursar, and two secretaries. Elsewhere around campus one could find a dean of men, a dean of women, a housemother, and a dietician. By McCain's final year the college had consolidated the old deans of men and women into the dean of students and had added an assistant to the president (or development officer), a director of publications, an admissions office consisting of a director and three counselors, a campus nurse, a business office staff, and a crew of half a dozen grounds and maintenance workers. Each major office boasted at least one secretary. Although the endowment had barely doubled since 1952, there were promises of unsettled wills that could double it yet again, and the annual operating budget had ballooned from less than $150,000 to more than $1 million. Demographic shifts and national cultural trends had brought about a monumental change in student social life. The introduction of televisions to classrooms and computers to the business office reflected attempts to keep pace with rapid technological advances.

The McCain years of the 1950s and 1960s, then, were abounding in growth, development, change. Nevertheless, in many fundamental respects Arkansas College in the late 1960s resembled the impoverished, ambivalent, searching institution that had stood as Batesville's beacon of culture and higher education since the days of Reconstruction. Barring some sort of miracle—and Arkansas College, it seemed, had used up most of those in past struggles to stay afloat—the endowment goal of $10 million by 1972 was clearly unattainable. Although federal grants and fund drives had supplied a large percentage of the money needed for the furious-paced building program of the 1960s, much of the construction had also been undertaken on credit, and it would take the college years to pay off these building debts. The McCain administration had satisfied the basic goals of the 1951 merger committee, the same goals that had spelled the end of the Spragins era, but the college had made little progress toward the loftier aims of becoming a liberal arts institution on par with elite colleges such as Haverford or Swarthmore or even with regional elites such as Southwestern or Westminster. Furthermore, Arkansas College struggled to recruit any student, much less the intellectually and materially elite who Bill McMillan and the merger committee had hoped would come to fill the classrooms after accreditation. Enrollment in the spring of 1969, though almost twice the enrollment during McCain's first year in Batesville, remained less than half the centennial goal of 600; even worse, with each passing year the postwar baby boom provided fewer and fewer young men and women for the nation's college classrooms. Accreditation and the building of a modern campus had not been enough to entice large numbers of students to the little town of Batesville.[92]

Nevertheless, despite the obstacles, McCain's accomplishments had been considerable, and the decision to make the endowment fund largely dependent on wills held promise for brighter financial days to come. Furthermore, by the late 1960s Arkansas College benefited from a faculty and board of trustees as strong as or stronger than any in the institution's history. Unlike so many of his predecessors in the president's office, McCain's decision to leave Arkansas College did not take place in an atmosphere of instability and uncertainty over the future. In fact, compared with the experiences of most past presidents, McCain left during a moment of triumph. In the fall of 1968 construction crews began laying the foundation for the new physical education building, the final piece of the campus plan developed a decade earlier. For McCain, whose passion during the decade had been the successful completion of this master plan, this was as clear a sign as any that his days and duties at Arkansas College

McCain the builder, c. 1960s.

were drawing to a close. He had shepherded the little college through the arduous accreditation process and through its development into a modern college in the turbulent 1960s. It seemed like time for a change for the McCains from a personal standpoint as well. Although still young for a college president, and especially one with more than a decade and a half of experience under his belt, Paul McCain was quickly approaching his fiftieth birthday, and he and his wife, Eleanor, had just sent their youngest child away to college.

So when he received a call in early 1969 from the president of Agnes Scott College, his father's old institution and his boyhood home, McCain considered it perfect timing. After a visit to the Decatur campus in the spring, McCain accepted the position of vice-president for development at Agnes Scott and announced his resignation to the Arkansas College board in May 1969. Seventeen years was a long time to be president; only the Longs had devoted more time to the leadership of Arkansas College. When Paul Moffatt McCain officially left office at the end of August, the trustees' search committee had still not found his replacement, and veteran trustee Nels Barnett stepped in to serve as acting president until the committee completed its mission.[93] The college and its campus on the bluff, a monument to the vision and perseverance of the steady McCain, were in good hands with Barnett, one of the few still living who could lay claim in all honesty to having saved this little school from certain death. But Barnett's task in September 1969 called for no heroics, only the mundane chore of watching over an institution that faced no threat of immediate demise, no grand plans for merger, an institution with a life of its own. The days of saving the college had passed, thanks largely to McCain. The days ahead were filled with potential and, as always, a hint of uncertainty.

PART IV: 1969–1997

On 3 September 1981, nine members of the board of trustees' investment subcommittee gathered at the Little Rock Municipal Airport to discuss the investment of a few small gifts and to listen to updates on current financial projects from Arkansas College's vice-president for finance. To the surprise of Robert Young III, chairman of the subcommittee, a visitor appeared and asked for the floor. Young called the meeting to order and obliged the visitor, who was not a stranger but Gaston Williamson, prominent member of the Rose Law Firm, father of trustee Jim Williamson, and a noted friend of the college. The elder Williamson rose from his chair, stepped behind the podium, and informed his listeners that he had come to the meeting as the attorney for the executor of the will of Jean Brown. Miss Brown, one of the college's most faithful and generous friends for more than half a century, had died in Hot Springs one week earlier at the age of ninety-eight. The trustees listened intently as the theatrical Williamson, in full courtroom mode, made his way down the seemingly endless list of beneficiaries, enunciating every last cent and acknowledging even the smallest bequests. As the performance stretched into minutes and as Jean Brown's sizable estate shrunk with each new line, Young and the other trustees began to wonder if there would be anything left for Arkansas College at the end of this soliloquy. Finally, after another dramatic pause, Gaston Williamson delivered the news that would forever alter the destiny of Batesville's little college. Jean Brown, who had never attended a single class at Arkansas College, had willed to her beloved school $14,313,427.15. The bequest, which at the time was the largest gift ever made to an institution of higher learning in the state of Arkansas, was two and half times as large as Arkansas College's total endowment. Like all small, independent institutions, Arkansas College had for decades dreamed of such a gift. When the money was wired to Little Rock's Worthen Bank the following afternoon, the college immediately went from being a poor little school to one with a stable financial future.[1]

Few events in the history of the institution have had such a transformative effect as that exercised by the bequest of Jean Brown. For almost 110 years Arkansas College had, like so many small independent institutions, struggled from year to year on shoestring budgets and pitiful endowments. Now, in a development that could truly be described as overnight, the college community watched as the darkest of the financial clouds lifted from the Batesville sky and a new and promising future peaked over the horizon. Although, as we shall see, the Brown bequest would prove to be no panacea for all the college's woes, even the financial ones, the large endowment gift did provide the funds needed for the journey toward distinction. In the more than two decades since the bequest, the college has achieved substantial improvements in almost every facet of its existence: faculty and student quality, physical expansion and appearance, resources for academics, marketing, and further fund-raising, and, perhaps most dramatically, reputation among peer institutions.

The greatest luxury afforded by the Brown bequest and subsequent gifts inspired by it has been not an extravagant wealth that has enabled the college and its leaders to strike off into realms of educational fantasy with reckless abandon but a basic financial security necessary for an earnest evaluation of institutional mission and the courage to undertake fundamental change inspired for once by idealism, not practicality. As we progress into the twenty-first century, we await and observe the unfolding results of a small-town college's large aspirations, many of them envisioned in the days following the death of a devout old Presbyterian lady from Hot Springs.

Chapter 7

Arkansas College in the Wild West Years

At 11:15 on the morning of 19 April 1973 the president of Arkansas College was crouched beneath the bursar's desk, thoroughly bewildered and somewhat frightened. Leading a struggling little institution with an endowment of barely one million dollars was indeed an intimidating task, especially for an inexperienced thirty-three-year-old, but, as far as anyone knows, the demands of the presidency of Arkansas College had never before led a president to prostrate himself beneath office furniture. On this Maundy Thursday it was in fact a capricious Mother Nature, and not the stress of the job, that had convinced Dan C. West to fling himself beneath this desk. With no warning, beyond a menacing western sky the color of a shotgun barrel, a raging funnel dipped from the low-lying mass of clouds, fluttered like an angry hummingbird across rooftops and treetops, and released its fury upon the northwestern edge of the college campus before returning to the clouds whipping across the Miller Creek valley. And just like that it was over. Within minutes the sun's rays began to peek through the purple haze; shocked students and staff members stumbled out of precarious shelters that had almost become tombs to witness the devastation wrought by what locals called the worst storm in Batesville history. The steeple and two columns of the Brown Chapel lay in ruins. The swirling winds had uprooted trees, broken windows out of automobiles and dormitory rooms, and damaged the roofs of the dining hall and recreation building.[1]

The Masonic buildings, the center of campus activity since 1954, received the brunt of the attack. The westernmost structure, the Education and Psychology Building, was a heap of bricks, chairs, desks, and papers. Almost as severely damaged was the eastern building that housed the administrative offices. The tornado had removed part of the roof and the northern wall of the grand Long Memorial Building, former home of the library. Of all the structures on campus, only the Becknell Physical Education Building emerged completely unscathed. Miraculously, the storm had taken not a single life and had inflicted only a few minor bruises and abrasions. Students and faculty members in the science building and library realized that a tornado had passed over only when the subsequent power failure coaxed them toward the exits. President West canceled classes for the rest of the day as well as the following Good Friday, which inexplicably had been left off the holiday calendar for the year. After a frantic weekend of removing debris and estimating damage, classes resumed the following Monday. The college rented four small mobile homes to house administrative offices. Teachers whose classrooms had been destroyed wandered around campus much like Isaac Long and his pupils had drifted about town a century earlier, settling in empty rooms whenever possible or on grassy slopes and chapel steps on bright, warm days.[2]

While the tornado required more physical change and construction than President West had ever dreamed of when he came to Batesville in the fall of 1972, it was nevertheless a fitting symbol, albeit a violent one, of the general trauma of a new era at Arkansas College ushered in by the dawning of the 1970s and more specifically by the arrival of young Dan C. West. Although the college community had only begun to see the first clouds in the distance and hear the early rumbles of a storm by April 1973, the West era was just then on the cusp of bursting forth into the college campus's academic version of a tornado. The changes would come fast and furious in the 1970s. Dan C. West, mirroring the American Zeitgeist of the post–civil rights era, was no respecter of tradition for the sake of tradition; anything not bolted down was liable to be blown away in his onslaught. The Arkansas College campus during the West administration was no place for the faint of heart. Within a couple of years, more than a few students and faculty members would be huddled beneath their desks, figuratively of course, befuddled by a storm of innovation and staring out at an academic world turned upside down.

Reacting to tightening enrollment challenges and current trends in the world of higher education, Arkansas College in the 1970s moved rapidly to expand and diversify a curriculum that had been stripped of its utilitarian tendencies during the past decade and a half. In addition, under the leadership of Dan C. West, the college underwent a thorough bureaucratic transformation with the adoption of modern management and evaluation systems and the development of innovative fund-raising and marketing techniques. Nevertheless, even as the endowment experienced unprecedented growth, the college continued to struggle against the familiar nemeses, balancing the budget and filling classrooms and dormitories. Whether due to the myriad changes and innovations or in spite of them, by the late 1980s Arkansas College had risen into the top tier of small, independent institutions in the region, a remarkable accomplishment for an institution that had spent most of its existence teetering on the brink of collapse.

Regardless of one's interpretation of the events of the 1970s and 1980s, there is no denying the frenetic activity of the era. The hectic pace of change and innovation rendered the 1960s, the decade of constant physical expansion, tame and subdued by comparison. Despite the obvious similarities between West and McCain in terms of youth and inexperience, their respective administrations proved to be in many ways polar opposites. The West administration, which dominated the era in question, would have presented an even sharper contrast to the McCain years had it not been for the brief presidency of R. W. Wygle.

When McCain announced his resignation in the spring of 1969, board chairman

After the tornado, 1973.

Shuford Nichols appointed a presidential search committee chaired by Little Rock trustee Storm Whaley. Out of the four men interviewed for the position, the committee finally selected Ralph William Wygle, the forty-two-year-old dean of administrative affairs at Kansas State Teachers College in Emporia (now Emporia State University). Whaley had learned of Wygle while serving on a Presbyterian committee with the president of Kansas State Teachers College, and two Arkansas College faculty members, Roberta Dorr Brown and Stanley Reed, had met the Kansan a few years earlier when they were all going through the Ed.D. program at the University of Arkansas.[3] Arkansas College was no stranger to selecting presidents who seemed rather odd choices, but the appointment of R. W. Wygle as the institution's thirteenth president may have been the most uncharacteristic result of all presidential searches. Although Wygle was Presbyterian and had more than a decade of experience in a variety of faculty, staff, and administrative roles in higher education, he was the first nonsoutherner elected president of Arkansas College. More important, he was a newcomer to the world of the independent liberal arts college. His entire educational experience, as a student, teacher, and administrator, had been in the state-supported system, and this fact was bound to have an influence on his decision making and performance at Arkansas College.

Raised in central Kansas, Wygle served a stint in the army during the final year of

World War II, though his youth prevented him from seeing front-line action, and returned home afterward to earn a degree from Kansas State Teachers College in 1950. He spent most of the 1950s as a high school teacher and football coach, earned a master's degree from his alma mater in the meantime, and in 1958 joined the faculty of Kansas State Teachers College. For most of his eleven years in Emporia, however, he served in staff and administrative posts, rising from director of field services to administrative assistant to the president and finally to dean of administrative affairs.[4]

In several respects Wygle's arrival on the Batesville campus in October 1969 signaled the beginning of a new era for Arkansas College. The new first lady, Peggy Orine Wygle, was the first president's wife who was also a career woman. Although she slipped into the traditional role of nonworking first lady during their years in Batesville, Peggy Wygle was a trained librarian who had taught school for several years, and she would resume her out-of-home activities once the Wygles left Arkansas College. From the standpoint of appearance and personality, Bill Wygle contrasted sharply with his predecessor. A tall, broad-shouldered man, taller even than "Tall Paul" McCain and about twice as wide, Wygle, like his predecessor a former college football player, made quite a physical impression upon entering a room. And Arkansas College's new president had a personality to match his size. Outgoing and gregarious, the smiling, back-slapping Wygle put teachers and students alike at ease, and his loud, plaid suits contrasted with the traditional dark and solid attire of both his predecessors and successors. With his style of dress and casual demeanor, according to one faculty member, Bill Wygle looked more like an insurance salesman than a college president.[5]

At the end of the turbulent 1960s Arkansas College could certainly have used a good salesman. After peaking in mid-decade, full-time enrollment had dropped and then stabilized at around three hundred students; part-time students were almost unheard of, and most dormitory residents were natives of the Northeast, creating an increasingly sticky situation with board members and Batesville's business owners. The endowment had yet to break the one-million-dollar mark; the goal of $10 million by the fall of 1972 was almost too far-fetched to even consider without a chuckle or a sigh. Arkansas College also suffered image problems that hampered recruiting and denominational support. Many Presbyterian families in the state continued to view the Batesville school as a second-rate institution, and most sent their children elsewhere to college. Ironically, at the same time recent tuition raises and slacking efforts to recruit regional students contributed to the college's developing elitist image within north central Arkansas, and the large numbers of northeastern students further exacerbated the growing rift between Arkansas College and its geographical region. Despite such image problems, the declining number of local students was primarily attributable to the stringent (by Arkansas standards) liberal arts curriculum offered on the bluff, a curriculum that offered little in the way of professional training and career preparation.

Wygle attempted to address Arkansas College's challenges through his 3-F Program: Friends, Funds, and Freshmen.[6] Wygle's strategies for attracting the former two differed little from those that McCain had used in recent years: lots of fund-raising trips and Progress Fund dinners, instruction on the value of including the college in wills, and an increasing reliance on federal funds, especially the Title III, or Developing Institutions, grants that had paid for significant faculty expansion in the late 1960s. Direct federal grants were still relatively new phenomena in the fall of 1969, and their existence and proliferation both attributed to and mirrored a movement in the late 1960s and early 1970s whereby independent liberal arts colleges came to more closely resemble state-supported institutions. In his efforts to attract more freshmen, the final and most important part of the 3-F trio, Wygle brought his background in public education to bear on Arkansas College's gradual separation with tradition and embrace of experimentation.

The chief products of Wygle's brief administration, which would encompass less than three calendar years, were all rooted in the president's personality and his background in a regional, state-supported institution. They also owed something to the particular era in which Wygle directed the college. The Wygle administration's legacy at Arkansas College consisted of a new spirit of openness and cooperation manifested in the college's first internal governance system, a loosening of the social restrictions placed on residential students, and the beginnings of a process designed to expand the curriculum into nonliberal arts areas in an attempt to serve and attract more students from Batesville and the surrounding region. All of these developments share some sort of connection with a broader spirit of experimentation and willingness to forego tradition that would come to define the dawning age in the life of Arkansas College.

The old system whereby administrative mandates had been handed down to the faculty from on high, the system that had offered only a modicum of faculty input in most major college decisions, was contrary to everything that Wygle was and had known. During his first year in Batesville, the new president led a group of faculty, administrators, and students who drafted the constitution for a new system of governance, one that would greatly increase the input and power of both teachers and pupils. Under the "council system" put in place during the 1970–1971 academic session, the college community, or Council of Eligible Voters (later renamed the College Senate), was divided into three governmental bodies: the College Council, the only body on which the president sat, the Academic Council, and the Student Affairs Council. Each council contained voting members from the administration, the faculty, and the student body, and each exercised near autonomy within its own sphere. Faculty members hailed the new system as modern and inclusive, although an unintended byproduct of the council system was a severe curtailment of the power of the deans of academics and students, an oversight that drew criticism from the North Central Association. The new council system also created confusion among the student body, but most associated with the college saw it as a step in the right direction.[7]

The council system heralded a new spirit of openness on campus and within the college community. In an attempt to improve alumni support and participation, an Alumni Council was formed in the fall of 1969; two years later a Board of Ministers was organized to facilitate cooperation between the college and the church. In the summers of 1970 and 1971 Wygle organized "leadership retreats" on Greers Ferry Lake, informal gatherings that sparked conversation among faculty members, students, administrators, and trustees. Activities associated with the American Association of University Professors and American Association of University Women intensified, and in 1971 the trustees, acting on Wygle's request, voted to allow nonvoting representatives from the faculty and student body to attend board meetings for the first time. A new student court system gave students a greater degree of participation in disciplinary matters. It took only a few months for students to realize that Wygle was much more amenable to their entreaties than McCain had been. One particularly telling example involved the administration's decision to close down old Independence Hall and transfer its two dozen residents to other dorms after the fall 1969 semester. However, when Bill Bristow, a sophomore from Strawberry, circulated a petition and led a drive to encourage Wygle to reconsider, the president reversed his decision and the young men spent the spring of 1970 in the old dormitory. (It was abandoned at the end of the academic year.)[8]

Students also had input in the most important development in on-campus life in the early 1970s, the liberalization of visitation and alcohol policies in the dormitories. Wygle almost immediately began redesigning the dormitory system to bring it in line with more modern systems on nondenominational campuses. Student resident assistants gained greater authority, and the Student Affairs Council adopted controversial policy changes that approved open visitation on weekends, which meant that students could host members of the opposite sex in their dorm rooms subject to certain guidelines, and allowed students who were twenty-one or older to keep and consume alcoholic beverages in their rooms. Female students won a victory in the spring of 1971 when the Student Affairs Council voted to suspend dormitory curfews for students in good academic standing who had obtained letters of permission from their parents. Curfews for male students had been dropped years earlier. As might be expected, abuse of the new policies on alcohol and visitation ran rampant, a situation made worse by the increased reliance on student disciplinarians. Interestingly, to the chagrin of some students other campus rules survived, such as the prohibition toward going shoeless or sleeveless in the dining hall.[9]

The same spirit of experimentation and openness to new ideas infused Wygle's philosophy concerning the curriculum and the college's responsibility to its most accessible constituency, Batesville and the surrounding area that the president referred to as "a ten-county-wide laboratory." It was in the area of curricular expansion and innovation that Wygle's presidency held the most promise for fundamental change. In his 1971 report to the college community Wygle trumpeted a new era: "We must be willing to give up many of the traditional concepts about education. We must continue to examine our ideas that certain courses are required for the 'educated' person." During the first year of the Wygle administration, Arkansas College announced that it was reducing the general education requirement by seven hours, that it was dropping the religion major (at the behest of theological seminaries who sought ministerial students with a firmer foundation in the secular liberal arts), and that it was adding four new majors over the next two sessions: sociology-social work, political science, chemistry, and physical education, health, and recreation. Chemistry had been a popular major at Arkansas College in the past but had lost ground to biology after World War II; the addition of Roberta Bustin to the faculty in the late 1960s gave the college two chemistry professors and paved the way for an expansion of courses to support the new major. The other three were new majors in Batesville and represented fields that were either partially or wholly outside of the traditional liberal arts canon. All three could be justified for their practical value. The new James C. Becknell Physical Education Building, named for a Little Rock businessman and benefactor, was scheduled to be ready for use by the fall of 1970, and its modern facilities and equipment would support an expanded physical education program. Sociology and political science were increasingly popular fields of study on university campuses, and rural, impoverished north central Arkansas demanded more social workers and additional training for those already in the field. During the 1971–1972 year the Academic Council further expanded the curriculum to include programs in elementary education and medical technology, the latter of which included a year-long internship at an approved hospital. The council also adopted education professor Stanley Reed's draft of an experimental new major called Modern Cultural Institutions, a nebulous, and short-lived, course of study that combined a number of nontraditional methods of study such as internships, self-paced work, and interdisciplinary courses. Although it would be several years before the new elementary education program would be accredited by the National Council for Accreditation of Teacher Education (NCATE), in the fall of 1971 Arkansas College became the smallest institution in the United States to have its secondary education program fully accredited by NCATE. Wygle, the faculty, and trustees expected the addition of these new majors to bolster enrollment. In the fall of 1971 full-time enrollment reached its highest level since the postwar G.I. boom with 341 students.[10]

Other curricular and structural changes during the era represented an attempt to adopt popular innovations in higher education and a willingness to approve widely accepted programs in American colleges and universities. The 1969–1970 academic year was the first in which Arkansas College utilized the increasingly popular 4–1–4 calendar, which consisted of fall and spring semesters sandwiching a four-week January term in which students enrolled in only one intensive course. The January term was designed to foster faculty research and to enhance the regular curriculum by offering innovative, sometimes unusual courses into which students and professors could pour all their energies. Offerings in the early 1970s included War in Modern Literature, The Black Man in Modern Literature, The German Lieder, History of Social Welfare, Poverty in Arkansas, and The South: Problems & Perspectives. The January interim also provided Arkansas College its first opportunities for travel courses, both within the United States and abroad. One early example was a course that took students on a ten-day trip to study historical architectural styles along the South Atlantic coast. A variety of science, social science, and humanities offerings featured field trips within the region. In the college's first foreign class excursion, religion professor Fitzhugh Spragins led a group of students on a two-week tour of the Holy Land during the January term in 1970. One year later Charles Oliver directed a three-week workshop in Paris. Another development that appealed to students was the college's decision to offer Advanced Placement credit and College Level Examination Program (CLEP) tests beginning in the fall of 1971. Although most Arkansas high schools featured no Advanced Placement programs in the early 1970s, incoming freshmen could earn up to twenty-six hours through CLEP tests. Arkansas College received its first trio of "instant sophomores" in the fall of 1971 when Deborah Fulbright and Mark Wood of Batesville and Phillip Rains of Dennard passed enough tests to in effect complete their freshman years.[11]

Perhaps even more important than curricular expansion and innovation to student recruitment in the early 1970s was Wygle's emphasis on service to the region, a concept that was rooted in his experience at Kansas State Teachers College. He could point to at least one precedent in his drive to address the educational needs of north central Arkansas. Although McCain had shunned any kind of utilitarian catering to the needs and demands of the surrounding area in favor of a more traditional liberal arts college mission, Arkansas College had in the summer of 1967 received a federal grant to establish an Upward Bound program on campus. Directed by education professor Stanley Reed, the Upward Bound program brought rising high school seniors from low income families to the campus for an eight-week summer session designed to motivate them to continue their education beyond the secondary level. The students, who were recruited from a six-county area surrounding Batesville, then returned to campus about once a month during their senior years in high school. Upward Bound ultimately had only a minimal effect on recruiting, but the program proved important as a first step in connecting the college to its geographical region and in paving the way for the development of college-level programs aimed at a local clientele.[12]

Statistics revealed that by the early 1970s the once-plentiful supply of teenagers was beginning to dwindle as the baby boomers entered their twenties. Statistics also revealed that the fastest-growing segment of the college population consisted of students over the age of twenty-five (nontraditional students), and that it was this group that was helping fuel the furious expansion of community colleges across the nation. Just as Arkansas College had looked to the suburbs of the Northeast to solve its enrollment problems almost a decade earlier, in the early 1970s the Wygle administration hoped to bolster the school's head count by attracting large numbers of nontraditional students from Batesville and the surrounding region. The first two years of Wygle's tenure evinced a new willingness to serve the area with programs that lay outside the college's historical mission. In the spring of 1970 the college received a federal grant to assist with training a group of social workers for a five-county area. In the following summer Arkansas College catered to the growing fascination with Ozark folklore and music by hosting the first annual Ozark Folklore Workshop. Directed by folklorists and alumni John Quincy Wolf Jr. and Bess Millen Wolf and featuring a lecture and demonstration by noted musician Jimmy Driftwood, the Ozark Folklore Workshop attracted almost forty adult students from seven states. Arkansas College continued to sponsor the workshop for several more years, even after it moved to the newly opened Ozark Folk Center in 1973. In the fall of 1970 the college worked out an arrangement that allowed Arkansas State University in Jonesboro to offer extension graduate classes on the Arkansas College campus, thereby answering a popular demand among the region's teachers.[13]

When Wygle implored readers of the *Arkansas College Bulletin* to "seriously question the idea that 'college' means four years of study immediately following high school," he had two programs in mind that would or could alter that old notion: the Continuing Education program and a proposed junior college known as the Human Resources Center. Inaugurated during the 1971–1972 academic year, Continuing Education was (at least initially) a noncredit program designed for nontraditional students who sought improvement of job skills or simply looked to enrich their lives through learning. Offering weekend and evening courses on subjects as varied as sewing, yoga, and Morse code, Continuing Education attracted more than six hundred students during its first year, many of them drawn to one of the popular seminars on real estate appraisal. The program also included extension courses aimed at senior citizens in nearby retirement communities such as Cherokee Village and Fairfield Bay. Although Continuing Education was to become a key component of the college's mission for the next two decades, the Human Resources Center failed to get off the ground. Motivated by the State Board of Higher Education's suggestion that Batesville establish a community college, Wygle and his staff obtained a $20,000 grant from the Ozarks Regional Commission to conduct a feasibility study concerning the proposed junior college. Under the Human Resources Center plan that evolved during the 1971–1972 year, Arkansas College and Independence County would have cooperated in establishing what would have amounted to a two-year technical branch offering everything from secretarial training to plumbing and welding classes.[14]

Despite a flurry of activity, the Human Resources Center never materialized, and Wygle did not wait around to witness its demise. In January 1972, after less than twenty-eight months on the job, R. W. Wygle announced that he was resigning effective 30 June 1972 in order to assume the presidency of Northwestern State College in Alva, Oklahoma.[15] Praised by students and faculty for introducing a refreshing spirit of openness and cooperation to the little campus during his three years in Batesville, the president had nonetheless watched in amazement as the annual debt rose to a record-breaking $150,000 in the summer of 1971 before subsiding the following term.[16] Exhausted from the relentless demands of fund-raising and likely exasperated by the institution's lack of financial progress, Wygle was returning to familiar territory in the state university system on the Great Plains. His brief administration at Arkansas College would prove to be Wygle's first and last brush with the peculiar universe of independent liberal arts colleges. It had been an unseemly fit from the beginning. Strangely enough, however, the spirit of the Wygle years would live on in the wild and woolly days that followed.

Considering that the search for Wygle's replacement was the most thorough in the college's history to that time, it is quite surprising that it was also one of the quickest. Of course, it had been only three years since the last search, and the experience was still fresh on the minds of most trustees. In February 1972 chairman Shuford Nichols appointed longtime board secretary H. Carter Jeffery to chair the search committee. By the time the board got through appointing three subcommittees to help with the process, almost all the trustees, as well as a few faculty members, were involved with the search. Four months later Nichols introduced the new president to the full board of trustees. Dan Carlos West was a dapper, mustachioed young Texan, at thirty-three the youngest college president in Arkansas and the youngest in Batesville since a thirty-two-year-old Paul McCain had arrived in town two decades earlier. Despite his lack of experience, West appeared to be tailor-made for the presidency of this still small and still struggling institution. Born in Galveston during the waning days of the depression, West graduated high school in Dallas and attended the University of Texas for a year before making his way to the U.S. Naval Academy. He left Annapolis three years later without having taken a degree and earned his B.A. from Austin College, one of Arkansas College's sister institutions, in 1962. After receiving the B.D. degree from Union Theological Seminary in Virginia in 1965, West entered the ministry, spending more than three years as pastor of a Presbyterian church in suburban Nashville. In the meantime he pursued graduate studies in the Divinity School at Vanderbilt University. Shortly before taking his doctorate in divinity from Vanderbilt, West returned to Austin College to become director of church relations. When the Arkansas College search committee found him at Austin College in the spring of 1972, he was one of the busiest men on campus. Having recently been elevated to faculty status as an assistant professor of interdisciplinary studies, West also served as interim campus minister and as coordinator of an expansive, new educational project that would eventually overhaul almost every facet of life at Austin College. This was quite a burden for a young man, but, as the Arkansas College community would quickly discover, Dan C. West was no ordinary young man.[17]

The president who arrived on campus in August 1972 was, like McCain, a no-nonsense fellow who approached his job with a serious and dutiful mind. In contrast to the casual Wygle, West was a model of solemnity who brought back the dark suits and solid ties of Presbyterian college presidency. In later years faculty and students would joke that even in baby pictures Dan C. West was wearing a three-piece suit. The new first lady, Sidney Childs West, was therefore the perfect companion and ambassador. Batesville society had not seen the likes of Sidney West. Beautiful and outgoing, the vivacious Sidney struck up new and lasting friendships with the ease of walking across a room. Nevertheless, like her predecessor Sidney West, an Austin College alumna who held a master's degree from Vanderbilt, represented a new and modern breed of first lady. Her petite frame belied a fierce independence and an outspoken nature. Together the Wests exuded an intelligence and a passion for the cause of independent higher education that was contagious, especially within the broadening circle of the college's trustees and friends.[18]

Although an ordained minister, West was not cut from the mold of the minister-president of an earlier era. He was first and foremost an educational innovator and a resolute leader possessed of an acute business savvy. West came to Arkansas College brimming with ideas. Impressed with his self-confidence and his mastery of current trends in higher education, the trustees gave the young president near carte blanche to

The new president meets the press. *Pictured left to right:* H. Carter Jeffery Sr., Shuford Nichols, Dan C. West, and Sidney West.

jumpstart the struggling college. West's palette revealed a mixture of potential and ominousness. Only one-third of the college's full-time faculty members possessed terminal degrees, and only one tenured professor held a doctorate. Arkansas College and other independent schools faced increasing competition from less expensive state-supported institutions, and Arkansas was one of only a handful of states that offered no scholarship or grant money to students attending independent colleges. The endowment, just over $800,000, had been in stagnation for a decade, and the college had been forced to take out several short-term, high-interest loans to cover almost $175,000 in operating deficits during Wygle's first two years. In addition, Arkansas College still owed more than $2 million in low-interest federal loans from McCain-era building projects. In recent years the Nixon administration had slashed federal student aid funds, meaning that schools like Arkansas College, those that enrolled large numbers of low-income students, were forced with providing a higher percentage of financial aid out of strained institutional coffers. One immediate result of this situation was a drastic increase in Progress Fund goals, which reached half a million dollars in 1973–1974. And Arkansas College appeared no closer to attracting significant numbers of the coveted affluent students than it had been more than twenty years earlier when the merger committee had begun formulating plans for a first-rate liberal arts institution. Perhaps most foreboding of all was the recent flood of higher education literature forecasting the demise of dozens, perhaps hundreds of small, independent schools. Arkansas College was lumped among these "invisible colleges," as they came to be called by self-appointed experts, and because of this classification the Batesville institution was not expected to live long beyond its one-hundredth birthday.[19]

But not everything was doom and gloom. Despite the relative dearth of doctorates, the faculty in the early 1970s already contained a number of professors who would together comprise a foundation around which West would build the strongest group of educators in Arkansas College's history. The institution's endowment-building strategy, which relied heavily on benefaction, promised to pay off sometime down the road. The establishment of the McCain Scholarships in 1970, recipients of which had to show a B average in high school and a minimum of 1,000 on the SAT, had already begun to attract greater numbers of excellent students, and an overall increase in the college's financial aid offerings boosted full-time enrollment in the fall of 1972 to an all-time high of 391, 75 percent of whom were Arkansans.[20] Under the direction of chairman Shuford Nichols and vice-chairman Frank Lyon Sr., leadership potential on the board of trustees was stronger than ever before. And, perhaps most significant of all, the campus was in excellent condition and offered an effective mixture of tradition (the Masonic buildings) and modernity (most other structures had been completed within the past decade). The fact that the physical plant was complete and adequate for an even larger student body, with the possible need of adding a dormitory or two, was especially important to West. He had been recruited to Arkansas College to provide innovation and ideas, not to build. But we know how nature treats the best laid plans.

Dan C. West's initial year at the helm of Arkansas College was a whirlwind of activity. It would have been a breathless year even had West stayed in Texas, but the young president's presence contributed to the general hurly-burly. The 1972–1973 session was Arkansas College's centennial year. Technically, the previous academic year had been the one-hundredth in Batesville, but the centennial anniversary of the chartering of the college would not occur until October 1972, and the administration and faculty planned a full year of events centered around this milestone. During Wygle's final year on campus, a faculty committee chaired by history professor Dan Fagg and mathematics professor Ed Mosley selected the centennial theme: "*Humanitas*—A Continuing Ideal." Although Arkansas College had only periodically hosted a Latin class since Eugene Blandford retired twenty-one years earlier, Humanitas, whose many translations included humanity, culture, refinement, and civilization, was a fitting theme, both humble and noble at once. Considering the curricular changes then on the horizon, the theme of Humanitas, as we shall see, also contained a dose of irony. The year kicked off with a Centennial Convocation in September, West's first opportunity to address the full student body and faculty together. The college celebrated its Charter Day Commemoration in October by gathering on the downtown lawn in front of the institution's original building, now called Morrow Hall and owned by the First Presbyterian Church. West was joined on this occasion by the college's living former presidents, Wygle, McCain, and Thomas Lowry. Spectators witnessed the unveiling of a histori-

Four Arkansas College presidents at the centennial celebration in 1972. *Pictured left to right:* Paul McCain, R. W. Wygle, Thomas M. Lowry, and Dan C. West.

cal marker on the old downtown campus, identifying the location as the original home of Arkansas College, and on the present campus the presentation of a sundial containing the cornerstone from the old Isaac J. Long Memorial Building. Harlequin Theatre presented a special multimedia program entitled "AC/One C," which featured slides, film, and student portrayals of historical Arkansas College personalities.[21]

The highlight of the spring was the inauguration of Dan C. West on 12 April 1973. The celebration began the day before with a performance by the Austin College Concert Wind Ensemble and Harlequin's production of the Tennessee Williams play, "The Glass Menagerie," followed by a formal ball. The actual inauguration featured the singing of the Philander Smith College Gospel Choir and an address by West's mentor, Austin College president John D. Moseley. The inauguration festivities were designed to lead into the Centennial Commencement in May, but the tornado that strafed the campus one week later put a damper on the graduation exercises despite the address given by former secretary of state Dean Rusk, one of the most notable figures to ever appear on the Arkansas College campus.[22]

West contributed to the frenzied atmosphere during his first year on campus by launching an exhaustive nine-month study of all phases of the college's existence. Directed by two young newcomers to the faculty, economist Dennis Jacobe and social work professor and alumnus Robert Frank, the Arkansas College Evaluation and Planning Process was designed to evaluate and reorganize the college's aims for the next century by subjecting every facet of the institution, from its mission statement down to the budget of the maintenance department, to the intense scrutiny of modern economics and models of evaluation. The Evaluation and Planning Process in many ways resembled the planning effort that West had only recently taken part in at Austin College, though the outcomes and recommendations of the two studies would differ considerably. The result of all this evaluating and planning, a process that involved almost all faculty and staff in at least one committee, was what West called the "New Plan." The trustees approved this long-range guide at their May 1973 meeting.[23]

As West looked forward to his second year in the president's office, he itched to put into action the innovative New Plan but faced the more pressing question of sustaining a wounded institution and replacing the buildings destroyed by the tornado. Throughout the spring and summer of 1973 trustees and administrators haggled with the insurance company, considered building options, raised money for the emergency fund established soon after the tornado hit, and approached governmental agencies and private foundations to seek funds to help rebuild part of the campus. In the fall of 1973 the board approved a recommendation to demolish all three Masonic buildings. The two smaller structures were quite obviously beyond repair, but West's request for the destruction of the Long Memorial Building, the stateliest on campus and the one that appeared salvageable, elicited protests from some professors and students and attributed to a laggard insurance settlement that took more than two years to conclude. In the meantime, with the assistance of First District congressman Bill Alexander, the college secured a low-interest disaster loan of $900,000 from the Small Business Administration in addition to a $350,000 challenge grant from the Mabee Foundation in Oklahoma, at the time the largest gift the college had received from a private foundation.[24]

Given the scarcity of funds and the college's precarious financial situation, the board decided to replace the three razed buildings with a new administration building and an instructional annex to the library. Both new structures were ready for use by the time the fall 1975 semester got under way. The instructional annex, a U-shaped addition on the eastern side of the library that left an open courtyard in the middle, was partially funded by the Mabee grant, which prompted the board to christen the entire complex the J. E. and L. F. Mabee Learning Resources Center. The administration building, a ground-level, 10,000-square-foot structure, was located near the old Masonic buildings on the rise overlooking the Miller Creek valley on one side and Brown Chapel and the dining hall on the other. The college public relations department boasted that the new building was one of the first college structures in the country to use the "open office" concept, which involved movable modular partitions and furniture within a cavernous space in the middle of the building surrounded by a series of walled-in offices. Students were less enthusiastic about the new cubicle arrangement, a malady of architectural efficiency that would soon become synonymous with bureaucratic mundaneness. In the first *Highlander* critique of the new building, editor Gregory Cooper described the administration building as a "giant shoebox with a couple of sets of McDonald's 'golden arches' attached to the back." By the following fall, after students had come face to face with the cubicle partitions during registration, some took to referring to the institution's new center of operations as the "Money Maze." From the standpoint of aesthetics and tradition, the replacement of the Long Memorial Building with the new administration building was unfortunate indeed, but both structures were products of their respective eras and, in that sense, Arkansas College's administration building owed its design to the same spirit that gave the world Formica and Astroturf.[25]

The administration building and instructional annex turned out to be the first products of a flurry of building activity in what was supposed to have been a presidential administration devoted to other matters. The fall of 1975 also witnessed the dedication of the Charles W. Brown Student Housing Complex. Burgeoning enrollments during West's first years at Arkansas College forced the administration to move two mobile homes onto the eastern edge of campus and to maintain two off-campus houses for resident students. Faced with the need for more on-campus housing, the college and its architects followed the trend of eschewing traditional dormitories in favor of apartment-style housing structures. The Brown Complex, known to students as the Brown Apartments, consisted of six connected, two-story apartments, each housing six students. Constructed just east of the Morrow Quadrangle, the new housing complex was funded primarily through a gift from Clark N. and Mary Perkins Barton of El Dorado and at their request was named in honor of their pastor. Three years later the college completed another cluster of apartments adjacent to the Brown Complex, some of which were reserved for married students. This set of apartments was later named in memory of the recently deceased Clark N. Barton.[26]

By the time the Barton Apartments opened in the fall of 1978, Arkansas College students enjoyed a new student union. Plans for a student union, which was originally supposed to be built on to the eastern side of the dining hall, had languished in limbo for more than a dozen years before construction began in the summer of 1976. When students balked at the idea of building on to the dining hall, the administration and board agreed to construct a separate structure. Once again Arkansas College benefited from another substantial challenge grant from the Mabee Foundation, this one for $450,000. Erected on the knoll northeast of the Becknell Building, the new student union opened for business in the fall of 1977. In the meantime, the construction on and near what had been the intramural field east of the learning resources center spurred the relocation of outdoor intramural events to the hillside on the extreme southeastern corner of the campus, which in turn necessitated extensive landscaping on the "back forty" and around Bryan Lake. By this time the loop on the eastern side of campus connecting Highland Drive with College Street had also been completed.[27]

While brick and mortar necessities demanded much of West's attention during the 1970s and into the 1980s, it was curricular and organizational innovation that appealed most to the young president and that generated the most response, both on campus and in the media and in lights both negative and positive. The centerpiece of West's innovative design for the future of Arkansas College was the New Plan. Just as Franklin D. Roosevelt's New Deal (the simplicity of its title often shrouding the revolutionary effects of its particulars) had inspired both blind loyalty and rabid distrust four decades earlier, West's New Plan tended to polarize the college community into proponents or detractors. It was hard not to have an opinion on a plan that promised to make such sweeping changes.

We have already seen that Dan C. West was recruited to Arkansas College for the express purpose of restructuring a moribund curriculum and revitalizing a college in search of a purpose. Even before the official announcement of his hiring in the spring of 1972, religion professor Fitzhugh Spragins, the faculty's representative on the search committee, had written to West to assure him that "we are not tradition-bound in any way." Arkansas College was open to change, in fact needed change, and change is what it would get across the board. Citing the demand to "innovate or die," the New Plan attempted to stay "in the forefront of the educational community" through "managed innovation." From a management perspective, this entailed instituting modern techniques of zero-based budgeting and a system of management by objectives. From a curricular perspective, the one that affected the greatest number of people, this meant the expansion of the curriculum into professional, even technical, career-related areas, or the development of what the New Plan referred to as a "hybrid curriculum."[28]

Given the curricular expansion and modification that followed, the centennial theme of "Humanitas—A Continuing Ideal" seems both curious and curiously fitting. While the humanistic studies, to which the Latin humanitas refers implicitly, remained an integral component of the new core curriculum, the humanities suddenly found themselves on the periphery when it came to upper-level studies in the 1970s. Yet, Arkansas College had never held too tightly to the ideal of maintaining a focus on humanities or even on the "pure" and traditional liberal arts. The traditional curriculum had always been somewhat of a "continuing ideal," a goal frequently compromised out of necessity and pragmatism. As early as the 1880s, the curriculum reflected an attempt to provide for the more practical and utilitarian educational needs of a rural region largely unserved by normal schools and land-grant universities. During the two major postwar periods of the twentieth century, college administrators had been motivated by economics and practicality to institute such nonliberal arts studies as home economics and secretarial training.

If the past two decades had proven anything, it was that Batesville provided a poor laboratory for experimenting with a stripped-down liberal arts curriculum. Even after gaining accreditation and building a modern campus, Arkansas College, or so it seemed, lay too far off the beaten path to attract the affluent suburbanites that Bill McMillan and his merger committee had set their sights on in the early days of America's postwar boom. Batesville not only lacked access to the suburban enclaves that had in recent years sustained the expansion of Southwestern at Memphis, Austin College, Westminster College, and even Hendrix in Conway, but the state of Arkansas lacked any widespread historical commitment to the superior education that independent liberal arts colleges claimed to impart. For most parents and students living within the orbit of Arkansas College and Batesville, there was no distinction between an Arkansas College or a Hendrix on the one hand and an Arkansas State University or a University of Central Arkansas on the other. College was college, plain and simple, and it cost a great deal less to send a child to Jonesboro than to Batesville. Compounding matters locally was a movement on the part of state legislators to develop a community college system in Arkansas, and one of the potential sites targeted by state education officials was Batesville. West and other college leaders understood the dire implications such a development would hold for Arkansas College. Like so many small, poor colleges of the era—the "invisible colleges"—Arkansas College found itself in an unenviable predicament, caught somewhere in the limbo between maintaining the liberal arts ideal and catering to a wider public in an effort to keep the doors open.[29]

Arkansas College reacted to this predicament, then, in much the same way that dozens of other similar schools did in the 1970s: it tried to achieve a happy medium somewhere between the two extremes. According to one study, many small institutions in Arkansas College's class (Carnegie Category II colleges) compromised their traditional liberal arts missions in the 1970s by expanding into professional and occupational programs and by trying to become in effect small, comprehensive, regional universities.[30] This was a survival strategy, a response to the demand to "innovate or die," and Arkansas College and Dan C. West proved to be innovators. Given Arkansas College's historical flirtation with the attractive yet fickle utilitarianism, it would be easy to overstate the degree to which the New Plan actually compromised the institution's liberal arts tradition. Nonetheless, the New Plan certainly went beyond anything that West's predecessors had ever imagined. Whereas previous administrations had waded around the edges of the pool of professional and nonliberal arts education, always avoiding the forbidden waters further from shore, under the New Plan West and his administrators were preparing to dive headfirst into the deep end.

The New Plan did not propose to completely abandon the liberal arts focus at Arkansas College. Instead, it called for the addition of career preparation options to the existing curriculum, including some nondegree programs that would require only one or two years to complete. Much of West's vision was built around the dictum: "He is not a failure in life if he does not continue for four years of college," a statement that could have come from the mouth of R. W. Wygle. The motivation for that dictum was a set of statistics that revealed that the vast majority of high school students from the ten-county region surrounding Batesville who planned to pursue some kind of post-secondary education had in mind training for a job. Furthermore, in recent years four in five of Arkansas College's graduates had entered the job market immediately after graduation, and a large percentage of those entered the teaching field. Few used their Arkansas College education in a traditional liberal arts manner, as a steppingstone to graduate or professional school.[31]

The feasibility study conducted for Wygle's proposed Human Resources Center showed that the three most popular areas of study among students from north central Arkansas were business, community service (which included teaching), and health science and service. With programs in secondary, elementary, and physical education as well as the beginnings of a social work program, the college already had a good start in the area of community service education, but only the recently instated medical technology program and the old business and economics major addressed the other two areas. Thus the New Plan identified business management and health services as the top priorities for expansion. Between 1973 and 1975 Arkansas College added majors (now renamed concentrations under the New Plan) in business administration, business finance, public administration, office administration, data processing, community health administration, environmental health, health care administration, and medical office administration. In the late 1970s the college instituted concentrations in accounting, media arts, and health education. In addition, two-year programs were inaugurated in secretarial administration, data processing, environmental health technology, hospital unit management, and medical office assistance. Although the college granted a number of certificates to students who completed one of the two-year courses of study, differences of opinion on the board prevented the trustees from ever approving West's recommendation to issue the associate of arts (A.A.) degree.[32]

The new concentrations in the areas of business and health also received their own divisions under the New Plan. Among the structural changes enacted by the New Plan was a reformulation of the old three-division curriculum (science, social science, and humanities) into five programs: business management, health science, community service, humanities, and the core curriculum. The new curricular structure proved a bit confusing to students and faculty at first, and the shuffling of old and new concentrations from one program to another often made for strange bedfellows, as when history professor Jane Fagg found herself in charge of the business management program. Of the five programs, business management and community service represented the most obvious departures from the traditional liberal arts curriculum; nevertheless, throughout the preceding decade business and education had consistently ranked as the two most popular areas of study at Arkansas College. The health sciences program offered technical and professional concentrations alongside standards such as biology and chemistry, which were reduced to tracks within the new life sciences concentration. Likewise, within the community service program, the fields of psychology, sociology, and social work were lumped into a new concentration in behavioral science. The humanities program, once the center of academic life at Arkansas College, was reduced to peripheral status with concentrations in history, literature, and theatre as well as a new one in American Studies, a hodgepodge of humanities and social sciences that gained widespread acceptance on American campuses following the folk explosion of the 1960s. Two longtime majors, music and mathematics, found themselves in unfamiliar programs and relegated to tract status within teacher education.[33]

No area of the curriculum experienced more change at the hands of the New Plan than did the college's traditional general education requirements. Renamed the core curriculum and reduced from forty-four to thirty-one hours, this fifth program received a thorough overhaul. Again, West's recent experience at Austin College, which had just undertaken a massive restructuring of its core, influenced the process. Under the New Plan, the core curriculum was divided into three parts—Communications, the Contemporary World, and the Western Tradition—and within each part traditional general education courses were altered to fit the college's new broader mission and to make use of current classroom innovation. Communications basically consisted of courses in speech and composition. The Contemporary World offered students limited choices among introductory courses in the sciences, mathematics, world history, comparative government, human behavior, literature, the arts, and Christianity. An unheralded byproduct of the new core, and one that reflected the continuing secularization of the denominational college curriculum, was the absence of a Bible course, which meant that for the first time in the history of the institution freshmen were not required to take the course that had years earlier been at the center of an Arkansas College education. The discarding of the mandatory Bible course, combined with the disappearance of required chapel attendance, reflected Arkansas College's quarter-century evolution from conservative Presbyterian college to "church-related college" in the broadest sense. Like most mainstream Protestant institutions, Arkansas College since midcentury had undergone the gradual "shift from a relatively narrowly defined Christianity to a broadly defined liberal Christianity that could be equated with civilization itself," according to historian George M. Marsden. The most innovative part of the new core curriculum was a series of three courses concentrating on Christianity's secular replacement as the "source of coherence" in the modern liberal arts curriculum, the Western humane tradition. Designed for juniors and seniors as a capstone to the undergraduate education—a secular descendant of the nineteenth century's moral science course—the Western Tradition courses were interdisciplinary and allowed students to work at their own pace. Some of the other core courses also required interdisciplinary approaches such as team teaching, and all embraced the popular innovations and experimental teaching methods of the day such as audiovisual aids, independent study, and peer review and instruction.[34]

While the changes to the core curriculum represented a sharp and conscious break with the institution's immediate past, other parts of the New Plan simply called for expansion of programs put into place or proposed during the Wygle administration. With the help of a federal grant, one of only six of its kind issued to independent colleges, Arkansas College established a Cooperative Education program, which allowed students in a variety of concentrations to earn up to twelve credits (as hours became known in the West era) for off-campus, on-the-job training. Cooperative Education embodied an extension of the hands-on career preparation concept already utilized in student teaching and in the year-long medical technology practicum. The West administration also pursued Wygle's Human Resources Center/community college proposal. Arkansas College and the education committee of the Batesville Chamber of Commerce asked the state attorney general's office to consider the constitutionality of setting up a publicly funded two-year institution under the control of a private college; however, when the attorney general's office took more than a year to reply, local leaders spearheaded the establishment of Gateway Vocational-Technical School in Batesville, a development that, according to a relieved West, "obviated the need for a community college."[35]

Of more lasting and significant impact to the West years at Arkansas College was the Continuing Education program, which had been inaugurated during the final year of the Wygle administration. West saw several possibilities in Continuing Education. Statistics showed that more than 60 percent of all American college students attended on a part-time basis, and most of these were nontraditional working adults who filled evening classrooms. By catering to this growing body of students, the college stood to increase revenue and possibly recruit a few into the ranks of full-time students. Furthermore, Continuing Education provided a system and schedule that separated the technical and career-related offerings from the regular curriculum. In 1975 Arkansas College began offering college credit for some of its Continuing Education classes at the same time that a series of federal grants allowed for an expansion of course offerings designed for senior citizens, women, and health care personnel. As a result, the number of Continuing Education classes more than doubled to thirty-five and in 1976–1977 reached forty-four. Nevertheless, throughout the decade the college experienced mixed success with the program; evening credit courses tended to be among the least popular, while noncredit real estate seminars and courses designed for specific occupational groups at one or more of the local manufacturing plants drew the largest crowds. In 1976 the college announced a new senior citizen rate of five dollars per credit. The cheap tuition available to those over fifty-five attracted more students but less revenue, and West, the trustees, and the faculty worried that the wide range of Continuing Education offerings—from Preventive Medicine for Cattle to macrame and guitar lessons—tarnished the college's already less-than-phenomenal image. In spite of image concerns, the Continuing Education program became an integral component in the college's growth strategy in the 1980s, and, under the direction of Arkansas College's jack-of-all-trades Jim Mitchum, by the mid-1980s the program attracted more than three hundred part-time students each year.[36]

By the time the tornado called the New Plan got through with Arkansas College much had been changed, both cosmetically and fundamentally, and the things that had escaped alteration had nonetheless undergone thorough evaluation. West installed Roberta Dorr Brown in the new office of institutional research and development (later planning) and recruited young mathematics professor and alumnus Ed Mosley to replace her as dean of instruction (formerly academic dean.) The New Plan replaced the dean of students with the director of guidance services, a position that took on extra administrative duties with the introduction of a campus minister and a director of evaluation and placement. The changes in almost every area of the college struck many faculty members, especially veteran ones, as too much too quickly. In the spring of 1973 Fitzhugh Spragins warned the board of trustees that the New Plan had demoralized the faculty, many of whom felt there had been too little faculty input in the evaluation and planning process that produced the plan.[37] These nascent protests would intensify soon enough.

By the end of West's second year in Batesville, the young president had a budding insurrection on his hands. A corps of veteran professors protested almost every facet of the New Plan, from its restructuring of academic divisions down to its rapid expansion of the curriculum in career-oriented directions. West had also directly contributed to the growing disaffection by placing a moratorium on tenure while a committee undertook a thorough evaluation of the college's outmoded procedures, by eliminating merit pay increases, by awarding the largest raises to low-ranking professors, and by reducing others, including popular music professor Dorothy Landis Gray, to part-time status. Most of the faculty's resentment, however, stemmed from what they viewed as West's haughty, dictatorial management style. West openly chafed under the inclusive governance system that Wygle had introduced, claiming that the unwieldy council system hamstrung his efforts by placing too many needless checks on presidential prerogative. With a stubbornness that so often accompanies the visionary and the young, he was determined to see his program through, even in the face of widespread faculty discontent. From the standpoint of veteran professors who had labored in silence during the McCain administration, Wygle's council system had provided the faculty a new and powerful voice in college affairs, one that they would not give up without a fight. In May 1974 the discontent bubbled over and produced two closed-door faculty meetings at which some professors called for West's immediate resignation. The president, who enjoyed the unwavering support of the board of trustees, remained at the helm. He would face his toughest challenge yet in the coming year.[38]

The 1974–1975 academic year delivered the coup de grace of the controversial New Plan, at least as far as most students and many professors were concerned. Students who enrolled in the fall of 1974 found a strange new calendar for the coming year. The Arkansas College Diversified Calendar abandoned the 4–1–4 setup that had been in use for the past five years and in the process, argued some students and faculty, abandoned common sense. Developed by a faculty committee, the diversified calendar sought to combine the advantages of a quarter system with the "Colorado System," a recent innovation at Colorado College that featured nine one-month blocks within a school year. Another product of the spirit of educational experimentation that permeated the era, the diversified calendar, a unique hybrid of sorts, divided the year into quarters, with the winter and summer quarters broken into one-month modules. This translated into the clumsy numeration 3–1–1–1–3. It also translated into immediate student and faculty protest. Although designed to provide scheduling flexibility, a greater opportunity for innovative and self-paced course work, and more faculty released time for research, when put into practice the diversified calendar turned into a nightmare. Professors struggled to adapt traditional, semester-long courses to quarters, or even to one-month modules, and students struggled to collect a sufficient number of credits. An article in the *Highlander* argued that "the [New Plan] forces students to take fewer classes, pay more for them and get less out of them." The self-paced nature of some modular courses overlapped with more structured classes, creating a confusing and difficult system for students and teachers alike. Furthermore, the innovative calendar, the only one of its kind in the state, wreaked havoc on extracurricular activities, especially varsity sporting events.[39]

This time both faculty and students protested. In the spring of 1975 the faculty adopted a resolution criticizing West's dictatorial leadership style and the board of trustees for granting raises that failed to cover the increase in the cost of living. Most also voiced complaints against the new calendar. Students were even more vehement in their protests, many of them motivated by a simultaneous struggle with the president over dormitory regulations. Claiming that the liberal alcohol and visitation rules put in place during the Wygle administration had resulted in anarchy in the dormitories, West banned alcohol from campus and restricted visitation privileges beginning in 1974–1975, the same year the diversified calendar went into effect. When the College Council declared West's unilateral rules unconstitutional according to the governance system, the president vetoed the council's ruling, earning a fresh wave of faculty and student resentment. Furthermore, in October 1974 West informed all students under the age of twenty-one who were living in apartments off campus that they would be required to move back on to campus or back home. The succeeding months produced a barrage of *Highlander* editorials critical of the president and a constant stream of informal and formal campus discussions of the administration and the New Plan. Student editors referred to the campus under West's direction as a "police state" and complained that the administration was "more concerned with finances and favorable publicity than the needs and interests of the students." The spirit of dissent reached its peak on the evening of Wednesday, 9 April 1975, when about fifty students, led by the Student Government Association's treasurer-elect Misty Thillen, converged on the Wests' front lawn to protest the diversified calendar, by now a lightning rod for all campus controversies. Two weeks later the College Council voted to reinstate the 4–1–4 calendar, and this time the president did not use his veto.[40]

With the return to the comfortable calendar and with the arrival of the personable and popular Robert Knott to occupy the newly created office of dean of the college, the most serious student protest abated. Nevertheless, students continued to agitate for greater SGA authority and a return to more lenient dormitory regulations for two more years. In the spring of 1977 West vetoed a proposed Student Affairs Council policy that would have liberalized visitation hours and allowed twenty-one-year-olds to keep alcohol in their rooms; the issue would not come up again, at least in a formal manner, for the rest of the West administration. Fortunately for West, his relationship with the board of trustees suffered none of the low points of his relationships with the student body and the faculty. In the final estimation, the ability to sell his vision to the board and to the college's various constituencies may have been West's greatest talent. For the first four years of the West administration, Shuford Nichols served as chairman of the board and mentor to the young president. Nichols's experiences at Arkansas College in the late 1920s, a golden age of sorts in terms of student quality and activity, and his later years at Washington and Lee had left an indelible impression on him. His vision for what the college could become, a first-rate, residential institution focusing on the liberal arts, sprang largely from those early experiences. Nichols's confidence in the college's ability to one day achieve this vision carried the board through the difficult days of the late 1960s and early 1970s and inspired discouraged trustees and friends to stick with the little school. Sophisticated, intelligent, and well traveled, Nichols led with a quiet and understated authority. He would remain a faithful and influential member of the executive committee and counsel to West even after he relinquished the chairmanship.[41]

When Nichols stepped down after eleven years as chair in 1976, the trustees elected the logical choice, the humble yet firm leader who had served on the board

The president and the chairmen of the board. *Pictured left to right:* Dan C. West, Frank Lyon Sr., and Shuford Nichols.

since the days of the Spragins presidency, the master salesman and successful businessman who had devoted much of his nonprofessional life to raising money for and advancing the cause of Arkansas College. Frank Lyon Sr. and Dan C. West forged a professional and personal working relationship as close as or closer than any between an Arkansas College chairman and president since the days of Thomas Welch and Isaac Long. Surpassing mere friendship and collegiality, Lyon became a father figure to the young president and became intimately involved in the college's affairs. Marion Bradley Lyon and Sidney West became even closer friends. Almost inseparable, the two traveled together and became de facto interior designers for each new building project on campus. Both were instrumental in inspiring an unprecedented level of interest in the college among the wives of the mostly male board of trustees. And it was through the influence of Marion Lyon's mother, who had helped establish the Women of the Church's Loving Hearts Scholarships, that Frank Lyon Sr. had first gained an interest in Arkansas College years earlier.[42]

By the time he assumed the chairmanship of the board in 1976, Lyon had already established himself as a statewide proponent of private higher education. In the early years of West's administration, Lyon and the young president worked side by side to influence the state legislature to establish a scholarship fund, similar to programs already in existence in most other states, that could be used at either state-supported or independent institutions. In 1973 West spearheaded a movement that resulted in the founding of the Arkansas Council of Independent Colleges and Universities (ACICU), an organization whose primary purposes were to defeat the proposed community college system and to pursue scholarship legislation. In the following year Lyon served as chairman of the Committee for Greater Access to Higher Education, which brought the power and influence of members of the state's business and professional classes to bear on the state assembly and other politicians. The community college proposal was eventually replaced with a bill providing for the creation of vocational-technical schools. The ACICU and the Committee for Greater Access convinced 1974 gubernatorial candidate David Pryor of the value of their campaign, and in 1975 the state legislature passed a bill establishing the State Scholarship Program, which provided up to $300 for eligible, first-time college students from Arkansas. The State Scholarship Program was declared constitutional by a federal district court two years later. By the early 1980s Arkansas College was receiving more than $40,000 annually from the program.[43]

Lyon's involvement in the push for the State Scholarship Program reflected a developing sensibility among board members during the West years. Trustee interest and participation grew rapidly during the 1970s, so much so that West praised the board as the best in the college's history. The young president realized that an active, powerful, and enthusiastic board was a necessity for the growth and survival of any small college. Through a combination of restructuring the committee system, wise recruiting of new members, and increased cultivation of the time and efforts of veteran trustees, West, Nichols, and Lyon molded a lively board whose meetings ceased to revolve around rubber-stamping the various articles of the president's report. During the early years of his administration, West enjoyed the advice and experience of a strong block of veteran local trustees: H. Carter Jeffery Sr., John P. Morrow Jr., Nels Barnett, W. D. Murphy Jr., and Stanley Wood Sr. In later years other Batesville residents, including attorney Sam Highsmith and Arkansas Eastman head M. L. Gernert, and Newport trustees P. K. Holmes and Kaneaster Hodges Jr. stepped in to carry on the tradition of strong local leadership.[44]

But, as had been the case for many years, the prestige and power of the board came primarily from outside of Arkansas College's region, and the trend toward non-Batesville control continued. West urged the board to rethink its committee structure; one of the key results was abandoning the old system whereby the executive committee was composed only of Batesville trustees and the chairman of the board. Under the influence of Little Rock residents Nichols and especially Lyon, more and more board meetings and functions found their way to the state capital. West inherited a number of seasoned and valuable trustees from around the state: W. C. Brown Jr., Violet Miller, and William T. Couch of Hot Springs; William H. Dunklin of Pine Bluff; Harold Ohlendorf of Osceola; Bill McMillan of Arkadelphia; and Frank Sloan of Jonesboro. The president, as well as other board members, recruited a number of others who proved valuable assets to the college: Robert A. Young III of Fort Smith, Ferd A. Bellingrath of Pine Bluff, Charles J. Hoke of El Dorado, Herbert C. Rule III of Little Rock, Larry Derby of Warren, R. Sloan Wilson of Little Rock, and James G. Williamson Jr. of Conway. By the time West arrived in Batesville the board had expanded its boundaries beyond the state of Arkansas. The merging of the Synods of Arkansas and Oklahoma had brought the first non-Arkansans to the board in 1969, and the creation of the Synod of Red River during the first year of West's presidency expanded the college's synodical area to also include Texas and Louisiana. Within a few years Arkansas College counted among its trustees Texans Graham Holloway, Anne Stewart, and Hugh M. Patterson (also an alumnus), Elizabeth Hicks of Louisiana, and Oklahoman J. Marshall Huser.[45]

West also utilized his background in church relations to maintain a strong bond with the college's shifting synodical and denominational bodies. The young president inherited the newly established Board of Ministers (later renamed the Board of Visitors), and during West's initial year in Batesville, Arkansas College signed a covenant with the new Synod of Red River that allowed the synod to elect to the college's board of trustees only people nominated by the board. This, in essence, created a self-perpetuating board of trustees. Although the establishment of self-perpetuating boards was one of the trends of a decade in which many private colleges distanced themselves from denominational traditions or severed those ties completely, under Dan C. West Arkansas College actually strengthened its ties to the church. In the fall of 1973 Bob Lively arrived in town as the college's first campus minister. Lively established the Campus Ministry Board and inaugurated that organization's annual Hunger Walk during his two years at Arkansas College, and his popular replacement, Charles "Buddy" Hughes, continued to spark both spiritual and secular interest with his Coffee Pot Chapels and other programs in the post-mandatory-chapel era. Ben Collins, Ed Bayless, and others maintained a ministerial presence on the board of trustees, while various college personnel took active roles in Presbyterian affairs.[46] West, himself an ordained minister, played a leading role in the merging of the southern Presbytery of East Arkansas with the northern Presbytery of the Ozarks to form the Presbytery of Arkansas (Union) in 1973 and helped convince the new body to contribute $10,000 annually to the scholarship funds of Arkansas College and the College of the Ozarks. And, despite the fact that synodical and presbyterial donations accounted for an increasingly minute portion of the annual budget, Arkansas College continued to draw the largest number of its trustees and significant donors from the Presbyterian Church. Observing the college's maintenance of denominational ties and strengthening of church relations is not to say that Arkansas College somehow turned back the tide of the secularization of higher education. By the mid-1970s mandatory chapel was a relic of the past, and the core curriculum had been purged of traditional Bible courses. Nevertheless, the revised core that took effect in 1979 reinstated a mandatory one-semester introductory Bible class.[47]

The often confusing consolidations and discussions of cooperation among the various Presbyterian organizational bodies in the 1970s also resurrected an old bugaboo that had been buried for more than two decades—the looming specter of merger with the College of the Ozarks. At the very moment Arkansas College was celebrating its centennial year and before the Wests could get everything unpacked in the president's house, the Presbyterian Synods of the Sun (northern church) and Red River (southern) began discussing a possible union. Although such cooperation at the synod level would wait another decade, back-room discussions ultimately turned to the subject of the little state of Arkansas and its two struggling Presbyterian colleges. As early as West's first semester at Arkansas College, the young president began correspondence with Ozarks president Don Davis regarding methods of cooperation between the two schools. Both institutions appeared particularly vulnerable. Arkansas College was struggling to pay its mounting bills in what West referred to as "a critical juncture in its development," and the Synod of Red River had recently announced its intentions to cut off the $40,000 it paid to the institution each year. The tornado of April 1973, and the extensive rebuilding the college faced as a result, provided further impetus for West to seek a merger. The financial situation for the College of the Ozarks was even more grim. Beginning with the 1973–1974 academic year the Clarksville school would no longer receive the $300,000 previously given by the Board of Missions of the United Presbyterian Church in the U.S.A.[48]

The discussions between West and Davis sparked a strategy meeting in early 1973, and the following months produced a stream of scenarios and conjecture. The union of Arkansas's two presbyteries in October 1973 punched cooperation efforts into high gear. Shortly before Christmas, representatives from the two institutions met in Little Rock and discussed, among other things, the possibility of merging the colleges and building a new campus at Ferncliff, a Presbyterian retreat and conference center on the western edge of Little Rock. By the spring of 1974 merger talks had advanced to the point where West had drafted a broad blueprint for "A Presbyterian College in Little Rock, Arkansas." Although the merger matter had not yet come before the entire board, the leaders of Arkansas College tacitly approved the basic concept of merging and relocating to central Arkansas. Nichols and Lyon, the two most influential trustees, lived in Little Rock, and Lyon had long liked the idea of a Presbyterian institution in Arkansas's largest city. Echoing the failure of an earlier day, however, talks came to an abrupt end in the summer of 1974 when President Davis of Ozarks resigned and the executive committee of that college's board shot down the merger proposal.[49]

The merger talks refused to go away this time, however. Two years later "cooperation" talks resumed between West and new Ozarks president R. L. Qualls, and a grant from the Winthrop Rockefeller Foundation funded an in-depth study into the possible means of cooperation between or union of the institutions. Once again the resignation of an Ozarks president cooled the discussion when Qualls stepped down, and merger talks smoldered beneath the surface for a couple of years before rising phoenix-like in the summer of 1980. Urged along by officers of the Synod of Red River, by West, and by former Ozarks president Qualls, board chairman Frank Lyon Sr. met with Ozarks chairman Tracy Kelly to discuss the possibility of a "merger/takeover by Arkansas College of the College of the Ozarks," whose enrollment had dipped below 150 during the previous session. By the fall, however, an improved enrollment, the arrival of a new president, and an obstinate board of trustees had diminished the appeal of merger in Clarksville.[50] Even the permanent reunion of the two general assemblies three years later failed to rekindle the issue. The champions of merger had come up short again. Their dream for a nationally recognized college on the outskirts of Arkansas's largest metropolitan center, an institution that would finally be able to compete with Hendrix for students and publicity, waned as the administration of Jimmy Carter came to an end. But the champions of merger had also learned a lesson from the 1951 event; the talks of the 1970s and 1980 had been restricted to high-level, confidential meetings. No educational experts painted glowing visions of a potential elite institution. No trustees publicly criticized the poor quality of education offered at either school. Life would continue on in Batesville and Clarksville as if the merger discussions had never taken place.

One of the primary reasons for the subsequent declining interest in merger on the part of Arkansas College was its increasingly stable financial situation, which received an unexpectedly large ballast less than a year after the most recent discussion with the College of the Ozarks when aged Jean Brown left the Batesville institution more than $14 million in her will. In Dan C. West's nine years before the Brown bequest of 1981, the college had witnessed a slow but steady rise in the endowment, a successful capital funds campaign, and frequent cash flow problems. For years the two biggest challenges for Arkansas College had been the enrollment and finances. West inherited a school with a paltry endowment of some $820,000. Thanks to a few large bequests, that figure almost doubled during the first year of West's administration; nevertheless, the endowment continued to cover less than 10 percent of the annual budget, and it was a far cry from the $10 million goal adopted during the McCain years. In 1974 the college approved a more reasonable goal of reaching $5 million by the end of the 1980–1981 academic year. Furthermore, in

1973 the board of trustees amended its endowment policy to create a reserve endowment, officially the Arkansas College Reserve Fund, the principal from which could be spent to cover deficits and other immediate costs. This new endowment agreement gave trustees the authority to place unrestricted gifts (those not specified for a particular use) into the reserve fund instead of into the permanent endowment.[51]

In December 1974 Arkansas College launched its most ambitious fund-raising project to date, the $3 million Challenge of the Decade Campaign. Directed by vice-president for development John Mays and trustee William T. Couch, an engineer and businessman from Hot Springs, the campaign received an enthusiastic response within the church and among the college's longtime friends and ended three years later having exceeded the goal by $250,000. Although most of the proceeds from the campaign were funneled into building projects, more than a quarter of the money earned found its way into the permanent endowment, which by the end of 1977 exceeded $3.5 million. The growing endowment found itself in increasingly able and savvy hands as new trustees such as Ferd Bellingrath and Robert A. Young III, and later Graham Holloway, lent their financial acumen to the investments subcommittee. In spite of the endowment's growth and higher earning rates, however, skyrocketing costs increased the annual budget to such an extent that the earnings from that $3.5 million accounted for only 5.6 percent of the college's revenue during 1976–1977.[52]

By the summer of 1981 additional efforts had raised the endowment to approximately $6 million. Nevertheless, the endowment continued to contribute a relatively small amount to yearly income, leaving the college in a vulnerable state. By the late 1970s Arkansas College's number-one source of revenue was the government; close to 30 percent of the school's income came from federal programs and state scholarship monies. During the decade the institution experienced an unusual amount of success in securing a variety of government educational grants, mostly due to the untiring efforts of vice-president for planning Roberta Dorr Brown. Brown's efforts proved so lucrative, in fact, that as early as 1976 trustees began to openly question the college's growing reliance on federal largesse. Still, the combination of annual gifts and tuition covered more than half the budget; consequently, Arkansas College was susceptible to the whims of the economy and the vicissitudes of enrollment. When the Challenge of the Decade Campaign deflected interest and energies away from the Progress Fund drive in the mid-1970s, annual fund-raising fell off sharply; this, combined with an unexpected drop in enrollment, produced a deficit for 1977–1978 and constant cash flow problems in succeeding years that required the board to dip into the Reserve Fund on a few occasions. Annual financial struggles peaked during the 1979–1980 year. Reduced tuition receipts due to another unexpected drop in enrollment, soaring utility costs, and high interest payments on recent short-term loans—at one point the college faced $335 per day in interest charges alone—resulted in a projected budget deficit of $225,000, which was in addition to more than $260,000 in deficits accrued in past years. The business committee of the board of trustees slashed more than $100,000 from the next year's budget, much of it in the area of faculty salary and raises. Ultimately, it was a combined gift of $1 million from siblings Jean and W. C. Brown Jr. that helped balance the budget and reduce short-term debt.[53]

The years surrounding the switch from the decade of the seventies to the decade of the eighties marked a time of reckoning for Arkansas College. Within the Arkansas College community, the tremendous bequest of Jean Brown has often been viewed as a watershed, a single event that so altered the current of events as to be identified forever with history's other crucial moments. The Jean Brown bequest can also be seen as something of a capstone on a process already in motion. And this altered description of one of the college's most important events does not imply that the institution's greatest bequest was somehow unworthy of watershed status; rather it suggests that the events of August and September 1981 assume an even greater importance when considered in the context of the college's immediate past.

It did not take long for reality to set in for the West administration. The furious professional and career-focused curricular expansion of the early and mid-1970s did not burgeon class rolls as planned. Enrollment during the decade peaked in the fall of 1974 at 462 full-time equivalent (FTE) students. With five years of steady growth bolstering confidence, Arkansas College prognosticators predicted that the number of on-campus students would more than double to 406 by 1979 and that FTE enrollment would exceed 600 by the end of the decade. A sudden and unexpected decline in enrollment at mid-decade laid waste to the college's goals, exacerbated financial struggles, and forced a reevaluation of the mission and programs generated by the New Plan. Beginning in 1977 an increased emphasis on expanding Continuing Education offerings and local recruiting swelled the student body's total head count, but full-time attendance stagnated. West witnessed a succession of short-term admissions directors pass through campus throughout the decade, and, with no other solution in sight, in 1979 hired a private firm, D. H. Dagley and Associates of Atlanta, to manage the admissions office.[54]

Dagley and Associates faced the unenviable task of boosting enrollment at a college that had historically struggled to recruit large numbers of students. Compounding this difficulty was statistical evidence showing that the college-age population would decline sharply in the 1980s. As if these two major obstacles were not enough, statistics also revealed that Arkansas, second only to Mississippi in terms of poverty, ranked last among all southern states in the percentage of its college-age inhabitants enrolled in higher education. The college injected yet another factor that would prove a challenge to any massive recruiting campaign, stricter admissions standards. The growth in enrollment of the early 1970s had been accomplished in a way that frequently sacrificed student quality. Consequently, by mid-decade the overall quality of the student body had suffered a noticeable decline. In most years a majority of incoming freshmen at Arkansas College scored below the national average on the American College Test (ACT), and a study of the Graduate Record Examination (GRE) results of the class of 1976 revealed that Arkansas College graduates ranked in the twenty-second percentile in humanities and in the thirty-sixth percentile in natural sciences. The poor quality of the student body also contributed to a bloated attrition rate, as many of the most ill-prepared lasted only a semester or less before dropping out.[55]

In an attempt to reduce attrition and improve the overall quality of the student body, the college developed a new orientation program and began to revise its relatively open admissions policies. Under the direction of associate dean Robert Husband, in 1976 Arkansas College inaugurated its Mentor Program, a year-long, mandatory orientation program designed to assist freshmen in the transition to college life by providing discussion groups, activities, and mentors from the student body and the faculty. Beginning in the fall of 1977, no one with a high school grade point average of less than 2.0 was admitted as a full-time student. In addition, during the 1970s the West administration gradually transformed its scholarship program from one based primarily on need to one based almost exclusively on merit. This policy received a boost in 1976 when W. C. Brown Jr. made a $350,000 donation to the endowment for the establishment of a scholarship named in memory of his father and his brother, Allan. The Brown Scholarship, which has become the college's most prestigious, was first awarded the following year to two students who had maintained a minimum high school grade point average of 3.5 and who were required to maintain a 3.3 grade point average at Arkansas College. Another key component of the effort to improve student quality involved recruiting strategy. Echoing similar decisions dating back more than two decades, in the late 1970s the West administration redoubled its efforts to recruit in urban areas, especially in regional cities such as Little Rock, Memphis, and St. Louis. Dagley and Associates even assigned a full-time worker to Little Rock, with an office in the Second Presbyterian Church. The implication, of course, was that urban, or at least suburban, kids would enter college better prepared than the small-town and rural kids of north central Arkansas. Perhaps even more important, they would also be able to pay for a higher percentage of their education. By the mid-1970s students from the ten-county area surrounding Batesville accounted for more than two-thirds of the college's enrollment, a figure that the West administration hoped to reduce to two-fifths by the 1980s.[56]

The decision to once again court the suburban student suggests an important change of focus in the late 1970s, or at least an intensification of previously stated goals. As we have seen, the proliferation of courses and concentrations under the New Plan failed to attract large numbers of students. Within a couple of years a few of the experimental and career-focused concentrations died natural deaths due to lack of student interest. Widespread student and faculty displeasure also brought the core curriculum under fire. In the spring of 1976 new dean of the college Robert Knott began evaluating the core curriculum, as well as the college's overall curriculum and mission. His report issued the following summer called for reforming the core, reducing the number of concentrations, developing more two-year programs to serve area students, and placing recruiting emphasis on rural and small-town students within the college's immediate region. Knott's sudden departure a year later points to a marked difference of opinion over the final two issues within the administration. Nevertheless, his first two suggestions (reworking the core curriculum and reducing the number of concentrations) became immediate priorities. After trusty Roberta Dorr Brown filled in as interim dean during the 1977–1978 session, Arkansas College reconfigured its administrative structure, abolished the position of dean of the college, and hired John T. Dahlquist as dean of the faculty in the spring of 1978. A New

Englander educated at Boston University, Dahlquist brought with him from little Kansas Wesleyan College a strong personality, a drawer full of bow ties, and a sincere commitment to the liberal arts. As a historian, he was also the first scholar from the humanities to hold the deanship since the late 1950s. This was an important distinction, for the first task of the new dean would be to oversee a thorough reconsideration of almost the entire curriculum.[57]

Dahlquist shepherded the faculty through an extensive revision of the core curriculum during his first year in Batesville, and helped put the new core into operation during the 1979–1980 session. The 1979–1980 academic year at Arkansas College was a momentous one. We have already witnessed the myriad financial problems that plagued West and the board throughout the year. These problems were particularly vexing considering the extent of changes on campus and within the college community. In addition to the new core, the 1979–1980 session featured a slimmed-down curriculum and the first phase of the college's largest capital campaign to date. In many respects the new core curriculum resembled the old general education requirements of the pre–New Plan days. Reflecting Dahlquist's preference for tradition as well as the influence of the new core curriculum revealed by Harvard a year earlier, Arkansas College's new core retained the thirty-one-hour structure, including the Mentor Program (or Personal Development Seminar), but abandoned most of the experimental and cross-disciplinary aspects of the core under the New Plan. Divided into a skills curriculum and a liberal studies curriculum, the new core reinstated the old western civilization classes, the traditional English composition courses, one semester of literary masterpieces, and classes in basic mathematics and either biology or physical science. The only direct descendant of the New Plan was the U.S. Government in Perspective course, and the new core curriculum established a link with the past by creating a mandatory, one-semester Bible class. With the addition of American Economic Life and Approaches to the Fine Arts in 1986, the core curriculum established in the fall of 1979 remained in place throughout the rest of the West administration.[58]

By the late 1970s the enthusiasm for career-oriented concentrations had begun to wane on all fronts. In addition to the revision of the core curriculum, the college saw half a dozen of its recently established concentrations expunged from the catalog in 1979 and 1980: public administration, medical office administration, health education, environmental health, political science, and office administration. Nevertheless, as the 1980s dawned Arkansas College maintained its most popular and successful nonliberal arts concentrations and focused energies into strengthening these programs. The medical technology program underwent significant expansion in the early 1980s and eventually received national accreditation. Under the direction of Anne Summers, the social work program received accreditation during the 1984–1985 session; again, Arkansas College became one of the smallest institutions in the country to achieve that distinction. In the field of education, David Bell directed the elementary program through its accreditation process during 1979–1980; six years later Arkansas College's special education program joined the ranks of the accredited.[59]

The curricular changes of the late 1970s and early 1980s were accompanied by a new resolve to strengthen faculty quality. As early as the fall of 1978 the board of trustees began discussing the need for a stronger and better-paid faculty, possibly through the use of endowed positions. These discussions bore fruit the following April when the First Presbyterian Church of Pine Bluff announced its intention to raise a quarter of a million dollars for the establishment of the W. Lewis McColgan Endowed Professorship in Religion, Arkansas College's first endowed position since the James Wilson Moore Professorship of Bible faded out of existence after the death of Eugene Long in 1931. Named in memory of First Presbyterian's longtime pastor and former Arkansas College trustee, the W. Lewis McColgan Endowed Professorship spurred the college to seek similar gifts from other sources. The establishment of the Lamar Williamson Prize for Excellence in Teaching in December 1979 also provided a boost to faculty improvement efforts. Founded by Little Rock attorney J. Gaston Williamson in memory of his father, a Monticello attorney who had attended Arkansas College briefly in the early part of the century, the Williamson Prize provided a silver cup and an annual award of $1,000 for the faculty recipient, who was then required to prepare a scholarly paper to be presented to the college community in a special convocation. The first Lamar Williamson Prize was awarded to chemistry professor Roberta Bustin in the spring of 1980, and the first Williamson Prize lecture was her presentation on acid rain the following fall.[60]

Injecting even more activity into the turbulent 1979–1980 session, in the fall of that year the board launched a campaign designed to add $4 million to the endowment by June 1983. The endowment drive was just the first phase of an ambitious, decade-long campaign for $11 million, about half of which was destined for the endowment, with the other half to cover building and renovation projects as well as a maintenance endowment to assure the upkeep of the new buildings. Most of the endowment goal was earmarked for faculty improvement; in the spring of 1980 the board of trustees announced plans to establish ten endowed professorships and four endowed chairs. The college got off to a good start on its endowed professorship drive that very spring when old friend and now advisory trustee W. C. Brown Jr. established a professorship in English, which the board then named in his honor. Arkansas College received its first endowed chair gift in late 1980 when Mary Perkins Barton of El Dorado established the Clark N. and Mary Perkins Barton Chair of Business. Within five years of launching the endowment drive Arkansas College had established eleven new endowed professorships and two endowed chairs. Before the end of the decade the college would add a chair of education and an endowed professorship in biology, raising the total number of endowed faculty positions to fifteen.[61]

No fewer than five of the endowed positions owed their existence to Jean Brown and W. C. Brown Jr. Jean Brown's bequest of more than $14 million upon her death in August 1981 provided the financial clout needed to carry out the various efforts launched in recent years. The board's decision to place the entire bequest in the permanent endowment fund not only raised the endowment to more than $20 million and made it the largest in the state, it also bred confidence in the stability of the institution and in its future. It is difficult to overestimate the impact the Brown bequest had on Arkansas College. Almost every facet of the institution's existence was eventually affected in some way. Income from the bequest allowed the college to get out from under its short-term debt. The massive new flow of money also found its way into scholarship funds, a recruiting tool whose power and necessity West had gradually come to appreciate, and into a new international studies program. The deficits of recent years disappeared, and for the first time in recent memory the college experienced budget surpluses in 1982 and 1983. The money seemed so plentiful that the board voted to use part of the bequest income to replace the approximately $86,000 of endowment principal that had been spent in the dark days of the 1920s and 1930s. Psychologically, the bequest lifted the spirits of a faculty and staff that had learned to live on shoestring budgets, and the gift and its publicity proved a valuable recruiting tool. By the fall of 1982 the board found itself in the unprecedented position of heralding the college's "excellent financial condition." The endowment's income of almost $5.4 million during the 1982–1983 fiscal year was 90 percent as great as the total endowment fund on the eve of the Brown bequest. And despite a momentary lag in giving to the college—a frequent byproduct of such a large gift—by the end of 1983–1984 the endowment was approaching the $30 million mark, almost unfathomable for an institution that little over a decade earlier had less than $1 million.[62]

The timing of the gift was significant also in that it boosted morale at the beginning of the college's year without its president. In a move almost unprecedented in higher education, Dan C. West had decided to take a year's sabbatical to pursue studies at Harvard University toward a doctorate in higher education administration, and chairman Frank Lyon Sr. had heartily approved. In fact, the Wests were on their way to Massachusetts when they found out about Jean Brown's death, and when the will was probated a few weeks later the president would have to offer prayers of thanks from Cambridge instead of Batesville. By the spring of 1981, his ninth year at the helm, West had grown worried "about staying too long, running out of ideas, [and] growing stale." He had been in perpetual motion for as long as he could recall, raising money, delivering sermons, giving speeches, conducting meetings, creating ideas, and generally trying to improve the college while at the same time seeing to it that the institution simply stayed afloat. He hoped that a year of intensive study at one of the nation's best graduate schools for education would reinvigorate the innovative mind that had first tackled the challenge that was Arkansas College in 1972. West also realized that earning an Ed.D. would improve his and the college's stature within the community of liberal arts schools. And he promised Lyon that he would devote at least five more years to the college upon his return.[63]

The sabbatical year was unusual and remarkable on several accounts. Not only was it uncommon for a college president to leave his institution for an entire year, it was also almost unheard of for a president to entrust his job to a trustee. West did just that when he convinced William H. Dunklin to take the reins in the fall of 1981. A semi-retired Pine Bluff businessman and owner of an extensive farming operation, Bill Dunklin was a graduate of Princeton and had attended Harvard Law School before earning his law degree at the University of Arkansas. Dunklin had been among the earliest trustees recruited to the board by West. Throughout the sabbatical year, the acting president benefited from the expert advice of a group of veteran administrators including Roberta Dorr Brown, dean John Dahlquist, dean of students Dennis Wright, registrar Frances Burks (Rodgers), and vice-president for finance Richard Thomas. Dunklin also inherited West's administrative assistant, Sylvia Spencer.[64]

Accustomed to the rigors of a college presidency, West found graduate school relaxing and enjoyable, even though he convinced his advisors to allow him to take severe overloads during his year at Harvard. The persistent and persuasive West managed to squeeze almost two years worth of course work and writing into twelve months and arranged to complete the remainder of his requirements through the mail. As he had hoped, the sabbatical recharged West's creative batteries and sent him home full of ideas for improving Arkansas College and for setting it on a firm financial footing. The Wests returned to Batesville in the late summer of 1982 and moved back into their newly renovated and redecorated president's home, thanks to the generosity of Frank and Marion Lyon. Upon West's return to Batesville, Dunklin agreed to remain in the partial employ of the college as the special assistant to the president, a position that he held until West completed his degree in 1984.[65]

The result of West's sabbatical year was something of a two-part presidency. Just as the McCain years can be divided into the period leading up to accreditation and the decade following it, the West administration in many ways divides nicely into pre-sabbatical and post-sabbatical stages. Among the issues that had occupied much of the president's thought during his year in Cambridge were the continuing conundrum of strengthening the liberal arts heart of the institution while meeting regional needs with career-oriented and professional programs and the ongoing concern (even after the Brown bequest) of ensuring the college's long-term financial security. West believed he had plans that could prove to be the solution for both problems. The developments during the two years before the sabbatical reflected the board's desire to move the college into the front ranks of small liberal arts schools in the region. Yet Arkansas College's historical inability to recruit large numbers from outside the immediate Batesville area forced a curricular flexibility that could react to market demands and that was at the mercy of "the many deficiencies in the Arkansas public school system." Before West left for Harvard, Arkansas College had tried to address a part of this need by establishing the Learning Enrichment Acceleration Program, or LEAP Center, which was in effect a remedial program designed to bring unprepared students to the level required for satisfactory freshman work. But West realized there was a need for a much broader program to address the multifaceted needs of the Batesville area without sacrificing quality and without abandoning the liberal arts tradition.[66]

West's answer to this problem was a "cluster college concept" that would include everything from a secondary academy to a couple of graduate programs. Under this concept a wide range of programs, in addition to the liberal arts college at the center, could be developed under one umbrella. An academy could provide quality, private secondary education in a state and region sorely lacking such facilities, and it could serve as a source of recruitment for the college. An expanded Continuing Education program could meet the needs of local people who had no desire for a traditional liberal arts education and who had no access to a community college. Furthermore, the development of such a program at Arkansas College, West reasoned, might stave off the establishment of a community college in Batesville. The state had just recently opened one in nearby Newport, and West feared it was just a matter of time before the movement stirred in Batesville again. There was still a need for access to graduate study in north central Arkansas, especially in education, and the cluster college concept left room for expansion into the master's degree level. All of this would be done in a way that would leave the liberal arts intact, perhaps even strengthen Arkansas College's liberal arts focus by putting more distance between the standard undergraduate education and the more utilitarian aims that the college had long pursued.[67]

To the president's dismay, the reception for his broad plan was cool at best. A few trustees, including Lyon, thought it workable, but veteran faculty members opposed the plan as too radical and unpractical in scope. West quickly abandoned the academy plan but continued to pursue other parts of his vision, including an expanded Continuing Education program and a limited foray into graduate studies. West called for the expansion of the Continuing Education program into an affiliated entity called the School of Independent Living or Independence College. Recognizing that "the effort to move Arkansas College into the ranks of 'quality' liberal arts colleges is somewhat contradictory to the demand for the non-traditional part-time program," West proposed to separate the most utilitarian offerings from the college's liberal arts degree programs. The School of Independent Living would be available only to part-time, nontraditional students and would offer courses at one-third the standard tuition rate. When North Arkansas Community College in Harrison announced plans to offer extension courses at Batesville High School in the fall of 1983, West became even more convinced of the efficacy and necessity of the School of Independent Living. The faculty continued to oppose the plan, however, as did many trustees until the board killed the proposal a year later.[68]

West also raised the possibility of establishing a nursing program as well as graduate programs in business and education. Neither the faculty nor the board evinced much interest in nursing or an M.B.A. program, but the master's in education seemed more feasible. Although the board's education committee approved plans for an experimental graduate program in education, the faculty, led by veteran education professor Stanley Reed, repeatedly voted down the proposal. Opponents of the graduate program argued that enrollment was too small, that the library was inadequate for graduate-level research, and that the undergraduate education program was still in a developmental stage. West brought the issue up again after mid-decade but found little support and eventually abandoned the graduate program idea.[69]

West's other post-Harvard ideas, an honors program with an international study component and an innovative endowment strategy, proved more successful. Dan and Sidney West were enamored of world travel and understood its educational value, especially for the rural and small-town kids who made up a majority of the student body at Arkansas College. Beginning in the late 1970s, the Wests led students on two-week, January term tours of foreign locations. A West family vacation to England in the summer of 1977 provided the spark of inspiration, and the president promptly scheduled a 1978 January term course on Historic London. The arrival later that year of new academic dean John T. Dahlquist, another champion of international study who had even conducted class tours as a faculty member at Kansas Wesleyan College, provided another authoritative and convincing voice. The inaugural trip to London was followed by tours of Italy and Austria. The president and dean considered the excursions successful and began lobbying the board for the inauguration of a foreign travel program. In 1983 the trustees adopted the Honors International Studies Program, a selective program designed by Dahlquist and history professor Jane Fagg that required twenty-four hours in cross-cultural studies, foreign language, and a period of foreign study ranging from a month to a whole semester. The year 1984 featured the Summer in Austria program, the first foreign study program designated as part of Honors International Studies. Heidi Helmke, a Brown Scholar from Yellville, became the first Arkansas College student to complete the program after her month in Paris in 1985. Two years later Joe Key of Sheridan enjoyed one of the most interesting foreign study experiences when his semester in London led to work as a research assistant for David Owen, a founder and leader of Great Britain's former Social Democratic Party. In 1988 trustee Shuford Nichols and his wife, Laura, donated $1 million for the establishment of a foreign travel program that would eventually become available to all juniors and seniors in good standing. The Nichols Study-Travel Program provided transportation and lodging for two-week foreign trips in conjunction with specially designed study travel courses.[70]

The most innovative of West's post-Harvard plans, as well as the most publicized, involved the decision to pursue nontraditional avenues of money making in an attempt to offset rising educational costs and ensure the institution's future financial stability. The president realized that even with the sizable endowment, which by the mid-1980s ranked in the top 120 among all U.S. institutions, rising costs would outpace income and the college would need alternative sources of revenue in years to come. The idea that West and Richard Thomas, vice-president of finance, eventually developed placed Arkansas College in the forefront of innovation in higher education finance and elevated both men to expert status on matters of small college finance. But the journey toward innovation had an unlikely beginning.

Using proceeds from the sale of old Williams Gymnasium and other property, in early 1978 Arkansas College purchased forty-five acres about thirteen miles west of Batesville, a plot that included lock and dam number three on the White River near Walls Ferry. The original plan was to develop the site into a student recreation area and faculty retreat. A law passed by Congress that same year that required utility companies to buy electricity from small producers went unnoticed at Arkansas College. In 1980, however, a Tennessee company contacted the college to inquire about developing a hydroelectric plant at lock and dam number three; the company hoped to take advantage of the recent federal law. Initially uninterested in selling or renting the land or in developing a hydroelectricity plant, college officials began considering the idea only when Thomas discovered a loophole that would have allowed the state's major utility company, Arkansas Power & Light, to requisition the lock and dam for development. After a series of studies and licensing negotiations with local civil authorities that resulted in cooperation between the college and Independence County, in early 1983 Thomas announced plans to construct a 5.6 megawatt-producing hydroelectric plant (very small by modern standards) at an estimated cost of from $14 to $20 million.[71]

The dam project was only the first of several nontraditional investments. In September 1982 Richard Thomas and some trustees began negotiations with a group of Arkansas investors planning to purchase a new Kroger supermarket in Huntsville, Alabama. Such an investment offered a risk factor much higher than that of traditional blue-chip stocks and bonds and was therefore out of the question for a college board of trustees. Consequently, West, back from Harvard with a fresh perspective on national trends, suggested that Arkansas College follow the example of Oklahoma Christian College and set up a subsidiary to handle "equity investment opportunities and remove the tax consequences from the college." Oklahoma Christian College had recently established an investment subsidiary to develop retail stores in shopping malls, and, West said, a similar body at Arkansas College could manage the dam project, the grocery store, and any other unusual investment opportunities that might arise. Although not all the trustees favored Thomas's risk taking, all agreed that if undertaken it should be accomplished through a subsidiary; in October 1982 the board approved West's and Thomas's blueprint for this new for-profit branch of the college, the Aberdeen Development Corporation, and voted to supply the subsidiary with $200,000 seed money from the reserve fund or from endowment income.[72]

According to the Aberdeen Development Corporation's charter, the subsidiary's board was to be composed of six Arkansas College trustees, with the college's board chair doing double duty as the corporation's chair. Likewise, West would serve as president of Aberdeen, with Thomas handling everyday operations. All earnings not reinvested would go to the college. West and Thomas almost immediately began looking for additional investment opportunities. In 1983 Thomas began developing a condominium project in Little Rock and brokered the college's purchase of more than 1,500 acres of undeveloped land east of Batesville for $1.5 million. For the latter venture, which became the college's most ambitious, the Aberdeen Development Corporation established its own subsidiary, Stirling Realty Corporation, just to handle the land purchase. Stirling promptly sold a one-half interest in the land to a subsidiary of Batesville's Independence Federal Bank, which retired Aberdeen's debt and netted a significant profit. In the spring of 1984 Aberdeen announced plans to develop its Batesville-area property, soon to be named Eagle Mountain, both residentially and commercially, and hired a contractor to construct a road into the heart of the property. The Eagle Mountain project eventually earned Aberdeen, and Arkansas College, proceeds through the sale of house lots and commercial sites, including a large Wal-Mart complex later in the decade. Under the direction of Johnny Mitchum, a Batesville native who took over management of Aberdeen when Thomas left in 1985, the

Aberdeen Services Corporation was established to handle the college's accounting and computer work.[73]

The Aberdeen Development Corporation sold off its interest in the Kroger store within a couple of years, and the hydroelectricity project never got off the ground. Nevertheless, Arkansas College continued to pursue new revenue sources. In 1986 the college became the first independent institution in Arkansas to sell tax-exempt public improvement bonds under the state's Act 142 of 1984. The bond issue generated $2.5 million for campus improvements and renovations.[74] Almost as important as the money generated from Arkansas College's creative financial strategies, however, was the publicity it yielded. Before the 1980s Arkansas College stayed tucked away in the isolation of the eastern Ozarks. The statewide press centered in Little Rock, much less regional and national media, rarely focused attention on any part of Arkansas outside of a fifty-mile radius surrounding the capital, and for most people living outside of north central Arkansas Batesville remained a remote little town well off the beaten path. The 1970s had produced some improvements in this area, however. In 1976 Arkansas College received regional recognition when it was awarded generous grants from the National Endowment for the Humanities and the Rockefeller Foundation for the purpose of establishing the Arkansas Folklore Education Consortium. The Consortium, directed by folklorist George E. Lankford, helped bring an academic point of reference to the new Ozark Folk Center in Mountain View, spawned an American Studies program within the Arkansas College curriculum, collected a large and valuable folklore and folk music archive, and produced the journal *Mid-America Folklore*. In addition grant money sponsored the establishment of the Arkansas College Monograph Series, the first academic press in the state.[75]

Two events in 1978 gained statewide publicity. In May of that year Arkansas College held its first annual lecture in the Hugh B. Patterson Sr. Lecture Series. Founded in memory of the father of the longtime publisher of the *Arkansas Gazette*, the Patterson Lecture Series provided stipends to bring prominent figures in the world of journalism to the campus of Arkansas College. Fred Graham, a legal correspondent for CBS News and son of Arkansas College alumni Otis and Lois Patterson Graham, delivered the first lecture in 1978. Later Patterson lecturers included such noted journalists as Seymour Hersh, Harry Ashmore, Helen Thomas, and Hodding Carter III. The fall of 1978 witnessed the inauguration of the Kaneaster Hodges Sr. Lecture Series, founded by Senator Kaneaster Hodges Jr., an Arkansas College trustee from Newport, in memory of his father. Massachusetts senator Edward "Ted" Kennedy, the first senator to speak on campus since J. William Fulbright defended his anti-Vietnam stance before the student body eight years earlier, delivered a speech on education to a crowd of seventeen hundred in Becknell Gymnasium, an event that drew to campus a number of the state's dignitaries including Governor David Pryor and young attorney general Bill Clinton. Former president Jimmy Carter's talk on foreign policy five years later attracted an even larger crowd and press representation.[76]

The Brown bequest, which was trumpeted on the front page of the *Arkansas Gazette* as the largest gift ever given to an institution of higher education in the state, kicked off a decade that saw little Arkansas College receive more statewide and national publicity than it had received in the previous 110 years of its existence *combined*.[77] Following the statewide press coverage created by the Brown bequest in 1981, the Aberdeen Development Corporation kept tiny Arkansas College in the regional and even national spotlight through mid-decade. The *Arkansas Gazette* ran a front-page feature on the college's nontraditional investments in June 1983, the same month that a lengthy article on the same topic appeared in the *Chronicle of Higher Education*. An even more thorough treatment appeared in the *Arkansas Magazine* section of the Sunday *Arkansas Democrat*. In the following months articles on and mentions of Arkansas College's financial innovation appeared in publications as prominent as the *Wall Street Journal, Business Week,* and the *New York Times*. The value of such publicity is probably unmeasurable, especially for a small, out-of-the-way institution such as Arkansas College. The administration and trustees understood the power of publicity and looked to capitalize on the college's most visible era.

The publicity generated by the college's investment schemes was simply a valuable byproduct of efforts to secure the institution's financial future. Another development of the 1980s that created a great deal of publicity, the Scottish Heritage Program, was the result of a calculated effort to increase Arkansas College's visibility within the state and the region. As we have seen, the college had made use of the trappings of Scottish history and lore since John D. Spragins first introduced the theme during World War II. Since that time Arkansas College athletic teams had been known as the Highlanders, Scots, and Pipers, the yearbook had been changed from the *Index* to the *Scot*, and the student newspaper had carried the title *Highlander*. For several years the freshmen beanies, popular at schools across the country, found on the heads of Arkansas College students were actually tam o'shanters. And since the late 1960s a highlight of freshman orientation week had been a modified highland games competition. Nevertheless, Arkansas College had made little effort to develop an image using the Scottish roots of Presbyterianism.

When Dagley and Associates came on board in 1979 to direct the admissions office for Arkansas College, the private firm quickly realized that Arkansas College suffered from image problems, the primary one being that the school *had* no identifiable image, no hook to relay a sense of uniqueness to prospective students. Dagley and Associates recommended strengthening and publicizing the institution's Scottish elements to improve marketability among the growing body of high school students. The timely and unrelated arrival of a new vice-president for development shortly afterward provided just the person to undertake such a mission. Ralph M. Graham, a native of Texas who arrived in Batesville in the fall of 1980, brought with him a deep, almost fanatical love for all things Scottish. A former Presbyterian minister and professor of religion at Trinity University in San Antonio, Graham was the grandson of Scottish immigrants, and he developed a deep appreciation for Scotland while earning a Ph.D. at Glasgow University.[78]

Once he received West's approval to begin developing a Scottish image at Arkansas College, Graham wasted no time. In the fall of 1980 he founded the Pipes and Drums of Arkansas College, made up of freshman pipers Glen Glaros and Mary DuBose and senior drummer Chris Thuneman. The trio performed at basketball games and in special events around the state that first year, and as the 1980s wore on the Pipes and Drums, whose players received scholarships to attend Arkansas College, supplanted the Lassies as the college's busiest musical ambassadors. In April Arkansas College hosted the first annual Ozark Highland Games on the new J. Marshall Huser Track and Field. Developed by Graham and dean of students Dennis Wright with assistance from the Arkansas Scottish Cultural Society, the Ozark Highland Games featured an assortment of events quite unusual to most visitors: the caber toss, flinging bats of oats with a pitchfork, and various weight tosses. The games also brought to Batesville professional highland dancers and bagpipers as well as Scottish and Ozark crafts and foods. Renamed the Ozark (later Arkansas) Scottish Festival, the games attracted larger and larger crowds to the Arkansas College campus throughout the decade and generated publicity within the state and region and among Scottish heritage groups worldwide. Within a few years the Scottish Heritage program at Arkansas College had landed Graham and his Pipes and Drums on the front cover of *Grit* and had earned the Batesville school recognition on NBC's *Today* show and on Atlanta's WTBS superstation.[79]

Determined to develop a broad-based Scottish Heritage program that would provide year-round entertainment and events, Graham also inaugurated Burns Nicht and Kirkin o' the Tartans celebrations at Arkansas College. The kilted vice-president of development hosted the college's first annual Burns Nicht Supper, a celebration honoring the birthday of Scottish poet and icon Robert Burns, in January 1982. Three months later the campus held its first Kirkin o' the Tartans, a "traditional" Scottish religious service founded by an American clergyman during World War II as a prayer service for besieged Britons. The Kirkin o' the Tartans service was eventually moved to the fall of the year. Graham even initiated an annual summer tour of Scotland in 1982, in which he chaperoned any faculty, trustees, or friends who wanted to visit Presbyterianism's mother land. By the late 1980s the college offered classes in bagpiping and highland dancing.[80]

Frequently, the Scottish Heritage Program inspired the college's public relations department to take liberties with the institution's background. Such public relations events rarely see the need for historical authenticity. For instance, a brochure advertising the 1982 highland games claimed that Arkansas College had been founded by "Scottish Presbyterians," and much was made of the Ozark region's Scottish roots. Although a Scotch-Irish heritage program would have been more historically accurate, such a program would have found little to celebrate except a history of religious violence and a conquering of the American frontier. And Scottish music, particularly the bagpipes, often inspires either intense love or loathing. After attending an event at which the Pipes and Drums were featured, trustee and alumnus Hugh M. Patterson wrote a fellow trustee: "(C)andor commands my admission that the pipes are not my favorite sound-maker, and I have heard them from the Castle at Edinburgh on down. I wonder how in the world such a device ever came into being?" Many continue to wonder, and the Scottish Heritage Program continues to lend the college a distinctiveness, albeit a contrived one, within the region.[81]

The publicity boom at Arkansas College in the early 1980s played a key role in a sudden enrollment surge, just at the time when statistics warned of a shrinking base of teenagers. Other factors spurring the growing recruiting success included an expansion of the Continuing Education program beginning in 1983 and the creation of more than one hundred new merit scholarships using money from the Brown bequest. When the Wests returned from Massachusetts in the fall of 1982, they were greeted by the largest student body in Arkansas College history to that time. The total number of full- and part-time students enrolled in credit courses exceeded 600 for the first time ever, and full-time equivalent enrollment stood at 490, an increase of 13 percent over the previous fall. The following autumn brought another record crowd of students to campus, with more than 650 total and an FTE of 527. As usual the numbers could be interpreted in different ways, both promising and foreboding. College officials boasted that the Batesville institution had experienced the most dramatic enrollment increase of all four-year schools in the state over the past two years. Nevertheless, a couple of statistics bothered the administration and the trustees. Arkansas College contained the largest percentage of part-time students of any independent institution in the state, a fact that pointed to an unhealthy dependence on nontraditional students, especially for a college with dreams of becoming a first-rate residential campus. Many college officials also worried about the continuing inability to recruit outside of north central Arkansas; fully 60 percent of freshmen in the fall of 1983 hailed from the ten-county area surrounding Batesville, and only 8 percent were non-Arkansans.[82]

Perhaps the most encouraging aspect of the sudden enrollment growth of the post-Brown bequest era was the fact that it took place at the exact time when the college was instituting more stringent admission requirements. Beginning in the fall of 1982 all new enrollees had to have had at least a 2.5 high school grade point average. The faculty further tightened requirements the following year by adopting a minimum American College Test score of 18, roughly the national average, for automatic admission. Students who failed to meet the g.p.a. and ACT minimums had their cases decided by the admissions committee. The other component of the new resolve to strengthen the quality of the student body was a dramatic increase in the number and value of merit scholarships and stricter qualifications for the institution's most valuable and prestigious scholarships. By the fall of 1983 Arkansas College boasted more than two hundred different merit-based scholarships, compared to less than one hundred before the Brown bequest. Beginning in the fall of 1982 the college increased the number of Brown Scholarships from two for each freshman class to six; competition for the Brown Scholarships also grew more intense as the faculty approved minimum requirements of a 25 on the ACT (or 1,145 on the SAT) and a 3.75 high school g.p.a. Minimum requirements for Arkansas College's second most valuable scholarship, formerly known as the McCain Scholarship, were raised to a 22 ACT score and 3.5 g.p.a. The result of the college's new admissions policies and larger scholarship endowment was a noticeably stronger student body. The freshman class of 1984, though smaller than the previous two freshman classes, proved to be the strongest to date during the era of college entrance tests and also the strongest of the entire West administration. The class's average ACT score of 22.1 represented a 30 percent increase in just three years, or since the initiation of the new admissions policies.[83]

Not surprisingly, as the administration and board had feared when accepting the more stringent admissions policies, full-time enrollment fell off in mid-decade, perhaps in part due to slacking publicity. Despite an enrollment explosion in the Continuing Education program that catapulted the total number of students to more than 750 by the fall of 1985, smaller freshman classes and continuing retention problems resulted in another period of enrollment stagnation, a period that watched full-time enrollment dip below the 400 mark during four different semesters between 1984 and 1987. Arkansas College also struggled to reach dormitory capacity during the mid-1980s. The enrollment challenges of this era vexed the West administration. Even with the state's largest endowment and a half decade of more publicity than the college had enjoyed in the whole of its first 110 years, recruiting and retention continued to serve as obstacles on the road to regional distinction. Yet, West could point to a promising and permanent increase in the quality of the student body. In the fall of 1981, 57 percent of all Arkansas College freshmen scored below the national average on the ACT; six years later only 15 percent failed to reach the national average. After 1985 no freshman class at Arkansas College would carry an average ACT score of less than 21, and by the end of West's tenure in Batesville his school's freshmen regularly exceeded the national average score by at least 10 percent and the state average by 20 percent.[84]

By the late 1980s the quality and ability of Arkansas College's student body was as strong as, probably stronger than, it had ever been. The same could be said of the faculty. Since leaving Arkansas College, Dan C. West has often observed that the one thing he was most proud of by the end of his days in Batesville was the unsurpassed quality of the faculty. Faculty improvement at such a small and low-paying institution required constant vigilance, and the process took place in fits and starts. West's first decade at Arkansas College was marked by a wave of retirements and the flux of rapid turnover. By the end of the young president's first five years at the helm, retirements—some of them the result of the president's urging—had purged the faculty of all professors whose service dated back beyond the mid-1960s, such popular personages as Ellis G. Mosley, James Vernon Balch, Doris Hammett, Virginia Kirk, and Thelma Pickens. This process also rid the faculty of many of its members who did not hold a doctorate. By the fall of 1975 more than half the full-time faculty held doctorates, and that percentage would grow steadily into the 1980s. Low salaries, internal conflict, and curricular turmoil resulted in frequent turnover during the 1970s as a succession of young academics seasoned for a brief time at Arkansas College before moving on to other colleges or universities.[85]

The volatility began to give way to stability during the second half of the West administration, however. The arrival of John T. Dahlquist as dean of the faculty in 1978 ushered in a period of academic leadership stability rarely matched in Arkansas College history. Dahlquist's ensuing fourteen-year deanship, the longest consecutive term as dean in the school's history, was a major reason for the consistent and deliberate strengthening of the faculty during the 1980s. Even more crucial was the board's decision to establish a number of endowed professorships and chairs with money from the Direction Toward Distinction Campaign of the 1980s. The endowed positions not only provided competitive salaries but also reflected the trustees' determination to build and retain a strong faculty. The endowments improved the faculty in two ways: by attracting highly qualified scholar/teachers from other institutions and by rewarding outstanding current members of the Arkansas College faculty.

Among the first to be rewarded in the latter fashion were Dorothy Landis Gray, named the Jean Brown Professor of Music, and Fitzhugh Spragins, who assumed the title Josephine Emily Brown Professor of Religion. Soon thereafter three other veteran professors received endowed positions. Roberta Bustin became the J. Paul Smith Professor of Chemistry, Dan Fagg the Paul M. McCain Professor of History, and Terrell Tebbetts was named the W. C. Brown Jr. Professor of English. Among the first recruited to Arkansas College to fill endowed positions were Donald V. Weatherman, Robert K. Holyer, and Bert E. Holmes. Weatherman, a native of southern California with a Ph.D. from Claremont Graduate School, came to Batesville in the fall of 1983 as the John D. Trimble Sr. Professor of Political Philosophy, and Holyer carried a Ph.D. from the University of Cambridge (England) when he arrived the following year to assume the W. Lewis McColgan Professorship of Religion. Holmes, a Kansas State University Ph.D., was named to the college's first endowed chair when he became the William Clark Brown Sr. Distinguished Professor of Chemistry in 1983. Holmes quickly established himself as a conscientious and vocal leader of the faculty and began developing the science division into a first-rate program stressing collaborative research between faculty and students. Arkansas College filled its other endowed chairs later in the decade with the arrival of William H. Weber III in 1986 and Clara M. Jennings in 1988. Weber, a Columbia Ph.D., assumed the Clark N. and Mary Perkins Barton Distinguished Professorship of Business, and Jennings, who was also notable as Arkansas College's first black faculty member, was appointed the Rountree Caldwell Bryan Distinguished Professor of Education. Weber and Jennings ultimately had short tenures in Batesville, but biologist Scott W. Peterson and economist Thomas E. Cooper, both lured to Arkansas College by endowed positions, enjoyed longer terms of service. By the time West left the college in 1988, the faculty boasted three endowed chairs and eight endowed professorships or associate professorships.[86]

In addition to the professors in endowed positions, Arkansas College benefited from an extraordinarily experienced and dedicated faculty by the late 1980s. By the time West left, several, such as Veryl V. Board (biology), Charles R. Oliver (languages and literature), Ann Adams Rhodes (psychology), Jane Fagg (history), and Fred Wann (physical education), had devoted two decades or more to Arkansas College, and others were nearing twenty years of service. Ed Mosley (mathematics), George E. Lankford (folklore), L. J. Summers (theater), and Anne B. Summers (social work) were among those who joined the faculty in the 1970s and remained when West resigned.[87]

Building on the trend started during the latter years of the McCain administration, the personnel additions of the 1970s and 1980s produced a much more qualified and educated faculty. By the time West departed Batesville, 75 percent of the faculty held terminal degrees. Reflecting a growing openness in society following the civil rights movement, the 1970s and 1980s also watched as the faculty gradually assumed a more diverse cast. In 1974 political scientist George Zilbergeld became the first Jewish member of the faculty. Four years later accounting professor Khursheed Omer, a Muslim and native of Pakistan, became the first foreigner appointed to a tenure-track position at Arkansas College. It took another decade, however, before education professor Clara Jennings joined the faculty as the first black educator at Arkansas College.[88]

The student body achieved a significant level of racial diversity well before the faculty did so. The face of the student body began to change in the 1970s to more closely approximate Arkansas's racial makeup. At the same time, the attitudes and appearances of Arkansas College students underwent a transformation as the inclusive spirit of the 1960s belatedly made its way southward in the early 1970s. Arkansas College contained little more than a token black population at the end of the McCain era, and by 1970–1971, the final year under the guidance of Coach Dick Winningham, the Scots were the only all-white basketball team in the state. But the rapid desegregation of the team after the arrival of Lavaughn Robertson in the fall of 1971 mirrored a substantial increase in the number of black students and a rise in black consciousness in the early and mid-1970s. One of the first assembly speakers of the West era in the fall of 1972 was black activist Queen Mother Moore. Arkansas College's Black Student Association (BSA) was established in the fall of 1973, and the BSA sponsored its first Black Emphasis Week the following April. By the mid-1970s more than half the members of the men's varsity basketball team were black while the number of black students enrolled at Arkansas College had increased to more than fifty. In 1975 William Adair became the first African American elected president of the Student Government Association, and in 1976 Adair and Darlene Crow became the first black Mr. and Miss Arkansas College. As usual the students proved a step ahead of the board and administration in such matters. There was not an active African American trustee until Little Rock educator Roland Carpenter came on board in 1984, four years before Clara Jennings joined the faculty.[89]

The students of the 1970s also brought to campus the trappings of their generation's youth culture. Encouraged by the relative freedom of the Wygle administration, long hair and afros quickly replaced the crew cuts of the McCain era, and hippies made their first appearances in Batesville, to the chagrin of most on the still-conservative campus. Folk music held on for one last season of triumph, rooftop sunbathing became a favorite pastime, and drugs began to infiltrate campus. By 1971 *Highlander* editors printed the administration's warnings of the consequences of drug arrest. In the spring of 1974, just one year after an Arkansas College student was arrested for drug possession by local authorities, a student editorial proclaimed: "Marijuana, as well as other illegal intoxicants, can be found in abundance on this campus." The new West administration policies against alcohol on campus rekindled that touchy issue as well. For the most part the activism of the 1960s had dissipated by the Watergate era. *Highlander* editors blamed the sporadic publication of the school paper on widespread student apathy during the Wygle administration. On the surface it certainly seemed that the student engagement of the 1960s was on the wane. For every Bill Bristow, a Strawberry farm boy whose acceptance into Harvard Law School the whole college celebrated, there was a Carl Farina, a New Jersey native whose most notable achievement at Arkansas College was spending a Guinness world record of more than seventy-two hours in the shower, a feat that earned him sarcastic praise from the *Highlander* and a water bill of fifty-five dollars from the administration. Apathy gave way to a combination of anarchy and exhibitionism in 1974 as the fad of streaking found its way to the Arkansas College campus. By mid-decade most student unrest stemmed from the New Plan and protest over West's stricter dormitory regulations, and by the 1980s student life had followed Reagan-era America into a conservative torpor reminiscent of the Eisenhower fifties.[90]

The pace of extracurricular change and expansion in the 1970s and 1980s often served as a gauge of student interest and commitment. The most prominent extracurricular development of the early 1970s grew in part from the cultural ferment of the latter McCain years at Arkansas College. By the time R. W. Wygle arrived in Batesville in 1969 the campus contained four Greek organizations, none with a national affiliation. Both fraternities, Chi Beta Phi and Gamma Delta Iota, had been founded by and heavily composed of northeastern students in the 1960s. In the fall of 1970 the largest fraternity, Chi Beta Phi, won acceptance as a colony of Tau Kappa Epsilon, a national fraternity headquartered in Indianapolis. Spurred by their competitor's success, Gamma Delta Iota, which was renamed Omicron Eta Sigma in memory of Otto Henry Schwarz, who died of a heart attack in May 1971, gained colony status within one of the South's most successful fraternities, Kappa Sigma, in the spring of 1972. Both became full-fledged chapters of their respective fraternities in early 1973. Although it got a late start in the game, an Arkansas College sorority actually achieved national status shortly before the fraternities did so. In the fall of 1972 Sigma Alpha Sigma gained recognition from Alpha Xi Delta as a pledge affiliate, and in January 1973 the national body granted full privileges to the Zeta Iota chapter. The newly minted Alpha Xi Delta thus became the first nationally affiliated Greek organization at Arkansas College since the 1930s.[91] Kappa Kappa Alpha sorority, the oldest Greek organization on campus, was the only one without national ties by the end of 1972–1973 and would remain so until the rise of a new sorority, Zeta Omega, during the late 1980s.

As on most college campuses, the sororities and fraternities assumed distinctive personalities of their own, albeit ones that could shift with the changing characteristics of the general student body. Whereas both fraternities counted significant numbers of non-Arkansans on their rolls in the early 1970s, by mid-decade they had, like Arkansas College's populace, come to be comprised primarily of natives of the state, and Tau Kappa Epsilon even maintained a significant African American contingent for a few years. The image of Tau Kappa Epsilon's membership gradually shifted from "obnoxious northerners," in the words of one early Kappa Sigma, to locals and rednecks, while Kappa Sigma, with its mandatory dress-up days and higher grade point averages, generally cultivated a more positive reputation as the fraternity of campus leadership and scholarship, an image interpreted by the competition as rich kids and preppies. The distinctions and direct competition between the two sororities abated somewhat due to the national/local divide, but Tau Kappa Epsilon and Kappa Sigma remained fierce competitors and utilized both real and perceived differences to sustain

The members of Kappa Kappa Alpha, the college's oldest Greek organization, pose for the yearbook photographer, c. 1983.

interest in the small fraternity system, no mean feat considering the lack of fraternity houses and other common trappings of the Greek life on typical university campuses.[92]

Other extracurricular activities of the era grew out of the spirit of cooperation rather than competition. One of the more interesting was the founding of Arkansas College's first, and last, radio station. In the early 1970s a group of students calling themselves the A.C. Crazies began discussing plans for a campus radio station. The Crazies raised their own funds and developed a proposal for a ten-watt (barely campus-wide) FM station, which the Federal Communications Commission approved in the spring of 1974. KGED-FM went on the air during the following academic session. Operated out of Brown Chapel originally, before moving to the basement of the Learning Resources Center in early 1976, most of the air time was occupied by volunteer students playing their own records. The radio station remained active, though almost in an underground fashion, until financial problems and potential licensing issues closed it down in the early 1980s.[93]

Much of the extracurricular expansion that took place in the 1970s was a direct result of the "hybrid curriculum" produced by the New Plan. Each new career-oriented concentration generally produced a new student organization. By the mid-1970s Arkansas College students could join any number of clubs, societies, and organizations affiliated with specific disciplines: the Physical Education Club, the Mental Health Club, the Student National Education Association, Phi Beta Lambda (business), and

Eta Sigma (education). In addition to membership in regular organizations, students in career-oriented concentrations sometimes found themselves engaged in unusual activities outside the classroom. As part of their University Year in Action project in December 1979, Anne Summers and a group of her social work students sponsored a Vietnamese refugee family. The project quickly outgrew the boundaries of the campus and spread into the community; as a result four Batesville churches and a local group calling themselves the Friends of Refugees helped relocate to Batesville an entire extended Vietnamese family of more than forty individuals.[94]

The reduced emphasis on the arts under the "hybrid curriculum" of the 1970s took its toll on the theater and music programs. Frequent faculty turnover following the health-related resignation of Johnny Homesley in 1970 hurt Harlequin Theatre. This combined with budget cuts, reduced offerings in speech and theatre, and an increased emphasis on co-productions with the Batesville Community Theater to dampen on-campus enthusiasm and ultimately resulted in a lower profile for student theater productions. The arrival of L. J. Summers as a full-time faculty member and director of Harlequin Theatre in 1977 brought a sense of stability back to the department. Summers gradually backed off the previous close cooperation with the Batesville Community Theatre, and in 1984 Harlequin Theatre reentered competition for the first time in years at the Arkansas Kennedy Center American College Theatre Festival.[95]

While the Harlequin Theatre survived the West years, albeit in a reduced role, the era witnessed the demise of another extracurricular mainstay, the Lassies. The most visible extracurricular product of the 1960s began to lose its luster in the 1970s. Despite USO tours to the Caribbean in 1972 and to West Germany in 1974, by the early 1970s the era's anti-establishment spirit had turned on the Lassies. In a time when school spirit and achievement were often viewed as blasé by skeptical students, the perky, world-traveling Lassies made a good target for derision by *Highlander* editors and disenchanted students of any stripe. Furthermore, the rekindling of the Equal Rights Amendment movement suddenly cast the Lassies—all of them attractive, impeccably groomed, and usually dressed in short skirts—in a new and anachronistic light. The Lassies, eventually joined by the Lads, held on for the remainder of the decade, but the rise of the Scottish Heritage Program in the 1980s substituted the Pipes and Drums as the institution's new musical ambassadors. By the time Dorothy Landis Gray went on sabbatical in 1984, her first year away from Batesville in almost four decades, the music department had been reduced to the college choir with its annual Christmas and spring concerts. Gray's replacement, William H. Braun, injected new life into the music department when he inaugurated the Madrigal Dinner in December 1984. The Madrigal Dinner, a Christmas-season, Renaissance-themed musical presentation, attracted larger and larger crowds to the new Edwards Dining Hall until Braun left Arkansas College in 1991. The music scene at Arkansas College also benefited from the endowment of two concert series in the 1980s. The Ashley-Lewis Concert & Recital Series, funded by a Newport woman, was inaugurated in November of 1983; three months later the Elysian Trio performed in the first West Endowed String Concert, established by the president and first lady of Arkansas College.[96]

One result of the expansion of extracurricular activities in the 1970s and 1980s was that the athletic program, specifically basketball, lost its central role in the social life of the college. The two decades following the resignation of Paul M. McCain brought about a succession of major changes within the varsity program, from the introduction of women's athletics to the development of a top-notch track and field team. As the 1970s dawned, Arkansas College maintained its traditional focus on men's basketball, with token Arkansas Intercollegiate Conference competition in tennis, bowling, golf, and cross-country. The college also fielded a winless soccer team, though that international sport was not officially recognized by the conference. By the end of the West era, varsity sports consisted only of men's and women's basketball, track, and cross-country. The eighteen years in between, however, witnessed significant alterations within the varsity program and in some respects represents a sort of golden age for athletic success at Arkansas College.

The completion of the Becknell Physical Education Building in 1970, with its Olympic-size swimming pool, allowed Arkansas College to form its first swimming team. In the spring of 1971 baseball returned as a varsity sport under the tutelage of Fred Wann. Facing a shrinking budget and forced to play off campus because of the lack of a field, the baseball program was discontinued four years later. By the end of the decade bowling, swimming, tennis, soccer, and golf had all followed baseball into the varsity sports dustbin. An effort by Dan C. West to start a new soccer program in the early 1980s failed as well. Despite the high attrition rate for varsity athletic teams, those that survived the trying 1970s and 1980s generally fared well in competition.

The West era's most successful varsity sport languished in obscurity, just like every other sport not played on a basketball court, at the same time that it dominated statewide competition. The completion of the J. Marshall Huser Track and Field in 1980 gave Arkansas College a facility as good as any in the AIC, and young coach Larry Rogers arrived in the fall of that year to make good use of it. During his five years as track and cross-country coach, Rogers led his women's squads to four district cross-country championships and three first-place finishes in AIC track and field competition. In the process of garnering several coaching awards, including Southwest Regional NAIA Women's Track Coach of the Year in 1982, Rogers groomed numerous all-district and all-conference runners as well as two NAIA All-Americans, Diane Marshall in cross-country and the 1,500 meter run and Brenda Jones in the heptathlon. Arkansas College continued to make strong showings in women's cross-country until Rogers's replacement, Jerry Hutchison, left in 1989.[97]

Although it remained the best funded and most popular spectator sport on campus, men's basketball lost the centrality of wintertime social activity that it once had held. The increasing popularity of major college and professional basketball during the 1970s and 1980s and the proliferation of televised sporting events due to cable television contributed to the loss in popularity. Despite the fact that fewer and fewer students attended games under normal circumstances, the era in question generated several significant events in Arkansas College athletic history and produced some of the best teams Batesville had ever seen. The Scots greeted the 1970s with the AIC's dean of coaches, R. C. "Dick" Winningham. The old coach stayed in Batesville just long enough to break in the new gymnasium. By the time he resigned in the spring of 1971, Winningham had already outlasted his era. Although Charles Jackson, a black player from Helena, had suited up for the Scots from 1968 to 1970, during Winningham's final season Arkansas College featured the only all-white team in the state, and the Scots' record of 8–18 was the worst in the coach's twenty-year career.

Winningham's replacement was his greatest scorer, Lavaughn Robertson. Robertson, a 1964 alumnus who had just completed his second year as assistant coach at Arkansas State University, brought a spirit of change and experimentation to the basketball program that fit well the times in the early 1970s. Robertson quickly integrated the team and used his considerable recruiting skills to gather as talented a group of players as any Arkansas College had ever seen. By the mid-1970s the recently all-white Scot roster contained a majority of black players. After a last-place conference finish in 1971–1972, the fast-paced, athletic style of play ushered in by Robertson produced a winner the following season. The Scots drew record crowds of more than two thousand fans to Becknell, a local radio station began broadcasting games for the first time ever, and Little Rock television stations sent camera crews and reporters to film the exploits of all-AIC performers Milton Sullivan and Elliott Jackson for the sports report on the ten o'clock news. In what would become a familiar story in the 1970s, Robertson's Scots in 1972–1973 could not ride their talent to a championship. In succeeding years Robertson continued to recruit all-conference-caliber players, but due to a lack of chemistry or consistency the Scots never vied for a title of any kind. Robertson's successor, a "ball of fire" from Louisiana named Dwain Roark, inherited a talented squad and led the Scots to a second-place AIC finish and a 23–8 season in 1979–1980 before losing in the semifinals of the District 17 tournament.[98]

When Roark unexpectedly resigned after only two years, Terry Garner arrived in Batesville to usher in the most successful string of seasons in Arkansas College basketball history. Like his predecessor, Garner was a "ball of fire" on the sideline, stout and red-faced with a fiery, competitive spirit. A former basketball and baseball player at Little Rock University (University of Arkansas at Little Rock) and a protégé of legendary Ouachita Baptist coach Bill Vining, Garner led the Scots to a 21–10 record in 1980–1981, a season in which star guard Charlie Howard became Arkansas College's first ever all-American selection. The campaign also earned Garner both district and regional coach of the year honors. Two years later Garner was named AIC coach of the year after leading the Scots into a first-place, regular-season tie with Henderson State University, the first ever conference title for Arkansas College. The Scots made history a year later, in 1984, when they won their first District 17 tournament, thereby earning a berth in the NAIA national tournament at Kansas City. Led by honorable mention All-American Kelvin Blevins of East St. Louis, Illinois, and academic All-American Kevin Johnson, a local boy from Mount Pleasant, the Scots made the journey from "AC to KC" and won their opening round game before falling to eventual national runner-up Wisconsin-Stevens Point. By mid-decade, however, the institution's more stringent admissions policies began to exercise a negative effect on recruiting, and by the end of the decade the Scots had returned to more familiar territory in the middle of the AIC field.[99]

Shortly after West's arrival in Batesville, the Scots had company in the gymnasium. In 1972 Congress enacted a series of educational amendments, one of which, Title IX, prohibited sexual discrimination in any program or activity at an institution receiving federal funds. This category included Arkansas College. Although subsequent amendments delayed mandatory compliance, Arkansas College wasted no time in establishing women's varsity sports. In the spring of 1973 a group of the top girls from the intramural league formed a college team to compete in the Arkansas Women's Extramural Sports Association (AWESA) tournament in Little Rock. The following year men's assistant coach Don Boen formed Arkansas College's first official varsity women's team; the Scots, as they were then known, won two of seven games with victories over Arkansas State University and John Brown University.[100]

The arrival of young Van Gore Compton, formerly a high school teacher and coach at Forrest City, in the fall of 1974 brought Arkansas College its first full-time women's varsity coach and first complete women's basketball schedule. The women finished the season with eight wins and thirteen losses and boasted one of the Arkansas Women's Intercollegiate Sports Association's top players in Beth Haizlip of Paragould. With the addition of all-conference players Beverly Bass of Palestine and Debbie Wheeler of Pleasant Plains, the Pipers (taking their new name from the title of the college's alumni magazine) posted a winning record of 14–8 the following year. The Pipers remained competitive until exploding to the top of the league in 1980–1981. At one point that season Compton's Pipers reached the top ten in national rankings before a rash of injuries ended their season with a disappointing loss in the second round of the conference playoffs but a school-best record of twenty wins and only four losses. Compton, who also coached the women's volleyball team from its inception in 1974 until its demise in 1983, left Arkansas College in 1986 and was replaced by cross-country and track coach Jerry Hutchison. Hutchison's Pipers, now competing in the women's AIC, remained, like the Scots, competitive but too bereft of talent to challenge for a championship.[101]

The last half of the 1980s was in many respects a time of success for Arkansas College and Dan C. West. On 31 December 1986 college officials proclaimed the end of the Direction Toward Distinction Campaign. Exceeding the goal by more than \$2 million, the campaign raised almost \$12.5 million for physical expansion and endowment, more money than Arkansas College had raised in all previous campaigns *combined*. The physical expansion generated by the campaign consisted mainly of an addition to the student union and the major renovation of another building. In the fall of 1983 the new Edwards Dining Hall addition to the student union was opened to students. Local businessman and former trustee John W. Edwards had earlier given the largest gift for the dining hall project and the largest ever by a Batesville resident. Having served as a dining hall for two decades, the Alphin Building sat idle for two years while work crews, funded in part by grants from the National Endowment for the Humanities and the Kresge Foundation, transformed the interior to accommodate classrooms and

It's AC to KC. Two-time Academic All-American Kevin Johnson cuts down the net after the Scots win the 1984 District 17 tournament championship, thereby earning their first trip to the NAIA national tournament in Kansas City.

an art studio downstairs and faculty offices on the new second floor. By the beginning of classes in the fall of 1985, the Alphin Humanities Building contained a spacious art gallery, named in honor of the Kresge gift, and attractive Georgian furnishings and decor designed by Marion Lyon and Sidney West and donated to the college by trustee Robert A. Young III. Accompanying the renovated Alphin Building was Arkansas College's first major in art. Other construction projects of the era included a new bridge across and path around Bryan Lake, an intramural softball field on the hillside above the lake, the transformation of the old recreation hall into an admissions office, and the renovation of two college-owned houses near campus for use by faculty members and visitors. The college also purchased an airplane in the early 1980s and undertook an extensive expansion of computer facilities, including the establishment in 1981 of the Apple Orchard, a computer center containing sixteen Apple personal computers.[102]

Enrollment began to rise once again late in the decade. After full-time enrollment dropped below 400 in the fall semesters in 1985 and 1986, it climbed to 440 in the fall of 1987 and to a record of more than 500 in 1988. The total count, including part-time students, exceeded 800 for the first time ever during that same semester. This enrollment boom, which necessitated the use of three mobile homes and converted dormitory lounges for student lodging, was especially promising given the college's recent decision to accept no one with an ACT score below twelve, a minimum that was raised to fourteen the following year in keeping with the mission to improve student quality. The administration also pointed to the rising percentage of non-Arkansans in the freshman class—up from 2.5 percent in 1986 to 18.6 percent in 1988—as proof of Arkansas College's growing regional reputation and as evidence of the admissions office's effective recruiting practices in neighboring states. The successful recruiting years in 1987 and 1988 suddenly made the stated goals of 600 full-time and 400 part-time students by 1990 seem attainable.[103]

The rise in enrollment of the late 1980s probably had at least a little something to do with the recent national recognition of the strides made by Arkansas College during the West years. In 1983 and 1984 the Brunswick Foundation rated Arkansas College one of the top-five colleges with enrollments under one thousand in the United States, ranking the Batesville institution above such colleges as Centre, Culver-Stockton, and Belhaven. Although Brunswick's rating system was geared heavily toward services for nontraditional students and financial innovation, two areas in which Arkansas College excelled, the measurement system used by *U.S. News and World Report* was more inclusive. In November 1986 that magazine's annual ranking of American institutions listed Arkansas College as the eighth-best small, comprehensive (Carnegie Category II) college in the South, a geographic region containing 168 such schools. Two years later Arkansas College cracked the top ten once again, a position that would become familiar territory in the following decade.[104]

Dan C. West had much to be proud of by the late 1980s, in addition to this recognition. Despite the momentary setback caused by the stock market crash in October 1987, the endowment was approaching $40 million; the income generated by the endowment now accounted for more than one-third of the annual budget, compared to less than one-tenth in the 1970s. Alumni relations were in their best condition in years. West had supervised the passing of the torch on the board of trustees as Robert A. Young III replaced Frank Lyon Sr. as chairman in 1987. Behind the capable leadership of John T. Dahlquist the faculty was at its strongest and most seasoned level in the history of the college, and Bert E. Holmes's direction of the science division had begun to bring thousands of dollars of grant money into Batesville along with regional acclaim for the biology and chemistry programs. Shuford Nichols's gift of $1 million in 1987 funded the establishment of a foreign travel program that would eventually send hundreds of Arkansas College students on two-week journeys to Europe, Asia, and elsewhere at the college's expense. West's personal lobbying efforts had helped get a new state scholarship program passed through the legislature in Little Rock. Independent institutions such as Arkansas College especially benefited from the new Governor's Scholar program, which provided substantial scholarships for outstanding Arkansas students for use at any college in the state. West's personal suggestion to Governor Bill Clinton also resulted in the founding of the Arkansas Governor's School, a six-week summer program for gifted and talented high school seniors modeled on a similar project in North Carolina. The college's inability to secure Batesville as the site of the Governor's School, which continues to be held on the campus of Hendrix College, proved unfortunate, especially for recruiting purposes. The Continuing Education program was drawing more part-time students to campus than ever before and, largely through the efforts of the affable Jim Mitchum, had fostered an environment of cooperation between Arkansas College and the local area that had fallen off before the 1970s.[105]

Like all good Calvinists, however, West and the trustees knew that things could always worsen. They usually had in the college's past. Perhaps the enrollment boom of the late 1980s was simply an aberration, a temporary spike in the graph that could not be sustained. While the endowment was at its highest point in history, the college continued to face budget challenges, and the trustees found themselves forced to dip into the reserve fund even as the decade neared its close. The annual fund drive remained a problem area, due in no small part to the low rate of alumni giving, and the college continued to cover more than a quarter of the average student's tuition and fees. And by the late 1980s dark clouds had begun to gather in the legislature as politicians began to discuss the possibility of expanding the community college system in Arkansas, a serious threat that West and other independent college leaders had fended off years earlier. Around the nation, scholars and bureaucrats continued to predict the demise of the small independent college, a favorite pastime of university-supported education specialists for almost a century.

Fortunately, Presbyterianism and pessimism are not synonymous. In spite of the negatives that could be dredged up, Arkansas College was in good shape in the late 1980s. When compared with the institution's status in 1972, the college looked downright marvelous. By the fall of 1987 the trustees were confident enough in the institution's progress and direction to begin confidential discussions of a proposed $50 million campaign. Almost half that goal would be earmarked for the endowment, and more than $14 million would be used toward construction projects outlined in the new campus master plan: two new dormitories, three instructional buildings, including one for the growing business division, and a theatre along with additions to several other campus structures. In order to avoid the possibility of an embarrassing public failure, the board voted to delay official announcement of the new drive, the Universal Campaign, until pledges could be secured for at least a third and perhaps one-half of the total goal. In the spring of 1988, however, the board was given another reason to delay public announcement of the Universal Campaign—the need to wait on the arrival of a new president.[106]

In March 1988 Dan C. West informed the board and the college community that he would be stepping down as president of Arkansas College on 1 August 1988. For many it was hard to imagine Arkansas College without Dan and Sidney West. Others were more than happy to see the controversial president go; a few elated faculty members even made and donned buttons trumpeting their survival of the West years. In the modern world of higher education, sixteen years was a very long presidency. As far as Arkansas College was concerned, the West administration had been at once the most turbulent, the most exciting, the most confusing, the most successful in the institution's 116-year history. But the very elements that created such turbulence, excitement, and success had made West a sought-after leader. The president's innovations, from the New Plan to Aberdeen Development Corporation, generated publicity not only for Arkansas College but also for Dan C. West. By the mid-1980s West was nationally recognized as a leading spokesman for small college affairs and as an expert on innovative methods of finance. In fact, his Harvard dissertation, "Additional Resources for Financing Small Colleges in the 1990s," spawned several important book and journal articles that further improved his stature in the world of small independent colleges. For several years before 1988 West had been courted by various institutions across the country, including such Presbyterian stalwarts as his alma mater Austin College and Mary Baldwin College in Virginia. Before 1988 he had consistently turned other offers down.[107]

When an offer from another Presbyterian institution, Carroll College of Wisconsin, came in early 1988, the time seemed right for leaving Batesville. Like Paul M. McCain nineteen years earlier, West was nearing fifty and his children were either in college or nearing college age. Also like McCain, West felt that he had accomplished about as much as he could have expected; it was time for a leader with new blood and a fresh approach, especially with the impending fund-raising campaign to top all Arkansas College campaigns. Dan C. West, like McCain before him, knew he was leaving Batesville's little college in much better shape than he had found it. Many of those who had helped him in this process would stay behind to lead Arkansas College into the new administration, into the next decade, into the next as-yet-undetermined vision of the future.

Chapter 8

Tossing Our Hats Over the Wall: The Griffith Years

As a middle-aged man living in the United States, writer Frank O'Connor reflected on the days of his boyhood in pre–World War I Ireland. In one of his more trivial yet exhilarating memories, O'Connor discovered a metaphor for courage and risk taking in the face of seemingly insurmountable odds. Among the happiest days of O'Connor's childhood were occasions when he and his friends were able to escape the slums of Cork and explore the green fields and rocky slopes of the Irish countryside. When the lads encountered "an orchard wall that seemed too high to climb," they took off their caps and flung them over the wall. "(T)hen we had no choice but to follow them." Speaking on the day of his inauguration as Arkansas College's fifteenth president, John V. Griffith evoked O'Connor's metaphor to convey the challenges that lay ahead and the way in which his administration would go about meeting those challenges.[1] It was an apt use of symbolism. By the late 1980s Arkansas College had become a very good regional liberal arts college. In the months and years ahead Griffith and the college community would toss their hats over the wall that separated good regional colleges from high-profile, nationally respected institutions. The goal of lifting little Arkansas College into the ranks of the country's elite colleges, first articulated almost four decades earlier by Bill McMillan and Frank Lyon Sr., would become the driving force in the development of the institution during the 1990s.

The decade following the resignation of Dan C. West was one of constant, deliberate, and often sweeping change. In fact, by the late twentieth century, change, frequently confused with progress, had become the norm in a society so enamored of transformation that even conservatives faced requirements of proactivity. The age of the status quo, passive presidency, even in the small denominational college, had long since passed. Of course, as we have seen, Arkansas College had never been able to rest on its laurels. For most of the post-West decade, the college went forward under the watch and care of John V. Griffith. The Griffith years, though barely more than half as long as the West administration, were nevertheless marked by an almost delirious whirl of activity, all of it emanating from the central goal of elevating Arkansas College to the status of such respected midcontinent institutions as Rhodes, Austin, Millsaps, Hendrix, and Grinnell. Meeting this goal would mean transforming the college into a selective, expensive, residential institution with a more diverse student body and a more positive reputation within the state and region. Like his predecessor, Griffith would reevaluate, refurbish, restructure almost everything in this hat-tossing process.

Hat tossing of a different variety was on the minds of some in the Arkansas College community in the late summer of 1988, however, when a record number of freshmen reported for orientation week. The Wests had been gone less than two weeks, and greeting the matriculates in their place were Graham and Carolyn Holloway. Following the precedent set earlier in the decade when Bill Dunklin filled in for the absent West, the trustees appointed one of their own to serve as interim president in the fall semester of 1988. Graham Holloway, a Texas businessman and University of North Carolina graduate whose late son had graduated from Arkansas College in 1980, had served on the board since 1978. From a public relations standpoint, the Holloways' semester in Batesville got off to a strong start. Enrollment reached record levels, with the number of full-time students exceeding 500 for the first time ever. The freshman class of 188 continues to stand as the largest in the institution's history. The unexpected freshman windfall strained campus housing to the breaking point, forcing the renovation of some dormitory lounges into student rooms and the use of three mobile homes for student housing. The growth in on-campus enrollment also spurred the trustees to begin construction on two new dormitories in the fall semester. In addition to the enrollment boom, Arkansas College made its second appearance on *U.S. News and World Report*'s list of the top-ten regional liberal arts colleges in the South.[2]

Holloway's sojourn in Batesville was not without its challenges. One of Holloway's primary responsibilities was maintaining the momentum of an effort to raise $6.7 million by April 1989 in order to receive a $1 million grant from the Mabee Foundation. Furthermore, in spite of the record enrollment and the relatively hefty endowment, the familiar specter of economic distress reared its head once again. Early in the year the board's executive committee realized that Arkansas College faced its third consecutive session with a budget deficit. Interest payments alone from the short-term debts accrued during the final years of the West administration exceeded $500,000 by 1988–1989. By the time dean of the faculty John T. Dahlquist relieved Holloway as interim president in February 1989, the college's financial troubles demanded immediate attention. At their spring meeting the trustees took several steps to shore up the budget. In addition to eliminating a dozen staff positions, the board voted to increase the endowment spending rate to 10.75 percent, more than twice the desired rate, in order to balance the coming year's budget and to reduce debt. The trustees also agreed for the first time to assume responsibility for a portion of the annual fund. Most importantly for the student body, the board accepted a tuition hike of more than 10 percent.[3]

A different issue occupied the minds of most trustees in 1988—the search for Arkansas College's next president. The hunt for Dan C. West's successor marked the

The hat is tossed. President John V. Griffith delivers his inaugural address from the back steps of Brown Chapel, 1989.

first nationwide, professional presidential search in the institution's history. Upon receiving West's resignation in the spring of 1988, the board appointed a search committee composed of trustees, faculty, students, and alumni. Headed by board chairman Robert A. Young III, the committee promptly hired a Washington, D.C., consulting firm to survey the college's situation and make recommendations for future development, as well as to assist in the process of finding candidates qualified to lead the school into its next phase. The search turned out to be an easy one for most on the committee. By the fall of 1988 they had found their man in John Vincent Griffith. In fact, the committee members were so certain of Griffith's abilities and potential that they decided to invite no other candidates for campus visits.[4]

When he was first contacted by Arkansas College in the spring of 1988, John V. Griffith was completing his third year as vice-president of institutional advancement at Davidson College in North Carolina, an institution that he had first served as dean of admissions and financial aid. Like Paul McCain, Griffith had spent most all his life on or around a small liberal arts college campus. Born in the town of Hamilton in upstate New York, he grew up on the campus of Colgate College, where his father served as dean of students. After graduation from another elite liberal arts institution, Dickinson College in Pennsylvania, Griffith and his new wife, Nancy, also a Dickinson graduate, moved to Massachusetts, where he earned a master of divinity degree at Harvard Divinity School in 1972. Ordained to the ministry by the American Baptist Convention, Griffith spent the mid-1970s as chaplain of a girls' boarding school in Massachusetts before he and Nancy moved back to upstate New York to pursue graduate studies at Syracuse University. After a year as a research faculty member at the University of Michigan, he received his Ph.D. in the psychology of education from Syracuse in 1979. Soon thereafter the job as dean of admissions and financial aid at Davidson first brought the Griffiths to the South and into the realm of Southern Presbyterian higher education.[5]

Despite having never served as a college president before, John V. Griffith was probably the most experienced administrator to ever take the reins of Arkansas College. At forty-two, he was a decade older than Dan West had been when he first came to Batesville, and Griffith's Davidson experience proved particularly appealing to the board of trustees. Not only had his tenure in North Carolina introduced Griffith to the ins and outs of Presbyterian higher education, but his particular familiarity with student recruiting and fund-raising seemed to equip the new president to tackle the two areas that had traditionally been the greatest challenges at Arkansas College. This strong record of service and experience helped to compensate for the fact that Griffith was the first president at Arkansas College who was not a product of the Presbyterian tradition as well as the first from the northeastern United States.

Even more striking than Griffith's liberal arts pedigree was his exuberant personality. Engaging, charismatic, and idealistic, the new president represented a sharp contrast with more reserved predecessors such as West or McCain. Griffith moved effortlessly among the various constituencies in the college community, seemingly at ease whether at bow-tie trustee affairs, faculty meetings, or hamburger cookouts with freshmen. Whereas Dan C. West often seemed to students a distant figure who appeared before the college only on special occasions, a casually dressed Griffith accompanied by his golden retriever would soon become a familiar and welcome sight to campus residents. With the skill of a politician and the voice of an orator, Griffith also possessed an ability to connect with audiences that few if any of his predecessors had displayed. Like the Wests before them, the Griffiths complemented each other to form an effective first couple. Through the force of her effervescent personality, Sidney West had balanced the seriousness and unrelenting professionalism of her husband. Nancy Griffith was a different first lady altogether, though in many ways as effective as her predecessor. Scholarly, reflective, and insightful, Nancy Griffith proved a valuable advisor and confidante. Reflecting the changing times, she also became the first Arkansas College president's wife to maintain a career when she assumed the directorship of the institution's regional studies center.

The search committee's insistence on bringing John V. Griffith to Arkansas College represented much more than infatuation with a dynamic personality. In the late 1980s a variety of developments appeared to be moving Arkansas College in the direction of some vague, loosely defined future, a future or vision that Griffith was uniquely suited to articulate. During the last half of the West administration, and especially following the Jean Brown bequest in 1981, the college had made great strides toward becoming an institution of distinction within the state and region. The past few years had witnessed the beginnings of selective enrollment, the foundation of scholarships designed to attract first-rate students, and the gathering of a talented and highly educated faculty. The momentum generated by these changes and the rapid enrollment growth of recent years suggested to many that Arkansas College stood on the precipice of something grand, something akin to the vision of Bill McMillan, Frank Lyon Sr., and their supporters almost forty years earlier. Just what form this future would take remained to be seen in the days after West's resignation. In the process of finding a new president the college received a series of strong recommendations from two academic consultants. At the top of the list were suggestions to increase the residential focus on campus and to develop a stronger curriculum in the traditional liberal arts. These suggestions played a key role in shaping the search criteria that eventually brought Griffith to Batesville.[6]

There were other factors influencing the emerging vision of Arkansas College's future as well. Politicians had once again raised the issue of expanding the state's community college system; their efforts would bear fruit two years after Griffith's arrival. Perhaps most important, among Arkansas College's trustees and friends were a core group of supporters whose personal experiences at elite liberal arts institutions had convinced them of the superiority of such an education and of the need for Arkansas College to enter the ranks of such schools. Chief among this group were outspoken faculty members such as academic dean John Dahlquist, Bert E. Holmes, Donald V. Weatherman, Robert K. Holyer, and George E. Lankford as well as the college's three most recent board chairmen, all of whom shared some sort of connection with Washington and Lee University in Lexington, Virginia. As a young man Frank Lyon Sr. had come away from his first visit to Washington and Lee with an indelible impression of the ideal college environment, an impression that stayed with him throughout his life. Robert A. Young III, who had succeeded Lyon during the last year of West's administration, was a graduate of Washington and Lee whose college experience had convinced him of the superiority of a high-quality liberal arts education. The president of Arkansas Best Corporation and Arkansas Best Freight System in Fort Smith, Young also shared a strong connection to Arkansas College's past through the family of his wife, Mary McRae Young, daughter of alumnus Carleton McRae and great-granddaughter of former board chairman Thomas C. McRae. More than anyone else, however, it was Shuford Nichols, another Washington and Lee alumnus, who conveyed this vision to John V. Griffith. Shortly after being hired by the search committee, Griffith received an unexpected phone call from Nichols. It was to be the last conversation between the old chairman and the new president, for Nichols would die a few months later. Opening the discussion in typical light fashion by reassuring Griffith, "I always like a man that wears a striped tie," Nichols extolled the virtues of the country's top liberal arts colleges and spoke of a day when Arkansas College would join the ranks that included his Virginia alma mater. Griffith listened intently. He recognized the challenges ahead, but shared the old man's unshakeable faith in the intrinsic value of an education absorbed in the residential, liberal arts college setting.[7]

The conversation with Nichols was still fresh on Griffith's mind when he arrived in Batesville with his family on the two-hundredth anniversary of the storming of the Bastille. It was a typically hot and humid mid-July day that greeted the new first family. As they crested the hill on Highland Road, the Griffiths noticed a flashing yellow sign perched on the front lawn of the president's home. It read: "Welkum to Arkansaw Doc Griffin and Fambly!" The front lawn contained other adornments as well—an old car seat, a worn tire sheltering a plastic floral arrangement, and a bottle tree. It was obvious to the new president that his faculty and staff could poke fun at Arkansas's backward image; it was also obvious that they understood the deep-rooted ambivalence that such an image must have stirred in a New Yorker whose career had never before taken him so far from the citadels of American academe. Whatever ambivalence the new president may have had largely dissipated a few weeks later when Griffith received a most unexpected announcement from one of the college's most loyal families. Frank and Marion Lyon used the occasion of a quiet dinner and visit in their Little Rock home to inform the Griffiths of their intention to give Arkansas College $5.25 million, at the time the largest nonbequest gift the institution had ever received. Most of the money would be used toward the construction of a new business and economics building, completed in the summer of 1993, with the remainder earmarked for the renovation of the Bevens Music Room in Brown Chapel (long a favorite project of Marion Lyon), the establishment of a president's discretionary fund that could eventually be put toward the construction of a new president's home, and the creation of an endowment for the library. John V. Griffith's welcome to Arkansas was complete and offered the best of both worlds—a tire turned lawn ornament and a generous gift from one of the state's most successful families.[8]

Nevertheless, Griffith's primary focus remained the development of a plan that would catapult the college into the ranks of the elite liberal arts schools with which he was so familiar. This straightforward goal would serve as a guiding beacon for the disparate developments of the Griffith administration. Shortly after the beginning of classes in the fall of 1989, board chairman Robert A. Young III convened a Little Rock meeting of the executive committee at which the new president outlined both the spirit and the specifics of his upcoming "hat-tossing" inaugural address. It was at this meeting that Griffith first shared his long-term vision for Arkansas College with the leaders of the board. The new president's overarching goal was to lift the college to Carnegie Liberal Arts Category I status, which translated into a highly selective, mostly residential college with a heavy curricular concentration on the liberal arts and sciences. Within Arkansas only Hendrix boasted such a classification, and within the surrounding region Rhodes College (formerly Southwestern) in Memphis, Millsaps in Jackson, Mississippi, and Centenary in Shreveport, Louisiana, were the most prominent. In order to achieve such status, Griffith suggested, Arkansas College would need to remove the narrow professional programs installed during the 1970s, triple the size of the library's holdings, focus on the growth of the residential student body (with a goal of seven hundred on-campus students by the turn of the millennium), and revamp an outdated tenure and promotion system to ensure the recruitment and retention of a superior faculty.[9]

At Griffith's urging the executive committee agreed to charge the new president with the task of overseeing a strategic planning process that would articulate, institute, and monitor the changes necessary for realizing the college's new vision. Interestingly, the development of a strategic planning process had been the first recommendation offered by the search consultants in the spring of 1988. Chairman Young delivered the official charge to the president after Griffith's inaugural address in October 1989. Griffith wasted no time in appointing a Strategic Planning Task Force made up of faculty, staff, trustees, students, and alumni and co-chaired by chemistry professor Bert E. Holmes and political philosophy professor Donald V. Weatherman. With the assistance of a professional consultant, the task force worked feverishly through the winter of 1989–1990 to draft a bold yet succinct "Strategic Plan for Arkansas College."[10]

Griffith was able to avoid the pitfalls that had plagued the drafting and implementation of the New Plan in the early 1970s. Like West, Griffith utilized a "constituent-based" approach by involving large numbers of people in the planning process; unlike his predecessor, Griffith successfully communicated his vision to the college community and found, for the most part, agreement among the faculty. All division chairs, as well as the dean and other veteran educators, were appointed to the task force. By February 1990 the task force had completed its Strategic Plan, which was promptly and unanimously adopted by the board of trustees at its winter meeting.[11]

The most important document yet generated on the college campus, the Strategic Plan became the blueprint for the growth and development of the institution in the 1990s and beyond. Built upon the daunting promise "to lead the south central region in undergraduate, liberal arts education," the Strategic Plan presented a new mission statement and outlined nineteen key priorities that would render Arkansas College a "highly selective, independent liberal arts college serving Arkansas, the region and the nation" by the year 2000. At the top of the list was the need to "strengthen and expand traditional liberal arts offerings." Other curricular goals included the enrichment of the core curriculum and the fortification of such distinctive elements as student-faculty research and the international travel program. The plan also called for the development of a strong residential program in which at least three-quarters of the projected eight hundred full-time students would live on campus. If the desire to raise the average American College Test score to twenty-six (from twenty-two) seemed to fly in the face of these lofty admissions goals, the plan recommended strengthening the financial aid program to meet the needs of all students. The faculty-related goals predicted that the number of faculty would almost double to eighty, 90 percent of whom would hold a doctorate. The faculty workload would be reduced from eight to six courses per year, and salaries would be upgraded to the level of those in the upper tier of highly selective liberal arts institutions. As far as money was concerned, the Strategic Plan suggested raising tuition costs to approximate the fees charged by other highly selective colleges, completing a physical expansion estimated at $30 million, expanding the endowment to $185 million with a 5 percent spend rate, and increasing the Annual Fund to $1.75 million. Finally, the plan called for a reappraisal of town-gown relations and an emphasis on public relations in general, which "may lead to a reconsideration of the College's name."[12]

The task force's process, which coincided with the beginning of the decennial self-study for reaccreditation, convinced most faculty members of the value and rightness of the Strategic Plan. By involving almost every faculty member, as well as many students, trustees, alumni, and staff, the process also lent the Strategic Plan a kind of common property quality that resulted in a widespread vested interest on the part of large numbers of Arkansas College personnel. By the end of the 1989–1990 academic year, the flurry of ground-level activity coupled with Griffith's stirring rhetoric and sincere salesmanship had convinced most people on campus that the new vision for the college was not only appropriate but necessary.

Obviously, the Strategic Plan promised to alter almost every facet of the college's program, from the core courses required of all students down to the design of the college catalog. Never before had Arkansas College undertaken so monumental a task as was called for in the Strategic Plan. Dan C. West's New Plan had tried to force innovation and change on a largely unwilling faculty and student body, but the New Plan had also reflected a hint of desperation, a wild attempt to stay afloat by responding to the educational marketplace. The institution that Griffith inherited was in much better shape (academically and financially) than Arkansas College had been in two decades earlier, which meant that in many ways the goals of the Strategic Plan represented a more radical undertaking—the gamble of forsaking a path that had produced at least a limited amount of success in recent years for a course of action which had rarely been completely successful for American institutions of higher learning, even less so those in poor states like Arkansas. Nevertheless, whereas in the 1970s dozens of small independent colleges like Arkansas College had expanded their curricula as a survival strategy, by the late 1980s the advice de jour for these same institutions was niche marketing. Instead of trying to be all things to all people—little regional universities in effect—the small colleges should, said the experts, concentrate on doing one or two things extremely well, thus occupying a "niche in the academic market place."[13] Sensing the imminent expansion of the community college system in Arkansas and already beset by more stringent and aggressive competition from the state university system, Griffith, the trustees, and most of the faculty made the conscious choice to hitch onto the train of the selective liberal arts college and to see where the ride would take them.

In the months and years after the trustees' vote of confidence in the Strategic Plan, Griffith appointed a succession of commissions and committees, each charged with hammering out the details of a specific phase of the Plan and overseeing its implementation. By mid-decade this broad-based effort had drawn every member of the faculty, administration, and board, as well as significant numbers of student leaders, into the process of defining the vision for the college's development. Broadly speaking, the Strategic Plan addressed myriad issues and areas that fell under one of three categories: the academic program, the student body and residential life, and public relations and financial development.

From the beginning Griffith viewed the academic component of the Strategic Plan as the heart and soul of the long-term vision and the key to achieving Carnegie Category I status. At the center of the academic program was the curriculum, which by 1990 reflected a combination of traditional liberal arts studies with more narrowly focused professional programs. In the fall of 1990 the president established two study commissions to analyze facets of the current curriculum and to make recommendations for change based on the mandates of the Strategic Plan. One commission, under the leadership of George Lankford, was charged with a thorough reconsideration of the core curriculum, while the second commission, co-chaired by Terrell Tebbetts and Donald V. Weatherman, was instructed to develop a list of academic majors that would bring Arkansas College in line with highly selective liberal arts institutions such as Rhodes and Austin. The work of both commissions over the next two years proved "far more complex, controversial, and demanding than [the president] anticipated." Discussions of serious curricular alteration peeled back the layers of idealism and anticipation that had been part and parcel of the electric optimism of Griffith's first year on campus. The gradual realization that matching the rhetoric with action threatened faculty positions and challenged a core curriculum that had been in place for more than a decade resulted in a "loss of morale among some faculty members." Nevertheless, in November 1992 the faculty assembly approved the report of the Majors Study Commission; two months later the faculty adopted a similar report from the Core Curriculum Study Commission.[14]

By the time the controversial report on majors was issued, the faculty had already begun to trim the more utilitarian components of the curriculum. Shortly after adoption of the Strategic Plan, the Clark N. and Mary Perkins Barton Distinguished

Professor of Business, Clarence Adams, oversaw an extensive restructuring of his division that included dropping majors in management, marketing, and computer studies in business as well as the two-year data-processing certificate, a relic of the 1970s movement to append a junior college affiliate to Arkansas College. Adams's committee also recommended replacing the B.S. in economics with a B.A., reflecting an increased emphasis on the philosophical over the practical. At the same time the Science and Mathematics Division agreed to discontinue the health care administration major and completed the phasing out of the medical technology program, a process that had been put in motion before West's departure. The music major also underwent a transformation; befitting the college's movement toward the traditional liberal arts, faculty in the Arts and Humanities Division agreed to abandon the university or conservatory model of music education in favor of a curriculum emphasizing history and theory.[15]

Even after such significant tinkering with the curriculum, the report on majors in the fall of 1992 struck many as extreme. Attempting to adhere as closely as possible to the Strategic Plan's vision of the liberal arts institution, the Majors Study Commission produced a set of recommendations that removed professionally oriented courses of study from the Arkansas College curriculum, or at least subsumed them within a major that more closely approximated the liberal arts ideal. Those critical of the Majors Study Commission's work pointed to the controversial decision to eliminate social work and physical education, two of the most popular majors on campus, and the determination to "reconceptualize" professional areas of study as concentrations within liberal arts disciplines. This reconceptualization ultimately eliminated four additional majors: accounting and management (both of which became concentrations within the economics major), communications (which was reduced to a journalism concentration within English), and elementary education. Beginning in the fall of 1995 all teacher education students, even those planning to pursue careers in elementary education, were required to complete a major in one of the liberal arts. In addition, the report suggested replacing the old speech and theatre major with a simple theatre major and recommended the addition of major fields of study in Spanish, French, politics, physics, and anthropology/sociology. By the time Griffith left the college five years later, only Spanish and politics had been elevated to the status of major.[16]

For decades the teacher education program had produced more Arkansas College graduates than any other major or educational program. Although teacher education survived the curricular purge of the early 1990s, the program underwent a radical and innovative overhaul under the guidance of George Stone, a veteran small college educator who joined the faculty in 1990 as the Rountree Caldwell Bryan Distinguished Professor of Education. Utilizing his own research and experience, as well as theories of teacher training developed by John Goodlad of the University of Washington's Center for Educational Renewal, Stone directed the design of the college's new Liberal Arts Teacher Education Program during the 1992–1993 session and secured a $150,000 grant from the Winthrop Rockefeller Foundation to fund its implementation. Based on Stone's dictum that "what to teach is as important as how to teach," the innovative program shifted the focus in teacher training from a heavy reliance on standard pedagogical and theoretical courses toward a concentration on classroom study in the liberal arts. At the same time, the Liberal Arts Teacher Education Program placed a greater emphasis on classroom experience, including the expansion of the student teaching requirement from roughly three months to a full academic year. By limiting student teaching to only two local school districts, Batesville and Southside, the new program also allowed the college's educational faculty and students to work more closely with administrators and teachers in the development of an instructional team concept, whereby each student benefited from the guidance and supervision of a team of professional educators. The Liberal Arts Teacher Education Program was in full operation by the fall of 1995 and received glowing reviews from the National Council for the Accreditation of Teacher Education the following spring. In the summer of 1997 the unique program received an unexpected vote of confidence and publicity boost from Pulitzer Prize-winning columnist Paul Greenberg, who praised the college's teacher training methods in his syndicated *Arkansas Democrat-Gazette* column.[17]

Although the new teacher education program affected a shrinking number of students as the college drifted toward a student body concentrating more heavily on pre-graduate and pre-professional school study, the alterations in the core curriculum impacted each student and most faculty members. Not surprisingly, the process of revising the core proved more difficult and the results less universally popular. The core curriculum, which at Arkansas College had been known as general education before the 1970s, had long been a rather fluid concept and had undergone two major revisions during the previous administration, the last one taking place midway through West's tenure under the direction of dean John T. Dahlquist. The new design for the core that the faculty approved in early 1993 required a minimum of thirty-five hours, with a possibility of fifty hours of mandatory course work. George Lankford's Core Curriculum Study Commission recommended dividing the core into three parts: a proficiency component, a distribution component, and a common core in western heritage and history. The proficiency component featured courses in English composition and college algebra and reinstated a universal one-year foreign language requirement for the first time since the 1950s; incoming freshmen were given the opportunity to bypass any of these requirements through proficiency examinations. The distribution component, designed to expose students to a variety of disciplines, offered a range of electives within each academic division. Every student was required to complete three hours each in fine arts and religion and philosophy, six hours in social sciences, and eight hours in natural science and mathematics. The most significant departures for the new core involved a four-year physical education requirement, harking back to pre–World War II general education mandates, and a sophomore year block in which all students studied western civilization, philosophy, and literature. The latter requirement, which initially implied an interdisciplinary team-teaching approach, proved the most contentious among the faculty and thus the most difficult to implement. After a protracted debate over the Western Thought requirement of the common core during the 1994–1995 academic year, the new core curriculum put in place for the fall of 1995 maintained separate courses for history, philosophy, and literature. Nevertheless, an "undercurrent of anxiety among students and faculty" hampered the Western Thought core throughout its first two years, and in 1997 further (and ultimately unsuccessful) attempts were made to integrate western civilization and western philosophy into a single course.[18]

Beyond the revisions of the core curriculum and major fields of study, the Strategic Plan called for an increased emphasis on the curricular activities that were unique, or at least partially so, to Arkansas College. In 1990 the two most prominent features of this category were the recently developed programs of student-professor research, especially in the sciences, and foreign travel and study. By the time Griffith arrived in Batesville the science faculty had already established a reputation for strong student-teacher research. By the early 1990s projects directed by biology professor Scott Peterson and chemistry professor Bert E. Holmes were generating more than $100,000 in grant money annually from such foundations as W. M. Keck in Los Angeles and Frost in Denver. In 1992 Holmes, chair of the division, received national recognition for his student research program when the Chemical Manufacturers Association named him one of only six National Catalyst Award winners in the country. The honor was further sweetened when the National Science Foundation granted Holmes and Arkansas College $136,000 for student research on chlorofluorocarbons. Research grants regularly provided funds to employ biology and chemistry majors as summer research interns, and Peterson developed a program in which one or two biology majors conducted research in Rome during the summer.[19]

Peterson's Italian research trips were in keeping with the growing emphasis on foreign travel and study during the West administration. Although the Honors International Program had been in existence at Arkansas College since the early 1980s, due to the cost and substantial course requirements few students took advantage of the opportunity for foreign study. With the establishment of the Nichols Travel Program in 1988, endowed through a gift from former board chairman Shuford Nichols, foreign study took on a different and much more accessible form. Under the Nichols Program, students who completed sixty hours at Arkansas College while remaining in good academic and financial standing qualified to receive free round-trip airfare and lodging for a two-week trip capping off a designated study-travel course. Initially all the Nichols travel courses were offered during the January term and featured two weeks of classroom work on campus followed by an educational travel experience. Matriculates in the freshman class of 1988 were the first to benefit from the program, and in January 1991 twenty-two of them enrolled in one of two Nichols Travel Program courses: John T. Dahlquist's "London in the History of Britain" and George Chlebak's "Tour de France," which featured no bike rides through the Pyrenees but plenty of examination of Gothic art and architecture. The low turnout for travel courses was primarily due to students' and parents' anxiety over recent and current world events, which included the international uncertainty following the downfall of communism in eastern Europe and the possibility of danger to Americans traveling abroad as a result of the Gulf War. The Nichols Travel Program hit full stride, however, the following January when dozens of students headed for destinations as diverse as Scotland, Turkey, and the Caribbean.[20]

The success of the Nichols Travel Program led to the abandonment of the Honors International Program in 1992. That same year the Nichols family donated another half million dollars to fund a full-time director of the travel program. Dahlquist stepped down after fourteen years as dean of the faculty to assume the new position, taking over for Fitzhugh Spragins, who had directed the program on a part-time basis for the first two years. To replace the valuable longer-term foreign study experiences offered by the defunct Honors International Program, Dahlquist led the college's efforts to establish exchange programs with individual institutions. In 1995 Russ Galbraith of Bryant traveled to England to attend University College of Scarborough as Lyon College's first exchange student under the new arrangement. Soon thereafter, formal agreements were signed with universities in Scotland, Northern Ireland, and Mexico, and by 1996 the college catalog boasted a minor in international studies. In 1995 math professor Ed Mosley succeeded Dahlquist as director of the newly renamed Nichols Study-Travel Program; Mosley's chief effort was to move the program away from the January term format toward the development of semester-long courses featuring a two-week travel component at the end.[21]

Although student-faculty research and foreign travel and study were the first things that came to mind when considering distinctive elements of the curriculum in the early 1990s, the Griffith years witnessed the development of additional programs that promised curricular distinctions. Capitalizing on the West-era adoption of Highland Scottish trappings as a key element in the college's public image, the director of the Scottish Heritage Program collaborated with the music department to develop a minor in Scottish Arts with a concentration on bagpiping and the history of Scottish music. It was also during the 1990s that the college developed the resident artist and executive programs. With the completion of the Lyon Building in 1993, the college inaugurated the Executive-in-Residence program as part of the business and economics faculty. Board vice-chairman Graham Holloway, who as interim president five years earlier had launched the Arkansas Business Leaders Symposium, returned to campus that fall as Arkansas College's first Executive-in-Residence.[22]

In the fall of 1993 Andrea Budy, an award-winning poet who had settled in nearby Mountain View, became Arkansas College's first Artist-in-Residence. Budy developed the successful and popular Visiting Writers Series and resurrected the literary society tradition with the reincarnation of the Erosophic Society, which sponsored monthly, public poetry readings. In the summer of 1995 Budy organized the first White River Writers' Workshop, a week-long conference in which invited poets took part in seminars, public discussions, and poetry readings. The workshop attracted several accomplished poets from around the nation and generated enough positive reaction and publicity that a second one was held the following summer. With no endowment and only a slim hold on the budget, however, both the Writers' Workshop and Artist-in-Residence programs fell victim to budget cuts in 1997. Nevertheless, the Visiting Writers Series continued into the new millennium, bolstered by alumna and John Steinbeck scholar Martha Heasley Cox's endowment of the Leila Lenore Heasley Lecture Series in 1996. Novelist Rosellen Brown appeared on campus for two days in

Tour de France. Professors George Chlebak (*bottom left*) and Ed Mosley (*bottom right*) and students in one of the first Nichols Travel courses pose beneath the Eiffel Tower.

The Pipes and Drums cross the bridge over Bryan Lake during the Ozark Scottish Festival, 1991.

March 1997 as the first Heasley Lecturer; since its inception the Heasley Lecture has attracted to campus such critically acclaimed writers as Donald Harington and William Least Heat-Moon.[23]

The Artist-in-Residence and Executive-in-Residence programs were designed to complement a faculty that Griffith hoped to build into one of the strongest of any liberal arts college in the region. The president was well aware that the ultimate success or failure of the academic phase of the Strategic Plan hinged on the institution's ability to build and maintain a first-rate faculty. As we have seen, the West administration made great strides in this direction, especially with the proliferation of endowed professorships in the 1980s. By the time Griffith arrived at the end of the decade, Arkansas College boasted a solid corps of experienced and dedicated professors around which to build the kind of faculty expected of a Category I institution. Nevertheless, there were challenges to be addressed. Research for the Strategic Plan revealed that faculty salaries at Arkansas College lagged significantly behind those offered by other selective liberal arts colleges in the south central region. Furthermore, the college's tenure and promotion system, introduced in the McCain administration and updated during the West years, was outdated and failed to meet the minimum requirements set forth by the American Association of University Professors (AAUP). Finally, the small size of the faculty (fewer than fifty full-time professors and instructors in 1989–1990) limited the school's ability to expand course offerings and curricular programs.[24]

Griffith attempted to improve opportunities for faculty when in the spring of 1990 he used a portion of the president's discretionary fund to create the Lyon Faculty Fellowships, small stipends designated for summer research or professional development and aimed specifically toward new tenure-track faculty. The Lyon Faculty Fellowships signaled a movement toward increased emphasis on faculty scholarship, a direction that was affirmed two years later when the board of trustees adopted a new tenure and promotion policy that brought professional expectations at Arkansas College in line with those at peer institutions across the country. Although not of the "publish or perish" variety found on large university campuses, the new tenure and promotion system carried modest professional development requirements and contained an "up or out" clause, which prevented the college from retaining faculty members for whom tenure had been denied. The Strategic Plan also reinforced the college's new scholarship expectations by promising to reduce the annual course load from eight to six, although the course goal was raised to seven at the plan's midterm reevaluation in 1995. In keeping with the plan's concentration on the liberal arts, the Griffith years saw the addition to the faculty of positions in Spanish, French, history, theatre, physics, philosophy, and chemistry, and the faculty approved new professorships in art history and anthropology, positions that, due to budget restraints, were filled only after Griffith's departure.[25]

Against the backdrop of curricular reform and frequent divisional shuffling, the faculty relied on stability and able leadership in the dean's office, which remained under the care of John T. Dahlquist or Robert Holyer throughout most of Griffith's tenure. By the mid-1990s the college possessed its most experienced, talented, and scholarly faculty in its more than 120 years of existence. Within the first three years of Griffith's presidency the number of endowed professorships had grown to eighteen. Included in this number were two positions funded by a million-dollar gift from the family of the late Shuford Nichols in 1992: the William Jefferson Clinton Professorship in International Politics, first occupied by Bradley Gitz in 1994, and the J. William Fulbright Professorship of Modern Languages, which Spanish scholar Bart L. Lewis filled in 1993. The Griffith administration also witnessed a wave of positive publicity generated by the faculty. In addition to the accolades for student-faculty research in the sciences, professors on the Batesville campus laid claim to the state's most prestigious higher education teaching award. In 1997 Lewis was named Arkansas Professor of the Year by the Carnegie Foundation for the Advancement of Teaching and the Council for Advancement and Support of Education (CASE). By this time, Griffith's last year at Lyon College, the CASE award had become almost commonplace among the faculty, having been bestowed upon Roberta Bustin (chemistry) in 1989, George Lankford (folklore) in 1991, Terrell Tebbetts (English) in 1992, and Scott Peterson (biology) in 1994. In spite of the obvious successes of the faculty, however, the college's inability to reach and maintain the salary level of highly selective residential institutions in the region, due primarily to budget restraints resulting from declining enrollment and overspending on financial aid, continued to concern veteran faculty members and hamper recruitment of highly qualified scholar-teachers. By 1994 the faculty identified the effect of the college's low salary scale on recruitment as one of the primary hindrances to progress. In October 1996 the board of trustees adopted a plan to establish a salary increase pool of 1–2 percent above the rate of inflation, but the situation had improved little by the time Griffith left a year later.[26]

With the increased demands on faculty scholarship and the general movement toward selective college status, the quality and size of the library became a pressing issue. The Strategic Plan called for expanding the library's holdings to 200,000 volumes by the year 2000, which represented an increase of almost 200 percent over current collections in 1990; declining enrollment and budget tightening in the mid-1990s influenced the decision to reduce the goal to 150,000 volumes. In the process of trying to reach this goal, the library underwent several important changes in the 1990s under the direction of Dean Covington. The switch from a traditional card catalog system to a computerized one was accomplished during the 1990–1991 session, resulting in an increase in book circulation of almost 75 percent in the first year alone. The rapid growth in collections necessitated physical expansion for the library. In 1994–1995, with funding from the Mabee Foundation and a major donation by the family of trustee J. D. Simpson III, the educational annex on the east side of the Mabee Learning Resources Center was renovated and merged with the library to form the re-christened Mabee-Simpson Library. This major addition to the library provided more space for collections as well as faculty offices and student study rooms. By the time Griffith left in late 1997, the library's holdings had doubled to approximately 140,000 volumes, and the improvement of interlibrary loan and development of on-line databases promised to provide even more services for the faculty and the student body.[27]

Although faculty composition and expectations, library quality, and the curriculum underwent significant alterations during the Griffith administration, the first element of the Strategic Plan's academic program to be implemented was the Honor System. As we have seen, Arkansas College developed an honor system during the 1920s, but by midcentury it was defunct. The creation of an honor system had long been on the mind of board chairman Robert A. Young III, whose alma mater, Washington and Lee, maintained a simple code of honesty and integrity introduced by General Robert E. Lee and based on the code of honor at West Point. The new president shared Young's regard for an honor system and wasted no time before championing the cause to the college community. Shortly after assuming the presidency, Griffith convinced the Student Government Association to appoint an Honor Code Committee. The committee, chaired by junior Jim Endrihs, studied honor codes from elite institutions such as Washington and Lee and the University of the South and interviewed Arkansas College students to assess local interest in such a system. In the spring semester of 1990 the Honor Code Committee completed its draft of a proposed honor pledge and urged the student body, faculty, and administration to adopt the pledge. Overshadowed and slowed by the completion of the self-study and general implementation of the Strategic Plan, the honor system took two years in coming to fruition. On 11 March 1992 Griffith cancelled classes and requested that all students, faculty, and staff participate in a day-long program on the value and meaning of an honor system, including a panel discussion with student and faculty representatives from Davidson, Rhodes, and the University of the South. In a plebiscite held one month later, Arkansas College students formally adopted the honor pledge and honor system, which received the approval of the board of trustees soon thereafter.[28]

Designed to foster a sense of integrity, responsibility, and community among students and faculty, the Honor System consisted of a brief, four-sentence pledge, to which new students and faculty demonstrated their acquiescence by signing the Roll of Honor each fall at the matriculation ceremony, and an Honor Council made up of a dozen students elected by their peers. The Honor Council was given the authority to try students accused of code violations and to penalize those found guilty, with a maximum sentence of expulsion from school. The first major challenge to the new system came in 1996 when a suspended student filed a lawsuit in Independence County Circuit Court. Although the ruling did nothing to challenge the legality of the Honor System, the case did serve as something of a temporary impediment to the development of the system when in 1998 the jury ordered the college to pay the plaintiff more than $20,000, a verdict that was eventually overturned on appeal.[29]

An offshoot of the Honor System and its Honor Council was the Social Council, which was implemented during the 1994–1995 academic session. The Social Council, whose duty was to hear cases involving potential violations of social policies dealing with such issues as alcohol and dormitory visitation, represented only one facet of the work accomplished by the Student Life Study Commission, one of a half dozen groups appointed by Griffith to fill in the broad outlines of the Strategic Plan. And the Student Life Study Commission focused on just one area within a wide range of student and campus life affairs addressed by the Strategic Plan: financial aid and recruiting, student body demographics, residential issues, and campus activities.[30]

The first area approached by the Student Life Study Commission—and the one that eventually led to the establishment of the Social System and Social Council—was the issue of social responsibility and ethics. One result of the commission's work was a gradual liberalization of dormitory visitation policies. Even more important, especially in terms of student interest and public relations, was the reopening of a dialogue concerning the college's alcohol policies. Alcohol had been banned from dorm rooms and the college campus since the mid-1970s, even for students twenty-one and older. By the 1980s explicit student protest over these restrictions had all but disappeared, replaced instead by widespread, barely covert disregard for school rules. The trail to Newport had become something of a tradition at an institution lacking in traditions. Nevertheless, some students and faculty denounced the college's policies as hypocritical because alcohol was regularly served to trustees and guests attending receptions at the president's home as well as at special functions held at the Faculty House on 23rd Street. Others claimed that the no-alcohol policies were simply outdated in late-twentieth-century America, and, perhaps even more serious for a school like Arkansas College, might hamper recruitment and retention.

Both chairman Young and Griffith agreed that the time had come to at least reappraise the college's stance. Consequently, in 1990 Griffith, at the behest of the

Student Life Committee of the board, appointed a Presidential Task Force to study and evaluate the policies regarding alcohol. Under the direction of new dean of students Bruce Johnston, the Task Force recommended revising the alcohol policies to allow students twenty-one or older to store and consume alcoholic beverages in their dorm rooms. In an attempt to head off criticism from local church groups and leaders, the Task Force also designed an alcohol education program to accompany the altered policies. The board of trustees adopted the Task Force's proposal in the spring of 1991 and approved its implementation beginning the following fall semester. In spite of the efforts to circumvent protests to the new policies, Griffith spent much of the 1991–1992 year defending the Task Force and its new alcohol program from vocal critics in the community. The Task Force continued to refine the system until the fall of 1994 when the board adopted a new alcohol policy that placed greater stress on teaching abstinence through the continuing alcohol education program.[31]

The Honor System and Social System were important components of many selective residential institutions, and thus the adoption of these programs was an integral step in the march toward Carnegie Category I status, a journey that frequently saw the college emulate schools that it hoped one day to compete with on a level field. Perhaps nowhere was this imitation more evident than in the area of recruitment and student body development. Much of the focus of the Strategic Plan centered on improving admissions selectivity and transforming the student body from one dominated by commuters to one in which the vast majority of students lived on campus. Specific goals in the Strategic Plan included raising the average ACT score by more than 15 percent to 26 and increasing the number of residential students to six hundred by the end of the millennium, both of which would place the college within closer proximity to Carnegie Category I institutions in the region.

In order to attract the high-quality, residential students on which a selective liberal arts college depended, the Griffith administration overhauled admissions policies and recruiting strategies. Under the direction of new dean of admissions Jonathan Stroud, in 1990–1991 the admissions office instituted a number of changes designed to "increase diversity and quality" among incoming freshmen and to attract increasing numbers of out-of-state students. The new approach included a fifteen-dollar application fee, a common practice at selective institutions, as well as a more complex system used to evaluate applicants, one that relied on more than standardized test scores and high school grade point averages. A brand-new series of admissions publications, most of them featuring student and faculty portraits taken by a professional photographer from North Carolina, signaled the college's changing image to prospective students. Furthermore, the admissions staff attempted to broaden the institution's regional presence by intensifying recruiting efforts in urban centers such as St. Louis, Memphis, and Dallas-Fort Worth. All of these changes were designed to enhance the perception of Arkansas College as a more prestigious institution, which in turn, it was expected, would attract greater numbers of the academically superior and financially affluent students whom the college had coveted since the 1950s. By the spring of 1993 the college also boasted a professionally designed, thirty-minute recruiting video.[32]

The arrival of a new dean of admissions (now vice-president for enrollment services) in mid-decade resulted in an intensification of selective, liberal arts recruiting strategies. In 1995–1996 the admissions and alumni offices cooperated in the development of the Lyon Admission Team, a program that relied on active alumni to contact prospective students in Little Rock, Batesville, Jonesboro, and other cities. The following year the admissions office completely revamped the college's application, requiring for the first time an essay from potential matriculates and requesting that faculty members personally respond to students whose essays dealt with their particular academic strengths. The attempt to cultivate an image of selectivity must have worked, for by the latter years of the Griffith administration a sort of natural selection had winnowed out most unqualified applicants and in the process had thinned the total applicant pool considerably.[33]

Although, as we shall see more fully later, the overall enrollment goals adopted in the Strategic Plan proved well beyond reach, the Griffith administration did witness significant strides toward the goals of improving student quality and cultivating a primarily residential student body. The percentage of non-Arkansans in the freshman class more than doubled between 1991 and 1992, and by 1993 more than 90 percent of freshmen resided on campus, up from fewer than 75 percent just two years earlier. The higher percentage of residents reflected the declining number of students from the Batesville region, a goal of the Strategic Plan whose rapid realization in the 1990s was spurred by among other things competition from community colleges, rising tuition costs, decreasing recruitment efforts in the area, and a backlash toward the college's developing elitist image. The aptitude of incoming freshmen continued to improve into the mid-1990s. Beginning in 1993 the college accepted no one with an ACT score below 18; by 1995 this policy had helped raise the average test score of freshmen on campus to just under the goal of 26. The residential population also increased steadily until mid-decade. With the completion of McRae and Wilson and Rogers halls in 1989 and Hoke-McCain Hall in 1994, the Griffith years saw housing capacity expand by more than 160 beds. Consequently, by the fall of 1995 the on-campus population had surpassed 400 for the first time, prompting dean of students Bruce Johnston's observation that the "residential college is quickly becoming reality."[34]

A major priority of the Griffith administration was the enhancement of student life and the campus experience for the increasingly residential college. In addition to encouraging the development of the Honor and Social systems, the president championed greater student participation in extracurricular activities and athletics. In his first year in Batesville, Griffith urged students to form a pep band for home basketball games (even volunteering to wield the cymbals himself) and arranged for the construction of a beach volleyball court east of the gymnasium. In an attempt to encourage excellence, community service, and friendly competition, he established the President's Cup in the spring of 1990. Awarded to the top Greek organization based on a formula that assigned scores in areas such as intramural athletics, academic achievement, and community service, the President's Cup consisted of a silver trophy and cash stipend provided by trustee P. K. Holmes. By the time the first President's

Cup was awarded to Kappa Sigma fraternity in 1991, Arkansas College contained two new Greek organizations. In addition to older fraternities and sororities such as Tau Kappa Epsilon, Kappa Kappa Alpha, and Alpha Xi Delta, a group of female students founded Zeta Omega during the latter part of the West administration, a sorority that became a colony of Phi Mu in 1992. The Griffith years also witnessed the brief existence of a small Arkansas College chapter of the fraternity Delta Upsilon as well as the creation of a new local fraternity, Phi Theta Gamma.[35]

Community service became a hallmark of campus activities during the Griffith administration. In 1990 members of the Campus Ministry Board made the first of many trips to labor on house-building projects for Habitat for Humanity. In September 1991 Griffith inaugurated Service Day, a day in which the college cancelled classes to allow and encourage students and faculty to participate in organized community service activities around the Batesville area. Community service projects continued to occupy a key position in the social programs of Greek organizations as well.[36]

Students of the 1990s enjoyed access to a variety of new academic and social organizations, such as Omicron Delta Epsilon (economics honor society), Phi Alpha Theta (history honors society), and the Erosophic Society. Traditional extracurricular activities—music, theatre, intramurals—also attracted participants. The Harlequin Theatre was perhaps the chief beneficiary of the Griffith administration. The completion of Holloway Theatre in the spring of 1991 provided the troupe with a modern, black box experimental theatre. Michael Counts arrived a year and a half later to develop the college's newly focused theatre major and to help Harlequin Theatre reconnect with the glory days of its past.[37]

Athletics remained among the most popular extracurricular activities on campus during the Griffith era. The athletic program underwent significant changes. Realizing the need for more varsity team sports, both for purposes of student participation and entertainment, Griffith supported the expansion of women's and men's programs during the 1990s. In the fall of 1991 the president used a portion of his discretionary fund as seed money to help kick-start a new soccer club. Although a favorite project of Griffith's, the Rowdies, as members of the soccer team referred to themselves, never advanced to varsity status. Two other team sports did, however. The 1992–1993 academic year saw the reestablishment of two former Arkansas College sports: baseball and women's volleyball. The baseball Scots resumed play in February 1993 after a hiatus of nearly twenty years. Under the tutelage of coach Kirk Kelley, the Scots posted a respectable 23–27–1 record in their first year of competition. The baseball team, in true Arkansas/Lyon College fashion, remained competitors, though rarely challengers, over the next few seasons. One of the biggest milestones for the baseball program happened a few months after Griffith's departure when the Scots played their first home game on the new campus baseball field on 6 February 1998, a 14–8 victory over Hillsdale Baptist College.[38]

Although the college continued to field varsity teams in cross-country, golf, and tennis, basketball remained the preeminent sport on the Batesville campus. The Scots never regained the form, or talent level, that had taken them to the top of the Arkansas

Intercollegiate Conference in the early and mid-1980s. Their best finish in the Griffith era came in 1991 when the Scots reached the semifinals of the District 17 tournament. Coach Terry Garner marshaled the team for four more years before stepping down to serve as athletic director in 1995; his successor was assistant coach and former Scot player Kevin Jenkins. Despite the lack of team success, the Scots did produce two honorable mention all-American post players in the 1990s, Lyle Middleton in 1992 and Ryland Kieffer in 1997. The Pipers, who played the first half of the 1990s in one of the nation's toughest small college conferences, won no championships but experienced more team and individual successes than the Scots. Behind the coaching of Randy Gatling, who replaced Jerry Hutchison in 1989, the Pipers developed into one of the AIC's best women's teams in the early 1990s. Their best finish came in 1992 when they lost in the district finals to Arkansas Tech, the eventual national champions. Individually, five different Pipers received all-conference or all-region awards, including three-time all-AIC performers Grace Catt and Brandi Love and Lyon College's first and only women's basketball all-American Stephanie Rowton, who was named to the NAIA's second team in 1998. Catt finished her career in 1991 as the school's all-time leading scorer and rebounder; she also earned the distinction of being the first female athlete in the AIC to earn all-conference honors in three different sporting events when she excelled in basketball, cross-country, and track during 1988–1989.[39]

One critical development overshadowed all others in the realm of collegiate athletics during the 1990s—the dissolution of the AIC. Arkansas College was a charter member of the Arkansas Intercollegiate Conference upon its founding in 1928. For more than sixty years the AIC pitted tiny liberal arts colleges like Arkansas College and College of the Ozarks against larger state colleges and universities such as the University of Central Arkansas and Arkansas Tech University. Although differing enrollments, athletic budgets, and admissions standards had frequently placed schools like Arkansas College and Hendrix at a disadvantage, the AIC was valuable in many regards. It provided traditional, in-state rivalries that in some cases were nearly one hundred years old. For institutions with limited athletic budgets, the conference also saved money because all the member schools were in the state. And just as important to an institution like Arkansas College, competition against in-state opponents, and especially larger universities, generated much-needed publicity throughout Arkansas through local and state newspaper and television coverage.

Rumors had been forecasting the demise of the old conference for years. The prospect of breaking up the AIC was particularly appealing to the institutions with strong football programs who looked to improve their level of competition by playing more schools outside the state. The small schools were not above looking toward other options either. As early as 1991–1992 Griffith and Garner had begun discussing the possibility of leaving the expensive NAIA for Division II of the National Collegiate Athletic Association (NCAA). Although it did not come as a shock to anyone involved in the conference, the announcement in the summer of 1994 that the AIC would come to an end after the 1994–1995 season was still hard to accept. Hendrix's decision to enter Division III (nonscholarship) of the NCAA coupled with the decision of three football teams to leave the conference left the AIC with only half a dozen teams in its final year. The college held joint membership in the NCAA (Division II) and the NAIA from 1994 to 1997 while trying to find a new home. In the latter year the Scots and Pipers joined the TranSouth Athletic Conference, a collection of twelve NAIA institutions in Arkansas, Tennessee, Mississippi, Alabama, and Georgia and began the process of trying to forge new rivalries with colleges that many people in Arkansas had never heard of.[40]

The most ambitious undertaking in the area of campus life was the development of the house system, a strategy designed to promote intellectual and social development by intermingling academics with residential life. The house system, whereby dormitories are arranged into clusters called houses and the houses contain faculty residences, developed as a response to the college's poor retention rates. The first step in this direction occurred in the fall of 1991 when the administration decided to house all freshmen together in the dormitories on the old Morrow Quadrangle in hopes of stemming freshman-to-sophomore attrition rates that often exceeded 30 percent. When freshmen retention rates improved under the new arrangement, Griffith, trustees, and others in the college community began to consider the development of a full-fledged house system similar to the famous programs maintained at elite institutions such as Harvard and Princeton. As a result of these discussions, the college's newest residence facility was designed to accommodate a live-in faculty member. When Young House, consisting of Hoke and McCain halls, opened in the fall of 1994, the college brought in a young philosophy professor, Michael Glass, to serve as the first preceptor in the fledgling house system. Retention fell off again in the mid-1990s, however, prompting Griffith to appoint a committee headed by Spanish professor Bart Lewis to design and implement a campus-wide house system. After a group visit to observe Harvard's house system firsthand, the committee drafted its plan in the spring of 1997. Alumnus and math professor Ed Mosley agreed to serve as the first Mary and Robert A. Young III House Master of the freshman complex, and he and his wife moved into the new Spragins House, which was constructed as an addition to the Morrow Quadrangle building, the following fall.[41]

Perhaps the most significant outcome of the various Griffith-era campus programs and attempts to promote a residential atmosphere was a heightened degree of student involvement in social and academic affairs. Through their positions on the Strategic Planning Task Force, NCA self-study committees, and the various commissions appointed to flesh out the specifics of the Griffith administration philosophies, students of the 1990s experienced an unprecedented level of input and participation in the college's affairs. Students played key roles in the design and implementation of the Honor and Social systems. Many students also responded to the president's open-dialogue policies and engaging personality by voicing complaints and opinions. In the fall of 1990 a group of students responded to faculty desires to eliminate the January interim term by carrying out a "Save Jan Term" campaign. The campaign proved successful, though the faculty succeeded in abandoning the January term after 1998. The spring of 1991 brought another round of protests when many upperclassmen reacted unfavorably toward the plan to maintain separate housing for freshmen. Many students also voiced disapproval of the frequent and substantial tuition and fee increases of the early 1990s. The central role of students in both the Honor System and the Social System assured the continuation of the newer, more stringent demands on student activity and participation. Students were also among the detractors of the Strategic Plan and its eventual elimination of several major areas of study; one of the most common worries was that the curriculum's stricter emphasis on the liberal arts and pre-graduate study would hinder opportunities for those seeking immediate employment following graduation.[42]

For the most part the discontent of the 1990s was healthy and even refreshing, a sign of concern on the part of the student body. And as in past eras when student participation had risen, the atmosphere reflected the presence of many promising young men and women on campus. Once the college embarked on its journey toward Carnegie Category I status, Griffith never missed an opportunity to laud special student achievements and to celebrate the growing lists of prominent graduate and professional schools to which Arkansas/Lyon College graduates were being accepted. In 1989 sophomore LaVerne Cox became the first Arkansas College student, and the only Arkansan that year, to receive the prestigious Truman Scholarship, which provided money for two years of graduate or professional education after completion of the bachelor's degree. Five years later senior Brad Austin, who in 1990 had been named the college's first Alumni Council Scholar, was awarded a valuable Rotary Fellowship for a year's study in Scotland. As an increasing percentage of the college's graduates in the 1990s looked to continue their education beyond the bachelor's level, the expanding list of destinations came to include graduate and professional schools at Harvard, Yale, Rice, Vanderbilt, Duke, and other institutions.[43]

Such student success stories could work wonders for the college's image. The practice of image development was integral to the Griffith administration and to the realization of the Strategic Plan's Carnegie Category I dreams. In many respects, image building was the institution's primary activity throughout much of the 1990s. Even such seemingly straightforward tasks as curriculum revision and campus life innovations were often undertaken with one eye gauging the public's response. This is not surprising when one considers that at the heart of the Strategic Plan lay a concern over the public's image of the little Batesville college, an anxiety that had been present among the school's leadership for at least forty years by the time Griffith arrived in town. When it came right down to it, the quest for Carnegie Category I status was the quest for a new image, a perception of exclusivity and excellence that would assure the college a secure place, a niche, in the churning marketplace of higher education. Because many other colleges had already secured such an image, and the academic ranking that accompanied it, Arkansas College would not have to rely on innovation as much as on emulation. Adopt the trappings of the elite institutions—a dangerous label in Arkansas—and the honor students from the suburbs, the money from the wealthy donors and foundations, and the press coverage trumpeting success would follow.

Even before Griffith's arrival Arkansas College had begun to cultivate an image of academic excellence, at least within the realm of comprehensive, regional institutions, those maintaining a dual focus on liberal arts education as well as professional and pre-professional training. Arkansas College first appeared in the top ten of *U.S. News and World Report*'s list of the best regional small colleges (Carnegie Category II) in the South in the fall of 1986. This strong showing was due in no small part to the school's unusually large endowment (at the time) for such a small institution. Two years later Arkansas College made a second appearance on the list; although a third waited until 1991, by mid-decade the school was a fixture among the top-ten southern institutions in its category.[44] Although the ratings of magazines owed little to an institution's ability to market an image, the new president promptly displayed his skill and determination in this area when he helped orchestrate a publicity-generating backlash against the editor of the *Arkansas Democrat* in the winter of 1990. In a rare editorial that appeared to skirt controversy, John Robert Starr praised recent developments at Ouachita Baptist University and urged the Arkadelphia institution to challenge Hendrix as the best small college in the state. His failure to so much as mention the existence of Arkansas College elicited a deluge of impassioned letters to the editor, many of them influenced by Griffith's comments in reaction to the perhaps inadvertent slight. In response, Starr dispatched a young reporter to do a front-page feature on the Batesville college, an article that produced some of the school's best publicity in years.[45]

The compliments from the *Arkansas Democrat*, *U.S. News and World Report*, and other publications made good grist for the college's publicity mill. And an effective mill it was. Behind the leadership and vision of talented Independence County native and alumnus Mark Wood, the college's public relations office worked closely with Griffith and other administrators to transform the institution's image during the 1990s. The development of an image of selectivity and excellence anticipated the rise to Carnegie Category I status and also helped to ensure and maintain that rise. Following in the wake of the Strategic Plan, Wood and his assistants helped alter the look and persona of Arkansas College in the early 1990s. Using professional photographs and cutting-edge desktop-publishing techniques, Wood's office designed an award-winning new viewbook, "Faces and Voices," in 1990–1991. In the fall of 1991 the *Piper*, which Wood edited, revealed its watershed "Out of the Shadow: Becoming a National College" issue, which featured a lengthy interview with Griffith as well as candid discussions of the demanding road to academic prominence. Two years later Wood redesigned the layout and format of the *Piper*, reflecting the more mature and serious academic tone that had come to dominate the alumni magazine in recent years. The magazine's feature articles in the early and mid-1990s frequently touched on the issue of image or public identity, almost always in a light that supported the lofty goals and initiatives of the Griffith administration.[46]

That landmark fall 1991 edition of the *Piper* also alluded to an issue that would dominate much of the public's and college community's perception and analysis of the Griffith years, the name change. The movement to adopt a new name for Arkansas College became the centerpiece of the campaign of image development during the first half of the 1990s; in the process it became the single most controversial and memorable episode of the Griffith administration, perhaps in the long history of the institution as well.[47]

Although most alumni and students had remained blissfully unaware, the topic of changing the name of Arkansas College had been surfacing, sinking, and resurfacing at least since the immediate post–World War II era. The earliest record of an official discussion of the institution's name dates from November 1946, when members of the executive committee of the board mentioned the need to distinguish between Arkansas College and Arkansas State College in Jonesboro. Few within the circle of the college's leadership, including President John D. Spragins, favored a name change, and the issue lay dormant for almost a decade. The failed merger movement of the early 1950s rekindled name change discussions, and the advocates of adopting a new name found an ally in new president Paul M. McCain. As early as 1956 McCain broached the subject in a meeting of the board, arguing that the generic name bred confusion and led potential students and donors to believe that Arkansas College was a state institution. Although there is no clear reason why the topic died once more, it is likely that McCain and the trustees who favored a change met resistance from the obstinate chairman, John P. Morrow Sr., for it was only after his death that the trustees returned to the subject of a name change. In the fall of 1966, now under the direction of chairman Shuford Nichols, the board appointed a committee to study a proposed name change. The committee recommended changing the school's name and suggested that the board adopt Aaron Lyon College as the new title, a name that both evoked the heritage of the community and institution (longtime Batesville resident Aaron Lyon had served as the first vice-president of the board) and promised to place the college at the head of any alphabetized listing of institutions (a marketing justification that McCain, only partially in jest, championed vehemently). Once again, however, the proposal encountered too much opposition on the board; Batesville's little school would remain Arkansas College.[48]

Despite Dan C. West's support for the idea of a name change, discussions went nowhere in the 1970s and 1980s, so that it was Arkansas College that welcomed the Griffiths in 1989. The movement to change the institution's name became inextricably linked with the implementation of the Strategic Plan and the cultivation of a new image of distinctiveness in the following years. From the very beginning of the Griffith administration the name change became a priority of the college's leadership. In one of his first meetings with board chairman Robert A. Young III, Griffith expressed his desire to finally carry the odyssey of the name change to fruition. Young and other trustees agreed to reopen the matter. Consequently, one of Griffith's first presidential duties in the fall of 1989 involved a visit to Rhodes College, the former Southwestern at Memphis that had adopted its new name only five years earlier. Accompanied by Young and former board chairman Frank Lyon Sr., Griffith discussed the process of Rhodes's change with administrators in hopes of learning from the Memphis school's successes and regrets. Agreeing with Young that a change of name would benefit Arkansas College but that any such change should be accomplished through unilateral action of the board of trustees, Griffith oversaw the inclusion of a statement requesting consideration of a name change in the Strategic Plan.[49]

Two years later, after the curricular and social system restructuring programs called for in the plan were well under way, the Alumni Council unanimously adopted a resolution endorsing "the purpose of joining together in supporting and implementing a name change." At its spring 1992 meeting, the board adopted a similar resolution and instructed Griffith to take the necessary steps to prepare for a name change and review potential new names. Griffith promptly appointed an Arkansas College Name Change Advisory Committee, chaired by vice-president for institutional advancement Darrell Loyless and composed of faculty, staff, trustees, students, and alumni, and the Advisory Committee hired a professional firm from Denver to conduct a comprehensive study of the effectiveness of the current name, the possibilities of a new name, and the potential challenges and rewards that would accompany the adoption of a new name. After interviewing faculty members, current students, alumni, and trustees and after conducting phone surveys, the firm issued its report in late 1992. By this time the issue had been debated thoroughly enough within the college community that the report offered few surprises. Arkansas College's name awareness was "extremely low" outside the state and perhaps even lower within the state than some might have believed. The reasons marshaled in support of a name change were by now familiar: confusion with state institutions, the lack of a "concise, high impact, one-word" name, the negative connotations of the word Arkansas and the impact this had on out-of-state recruiting, and the failure to convey a sense of uniqueness or dignity. Most of these reasons owed something to the Griffith administration's attention to the power of image. In fact, the report noted as its raison d'être the resolution of "certain image and identity deficiencies or perceptual problems."[50]

As one would expect, reaction within the college community toward such a personal and controversial issue was mixed. The report found alumni and students with any number of opinions, some supportive of a name change, some hostile, some quite unconcerned. Many current students and recent alumni expressed dismay over the college's lack of a positive image and blamed the situation on the name, while an older alumnus supportive of the name change proposal summed up his alma mater as possessing "a proud 120 year history with no tradition," again the implication being that the name Arkansas College contributed to the anonymity. Although much of the most vocal support for the name change emanated from such areas as the board of trustees and the admissions office, or the school's representatives most likely to encounter negative reactions to the name Arkansas College outside of the region surrounding Batesville, the most vociferous opponents to change came from the growing body of alumni. Graduates of the college informed the consulting firm that the confusion with other institutions in the state, perhaps the most common argument of the pro-change forces, was overblown and isolated. One alumnus expressed the common fear that abandoning the name Arkansas College would "unravel the historic fabric that the school has woven." Other alumni reacted strongly to what they viewed as an excessive concern with image. In a letter to Darrell Loyless, one alumnus warned that a name change would not magically cure the institution's long-running identity crisis, a challenge against which, the writer observed, almost all small schools struggled. Another criticized the proposed name change as "a marketing strategy, i.e., sell more Arkansas College, have more students, take in more money, and perhaps be bigger." Although the administration and board would never have used the language of crass commercialism, the name change movement was in essence motivated by the forces of image development and marketing, to both students and potential donors. It was a realistic reaction to the challenges inherent in the drive to achieve academic excellence and the reputation necessary to sustain it.[51]

Occasionally nonalumni voiced their opinions to college officials. In one of the more interesting reactions to the talk of name change, an elderly Little Rock man inveighed upon alumni director Lucy Yeager to "please gather a crowd and run that guy off who wants to change the name of the school." In the same letter the man, a high school classmate of Frank Lyon Sr., praised the longtime trustee: "I am so happy for what he has done for the college." The author of the letter must have had mixed reactions a year and a half later when the new name was finally announced. But the unveiling of a new name seemed far in the future even by the time the Name Change Advisory Committee submitted its report to the board in March 1993 recommending a definite name change and offering five possibilities for the new designation.[52]

Of the five names recommended to the board for consideration, three had been suggested by the consulting firm based on preliminary market research: Allanby, a Scottish-sounding name created by the firm; Longkirk, a combination of the college's founder with the Scottish Presbyterian word for church; and Makemie, name of the father of American Presbyterianism and a possibility that had been debated in the 1960s. In addition, the Name Change Advisory Committee also threw into the pot the current name, now more than 120 years old, as well as Lyon, a shortened version of Paul McCain's old favorite that satisfied the desire for a strong, one-word title and honored the Lyon family's half century of service and friendship to the college. After the executive committee of the board substituted Aberdeen for Makemie, which appears to have been dropped primarily because no two people could agree on its spelling or pronunciation, and added a sixth candidate, McRae, the consulting firm conducted a market research campaign through phone surveys with high school counselors and parents of college students during the summer of 1993. Using a variety of questions to determine name recognition and prestige within and outside the state and region, the surveys revealed Aberdeen to be the most popular and promising name, followed in most categories by Longkirk and McRae. Arkansas College consistently finished last among the six, though the decision not to test the current name in surveys conducted within 150 miles of Batesville likely rendered Arkansas College's apparent unpopularity a self-fulfilling prophecy.[53]

Once the survey results were complete, the executive committee asked Griffith, Young, and vice-chairman Graham Holloway to discuss further the potential names and make a recommendation to the full board. In the end Aberdeen College, the best testing of the candidates and a favorite among alumni and students because of the possibility of maintaining the acronym A.C., lost out due to legal concerns over rights to the name (because of Scotland's Aberdeen University) and the negative connotations of the old Aberdeen Development Corporation in the Batesville community. With Aberdeen out of the way, the "excellent graphics potential" of Lyon, as well as the promise of honoring one of the institution's most prominent leaders of the twentieth century, catapulted the four-letter word ahead of the other competitors. But the name change was easier discussed than accomplished. It took hours of pleading and reassurance by Griffith and Young on two separate visits to the Lyons' Little Rock home before the humble and reluctant former board chairman relented and agreed to approve the college's adoption of his family name. The Lyon family's primary concern, one understandably shared by the board and administration, was that the public and the college community might construe the change as the sale of the name to the highest bidder. It is quite likely that the quiet and unassuming Frank Lyon Sr., worried about the public's perception of his family's role in the name change process, never fully reconciled the immense and, most would probably agree, deserved honor with the trepidation it inspired.[54]

Some two months after convincing Frank Lyon Sr. and Marion Bradley Lyon to embrace the college's decision, Griffith and the trustees unveiled the new name to the public in an open session of the board in Brown Chapel on the morning of 23 February 1994, the one hundred and sixtieth anniversary of the birth of Isaac J. Long. In the moments before the carefully scripted affair, a typically exuberant Griffith joked with his staff that the new name would be Coffin College, in faux honor of longtime chairman of the board James P. Coffin, and that the new motto would be, "Preparing people for life's undertakings." But the atmosphere in Brown Chapel was much more sober, as one by one the trustees cast their voice votes in favor of Lyon College. (In addition, at the behest of English professor Terrell Tebbetts and the members of the Name Change Advisory Committee, the board also voted to reinstate the college's original Latin motto that had been abandoned during the McCain administration: "*Perseverantia Omnia Vincet Deo Volente*.") The unveiling elicited a few approving cheers from the audience of students, faculty, alumni, and college friends as well as a few groans of dissatisfaction. As the Lyons had feared, there were those who left the convocation convinced that the college had auctioned its name; others, many idealistic young students among them, were simply disenchanted with a process that seemed to be tied too closely with the institution's feverish image-crafting efforts. The fact that Griffith, the Lyons, and a delegation from the college left the convocation immediately to fly to a Little Rock press conference attended by the governor and both Arkansas senators did little to assuage such suspicions. Perhaps one veteran faculty member was correct when he claimed that in between the lovers and haters of Lyon College, the vast majority would come to accept the new name, though without a lot of enthusiasm.[55]

In the days and weeks immediately following the name change announcement the college moved to take advantage of the unprecedented opportunity for publicity by taking out large advertisements in the state's major daily newspapers as well as urban dailies from as far away as New Orleans, St. Louis, and Oklahoma City. Arkansas College had labored in differing degrees of anonymity for almost 122 years; the Griffith administration was determined that obscurity would not hound Lyon College. The official implementation of the new name on 1 July 1994 was anticlimactic; in fact, the president, exhausted from five of the most breathless years in the institution's history, was at the time thousands of miles away on sabbatical in Europe with his family. By the time he returned for the beginning of the fall semester, granite Lyon College signs sat at the two entrances to campus where the old wooden Arkansas College signs had stood for years. Crisp new letterheads and envelopes flashed the Lyon College crest in red, yellow, blue, and white ink. Podiums and lecterns evinced recent tampering and smelled of glue and paint. An electricity of promise filled the air, as it usually did in the Griffith years. Shortly before classes commenced, the board's executive committee reaffirmed its support for the direction of the college under the Strategic Plan. The Griffiths began their first fall semester in the new president's home, Bradley Manor, built on the bluff in the northeastern corner of campus; the admissions and alumni relations offices moved into their new quarters in the renovated old president's home. And in November 1994 Griffith received word that Lyon College had tied with Roanoke College of Virginia as *U.S. News and World Report*'s best regional college in the South, prompting features on the old school with the new name by the *Arkansas Democrat-Gazette*, the Memphis *Commercial Appeal*, and the *Atlanta Constitution*.[56]

Unfortunately for Lyon College, while the name change seemed to work magic in terms of generating press coverage, it exercised no immediate effect on the institution's two most troubling areas—enrollment and finances. Full-time enrollment in the fall of 1994 declined by more than 10 percent from the previous fall. Lyon's 476 students represented the smallest autumn enrollment since the final year of the West administration. To make matters worse, the admissions office and administration had expected no such decline and instead had forecast a 5 percent growth. The result was a budget that depended on eighty-one more students than the registrar counted, which translated into a shortfall of $950,000, and that on top of an even larger deficit already worked into the 1994–1995 budget. When the college celebrated its first LyonFest on founders' weekend in October, Nancy Griffith organized an impressive photographic and artifactual exhibit of the institution's 122-year history. Displayed in the original building of Arkansas College, now called Morrow Hall by the First Presbyterian Church, the exhibit contained no overt treatment of the college's long tradition of recruiting and economic struggles. Maybe it should have. After five years in the saddle, Griffith knew as well as his predecessors had these seemingly endemic challenges, the dominant themes in the history of Isaac Long's little school.[57]

One of the factors that made Griffith's election as president such an easy decision was his extensive experience with both admissions and fund-raising. But Arkansas/Lyon College was a much different place than Davidson College, and the curricular exigencies of the Strategic Plan and unforeseen developments within higher education often proved antithetical to the achievement of the Plan's recruiting and

Bradley Manor, the president's home named in honor of the family of Marion Bradley Lyon, became the residence of the Griffiths in 1994.

fund-raising goals. Even more so than fund-raising, recruiting had proven to be a persistent and unconquerable challenge. By the Griffith era the litany of reasons and excuses had become quite familiar to most within the college community. Batesville was too small and isolated to attract the affluent suburban kids who populated the country's and region's selective and prestigious college campuses, and the town and its dry county offered little in the way of entertainment and diversion. Arkansas, among the most laggard states in almost every aspect of education, had long provided a poor atmosphere for the liberal arts, and few Arkansans differentiated between an independent liberal arts education and the much cheaper courses of study offered by the state's dominant public universities. Fewer still recognized the contrasts between the liberal arts approach of a Hendrix or Lyon and the conservative evangelicalism of the state's more populous denominational campuses. Arkansas's minuscule Presbyterian population had been too weak to support one institution, much less two now that the union of northern and southern branches brought the College of the

Ozarks into denominational sisterhood, and competition, with Arkansas College. Furthermore, many of Arkansas's prominent Presbyterians who possessed ample financial means had long preferred to send their children "back east" for a proper education at a school like Davidson or Washington and Lee, or at least across the river to Rhodes College. By the late 1980s Presbyterians accounted for an increasingly insignificant minority of the student body at Arkansas College. Taken out of context, the Strategic Plan's goals of 800 full-time students and 600 campus residents by the year 2000 appears far-fetched, especially with the benefit of hindsight. Yet in the late 1980s and early 1990s there was reason for optimism on both fronts. Even while stiffening admissions requirements during the 1980s, the West administration had succeeded in growing the enrollment during the latter half of the decade. The most dramatic jump occurred the fall after West's departure when a record freshman class swelled full-time enrollment beyond the 500 mark for the first time in history, almost half of whom resided on campus. With the completion of two new residence halls by the fall of 1989, another record-sized student body greeted the onset of the Griffith era. Despite a drop in freshman enrollment from 188 to 162, the new president welcomed 539 full-time students—with a full-time equivalency of 640—and 290 campus residents. When the size of the freshman class rebounded to 181 and full-time enrollment reached an all-time high of 567 in 1990, it strained campus housing to the limit. The residential population surpassed 300 for the first time ever, and for the first time since the early 1970s more than half the college's full-time students lived on campus. With almost 300 part-time students, Arkansas College's total enrollment stood at 855 in the fall of 1990. And all of this had been accomplished without sacrificing standards; the freshman class of 1990 boasted an average ACT score of 23, highest to date for the institution. The campus was a hive of activity, with record numbers of dormitory residents and a constant stream of commuters and Continuing Education students moving in and out of crowded buildings and parking lots. When fused with the buzz generated by the Strategic Plan and the infectious optimism of the president and his crusade, Arkansas College did in fact appear to be emerging "out of the shadow," as one cover of the alumni magazine, the *Piper*, described it. Even after two successive years of severe tuition hikes the students continued to come, and the four consecutive years of enrollment increases represented the longest string of growth years that just about anyone could remember.[58]

But just as any good Presbyterian knows—and any Baptist for that matter—if it seems too good to be true, then it probably is. Little did John V. Griffith and the rest of the college community know that 1990–1991 was a banner year never again to be duplicated in the millennium. The freshman class in the fall of 1991 turned out to be the smallest at Arkansas College since 1986, a full 78 students short of the 200 counted on in the budget. The fact that this was the institution's most qualified set of matriculates yet—less than 3 percent scored below an 18 on the ACT while the average score improved to 24—provided only a meager salve to the bottom line. With the loss of a record graduating class in May 1992—the 113 seniors that May ranks second only to 1993's 118—and with another disappointing recruiting year, total full-time enrollment dipped below 500 for the first time in five years in the fall of 1992. A large and highly qualified freshman class in 1993 boosted full-time enrollment by more than 6 percent, but the year's success proved aberrant as enrollment declined by more than 10 percent in the fall of 1994 and stagnated in mid-decade.[59]

The reasons for the decline in enrollment were numerous. In addition to the standard challenges mentioned above, such as Batesville's isolation and distance from the mid-South's urban centers, the 1990s ushered in a new set of barriers that prevented the fulfillment of Strategic Plan enrollment goals. Declining numbers of high school graduates pushed schools across the nation to step up recruitment efforts, but the college-age population had been dropping since the late 1980s. A more immediate factor in the college's admissions struggles was the expansion of the community college system in Arkansas. In the summer of 1991 the state legislature passed a law transforming most vocational technical schools into two-year colleges. Within two years Arkansas College faced competition for freshmen and sophomores from three such institutions within a thirty-five-mile radius. Most foreboding was the development in the Miller Creek valley a mile north of campus, where the former Gateway Vo-Tech became Gateway Technical College (and eventually the University of Arkansas Community College at Batesville).

At the same time that area technical schools were developing into community colleges, Arkansas College's board of trustees, administration, and admissions office were taking steps to move recruitment practices in line with those of Carnegie Category I colleges in the region, steps that often made the community colleges more attractive alternatives to underclassmen within the Batesville orbit. In a dual attempt to shore up a faltering budget and to enhance the college's developing image as a selective liberal arts institution, in the spring of 1990 the board voted to increase annual tuition by 20 percent to almost $6,500, the steepest one-year hike in Arkansas College's history. The following year brought another 10 percent raise in tuition accompanied by a 5 percent increase in room and board costs. Substantial yearly increases in student fees continued until 1995 when the board of trustees agreed to limit annual expense hikes to no more than 1 percent above the rate of inflation. By that time a year's worth of tuition, room and board, and fees amounted to more than $13,000. Despite the fact that increases in institutional financial aid more than made up for the rising student costs, the obviously ballooning tuition costs (which more than doubled during the Griffith years) took a toll on recruiting efforts. Increasing numbers of local students found the cheap tuition and flexible schedules of the burgeoning community colleges more to their liking. The community colleges proved particularly damaging to Lyon's Continuing Education Program and summer school, and enrollment in both dwindled precipitously throughout the decade. Others were lured to state universities by the greater number of curricular offerings and by a growing number of scholarships and by the practice of "stacking" scholarships, a method of financial aid and recruitment that often resulted in students receiving more money than they were required to pay in tuition and fees.[60]

A less tangible factor in the college's enrollment struggles in the 1990s was a byproduct of the institution's image development efforts. Carried out in hopes of attracting larger numbers of students from beyond the Batesville region, the conscious cultivation of an image of selectivity and academic distinctiveness helped accomplish a sort of demographic transformation in the student body, though in somewhat reverse fashion. By mid-decade, in spite of the Regional Advisory Board's efforts to improve relations between the college and the local area, Lyon College had developed a reputation within north central Arkansas as an elitist school for children of the wealthy. As we shall soon see, that image bore little resemblance to the reality on campus, but the power of reputation often owes scant tribute to reality. The name change, appearing as something of a capstone to the years of image development, supplied skeptics with further proof that the college was moving rapidly to abandon area students in favor of an amorphous cadre of overachievers and suburbanites from the mid-South's metropolises. When the community colleges sprang to life as cheaper, less rigorous alternatives, the percentage of students from within Batesville's trading region declined sharply. By the fall of 1993 fewer than 30 percent of the college's matriculates lived in the ten-county region surrounding Batesville; four years later that figure had dropped to 16 percent. By the latter days of the Griffith administration the college had, in the words of trustee and interim Lyon president Ruth Schmidt, "built up an exaggerated—and, from its perspective, undesirable—reputation . . . for only being interested in students who have certain concrete, quantifiable credentials that suggest that they can succeed here." The result, concluded Schmidt, was "a highly idiosyncratic" self-selection among high school seniors that severely reduced the college's pool of applicants.[61]

Despite persistent recruiting shortfalls and nagging retention problems that reduced full-time enrollment to below 430 by the end of the Griffith administration, the era witnessed the development of a primarily residential student body, albeit on a smaller scale than the Strategic Plan had called for. Between 1989 and 1996 the number of students living on campus increased by almost 40 percent. The 404 dormitory residents in the fall of 1996 represented almost 90 percent of the current full-time student population. This emergence of a residential college gave the administration, faculty, and trustees reason for optimism and moved the institution closer to Category I status.[62]

Just as the annual admissions reports contained elements both promising and foreboding, the financial situation of the Griffith years offered a mixed bag. The late 1980s and 1990s brought almost annual budget deficits and unprecedented endowment spending levels at the same time that the college made progress on one of the most ambitious fund-raising campaigns ever undertaken by a small, independent institution. And because the college's budget difficulties and subsequent endowment spending reacted to declining enrollments, financial struggles—the bane of many a small college president and board—intensified as the decade of the 1990s wore on.

Although most people in Arkansas and many within the college community would have reacted to the claim with incredulity—given the college's endowment of almost $40 million—by the late 1980s the institution's year-to-year financial health had begun to falter. The three years previous to Griffith's election as president had produced budget deficits, which had been buried in creative accounting procedures;

by the time Griffith took office in August 1989 this "black hole" deficit had grown to approximately $3 million. Reacting to the decline in endowment earnings set off by the stock market crash of October 1987, the board had raised the endowment spending level to 10.75 percent, more than twice the rate the trustees had set as a goal in the mid-1980s and well above market dividends. This excessive draw on earnings and principal resulted in a declining endowment corpus by the late 1980s. Working with John Logan and Darrell Loyless, vice-presidents for finance and institutional advancement respectively, Griffith managed to cap off his first two years as president with balanced budgets. Furthermore, a $6.9 million bequest from the late W. C. Brown Jr. helped erase the black hole, and for the first time in the college's history the trustees adopted a 100 percent policy of contributing to the annual fund, whose intake increased from less than $350,000 before Griffith's arrival to almost $1 million by the end of his administration.[63]

Nevertheless, financial aid policies adopted in the early years of Griffith's presidency, coupled with declining enrollments, set the college on a course that led to overspending and annual operating deficits. In the spring of 1990 the board of trustees adopted Griffith's plan to curtail the number of merit-based scholarships and implement a primarily need-based financial aid program that would meet 100 percent of a student's federally established need through a combination of scholarships, work study, and loans. An increasingly popular financial aid strategy utilized by selective institutions, the need-based program was generally considered a wise financial move. Cutting out all institutional merit scholarships except the Brown, Anderson, and one-half tuition awards promised to increase college revenues by requiring students from more affluent families to pay for a larger percentage of their expenses. The administration also hoped that abandoning most merit scholarships would improve retention rates, since a leading cause of attrition was the loss of scholarships due to failure to meet minimum grade point averages.[64]

But the need-based financial aid program depended upon the admissions office's success in luring greater numbers of affluent students to campus, and, as we have seen, the college had never been completely successful in this endeavor. As a result of the college's promise to meet the full amount of a student's established need, financial aid expenditures soared in the 1990s. In the first four years under the new program the institution's financial aid bill increased by an average of 18 percent annually, while student costs grew by only 13 percent per year. Simultaneously, the amount of federal aid available to students continued to decrease, forcing institutions to foot an ever larger portion of financial aid packages. The immediate result was mounting operating deficits that led to short-term loans and a growing annual debt service. As enrollment fell off in mid-decade, the administration and board reacted by limiting annual student fee raises to no more than 1 percent above the rate of inflation and by instituting loan caps, whereby the college limited the amount of federal loans a student could amass. Griffith and the board also addressed falling enrollments by instituting a series of new scholarships aimed at specific constituencies: local students (Long Scholarship), Presbyterians (Presbyterian Fellowship), and minorities (Dean's

Scholarship). All these efforts entailed offering still more institutional aid to students. By the mid-1990s, 95 percent of Lyon College students received some form of financial aid, an alarmingly high percentage for an institution bent on joining the ranks of the selective and prestigious residential colleges of the mid-South. The continued inability to attract significant numbers of students from families willing and able to cover the full cost of a liberal arts education translated into escalating endowment spending rates. By the end of Griffith's term as president, the endowment spending rate had increased to more than 13 percent, a figure more than two and a half times larger than the 5 percent rate the college had hoped to achieve years earlier, and the endowment had stalled at $45 million, a far cry from the Strategic Plan's $185 million goal for 2000 or even the revised goal of $114 million adopted at mid-decade.[65]

As implementation of the Strategic Plan got under way in the early 1990s, Darrell Loyless, vice-president for institutional advancement, noted that money, and specifically the institution's ability to raise money, would be the key to the success of the plan. He was right. It was Loyless's primary duty to oversee a decade-long effort that was to generate sufficient funds to support an extensive building plan while at the same time increasing the endowment by four and a half times. Even if ballooning financial aid expenses and declining enrollments had not placed undue pressure on the existing endowment, this ambitious plan would have necessitated the raising of more than $100 million. Loyless and Griffith devoted their first couple years in Batesville to wrapping up the West administration's final fund-raising effort, the Universal Campaign, and to ironing out inherited budget problems.[66]

In the summer of 1991 the board's executive committee authorized the president to launch a three-year "silent" campaign that would collect money earmarked for immediate priorities and would lead into a larger public phase of a decade-long campaign. This Past as Prologue Campaign generated more than $14 million in gifts and pledges, including substantial donations from trustees Charles Hoke, Robert A. Young III, J. D. Simpson III, and Henry L. Nichols and a $4 million gift from Frank Lyon Jr. that established the Lyon Fellowship Program, which eventually provided up to ten new full-tuition scholarships annually for students planning careers in business, banking, or public service. The successful campaign also helped earn the college a $6.5 million challenge grant from the generous Mabee Foundation; the grant helped defray costs on several building projects, including construction of the new president's home and Young House containing Hoke and McCain halls and renovation of the old president's home. The success of the campaign helped earn Loyless an award as National Fund-Raiser of the Year by the National Society of Fund-Raising Executives in 1993.[67]

The public phase of the fund-raising campaign, entitled Fulfilling the Promise: The Campaign for Lyon College, finally got under way in October 1995. Despite recent budget problems due to declining enrollments and skyrocketing financial aid expenses, high spirits prevailed at the Gala Scottish Evening that kicked off the campaign at the second LyonFest. Declaring the campaign retroactive to January 1990, which allowed the college to claim several large gifts and benefactions from Griffith's first two years in office as well as the years of the Past as Prologue effort, the executive committee of the board could announce that more than half the $80 million goal had already been raised in the form of gifts or pledges. Robert A. Young III, board chairman since 1987, relinquished his duties to Graham Holloway in 1995 in order to become co-chair, along with trustee J. D. Simpson III and honorary chairman Frank Lyon Jr., of the campaign, which at the time was the most ambitious per-student fund-raising drive ever undertaken by an American institution of higher learning. The board established 1999 as the target date for reaching the $80 million mark while developing plans for yet another phase that would push the amount beyond $100 million by 2005. As usual the proceeds were to be directed toward strengthening the endowment, creating new faculty positions and scholarships, supplementing operating costs, and funding capital projects.[68]

Young, Simpson, Lyon, and Loyless orchestrated a truly national campaign, featuring socials around the state and in cities from San Antonio and Dallas to New York and Washington, D.C. Within two years the public campaign had generated $20 million. A successful year of fund-raising in 1996, capped off by a $5 million gift from Larry and Marilyn Derby of Warren to be used toward the construction of a new science building, helped the college claim another million-dollar Mabee grant. As we have seen, however, endowment spending continued to grow despite the impressive progress on the campaign. The primary reason for this was that the bulk of the campaign's production consisted of pledges and deferred gifts, many in the form of planned bequests. In his last presidential report to the board in 1997 Griffith lamented the college's inability to attract a sufficient number of large current gifts. Ironically then, twice during the 1990s, in the midst of the most extensive fund-raising project in the history of Arkansas higher education, the board and the administration found themselves issuing tax-exempt bonds for the purpose of raising money for current needs such as physical repair, construction, and debt restructuring. The resignations of both Griffith and Loyless in 1997 took the wind out of the campaign's sails temporarily and threatened to capsize it altogether.[69]

Shortly before commencement exercises in May 1997 Griffith informed board chairman Holloway that this graduation ceremony, his eighth as president, would be his final one at Lyon College. Griffith had recently accepted the presidency of Presbyterian College in South Carolina, and his duties there were to start the following January. The Griffiths left Batesville and Bradley Manor at the end of October, leaving Lyon College in the hands of new academic dean and acting president J. William Moncrief for two months before the arrival of trustee and interim president Ruth Schmidt in January 1998. A veteran of small college affairs—she had recently served for a decade as president of Agnes Scott College—Schmidt's task was to manage the college until Frank Lyon Jr. and his search committee could find the sixteenth president of the institution.[70]

The last couple of years had been difficult ones for Griffith, and especially his last full academic session, which he referred to as "the most challenging year of my presidency." The final years had produced triumphs and signs of progress toward achieving the goals of the Strategic Plan—the implementation of the house system, the expansion of the faculty, the development of the college's first website, the successful completion of the latest Mabee challenge drive, the breaking of ground for the new baseball field, and the passage of valuable state scholarship programs by the legislature. In the fall of 1996 *U.S. News and World Report* ranked Lyon number one among small regional colleges in the South for the second time in three years; the college also received its first top ranking in the "best value" category and appeared in *Money*'s list of the one hundred best buys in American higher education. But Griffith's final years were also peppered with challenges both trivial and substantive. Lyon's failed bid to have the Arkansas Governor's School relocated to Batesville from Hendrix was a disappointment, especially from a recruiting standpoint. This seemed to compound an earlier failure by the Batesville community and surrounding region to secure the Arkansas School for Math and Sciences. Beginning in 1995 a string of retirements and resignations removed from the faculty and staff several veteran members of the college family, including John T. Dahlquist, Veryl Board, and alumni Fitzhugh Spragins, Jim Mitchum, Frances Rodgers, and Roberta Bustin. The core curriculum continued to cause concern among some faculty members, while the tenure system and the failure to secure meaningful salary raises created consternation. Furthermore, the inclusiveness of the Griffith administration, while refreshing after the West years, also proved exhausting to many professors, whose various committee and commission assignments ate up the hours made available by class load reductions. As early as 1992 a team of inspectors from the North Central Association observed that problems stemming from overwork and "oppressive" out-of-class duties had "been disguised by the energy that comes from the sense of possibility, promise, and change." By the latter half of the decade that energy level had begun to subside.[71]

The two primary challenges facing Griffith, the same ones that not one of his predecessors had found a way to conquer, were the interrelated issues of money and enrollment. New Category I–type recruiting strategies implemented in 1995–1996 and increased competition from state-supported universities and community colleges resulted in a "tragic situation" for the admissions office and the annual budget. The freshman class of 130 students in 1996 marked a 23 percent decline over the previous year's incoming class. An even smaller class the following fall, combined with declining retention rates, resulted in the smallest full-time enrollment since 1986. The economic effects of the drop in enrollment were a continuing drain on the endowment and budget shortfalls necessitating cuts that not only threatened jobs and salary raises but that also threatened the very health and continuation of the Strategic Plan.[72]

Although it is still too early to assess many of the developments of the Griffith administration—some will take perhaps a generation to play out fully—a number of the accomplishments of the 1990s seem quite clear. Building projects produced new academic and residential facilities; the Lyon Business and Economics Building, Holloway Theatre, Young House, and Bradley Manor continued the college's architectural scheme that was introduced by Paul McCain in the 1950s. Perhaps the two areas in which the Lyon College of the Griffith era came closest to achieving its lofty goals were the residential college and the image of selectivity. By the end of the millennium almost 90 percent of Lyon's full-time students resided on campus, a development that reflected the wider range of student origins and the complex winnowing of students that is a major product of modern America's stratified higher education system and Arkansans' poor history of support for independent liberal arts education. The house system, honor system, and social system all played key roles in this transformation. The Griffith administration's crafting of a new image for the college, highlighted by the adoption of a new name, has had more mixed results. While it would be difficult to argue that Lyon College became an institution of national import during the 1990s, it is nonetheless evident that public perception of the school did undergo significant reworking. This new image of prominence and excellence has perhaps had its greatest impact, however, not in neighboring states or in the mid-South's metropolitan centers but in north central Arkansas, an impact that has not always been a positive one for recruiting efforts in this egalitarian and decidedly nonelitist region. And from the discussions and plans of the early 1990s, it is evident that the new image had not been crafted with the region around Batesville in mind.

At the end of a feverish eight and a half years as president of Lyon College, Griffith discovered, as had most of his predecessors, that a major part of his legacy, the memories of the 1990s, rested not so much on the innovations and transformations as on the age-old foci of concern—students and money. In his final report to the board Griffith admitted his frustration with "the fact that all this change, exciting as it has been, has so far failed to produce a tangible improvement in student enrollment, thus preventing us from tackling many of the College's pressing budgetary and financial problems." The Strategic Plan had attempted too radical a makeover in such a relatively brief amount of time, resulting in an image-over-substance quality that seemed to hover cloud-like over recent campus developments. In retrospect Griffith himself acknowledged that a twenty-year plan, instead of a ten-year plan, would have been more realistic and achievable.[73] If the college were to remain on the path toward national, or at least regional, distinction, the Griffith years would be seen as yet another step in the long journey, a catalyst perhaps but not a culmination. Nevertheless, it was a testament to the tremendous progress and continued promise of Lyon College that one could discuss the triumphs and failures of the decade without so much as a mention of the issue that had for so long dominated analyses, the question of survival. Perhaps the most elementary but crucial summation of the era was that, despite the many differences in spirit and action between this latest administration and the tenures of McCain and West, John V. Griffith carried on one major tradition—the college was a much different place in 1997 than it had been in 1989. The college's hat had certainly been tossed over the wall. Yet beneath the sound and fury much that had been fundamental to the institution's existence remained.

Epilogue

Charlie Handford never attended Arkansas College, but he spent most of his life in Batesville. A sign painter by profession, Handford was a gifted and sometimes disheartened artist who combated the tedium of sign painting and satiated his creative impulses by painting local landmarks. In the 1960s the middle-aged Handford undertook his most ambitious project, at least in terms of physical scope. Working from an old photograph and from his own memory, he began to render on a giant canvas a picture of the old downtown campus of Arkansas College as it would have appeared around the beginning of the twentieth century. With meticulous care, he attempted to recreate the buildings' characteristics and colors, from the shingles atop the old music building to the choppy, unstandardized sandstones of Alumni Hall. In 1983 the old Powell's Restaurant, where Handford's "Arkansas College" was displayed, closed its doors. The massive painting remained in the building, however, hidden from view until the year 2000 when the restaurant reopened as Kelley-Wyatt's.[1]

Anyone visiting Kelley-Wyatt's who gives the painting more than a fleeting glance will realize that the work is unfinished. After months of careful labor on the project, the eccentric Charlie Handford had grown tired of his monstrous canvas. In the 1970s he grew tired of his home town and his life as a sign painter and headed to New Orleans, where he found success and fulfillment drawing portraits for passersby at Jackson Square. His painting of Arkansas College's original campus still hangs in the restaurant. Handford painted the three old buildings from right to left, or south to north, so that the Isaac J. Long Memorial Building and Alumni Hall are relatively complete, while the college's oldest structure seems to fade out of existence as the eye scans from right to left. The shingles disappear midway along the roof, and the windows in the northern wing of the building stand gaping and colorless. The northern end of the building itself appears to be suspended in air, as if some great weight in the southern wing served as a counterbalance to prevent it from tipping over. It is almost as if Handford painted in reverse chronological order, and the further he delved into the college's past the more the painting was overtaken by a strange, opaque whiteness.

Although it is somewhat perplexing to find an uncompleted painting hanging in a restaurant, Handford's tribute to his hometown college is perhaps fitting. If there is one common characteristic that ties together the wide variety of institutions within American higher education it is change. Whether labeled progress, adaptation, strategic planning, or survival strategy, institutions of higher learning are living organisms that grow, contract, react, create, and compete in order to stay effective and stay alive.

As we have seen, the history of Arkansas/Lyon College is in many respects the story of a small, independent school's various efforts at adaptation and reaction to innumerable social, religious, economic, and educational forces. It is Isaac Long's decision to provide a "common school course" for students looking to teach in the public schools. It is the synod's and board's decision to make the curriculum "co-educational" by incorporating music and art as disciplines on an equal plane with languages and mathematics. It is William S. Lacy's experimentation with courses in home economics and business, and John D. Spragins's dream of a Christian college in which students earned their keep and their education. It is Paul McCain's vision of a campus on a bluff. It is Jim Mitchum convincing teenagers from New Jersey that there really is an Arkansas College and Roberta Brown finding federal grant monies in places no one else had thought to look. It is the New Plan and the Aberdeen Development Corporation and the myriad other ideas of a young Dan C. West. It is also John V. Griffith embracing the liberal arts tradition while Tom Lowry nods in approval, as does the spirit of E. B. Tucker and of Sam Williams and of Thomas Welch and of the father and son Long. Even after more than 130 years, Lyon College is still a work in progress, an institution and idea continuously evolving.

The few years since the departure of John V. Griffith have held true to the institution's tradition. There have been struggles and triumphs, age-old challenges and promises of future success. Administrators and trustees have worried more than anything else about enrollment and budget balancing; faculty have continued to set higher standards for excellence and have demanded effort and engagement from students; and students have, in the tradition of the liberal arts, found on Batesville's little campus an atmosphere that nurtures experimentation, self-discovery, and the quest for knowledge, truth, and beauty. Beneath it all, Lyon College continues to ponder its mission and its message to the public, its role in its region and state, and its place within the world of American higher education.

Although technically his presidency did not end until the final day of 1997, Griffith left Batesville at the end of October and left the management of Lyon College in the hands of one of its newest employees, provost and dean of the faculty J. William Moncrief. A Georgian with a Harvard Ph.D. in chemistry, Moncrief had relieved Robert K. Holyer as dean only a few months earlier and now found himself thrust into a two-month position as acting president. Faced with a fourth consecutive year of declining enrollment and the concomitant revenue shortfall, Moncrief spent most of November and December dealing with budget concerns. In addition, the admissions and institutional advancement offices began working with consultants to improve recruiting and refine Lyon's public image, respectively, while the faculty voted to abolish the January interim term that had been a key feature of the college's calendar for almost three decades. The 1998–1999 academic session would feature a traditional two-semester calendar for the first time since 1968–1969.[2]

Because the search committee only began work in the fall of 1997, Lyon College faced several months before the arrival of a new president. As had become the custom at Lyon, the board of trustees appointed one of their own, Ruth A. Schmidt, to serve as interim president for the first six months of 1998. Schmidt thus became the first woman to lead Lyon College (even on an interim basis), but she was no stranger to the small college campus. A scholar of Spanish literature, Schmidt had retired after a twelve-year stint as president of Agnes Scott College in Decatur, Georgia. Possessed of a strong resolve honed by years of experience facing the challenges of independent college leadership, Ruth Schmidt did not leave her Georgia home to spend half a year simply holding the fort at Lyon College. Instead, she used her time in Batesville to address some of the college's most vexing issues, such as enrollment, financial aid policies, endowment spending, curricular shortcomings, and the feasibility of certain facets of the Strategic Plan of 1990.[3]

Schmidt first tackled the most immediate challenges, recruiting and finance. Shortly after arriving on campus she removed the vice-president for enrollment services—under whose direction Lyon had suffered declining numbers of matriculates as well as declining numbers of applicants—and assumed personal direction of the admissions office. Schmidt made several recommendations concerning the need to shore up the college's financial situation. She pointed out the need for better spending control mechanisms for more efficient use of precious funds. Schmidt also convinced her fellow trustees to revise, rescind, or reconsider several financial aid policies (such as "scholarship stacking") adopted earlier in the decade that were designed to improve enrollment but apparently had contributed to a declining enrollment as well as a rising endowment spend rate.[4]

Addressing the perennial challenge of recruiting, Schmidt dismissed the assumption that Lyon College had to resort to "buying students" to fill its classrooms, an assumption that had implicitly underlain the admissions and financial aid policies of the 1990s and of previous eras. Schmidt argued that Lyon's lack of majors popular on most college and university campuses—such as business, education, and other non-liberal arts areas expunged by the Strategic Plan—kept more students away from the Batesville campus than the blossoming financial aid packages attracted. Consequently, Schmidt, as well as Griffith in his farewell remarks, urged trustees and future administrators to reassess the goals and actions of the Strategic Plan, to ground the plan in reality and make it "a true guide instead of a dream."[5]

A similar call for reassessing the college's direction and public image came from the report drafted by the presidential search committee's consultant in October 1997. Representing the Washington, D.C.-based Academic Search Consultation Service, Barbara E. Taylor surveyed the state of affairs at Lyon in the waning days of the Griffith administration. Her report provided a valuable snapshot of an institution that was a work in progress, a college that had made many strides in recent years but faced an uphill battle to reach the lofty (and frequently unrealistic) goals of the Strategic Plan. Taylor praised Lyon's able and dedicated faculty and board, its strong student body, its growing regional reputation, its attractive campus and large per capita endowment, and its valuable co-curricular developments, such as the honor system and the house system. She also pointed out the more sobering facts: that the college was on pace to fall far short of many crucial Strategic Plan goals, such as enrollment and endowment projections and retention rates; that the faculty, the heart and soul of any liberal arts college, remained underpaid by the standards of Lyon's peer institutions and unusually burdened by heavy committee assignments and an unwieldy governance system; and that, despite the sizable endowment ($52 million in October 1997) for such a small institution, Lyon College was nevertheless "financially pressed" and continued to spend too large a proportion of its endowment. Lyon's next president would have to deal with all these challenges. Perhaps most important, the search committee, the board of trustees, and their choice for president would face the task of reassessing the Strategic Plan and Lyon's place within the broad range of American colleges that lay claim to the description "liberal arts." According to Taylor's report, "The issue for Lyon College and its next president is the position on this [liberal arts] continuum that it wants to occupy and for which a market exists or can be developed."[6]

In the spring of 1998 this issue became Wallie Roettger's issue. After months of intense activity by the search committee and its chairman, Frank Lyon Jr., on 19 March 1998 the board of trustees named Walter Barackman Roettger the sixteenth president of Lyon College. No new president had ever taken the reins of the institution with more teaching and administrative experience in higher education. A native of Champaign, Illinois, where his father served as head coach of the University of Illinois baseball team, Roettger graduated from Stanford University in 1963 and served as an astrogeophysicist in the U.S. Air Force before resigning his commission in 1968. The following year he began graduate studies in political science at the University of Colorado, earning the Ph.D. in 1976. By the time he came to Batesville, Roettger had almost two and a half decades of teaching and administrative experience. After brief faculty appointments at Central College in Iowa and Emporia State University in Kansas, Roettger rose to the rank of associate professor of political science and directed the Institute of Public Affairs and Administration at Drake University in Des Moines, Iowa. In 1982 Roettger made his way to New England and an associate provost's position at the University of Hartford in Connecticut. His years at Hartford found Roettger wearing a variety of hats at one time or another, including the deanships of the college of technology and the school of business and public administration. After four years as executive vice-president and provost at Bryant College in Rhode Island, he came back to the Midwest to become vice-president and dean of the faculty at one of Lyon's sister institutions, Westminster College in Fulton, Missouri. He was completing his third year at Westminster when called to Lyon's presidency. When Wallie, as he would quickly become known around campus, moved into Bradley Manor in late June 1998, he was accompanied by his wife, Peggy, and young son, Daniel. Like her predecessor, Peggy Roettger was a career woman, having worked in public relations in New England before directing the Winston Churchill Memorial and Library at Westminster. She, too, would prove an invaluable advisor and extension of the president's office.[7]

In most respects, Roettger's directive was different from that of his predecessor. His mission was not the articulation of a grand new vision for Lyon College. Rather, Roettger's broad range of experiences within higher education convinced the search committee that he was the right man for a new phase in the college's development,

Pictured left to right, c. 2000: President Walter B. Roettger, Carolyn Holloway, former chairman of the board Graham Holloway, former trustee Rev. J. Layton Mauzé, and board chairman Robert A. Young III.

a phase that would require sound management, critical reappraisal of the Strategic Plan, timely rekindling of the moribund Campaign for Lyon College, dynamic yet stable leadership, and maintenance of the momentum that had been generated during the ongoing quest toward distinction.

Roettger's first years as Lyon's president were full of challenges. Despite the efforts by Schmidt and the consultants from Noel-Levitz during the previous year, full-time enrollment in the fall of 1998 was the lowest since 1984. The freshman class of 107 students was the smallest since the McCain administration, and the residential student population of 362 represented a 10 percent decline since 1995. Compounding misfortune with tragedy, just a couple of weeks into the fall semester the college community received word that Frank Lyon Sr. had died at the age of eighty-eight. And as so often happens amid the confusion and uncertainty of major administrative change, fund-raising fell off considerably during the 1998–1999 session. Although the alumni giving rate rose to an all-time high of 26 percent, collections in the annual fund fell by more than a quarter, and, facing both a change in administration and the prospect of falling far short of the $80 million goal, the board of trustees voted to extend the Campaign for Lyon College (or Fulfilling the Promise campaign) by eighteen months through the year 2000.[8]

In another development not uncommon during times of administrative transfer, the college saw several veteran administrators and faculty leave for positions elsewhere. In 1999 alone four veteran faculty leaders—Robert Holyer, Donald Weatherman, George Stone, and Tom Cooper—left Lyon College, and several others retired or resigned one year later, including veterans George Chlebak and Fred Wann and CASE Professors of the Year Jim Rulla and Bart Lewis. When combined with the retirements of the mid-1990s and a few high-profile departures of the latter Griffith administration—including chemistry professors Roberta Bustin and Bert Holmes—the high rate of turnover removed a significant segment of Lyon's veteran faculty by the end of the millennium. Likewise, the administrative staff underwent an almost complete overhaul in the years between 1997 and 1999. By the time the fall 1998 semester got under way, Griffith-era stalwarts Mark Wood, Darrell Loyless, and John Logan were gone; by the fall of 1999 only vice-president for student life and dean of students Bruce Johnston remained from John Griffith's cabinet.[9]

Nevertheless, these same years also witnessed triumphs and developments that promised to reap dividends for Lyon College in decades to come. The growing number of international students led to the formation of the International Student Organization in the fall of 1998 and to the appointment of Lyon's first International Student Advisor. Conversely, Lyon continued to send students around the world in the Nichols Travel Program and through the Nichols Semester Abroad Program, featuring exchange agreements with universities in England, Northern Ireland, and France. The fall of 1998 also brought about the full implementation of the house system on campus. In 1999 the Reverend Pat Baxter, a native of South Africa, joined the staff as Lyon's first campus minister in five years. Baxter reinvigorated the nonsectarian spiritual emphasis on campus and, along with the Board of Church Advocates and director of church relations Claudia Marsh, helped strengthen old ties with the Presbyterian Church. The Scottish Heritage Program and its Lyon College Pipe Band, both directed by native Scot William Muirhead since 1992, continued to generate a unique brand of publicity for the institution.[10]

Working from the consultant's report on the state of affairs at Lyon, one of Roettger's emphases was on improving faculty morale and stemming the outflow of experienced educators. Toward this end in the spring of 1999 the board of trustees approved faculty and staff raises for the first time in three years; as the new millennium dawned the administration continued to champion merit raises and equity adjustments. The new president and board of trustees also moved to bring the college's tenure and promotion policies up to national standards and to address Lyon's cumbersome faculty governance system by vesting more decision-making power in the office of the dean of the faculty. These efforts helped reduce the faculty turnover rate and stabilize a young but talented corps of professors who led the college into the new millennium, among them Williamson Prize winners Russell T. Stinson, Teresa Murphy, and Barrie Bondurant and CASE Arkansas Professors of the Year David Stricklin, Robert Gregerson, and Helen Robbins.[11]

After the initial disappointments of the 1998–1999 academic year, the Roettger administration experienced improving fortunes in the crucial areas of enrollment and finance. After bottoming out in the fall of 1998 at 411 full-time students, enrollment began a steady ascension that produced an 18 percent increase over the next three years while maintaining recent gains in student quality. The 486 full-time students in the fall of 2001 constituted the largest enrollment at Lyon College since 1993. Several factors accounted for this rise: a revamped admissions office, a return to more traditional methods of recruiting such as high school visits and college day displays, new transfer agreements with area community colleges, expanded curricular offerings, and improvements in Arkansas's state scholarship program, especially the introduction of the Distinguished Governor's Scholarship, a full tuition, room, and board scholarship, in 1998. Even more crucial to the college's rising enrollments was a dramatic increase in retention rates. Between 1997 and 2001 the freshman-to-sophomore retention rate improved from 68 percent to a record 86.5 percent, much of the improvement undoubtedly attributable to the success of the house system.[12]

Lyon's financial prospects also began to improve. In the fall of 1998 the board approved Roettger's recommendations to drop Lyon's commitment to full demonstrated financial need, to eliminate the policy that limited annual student fee increases to no more than 1 percent above the rate of inflation, and to stop the practice of "loan-capping." Through these cost-containing measures, as well as through improved investments and the curtailment of tuition discounting, the Roettger administration reduced the endowment spend rate and improved the budget situation. The annual fund rebounded after a lackluster 1998–1999 effort, and, most significantly, the Fulfilling the Promise Campaign received a critical injection in January 2000. With only twelve months to raise several million dollars in order to reach the $80 million goal, Jane and Frank Lyon Jr. announced the Lyon Leadership Challenge, whereby the Lyons promised to match dollar-for-dollar all new gifts and pledges, up to $10 million, through the end of the year. As the Lyons and the college's leadership had hoped, the Challenge spurred a record number of alumni to contribute to their alma mater and secured several generous gifts from friends and foundations. Campaign gifts, combined with matching dollars from the Lyon Leadership Challenge, generated more than $19 million during 2000. The final, ten-year fund-raising total of more than $90 million made Fulfilling the Promise: The Campaign for Lyon College one of the largest per capita drives in the history of American higher education.[13]

Lyon College took another important step in early 2001 with Roettger's announcement that construction would soon begin on the largest, most expensive building project in the institution's history. In April college dignitaries broke ground on a new math and science center estimated to cost almost $12 million. Named in honor of trustee Lawrence H. Derby of Warren and his wife Marilyn Church Derby, whose lead gift breathed new life into a seven-year effort to fund the sorely needed structure, the 55,000-square-foot Derby Center for Science and Mathematics is scheduled for completion by August 2004. The first phase of the structure, the Bellingrath Wing, was completed in early 2003.[14]

Prosperity in the world of the small college remained a fickle and elusive goal, however. Even with gains in enrollment, modest student fee increases, and tighter controls on financial aid, Lyon College continued to subsidize an unhealthy proportion of its students' education. Of the 417 full-time students enrolled during the fall of 1999, more than 95 percent received some sort of institutional financial aid. Before the celebration of the successful Fulfilling the Promise Campaign was over, the declining economy had begun to take a toll on the college's endowment investments, and the precipitous decline in technology stocks combined with the backlash from the terrorist atacks in September 2001 provided the most severe blow to the endowment since the stock market crash of 1987. Enrollment prospects took a significant hit in the fall of 2001 when the Arkansas state legislature, faced with a severe budget shortfall, voted to suspend key state scholarship programs indefinitely beginning with the freshman class of 2002.[15]

Even Lyon's reclassification by the Carnegie Foundation for the Advancement of Teaching, a centerpiece of the Strategic Plan, did not go exactly as envisioned. By the time the Carnegie Foundation announced its new classifications in the summer of 2000, there was no longer a Carnegie I category to shoot for. Although Lyon was classified among the "national baccalaureate liberal arts colleges," a category that encompassed the former Carnegie I schools, the new system also included in this group a number of small, poor institutions. Consequently, the new system no longer provided an automatic claim to elite status. Lyon College could now claim to be ranked in a category with in-state rival Hendrix and such mid-South luminaries as Rhodes, Millsaps, and Austin, but so could Arkansas Baptist College and a number of other institutions of lesser repute.[16]

Undoubtedly, despite the immediacy of traditional challenges such as enrollment and budget balancing, the most fundamental issue for the Roettger administration and the board of trustees was locating Lyon College's rightful place somewhere within the diverse world of liberal arts education. This question of mission lay at the heart of the institution's history; in one form or another it had affected, sometimes dominated, every presidential administration going back to the days of Isaac Long. The Strategic Plan of 1990 had set the college on a path that diverged sharply from earlier efforts to bridge the divide between the ideal of the liberal arts and the utility of career-focused, even technical, programs of study. By the late 1990s Lyon College was the closest thing Arkansas had to a "pure" liberal arts college, with no majors in education or business and the state's only universal foreign language requirement. Even among liberal arts colleges nationwide, few held more tightly to the ideal than did Lyon. Among the institutions Lyon had been chasing for the past decade, Rhodes College maintained majors in education and business administration and Millsaps in accounting, business administration, education, and computer science; Centenary College in Louisiana boasted seven different education majors, including one in physical education, as well as major fields of study in such nonliberal arts areas as accounting and finance. Even an institution as vaunted as Swarthmore maintained departments in engineering and computer science.

The process of reevaluating the goals of the Strategic Plan had begun even before Griffith's departure. As early as 1992 investigators from the NCA had expressed reservations concerning the possibly unrealistic ambitions of the plan, given the demographic, economic, and philosophical challenges inherent to liberal arts education in north central Arkansas. In 1995 a midpoint review of the plan produced a new set of more modest goals while reaffirming the broad outlines of Lyon's new mission. Facing mounting enrollment and financial difficulties, in April 1997 Griffith organized a roundtable discussion of strategic issues, in which trustees, faculty, staff, and a few students voiced their support for the basic direction of the Strategic Plan but also raised concerns and questions over specific areas of the plan's implementation. Echoing occasional student complaints of recent years, many of the roundtable's participants expressed uneasiness over Lyon's increasingly rigid focus on the liberal arts and that focus's implicit dedication to the idea of undergraduate education as preparation for graduate or professional school. Although an increasing number of Lyon graduates pursued further study after leaving Batesville, a majority continued to enter the workplace after earning their bachelor's degrees and many worried that the lack of career preparation and career-oriented majors hindered job seeking. In many ways the message emanating from the roundtable discussion mirrored what may be seen as Arkansas's collective response to generations of idealistic educators: "A liberal arts education is fine, as long as it is also practical." Leaders of Hendrix and Lyon had always confronted this ambivalent and utilitarian demand.[17]

With the consultant's report, the results of the roundtable discussion, and Ruth Schmidt's recent recommendations providing some direction, in the fall of 1998 Roettger recommended, and gained faculty and trustee approval for, reinstating academic majors in accounting and business; by the end of the 1999–2000 academic session the board had approved further recommendations for establishing majors in computer science and environmental studies. The faculty and administration also moved to expand offerings in areas such as middle school and physical education. Roettger's first year in office witnessed serious efforts at partnerships and articulation agreements with the University of Arkansas Community College at Batesville and other regional community colleges. Addressing students' concerns related to career planning, the president strengthened Lyon's newly renamed Career Development Center. Through the work of the Career Development Center, Lyon students gained greater access to internships, and in 2000 the college joined the Washington Center for Internships and Academic Seminars.[18]

In January 1999 Roettger appointed a fourteen-person strategic planning steering committee, which he chaired, whose charge was to develop a five-year plan that would lead the college into the new millennium, a plan that would pay special attention to the "fit between the mission of the College and the students it serves." Combining the efforts of eight separate project teams that studied the major areas of college life and operation, from academics to administration and from enrollment to student life, the committee submitted its work to the college community in early 2000, and the board of trustees formally approved the new Strategic Plan at its spring meeting in April. Much of the new plan called for a continuation of the progress made toward the Strategic Plan of 1990: continued development of a superior faculty, extracurricular and campus-life opportunities, and trustee leadership and participation. The Strategic Plan also promised to build a strong relationship between the college and the regional community and to increase the college's visibility and positive image. Having learned a lesson from the public shortcomings of the 1990s, the steering committee adopted more modest and reasonable numerical goals to be achieved by 2005: a sophomore-to-freshman retention rate of 73 percent, a four-year graduation rate of 53 percent, a full-time enrollment of 550 without a decline in academic quality or in the percentage of residential students, and an endowment of $69.5 million with a spend rate of less than 10 percent. Most important for the future of Lyon College, however, the new Strategic Plan reasserted the fundamental direction of the previous decade when, with its number-one priority, it vowed to "ensure continuing excellence and distinction in the liberal arts."[19]

Thus, Lyon College entered the twenty-first century with an institutional vote of confidence in the liberal arts-centered goals that had helped transform the little school in the past decade. The college and its leadership also possessed an appreciation for the challenges that lay in the paths of those goals. The liberal arts ideal remained a valuable and honorable objective; nevertheless, achieving the ideal, as it always had in Arkansas, would likely require coming to terms with the forces and philosophies of an egalitarianism bred by the frontier and sustained by generations of poverty and poor education and only gradually overcome through persistent effort. Building an institution of "excellence and distinction" was no overnight endeavor; neither was it an undertaking that could be largely achieved within a decade. With rare exceptions, the perennial challenges for higher education in the foothills of the eastern Ozarks had mandated a slow and plodding advance, a perseverance befitting a college begat by Presbyterians in a land of Baptists and Methodists.

It has been some thirteen decades since Isaac Long and a handful of students first read Latin and Greek, figured equations, and pondered biblical and ecclesiastical history on the campus of an upstart college. In many respects Long's challenges are those same perennial challenges faced by Lyon College's leaders today, and by the caretakers of liberal arts colleges around the nation. Like any independent institution, Lyon College relies on the benevolence of friends and alumni, and, while thankfully the days of the president struggling to collect five dollars or ten dollars from a couple dozen donors has long since passed, rising costs and an increasingly competitive and crowded field in higher education continue to tax annual financial resources and an endowment that has experienced little growth in more than a decade. Despite the obvious growth in enrollment since the days of Isaac Long, Lyon College remains among the smallest four-year colleges in the country; overcoming the various recruiting obstacles in the effort to bring students to Batesville continues to require innovation, dedication, and the strengthening of a recognizable institutional mission and image. In the face of all these challenges, Lyon College, as it always has done, perseveres. More remarkably, that perseverance, as it always has been, is accompanied by progress, by excellence, and by the promise of greatness.

On the surface, there is little about Lyon College in the early twenty-first century that would be recognizable to Isaac Long. With only a minute scattering of Presbyterian students, with more non-Protestants on the faculty than Presbyterians, and with not so much as a required semester of Bible class, Lyon College, in Long's view, would seem to have fallen far from its original faith-centered mission. A southerner of the nineteenth century, he would most likely be shocked at the diversity of ethnicities and nationalities on the little campus. The blufftop campus filled with buildings—some as imposing and impressive as Brown Chapel, the Lyon Building, and the new Derby Center for Science and Mathematics—would look to Long like a great university fortress, not the modern descendant of the little college that began life in a twenty-by-forty frame building. Nevertheless, there are threads of a timeless quality that link the Lyon College of the early twenty-first century with the tiny school founded in Reconstruction-era Arkansas by a determined group of Presbyterians and Batesville citizens. Long would find fascinating, though not surprising, the stories of his college's near-death experiences. Although Latin declensions and recitations are long gone, he would recognize the earnestness and intellectual sanctity of the mentor-mentee relationship. And he would certainly understand the difficulties of selling an often unreceptive public on the frequently intangible benefits of a liberal arts education. Above all, in Lyon College, more than 130 years after its founding, he would recognize the perseverance and promise of an Arkansas college.

Appendix I

Life after Lyon: Post-Presidential Careers

With the exception of founder Isaac J. Long, whose death on 10 December 1891 ended his nineteen and a half years as Arkansas College's leader, all the presidents of the institution had careers of varying lengths and accomplishments after the completion of their tenures in Batesville. Following is a brief synopsis of the post-presidential careers of the college's past presidents.

EUGENE R. LONG—One of two Arkansas College presidents to serve two nonconsecutive terms as president, the younger Long left Batesville for the first time in 1895 to accept a faculty position at Southwestern Presbyterian University in Clarksville, Tennessee, where he remained for only two years before returning to his alma mater for a sixteen-year stint as president. Long left Batesville again in 1913 to become professor of Bible at Austin College in Sherman, Texas. After three years at Austin, Long joined the faculty at Hampden-Sydney College in Virginia in 1916. Long returned to Arkansas College one year later to accept his alma mater's first endowed professorship—the James Wilson Moore Chair of Biblical Instruction—and remained on the institution's faculty until his death at the age of sixty-eight on 29 June 1931. Eugene Long and his wife, Sallie Meek Long, had no children, but they raised Sallie's niece, Margaret Goodwin, who graduated from Arkansas College in 1930 and later married Thomas M. Lowry Jr.

JOHN I. CLELAND—Although not a clergyman at the time of his presidency at Arkansas College, John I. Cleland entered the ministry after leaving Batesville. Cleland resigned his presidency in the spring of 1897 and soon thereafter enrolled in the McCormick Theological Seminary in Chicago, from which he graduated in 1901. Ordained by the Buffalo (New York) Presbytery of the PCUSA (Northern Presbyterian Church), Cleland served congregations in New York, Minnesota, and Wisconsin before moving his family to the Pacific Northwest in 1912. For the next eight or nine years he served as a minister and evangelist in the Seattle, Washington, area. Little is known of the last years of his life except that he was ordained in the Congregational Church in 1922 and served a brief presidency at a college in California. John I. Cleland died in

Phoenix, Arizona, on 20 April 1927 at the age of sixty-three. He was survived by a son and three daughters, all of whom remained on the West Coast. Cleland's widow, the former Mabel Goodwin of Batesville, later gained regional recognition as a writer of adventure stories aimed at an adolescent audience.

JEROME P. ROBERTSON—Robertson's brief presidency at Arkansas College proved to be his only foray into higher education. Upon his resignation in 1915, he reentered the Presbyterian ministry, holding pastorates at Morrilton, Arkansas; Galveston, Texas; Shelbyville, Tennessee; and Memphis. Robertson was serving as pastor of the church in Corinth, Mississippi, when he died at the age of seventy-three on 5 March 1936.

WILLIAM S. LACY—Like Eugene R. Long, Lacy served two nonconsecutive terms as president of Arkansas College. In the nine years between his two presidential tenures (1923–1932), Lacy served first as executive secretary for Southwestern at Memphis and then as superintendent for schools and colleges in the Synod of Mississippi. Sixty-two years old upon his final resignation in 1937, Lacy spent most of his final days living in Batesville and serving the Southern Presbyterian Church as a stated supply and evangelist. Having contracted tuberculosis, William S. Lacy died in the state sanatorium at Booneville on 27 January 1943. He was sixty-eight years old. Lacy was the father of four children. His only daughter, Elizabeth, graduated from Arkansas College in 1923 and married fellow alum J. Courtney White, who later served the school briefly as head football coach.

E. B. TUCKER—Tucker left Arkansas College in February 1931 to assume the presidency of Austin College in Texas. Interestingly, life got no easier for the harried Tucker in Texas. In more than a dozen years as president of Austin, Tucker faced severe financial problems, threats of closure and merger, and divisiveness among the college's various constituencies. Tucker also introduced a more modern, youth-oriented spirit at the staid institution, much as he had done at Arkansas College in the 1920s. Upon his retirement from Austin's presidency in 1943, E. B. Tucker returned to his native Tennessee. In 1946 he came out of retirement to join the faculty of the Webb School, a private academy in Bell Buckle, Tennessee. Tucker retired for good in 1960 and in 1963 was awarded the Austin College Founders Medal. He died at the age of ninety-one on 17 November 1972, less than one month after Arkansas College celebrated its centennial.

URY MCKENZIE—McKenzie, noted both for serving the briefest presidency in the institution's history as well as for helping save the college from closure, served briefly as superintendent of the Batesville schools after his 1932 resignation from Arkansas College. Like J. P. Robertson, McKenzie never again worked in the field of higher education; instead, he spent most of the Great Depression as an insurance salesman in Hot Springs before buying a Lincoln County farm in 1938. With the exception of one year as a school principal, McKenzie spent the rest of his life farming. He died on his farm near Hope, which he had purchased at the end of World War II, on 1 February 1953 at the age of seventy-eight.

JOHN CROCKETT—Even in advanced age, John Crockett never shook the wanderlust that affected his early career. Crockett resigned the Arkansas College presidency in 1939 to become evangelist for the West Texas Presbytery, a position he held for three years. During the mid-1940s he served brief pastorates in San Antonio, Texas; Fayetteville, Tennessee; and southwestern Missouri before returning to Arkansas College as Bible professor in 1946. Crockett left Batesville again in 1951 and remained in the ministry in southern Missouri and northern Arkansas until his retirement in 1957. A lifelong bachelor, John Crockett died on 4 February 1964 at the age of eighty.

THOMAS M. LOWRY JR.—Although Thomas M. Lowry Jr. was never inaugurated as official president of Arkansas College, his tenure of almost three years eclipsed in longevity the terms of four earlier presidents. Lowry's resignation in April 1942 came as a result of his call to active military duty during World War II. He served most of the conflict stateside in the Army Air Corps, except for a brief tour of duty in India, and was honorably discharged after the war at the rank of major. Upon his return from military duty, Lowry joined the faculty at Southwestern at Memphis (now Rhodes College), where he taught history and political science until his retirement in 1970. Lowry and his wife, Margaret Goodwin Lowry, moved to Birmingham, Alabama, in 1986. After Margaret's death a few years later, he married Beatrice Roberts Harris. Lowry died in Birmingham at the age of ninety-five on 28 March 1997.

JOHN D. SPRAGINS—The last Arkansas native and alumnus to serve as president, John D. Spragins resigned in 1952 to assume the position of executive secretary for home missions in the East Arkansas Presbytery, a job that allowed him and his family to remain in Batesville. His tireless efforts over the next thirteen years resulted in the founding and strengthening of numerous Presbyterian congregations and missions in north central Arkansas. Spragins retired in 1965 and died on 14 May 1967 at the age of sixty-nine. Four of Spragins's five children graduated from Arkansas College, and his eldest son, C. Fitzhugh Spragins, served the institution for thirty years (1965–1995) as professor of religion.

PAUL M. MCCAIN—In 1969 McCain concluded the second-longest consecutive term as president in the history of the college in order to return to his hometown of Decatur, Georgia, and a new position as vice-president for development at Agnes Scott College. He remained in this position until his retirement in 1989. In 1979 Eleanor McCain, first lady of Arkansas College during most of the 1950s and 1960s, died of cancer. Paul McCain later remarried and after his retirement he and his wife, Dot, moved to a Presbyterian retirement village in Clinton, South Carolina. McCain died on New Year's Day, 2003, at the age of eighty-two.

R. W. WYGLE—After three years as president of Arkansas College, R. W. Wygle resigned in 1972 to assume the presidency of Northwestern State College in Alva, Oklahoma. Wygle remained in that position for three more years before leaving the higher education field to enter the insurance business in Wichita, Kansas. Now retired, the Wygles reside in a small town in central Kansas.

DAN C. WEST—In 1988 West resigned the presidency at Arkansas College to accept the same position at Carroll College, a Presbyterian institution in Waukesha, Wisconsin. After four years at Carroll College, West left to become vice-president for college relations at Union College in Schenectady, New York, the alma mater of Aaron W. Lyon, one of Arkansas College's original trustees. In February 1999 West left Union to take the position of vice-president for development, alumni, and public relations at Swarthmore College in suburban Philadelphia, perennially ranked among the nation's top liberal arts colleges. Dan C. West and Sidney Childs West remain in Swarthmore at the time of this book's publication.

JOHN V. GRIFFITH—Griffith resigned the presidency of Lyon College in 1997 and assumed the presidency of Presbyterian College in Clinton, South Carolina, in January 1998. At the time of publication the Griffiths are still at Presbyterian.

Appendix II

Lists of Leaders and Honors

COLLEGE LEADERSHIP

Presidents of Arkansas/Lyon College

1872–1891	Isaac J. Long
1891–1895	Eugene R. Long (acting)
1895–1897	John I. Cleland[1]
1897–1913	Eugene R. Long
1913–1915	Jerome P. Robertson
1915–1916	Daniel Frierson (acting)[2]
1917–1923	W. S. Lacy
1923–1931	Everett Brackin Tucker
1931–1932	Ury McKenzie
1932–1937	W. S. Lacy[3]
1937–1939	John Crockett
1939–1942	Thomas M. Lowry (acting)
1942–1952	John D. Spragins[4]
1952–1969	Paul M. McCain[5]
1969–1972	R. W. Wygle
1972–1988	Dan C. West[6]
1989–1997	John V. Griffith[7]
1998–present	Walter B. Roettger

Presidents/Chairmen of the Board of Trustees

1872–1886	Thomas R. Welch	Little Rock
1887–1890	A. R. Kennedy	Little Rock
1890–1893	J. W. Butler	Batesville
1893–1899	H. G. Bunn	Little Rock
1899–1901	Charles F. Penzel	Little Rock
1901–1926	James P. Coffin	Batesville
1926–1929	Thomas C. McRae	Prescott
1929	Stuart R. Oglesby Jr.	Hot Springs

1930–1933	Vann M. Howell	Little Rock
1934–1938	H. L. Paisley	Fayetteville
1939–1940	David Shepperson Sr.	El Dorado
1941–1944	J. Herndon McCain	Arkadelphia
1944–1956	S. Marcus Bone	Batesville
1956–1965	John P. Morrow Sr.	Batesville
1965–1976	Shuford R. Nichols	Little Rock
1976–1987	Frank Lyon Sr.	Little Rock
1987–1995	Robert A. Young III	Fort Smith
1995–1998	Graham Holloway	Dallas, Texas
1998–present	Robert A. Young III	Fort Smith

Academic Deans

1916–1917	Evander D. Brown
1917–1920	Eugene R. Long
1920–1925	R. K. Timmons
1925–1929	Lincoln Barker
1929–1933	Samuel W. Williams
1933–1934	Lincoln Barker
1934–1936	Thomas M. Lowry Jr.
1936–1946	Samuel W. Williams
1946–1954	Harry King
1954–1957	Lorne K. McAdam
1957–1958	Harry King
1958–1961	Roland B. Dickison
1961–1963	Roberta Dorr Brown
1963–1966	Glen Haddock
1966–1973	Roberta Dorr Brown
1973–1975	Edward N. Mosley
1975–1977	Robert E. Knott
1977–1978	Roberta Dorr Brown
1978–1992	John T. Dahlquist
1992–1997	Robert K. Holyer
1997–2000	J. William Moncrief
2000–present	John M. Peek

STUDENTS

Recipients of the Charles H. Coffin Scholarship Medal

YEAR	RECIPIENT	HOME
1907	George T. McKee	Little Rock
1908	Horace Sloan	Portia
1909	Stuart R. Oglesby	Hope
1910	E. B. Paisley	Gurdon
1911	none given	
1912	Christine Murphy	Jefferson County
	Eugene Sloan	Black Rock
1913	none given	
1914	Malcolm E. Evans	Batesville
1915	M. S. Smith Jr.	Batesville
1916	Fred Maxfield	Batesville
1917	none given	

1918	no record	
1919	none given	
1920	none given	
1921	Ira Nelson Barnett III	Batesville
1922	John Quincy Wolf Jr.	Batesville
1923	none given	
1924	none given	
1925	William A. Sensabaugh	Pfeiffer
1926	Etta Brewer	McAlester, Oklahoma
1927	Lillian Jimerson	Sulphur Rock
	Avon Shannon	Stuttgart
1928	Marguerite Glant Shannon	Stuttgart
	Stuart H. Salmon	Stamps
1929	Marjorie Norton	Star City
1930	Bess Millen	Malvern
1931	none given	
1932	none given	
1933	Ella Myrl Dobson	Batesville
	Wilma Stanley	Strong
1934	Allie Beth Dent	Batesville
	Doris Wray	Batesville
	Lois Thomas	Batesville
1935	Leila Heasley	Batesville
1936	Martha Cantley	Hope
	Dorothy Ross	Batesville
1937	none given	
1938	none given	
1939	Lillie Mae Martin	Batesville
	Frances Ross	Batesville
1940	Frances Chaney	McCrory
1941	none given	
1942	Betty Wasson	Batesville
	M. E. Wasson	Batesville
1943	no record	
1944	Mary Engels	Moorefield
1945	none given	
1946	Charline Bryant	Batesville
1947	Kathleen Sharp	Hoxie
1948	Lowell Southerland	Independence County
1949	James Vernon Balch	Independence County
1950	Gary Jones	Bargoed, Wales
1951	Pearl Ottinger	Batesville
1952	Joan Creason	Hot Springs
1953	Joyce Virginia Shillcutt	North Little Rock
1954	Evelyn Willard	Dallas, Texas
1955	Von Dean Gray	Batesville
1956	Marjorie Stuart	Batesville

1957	James Gillaspy	Batesville
1958	Ernestine Teeter	Tillar
1959	Barbara Buford	Forrest City
1960	Jacob C. Turner	Warren
1961	Mike Collins	Batesville
1962	James Logan Morgan Jr.	Newport
1963	Moorene Goff Newton	Moorefield
1964	Roberta Mae Bustin	Batesville
1965	Mary King	Newport
1966	Lamar Middleton	McGehee
1967	Mayola Satterfield	Brinkley
1968	Clifford Jackson	Donaldson
1969	Lance Jones	Hope
1970	Ronnie Brogdon	Batesville
1971	Ray Hamlett	McHue
1972	Billy Wayne Bristow	Strawberry
1973	Peggy Reynolds	Batesville
1974	Mary Ann Gray	Batesville
1975	Mark Wood	Floral
1976	Mara Marlin	North Little Rock
1977	Joan Rodella Chisam	Batesville
1978	Jeannie Dacus Whitener	Batesville
1979	Keith Stillwell	Batesville
1980	Karen Sue Calaway	Batesville
1981	William L. Garner	St. Ann, Missouri
1982	John Collins	Bonham, Texas
1983	Doug Punke	Enid, Oklahoma
1984	Marsha Allen	Drasco
1985	Cynthia Britton Barber	Batesville
1986	Patty L. Keeton Burks	Yellville
1987	David Wesley Duke	Newport
1988	Benjamin Blount	Allerton, Iowa
1989	Jennifer Smith	North Little Rock
1990	Leroy Roberts II	Batesville
1991	Roger Weitkamp	Batesville
1992	Benjamin Weston	Cave City
1993	Shane Robert Smith	Jonesboro
1994	Heather James	Batesville
1995	Rebecca Osborne	Newport
1996	Robert Gregory Tebbetts	Batesville
1997	Elizabeth Susan Neelly	Russellville
1998	Leslie Lynn Chambliss	Diaz
1999	Brandon Colby Flygare	Kingston, Missouri
2000	Kimberly Dickerson	Little Rock
2001	David McCullars	Conway
2002	Jonathan Thompson	Ozark

Campus Leaders

YEAR	YEARBOOK EDITOR	STUDENT BODY PRESIDENT	NEWSPAPER/LITERARY MAGAZINE EDITOR
1890			W. A. Ramsey
1891			W. A. Ramsey
1892			G. H. Lacy &
			A. Syd. Gibson
1893			A. Syd. Gibson
1896			C. P. Radford
1897			H. L. Paisley
			H. R. Keeble
1898			H. R. Keeble &
			J. L. Bevens &
			Thomas L. Green
1907			Horace Sloan
1908			Leo Partlow
1909			S. R. Oglesby Jr.
1910			T. D. Murphy
1911			Eugene Sloan
1912			Paul Ward
1913			Victor Wade
1914			Malcolm Evans
1915			F. Reginald Young
1919	John Quincy Wolf Jr.		
1920	John D. Spragins		Henry Sanderson Jr.
1921	John Quincy Wolf Jr.		Annie Frierson
1922	John W. Patterson		Helen J. McMurtry
1923	Marshall Hickman		Horace Casey
1924	Horace Casey		Elizabeth Osborne
1925	Jacob Meadow		J. Keith Morrow
1926	J. Herndon McCain	Harry Maxfield	Harriet Elcan
1927	John Parse	Harmon Ramsey	Meriam Anderson
1928	Stuart Salmon	John Benish	Shuford Nichols
1929	Harvey Booth	Alexander Henry	John Benish
1930	Mac Trimble	Eugene Poindexter	Blake Downie
1931	Elliott Hunter	Hugh M. Patterson	Harriet Sue Downie
1932	no yearbook	George Robinson	Ewing Orr

1933	no yearbook	Chester Crawford	no paper
1934	Mary Katherine Irving	J. W. Collier	no paper
1935	Carolyne Hipolite	Hubert Blakely	no paper
1936	no yearbook	no record	Thurston Masters
1937	Margaret Terry	Hugh Baty Proctor	Thurston Masters
1938	Mattie Louise McNutt	Charles Taylor	Carl Ray
1939	Lillie Mae Martin	Troy Gray	Eugene Bartlett
1940	Jane Wasson	Charles Bensberg	Ruth Horne
1941	Curry Patton	Howard Welborn & C. E. Gray	Ruth Horne
1942	no yearbook	Ben Evan Gillespie	no paper
1943	no yearbook	Bertis Nix	Edgar Brown
1944	Doris Tosh	Roberta Dorr	John T. Barr Jr.
1945	Emily Boehler	Ura Fae Burks	Doris Kimbrough
1946	Edith Clarke & Frances Holloway	Emma Lou Bridgman	Charline Bryant
1947	Marvin Shaw	Conway Lawrence	Billie Ruth Stokes
1948	Lawrence Eighner	Hugh Shell	Jean Westbrooke
1949	Lim Parks Jr.	James Vernon Balch	Alice Coleman
1950	H. Gary M. Jones	Benjamin F. Kelley	Herbert Meharg
1951	James Hall	Dave Becton	Vern Wheeler
1952	Joan Creason & Bob Doom	Lavene Ransom	no paper
1953	Marian Beth Pegg	Doin Hicks	no paper
1954	Emma Lee Lewis & Sarah Longley	Gordon Boyer	no paper
1955	Norma Black	Allen Porter	Billy Hobbs
1956	Fitzhugh Spragins	John Sharman	Marjorie Stuart
1957	Charlene Conner	Fitzhugh Spragins	Curt Avery & Sylvia Buercklin
1958	Ernestine Teeter	Jimmy Williams	Barbara Buford
1959	Betty Sue Hall	Fred Gray	Jane Mabry & Betsy Spragins
1960	Maury Stotts & Knoxie King	Jim Mitchum	Betsy Spragins & Doug Brodie
1961	Knoxie King	Ed Huff	Betsy Spragins
1962	Linda Green	Howard Hopkins	Julia Ellis
1963	Earnest Allen	Bill Walmsley	J. A. Huddleston
1964	Ginni Tucker	Jim Balch	J. A. Huddleston
1965	Peggy Pegg	Clarence Cash	Clarence Cash
1966	Cliff Jackson	Clarence Whichard	Bill Neal

1967	Cliff Jackson	Robert Mitchum	Drew Ponder
1968	Kathy Pardue	Cliff Jackson	Tom Arnold
1969	Dale Anderson	Harley Chappell	Tom Arnold & Herman Hammerschmidt
1970	Ronald Davidson	Ronnie Brogdon	Herman Hammerschmidt
1971	Billy Wayne Bristow	Ed Holmberg	Danny Brightwell
1972	Mike Gunter	Billy Wayne Bristow	Mike Bowlan
1973	Mark Wood	Suzanne Snelson	Bob Davis & Jim Lipscomb
1974	Anna Marie Hardin & Barbara Blessing	Charlie Barber	Larry Welch
1975	Anna Marie Hardin & Greg Nelson	Tom Rau	Greg Cooper
1976	Barbara Blessing	William Adair	Vickie Dunigan
1977	Ben Dickens	Donald Hurley	Debra Ann Holmes
1978	Sarah Stephenson	Eric Hance	Tom Ekman
1979	Melissa Seay	Ron Orick	Cheri Wright
1980	Laurie Wirthlin	Melissa Seay	Gerald Kimbrough
1981	Dawn Melton	Clay Sloan	Myra Yates
1982	Regina Craig	Wayne McKnight	Tripp Franks
1983	James Earl Pool	Chuck Jeffery	Tim Bateman
1984	Sandra Cannon	James Earl Pool & Lisa Lawson	Heidi Helmke
1985	Deborah Sisson	Steve Dixon	Lori Berry
1986	Loretta Barnett	Curt Bessette	Scott Coffin & Brad Dilday
1987	Kimberly Bessette & Curt Bessette	Joe Key	Lesa Thompson
1988	Robert Blount & Mike Kemp	John Forkner	Michelle Erwin & Valerie Vallance
1989	Lori Kirchens	Tammy Friel	Michelle Erwin & Kathy Clements
1990	Mark Light	Lori Kirchens	Mary Leslie
1991	Crystal Brown	John Treat	Len Rayburn
1992	Jennifer Stroud	Brien Hall	Meredith Bemis
1993	Gina Block	Shane Smith	Jennifer Stroud
1994	Kevin Hamilton	Mark Woods	Karen Culp
1995	JoAnn Adcock & Kevin Jumper	Tiffany Runyan	Gwen Green

1996	Brad Young & Monica Alexander & Mandy Weaver	Jason Caldarera	Ron Hanks
1997	Mandy Weaver & Robyn Christian & Frances Titsworth	Brad Young	Tony Abney
1998	Frances Titsworth & Ginny Kordsmeier & Bahar Frantz	Holly Payne	Leah Vest
1999	Bahar Frantz & Natalie Pruitt	Kenneth Slifer	Kelly Burns
2000	Casey McNally	Kenneth Slifer	Elizabeth Mazar
2001	Scott Shelby	Teryn McDuff	Josh Baugh
2002	Scott Shelby	Teryn McDuff	Kevin Vornheder & Jeremy Haggard
2003	Scott Shelby	Emilie Brady	Kevin Vornheder

Brown Scholars

YEAR GRADUATED	STUDENT	HOMETOWN
1982	Dawn Melton	Newport Beach, California
1983	Charles Jeffery	Batesville
1984	Terri Jan Leslie	Warren
1985	Susan Thomas	Traskwood
	Heidi Helmke	Yellville
1986	Patty Keeton	Yellville
1987	David Wesley Duke	Newport
	Anne Schrad	Fairfield Bay
	Debbie Tipton	Lonoke
1988	Yukari Jones	Jacksonville
	Brian Oxner	Memphis, Tennessee
	John Paul Zimmer	Jonesboro
1989	John Forkner	Shell Knob, Missouri
	Jennifer Smith	North Little Rock
1990	Damon Bolton	Sheridan
	Mark Bedford	Royal
	KaLyn Muncy	Melbourne
	Anne Williams	Pine Bluff
1991	Laverne Cox	Earle
	Bonnie Michele Holloway	Rogers
	Be Pham	Batesville
	John Treat	Searcy
1992	Scott Jackson	Valrico, Florida

	Terence James	Batesville
	Catherine Parrish	Murfreesboro
	Dharmesh Patel	Little Rock
	David R. Stipp	Hot Springs
1993	Noel Mace	Batesville
	Amy Seymour	Fort Worth, Texas
	Shane Smith	Jonesboro
	Ginger Townsend	Stuttgart
1994	Mary O'Sullivan	Fort Smith
	Brian Bailey	Pocahontas
	Shera Baldwin	Rapid City, South Dakota
	Greg Buxton	Pocahontas
	Christopher Cochran	Mammoth Spring
	Kristi Nikkel	Benton
1995	Gwen Green	Hoxie
	Kacie Richardson	Gassville
	Wayne Southwell	Lonsdale
	Sarah Taunton	El Dorado
	Gina Wake	Henderson, Tennessee
1996	Lori Carpenter	Hamburg
	John Russell Galbraith	Bryant
	Chase Gipson	Owasso, Oklahoma
	Ginger Sipes	Little Rock
	Christine Wallace-Hudson	Pettigrew
1997	Heather Henderson	Heber Springs
	Jessica Hesse	Weiner
	Elizabeth Neelly	Russellville
	Kristi Thompson	Pocahontas
1998	Shannon Blackwell	Zachary, Louisiana
	Justin Bumgardner	Guthrie, Oklahoma
	Johnathan Horton	Marshall
1999	Heather Suzanne Wade	Yellville
	Brandon Flygare	Kingston, Missouri
	Joshua Hanson	Little Rock
	Chris Musselman	Perryville
	Holly Payne	Berryville
2000	Stephen Bell	Bismarck
	Lori Colburn	Osceola
	Elizabeth Mazar	Blytheville
	Andrea McCollum	Malvern
2001	Shelia Borgognoni	Monticello
	William Cooksey	Jonesboro
	Maria Kaloghirou	Jonesboro
2002	Richard Ambler	Magnolia
	Amanda Price	Gravette
	Elizabeth Rowe	Hot Springs
	Jonathan Thompson	Ozark

Recipients of the Distinguished Alumni Award

YEAR OF AWARD	RECIPIENT AND CLASS
1950	Paul K. Calaway '31
1950	Laman A. Gray '28
1950	Harry U. Maxfield 1882
1951	Bess Maxfield '09
1951	Karr Shannon '32
1952	Chester C. Crawford '33
1972	Stuart R. Oglesby Jr. '09
1972	John Quincy Wolf Jr. '22
1973	George T. McKee '07
1974	Hugh M. Patterson '31
1975	Allie Beth Dent Martin '34
1976	Doin E. Hicks '53
1977	Martha Heasley Cox '38
1978	Gerard J. Bensberg '49
1979	Ira Nelson Barnett III '21
1980	Jabez F. Jackson Sr. '30
1981	Helen Sullivan Knight '31
1982	Bess Millen Wolf '30
1983	W. D. Murphy Jr. '33
1984	Gilbert Ford Kinney '28
1985	W. Joe Frierson '27
1986	James W. Headstream '34

YEAR OF AWARD	RECIPIENT AND CLASS
1987	George M. Gibson '28
1987	Amelia Samano Bishop '27
1988	Evalena Hollowell Berry '42
1989	W. Carl Garner '38
1989	Roberta Dorr Brown '44
1990	Thelma A. Pickens '22
1990	Fred Wann '59
1991	Edward Love '51
1991	Marvin Shaw '47
1992	Bill W. Bristow '72
1993	J. W. Collier '34
1994	Deborah Willhite '74
1995	Mary Helen Fallis Dobbins '48
1996	Ella Myrl Dobson Shanks '33
1997	Arvil Burks '53
1998	William F. Rogers '33
1998	Wilbur Gilbert '56
1999	Victoria Scritchfield Crittenden '78
1999	Adam D. Robertson '63
2000	Wanda Allender Rider '54
2000	H. Gary M. Jones '50
2001	Lucy Jeffery Yeager '67
2002	Jim Rollins '69

Recipients of the Alumni Service Award

YEAR OF AWARD	RECIPIENT AND CLASS
1983	Marjorie Dowzer '34
1985	Evalena Hollowell Berry '42
1986	Josephine Cook Beck '41
1989	Betty Morrison Sloan '23
1997	Roberta Bustin '64

Recipients of the Patterson Alumni Decade Award

CLASS	RECIPIENTS
1966	Karen Webb Blaesing and Larry M. Gerber
1967	Robert Mitchum
1968	Joy Powers Simonson and Seth Willets
1969	Lindy Mason Hodges and Jimmy Don Rollins
1970	No award given
1971	Frances Layne Duke and James Pearson
1972	Mary Jane Pierce Norton and Bill W. Bristow
1973	Martha Miller Harriman and Tommy L. Hicks
1974	Judy Campbell McDaniel and David E. Parker
1975	Deborah Kay Fulbright and Marvin E. Holtz
1976	Denise R. Nemec and Charles D. Morris
1977	Peggy Franks Pierce and Greg Golden
1978	Melissa Hicks and Roger Gaylon Franks
1979	Renee Jeffery and Keith D. Stillwell
1980	Karen Calaway Hester and Kenny Hutson
1981	Laurie Wirthlin Lewis and Paul Wesley Hance
1982	Dawn Melton Mulkern and John R. Way
1983	Patricia Seibert and Doug Punke
1984	Julea Garner and Alan Bufford
1985	Heidi Helmke Von Hoffman and Roy Goetz
1986	Tracy L. Stewart and Steve Seaman
1987	Jeanne Forkner and Greg Mohlke
1988	Penney Wood Rector and Ben Blount
1989	Jacqueline Howard Bedford and Michael Morse
1990	Kelly Hunt Lyon and Dennis Ciecielski
1991	Crystal Brown Kemp and Derek McDowell
1992	Cheri Engle Weitkamp and Jason Finney

All-Conference, All-District, and All-American Athletes

The following is a list of decorated Arkansas/Lyon College athletes. Unless otherwise noted, the athletes listed as All-AIC or All-State were first team selections. (In 1969 AIC basketball abandoned the first-team–second-team format in favor of a ten-member All-AIC squad.) Because of the disorganized nature of small college athletics in the early twentieth century—and in some sports even into midcentury—the list does not include any athletes from the era before World War I. It also excludes athletes who excelled in nonintercollegiate sports; one example of an athlete not recognized here would be Bernis Duke, an Amateur Athletic Union state heavyweight boxing champion in the early 1950s. In other instances, the lack of thorough records may have led to the unintentional omission of all-conference performers.

Men's Basketball

ALL-AMERICAN	YEAR
Charlie Howard (Second Team)	1981
Kevin Johnson (Academic)	1984 & 1985

ALL-AIC—FIRST TEAM	YEAR
James "Slim" Carvell (All-State)	1930
Travis "Pete" Creed (All-State)	1930
Lonnie Etheridge (All-State)	1931 & 1932
Charles Taylor (All-State)	1938
Kohn Bray (All-State)	1939 & 1940
Vic Stewart	1941 & 1942
Bob Rutherford	1948 & 1949
Harry Neff	1952 & 1953
Bobby Smith	1955 & 1956
Jim Harris	1957
Corbett Passmore	1958 & 1959
Francis "Birdie" Rogers	1960 & 1962
Lavaughn Robertson	1962, 1963 & 1964
Jim Haney	1966, 1967 & 1968
Bill Cossey	1969
Elliott Jackson	1973
Milton Sullivan	1973
Martin Jacobs	1974
Ed "Goose" Tatum	1974
Jim Hansen	1975
Clifton Avant	1978

Lee Andrew Smith	1978
Joe Holt	1979 & 1980
Charlie Howard	1980 & 1981
Rodney Tunson	1982
Kevin Johnson	1983 & 1985
Charlie Grant	1984
Charlie Traub	1988
Danny Daniels	1989
Lyle Middleton	1992
Steve Scherrey	1994

ALL-DISTRICT 17	YEAR
Elliott Jackson	1973
Martin Jacobs	1974
Calvin Breedlove	1974
Ed "Goose" Tatum	1974
Lee Andrew Smith	1978 & 1979
Joe Holt	1979 & 1980
Charlie Howard	1980 & 1981
Rodney Tunson	1981 & 1982
Kevin Johnson	1983
Lyle Middleton	1992

POST-AIC AWARDS		YEAR
Ryland Kieffer	All-Southwest Region	1996 & 1997
Jake Newton	All-TranSouth Conference	1998
Clint Reed	All-TranSouth Conference	1999
Brandon Byrd	All-TranSouth Conference	2002

Women's Basketball

ALL-AMERICAN	YEAR
Stephanie Rowton (Second Team)	1998

ALL-CONFERENCE (AWISA OR AIC)	YEAR
Beverly Bass	1976
Debbie Wheeler	1976
Lou Riley	1977
Billie Willett	1978 & 1979
Brenda Olive	1980, 1981 & 1982
Susie Fudge	1980, 1981 & 1982
Alice White	1981 & 1982

Rena Shaver	1983 & 1984
Sharon Scott	1984 & 1985
Tracy Stewart	1985
Carol Small	1986
Tanya Britt	1987
Annie Harris	1989
Grace Catt McDowell	1989, 1990 & 1991
Brandi Love	1992, 1993 & 1994
Olivia Malland	1995

ALL-DISTRICT 17	YEAR
Rena Shaver	1984
Sharon Scott	1984
Grace Catt McDowell	1989, 1990 & 1991
Brandi Love	1992

POST-AIC AWARDS		YEAR
Stephanie Rowton	All-Southwest Region	1996
Stephanie Rowton	All-TranSouth Conference	1998
Daisy Dyer	All-Southwest Region	1997
Sarah Meier	All-TranSouth Conference	2000 & 2001
Amy Shue	All-TranSouth Conference	2000
Melissa Allen	All-TranSouth Conference	2001

Football

ALL-STATE OR ALL-AIC (FIRST TEAM)	YEAR
J. Courtney White	1922
Lowell Manning	1925
Earl Stokes	1927
Paul Fiser	1929
Lloyd Berry	1934
Ray Brown	1949 & 1950

Baseball

ALL-STATE, CONFERENCE, OR DISTRICT	YEAR
Sonny Conine	1950 & 1951
Linn Garner	1950
Frankie Shell	1951
Wendell Hawkins	1972

James Andrews	1974
Foster Ward	1993
Dennis Amaral	1996
Patrick Kircher	1996
Ricky Strole	1996
Ryan Rana	1998
Brant Owens	1999
Jason Livernois	2002

Volleyball

ALL-CONFERENCE, DISTRICT, OR REGION	YEAR
Suzzette Knowles	1977
Johanna Turimave	1977
Erma Kelley	1980
Jennifer Walls	1998
Jaime Bedard	2000
Courtney Guziewicz	2000
Jessica Cline	2001
Ceca Brckalo	2002

Women's Cross-Country

ALL-AMERICAN	YEAR
Diane Marshall	1981

ALL-CONFERENCE OR DISTRICT	YEAR
Diane Marshall	1981
Sheila Murphy	1981
Linda Ramsey	1981
Lois Hudson	1983 & 1984
Laura Abbott	1983
Brenda Jones	1983 & 1985
Paula Johnson	1983 & 1985
Michele Melton	1983
Tina May	1984
Lili Hughes	1984
Kathy Buchanan	1984
Angie Gobel	1984 & 1986
Kim Brown	1985 & 1986
Michelle Thompson	1985
Danea Hall	1985

Grace Catt McDowell	1988
Kristie Gay	1989
Robin Webb	1990, 1991 & 1992
Lavel Buck	1990
Alisa Hook	1990
April Schneider	1992
Tricia Collins	1992
Jennifer Presley	1993 & 1994
Michele Smart	1994

Men's Cross-Country

ALL-CONFERENCE OR DISTRICT	YEAR
Oneal King	1983
Johnny Reed	1984
Chris Marcak	1984
Tim Martin	1984
Shane Garrett	1987
Justin Hawkins	1993 & 1994
Justin Bumgardner	1994

Women's Track and Field

ALL-AMERICAN	YEAR
Diane Marshall	1982
Brenda Jones	1983 & 1984
Lois Hudson (Academic)	1984
Tammy Peten	1990
Robin Webb	1991

ALL-CONFERENCE OR DISTRICT	YEAR
Brenda Frerker	1981
Kimmie Kirkpatrick	1981
Barbara Perk	1981
Linda Ramsey	1981
Krystal Kuyper	1982
Diane Marshall	1982
Jerri Gleghorn	1983
Lois Hudson	1983, 1984 & 1985
Paula Johnson	1983
Michele Melton	1983 & 1984
Terri Robertson	1983

Shelby Williams	1983
Brenda Jones	1983, 1984 & 1985
Sharon Scott	1984 & 1985
Laura Abbott	1984
Tina May	1985
Carol Small	1985 & 1986
Rochelle Patterson	1985
Kim Brown	1986
Annie Harris	1989
Tammy Peten	1988, 1989 & 1990
Robin Webb	1991 & 1992
Susan Kirk	1991

Men's Track and Field

ALL-CONFERENCE OR DISTRICT	YEAR
Tillar Conner	1924
Cecil "Red" Justus	1926
George Heard	1930
Todd Smithhart	1982
David Hicks	1984
Oneal King	1984
Chris Marcak	1984
Richie Thomas	1984
Rob Garner	1991 & 1992

Other All-American Performers

Adriane Barnett — Women's Golf 2002

Other All-Conference Performers

STUDENT	SPORT	YEAR
O. J. Broadwater	Men's Tennis	1950
Bob Lotridge	Men's Tennis	1950
John Nash	Bowling	1966
Thomas Koc	Bowling	1969
Steve Schwafferman	Bowling	1970
Steve Purdy	Men's Golf	1976
Joe Cooper	Men's Golf	1994
Tara Reynolds	Women's Tennis	1995
Adriane Barnett	Women's Golf	2002
Julie Church	Women's Golf	2002

Inductees in the Lyon College Athletic Hall of Fame

YEAR OF AWARD	INDUCTEE AND CLASS	YEAR OF AWARD	INDUCTEE AND CLASS
1983	Bernis Duke '53	1992	John Cook '53
	William H. "Spider" Irving '31		Jim Harris '58
	Coach R. C. "Dick" Winningham		Lee Andrew Smith '79
1984	Jim Haney '68	1993	Fred Wann '59
	Bob Rutherford '49		David Seward '65
	Charles Taylor '38		Clifton Avant '78
1985	Kohn Bray '40	1994	Prior Evans '30
	Robert Lee Calaway '39		Arvie "Bubba" Burks '54
	Lowell Manning '29		Rena Shaver Thomas '84
	Lavaughn Robertson '64	1995	Edwin "Sonny" Conine '51
	Victor E. Stewart '50		Donald L. Hedden '50
1986	Paul "Red" Fiser '31		Kevin Johnson '85
	W. Carl Garner '38	1996	Bill Baxter '66
	Harry Neff '53		Coach Van Gore Compton
	Bobby Smith '56		Elmer Hogg '37
1987	Wesley Carpenter '35	1997	Coach Terry Garner
	Bill Cossey '69		Charlie Grant '84
	George Heard '33		Myron "Butch" Schlater '31
	Chaney Taylor '39	1998	Clyde C. Berry
1988	Corbett Passmore '59		Fred Lamb '66
	Joe Elton Martin '42		Diane Marshall Treadway '82
	Lonnie Etheridge '36	1999	Jack Haney '64
	Hayden Estes '41		Jim Hansen '76
1989	Linn Garner '53		David McDaniel '75
	Curtis King '52		John P. Morrow Jr. '28
	Francis "Birdie" Rogers '62	2000	Kelvin Blevins '85
	M. D. "Doc" Williams '42		Jim Canada '68
1990	Paul Bone '56		Tracy Stewart-Lange '86
	Allen Ray Brown '51		William "Chubby" Menard '17
	Charlie Howard '81	2001	O. J. Broadwater '50
	Henry Lee "Porter" Stewart '51		Wendell Hawkins '74
1991	Enid Barron '37		Tanya Britt Taylor '87
	Ronnie Brogdon '70	2002	Beverly Bass '77
	Elliott Jackson '74		Nathaniel VanPelt '75
	Hugh Baty Proctor '36		Gary Weeks '71
	James L. "G. G." Rutherford '42		Ed Mosley '60

Recipients of the Lamar Williamson Prize for Faculty Excellence

YEAR	RECIPIENT	ACADEMIC FIELD
1980	Roberta Bustin	Chemistry
1981	Terrell Tebbetts	English
1982	George Lankford	Folklore
1983	Dorothy Landis Gray	Music
1984	Jane Bush Fagg	History
1985	Daniel W. Fagg Jr.	History
1986	Donald V. Weatherman	Political Philosophy
1987	Bert E. Holmes	Chemistry
1988	Ann A. Rhodes	Psychology
1989	Edward N. Mosley	Mathematics
1990	Robert K. Holyer	Religion and Philosophy
1991	Virginia F. Wray	English
1992	Scott Peterson	Biology
1993	Thomas E. Cooper	Economics
1994	George Chlebak	Art
1995	Bart L. Lewis	Spanish
1996	John T. Dahlquist	History
1997	James L. Rulla	Mathematics
1998	Andrea Hollander Budy	English
1999	Russell T. Stinson	Music
2000	Teresa B. Murphy	Education
2001	Cassie L. Creighton	Accounting
2002	Barrie Bondurant	Psychology

Recipients of the CASE Arkansas Professor of the Year Award

YEAR	RECIPIENT	ACADEMIC FIELD
1989	Roberta Bustin	Chemistry
1991	George Lankford	Folklore
1992	Terrell Tebbetts	English
1994	Scott Peterson	Biology
1997	Bart Lewis	Spanish
1998	James Rulla	Mathematics
1999	David Stricklin	History
2000	Robert Gregerson	Biology
2001	Helen Robbins	English

Recipients of the Arkansas/Lyon College Medal

YEAR	RECIPIENT
1980	Jean Brown
1984	Shuford Nichols
1988	Frank Lyon Sr.
1990	W. C. Brown Jr.
1990	Marion Bradley Lyon

Recipients of the Honorary Alumnus Award

YEAR	RECIPIENT
1986	Frank Lyon Sr.
1988	M. L. Gernert
1988	Dan C. West
1988	Sidney Childs West
1989	Graham Holloway
1990	Hugh B. Patterson
1990	Dorothy Landis Gray
1991	William Dunklin
1993	Violet Miller
1994	Carolyn Holloway
1995	Mertie Harris
1995	Charles Hoke
1996	P. K. Holmes
1996	Virginia Holmes
1997	Elmer Kirk
1999	David Itkin
2000	Ferd Bellingrath
2000	Frances Bellingrath
2002	Herbert Rule III

Recipients of the Friend of Education Award

YEAR	RECIPIENT
1986	Catherine "Kitty" Barnett
1987	Marian McGinnis
1988	Dorothy Sydenstricker
1989	Billie L. Porter
1990	Abbie Snapp Arnold
1991	Annie Mae Miller
1991	Asbury Mansfield Miller
1992	Virginia Kirk
1993	Craig Johnston
1993	Lucille Pearson Johnston
1994	Doris Hammett
1995	Ruth G. Blair
1996	Nettie Bustin
1997	Jim Rollins
1998	Eugene McKay
1999	Madeline N. Burns
2000	Richard Galbraith
2001	Cassie Creighton
2002	Deborah Frazier

Appendix III

Brief Historical Sketches of Selected Arkansas Institutions, Past and Present

Arkansas Baptist College

Founded as the Baptist Institute in a Little Rock church in 1884, Arkansas Baptist College is one of three historically black, four-year colleges in Arkansas. After a brief closure, the institution reopened in the fall of 1885 as Arkansas Baptist College and has provided an education to a small number of the state's African Americans continuously since that time.

Arkansas College (Fayetteville)

The original Arkansas College, the state's first institution of higher learning, was chartered in December 1852 and accepted its first students shortly thereafter. Affiliated with the Disciples of Christ (or Christian Church), the small college awarded the first bachelor's degrees in Arkansas before closing its doors at the onset of the Civil War. The college building was burned in 1862, and Arkansas College did not reopen after the war.

Arkansas State University

One of four agricultural high schools established by the legislature in 1909, the First District State Agricultural School in Jonesboro admitted its first students in 1910. By the end of World War I, the institution had begun offering junior college-level instruction, and in 1930, five years after being renamed First District Agricultural and Mechanical College, it became a baccalaureate-granting school. The name was changed to Arkansas State College in 1933 and to Arkansas State University in 1967.

Arkansas Tech University

Another of the agricultural high schools, Arkansas Tech began life as the Second District Agricultural School in 1910. The institution achieved junior college status in 1922 and was renamed Arkansas Polytechnic College three years later. Russellville's college became a four-year institution shortly after World War II and assumed university status in 1976.

Cane Hill College

Chartered in 1852 one day after the founding of Fayetteville's Arkansas College, Cane Hill College was a Cumberland Presbyterian institution located in the Washington County town of Cane Hill. The college closed its doors in the spring of 1861 due to the Civil War but reopened in 1868 with a new frame building. Cane Hill's resurrection was to be short-lived, however, once nearby Fayetteville became home to the state university. Cane Hill College awarded a handful of bachelor's degrees before its demise in 1889.

Crescent College

Founded in Eureka Springs's grand Crescent Hotel in 1908, Crescent College operated for a number of years as a Baptist-supported junior college for young women before succumbing to the financial constraints of the Great Depression in 1933.

Galloway College

Chartered in 1888 by the Methodist Episcopal Church, South, Galloway College opened its doors in Searcy the following year. From that time until 1929 it served as Arkansas Methodists' women's institution of higher learning; in the latter year Galloway was merged with the Methodists' two other colleges on the Hendrix campus in Conway, leaving Searcy without a college for the next five years.

Harding University

Founded in 1924 in Morrilton as a Church of Christ institution, Harding College was moved to the Searcy campus of the former Galloway College ten years later. In 1979 the college became Harding University.

Henderson-Brown College

Founded in Arkadelphia in 1890 as Arkadelphia Methodist College, the school was renamed Henderson College in 1904 and, finally, Henderson-Brown College in

1911. Like Galloway College, Henderson-Brown was merged with Hendrix in 1929. The new institution was briefly known as Hendrix-Henderson College before it reverted to Hendrix College.

Henderson State University

When Arkansas Methodists moved to merge their three institutions, the state acquired the old Henderson-Brown campus in Arkadelphia and in 1929 established Henderson State Teachers College. Renamed Henderson State College in 1967, the school became Henderson State University in 1975.

Hendrix College

Opened in Altus in 1884 as Central Collegiate Institute, the college grew out of an academy founded eight years earlier by Methodist minister and teacher Isham Burrow. Renamed Hendrix College in 1889, the institution moved to its current location in Conway the following year. In 1924 Hendrix became the first independent college in the state to receive accreditation from the North Central Association. Five years later the Methodist Episcopal Church, South, of Arkansas merged its other two institutions (Galloway and Henderson-Brown) with Hendrix on the Conway campus. The altered institution was known as Hendrix-Henderson College for two years before reverting to the name Hendrix.

John Brown University

Founded in Siloam Springs by Salvation Army leader John E. Brown Sr. in 1919, John Brown University (originally known as Southwestern Collegiate Institute) was designed as an interdenominational, evangelical college with a strong emphasis on student manual labor.

Little Rock College

One of a handful of now-defunct colleges founded in the state's capital, Little Rock College opened its doors as a Catholic institution in 1908. By the time Little Rock Junior College was founded in 1927, Little Rock College had faded out of existence.

Lacrosse Collegiate Institute

Chartered as a junior college in a small Izard County community in 1881, Lacrosse Collegiate was an outgrowth of an academy established more than a dozen years earlier by former Batesville resident M. Shelby Kennard. Rebuilt as an academy after it was destroyed by a tornado in 1883, Lacrosse Collegiate closed its doors in the late 1880s.

Mountain Home Baptist College

Founded by the White River Baptist Association in 1893, the college limped into the twentieth century before closing in 1901. One year later it was reopened as an academy affiliated with Ouachita Baptist College. In 1916 Mountain Home Baptist College was elevated once again to junior college status, although many of its students remained on the academy level. Enrollment and financial problems proved too much to overcome, and the college closed its doors for the final time in 1934.

Ouachita Baptist University

Chartered by the Southern Baptist Church of Arkansas, Ouachita Baptist College opened in Arkadelphia in 1886. Accredited by the North Central Association in 1927, the institution was also popularly called Ouachita College until it became Ouachita Baptist University in 1965.

Quitman College

Growing out of a Cleburne County academy known as Quitman Institute, Quitman College opened in 1870 under the aegis of the Arkansas Conference of the Methodist Episcopal Church, South. In 1881 the Methodists erected a modern two-story building to house the college; however, six years later the Arkansas Conference withdrew its financial support from Quitman College in favor of Central Collegiate Institute (later Hendrix). Quitman College continued to educate students until it closed in 1898.

Philander Smith College

Walden Seminary, the earliest incarnation of the college, was founded in 1877 in Little Rock by a conference of African American ministers of the Methodist Episcopal Church. Designed to educate freedmen, the school closed in 1881 but reopened two years later as a chartered, four-year institution, Philander Smith College. The college is now also affiliated with the United Negro College Fund.

St. John's College

Although incorporated by the Arkansas Masonic Grand Lodge in 1850, St. John's College did not open until 1859. The Civil War cut short the Little Rock institution's life, and an effort to resuscitate the college after the war proved short-lived and unsuccessful.

Southern Arkansas University

Opened in Magnolia in 1911 as the Third District Agricultural School, the institution achieved junior college status in 1925 and was subsequently renamed Third District Agricultural and Mechanical College. In 1951, two years after becoming a four-year institution, the school was renamed Southern State College. The name was changed to Southern Arkansas University in 1976.

University of Arkansas, Fayetteville

Established as Arkansas Industrial University in 1871 and first opened for classes in January 1872, it is the oldest surviving institution of higher education in the state. The first permanent building, Old Main, was completed in 1875. In 1899 AIU became the University of Arkansas.

University of Arkansas, Little Rock

Founded in 1927 as Little Rock Junior College, the institution was renamed Little Rock University in 1957 in recognition of the move to four-year status. The university became a part of the University of Arkansas system in 1969.

University of Arkansas, Monticello

Founded by the state legislature as the Fourth District Agricultural School in 1909, the institution achieved junior college status in 1928, three years after being renamed Arkansas Agricultural and Mechanical (A & M) College. Arkansas A & M began awarding bachelor's degrees shortly before the outbreak of World War II. It was absorbed by the University of Arkansas system in 1971.

University of Arkansas, Pine Bluff

Founded in 1873 as Branch Normal College, a branch of the state university designed for black students, the institution served at times as a four-year and two-year college before achieving permanent four-year status in 1929. By that date the name of the institution had been changed to Arkansas Agricultural, Mechanical & Normal College (AM & N). In 1972 AM & N became a part of the University of Arkansas system.

University of Central Arkansas

Having opened its doors in 1908 as Arkansas State Normal School, the Conway institution first began awarding bachelor's degrees in the early 1920s. Renamed

Arkansas State Teachers College in 1925, the school established its first graduate program in 1955. In 1966 the institution was renamed the State College of Arkansas; the current name was adopted nine years later.

University of the Ozarks

Founded in Clarksville in 1891 by the Arkansas Cumberland Presbyterian Church, the institution began its life as Arkansas Cumberland College. After the Cumberland Presbyterian Church and the Presbyterian Church, U.S.A., officially united in 1906, the Presbyterian Church, U.S.A., and a reorganized remnant of Cumberland Presbyterians struggled for control of the institution for a number of years. Shortly after World War I the school became known as the College of the Ozarks, reflecting the takeover of non-Cumberland leaders. The name was changed to University of the Ozarks in 1987.

Williams Baptist College

Founded in 1941 as Southern Baptist College, the school was originally located in Pocahontas but moved to Walnut Ridge in 1946. Beginning in 1948 the two-year college received modest financial assistance from the Arkansas Baptist State Convention (ABSC); in 1968 the ABSC fully adopted the college. In the late 1970s Southern Baptist College began moving toward four-year status and in 1986 awarded its first bachelor's degrees. Five years later the college was renamed Williams Baptist College in honor of the school's founder, H. E. Williams.

NOTES

PREFACE

1. Goodspeed, *The Goodspeed Biographical and Historical Memoirs of Northeast Arkansas* (Chicago: Goodspeed Publishing Company, 1889), 952.

2. Frederick Rudolph, *The American College and University: A History* (1962; Athens: University of Georgia Press, 1990), 48.

3. C. Vann Woodward, *Origins of the New South, 1877–1913*, Volume IX of the History of the South Series (Baton Rouge: Louisiana State University Press, 1951), 438.

PROLOGUE: "The destitute and more isolated portions of the Master's vineyard"

1. I. J. Long, *A Discourse Commemorative of the Life, Character and Services of the Rev. Thomas Rice Welch, D. D. Delivered Before the Synod of Arkansas at Camden, Ark., November 17, 1886* (St. Louis, Mo.: Farris, Smith & Co., 1886), 16.

2. At the outset of war in 1861 most of the Presbyterian churches in the South broke with their northern brethren to form the Presbyterian Church in the Confederate States of America. At the close of the war the PCCSA was renamed the Presbyterian Church in the United States (PCUS).

3. Though Hammond was born and raised in the upcountry, he married into the lowcountry elite, inherited a large plantation, and became perhaps the one antebellum South Carolinian most associated with Charleston society and the planter elite.

4. Biographical information on I. J. Long, here and afterward, gathered from the following sources: Goodspeed, *Biographical and Historical Memoirs of Northeast Arkansas*, 686–87; E. C. Scott, comp., *Ministerial Directory of the Presbyterian Church, U.S., 1861–1941* (Austin, Tex.: Von Boeckmann-Jones, 1942), 414; "Obituary," *Arkansas College Magazine*, January 1892, 258–60. For information on the Scotch-Irish in the South, see: James G. Leyburn, *The Scotch-Irish: A Social History* (Chapel Hill: University of North Carolina Press, 1962); Grady McWhiney, *Cracker Culture: Celtic Ways in the Old South* (Tuscaloosa: University of Alabama Press, 1988); and Rodger Cunningham, *Apples on the Flood: The Southern Mountain Experience* (Knoxville: University of Tennessee Press, 1987).

5. A common school education, or grounding in the three R's, was often referred to as an "English" education, as opposed to a classical education, which required the study of Latin and Greek.

6. One of the oldest colleges west of the Appalachian range, Centre was founded in 1819. Danville Theological Seminary was founded in 1853; today it is the Louisville Presbyterian Theological Seminary. Columbia Theological Seminary, founded in Lexington, Georgia, and currently in Decatur, Georgia, originated in 1828.

7. The groundwork for Union Theological Seminary was laid in Hampden-Sydney beginning in 1807; Richmond became the site of the institution five years later.

8. Long, *Discourse*, 4–7, 10 (quote); Fay Hempstead, *Historical Review of Arkansas*, Vol. I (Chicago: Lewis, 1911), 421; Scott, *Ministerial Directory*, 759.

9. Virginia Fitzhugh Jeffery and Lucy Jeffery Yeager, *A Rich and Lasting Blessing: A 150 Year History of the First Presbyterian Church of Batesville, Arkansas* (Newport, Ark.: Craig Printing, 1992), 14, 110–11. A stated supply is in essence a temporary pastor, though, as in Long's case, the length of a stated supply's service may stretch into years.

10. U.S. Department of the Interior, Office of the Census, *Ninth Census of the United States, 1870: Population* (Washington, D.C.: Government Printing Office, 1872), 13, 85.

11. Nancy S. Griffith, "Aaron Woodruff Lyon: Pioneer Educator, Citizen and Christian Gentleman," *Independence County Chronicle* 35 (October 1993–January 1994): 56; A. C. McGinnis, "A History of Independence County, Arkansas," *Independence County Chronicle* 17 (April 1976): 48; Robert Neill, "Reminiscences of Independence County," in *Publications of the Arkansas Historical Association*, Vol. III, ed. John Hugh Reynolds (Fayetteville: Arkansas Historical Association, 1911), 354; *Minutes of Arkansas Presbytery*, May 1857, 97, Box 1, Presbyterian Collection, Lyon College Archives (hereafter, LCA); *North Arkansas Times*, 23 February 1867, 3, and 29 June 1867, 3; Nancy Griffith, "Michael Shelby Kennard," *Independence County Chronicle* 38 (October 1996–January 1997): 41; Eugene R. Long, "Arkansas College," in *Publications of the Arkansas Historical Association*, Vol. II, ed. John Hugh Reynolds (Little Rock: Arkansas Historical Association, 1908), 91.

12. *North Arkansas Times*, 24 August 1967, 3; "Account for Private Tuition 1868," I. J. Long's Speeches/Essays and Account Book, Box 2, Long Family Collection, Lyon College Archives (LCA).

PART I: 1872–1916

1. S. J. Connolly, "Ulster Presbyterians: Religion, Culture, and Politics, 1660–1850," in *Ulster and North America: Transatlantic Perpsectives on the Scotch-Irish*, ed. H. Tyler Blethen and Curtis W. Wood Jr. (Tuscaloosa: University of Alabama Press, 1997), 35.

2. Donald G. Tewksbury, *The Founding of American Colleges and Universities before the Civil War* (1932; Hamden, Conn.: Archon Books, 1965), 93–95. Tewksbury identified forty-nine colleges founded before the Civil War with some connection to Presbyterianism. Methodists ranked second with thirty-four colleges; Baptists founded twenty-five, Congregationalists twenty-one, and Catholics fourteen.

3. Quoted from Arkansas Synod records in H. L. Paisley, ed., *Centennial History of Presbyterianism (U.S.) in Arkansas* (no place of publication or publisher, 1954), 4.

4. Ibid., 5; Virginia Fitzhugh Jeffery and Lucy Jeffery Yeager, *A Rich and Lasting Blessing*, 110–11.

CHAPTER 1: Isaac Long on One End of a Log

1. "Arkansas College," *Texas Republican*, 12 January 1877, reprinted in *Batesville News Review*, 20 December 1935; *Arkansas Gazette*, 21 December 1876. The male graduates included William H. Wycough and Charles W. Maxfield of Batesville, T. J. Horne of Des Arc, Le Roy D. Houston of Rockbridge County, Virginia, and W. K. Patterson Jr. of Rutherford County, Tennessee. It should be noted that the three female AC graduates were the first women to earn A.B. degrees. In his 1969 dissertation, Robert Harold Basham noted that Cane Hill College (Washington County) graduated its first female students in 1876 also, but, like many coeducational institutions of the day, Cane Hill did not grant the A.B. to women, instead conferring upon them "an equivalent degree." Basham, *A History of Cane Hill College in Arkansas* (Ed.D. Diss., University of Arkansas, 1969; Ann Arbor: UMI, 1970), 187. Arkansas College's unusual December graduation was the result of an experiment early in the school's existence. At the end of the first session in the spring of 1873, Isaac Long decided to immediately undertake the second session, moving the summer vacation period to winter, the time of year when sickness inflated absences. However, enrollment dropped precipitously in the summer of 1874 and the plan was abandoned. The long-term result of this scheduling anomaly was a December graduation in both 1876 and 1878. The first spring graduation took place in 1880. General Catalog of Arkansas College, 1872–1922, Lyon College Archives. The title for chapter 1 is a play on President James Garfield's once-famous quote: "The ideal college is Mark Hopkins [longtime professor and president of Williams College] on one end of a log and a student on the other."

2. Frederick Rudolph, *The American College and University: A History* (1962; Athens: University of Georgia Press, 1990), 48.

3. I. J. Long, "Sketch of Arkansas College," pamphlet of combined articles that originally appeared as columns in the *Arkansas Presbyterian* (Little Rock), 1890–1891, 4.

4. Dallas T. Herndon, ed., *Centennial History of Arkansas*, Vol. I (Chicago: S. J. Clarke, 1922),

566, 568, 570–71; Basham, *Cane Hill College*, 119, 126–27; John Hugh Reynolds and David Yancey Thomas, *History of the University of Arkansas* (Fayetteville: University of Arkansas, 1910), 57.

5. Reynolds and Thomas, *University of Arkansas*, 57–62.

6. Presbyterians were the premier college builders of the nineteenth century. According to historian Donald G. Tewksbury, by 1860, though ranking behind Methodists and Baptists in number of American communicants, the Presbyterians controlled more colleges than any other denomination. By the Civil War, more than one-quarter of all colleges in the United States were controlled by or had been founded by Presbyterians.

7. Long, "Sketch," 3 (quote); Clarence Warren Speight, *Brief History of the Campus and Buildings of Austin Peay State College and Southwestern Presbyterian University* (Clarksville, Tenn.: APSC, 1962), II-2; Samuel W. Davies, "A Brief Sketch of My Life and Work Written at the Bequest of My Wife and Children," Samuel W. Davies Biographical Material, University of Arkansas Special Collections, Fayetteville; E. C. Scott, comp., *Ministerial Directory of the Presbyterian Church, U.S., 1861–1941* (Austin, Tex.: Von Boeckmann-Jones, 1942), 63. Hampden-Sydney, which opened in Virginia in 1776, is the second-oldest college in the South and the oldest Presbyterian institution in the region.

8. In 1872 the Arkansas Presbytery covered roughly half the state, including Little Rock and everything north of the Arkansas River except for the sliver of eastern Arkansas lying east of the St. Francis River.

9. "Minutes of the Arkansas Presbytery, April 1872" (Little Rock, Ark.: Gazette Publishing, 1872), 7; Long, "Sketch," 3, 4 (quote); Isaac J. Long, "The Early Years of Arkansas College," *North Arkansas Pilot*, 29 August 1879. In addition to Long and Boggs the provisional board consisted of the following: Col. W. K. Patterson, W. W. Kerr, and W. J. Burt of Jacksonport; Dr. John F. Allen, M. A. Wycough, and W. L. McGuire of Batesville; and Elijah Mount of Powhatan. Long was elected president and W. W. Kerr treasurer.

10. This block that became the original campus is now the site of the First Presbyterian Church and its buildings.

11. A. C. McGinnis, "Arkansas College, 1872–1972," *Independence County Chronicle* 14 (October 1972), 17; Isaac J. Long, "Brief Sketch of the Early History of Arkansas College," handwritten essay in ledger entitled "Brief Records of Arkansas College located in Batesville, Arkansas, founded in A.D. 1872," A.C. History—General, LCA.

12. Long, "Brief Sketch."

13. Ibid.; Board Minutes, May 1871, October 1872, April 1873, November 1875, Minutes of the Board of Trustees, 1872–1907, Box 1, Board of Trustees Records, LCA.

14. Nancy S. Griffith, "Aaron Woodruff Lyon: Pioneer Educator, Citizen, and Christian Gentleman," *Independence County Chronicle* 35 (October 1993–January 1994), 52–67.

15. Goodspeed, *Biographical and Historical Memoirs of Northeast Arkansas* (Chicago: Goodspeed, 1889), 669.

16. Ibid., 632–33; John P. Morrow Jr., "The Dr. Allen House: The Building and Its Owners," *Independence County Chronicle* 5 (April 1964): 52–58; J. P. Coffin and E. R. Long, "Memorial of J. F. Allen," Minutes of the Board of Trustees, 1872–1907.

17. Goodspeed, *Biographical and Historical Memoirs of Northeast Arkansas*, 726 (quote), 727, 690; Harry Wesley Maxfield, "Samuel Butler Wycough," *Independence Pioneers*, Vol. II, ed. Nancy Britton (Batesville, Ark.: Independence Pioneers Committee, 1989), 106.

18. Due to occasional additions throughout the fall, by the end of December Arkansas College contained sixty students.

19. "Catalogue of Students Entering Presbyterial High School, Sept. 1872," I. J. Long's Speeches/Essays and Account Book, Box 2, Long Family Collection, LCA. It is difficult to determine the age range or educational attainment level of the three categories. For instance, Long's son Eugene was only nine years old in September 1872 but was listed as an "academic" student. Eugene's younger sister Irene, then seven, was in the primary department. The fact that it took four and a half years to produce the first graduates, though Arkansas College only had a three-year collegiate course, suggests that the school was in fact a "high school," at least for the first year.

20. *Weekly North Arkansas Times*, 20 September 1872.

21. "V. H. Henderson Account, 1872," I. J. Long's Speeches/Essays and Account Book.

22. Long, "Sketch," 5.
23. Long, "Brief Sketch"; Long, "Early Years."
24. *Batesville Republican,* 27 November 1872.
25. Paul B. Barringer, *University of Virginia: Its History, Influence, Equipment and Characteristics, with Biographical Sketches and Portraits of Founders, Benefactors, Officers and Alumni* (New York: Lewis, 1904), 443.
26. John S. Brubacher and Willis Rudy, *Higher Education in Transition: A History of American Colleges and Universities,* 4th edition (New Brunswick, N.J.: Transaction Publishers, 1997), 70; George M. Marsden, *The Soul of the American University: From Protestant Establishment to Established Nonbelief* (New York: Oxford University Press, 1994), 90. According to an 1877 newspaper article, board members included a Baptist, a Methodist, and a Lutheran. Historian David B. Potts has illuminated the role of local boosters, who were not members of a particular college's denomination, in the development of small, nineteenth century colleges. Potts, "American Colleges in the Nineteenth Century: From Localism to Denominationalism," *History of Education Quarterly* 11 (1971): 363–80.
27. Frederick Rudolph, *Curriculum: A History of the American Undergraduate Course of Study since 1636* (San Francisco: Jossey-Bass, 1977), 103; James Tunstead Burtchaell, *The Dying of the Light: The Disengagement of Colleges and Universities from Their Christian Churches* (Grand Rapids, Mich.: William B. Eerdmans, 1998), 124, 188; Long, "Early Years." By stating that Arkansas College was not formed in the "spirit of denominational fear," I am not implying that Long and the other founders were not concerned with the actual or perceived secularization of the higher education curriculum. Their concern, however, was more a reaction to the state of education in the country in general. Their attempts to limit the secularization of the curriculum—and specifically the decision to require biblical history—also represented a denomination-wide spirit that decried the secularization of education during this era. Ernest Trice Thompson, *Presbyterians in the South,* Vol. II (Richmond, Va.: John Knox Press, 1973), 362.
28. Joseph M. Stetar, "In Search of a Direction: Southern Higher Education after the Civil War," in *The History of Higher Education,* ASHE Readers Series, ed. Lester F. Goodchild and Harold S. Wechsler, 2nd edition (Needham Heights, Mass.: Simon & Schuster, 1997), 253, 254; Unidentified clipping from a Batesville newspaper, c. June 1890, Humphreys Scrapbook, A.C. History to 1890, LCA; Long, "Sketch," 13 (first quote), 14 (second quote).
29. Ibid., 13; AC *Catalogue,* 1883–1884, 2.
30. Long, "Sketch," 10; "Catalogue of Students Entering Presbyterian High School;" Brubacher and Rudy, *Higher Education in Transition,* 73.
31. Long, "Sketch," 11 (first quote), 10 (second quote).
32. Rudolph, *Curriculum,* 30; Marsden, *Soul of the American University,* 37; Richard Hofstadter and C. DeWitt Hardy, *The Development and Scope of Higher Education in the United States* (New York: Columbia University Press, 1952), 15; *North Arkansas Times,* 23 June 1882 (quote). See also Caroline Winterer, *The Culture of Classicism: Ancient Greece and Rome in American Intellectual Life, 1780–1910* (Baltimore, Md.: Johns Hopkins University Press, 2002), 2.
33. Board Minutes, November 1875.
34. *Centre College Catalog* (Danville, Kentucky), 1858, 10–12; AC *Catalogue,* 1883–1884, 2 (quote). At the first meeting of the provisional board of trustees in May 1872, Long and Elijah Mount of Powhatan were appointed to prepare the course of study. Mount never appeared again in college records, so one has to assume that his role in designing the curriculum was limited.
35. Long, "Sketch," 5.
36. Ibid., 6; Board Minutes, November 1875, May 1876. Though existing records do not indicate exactly what measures were taken to alleviate the debt, Long mentioned a second subscription and noted that "the first place on the roll of honor is justly due to J. F. Allen." Long, "Early Years."
37. Board Minutes, April 1877, December 1877, December 1878, June 1883; "List of Scholarships," Brief Records of Arkansas College (ledger); Michael B. Dougan, *Arkansas Odyssey: The Saga of Arkansas from Prehistoric Times to Present* (Little Rock, Ark.: Rose Publishing Co., 1994), 181.
38. Board Minutes, June 1885, June 1887, June 1889, June 1890.
39. Board Minutes, November 1875; Long, "Sketch," 7 (quote); "Endowment notes given to endow the Professorship of Ancient Languages and Moral Science in Arkansas College," Brief Records of Arkansas College (ledger). The method of collecting endowment income, and most other forms of college funding, in those days was somewhat different than modern methods. An individual

who subscribed $500 to a scholarship or endowment fund did not actually give the board or the college the $500. Instead, he paid a predetermined annual interest (usually 10 percent) each year on an agreed upon date, for instance, fifty dollars on 1 January. This method, by not demanding large outlays of money up front, proved to be the best device for securing pledges, but it also depended upon the financial and moral integrity of the subscriber. Needless to say, the college's annual contributions never equaled 10 percent of any subscription list.

40. Board Minutes, June 1884, November 1886, June 1887. Rev. R. W. Shive of Prairie Grove replaced Kennedy as financial agent in June 1888, but resigned the following year. By June 1889 the Welch Memorial Fund contained over $5,000; but this was deceiving. Almost half that amount had been generated by the sale of Little Rock lots deeded to the college by Welch. Of the remainder, John F. Allen, ever generous, had subscribed $1,600 and Isaac and Eugene Long combined for $700, leaving only $400 from other sources. Board Minutes, June 1889.

41. Board Minutes, June 1887, June 1888, April 1892. Perhaps the most interesting piece of real estate willed to the college by Welch was a ten-acre orange grove in southern California. After years of legal wrangling, the college finally sold the plot in the late 1890s.

42. Welch died in Ontario, Canada, while serving in a diplomatic position for the U.S. government. Suffering from declining health, he had taken the position in 1885, a post that may have been a reward for his assistance during the Poland committee's investigation of the Brooks-Baxter affair in Little Rock a decade earlier. Interestingly, he was seriously considering returning to Arkansas and assuming the presidency of Arkansas College at the time of his death. Hempstead, *Historical Review of Arkansas*, 421.

43. Goodspeed, *Biographical and Historical Memoirs of Northeast Arkansas*, 706; Fay Hempstead, *A Pictorial History of Arkansas* (St. Louis: N. D. Thompson, 1890), 874–75.

44. *AC Catalogue*, 1875, 1.

45. Goodspeed, *Biographical and Historical Memoirs of Northeast Arkansas*, 623; *Batesville Guard*, 18 March, 1913, 1; Eugene R. Long, "Arkansas College," in *Publications of the Arkansas Historical Association*, Vol. II, ed. John Hugh Reynolds (Fayetteville: Arkansas Historical Association, 1908), 100.

46. C. Fitzhugh Spragins, "Uriah Maxfield: Early Merchant," *Independence Pioneers*, Vol. I, ed. Nancy Britton (Batesville, Ark.: Independence Pioneers Committee, 1986), 63. Maxfield's wife, Sally, was the daughter of Dr. John F. Allen.

47. Goodspeed, *Biographical and Historical Memoirs of Northeast Arkansas*, 781–82; Mrs. Carter Jeffery, "Lt. Coffin and the Confederate Silver," *Independence Country Chronicle* 3 (July 1962), 35–36.

48. Jeffery, "Lt. Coffin," 38.

49. "A. R. Kennedy Memorial," Board Minutes, June 1890.

50. Barringer, *University of Virginia*, 444; *Batesville Guard*, 3 July 1879, 3; Hempstead, *Pictorial History*, 1223, 1224.

51. Board Minutes, November 1875, April 1880; *AC Catalogue*, 1875, 2.

52. Board Minutes, June 1881; Isaac Long, "Memorial Sketch of John E. McMillan," A.C. History to 1890.

53. Board Minutes, June 1884; Virginia Fitzhugh Jeffery and Lucy Jeffery Yeager, *A Rich and Lasting Blessing: A 150 Year History of the First Presbyterian Church of Batesville, Arkansas* (Newport, Ark.: Craig Printing, 1992), 95. Instruction in Hebrew continued into the mid-1890s using local Presbyterian ministers, including Rev. A. R. Kennedy and Rev. A. G. Jones. It appears that Hebrew instruction ceased after Jones left Batesville in 1895.

54. Board Minutes, June 1888; *AC Catalogue*, 1889–1890, 1. R. K. Green was not a full-time faculty member, of course, but was listed for French and algebra. Though existing records are not clear on this point, it is also possible that alumna Cynthia Scherer may have been the first woman to teach at the college level when she was appointed as an instructor during Stubbs's absence (as state representative) in the winter and spring of 1877. Board minutes do not explicitly state that she would be teaching collegiate subjects, but in the absence of Stubbs it seems likely.

55. *AC Catalogue*, 1891–1892, 4; Scott, *Ministerial Directory*, 83; "Prof. Ross K. Long," *Arkansas College Magazine*, October 1890, 29.

56. Hofstadter and Hardy, *Development and Scope of Higher Education in the United States*, 18.

57. *Arkansas Gazette*, 21 December 1876.

58. AC *Catalogue*, 1874, 2 (first quote); Long, "Sketch," 15 (second quote); italics included in original.

59. Handwritten copy of article by I. J. Long that appeared in the *Batesville Republican*, c. May 1873, in Eugene R. Long Scrapbook, LCA.

60. Brubacher and Rudy, *Higher Education in Transition*, 114.

61. Rudolph, *Curriculum*, 138; Board Minutes, December 1875; Stetar, "In Search of a Direction," 256; Brubacher and Rudy, *Higher Education in Transition*, 101; AC *Catalogue*, 1881–1882, 2–3. The B.S. degree, first awarded by Wesleyan College in Connecticut in 1838, had become popular in American colleges and universities by the late nineteenth century. Other degrees such as the Ph.B. (bachelor's of philosophy) and the B.Litt. (bachelor's of literature) were never used by Arkansas College.

62. Board Minutes, June 1885. From the information available in existing records it appears that certificates of proficiency were rarely awarded. Craig C. Williams of Hempstead County received the first in 1881; it was five years before another certificate was awarded. The last recorded certificate of proficiency was awarded to Harry G. Bunn of Little Rock, son of the president of the board, in 1894 due to his illness-induced absence from classes during the final month of school. One other point of interest concerns the first B.S. granted by Arkansas College. The board later changed Craig C. Williams's certificate of proficiency to a B.S., making him the oldest B.S. but not the first to be awarded the diploma during graduation ceremonies.

63. Board Minutes, June 1881, June 1883, June 1884, June 1890.

64. Board Minutes, December 1876, June 1881, June 1884, June 1889, June 1890, June 1891.

65. *Batesville Republican*, 25 June 1873, 3; Richard H. Johnson to Co. Peter Hanger, letter printed in *Arkansas Gazette*, 1 August 1875; Walter M. Adams, *The White River Railway: Being a History of the White River Division of the Missouri Pacific Railroad Company, 1901–1951* (Branson, Mo.: Ozarks Mountaineer, 1991), 7. Health conditions and care were also less than ideal in the nineteenth century, and the college community was not immune. Classes were frequently canceled on account of epidemics of some sort or another. A scarlet fever epidemic in the spring of 1879 became so severe that almost two-thirds of the student body withdrew from school, forcing Long to end the session two months early. Deaths among the student body, whether in Batesville or back home, were at least common enough for Isaac Long to maintain a "Mortuary List" in one of his ledgers. According to the list, cousins William and Jonathan Ingrum were the first active students to die when they drowned in the White River on 4 December 1873. Several of the students apparently died of malaria. Ledger entitled Brief Records of Arkansas College, A.C. History—General, LCA.

66. "Journal of Maud Dickson," photocopy and typewritten transcription of original, A.C. History to 1890, LCA.

67. Long, "Sketch," 12; Walter Scott McNutt, "First Graduate of Arkansas College," *Arkansas Gazette* (Sunday Magazine Section), 6 March 1938, 11; *Index*, April–May 1907, 3.

68. AC *Catalogue*, 1885–1886, 12.

69. Johnson to Hanger; Brubacher and Rudy, *Higher Education in Transition*, 123.

70. *North Arkansas Pilot*, 18 April 1879.

71. Walter Scott McNutt, "First Graduate of Arkansas College," *Arkansas Gazette* (Sunday Magazine Section), 6 March 1938, 11; Eugene Long, "Arkansas College," 11–12; Board Minutes, June 1885; Charles Coffin, Jay Boggs, and E. R. Long to Alumni, c. 1888, copy of form letter sent to members of Alumni Association in Eugene Long Scrapbook; C. F. Bizzell to John P. Morrow, 23 July 1958, Folder 7, John P. Morrow Papers, LCA.

72. *Batesville Republican*, 17 December 1873, 3.

73. Handwritten copy of clipping from unidentified Batesville newspaper in Eugene Long's Scrapbook, LCA.

74. Maud Dickson Journal; Rudolph, *Curriculum*, 98.

75. *Index*, April–May 1907, 9, 17; Eugene Long, "Arkansas College," 11; Brubacher and Rudy, *Higher Education in Transition*, 120.

76. *Index*, April–May 1907, 9; *Arkansas College Magazine*, March 1891, 25 and March 1890, 26; various Philomathean and L'Etoile program bulletins pasted in Eugene Long's scrapbook. Apparently, the Erosophic Society was not the first rival to the Philomatheans, but it was the first to survive for any length of time. The first issue of the *Arkansas College Magazine* in March 1890 mentions a rival organization called the Athaeneum Society (p. 18), but by March of 1891 it was no longer in

existence. For a more detailed look at the effects of the Lost Cause on late-nineteenth-century southern college and university campuses, see Dan R. Frost, *Thinking Confederates: Academia and the Idea of Progress in the New South* (Knoxville: University of Tennessee Press, 2000); and Paul M. Gaston, *The New South Creed: A Study in Southern Mythmaking* (New York: Knopf, 1970).

77. AC *Catalogue*, 1890–1891, 22, 23; *Arkansas College Magazine*, 22.

78. Unidentified clipping from Batesville newspaper, c. June 1885, Humphreys Scrapbook, A.C. History to 1890; AC *Catalogue*, 1888–1889, 1; 1890–1891, 23.

79. *Arkansas College Magazine*, March 1890, 21; November 1890, 24; July 1890, 27; December 1890, 23; *Index*, April–May 1907, 7. According to an article in the April–May 1907 issue of the *Index*, the YMCA was organized at Arkansas College during the 1893–1894 session, but notices of YMCA activities suggest that it was in existence at an earlier date.

80. *Arkansas College Magazine*, March 1890, April 1891.

81. AC *Catalogue*, 1890–1891, 24.

82. *Arkansas College Magazine*, October 1891, 184; November 1891, 213; November 1890, 27; *Index*, April–May 1907, 3.

Chapter 2: A Reluctant President in an Age of Change

1. *Arkansas College Magazine*, February 1897, 23–24.

2. AC *Catalogue*, 1885–1886, 5; Board Minutes, June 1884.

3. A. C. McGinnis, "Arkansas College, 1872–1972," *Independence County Chronicle* 14 (October 1972): 28. For a general look at financial straits in the state in the 1880s and early 1890s, see Carl H. Moneyon, *Arkansas and the New South, 1874–1929*, Histories of Arkansas Series (Fayetteville: University of Arkansas Press, 1997).

4. Eugene R. Long, "Arkansas College," in *Publications of the Arkansas Historical Association*, Vol. II, ed. John Hugh Reynolds (Fayetteville: Arkansas Historical Association, 1908), 103 (quote); Board Minutes, December 1891.

5. *Arkansas College Magazine*, April 1892, 51 (first quote); unidentified clipping from a Batesville newspaper, c. April 1892 (second quote), Eugene Long Scrapbook, LCA.

6. Long, "Arkansas College," 12–14; *Arkansas Gazette*, 22 April 1892; 23 April 1892.

7. Board Minutes, June 1892, June 1893; AC *Catalogue*, 1893–1894, 12; 1891–1892, 3.

8. Board Minutes, June 1892; "Resolutions of the Lawrence County Bar in Respect to the Memory of James H. Townsend," Townsend, James folder, A.C. History 1891–1900, LCA; E. C. Scott, comp., *Ministerial Directory of the Presbyterian Church, U.S., 1861–1941* (Austin, Tex.: Von Boeckmann-Jones, 1942), 329.

9. AC *Catalogue*, 1891–1892, 1, 3; 1892–1893, 11 (quote), 18.

10. Board Minutes, June 1892, October 1893 (quote), June 1894; unidentified clipping from a Batesville newspaper, c. May 1892, Eugene Long Scrapbook.

11. *Arkansas Gazette*, 21 January 1893, 3; 21 February 1893, 4; 25 February 1893, 2; "Petition to the General Assembly of the State of Arkansas," Batesville, Ark., 16 January 1893, SMC Box 66, No. 34, Arkansas History Commission, Little Rock. Batesville's Three Mile Act was just one of scores of similar legislative local prohibition bills passed at the behest of ministers, teachers, and others. The 1893 session of the legislature passed a law prohibiting the sale or advertising of liquor, as well as gambling and gaming, within five miles of Arkansas Cumberland College (University of the Ozarks) in Clarksville and another banning the "sale of intoxicants within certain territory in Baxter County within which is located the Mountain Home Baptist College." Ibid., 9 April 1893, 14.

12. Board Minutes, December 1893; *Davidson* (College) *Monthly*, June 1896, 329–31; Michael B. Dougan, "Henry Gaston Bunn," in *Dictionary of North Carolina Biography*, Vol. I, ed. William S. Powell (Chapel Hill: University of North Carolina Press, 1979), 270.

13. Board Minutes, October 1894, June 1895; E. R. Long to Presbyterian ministers, form letter, c. 1893, in Eugene Long Scrapbook.

14. Board Minutes, July 1895; Long's resignation letter to board of trustees, 22 February 1913, Board Minutes, February 1913.

15. Board Minutes, August 1895; Presbyterian Theological Seminary, *General Catalogue of the Presbyterian Theological Seminary* (Chicago, Ill.: Presbyterian Theological Seminary, 1939), 259.

16. Board Minutes, June 1896; *AC Catalogue*, 1893–1894, 5, 8; Scott, *Ministerial Directory*, 540, 393.

17. John I. Cleland, "Report of the President," Board Minutes, June 1896 (both quotes).

18. Ibid.; *AC Catalogue*, 1895–1896, 10, 12, 13 (quotes).

19. *AC Catalogue*, 1895–1896, 12, 15–17. Cleland's shift of curricular focus to Greek, and particularly secular Greek writings, reflects the wider American academic community's earlier shift from "words to worlds," according to Caroline Winterer. Beginning in the antebellum era, many classical scholars in the United States began to turn from a "love of Rome and a focus on classical grammar to a new focus on ancient Greece and the totality of its society, art, and literature." Had Cleland stayed longer at Arkansas College, Batesville's institution might have witnessed a much earlier transformation from the old college of mental discipline to the modern college of liberal culture. Caroline Winterer, *The Culture of Classicism: Ancient Greece and Rome in American Intellectual Life, 1780–1910* (Baltimore, Md.: Johns Hopkins University Press, 2002), 4.

20. Ibid., 19–20, 21, 25–26.

21. Board Minutes, June 1896.

22. Ibid.; *Arkansas College Magazine*, May 1896, 2 (quote); June 1896, 40, 46.

23. *AC Catalogue*, 1896–1897, 20; "Untitled Reminiscences of E. C. Blandford," c. 1947, in Historical Sketches file, A.C. History—General, LCA; "Untitled Reminiscences of William S. Lacy," undated, Historical Sketches file (quote).

24. *AC Catalogue*, 1896–1897, 4; *Batesville Bee*, 2 July 1896.

25. *Batesville Bee*, 2 July 1896.

26. Ledger labeled "Student Roll and Record, 1895–1897," A.C. History—1890–1900, LCA; *Arkansas College Magazine*, January 1897, 8; circular attached to back inside cover of February 1897 issue of *Arkansas College Magazine* (quote); James E. Lester Jr., *Hendrix College: A Centennial History* (Conway, Ark.: River Road Press, 1984), 43, 53; John Gladden Hall, *Henderson State College: The Methodist Years, 1890–1929* (Arkadelphia, Ark.: Henderson State College Alumni Association, 1974), 60; Patsy Gail Magouyrk, "Old Jamestown—Center of Learning," unidentified and undated newspaper clipping, Colleges and Universities—History Folder, Arkansas Vertical File, Independence County Library, Batesville, Arkansas.

27. Unidentified clipping from a Batesville newspaper, 7 February 1897, in Eugene Long Scrapbook.

28. *Arkansas Gazette*, 26 January 1897, 3. The argument over the Three Mile Act became a moot one in 1904 when a countywide election made Independence County a dry county. A. C. McGinnis, "Liquor Legislation and Independence County," *Independence County Chronicle* 18 (July 1977): 33.

29. Long, "Arkansas College," 107; Board Minutes, February 1897 (quote), April 1897; *Arkansas College Magazine*, February 1897, 27. It appears that Cleland had also left Presbyterian College on less than amicable terms. In his diary on 12 June 1894, William Plumer Jacobs, president of PC's board of trustees, recorded the following cryptic thought: "Goodbye, Cleland. You have been a sore thorn in my side but I forgive you. I thank God that I can say in all my dealings with you, I have acted like the Christian you ought to be—a Christian gentleman." Thornwell Jacobs, ed., *The Diary of William Plumer Jacobs* (Oglethorpe University, Ga.: Oglethorpe University Press, 1937), 311.

30. Board Minutes, April 1897.

31. Lester, *Hendrix College*, 64–70.

32. Board Minutes, June 1897.

33. *AC Catalogue*, 1896–1897, 12, 13, 14, 17. According to minutes of the board of trustees, the final master's degree awarded by Arkansas College was given to Rev. J. Franklin Lawson ('94) in 1900.

34. *AC Catalogue*, 1896–1897, 10.

35. Board Minutes, June 1899, June 1901, October 1901, September 1905. In this context the "Family," also known as the Dynasty, refers to the group of kinsmen and friends who dominated Democratic politics in antebellum Arkansas. Allen Johnson was the eldest son of newspaper editor and politician Richard H. Johnson, who ran unsuccessfully for governor in 1860. Arkansas College had other Family connections in the nineteenth century. Original board president Thomas R. Welch was related by marriage to two prominent Family friends, Chester Ashley and Edward Cross.

36. Board Minutes, June 1899, June 1902, June 1903, June 1908; Scott, *Ministerial Directory*, 386. According to board minutes, the presidency of Arkansas College was offered to Rev. Henry C. Evans

of Kirkwood, Missouri, in the fall of 1899, but his congregation refused to release him from his appointment.

37. Board Minutes, June 1908, June 1911; AC *Catalogue*, 1910–1911, 4; 1911–1912, 4; Scott, *Ministerial Directory*, 671, 768.

38. Board Minutes, June 1899, June 1900, June 1901, June 1903.

39. Board Minutes, June 1900, June 1901; *Arkansas CollegeCatalogue*, 1905–1906, 26.

40. Board Minutes, June 1904, June 1905, June 1906.

41. Board Minutes, July 1907, June 1908; *Index*, November 1908, 23 (quote); Board of Trustees, "Report to the Synod," October 1908, in Board Minutes; Board Minutes, June 1910.

42. Board Minutes, June 1908, November 1903, June 1910; *Arkansas CollegeCatalogue*, 1902–1903, 24, 25; 1909–1910, 36.

43. Board Minutes, June 1908; Board of Trustees, "Report to the Synod," October 1908. At its June 1908 meeting, the board also authorized the executive committee to undertake plans for the erection of a "Science Hall" just east of campus, but apparently this plan fell through.

44. *Index*, April–May 1907, 9, 11, 15, 17; "Untitled Reminiscences of E. C. Blandford," c. 1947 (quote), Historical Sketches, A.C. History—General, LCA. There appears to have existed a second literary society for young women in the first years of the new century. The Clionian Society, however, was already defunct by the time the *Index* appeared in 1906. The societies' colors included Philomathean, purple and white; Erosophic, crimson and gold; L'Etoile, red and white.

45. Handbill for "Open Session of Erosophic Society of Arkansas College, Dec. 6, 1897," in Eugene Long Scrapbook.

46. *Index*, October 1907, 1; *Arkansas CollegeCatalogue*, 1913–1914, 16; 1914–1915, 21; 1905–1906, 24; 1918–1919, 16.

47. *Index*, April–May 1907, 7; April–May–June 1915, 5; *Arkansas College Magazine*, September–October 1896, 6.

48. *Arkansas College Magazine*, June 1896, 47; *Index*, March 1909, 30; April 1909, 24 (quote).

49. Handbill for "Piano Recital," in Eugene Long Scrapbook; *Index*, November 1911, 24.

50. *Arkansas College Magazine*, May 1896, June 1896.

51. *Index*, December 1906, April–May 1907, 19.

52. "Untitled Reminiscences of E. C. Blandford." For a discussion of the rise of college athletics in the late nineteenth century, see Frederick Rudolph, *The American College and University: A History* (1962; Athens: University of Georgia Press, 1990).

53. *Arkansas College Magazine*, September–October 1896, 22; *Index*, March 1907, 33; October 1907, 34; AC *Catalogue*, 1906–1907, 28; 1914, 9.

54. AC *Catalogue*, 1906–1907, 28; 1914, 36.

55. *Arkansas College Magazine*, March 1890, 18; November 1892, 21; October 1892, 28 (first quote).

56. AC *Catalogue*, 1900–1901, 24.

57. *Index*, April–May 1907, 67 (quote), 68; March 1908, 16.

58. *Index*, May–June 1908, 40, 42, 43; May–June 1909, 57; March 1909, 34; May–June 1910, 49; May–June 1912, 40, 47 (quote); February 1913, 35; May–June 1913, 35, 36; April–May 1915, n.p. There is some confusion over the state championship of 1912. According to the May–June 1912 issue of the *Index*, Ouachita won two of three games in the state championship series with Arkansas College. But in February 1913 the *Index* mentions the arrival of the previous year's baseball championship trophy, which was placed on display in a Batesville merchant's window. And despite Arkansas College's accusation that other schools recruited "professional players," the Presbyterians, according to John P. Morrow Jr., were known to have used a few ringers of their own during their championship seasons. John P. Morrow Jr.–Betsy Shaw interview.

59. *Arkansas College Magazine*, January 1897, 22; February 1897, 23; *Arkansas Gazette*, 20 February 1938.

60. *Index*, January 1912, 27; November 1912, 31; December 1912, 17; March 1915, 20, 23 (quote); April–May 1915, n.p. (quote).

61. *Arkansas College Magazine*, January 1897, 21; *Index*, November 1908, 40; November 1912, 31; May–June 1912, 40.

62. *Arkansas College Magazine*, October 1891, 173; November 1891, 213; June 1896, 43 (quote).

63. *Index*, October 1911, 30; November 1911, 32; November 1912, 31; October 1913, 19, 22, 23; October 1914, 7; November 1914, 20, 21; December 1914, 13; McGinnis, "Arkansas College," 38. Christian Brothers College is in Memphis, and First District State Agricultural School was the forerunner of Arkansas State University. At the time First District was still basically a high school. The lineup for the Lambs during the season of 1914 included: center—Charles Ferrill of Batesville; right guard—Joel Rhodes of Wilmar; right tackle—Willie Menard of DeWitt; right end—Duane Swift of Batesville; left guard—Farris Purviance of Pottsville; left tackle—Fred Fitzhugh of Batesville; left ends—Hamilton Patton of Camden and Norwood Street of Lonoke; quarterback—Max Brown of Stamps; fullbacks—Floyd Stein of Batesville, Ray Johnston of Batesville, and J. Richard Brown of Stamps; right halfback—John Greenfield of Batesville; and left halfbacks—Ray Johnston and Hamilton Patton.

64. *Index*, December 1914, 21; April–May 1915, n.p.

65. *Arkansas College Magazine*, May 1896, 20; September–October 1896, 21; April–May 1897, 28; November 1897, 14; *Index*, November 1909, 23; March–April 1908, 18; March 1910, 21; May–June 1910, 49.

66. Board Minutes, June 1908.

67. Board Minutes, June 1904.

68. Board Minutes, June 1909; AC *Catalogue*, 1908–1909, 18. For a discussion of curricular changes at American colleges and universities during this era, see Frederick Rudolph, *Curriculum: A History of the American Undergraduate Course of Study since 1636* (San Francisco: Jossey-Bass, 1977).

69. *Arkansas College Magazine*, 1910–1911, 21–29.

70. Ibid., 21–30.

71. AC *Catalogue*, 1908–1909, 22; 1911–1912, 27.

72. Synod Board of Trustees to Constituency of the Synod of Arkansas, form letter in Eugene Long Scrapbook; *Arkansas College Monthly News Letter*, 2, 3.

73. Board Minutes, June 1911, special; AC *Catalogue*, 1910–1911, 18; 1911–1912, 4.

74. AC *Catalogue*, 1911–1912, 42 (first and second quotes), 43 (third quote), 44; 1915–1916, 20. Though it appears the board of trustees did not fully and officially adopt music and art as legitimate curricular studies until 1911, the 1910–1911 catalog indicates that there was some attempt to integrate music and art into the curriculum in 1910. Both Rutherford and Nesbitt appear on the faculty page for the 1910–1911 session, along with a voice teacher named Beulah Casey. AC *Catalogue*, 1911, 4.

75. Board Minutes, May–June, 1912; Eugene Long to Arkansas College Board of Trustees, 22 February 1913, letter of resignation in Board Minutes, March 1913.

76. Long to Arkansas College Board of Trustees; Eugene Long to Arthur G. Jones, 13 December 1912 (quote), Eugene R. Long Family Outgoing 1910–1919, Box 1 of 4, Family Correspondence, Arthur Gray Jones Papers, Stitt Archives, Austin Presbyterian Theological Seminary, Austin, Texas; Eugene Long to Arthur G. Jones, 2 January 1913, ibid.

77. Long to Arkansas College Board of Trustees.

78. Board Minutes, March 1913 (all quotes), May 1913; June 1913; Scott, *Ministerial Directory*, 263.

79. Scott, *Ministerial Directory*, 614.

80. AC *Catalogue*, 1912–1913, 4, 5–6; Board Minutes, June 1913.

81. AC *Catalogue*, 1912–1913, 4; 1913–1914, 8, 9. The college's report to the synod in October 1913 noted a teacher of expression named Adams, but no other record of her service is available.

82. *Batesville Guard*, 13 May 1913, 1; 9 May 1913, 1; 10 June 1913, 1; 25 April 1913, 1; Board Minutes, June 1913, informal meeting; Arkansas College Board of Trustees, "Report to Synod," October 1913, Board Minutes; AC *Catalogue*, 1913–1914, 11.

83. Board Minutes, June 1914; *Index*, October 1913, 17–18; March 1913, 28.

84. Board Minutes, June 1914, June 1915; AC *Catalogue*, 1914–1915, 9; AC *Catalogue*, 1914–1915, 12, 17, 18, 21, 25, 42, 54; 1915–1916, 25.

85. Board Minutes, June 1915.

86. Board Minutes, June 1915, special; *Batesville Guard*, 8 June 1915. Robertson may also have lost favor with the Batesville community by championing merger. Though there is no surviving proof that he was a proponent of merger, according to I. N. Barnett III, whose wife, Kitty, was a niece of J. P. Robertson, the president earned the enmity of local college supporters by advocating merging Arkansas College with Southwestern Presbyterian University in Clarksville, Tennessee.

87. Board Minutes, June 1915, special; February 1916.
88. Board Minutes, February 1916; June 1916.
89. Board Minutes, February 1916.

PART II: 1917–1937

1. A. C. McGinnis, "A History of Independence County, Arkansas," *Independence County Chronicle* 17 (April 1976): 104; John M. Barry, *Rising Tide: The Great Mississippi Flood of 1927 and How It Changed America* (New York: Simon & Schuster, 1997), 185–89. See also Pete Daniel, *Deep'n as It Come: The 1927 Mississippi River Flood* (1977; Fayetteville: University of Arkansas Press, 1996).

2. "Arkansas College: Its Future," pamphlet published by college (Batesville, 1927), 19.

CHAPTER 3: "Heroic and Pathetic in the Extreme"

1. A. C. McGinnis, "A History of Independence County, Ark.," *Independence County Chronicle* 17 (April 1976), 101; Board of Trustees Minutes, June 1916; *AC Catalogue*, May 1916, iii.

2. E. C. Scott, *Ministerial Directory of the Presbyterian Church, U.S., 1861–1941* (Austin, Tex.: Von Boeckmann-Jones, 1942), 386; Executive Committee of Christian Education and Ministerial Relief of the Presbyterian Church in the United States, *Our Presbyterian Educational Institutions* (Louisville, Ky., 1914), 145–46.

3. Board Minutes, December 1916; James P. Coffin to Henry Moore, 1 March 1917, "Letter to James P. Coffin, 1917" folder, A.C. History—1901–1920, LCA.

4. Board Minutes, December 1916; Coffin to Moore.

5. "Dour incivility" is the phrase historian S. J. Connolly uses to describe the personality that was a cultural inheritance of the lowland Scot. S. J. Connolly, "Ulster Presbyterians: Religion, Culture, and Politics, 1660–1850," in *Ulster and North America: Transatlantic Perspectives on the Scotch-Irish*, ed. H. Tyler Blethen and Curtis W. Wood Jr. (Tuscaloosa: University of Alabama Press, 1997), 31.

6. Scott, *Ministerial Directory*, 386; Synod of Arkansas, Presbyterian Church in the United States, *The History of Presbyterianism in Arkansas, 1828–1902* (Little Rock: Arkansas Democrat, 1902), 179–80; S. H. Chester, *Pioneer Days in Arkansas* (Richmond, Va: Presbyterian Committee of Publication, 1927), 22. William S. Lacy's older brother, George, was an 1892 graduate of Arkansas College and spent the majority of his adult life as a missionary in Mexico.

7. Board Minutes, February 1917, June 1916, June 1921, June 1922. In 1920 the board voted to reduce the responsibilities of Little Rock banker F. J. Schmutz, who had been serving as board treasurer despite not being a regularly elected member of that body, to overseer of the endowment fund. Thus, in 1921 Boggs became both college and board treasurer.

8. Board Minutes, February 1917; *Batesville Guard*, 15 June 1917.

9. Board Minutes, May–June 1917, June 1917 (Little Rock); Eugene R. Long to Arthur G. Jones, 27 December 1916, "Eugene R. Long Family Outgoing 1910–1919," Family Correspondence, Box 1, Arthur Gray Jones Papers, Stitt Library Special Collections, Austin Presbyterian Theological Seminary, Austin, Texas. E. D. Brown remained on the faculty for the 1917–1918 session as professor of mental and physical sciences before returning to the ministry in southern Arkansas.

10. Board Minutes, March 1918, June 1919. The four children of W. C. Brown Sr. were Allan, Jean, Josephine, and W. C. Jr., a member of the class of 1915. During his lifetime W. C. Brown Sr. of Stamps had been a financial donor to Arkansas College, and after his death Brown's widow, Adana, established the W. C. Brown Scholarship in 1916. Mrs. Brown funded the scholarship with an endowment of $1,800 and reserved the right to name the beneficiary each year. Board Minutes, June 1916.

11. Board Minutes, March 1918, March 1918 (Little Rock), June 1919; *Arkansas Gazette*, 13 December 1917. At the time of the fire in December the *Arkansas Gazette* reported a $4,500 insurance policy on the dormitory, but statistics available in the minutes of the board of trustees suggest that the policy actually produced only $2,500.

12. Carl H. Moneyhon, *Arkansas and the New South, 1874–1929*, Histories of Arkansas Series (Fayetteville: University of Arkansas Press, 1997), 96; Treasurer's Report, Board Minutes, May 1918.

13. David O. Levine, *The American College and the Culture of Aspiration, 1915–1940* (Ithaca, N.Y.: Cornell University Press, 1986), 27–28; Board Minutes, September 1918, June 1919; *Arkansas Gazette*, 18 September 1918.

14. Levine, *The American College and the Culture of Aspiration*, 28; *Index*, January 1919, 27–28; Board Minutes, June 1919; *AC Catalogue*, May 1919, 53–54. The four SATC men who earned degrees at Arkansas College were Raymond Johnson of Cave City, Horace Jones of Strawberry, Will A. Sensabaugh of Pfeiffer, and Carl Teter of Batesville.

15. Board Minutes, June 1919, October 1919; *AC Catalogue*, May 1920, 9–10; *Index*, April 1920, 2. The girls' dorm was named Welch Hall at the request of chairman James P. Coffin, one of the few college associates who could still remember Rev. Thomas Welch. The naming of the building was a conscious attempt to make amends for the liquidation of Welch's trust/endowment to the college years earlier.

16. Board Minutes, May–June 1921 (quote); June 1922; *AC Catalogue*, May 1923, 57–61; James E. Lester Jr., *Hendrix College: A Centennial History* (Conway, Ark.: Hendrix College Centennial Committee, 1984), 102; John Gladden Hall, *Henderson State College: The Methodist Years, 1890–1929* (Arkadelphia, Ark.: Henderson State College Alumni Association, 1974), 141; Robert A. Leflar, *The First 100 Years: Centennial History of the University of Arkansas* (Fayetteville: University of Arkansas Foundation, Inc., 1972), 391; Michele Roussel Wasson, "Gem of the Ozarks: A History of Mountain Home College, 1890–1934," M. A. thesis, University of Arkansas, 1982, 43.

17. Board Minutes, June 1920. More than half the $101,687.89 collected by the end of May 1920 came from the previously mentioned gifts of the Brown family and Henry Moore.

18. Board Minutes, May–June 1921, June 1922.

19. *Panther*, October 1921, 1; *AC Catalogue*, May 1922, 11–12.

20. *AC Catalogue*, May 1923, 12. Irene Ferrill became Arkansas College's first full-time librarian when the gymnasium was converted into a library in 1921. Up until that time one or more faculty members had pulled double-duty as librarian, with assistance from upper-division students.

21. *AC Catalogue*, May 1921, 49–50; May 1930, 62–63; Faculty Assembly Minutes, 3 September 1924.

22. *AC Catalogue*, May 1921, 23–25.

23. Ibid., May 1922, 22; May 1923, 23; Frederick Rudolph, *Curriculum: A History of the American Undergraduate Course of Study Since 1636* (San Francisco: Jossey-Bass, 1977), 236.

24. *AC Catalogue*, May 1920, 5; May 1923, 5. By 1922–1923 the college catalog listed Lacy and seventeen faculty members; but only seven of these were full-time, academic professors.

25. *AC Catalogue*, May 1920, 5; May 1921, 5; *Batesville Guard*, 2 June 1921, 1; Scott, *Ministerial Directory*, 719; *Mary Baldwin Magazine*, May 1990, 59. Sommerville served as president of Lewisburg Seminary in Lewisburg, West Virginia, from 1911 to 1916 and of Texas Presbyterian College in Milford from 1916 to 1918.

26. *AC Catalogue*, May 1921, 5; May 1924, 6.

27. Treasurer's Report, May 1917, Board Minutes, June 1917; Board Minutes, June 1920, June 1922.

28. Board Minutes, June 1923.

29. Board Minutes, February 1929; *Panther*, 24 April 1923, 1.

30. Board Minutes, June 1923 (first quote); June 1923, special, (second quote).

31. Eugene Long to A. G. Jones, 2 August 1923, "Eugene R. Long Family Outgoing—1920–1925 and undated," Family Correspondence, Box 1, Arthur Gray Jones Papers.

32. W. S. Lacy to Board of Trustees of Arkansas College, 26 June 1923, Board Minutes, June 1923 (special); *Panther*, June 1922, 3.

33. Board Minutes, June 26, 1923 (special).

34. Phil Coop, "Dr. Tucker Has Served Education Over 60 Years," *Shelbyville Times-Gazette* (Tenn.), 11 July 1968, 1, 10; assorted biographical information in E. B. Tucker file, A.C. People, LCA.

35. *Panther*, 18 September 1923, 1.

36. William Clyde DeVane, *Higher Education in Twentieth-Century America* (Cambridge, Mass.: Harvard University Press, 1965), 16; Levine, *The American College*, 119.

37. *Index*, January 1919, 20.

38. Ibid., 23, 29, 28. There is no accurate count on the number of Arkansas College alumni and former students who served in the military during World War I. The *Batesville Guard* reported on 8 June 1918 that eighty-five former students were in the service. The January 1919 issue of the *Index* stated that almost all male graduates since 1905 had served in war service, either as civilians or as military personnel.

39. *Panther*, 30 May 1924, 3; 2 May 1925, 1; 9 February 1926, 1.

40. Catherine Robertson to James Robertson, 20 February 1923, "Correspondence," A.C. History—1921–1930, LCA.

41. *Panther*, 30 October 1923, 1; 18 January 1926, 1; 11 October 1922, 1; 2 November 1927, 1; quote from Eugene Long to A. G. Jones, 12 January 1925, "Eugene R. Long Family Outgoing—1920–1925 and undated," Arthur Gray Jones Papers.

42. *Index*, December 1919, 1; February 1920, 6; *Panther*, June 1922, 1; 31 May 1923, 1; 8 March 1924, 1; Faculty Assembly Minutes, 15 December 1923; Long to Jones, 12 January 1925.

43. *Panther*, 4 May 1926, 1; 13 April 1927, 1; 11 April 1928, 1; *Index*, 1928, 85. McMurry College (now University) is in Abilene, Texas, and St. Edward's University is in Austin, Texas.

44. *Panther*, 29 September 1928, 1; 24 November 1931, 5; 15 March 1932, 1; President's Report, Board Minutes, February 1929; *Rostrum* (official publication of Kappa Gamma), Winter 1933–1934, 11, 15; *Index*, 1935, 63.

45. *Index*, February 1920, 2; *Panther*, November 1920, 5; April 1921, 2; October 1921, 3 (quote); *Index* (yearbook), 1920, 56, 57, 58; 1921, 69, 70, 71, 72; 1922, 56, 57.

46. *Panther*, 4 October 1927, 3; *Index*, 1928, 92, 94, 95, 96, 107; 1927, 73, 75, 76, 77, 96; Shuford Nichols and Hugh Mann (Delta Kappa Sigma) to Arkansas College Board of Trustees, n.d., included in Board Minutes, March 1928; President's Report, Board Minutes, June 1928.

47. President's Report, Board Minutes, June 1928.

48. "Arkansas College: Its Future," pamphlet published by the college in 1927 as part of the Arkansas College Expansion Program, A.C. History—1921–1930, LCA; AC *Catalogue*, May 1928, 89.

49. President's Report, Board Minutes, February 1929; *Panther*, 19 February 1929, 1. A case of mistaken identity may have accounted for the failure of Delta Kappa Sigma to obtain a national fraternity charter. John P. Morrow Jr., a member of Alpha Lambda Tau, recalled an incident in which members of his fraternity "disturbed" a professor who lived in the men's dormitory late one night. According to Morrow, believing that the disturbance was the work of Delta Kappa Sigma, the college administration blocked the fraternity's efforts to join a national body. John P. Morrow Jr.–Betsy Shaw interview.

50. *Panther*, 23 May 1928, 1; Faculty Assembly Minutes, 1 October 1928; 4 October 1928. According to the board of trustees' minutes for June 1925, the Erosophic Society had requested permission to erect a lodge on the new campus, but nothing ever came of this request.

51. President's Report, Board Minutes, February 1929; *Panther*, 7 May 1929, 1; 4 November 1930, 2; 26 November 1929, 1. One result of the demise of Greek organizations was the brief reestablishment of the Erosophic and Philomathean societies during the 1936–1937 session. Principally accomplished as a result of efforts by President Lacy, the reincarnated Philo and Soph were coeducational but apparently disappeared once again after Lacy's departure.

52. *Panther*, 26 September 1922, 2; 24 November 1925, 1; 20 April 1926, 1; 2 November 1927, 1; 11 October 1922, 2; AC *Catalogue*, May 1929, 87. Founded in 1889, the Epworth League is/was the youth organization affiliated with the old Methodist Episcopal Church, South.

53. Faculty Assembly Minutes, 10 May 1923 (quote). It could be argued that a leading reason for the rise in disciplinary cases in the 1920s was the absence of non-college social outlets in the Batesville community. One of the few off-campus social activities, according to John P. Morrow Sr. (a student at the college from 1924 to 1928), was the Monday night picture show. In that era the college held classes Tuesday through Saturday (it being considered improper to study on Sunday), which left Monday as date night. Students attending the picture show would gather at the dormitories and then proceed en masse, two-by-two flanked in front and back by college chaperones, to the theater downtown. The theater's owner took advantage of his captive audience's one night of pleasure by charging fifty cents admission on Monday nights, compared with only twenty-five cents every other night. John P. Morrow–Betsy Shaw interview.

54. "Faculty Report," Board Minutes, February 1926.

55. Faculty Assembly Minutes, 23 September 1926; 2 February 1928; 7 March 1929; 27 September 1928; *Panther*, 12 November 1929, 1.

56. *Index*, January 1919, November 1919; *Panther*, 12 February 1924.

57. *Panther*, November 1920; 12 September 1922; 25 March 1930, 2; Faculty Assembly Minutes, 11 December 1930.

58. Faculty Assembly Minutes, 10 January 1924; 17 January 1924; *Panther*, 12 February 1924, 1; "Constitution of Honor Committee," in Faculty Assembly Minutes. Members of the first Arkansas College Honor Council included seniors Catherine Robertson and William Rutherford, juniors Lois Hodge and William Sensabaugh, sophomores Harriet Elcan and Paul Edgar, and freshmen Annie Rush and Alfred Kelly. The names of the two preparatory representatives have not survived.

59. *Panther*, 9 March 1926, 2; President's Report, Board Minutes, March 1928, March 1930; Faculty Assembly Minutes, 31 January 1930.

60. *Panther*, 30 November 1927, 1; 13 December 1927, 1; 18 January 1928, 1; Faculty Assembly Minutes, 15 December 1927. The other officers were secretary Augusta Prather, a Batesville senior, and treasurer Ethel Robertson, a junior from Helena. Members of the Senate included seniors Mary Gray and George Gibson, juniors Kenneth Snipes and Harvey Booth, sophomores Shuford Nichols and Lyman Reeder, and freshman Madeline Youmans.

61. *Panther*, 7 March 1928, 1; 6 March 1929, 1; Faculty Assembly Minutes, 19 April 1928; 27 February 1928; 18 February 1929; 7 March 1929.

62. *Panther*, 7 March 1928, 1; 1 October 1929, 1; Faculty Assembly Minutes, 29 September 1932.

63. *Index*, January 1919, 28; June 1919, 7.

64. *Index*, April 1920, 1; *Panther*, November 1920, 3; Board Minutes, June 1924; AC *Bulletin*, May 1924, 7.

65. *Panther*, 20 March 1924, 1; 4 October 1924, 1; 29 November 1924, 1; *Index*, 1925, 86, 87.

66. *Panther*, 9 March 1926, 2; 23 March 1926, 1; AC *Bulletin*, May 1929, 76–80.

67. AC *Bulletin*, May 1918, 53; *Index*, 1928, 16; Michael L. Counts, "History of Harlequin Theatre," in *The 75th Anniversary of Harlequin Theatre at Lyon College* (Batesville, Ark.: Lyon College, 2000), 4.

68. Counts, "Harlequin Theatre," 4–5; *Panther*, 23 April 1924, 1; 7 March 1925, 1; *Index*, 1925, 54.

69. *Panther*, 24 November 1925, 1; 8 December 1925, 1; 7 March 1928, 1; 11 April 1928, 1; Counts, "Harlequin Theatre," 5–6.

70. *Panther*, 10 April 1929, 1; 25 March 1930, 1; 19 April 1932, 1; "First Annual State High School Theatre Tournament," brochure c. 1928, "Miscellaneous File," A.C. History—1921–1930; Counts, "Harlequin Theatre," 6.

71. *Arkansas Gazette*, 24 October 1915, 26 (quote); 2 November 1916; 1 December 1916, 11; *Batesville Guard*, 29 November 1916; 1 November 1916; A. C. McGinnis, "Arkansas College, 1872–1972," *Independence County Chronicle* 14 (October 1972), 42; James E. Lester Jr., *Hendrix College: A Centennial History* (Conway, Ark.: Hendrix College Centennial Committee, 1984), 109.

72. *Index*, 1920, 64–65; 1921, 79–83; 1922, 65–67; "Faculty Athletic Regulations," in Faculty Assembly Minutes.

73. Board Minutes, June 1922; *Panther*, 12 September 1922, 1; 26 September 1922, 1; *Index*, 1923, 13.

74. *Index*, 1923, 68; Board Minutes, June 1923 (special).

75. *Index*, 1927, 102–7; *Panther*, 28 November 1923, 1; 5 October 1926, 1 (quote).

76. "Panther Pep," pamphlet contained in Virginia Shanks—Memories of her life at A.C., 1923–1927, LCA; 21 September 1926, 1 (first quote); 5 October 1926, 1 (second quote). Other Panthers who made all-state teams under Morrison's tutelage included Louis O'Brien, Ewin Grisham, Herndon McCain, Clint Gray, and Earl Stokes.

77. *Panther*, 13 April 1927, 1.

78. Records and list of all-state players compiled partially from the *Index*, 1928–1931. Also *Panther*, 8 December 1931, 1. Other all-state performers under Patterson included Carroll "Bull" Durham, Lonnie Etheridge, Kelly Thompson, and George Heard.

79. *Batesville Record*, 22 October 1931, 1; *Panther*, 29 September 1931, 1; 13 October 1931, 1, 3; 27 October 1931, 1.

80. Board Minutes, June 1932, May 1934; *Index*, 1934, 50; 1935, 51.

81. John P. Morrow Jr.–Melissa Jobe interview, 21 November 1977; Board Minutes, May 1936.

82. *Index*, June 1919, 7; April 1920, 1; *Panther*, April 1921, 1; May 1921, 1.

83. *Panther*, 31 May 1923, 2; 7 May 1924, 1.

84. *Index*, 1931, 73 (first and second quotes), 75 (third quote).

85. *Index*, March 1920, 1; 1926, 65.

86. Board Minutes, October 1927; February 1929; *Panther*, 18 December 1928, 1; AC *Catalogue*, May 1929, 15; *Index*, 1930, 68–69; 1935, 56.

87. *Panther*, June 1922, 1; 31 May 1923, 6; 23 April 1924, 3; 30 May 1924, 1; 18 April 1925, 1; 25 May 1926, 4; 6 May 1930, 1; *Index*, 1931, 72.

88. *Panther*, March 1921, 4; 31 May 1923, 5; 14 April 1931, 1; 5 May 1931, 3; 7 May 1929, 5; *Index*, 1930, 71; 1931, 76.

89. *Panther*, 4 October 1927, 1; 23 October 1928, 1; 20 November 1928, 1.

90. *Panther*, November 1920, 6; May 1921, 7; 31 January 1923, 1; 30 November 1927, 7; 13 December 1927, 3; *Index*, 1928, 66.

91. *Panther*, 23 May 1925, 3; *Index*, 1925, 73.

92. *Panther*, 11 October 1922, 1; *Index*, 1923, 72; 1926, 68, 69.

93. Board of Trustees, May 1936; Faculty Minutes, 21 May 1936.

94. Information gathered from AC *Catalogs*, 1924–1931.

95. *Panther*, 12 October 1925, 3; 20 November 1928, 1. Bramlett held a master's degree from the University of Chicago and a Ph.D. from the University of North Carolina.

96. Interview with Bess Wolf, 7 November 2000. Although a "disciplinarian of the first school" who was reported to have once threatened a student by hanging him out a second-floor window, Long seems to have preferred airing his dissatisfactions with various student activities in public forums, especially at morning chapel (John P. Morrow Jr.–Betsy Shaw interview). The editorial staff of the *Panther* resented Long's practice of presenting his negative critiques at chapel instead of presenting them to the staff in private. Virginia Rose Johnson ('32) also recalled the morning that she was horrified to hear Long single out the yell leaders, of which she was one, for special derision due to the off-color language of one of their football-game yells. Interview with Johnson, 15 November 2000.

97. AC *Catalogue*, May 1925, 6; Board Minutes, March 1925, April 1929 (special). Little Dan Frierson died 31 October 1933 at the age of sixty-three.

98. AC *Catalogue*, May 1925, 6; interview with Franklin Williams.

99. AC *Catalogue*, May 1924, 6; Wolf interview. Catherine Barker published *Yesterday Today: Life in the Ozarks* in 1941. John Quincy Wolf Jr. is best remembered today for his folk song recordings, his "discovery" of noted 1950s and 1960s folk performers such as Jimmy Driftwood and Almeda Riddle, and for editing his father's reminiscences into *Life in the Leatherwoods*. See John Quincy Wolf, *Life in the Leatherwoods*, ed. Gene Hyde and Brooks Blevins (Fayetteville: University of Arkansas Press, 2000).

100. Laman A. Gray, M.D., to Paul McCain, 27 March 1957, Folder 4, John P. Morrow Papers, LCA.

101. AC *Catalog*, May 1927, 35–36; May 1928, 39–40.

102. Board Minutes, March 1930. Following is a list of the number of students in each major field in the spring of 1930: English—78; history—45; chemistry—19; mathematics—14; Spanish—9; psychology—6; education—5; philosophy—3; French—3; Latin—3; biology—2; German—1; Greek—0.

103. AC *Catalogue*, May 1924, 23; Board Minutes, June 1924.

104. Board Minutes, June 1928, June 1925, June 1926; AC *Catalog*, May 1927, 78–79; May 1929, 87.

105. Hugh Hawkins, *Banding Together: The Rise of National Associations in American Higher Education, 1887–1950* (Baltimore, Md.: Johns Hopkins University Press, 1992), 78.

106. Board Minutes, March 1924, June 1924, June 1925; AC *Catalog*, May 1929.

107. Board Minutes, March 1924, March 1925. By 1926–1927 the NCA had increased its minimum endowment requirement to $500,000.

CHAPTER 4: "Muddling through Somehow"

1. AC *Catalog*, May 1928, 57.

2. Board Minutes, June 1922 (special), December 1922, April 1923, June 1923.

3. Eugene R. Long to Arthur G. Jones, 2 August 1923, "Eugene R. Long Family Outgoing—1920–1925 and undated," Family Correspondence, Box 1, Arthur Gray Jones Papers, Stitt Memorial Library Special Collections, Austin Presbyterian Theological Seminary, Austin, Texas; Board Minutes, March 1924.

4. Board Minutes, March 1924, June 1924.

5. Board Minutes, June 1924. Historian Frederick Rudolph has called the GEB and the Carnegie Foundation the two most important vehicles for standardization in higher education. The Carnegie Foundation, because of its refusal to grant money to denominational colleges, remained off limits to Arkansas College and similar schools that refused to sever religious ties. Frederick Rudolph, *Curriculum: A History of the American Undergraduate Course of Study since 1636* (San Francisco: Jossey-Bass, 1977), 223, 226.

6. Board Minutes, March 1924, June 1924. The $40,000 that McRae loaned Arkansas College was actually money from a trust fund that had been established by his late son-in-law, Prescott businessman Horace E. Bemis, for his eight children.

7. Board Minutes, March 1925 (first quote), June 1925 (second quote); James Tunstead Burtchaell, *The Dying of the Light: The Disengagement of Colleges and Universities from Their Christian Churches* (Grand Rapids, Mich.: William B. Eerdman's, 1998), 192; James E. Lester Jr., *Hendrix College: A Centennial History* (Conway, Ark.: Hendrix College Centennial Committee, 1984), 91; James E. Roper, "Southwestern at Memphis, 1848–1981," *Tennessee Historical Quarterly* 41 (Fall 1982), 210.

8. Board Minutes, June 1925; Carl H. Moneyhon, *Arkansas and the New South, 1874–1929*, Histories of Arkansas Series (Fayetteville: University of Arkansas Press, 1997), 134–35.

9. Board Minutes, June 1925.

10. Board Minutes, March 1926.

11. Ibid.

12. Board Minutes, June 1926, November 1926.

13. Timothy P. Donovan, Willard B. Gatewood Jr., and Jeannie M. Whayne, eds., *The Governors of Arkansas: Essays in Political Biography*, 2nd ed. (Fayetteville: University of Arkansas Press, 1995), 157, 164.

14. Board Minutes, November 1926.

15. Executive Committee Minutes, 31 December 1926; 9 March 1927; Board Minutes, March 1927.

16. Board Minutes, March 1927.

17. "Arkansas College: Its Future," pamphlet published by Arkansas College, 1927, 2, 19 (quote).

18. Executive Committee Minutes, 28 July 1927; 12 August 1927; 23 September 1927; 18 November 1927; Board Minutes, March 1928. In June 1928 Tucker reported that about $100,000 had been pledged, but that was deceiving. Most of those who pledged money also agreed to honor their pledges only after the program had been completed.

19. Board Minutes, March 1928, June 1928.

20. Tucker to Board of Trustees, 13 February 1929, Board Minutes, March 1929 (quote); Executive Committee Minutes, 11 February 1929; 26 February 1929; 16 March 1929.

21. Tucker to Board of Trustees, 13 February 1929.

22. Ibid.

23. Board Minutes, 23 April 1929.

24. Board Minutes, 23 April 1929; June 1929.

25. Executive Committee Minutes, 27 April 1929; 22 June 1929; 7 September 1929; 24 September 1929; Board Minutes, June 1929; 26 November 1929.

26. Board Minutes, 26 November 1929.

27. Board Minutes, March 1930; E. B. Tucker to Vann Howell, 11 February 1930, letter included in Board Minutes, March 1930.

28. Board Minutes, March 1930 (quote), June 1930, October 1930.

29. Board Minutes, June 1929; June 1930; 16 October 1930; American Historical Society, *Arkansas and Its People: A History, 1541–1930*, Vol. III (New York: American Historical Society, 1930), 282.

30. Board Minutes, 8 October 1930; Executive Committee Minutes, 11 December 1930.

31. Board Minutes, 30 December 1930; Executive Committee Minutes, 31 January 1931.

32. I. N. "Nels" Barnett III interview with Barbara Lindsey-Allen, 6 November 1986.

33. *Batesville Guard*, 11 April 1988, 5; 19 October 1949.

34. Barbara Lindsey Allen, "The Death and Resurrection of Arkansas College," *Independence County Chronicle* 29 (October 1987–January 1988): 17, 19.

35. Ibid., 19; *Minutes of the Synod of Arkansas*, 13–15 October 1931, 1–4.

36. *Minutes of the Synod of Arkansas*, 13–15 October 1931, 5.

37. *Batesville Guard-Record*, 5 February 1931, 1.

38. Executive Committee Minutes, 7 March 1931; 7 April 1931; Board Minutes, 17 March 1931; 31 March 1931; June 1931.

39. Wayne Banks, *History of Yell County, Arkansas* (Van Buren, Ark.: Press-Argus, 1959), 263; Donovan et al., *Governors of Arkansas*, 191.

40. *Batesville Guard*, 21 July 1931, 1.

41. *Minutes of the Synod of Arkansas*, 13–15 October 1931, 16.

42. *Arkansas Democrat*, 27 January 1932; *Arkansas Gazette*, 27 January 1932, 1. Though minutes of the board of trustees suggest that Allan Brown eventually agreed to divert enough of his funds to cover the $6,000 interest payment, by the fall of 1932 there was discussion of past-due interest on the bonds.

43. Board Minutes, 19 April 1932; 5 May 1932.

44. E. C. Scott, *Ministerial Directory of the Presbyterian Church, U.S., 1861–1941* (Austin, Tex.: Von Boeckmann-Jones, 1942), 386.

45. Board Minutes, 16 August 1932; 30 May 1933; untitled contract, August 1932, Miscellaneous Papers, Folder 9, A.C. History—Death and Resurrection of Arkansas College. Surviving documents suggest that Nels Barnett and John P. Morrow Sr. each contracted to pay $5,000 of this $20,000. William S. Lacy pledged $2,000, while Batesville citizens J. F. Grammar, S. M. Bone, J. Rich, and Charles. W. Maxfield each promised $1,000. These seven are the only persons listed on the contract housed in the archives.

46. *Batesville Guard*, 26 August 1932; 28 August 1932; 5 September 1932.

47. Executive Committee Minutes, 15 September 1932; 27 October 1932; 18 November 1932; Citizens Committee to Friends of Arkansas College, 7 November 1932, Miscellaneous File, A.C. History—1931–1940, LCA; AC *Catalog*, May 1933, 76.

48. Faculty Minutes, 22 September 1932; 6 October 1932; 29 December 1932; 19 January 1933; Bess Wolf, interview with author, 7 November 2000. Bess Wolf also recalled that the old college car would only run twenty miles at a time. A local mechanic taught Wolf and the other drivers what to do each time the car died.

49. Board Minutes, 28 May 1934. I. N. "Nels" Barnett III recalled that in the darkest days of the depression, the college began accepting payment in kind from many local merchants and business leaders who had pledged money through the Citizens' Committee's campaign. For instance, a local gas station provided gas and oil for the college's automobile. A theater gave movie tickets to the college, which were in turn sold to students. Other payments in kind consisted of produce, general merchandise, and laundry services. I. N. Barnett III interview with Barbara Lindsey-Allen, 6 November 1986.

50. Executive Committee Minutes, 25 January 1934; October 1934; 17 April 1935.

51. *Arkansas Gazette*, 5 November 1935, 2.

52. *Arkansas Democrat*, 4 November 1935; *Arkansas Gazette*, 5 November 1935, 2; Board Minutes, 26 December 1935; 25 May 1936; *Arkansas College Bulletin*, May 1935, 1–4, photocopy in Miscellaneous Papers, Folder 9, A.C. History—Death and Resurrection of Arkansas College, LCA. The synod also voted to replace the old Educational Commission with a Debt Committee, also chaired by W. H. Williams.

53. Faculty Minutes, 13 September 1933 (first quote); 2 February 1933; 14 February 1933;

23 March 1933; 4 April 1933; 13 April 1933; 27 April 1933; 25 May 1933; 28 September 1933; 11 January 1934; 25 March 1937 (third quote); *Panther*, 26 March 1936, 2 (second quote).

54. Faculty Minutes, 9 January 1933; 16 April 1934 (quote); 17 May 1934.

55. Bramlett was Arkansas College's first Ph.D., having earned the degree at the University of North Carolina; Gregorie, the college's first woman Ph.D., earned her degree from the University of South Carolina.

56. Roper, "Southwestern," 212; AC *Catalog*, May 1937, 5–6.

57. Faculty Minutes, 16 March 1933; Board Minutes, 28 May 1934; 25 May 1936; 2 April 1937; AC *Catalog*, May 1937, 5–6.

58. Board Minutes, 23 June 1936; 31 July 1936; Williams interview, 21 November 2000.

59. Statistics gathered from annual catalogs, 1933–1937; David O. Levine, *The American College and the Culture of Aspiration, 1915–1940* (Ithaca, N.Y.: Cornell University Press, 1986), 196–98; Board Minutes, 25 May 1936; 31 May 1937. The NYA, which would eventually spend more than $10 million on about 620,000 students, initially limited a college's participation to a maximum of 12 percent of its 1934–1935 enrollment, a percentage that was finally reduced to four. By the late 1930s about one in eight American college students received some form of NYA assistance.

60. Levine, *The American College and the Culture of Aspiration*, 191, 195 (quote).

61. Faculty Minutes, 6 April 1933.

62. *Panther*, 19 May 1936, 1 (quote); Board Minutes, 25 May 1936.

63. Board Minutes, 25 May 1936; *Batesville Guard*, 27 February 1937.

64. Board Minutes, 2 April 1937; 31 May 1937.

65. William S. Lacy to John P. Morrow, 19 August 1937, resignation letter attached to Board Minutes, 24 September 1937.

66. *Minutes of the Synod of Arkansas*, 25–27 October 1938, 2–7; John P. Morrow Jr.–Melissa Jobe interview. Interestingly, the only member of the synod who asked that his opposition to the plan be recorded was W. S. Lacy. This was perhaps due to a byproduct of the plan—a reduction of the college's annual income of about $3,000.

Chapter 5:
Little Haverford or Maryville of the West: The College Seeks a Purpose

1. *Highlander*, 24 October 1947, 1.

2. J. C. Jordan to John Crockett, 26 January 1938, Box 13, John D. Spragins Papers (JDSP).

3. Scott, *Ministerial Directory*, 157; biographical information gathered from numerous unidentified and undated newspaper clippings, Kalen and Morrow Papers, private collection of Lynn Morrow, Jefferson City, Missouri.

4. Newspaper clippings, Kalen and Morrow Papers.

5. *Batesville News Review*, 3 December 1937, 1; Board Minutes, 9 March 1939; *Batesville Record*, 23 September 1937, 1.

6. *Batesville Guard*, 25 November 1938, 3; 11 February 1939, 1; *Index*, 1938, n.p.; *Index*, 1939, n.p.

7. *Index*, 1937, 49–51.

8. Garner interview.

9. *Index*, 1938, n.p.

10. Ibid.; *Batesville Guard*, 3 March 1938, 1.

11. *Index*, 1938, n.p.; *Batesville Guard*, 3 March 1938, 1.

12. "Agreement," Synod of Arkansas File, A.C. History—1931–1940, LCA; Alexander Henry to Friends, 26 February 1945, Folder 5, John P. Morrow Papers, Ibid.

13. *Batesville Guard*, 30 August 1938, 1; John Crockett to J. J. Yarbrough, 22 September 1938, "Government, NYA Independence Hall to July 1, 1942," Presidential Papers 1940s–early 1950s, LCA.

14. Faculty Minutes, 13 October 1938.

15. Faculty Minutes, 6 October 1938. Actually, the college had established a remedial spelling class the previous spring, but the classes in diction and sentence recognition were first introduced in the fall of 1938.

16. *Index*, 1939, n.p.

17. Board Minutes, 30 May 1938; 29 May 1939; W. H. Williams to John P. Morrow Sr., 22 September 1938, "Miscellaneous," A.C. History—1931–1940.

18. John Crockett to Board of Trustees, 26 June 1939, in Board Minutes, 7 July 1939.

19. John D. Spragins to John Crockett, 11 July 1939, Box 13, JDSP.

20. T. M. Lowry Jr. to Nancy S. Griffith, c. May 1993, Tom Lowry file, A.C. People, LCA.

21. T. M. Lowry Jr. to Rev. David Shepperson, c. 1940, Box 13, JDSP.

22. Ibid.; John D. Spragins to John T. Barr, 2 April 1940, Box 13, JDSP.

23. T. M. Lowry Jr. to John D. Spragins, 13 March 1940; Lowry to Spragins, 23 February 1940, Box 13, JDSP.

24. Spragins to Barr, 2 April 1940; Board Minutes, 4 April 1940. The summer of 1940 also brought another financial victory when a group of Presbyterians donated $4,500 to help pay $11,500 in unpaid faculty salaries from the past few years. The other $7,000 was covered by the college when the administration and trustees convinced faculty members to accept past-due student notes in lieu of cash.

25. President's Report, in Board Minutes, 27 May 1940; Faculty Minutes, 16 January 1941.

26. John D. Spragins to J. Herndon McCain, 14 April 1941, Box 13, JDSP; T. M. Lowry Jr. to Board of Trustees, 27 May 1940, in Board Minutes, 27 May 1940.

27. Stuart R. Oglesby to John D. Spragins, 12 August 1940; Spragins to Ogelsby, 7 August 1940; Spragins to J. Herndon McCain, 29 August 1940; Spragins to Lowry, 4 December 1940, Box 13, JDSP.

28. Spragins to McCain, 29 August 1940; Lowry to Spragins, 2 December 1940; Lowry to Spragins, 23 February 1940, Box 13, JDSP.

29. President's Report, Board Minutes, 1 October 1940; McCain to Spragins, 21 November 1940, Box 13, JDSP.

30. Executive Committee Minutes, 23 April 1941; "Student Financial Aid, 1940–41," Folder 32, Box 2, Presidential Papers 1940s–early 1950s, LCA.

31. Faculty Minutes, 30 April 1940; 22 May 1941; 8 September 1941; Board Minutes, 27 May 1940; 2 June 1941; 25 May 1942.

32. *Arkansas College Summer* (tabloid), 8.

33. Board Minutes, 25 May 1942; 26 March 1942; Executive Committee Minutes, 26 November 1941; *Batesville Guard*, 19 December 1941, 1.

34. "Survey Report—Arkansas College," 10 April 1942, typescript, Folder 32, Box 2, Presidential Papers, LCA.

35. Ibid.; Board Minutes, 25 May 1942.

36. Ibid.

37. Ibid.

38. Ibid. The "sword of Damocles," which is how Lowry described the debt committee in a letter to the *Batesville Guard* on 12 March 1942, refers to a story in Roman mythology in which a man enjoying a feast looks up to find dangling above his head a sharp sword held only by a single horse hair.

39. I. N. Barnett to John D. Spragins, 20 March 1942; L. A. Taylor to Spragins, 25 March 1942; Spragins to John P. Morrow Sr., 8 May 1942, Box 13, JDSP; Board Minutes, 26 March 1942; 25 May 1942.

40. Spragins interview.

41. Scott, *Ministerial Directory*, 677.

42. Spragins interview.

43. Will MacLafferty to John D. Spragins, 22 June 1942; John P. Morrow to Spragins, 24 June 1942; Spragins to Elizabeth Rutledge, 23 June 1942, Box 13, JDSP.

44. President's Report, Board Minutes, 31 May 1943; John D. Spragins to John Richardson, 24 October 1942, Box 13, JDSP; *Minutes of the Synod of Arkansas of the Presbyterian Church in the United States*, 20–22 October 1942, 21–22.

45. Spragins to Richardson.

46. President's Report, Board Minutes, 31 May 1943; Board Minutes, 5 January 1943.

47. "Budget Balancer Movement," Folder 30, Box 2, Presidential Papers, LCA; *Arkansas Broadcaster*, February 1943, 1.

48. *Index*, 1944, n.p.; 1945, n.p.; *Highlander*, 1 March 1944.

49. *Index*, 1945, n.p.

50. AC *Catalog*, May 1944, 11; Board Minutes, 22 May 1944.

51. AC *Catalog*, May 1944, 9–10, 21.

52. John D. Spragins to J. Leighton Scott, 13 September 1951, Box 18, JDSP. Maryville College is a small college in eastern Tennessee that was at the time affiliated with the Northern Presbyterian Church, or PCUSA. By the middle of the twentieth-century Maryville had developed a well-known work program for needy Appalachian mountain students.

53. John D. Spragins to John P. Morrow Sr., 8 May 1942, Box 13, JDSP; Scott, *Ministerial Directory*, 38; Spragins interview.

54. "Arkansas College: A Distinctive Institution," undated brochure, Box 3, JDSP.

55. AC *Catalog*, May 1928, 81–85; February 1948, 84–91; Executive Committee Minutes, 30 April 1943.

56. John D. Spragins to Ministers of the Synod, 6 April 1951, Box 3, JDSP; untitled and undated press release, Folder 30, Box 2, Presidential Papers, LCA; *Index*, 1948, n.p.

57. AC *Catalog*, May 1944, 21; Scott, *Ministerial Directory*, 54; President's Report, Board Minutes, 31 May 1943; 22 May 1944; "Self-Help Division," undated press release, Folder 30, Box 2, Presidential Papers.

58. AC *Catalog*, May 1944, 18–20; President's Report, Board Minutes, 31 May 1943; "Self-Help Division," undated press release.

59. AC *Catalog*, May 1944, 24; *Batesville Guard*, 21 October 1943, 1.

60. Faculty Minutes, 20 January 1944; Board Minutes, 9 March 1944; *Highlander*, 1 March 1944; W. John Bleckley to Arkansas College Faculty and Staff, n.d., Box 26, JDSP; *Batesville Guard*, 3 December 1946, 1.

61. Rudolph, *Curriculum*, 282; DeVane, *Higher Education*, 124, 129; Keith W. Olson, *The G.I. Bill, the Veterans, and the Colleges* (Lexington: University Press of Kentucky, 1974), 23–24; unidentified and undated newspaper clipping, Folder 29, Box 2, Presidential Papers.

62. Olson, *G.I. Bill*, 33; *Highlander*, 19 January 1945, 1; 4 February 1946; Ruby Barr to Alumni, 12 October 1945, Box 3, JDSP; AC *Catalog*, June 1946, 97; April 1947, 97; February 1948, 96.

63. Executive Committee Minutes, 29 November 1946; Board Minutes, 24 February 1949; 14 October 1948.

64. Howard Welborn to Thomas M. Lowry, 25 December 1941, Letters to President Thomas M. Lowry, A.C. History—1941–1950; Elsie Garner to "Ma" Butler, 13 November 1942, Letters to Ma Butler, A.C. History—1941–1950; Ruby Barr to Alumni, 12 October 1945, Box 3, JDSP; undated and unidentified newspaper clipping, Transfer of Masonic Home Property, A.C. History—1941–1950.

65. *Highlander*, October 1946, 1; 6 March 1948, 1.

66. AC *Catalog*, May 1946, 19.

67. Board Minutes, 26 May 1947; *Batesville Guard*, 12 March 1947, 1.

68. AC *Catalog*, April 1947, 7–10.

69. Ibid., February 1952, 8–10; February 1948, 7–9; Board Minutes, 11 March 1948.

70. President's Report, Board Minutes, 31 May 1943; 22 May 1944; Executive Committee Minutes, 16 August 1946; Faculty Minutes, 2 March 1943; 20 March 1947.

71. Board Minutes, 26 May 1947; Faculty Minutes, 20 March 1946; 6 January 1949. In 1947 Arkansas College awarded its first B.S. degrees in almost forty years to Charles Edmondson of Locust Grove and Evelyn May of Washington and the first B.S.E. degrees to William Conway Lawrence of Charlotte and Paul Sutherland of Mountain View. Despite the fact that it remained on the books for many years, only two B.M. degrees were ever awarded by Arkansas College: Christene Brewer of Batesville in 1951 and H. Gerald Ballard of England in 1952.

72. AC *Catalog*, February 1949, 6; Executive Committee Minutes, 22 August 1949.

73. AC *Catalog*, February 1949, 6–7.

74. Counts, "History of the Harlequin Theatre," 3–4; *Index*, 1952, 62–63; *Highlander*, 6 May 1948, 2, 3.

75. Faculty Minutes, 9–11 September 1948; 8–10 September 1949; 24 March 1948; Randall M. Crider, "G.I. Joe Goes to School: The World War II Veterans of Arkansas College," unpublished senior thesis, Lyon College, May 1994, 13; *Highlander*, 19 December 1947, 1.

76. *Highlander*, 20 November 1947, 2; 29 March 1949, 4; *Index*, 1949; 1952.

77. *Index*, 1948, n.p.

78. *Highlander,* 26 May 1950, 4; *Index,* 1949, n.p.; 1952, 102–3. Arkansas College's best all-purpose athlete of the late Spragins era may have been Bernis Duke of Hardy. A basketball and football letterman, Duke was also a three-time state amateur boxing champion in the early 1950s.

79. Board Minutes, 12 October 1944; *Highlander,* 16 March 1946, 1; 19 December 1947, 1, 4; *Index,* 1947, n.p.; 1949, n.p.

80. Executive Committee Minutes, 15 November 1946; Board Minutes, 14 January 1947.

81. Unidentified and undated newspaper clippings, Dorothy Brown's Scrapbook, LCA; *Index,* 1948, n.p.; 1949, n.p.

82. Dorothy Brown's Scrapbook.

83. Ibid.

84. *Batesville Guard,* 11 June 1945, 1; Alexander Henry to Dear Friends, 26 February 1945; Lamar Williamson to John P. Morrow Sr., 14 June 1945, Miscellaneous 1941–1950, A.C. History—1941–1950, LCA.

85. Board Minutes, 6 August 1946; 9 October 1946; Executive Committee Minutes, 1 October 1946; 11 November 1946.

86. Board Minutes, 6 August 1946; 9 October 1946; 27 February 1947; 26 May 1947; 14 October 1948; 30 May 1949; 22 February 1951; 28 May 1951.

87. Faculty Minutes, 28 January 1948.

88. Faculty Minutes, 4 February 1948; 3 March 1948; 10 March 1948; 31 March 1948; 7 April 1948; 28 April 1948; 22 March 1949; *AC Catalog,* February 1949, 14; Board Minutes, 30 May 1949.

89. Board Minutes, 11 March 1948; Executive Committee Minutes, 18 August 1948; "Proceedings of the Grand Lodge F & A Masons of Arkansas, 16–17 November 1948," Transfer of Masonic Home Property, A.C. History—1941–1950.

90. Mary B. Hetzel to Ralph Graham, 9 April 1987, Miscellaneous, A.C. History—1961–Present, LCA; Board Minutes, 29 May 1950.

91. President's Report, Board Minutes, 21 September 1950; *Highlander,* 19 January 1951, 1; *AC Catalog,* February 1952, 97.

92. Board Minutes, 21 September 1950; 22 February 1951; 5 April 1951; 20 September 1951. Although Blandford's tenure at Arkansas College covered an incredible span of fifty-five years, he was on the faculty only forty-four of those, from 1896 to 1913 and again from 1924 to 1951.

93. Board Minutes, 21 September 1950; 28 November 1950; 22 February 1951; 5 April 1951.

94. Board Minutes, 26 April 1946; John D. Spragins to Kenneth S. Keyes, 4 April 1950, Box 3, JDSP.

95. Board Minutes, 5 April 1951; 28 May 1951; "Minutes of the Synod of Arkansas," 25–26 September 1951, 4; untitled press release, 8 May 1951, Merger With College of the Ozarks, A.C. History 1951–1960, LCA.

96. *Arkansas Gazette,* 22 July 1951, 1A; *Batesville News Review,* 19 July 1951, 1; *Batesville Guard,* 20 July 1951, 1.

97. John Quincy Wolf Jr. to Nels Barnett, 15 July 1951, Merger With College of the Ozarks; Charley Robinson to John D. Spragins, 2 November 1951, Box 17, JDSP.

98. *Batesville Guard,* 1 June 1951, 1; 6 July 1951, 1; 13 July 1951, 1; 19 July 1951, 1; Nels Barnett to W. C. Brown, 14 July 1951, Merger With College of the Ozarks.

99. *Arkansas Gazette,* 22 July 1951, 1A.

100. Nels Barnett to H. W. McMillan and Frank Lyon, 18 September 1951, Merger With College of the Ozarks; John D. Spragins to Roy L. Davis, 10 August 1951; Davis to Spragins, 8 August 1951; Davis to Vernon S. Broyles Jr., 11 August 1951, Box 19, JDSP.

101. "Minutes of the Synod of Arkansas," 25–26 September 1951, 12; *Batesville Guard,* 18 October 1951, 1. Five years earlier a George Peabody College survey had also suggested merging the two institutions; the Peabody survey suggested relocating the consolidated college to Clarksville, however. Division of Survey and Field Services, *Arkansas College and the College of the Ozarks: A Survey Report* (Nashville, Tenn.: George Peabody College for Teachers, 1946).

102. Barnett to McMillan and Lyon; *Batesville Guard,* 27 September 1951, 1; Board Minutes, 20 September 1951.

103. *Batesville Guard,* 18 October 1951, 1; Board Minutes, 1 November 1951; John D. Spragins to J. Herndon McCain, n.d., Box 3, JDSP.

104. Charley Robinson to John D. Spragins, 2 November 1951, Box 17, JDSP; John D. Spragins to J. B. "Betts" Spragins, 4 January 1952; John D. Spragins to Kenneth Snipes, 5 March 1952, Box 3, JDSP.

105. John D. Spragins to Members of the Board of Trustees, n.d., Box 13, JDSP; Board Minutes, 18 March 1952.

Chapter 6: Bricks and Mortar: Paul McCain Builds a Campus

1. *Arkansas College Bulletin*, April 1954, 1.

2. Untitled and unpublished memoirs of Paul McCain, 1989, LCA, 47; Board Minutes, 3 September 1952. Though unfamiliar with the institution, McCain did have two tenuous Arkansas College connections. J. Herndon McCain, a cousin, was an alumnus and former trustee, and another relative, Dorothy Sydenstricker, was the college librarian. Social studies and Bible professor Ellis G. Mosley served as acting president from 1 July 1952 until McCain's arrival in early September.

3. McCain memoirs, 1–2, 21, 23, 26, 28, 35, 40, 42, 44, 45. At Duke, Paul McCain studied under legendary southern historian Charles S. Sydnor. McCain wrote his master's thesis on the military career of Confederate general William H. T. Walker and completed a dissertation on the county court system in colonial North Carolina, a work that was published by Duke University Press shortly after his arrival at Arkansas College.

4. Board Minutes, 26 May 1952; 3 September 1952; 23 September 1952; 26 February 1953; 25 May 1953.

5. Board Minutes, 15 January 1953; 26 February 1953; 25 May 1953; 23 July 1953; 13 January 1954.

6. Board Minutes, 15 January 1953; 25 May 1953; 26 February 1953. Four veteran members were removed from the faculty due to the sixty-five rule during McCain's first two years. In the spring of 1953, seventy-nine-year-old education professor Frank Harrin voluntarily relinquished his position. The following spring McCain recommended and received the retirements of Dean Harry King and language professor Stanley Rockwood. Math professor Samuel W. Williams, seventy-five years old in 1953, was retained, however. English professor Amos Herold, who was sixty-seven in 1953, protested his forced retirement and sued McCain and the college, unsuccessfully.

7. Dressel, "Survey of the General Education and of the Student Personnel Program at Arkansas College," no date, Folder 8, Box 2, Presidential Papers, LCA.

8. Faculty Minutes, 25 November 1952; 15 November 1954; Executive Committee Minutes, 23 April 1954; Board Minutes, 24 February 1955; 30 May 1955. The four-division format inaugurated at Arkansas College in the fall of 1955 was identified by Roman numerals instead of by titles. Division I consisted of mathematics and sciences, Division II of social studies, religion, and philosophy, Division III of literature, languages, speech, and music, and Division IV consisted of business, education, and library science. When McAdam left unexpectedly after the 1956–1957 session, Harry King came out of retirement to serve as dean the following year, although he taught no classes. King re-retired in the spring of 1958 when Arkansas College hired Roland Dickison as dean.

9. AC *Catalog*, March 1953, 6–7; March 1958, 6–8; Board Minutes, 26 February 1953; 25 February 1954; 23–24 February 1959; 29 May 1961.

10. Executive Committee Minutes, 15 December 1954; Board Minutes, 30 May 1955; John S. Brubacher and Willis Rudy, *Higher Education in Transition: A History of American Colleges and Universities*, 4th edition (New Brunswick, N.J.: Transaction Publishers, 1997), 394–95. In addition to Brown, Orville Jones (psychology and education), Glen Haddock (mathematics), and W. David Moon (mathematics) all completed doctorates in the early 1960s while teaching at Arkansas College. All three left within two years of completing their terminal degrees.

11. AC *Catalog*, April 1955, 10–11; McCain memoirs, 54, 55. The renovation of the new library building was made possible by a gift from Corinne McCombs Hardy of Little Rock. In 1955 the college sold the original campus and its buildings to the Presbyterian Church of Batesville for $30,000.

12. No author, "A Report on the Arkansas Experiment in Teacher Education," September 1960, Folder 9, Box 2, Presidential Papers, LCA.

13. David O. Levine, *The American College and the Culture of Aspiration, 1915–1940* (Ithaca, N.Y.: Cornell Univesity Press, 1986), 106; William Clyde DeVane, *Higher Education in Twentieth-Century America* (Cambridge, Mass.: Harvard University Press), 69–70; Frederick Rudolph, *Curriculum: A History of the American Undergraduate Course of Study since 1636* (San Francisco: Jossey-Bass, 1977), 258; Brubacher and Rudy, *Higher Education in Transition*, 295, 298, 302.

14. "Report on General Education Curricular Changes," Folder 7, Box 2, Presidential Papers, LCA; Board Minutes, 15 January 1953; 13 January 1954; 23–24 February 1958. The general education curriculum adopted by the faculty in 1953 included twelve hours in English and literature, twelve in social studies, twelve in math and sciences, six in a foreign language, three hours of speech, six each in Bible and psychology-philosophy, and four hours of physical training. Under this system the freshman and sophomore years were basically prescribed for all students. In 1954 Arkansas College replaced one of the required science courses with a health class and added the Introduction to Fine Arts class; Fine Arts, originally a noncredit requirement but later valued at one hour per year, was conducted during the Tuesday and Thursday chapel periods and was often referred to as the Humanities course.

15. Board Minutes, 24 February 1955; Faculty Minutes, 22 October 1952; 12 January 1954; 1 March 1954; *Arkansas College Bulletin*, May 1955, 1; "Progress Report on the Arkansas College Self-Study," Folder 8, Box 2, Presidential Papers, LCA; Donald M. Mackenzie to Paul McCain, 26 November 1955, Folder 2, Box 2, Presidential Papers, LCA.

16. In the mid-1950s the Synod of Arkansas dramatically increased the amount of benevolence funds directed to the college; by the 1955–1956 academic year the synod's contributions had increased from less than $40,000 to more than $60,000 annually. The middle and late 1950s marked the high point in relative synod giving, however, for by the latter years of the McCain administration the college was still receiving about $65,000 a year from the synod in spite of the fact that the budget was several times larger than those of the 1950s. Board Minutes, 25 September 1956.

17. Board Minutes, 7 May 1954; "Articles of Incorporation of Arkansas Foundation of Associated Colleges," 11 March 1954, Arkansas Foundation of Associated Colleges Folder, Box 1, Presidential Papers, LCA. The other members of AFAC were College of the Ozarks, Harding, Hendrix, John Brown University, Ouachita Baptist College, and Southern (now Williams) Baptist College in Walnut Ridge, then a two-year school.

18. Board Minutes, 25 September 1956; Faculty Minutes, 8 October 1956; *Arkansas College Bulletin*, November 1957, 1; Robert B. Downs, *Cooperative Library Program: Report of Survey* (1963), pp. 2, 6, 31, Folder 13, Box 3, Presidential Papers, LCA; McCain memoirs, 60–61. To avoid repetition in the cooperative library agreement, each of the seven colleges used its Rockefeller funds to purchase books in specific areas or fields. Arkansas College's fields of concentration included British and American philosophy, United States history and government, biology, sociology, and church history.

19. Board Minutes, 7 May 1954; 28 September 1954; 30 May 1955; 28 February 1956; 5 March 1957; 24 September 1957; 2 April 1957; 26 February 1963; Executive Committee Minutes, 16 June 1955; 7 July 1957; 10 June 1957; *Arkansas College Bulletin*, September 1955, 1; December 1955, 1; April 1957, 1; June 1958, 1; McCain memoirs, 57. According to McCain's memoirs, the anonymous donor experienced financial difficulties and was never able to pay the full amount pledged. Furthermore, campaign expenses ultimately exceeded $100,000, rendering the ADVANCE Arkansas College Campaign much less valuable than it appeared on the surface.

20. Board Minutes, 28 May 1956; Donald M. Mackenzie to Paul McCain, 22 September 1956, Folder 8, Box 2, Presidential Papers, LCA.

21. Board Minutes, 27 May 1957; Executive Committee Minutes, 8 August 1957.

22. Board Minutes, 5 March 1957; 27 May 1957; 30 August 1957; James H. Pilkinton to W. W. Campbell, 7 January 1957, Folder 13, Box 2, Presidential Papers, LCA; Mackenzie, et al., *Higher Education and the Synod of Arkansas*, 4. The Council of Christian Higher Education was established at a special synod meeting in April 1956. It was formed in response to a $5,000 gift from the Board of Christian Education of the PCUS to be used for a study of Arkansas College.

23. *Arkansas College Bulletin*, November 1957, 1, 6; Board Minutes, 24 September 1957; 25 February 1958; 26 May 1958; 23 September 1958; 29 September 1959.

24. Board Minutes, 30 August 1957; Faculty Minutes, 5 February 1958; *Arkansas College Bulletin*, November 1958, 1; April 1959, 1; June 1959, 1.

25. The College of the Ozarks in Clarksville lost its accreditation in the early 1960s but later regained it.

26. Board Minutes, 28 September 1954; 25 February 1958; 23–24 February 1959; *Arkansas College Bulletin*, June 1955, 1; November 1958, 1; February 1959, 1; Faculty Minutes, 17 November 1958.

27. *AC Catalog*, March 1961, 63; Board Minutes, 28 May 1956; *Arkansas College Bulletin*, April 1965, 1.

28. *Arkansas College Bulletin*, November 1954, 1; *AC Catalog*, April 1960, 72–73; Diane Tebbetts, *The West Years: 1972–1988* (Batesville: Arkansas College, 1990), 28–29.

29. *AC Catalog*, April 1960, 72–73; Paul McCain to H. M. Brinkley, 9 January 1957, Advance Campaign-1957 Folder, Box 1, Presidential Papers, LCA.

30. Tebbetts, *The West Years*, 5–6; Board Minutes, 26 September 1961.

31. Tebbetts, *The West Years*, 16–17; Lyon interview.

32. *Arkansas College Bulletin*, February 1960, 1. The first campus project undertaken after the college received news of its accreditation in April 1959 was actually the construction of Bryan Lake, a three-acre lake in the southeastern part of the campus named for late trustee R. C. Bryan. The 1958–1959 academic year witnessed the first significant effort to landscape parts of the new campus, a requirement due to the recent construction of the chapel; the college also paved the new drive and parking lot in front of the chapel and poured several new sidewalks.

33. McCain memoirs, 67; *Arkansas College Bulletin*, April 1962, 1; Board Minutes, 28 May 1962; 16 July 1963; 24 September 1963; 25 February 1964; Executive Committee Minutes, 21 July 1964. Arkansas College received about $93,000 from the United for Christ Campaign; in addition to the federal loan, in the summer of 1964 the college received a gift of $25,000 (or $22,000 according to the memoirs of Paul McCain) from Hazel Alphin, widow of prominent El Dorado oilman Hendrick Alphin.

34. McCain memoirs, 66–67; *Arkansas College Bulletin*, September 1962, 1; Board Minutes, 26 September 1961.

35. Board Minutes, 27 September 1960; 24 September 1963; 22 September 1964.

36. Board Minutes, 28 May 1962; Mitchum interview.

37. Board Minutes, 25 May 1963; 5 October 1965; *Arkansas Presbyterian*, June 1965, 1; Executive Committee Minutes, 21 April 1964; 19 August 1964.

38. Board Minutes, 5 October 1965; 27 September 1966. In May 1965 the board adopted names for all four of the quadrangle buildings as well as for the sandstone dormitory, the chapel, the gymnasium, and the central Masonic building. The entire quadrangle as well as the small headquarters building for the quad was named in memory of John P. Morrow Sr., who had died only three months earlier. Trustee Gordon Love had died on the same day as Morrow and was likewise memorialized by one of the dormitories. The other two residence halls were named in memory of longtime Latin and German professor Eugene Blandford and former trustee and benefactor R. C. Bryan. The central Masonic building, housing the library and chapel, was named the Long Memorial Building in memory of Isaac and Eugene Long, and Williams Gymnasium was named in honor of elderly Sam Williams, who had retired as professor of mathematics and Greek two years earlier. As a result of the substantial gifts of Jean and W. C. Brown Jr., Brown Chapel memorialized their father, W. C. Sr., as well as their siblings Allan and Josephine.

39. Executive Committee Minutes, 26 June 1965; 2 August 1965; Board Minutes, 5 October 1965; 27 September 1966; 26 September 1967. The recreation building cost the college about $30,000, and the facing featured the same Eureka Brick & Tile Company (of Clarksville, Arkansas) bricks that had been used on the dining hall and quadrangle buildings. The bricks used for the chapel came from the Hope Brick Company.

40. *Arkansas College Bulletin*, March 1966, 1; September 1966, 10; March 1968, 4; Executive Committee Minutes, 31 March 1966.

41. *Arkansas College Bulletin*, June 1967, 2; March 1968, 4; January 1969, 6; Board Minutes, 26 September 1967; 27 February 1968; 24 September 1968; 25 February 1969; Program for "Dedication of the Science Building and Library," 3 December 1968, Folder 28, Box 3, Presidential Papers, LCA. Although the science building was the first Arkansas College building constructed with air conditioning as part of its original design, the administration building, or east Masonic building, was the first on campus to receive air conditioning in the summer of 1964. The original interior of the library was partly designed and furnished by Arkansas College alumna Allie Beth Dent Martin

('34), a consultant with Library Design Associates of Tulsa, Oklahoma, and, at the time, director of the Tulsa City-County Library. The language laboratory on the bottom floor of the library was provided by a gift of Mary Fuller Holmes of Hot Springs and was named in memory of her husband, E. Fletcher Holmes.

42. *Arkansas College Bulletin*, March 1968, 4; January 1969, 3; McCain memoirs, 70.

43. McCain memoirs, 70.

44. Board Minutes, 26 February 1963; 23 September 1958; 23–24 February 1959; 27 September 1960.

45. Faculty Minutes, 14 February 1958; Board Minutes, 25 February 1964; 22 September 1964; Gordon Love to Paul McCain, 14 September 1956, Folder 1, Box 2, Presidential Papers, LCA; McCain to Love, 20 July 1962, Folder 1, Box 2, Ibid.

46. Mackenzie, et al., *Higher Education and the Synod of Arkansas*, 16, 73.

47. William A. Johns to "Dear Friend," no date, Folder 16, Box 3, Presidential Papers, LCA.

48. Paul McCain to Kenneth Snipes, 27 January 1959, Folder 23, Box 1, Presidential Papers, LCA; Board Minutes, 26 May 1952; 24 February 1955; 23 September 1958; "A Report on the Arkansas Experiment in Teacher Education," September 1960, Folder 9, Box 2, Presidential Papers, LCA.

49. Mackenzie, et al., *Higher Education and the Synod of Arkansas*, 37–38; Board Minutes, 23–24 February 1959.

50. *Batesville Guard*, 20 May 1953, 1; *Arkansas College Bulletin*, December 1953, 1.

51. Board Minutes, 23–24 February 1959; 29 September 1959; 27 September 1960.

52. Board Minutes, 23–24 February 1959. Among Arkansas's independent colleges, Harding had the highest tuition rate in 1958–1959 at $449 per year; despite its lower tuition costs, John Brown University was the most expensive overall, with total charges of $965. By comparison with Arkansas College, Agnes Scott College featured a total of $1,675 in student fees, and a year as a resident student at Mary Baldwin College cost $1,650.

53. Board Minutes, 23–24 February 1959; 29 May 1961; 26 September 1961; 28 May 1962; *AC Catalog*, March 1961, 72–73.

54. Mitchum interview; *AC Catalog*, March 1963, 87–90; Board Minutes, 22 September 1964; 5 October 1965; 27 September 1967.

55. Annual demographic reports on student body from 1964–1965 to 1968–1969, in Registrar's Records, 1927–1966, and Registrar's Records, 1966–1975, LCA.

56. Wann interview.

57. Demographic report on student body from 1965–1966, Registrar's Records, 1927–1966, LCA; *Scot*, 1966, 39; 1970, 37.

58. Board Minutes, 22 September 1964; 26 September 1967; *Arkansas College Bulletin*, February 1959, 2; DeVane, *Higher Education in Twentieth-Century America*, 124. By the late 1960s Arkansas College's total costs had reached the national average for independent colleges, and fees in Batesville almost doubled the average at state colleges within Arkansas.

59. *Scot*, 1966, 45; 1969, 49; *Highlander*, 22 March 1969, 4; 7 May 1969, 5.

60. *AC Catalog*, June 1918, 55; Board Minutes, 24 February 1949. From surviving records it appears that the first foreign student to enroll in Arkansas College was Absalom George, who is listed as being from Persia (Iran). The name suggests that George may in fact have been the son of missionaries, though his parentage remains unclear. George first enrolled during the 1917–1918 session.

61. Gordon D. Morgan and Izola Preston, *The Edge of Campus: A Journal of the Black Experience at the University of Arkansas* (Fayetteville: University of Arkansas Press, 1990), 172–73; Larry D. Ball and William M. Clements, *Voices from State: An Oral History of Arkansas State University* (State University, Ark.: Arkansas State University, 1984), 117–18; Brown interview. Dates for integration courtesy of archivists or librarians at the respective schools: Renee Le Beau-Ford at Arkansas Tech and Stuart Stelzer at the University of the Ozarks.

62. Brown interview; James E. Lester Jr., *The People's College: Little Rock Junior College and Little Rock University, 1927–1969* (Little Rock, Ark.: August House, 1987), 165. Dates of integration courtesy of archivists or librarians at respective schools: Randall Watts at Arkansas-Monticello, Donna McCloy at Southern Arkansas, Mary Helen Thomas at Hendrix, and Henry Terrill at Harding.

63. *Highlander*, 21 April 1967, 2.

64. *Highlander*, 17 December 1964, 1, 2, 3; 5 April 1965, 1; *Scot*, 1967, 108.

65. *Highlander*, 11 November 1960, 2, 3; 17 December 1964, 3; *Scot*, 1968, 62.

66. *Highlander*, 29 October 1965, 4; 21 April 1967, 1; 15 September 1967, 3; 26 January 1968, 1; 22 March 1968, 1; *Arkansas College Bulletin*, October 1967, 1; Faculty Minutes, 12 May 1969; Fagg interview.

67. Faculty Minutes, 4 October 1965; 9 May 1966; *Highlander*, 29 October 1965, 2; 3 December 1965, 2; 14 January 1966, 5; 21 October 1966, 2; 3 March 1967, 2; 15 September 1967, 1; *Scot*, 1966, 45; 1967, 4. Student dancing was no longer considered an issue by the 1960s. According to Paul McCain's memoirs, the ban on student dancing had been lifted quietly and without incident during the early days of his administration. McCain memoirs, 79.

68. Faculty Minutes, 12 January 1967; *Scot*, 1967, 3, 40.

69. *Highlander*, 3 December 1965, 2; 27 October 1967, 1, 2; 26 January 1968, 2; *Scot*, 1968, 22–23; McCain memoirs, 70, 73.

70. *AC Catalog*, April 1954, 11, 30; *Arkansas College Bulletin*, December 1953, 2; Mackenzie, et al., *Higher Education and the Synod of Arkansas*, 53.

71. *Highlander*, 11 November 1960, 2; 15 December 1967, 1; Faculty Minutes, 19 February 1962; 23 November 1964, 13 May 1965; 25 May 1968.

72. *Scot*, 1967, 43; 1968, 109; 1970, 49; Board Minutes, 17 May 1965; 26 September 1967; Mitchum interview.

73. *Highlander*, 21 April 1967, 2; *Scot*, 1967, 3–4; Wann interview.

74. Counts, "History of the Harlequin Theatre," 4; *Highlander*, 26 May 1967, 2; *Arkansas College Bulletin*, May 1967, 2; December 1967, 3; Board Minutes, 27 February 1968; McCain memoirs, 64.

75. *Arkansas College Bulletin*, June 1953, 3; January 1954, 1; November 1959, 6; November 1956, 3.

76. *Arkansas College Bulletin*, June 1969, 2; June 1965, 2; May 1966, 5; July 1967, 2; *Arkansas Presbyterian*, August 1963, 2; May 1964, 1; *Scot*, 1965, 39. Lassies who made the original USO tour included Lucy Jeffery, Mayola Satterfield, Sharon Floyd, Susan Hicks, Emily Turner, Judith Meserve, Paula Melton, Jennifer Engles, Ginni Tucker, and accompanist Charlotte Thompson. Other highlights of the Lassies in the 1960s included an appearance at the 1965 World's Fair in New York and a performance in front of President John F. Kennedy at the dedication to Greers Ferry Dam in October 1963. Dorothy Gray also created a similar men's group called the Lads.

77. *Scot*, 1967, 104–23; 1968, 56–58; *Highlander*, 26 January 1968, 1.

78. *Scot*, 1965, 34–35; 1967, 116.

79. *Scot*, 1966, 90. Although there was no intramural program for young women, female students continued to take physical education classes under Ruth Fulbright. One of the more colorful results of Fulbright's instruction was the organization in 1957 of the Crossbowettes, an octet of coeds clad in plaid who put on archery demonstrations using crossbows. The crossbow group grew out of a failed Stone County theme park called the Land of the Crossbow. *Highlander*, 24 October 1957, 1.

80. *Scot*, 1966, 91; 1967, 28–29; 1968, 36; James V. Balch to Paul McCain, 29 September 1966, Folder 1, Box 3, Presidential Papers, LCA; *Arkansas College Bulletin*, September 1968, 2. Soccer was not considered an official sport of the AIC. The college did not hire new coaches for its new varsity sports, relying instead on current faculty and staff members. Joining Arkansas College in the Arkansas Collegiate Soccer League were Hendrix, Ozarks, and Philander Smith.

81. Wann interview.

82. *Scot*, 1953, 86–87; *Arkansas College Bulletin*, April 1953, 1, 3; October 1954, 1; March 1955, 2; November 1957, 1; February 1958, 3. The Scots' opponents in the 1953 AAU tournament reflect the lack of college teams involved in the competition. Before beating Hendrix in the tournament finals, Arkansas College defeated the Camden Naval Depot, the Hot Springs Coca Cola Bottling Co., and Lion Oil of El Dorado.

83. Board Minutes, 23–24 February 1959; *Arkansas College Bulletin*, February 1960, 1; Mosley interview; McCain memoirs, 72; Jim Bailey, "Athletic History Chronicler Was Textbook Shooter," *Arkansas Democrat-Gazette*, 25 April 2000, C1.

84. *Arkansas College Bulletin*, November 1963, 2; April 1964, 3; May 1967, 4; March 1968, 3, 4; May 1968, 2, 4.

85. Board Minutes, 26 September 1961; 22 September 1962; *Arkansas Presbyterian*, May 1964, 1; *Arkansas College Bulletin*, March 1968, 2. In addition to giving more scholarships, Arkansas College began rewarding its graduates with fellowships and awards. The Williams Fellowship, named in honor of

Sam Williams and originally given to a senior who planned to attend graduate school, was first awarded in 1959. The Spragins Award, established in honor of former president John D. Spragins, was first given in 1962. By the late 1960s the board had established two new fellowships, the Margaret P. Lester Fellowship and the Faculty Fellowship, and the faculty had begun granting twenty-five dollar book awards to students who excelled in certain fields of study.

86. In addition to Winningham and Sydenstricker, the others who were members of the faculty during McCain's entire seventeen-year tenure were James V. Balch (economics and business), Doris Hammett (speech), Ellis Mosley (religion and Bible), Dorothy Landis Gray (music), and Roberta Dorr Brown (business skills and education). Those who served for more than half of the McCain administration included Ruth Fulbright (physical education and assistant librarian), Dick and Mary Kinser (Christian education), Virginia Porter Kirk (chemistry), Margaret Pruden Lester (history), Thelma Pickens (English and assistant librarian), Ann A. Rhodes (philosophy, humanities, and psychology), Samuel W. Williams (mathematics and Greek), Daniel Seibert (education and psychology), and Lyndell Watkins (music).

87. Faculty Minutes, 15 March 1954; 28 February 1955; Board Minutes, 30 May 1955; 25 February 1964; *Arkansas College Bulletin*, December 1966, 2.

88. Board Minutes, 17 May 1965; *Arkansas College Bulletin*, March 1966, 3; December 1967, 2; Executive Committee Minutes, 4 September 1963; Williams interview; Brown interview. Sam Williams died in February 1967 at the age of eighty-eight. Former students still recall his sly sense of humor and his favorite quote ("I'm just wasting my sweetness on the desert air") when confronted with a classroom full of "nubbinheads." Tragically, Margaret Pruden Lester died when her car rolled over her in the driveway of her home only half a year after her retirement. Although Lester had permanently joined the faculty only in 1947, she also taught a few years at Arkansas College during the 1930s. Independently financially secure, Lester often donated part or all of her salary to the college.

89. *Arkansas College Bulletin*, September 1966, 10; May 1967, 3.

90. Board Minutes, 13 January 1954; 22–23 February 1960; 27 February 1962; Faculty Minutes, 25 April 1955; 18 January 1960; 16 March 1964; 22 March 1968; Executive Committee Minutes, 15 April 1955; 15 March 1958; *Arkansas College Bulletin*, June 1954, 1; February 1958, 2; February 1963, 1, 3.

91. Faculty Minutes, 14 March 1957; 9 December 1960; 9 December 1963; *Arkansas College Bulletin*, September 1966, 10; July 1967, 8; February 1963, 1, 3; Board Minutes, 26 September 1963. In the spring of 1969 the faculty voted to replace the comprehensive senior examinations with senior projects.

92. Board Minutes, 25 February 1969.

93. McCain memoirs, 101–2; Board Minutes, 13 May 1969.

PART IV: 1969–1997

1. Minutes of the Investment Subcommittee, 3 September 1981, Investments Subcommittee 1979–1981, Box 4, Board of Trustees: Board and Committees, LCA; Robert A. Young III interview.

Chapter 7: Arkansas College in the Wild West Years

1. *Arkansas College Bulletin*, September 1973, 7; *Batesville Guard*, 19 April 1973, 1; Diane O. Tebbetts, *The West Years: 1972–1988* (Batesville: Arkansas College, 1990), 8; Dan C. West interview.

2. *Arkansas College Bulletin*, September 1973, 7; Tebbetts, *The West Years*, 8.

3. R. W. Wygle interview.

4. Ibid.; S. R. Nichols to Dear Friends, 7 October 1969, R. W. Wygle folder, A. C. People, Lyon College Special Collections.

5. Wygle interview; Jane Fagg interview. At six-feet, five inches tall and well over two hundred pounds, Wygle has the distinction of being the largest president in the history of the college.

6. *Arkansas College Bulletin*, September 1972, 1.

7. *Highlander*, 15 October 1971, 2.

8. *Arkansas College Bulletin*, January 1970, 3; *Highlander*, 21 May 1971, 1.

9. *Arkansas College Bulletin*, March 1970, 2; *Scot*, 1971, 5; Ed Mosley interview; *Highlander*, 2 May 1972, 2; Faculty Minutes, 6 May 1971.

10. *Highlander*, 6 November 1970, 1; *Arkansas College Bulletin*, September 1971, 1; September 1972, 4, 3; Faculty Minutes, 18 November 1969; 21 April 1970; AC *Catalog*, August 1972, 98, 116.

11. Interim Term Schedules, 1970, 1971, 1972, 1973, Spring Semester 1969–January Term 1977, Academic Services: Course Numbers and Descriptions, 1925–1976, LCA; *Arkansas College Bulletin*, March 1970, 4; October 1971, 4.

12. *Arkansas College Bulletin*, June 1968, 2.

13. *Arkansas College Bulletin*, June 1970, 6; Fall 1970 (President's Report, 1969–1970), 3.

14. *Arkansas College Bulletin*, September 1971, 1; October 1971, 3; September 1972, 6; *Highlander*, 29 October 1971, 1, 3; 10 December 1971, 1.

15. *Highlander*, 4 February 1972, 1; *Arkansas College Bulletin*, September 1972, 1.

16. *Highlander*, 18 Feburary 1972, 2; *Arkansas College Bulletin*, September 1971, 17.

17. "Biographical Data," 1 June 1974, Dan C. West folder, A. C. People, LCA; Light Townsend Cummins, *Austin College: A Sesquicentennial History, 1849–1999* (Austin, Tex.: Eakin Press, 1999), 324–30.

18. Jim Mitchum interview; Robert and Mary Young interview.

19. Board Minutes, 20 February 1973. The study most associated with the early 1970s doomsayers is Alexander W. Astin and Calvin B. T. Lee, *The Invisible Colleges: A Profile of Small, Private Colleges with Limited Resources* (New York: McGraw-Hill, 1971).

20. Faculty Minutes, 17 February 1970.

21. Tebbetts, *The West Years*, 3.

22. Ibid., 8.

23. Ibid., 3; *Arkansas College Bulletin*, June 1973, 2; September 1973, 3.

24. Tebbetts, *The West Years*, 8; *Arkansas College Bulletin*, September 1973, 7; December 1973, 2; September 1975, 2; Terrell Tebbetts interview.

25. Tebbetts, *The West Years*, 12; *Highlander*, 5 May 1975, 2; 10 October 1975, 4.

26. Tebbetts, *The West Years*, 12, 15; *Piper*, December 1979, 1.

27. Tebbetts, *The West Years*, 12, 15; *Highlander*, 21 January 1976, 2.

28. *Arkansas College Bulletin*, June 1973, 2; C. Fitzhugh Spragins to Dan C. West, 20 May 1972, unfiled materials, Box 6, Presidential Papers, 1972–1988, LCA; "The New Plan: Arkansas College Evaluation & Planning Process, 1972–73," in Academic Services: Planning: The New Plan, LCA, 1, 2, 8.

29. Dan C. West interview.

30. Mary Margaret Amsler, "The Changing Role of the Small, Private Liberal Arts College," Qualifying Paper, Harvard University, 1984, 48.

31. Tebbetts, *The West Years*, 3–4; "The New Plan," 9; *Arkansas College Bulletin*, September 1973, 4.

32. "The New Plan," 9, 12; Tebbetts, *The West Years*, 7, 9, 11, 14, 15; *Arkansas College Bulletin*, March 1974, 5; June 1976, 4. The college offered its first two-year certificates in 1976 to Linda Conner of Brockwell and Lillian Williams of Newport.

33. Jane Fagg interview; AC *Catalog*, 1974–1975, 24.

34. Cummins, *Austin College*, 324–25; AC *Catalog*, 1974–1975, 26; Tebbetts, *The West Years*, 9; *Arkansas College Bulletin*, September 1974, 5; Robert Lynn Wood, "'The Survival of Recognizably Protestant Colleges': Reflections on Old-Line Protestantism, 1950–1990," in *The Secularization of the Academy*, ed. George M. Marsden and Bradley J. Longfield (New York: Oxford University Press, 1992), 180; George M. Marsden, "The Soul of the American University: An Historical Overview," in *The Secularization of the Academy*, ed. Marsden and Longfield, 5, 23.

35. Tebbetts, *The West Years*, 4, 7; *Arkansas College Bulletin*, June 1973, 7; Interim Report of the Human Resources Center Study, no date; Dan C. West to M. Olin Cook, 17 September 1974, Folder 32, Box 2, Presidential Papers, 1972–1988, LCA.

36. Tebbets, *The West Years*, 4, 33; *Arkansas College Bulletin*, March 1974, 6; September 1976, 2; Donna Bryant, "Arkansas College Continuing Education: Program Review and Recommendations," 20 October 1977; Jim Mitchum to Dan C. West, 28 April 1983, Folder 38, Box 2, Presidential Papers,

1972–1988, LCA. In 1983 the college adopted a tuition schedule that charged fifty dollars per credit for all Continuing Education courses, regardless of the age of the student.

37. Tebbetts, *The West Years*, 4; Board Minutes, 14 May 1973.

38. Tebbetts, *The West Years*, 9, 10; *Highlander*, 10 May 1974, 1; Ed Mosley interview; Jane Fagg interview.

39. Tebbetts, *The West Years*, 9, 10, 11; Terrell Tebbetts interview; Dan C. West interview; *Highlander*, 24 February 1975, 1.

40. Tebbetts, *The West Years*, 11, 7; *Highlander*, 5 November 1974, 3; 20 January 1975, 2; 24 February 1975, 1; 17 March 1975, 2; 24 March 1975, 7; 21 April 1975, 1; 5 May 1975, 1.

41. Tebbetts, *The West Years*, 15, 1; Dan C. West interview.

42. Ibid., 13; Robert and Mary Young interview; Dan C. West interview; Frank Lyon Jr. interview.

43. *Piper*, Fall 1984, 4; Dan C. West to Presidents of Independent Colleges of Arkansas, 16 October 1973, Folder 29; Minutes of the Legislative Board Meeting of the ACICU, 19 September 1975, Folder 30; Max K. Jones to ACICU Presidents, 1 June 1977, Folder 31; Dan C. West to Arkansas Foundation of Associated Colleges Presidents, 10 June 1981, Folder 35, Box 1, Presidential Papers, 1972–1988, LCA; Memorandum: Dan C. West to Board of Trustees, 20 April 1976, "President's Memoranda, February 1976 through August 1988," President's Office, Lyon College.

44. Dan C. West interview.

45. *AC Catalog*, 1974–1975, 91; 1980–1981, 105.

46. Jerry R. Tompkins to Dan C. West, 28 September 1983, Folder 1, Box 6, Presidential Papers, 1972–1988, LCA; *Arkansas College Bulletin*, December 1973, 2; June 1974, 2; *Piper*, May 1978, 7; Tebbetts, *The West Years*, 11, 20; James Tunstead Burtchaell, *The Dying of the Light: The Disengagement of Colleges and Universities from Their Christian Churches* (Grand Rapids, Mich.: William B. Eerdmans, 1998), 50; Minutes of Stated Meeting, 21–22 May 1974, *The Presbytery of Arkansas (Union)*, *1974* (Little Rock), 29; *AC Catalog*, 1979–1980, 27.

47. Jerry R. Tompkins to Dan C. West, 28 September 1983, Folder 1, Box 6, Presidential Papers, 1972–1988, LCA; *Arkansas College Bulletin*, December 1973, 2; June 1974, 2; *Piper*, May 1978, 7; Tebbetts, *The West Years*, 11, 20; Burtchaell, *Dying of the Light*, 50; Minutes of Stated Meeting, 21–22 May 1974, *The Presbytery of Arkansas (Union)*, *1974* (Little Rock), 29; *AC Catalog*, 1979–1980, 27.

48. Tebbetts, *The West Years*, 10; Fritz H. Ehren to Don Davis, 21 December 1972; Dan C. West to Hugh Nelson, 18 May 1973, Folder 21, Box 2, Presidential Papers, 1972–1988, LCA; "A Proposal Submitted to the Planning Council of Arkansas Presbytery (Union) by Dr. Dan C. West, President, Arkansas College & Dr. Don Davis, President, College of the Ozarks, May 9, 1974," *The Presbytery of Arkansas (Union)*, *1974* (Little Rock), 40.

49. Minutes of a meeting between representatives of Arkansas College and College of the Ozarks in Little Rock, 14 December 1973; "Background Notes," no date; Dan C. West to Don Davis, William J. Fogleman, and Hugh Nelson, 31 March 1974; Don Davis to William J. Fogleman, 2 July 1974, Folder 21, Box 2, Presidential Papers, 1972–1988, LCA.

50. Dan C. West to Frank Lyon Sr., John Mays, Robert Knott, and Richard Thomas, 17 June 1976; R. L. Qualls to Dan C. West, 15 December 1976; John C. Merson to Bob Nash, 22 November 1978; Frank Lyon Sr. to Dan C. West, 26 June 1980; West to Lyon, 22 July 1980; William J. Fogleman to Tracy Kelly, no date; John F. Burhorn to William J. Fogleman, 3 October 1980, Folder 21, Presidential Papers, 1972–1988, LCA.

51. Tebbetts, *The West Years*, 7, 12, 14; *Arkansas College Planning Guide*, *1974–1980*, 1st edition, 34; *Arkansas College Planning Guide*, *1976–1982*, 84, Academic Services: Planning: Planning Guides, LCA; Board Minutes, 16 October 1973.

52. Tebbetts, *The West Years*, 7, 12, 14; *Arkansas College Bulletin*, June 1976, 2; September 1975, 3; September 1977, 4.

53. Tebbetts, *The West Years*, 21–22, 14, 18, 20; *Arkansas College Planning Guide*, *1974–1980*, 1st edition, 84; Board Minutes, 25–26 October 1976; 10–11 April 1978; 23–24 October 1978; 23–24 April 1979; 22–23 October 1979; 14–15 April 1980; Memorandum: Dan C. West to Special Friends of the College, 5 August 1980, "President's Memoranda"; John T. Dahlquist interview.

54. *Arkansas College Bulletin*, September 1974, 2; November 1974, 3; September 1975, 3;

September 1977, 1; *Arkansas College Planning Guide*, 1974–1980, 1st edition, 30, 31; *Arkansas College Planning Guide*, 1976–1982, 2nd edition, 16; Board Minutes, 22–23 October 1979.

55. *Arkansas College Planning Guide*, 1976–1982, 2nd edition, 29, 56, 60.

56. Ibid., 68; *Piper*, December 1979, 3; *Arkansas College Bulletin*, September 1976, 2.

57. Robert E. Knott, "Arkansas College Institutional Mission, Purpose and Program," August 1976, A.C. History—General, LCA; Tebbetts, *The West Years*, 15, 18.

58. Faculty Minutes, 22 March 1979; Tebbetts, *The West Years*, 18; John S. Brubacher and Willis Rudy, *Higher Education in Transition: A History of American Colleges and Universities*, 4th edition (New Brunswick, N.J.: Transaction Publishers, 1997), 414; John T. Dahlquist interview.

59. Tebbetts, *The West Years*, 19, 23, 32, 20.

60. *AC Catalog*, 1980–1981, 118, 123; Tebbetts, *The West Years*, 19.

61. Tebbetts, *The West Years*, 21, 23, 26, 30.

62. Board Minutes, 19–20 April 1982; 25–26 October 1982; 11–12 April 1983; 24–25 October 1983; 9–10 April 1984.

63. Tartan Society Newsletter/Memorandum, 8 May 1981, "President's Memoranda"; Dan C. West interview.

64. Tebbetts, *The West Years*, 22; Dan C. West interview.

65. Dan C. West interview.

66. Ibid.; Tebbetts, *The West Years*, 18.

67. Dan C. West interview.

68. Tebbetts, *The West Years*, 24, 25, 26, 31; "School of Independent Living," revised draft, September 1983, Folder 38, Box 2, Presidential Papers, 1972–1988, LCA; *Batesville Guard*, 18 October 1983, 1.

69. Tebbetts, *The West Years*, 30, 33; Dan C. West interview.

70. Dan C. West interview; John T. Dahlquist interview; Memoranda: Dan C. West to Board of Trustees, 27 January 1978; Dan C. West to Special Friends of the College, 14 February 1979, "President's Memoranda"; Tebbetts, *The West Years*, 24, 34; *Piper*, Spring 1984, 12, 24; Winter 1985, 8; Winter 1986, 7; Spring 1988, 2.

71. Tebbetts, *The West Years*, 15, 23; *Piper*, May 1978, 5; *Arkansas Gazette*, 10 April 1983, 1, 6; 22 July 1984, B1; Lawrence Beimiller, "Innovation and Jean Brown's Generosity Help Tiny Arkansas College Prosper," *Chronicle of Higher Education*, 29 June 1984.

72. Tebbetts, *The West Years*, 23; Richard S. Thomas to Executive Committee, Business Committee, and Investments Sub-Committee, 21 September 1982; Business Committee Minutes, 11 October 1982, Business Committee, 1982–Spring 1984, Board of Trustees: Board and Committees, 1982–Spring 1984, LCA; Board Minutes, 25–26 October 1982.

73. Tebbetts, *The West Years*, 21–22, 23, 31, 32, 35; Memorandum: Dan C. West to the Board of Trustees and Other Special Friends, 29 May 1986, "President's Memoranda."

74. Memorandum: Dan C. West to the Board of Trustees and Other Special Friends, 29 May 1986, "President's Memoranda"; Tebbetts, *The West Years*, 32; Board Minutes, 29–30 October 1984.

75. *Arkansas College Bulletin*, June 1976, 3; *Piper*, May 1978, 4; George E. Lankford, "Arkansas Folklore Education Consortium, 1 July 1976 to 31 June 1980, in Academic Services: Planning: NEH Challenge/Rockefeller, LCA. Four titles were eventually published under the Arkansas College Folklore Monograph Series, the first of which was Charles McRaven's *Building the Hewn Log House* in 1978. Series editor was Richard Tallman, who served as an assistant professor of folklore and folklore archivist from 1976 to 1979. Another unusual academic activity of the late 1970s was the Earthlander Project, in which students read about the experiments of the Viking Lander on Mars and then recreated those experiments on a small plot of land near the Smith Science and Mathematics Building.

76. Tebbetts, *The West Years*, 18, 31; *Piper*, May 1978, 2; March 1981, 2; June 1983, 5; Memorandum: Dan C. West to Trustees and Other Special Friends, 29 May 1986, "President's Memoranda."

77. *Arkansas Gazette*, 11 September 1981, 1A.

78. Tebbetts, *The West Years*, 22; "Distinguished Scottish American Award Presented to Dr. Ralph McCulloch Graham," Arkansas College News Release, 21 November 1989, Dr. Ralph M. Graham Folder, A.C. People, Lyon College Special Collections.

79. Tebbetts, *The West Years*, 22; *Piper*, June 1981, 5; October 1982, 6; December 1983, 7; Fall 1985, 6.

80. *Piper*, September 1981, 3; March 1982, 6; June 1982, 2; Tebbetts, *The West Years*, 33; Celeste Ray, *Highland Heritage: Scottish Americans in the American South* (Chapel Hill: University of North Carolina Press, 2001), 51, 50.

81. *The Scottish Connection*, March/April 1983, 4; Hugh M. Patterson to William H. Dunklin, 12 July 1982, Folder 47, Box 4, Presidential Papers, 1972–1988, LCA; Kenneth J. Bearden and Keith M. Alman, "The Ozark Scottish Festival and the Fluidity in Roles," *Mid-America Folklore* 25 (Fall 1997), 58; Ray, *Highland Heritage*, 6, 47.

82. Tebbetts, *The West Years*, 30, 24; Freshman Profiles, 1982, 1983, Admissions/Financial Aid: Admissions: Freshman Profiles, LCA.

83. *Arkansas Gazette*, 15 February 1983, no page; Faculty Minutes, 13 October 1981; 11 May 1982; Freshman Profile, 1984, Admissions/Financial Aid: Admissions: Freshman Profiles, LCA.

84. Tartan Society Newsletter, 27 January 1986, "President's Memoranda"; Tebbetts, *The West Years*, 31; Freshman Profiles, 1985, 1986, 1987, Admissions/Financial Aid: Admissions: Freshman Profiles, LCA.

85. Memorandum: Dan C. West to the Board of Trustees and Other Special Friends, May 1987, "President's Memoranda"; Dan C. West interview.

86. *AC Catalog*, 1984–1985, 126; 1988–1989, 137, 138.

87. *AC Catalog*, 1988–1989, 137, 138, 139.

88. *AC Catalog*, 1988–1989, 137, 138.

89. *Highlander*, 13 October 1972, 1; 22 March 1974, 1; 28 April 1975, 3; 13 May 1976, 1; *Piper*, Winter 1985, 6.

90. *Highlander*, 14 December 1970, 2; 22 March 1971, 1; 3 May 1971, 2; 21 May 1971, 2; 22 October 1971, 2; 22 February 1974, 3; 8 March 1974, 1; 15 March 1974, 1; *Arkansas College Bulletin*, February 1972, 5; Faculty Minutes, 7 February 1972; Ed Trattner–Jim Hamilton interview. In a rare case of too much publicity, at least one potential donor threatened to strike Arkansas College from his will after reading an *Arkansas Gazette* account of streaking on the Batesville campus. W. J. Dungan to Dan West, 8 March 1974, Folder 44, Box 2, Presidential Papers, 1972–1988.

91. *Highlander*, 6 November 1970, 3; 21 May 1971, 1; 28 April 1972, 1; 29 September 1972, 1; Tebbetts, *The West Years*, 7.

92. "History of the Lambda-Iota Chapter of Kappa Sigma," Lambda-Iota Chapter Alumni Association, *http://www.wlrcreative.com/Lyon.KappaSig/history.html*.

93. *Highlander*, 3 March 1972, 2; Tebbetts, *The West Years*, 10–11.

94. *Synergist*, Winter 1981, 53.

95. Counts, "History of the Harlequin Theatre," 4.

96. *Highlander*, 3 November 1972, 2; *Piper*, July 1973, 7; October 1982, 1; January 1984, 12.

97. *Highlander*, 4 February 1971, 3; *Arkansas College Bulletin*, June 1975, 6; Tebbetts, *The West Years*, 10, 20, 22, 26, 23, 31; Memorandum: Dan C. West to Trustees and Other Special Friends, 28 November 1984; 13 May 1988, "President's Memoranda"; *Piper*, June 1980, 4; September 1981, 2; March 1982, 4; June 1982, 3; June 1983, 11; February 1983, 4; December 1983, 3; Spring 1984, 3, 5; Fall 1985, 5.

98. Tebbetts, *The West Years*, 7, 20; *Highlander*, 3 May 1971, 2; *Arkansas College Bulletin*, March 1973, 2, 3; June 1973, 5; March 1975, 4; *Piper*, March 1976, 10; Memorandum: Dan C. West to Board of Trustees and Other Friends, 18 May 1978, "President's Memoranda."

99. Tebbetts, *The West Years*, 22, 26, 31; *Scot*, 1981, 112.

100. *Scot*, 1974, 86. Before the arrival of full-fledged women's athletics in the 1970s, the closest that Arkansas College had come to women's varsity sports was during the late depression era, when the Girls' Resident Training Project of the National Youth Administration (NYA) organized a basketball team known as the Royals. Coached by an Arkansas College student, the NYA Royals advanced to the district AAU tournament in 1940 behind the play of all-district performers Marie Horton, Aleene Wilkerson, and Marie Massey. *Index*, 1940, 38.

101. Ibid., 1975, 78, 79; 1976, 100–101; 1981, 106, 107; *Piper*, March 1981, 2.

102. *Piper*, June 1981, 1; Spring 1987, viii; January 1984, 10; Winter 1986, 2; September 1981, 2; Memorandum: Dan C. West to Trustees and Other Special Friends, May 1987, "President's

Memoranda"; Tebbetts, *The West Years*, 26, 32; *Arkansas College Planning Guide*, 1980–1989, 7th edition, 148–49.

103. Tebbetts, *The West Years*, 34; Memorandum: Dan C. West to the Highlander Association, October 1987, "President's Memoranda"; *Piper*, Spring 1988, vii.

104. Tebbetts, *The West Years*, 32, 34; *Piper*, Spring 1984, 25.

105. Tebbetts, *The West Years*, 33, 34; Testimony Before the Revenue and Taxation Committee, Arkansas House of Representatives," 28 February 1985, Folder 14, Box 4, Presidential Papers, 1972–1988, LCA; Dan C. West interview.

106. Board Minutes, 26 October 1987; 11–12 April 1988.

107. Board Minutes, 11–12 April 1988; Tebbetts, *The West Years*, 31, 33; Dan C. West interview.

Chapter 8:
Tossing Our Hats over the Wall: The Griffith Years

1. Frank O'Connor, *An Only Child* (1961; Syracuse, N.Y.: Syracuse University Press, 1997), 180; *Piper*, Fall 1989, 7.

2. Dan C. West Memorandum to Arkansas College Board of Trustees, Faculty, Staff, et al., 6 May 1988, Graham Holloway File, A.C. People, Lyon College Special Collections; President's Report to the Board of Trustees, August 1989, I-2.

3. *Batesville Guard*, 8 September 1988, 1; President's Report to the Board of Trustees, August 1989, I-3, I-4, I-5, I-8.

4. Helen McCallie, "Summary of the Presidential Search, 1988 Committee," Presidential Search, 1988, Presidential Papers 1989–1997, LCA.

5. *Piper*, Spring 1989, 7, 8; John V. Griffith interview.

6. McCallie, "Summary of the Presidential Search."

7. Griffith interview; *Piper*, Spring 1988, iii.

8. President's Report, August 1989, I-1.

9. *Piper*, Fall 1989, 2, 6, 7; John V. Griffith interview.

10. *Piper*, Fall 1990, 21; John V. Griffith interview; McCallie, "Summary of the Presidential Search."

11. President's Report, August 1990, I-4; McCallie, "Summary of the Presidential Search."

12. Strategic Planning Task Force, "Strategic Plan Prepared for the Board of Trustees of Arkansas College," 14 February 1990, Strategic Planning/Self-Study, LCA.

13. *Piper*, Spring 1989, 9.

14. President's Report, August 1991, I-4; August 1992, I-7, III-1; August 1993, I-3.

15. President's Report, August 1990, III-9, III-21; August 1991, III-24; August 1992, III-9.

16. President's Report, August 1993, I-3, III-3, III-5. By the mid-1990s Lyon College offered majors in fourteen areas of study: art, biology, chemistry, economics, English, history, mathematics, music, politics, psychology, religion and philosophy, Spanish, and theatre. The curriculum also featured six concentrations: accounting and management within economics, human resource management within psychology, and journalism, elementary education, and secondary education within any of the major fields. In addition to the above fields, minors included anthropology, computer science, French, international studies, Scottish arts, and physics.

17. *Piper*, Fall 1994, 11, 12, 13; Fall 1996, 6; *Arkansas Democrat-Gazette*, 30 July 1997, B1.

18. President's Report, August 1993, III-3; August 1994, III-2; August 1996, I-1, I-7, III-1; August 1997, III-1.

19. President's Report, August 1989, I-2, I-6; August 1992, I-8.

20. President's Report, August 1991, I-1, August 1992, I-4; *Piper*, Spring 1991, 4–11.

21. President's Report, August 1992, III-7; August 1996, I-7; *Piper*, Fall 1994, 16; Spring 1996, 5.

22. President's Report, August 1993, I-6.

23. President's Report, August 1994, I-3; John V. Griffith to the Board of Trustees, 5 February 1996, President's Correspondence: Memos, 1995–1997, LCA; President's Report, August 1997, I-8, III-2.

24. President's Report, August 1989, I-5; Minutes of Business and Finance Committee of the Board of Trustees, 27 April 1995, Committees, 1995, LCA.

25. Minutes of Business and Finance Committee, 27 April 1995; President's Report, August 1990, I-6; August 1992, I-7; August 1994, III-1; August 1996, I-6.

26. *Piper,* Fall 1997, 30; President's Report, August 1994, II-2; August 1997, I-1.

27. President's Report, August 1993, I-1; August 1991, III-28; August 1996, I-2; September 1998, III-6.

28. *Highlander,* 16 February 1990, 1; President's Report, August 1990, I-5; August 1992, I-5.

29. President's Report, August 1996, I-4; September 1998, I-11. The Arkansas Court of Appeals later rejected the local court's ruling in favor of the student/plaintiff, stating that, in absence of procedural shortcomings, a decision in an honor system case was not subject to judicial review.

30. President's Report, August 1995, I-4.

31. *Highlander,* 19 October 1990, 1; President's Report, August 1991, I-3; August 1992, I-3; August 1995, I-4.

32. President's Report, August 1991, VI-1; August 1993, I-5.

33. President's Report, August 1996, VI-2; August 1997, VI-1, VI-2.

34. President's Report, August 1991, VI-1; August 1994, VI-1; August 1996, I-2, VI-1; Bruce Johnston to Members of the Student Life Committee of the Board of Trustees, 29 September 1995, Committees: Fall 1995, Board of Trustees Records, LCA.

35. President's Report, August 1990, I-5; *Scot,* 1993, 130.

36. President's Report, August 1991, I-2; August 1992, I-3.

37. President's Report, August 1991, I-6.

38. President's Report, August 1992, I-3; August 1993, I-5, III-9.

39. President's Report, August 1989, III-32; August 1992, III-29; August 1993, III-9; August 1994, III-6; August 1997, III-7; September 1998, III-7.

40. President's Report, August 1992, II-2; August 1995, I-1; August 1996, III-8; August 1997, I-3; *Piper,* Fall 1994, 18.

41. President's Report, August 1991, I-7; August 1993, I-2; August 1995, I-2; August 1997, I-4, III-1.

42. President's Report, August 1991, I-5, I-7; September 1998, III-2; *Highlander,* 19 February 1993, 3.

43. President's Report, August 1989, I-6; *Highlander,* 6 April 1990, 1.

44. President's Report, August 1989, I-2; August 1994, I-1.

45. *Piper,* Spring 1990, 8.

46. *Piper,* Spring 1991, 2, 8; Fall 1993, 2. Another phase of image building in the 1990s involved the continuation of West-era efforts to cultivate Scottish arts and heritage. By 1989 the Ozark (later Arkansas) Scottish Festival had become financially self-supporting. That annual event continued to draw larger and larger crowds to campus each April into the 1990s. In 1991 Arkansas College became the second U.S. institution (South Carolina's The Citadel was the first) of higher learning to adopt its own tartan, which Russ Spaulding, director of the Scottish Heritage Program, helped design. President's Report, August 1989, I-7; August 1991, II-4.

47. *Piper,* Fall 1991, 10.

48. Executive Committee of the Board of Trustees Minutes, 27 November 1946, LCA; Board Minutes, 28 February 1956; 27 September 1966, LCA; Jim Mitchum interview.

49. Griffith Memorandum to "The File," 29 September 1989, Arkansas College Name Change Folder, LCA; Robert A. Young III interview; John V. Griffith interview.

50. Glenn Monigle and Associates, Inc., "Platform for Strategic Communications Planning and Name Development Prepared for Arkansas College," 12 December 1992, Arkansas College Name Change Folder, LCA.

51. Ibid.; J. Craig Ogilvie to Darrell Loyless, 28 January 1993; Tom Garner to Terrell Tebbetts, 25 January 1993, Letters Concerning the Proposed Name Change, Arkansas College Name Change Folder, LCA.

52. John Hollis to Lucy Yeager, 22 June 1992, Letters Concerning the Proposed Name Change; Name Change Advisory Committee Proceedings, 13 March 1993, Arkansas College Name Change Folder, LCA.

53. "Name Change Advisory Committee: Recommendations to the President," Name Change Advisory Committee Proceedings, 13 March 1993; Darrell Loyless to Name Change Advisory

Committee, 14 October 1993, Arkansas College Name Change Folder, LCA. One of the favorite pastimes of people who favored the name change was writing letters to college administrators or Name Change Advisory Committee members with suggestions for the new name. Alumni and friends of the college submitted dozens of names. Among the most common suggestions were names beginning with the letter "A," in order to preserve the familiar A.C. —Addington, Alba, Acton, Abingdon, and Ashby to name a few. Aberdeen was also a favorite. Some sought to maintain a link with the state or region: Arkansas Highland, Arkansas Presbyterian, Arkansas Christian, Ozark Highlands, Independence, and even the University of Arkansas at Batesville, from someone apparently unfamiliar with the motivations for change. Many suggested names that played off the college's renewed interest in Scottish heritage (Caledonia, Eliot, Edinburgh, Holyrood, Leeds, and Dumbarton) while others looked toward the heritage of the church and the college (Aaron Lyon, Long, and Makemie). Some even used the occasion for levity, or at least one hopes that the recommendation of Clann-na-Gaedheal was made in jest.

54. *Batesville Guard,* 24 February 1994, 1, 3; Young interview; Griffith interview; Frank Lyon Jr. interview.

55. Draft of Schedule and Time Line for Unveiling of Arkansas College's New Name, no date, Arkansas College Name Change Folder, LCA; *Batesville Guard,* 23 February 1994, 3; 24 February 1994, 1, 3; *Grace Notes,* April 1994, 1; C. Fitzhugh Spragins to Darrell Loyless, 19 February 1993, Arkansas College Name Change Folder, LCA.

56. President's Report, August 1995, I-1, I-2; August 1994, I-5; *Piper,* Fall 1994, 2.

57. President's Report, August 1995, I-1, I-4.

58. President's Report, August 1989, I-2; August 1990, III-31; August 1991, I-2, IV-2, VI-1; *Piper,* Fall 1991, cover.

59. President's Report, August 1992, I-1, III-32, III-33, VI-1; August 1993, I-2, VI-1; August 1994, I-1, III-4; August 1995, I-1, I-2, VI-1.

60. President's Report, August 1990, I-4; August 1991, II-3; August 1995, I-3; September 1998, I-7.

61. Tebbetts interview; Mitchum interview; President's Report, August 1994, VI-1; September 1998, VI-2.

62. President's Report, August 1990, III-31; August 1997, I-2.

63. President's Report, August 1989, I-3, I-8; August 1990, I-2, I-4, I-8, VII-2; August 1991, I-5, I-7; September 1998, I-12; *Highlander,* 18 January 1991, 1.

64. *Highlander,* 12 January 1990, 1; President's Report, August 1991, I-5.

65. President's Report, August 1992, VI-2; August 1993, I-6; August 1995, I-3, II-1; August 1997, I-6, II-3.

66. *Piper,* Fall 1990, 22; President's Report, August 1989, I-7, II-1.

67. President's Report, August 1991, I-7; August 1992, I-2; August 1993, I-1, I-4, VII-1; August 1994, I-2, I-3, VII-1.

68. President's Report, August 1995, I-3; August 1996, I-1, I-3; Minutes of Executive Committee of the Board of Trustees, 20–21 August 1995, Committees: Fall 1995, Board of Trustees Records, LCA.

69. President's Report, August 1997, VII-1, I-3, I-10, I-7; August 1995, II-1; August 1996, I-5.

70. Griffith interview; President's Report, I-10.

71. President's Report, August 1995, I-7; August 1996, I-6, I-1, I-7, III-2; August 1997, I-1, I-2, I-4, I-5, I-6, I-8; North Central Association, "Report of a Visit to Arkansas College, March 2–4, 1992, for the Commission on Institutions of Higher Education of the North Central Association of Colleges and Schools," LCA.

72. President's Report, August 1997, I-2; August 1998, I-2, I-3, II-3.

73. President's Report, August 1997, I-12; Griffith interview.

EPILOGUE

1. Interview with Armilda Brodie, 18 January 2002.

2. J. William Moncrief memorandum to Board of Trustees, 10 November 1997 and 9 December 1997, unprocessed presidential office materials, LCA.

3. Moncrief memorandum, 10 November 1997.

4. Ruth A. Schmidt memorandum to Board of Trustees, 12 May 1998 and 17 June 1998, unprocessed presidential office materials, LCA; President's Report to the Board of Trustees, September 1998, I-6, I-7, I-8, VI-3. As discussed in the previous chapter, loan-capping refers to the practice of limiting a student's accrual of federal student loans to a maximum that is below the federal maximum and by making up the difference with institutional financial aid funds. Scholarship stacking refers to the practice of awarding merit or nonmerit scholarships on top of other scholarships. This practice is especially common with student athletes, many of whom are not allowed full scholarships under NAIA regulations.

5. President's Report, September 1998, VI-3, I-4; Schmidt memorandum, 12 May 1998. The phrase "buying students" is not meant to be attributed to Schmidt, or for that matter to anyone specifically. Instead, it is a phrase used often to denote the practice of building enrollments through overly generous financial aid strategies.

6. Barbara E. Taylor, "Report From the Academic Search Consultation Service to the Presidential Search Committee of Lyon College," 21 October 1997, Presidential Search, President's Office, Papers and Correspondence, 1989–1997, LCA.

7. *Piper,* Spring 1998, 4–5.

8. President's Report, October 1999, PR-1, PR-3, BT-7.

9. President's Report, October 1999, AS-3; October 2000, AS-3, AS-4; *Piper,* Spring 1999, 8.

10. President's Report, October 1999, PR-2, AS-2, AS-7, SL-9; October 2000, PL-3; Roettger interview.

11. President's Report, October 1999, PR-3; October 2000, PL-2.

12. President's Report, October 1999, PR-1; September 1998, VI-4; "Lyon College Fall," 2001, seasonal bulletin published by Lyon College, 1.

13. President's Report, October 1999, PR-2, PR-4; October 2000, PL-4, PL-5; "Lyon College Reaches Lofty Goal," Lyon College press release, 21 February 2001.

14. "Lyon College Breaks Ground for New Derby Science and Math Center," Lyon College press release, 27 April 2001.

15. President's Report, October 2000, ES-7; "Lyon College Fall," 2001, 1.

16. President's Report, October 2000, PL-4.

17. President's Report, August 1992, I-12; "Roundtable Discussion on Strategic Issues, April 1997: Analysis of Survey Responses," report appended to John V. Griffith memorandum to Board of Trustees, 29 September 1997, unprocessed presidential office materials, LCA.

18. President's Report, October 1999, PR-2, BT-2, AS-2; October 2000, PL-4, BT-3, AS-1.

19. Strategic Planning Steering Committee, *The Strategic Plan for Lyon College: 2000–2005,* unprocessed presidential materials, LCA, 1, 2–9.

APPENDIX II:
Lists of Leaders and Honors

1. Rev. J. E. Latham served as acting president from the time of Cleland's departure in April 1897 until Long's return in the summer.

2. E. D. "Van" Brown served as interim president for the fall semester of 1916.

3. Dean Samuel W. Williams served as interim president from August to October 1937, and again from April to late June 1942.

4. Professor Ellis Mosley served as interim president from July to September 1952.

5. Trustee and alumnus I. Nelson "Nels" Barnett III served as interim president in September and October 1969.

6. During West's sabbatical year (1981–1982), trustee William Dunklin served as acting president. Following West's departure, trustee Graham Holloway served as interim president from August 1988 to January 1989; academic dean John T. Dahlquist then served as interim president until Griffith's arrival in July 1989.

7. Following Griffith's departure, academic dean J. William Moncrief served as interim president for the final two months of 1997; trustee Ruth Schmidt then served as interim president until the arrival of Roettger in the summer of 1998.

BIBLIOGRAPHY

PRIMARY SOURCES

Published Works

Centre College. *Centre College Catalog*. Danville, Ky.: Centre College, 1858.

Division of Survey and Field Services. *Arkansas College and the College of the Ozarks: A Survey Report*. Nashville, Tenn.: George Peabody College for Teachers, 1946.

Goodspeed. *The Goodspeed Biographical and Historical Memoirs of Northeast Arkansas*. Chicago: Goodspeed Publishing Company, 1889.

Jacobs, Thornwell, ed. *The Diary of William Plumer Jacobs*. Oglethorpe University, Ga.: Oglethorpe University Press, 1937.

Long, I. J. *A Discourse Commemorative of the Life, Character and Services of the Rev. Thomas Rice Welch, D. D. Delivered Before the Synod of Arkansas at Camden, Ark., November 17, 1886*. St. Louis, Mo.: Farris, Smith & Co., 1886.

———. "Sketch of Arkansas College." Pamphlet consisting of a combination of articles that originally appeared in the *Arkansas Presbyterian* (Little Rock) in 1890–1891.

Mackenzie, Donald, et al. *Higher Education and the Synod of Arkansas: A Report to the Council for Christian Higher Education of the Synod of Arkansas, Presbyterian Church in the United States*. N.p.: 1958.

Presbyterian Theological Seminary. *General Catalogue of the Presbyterian Theological Seminary*. Chicago: Presbyterian Theological Seminary, 1939.

Scott, E. C., comp. *Ministerial Directory of the Presbyterian Church, U.S., 1861–1941*. Austin, Tex.: Von Boeckmann-Jones, 1942.

U.S. Department of the Interior. Office of the Census. *Ninth Census of the United States, 1870: Population*. Washington, D.C.: Government Printing Office, 1872.

Periodicals

Arkansas Democrat

Arkansas Democrat-Gazette

Arkansas Gazette

Arkansas Presbyterian

Batesville Bee

Batesville Guard

Batesville News Review

Batesville Record

Batesville Republican

Chronicle of Higher Education

Davidson (College) *Monthly*

Mary Baldwin (College) *Magazine*

North Arkansas Pilot

North Arkansas Times

Rostrum

Scottish Connection

Shelbyville (Tennessee) *Times-Gazette*

Synergist

Texas Republican

Weekly North Arkansas Times

Lyon College Archives and Special Collections (LCA)

A.C. History Collection.
A.C. People Files.
Academic Services Records.
Admissions/Financial Aid Records.
Arkansas College Bulletin.
Arkansas College Catalogue.
Arkansas College Magazine.
Arkansas College Monthly News Letter.
Arkansas College Name Change Folder.
Arkansas College Summer (tabloid).
Board of Trustees Records.
Dorothy Brown's Scrapbook.
Eugene Long Scrapbook.
Faculty Assembly Minutes.
Highlander.
Index.
John P. Morrow Papers.
Long Family Collection.
McCain, Paul. Unpublished and untitled memoirs. 1989.
Panther.
Piper.
Presbyterian Collection.
Presidential Papers.
President's Reports, 1972–2001.
Registrar's Records.
The Scot.
Strategic Planning/Self-Study Records.
Unprocessed presidential office materials.
Virginia Shanks—Memories of her life at A.C.

Lyon College President's Office

President's Memoranda, February 1976 through August 1988.

University of Arkansas Special Collections

Samuel W. Davies Biographical Material.

Arkansas History Commission

Petition to the General Assembly of the State of Arkansas, Batesville, Ark., 16 January 1893. SMC Box 66, No. 34. Microfilm.

White River Regional Library

Arkansas Vertical File.

Stitt Memorial Library Special Collections, Austin Presbyterian Theological Seminary

Arthur Gray Jones Papers.

Presbyterian Historical Collection, Montreat, North Carolina

John D. Spragins Papers (JDSP).

Others

Kalen and Morrow Papers. Private collection of Lynn Morrow. Jefferson City, Missouri.

Interviews

CONDUCTED BY AUTHOR

Beary, Michael. Batesville, Arkansas. 6 March 2001.

Brodie, Armilda. By telephone. 18 January 2002.

Brown, Mitchael. By telephone. May 2001.

Dahlquist, John T. Batesville, Arkansas. 28 April 2002.

Fagg, Jane. Batesville, Arkansas. 16 May 2001.

Garner, Carl. Tumbling Shoals, Arkansas. 5 March 2001.

Griffith, John V. Clinton, South Carolina. 26 October 2000.

Haney, Jim. Highland, Arkansas. 27 February 2002.

Hicks, Basil. Little Rock, Arkansas. 5 February 2001.

Johnson, Virginia Rose (Davidson). By telephone. 15 November 2000.

Lyon, Frank, Jr. Batesville, Arkansas. 25 April 2002.

Mitchum, Jim. Batesville, Arkansas. 30 April 2001.

Mosley, Ed. Batesville, Arkansas. 10 May 2001.

Roettger, Walter B. Batesville, Arkansas. January 2002.

Rutherford, Virginia. By telephone. 14 November 2000.

Spragins, Fitzhugh. Batesville, Arkansas. 14 March 2001.

Tebbetts, Terrell. Batesville, Arkansas. 10 July 2001.

Trimble, J. D., Jr. El Dorado, Arkansas. 19 March 2001.

Wann, Fred. Batesville, Arkansas. 14 May 2001.

West, Dan C. Swarthmore, Pennsylvania. 31 July 2001.

Williams, Franklin. Batesville, Arkansas. 21 November 2000.

Wolf, Bess. Batesville, Arkansas. 7 November 2000.

Wygle, R. W. By telephone. 25 April 2001.

Young, Robert A., III, and Mary Young. Fort Smith, Arkansas. 18 July 2001.

CONDUCTED BY BARBARA LINDSEY-ALLEN

Barnett, I. N. "Nels," III. Batesville, Arkansas. 6 November 1986.

Edwards, Glenn. Batesville, Arkansas. 3 October 1986.

Murphy, W. D., Jr. Batesville, Arkansas. 4 November 1986.

IN FOLKLORE ARCHIVE, LYON COLLEGE REGIONAL STUDIES CENTER

John P. Morrow Jr. interviewed by Betsy Shaw. Batesville, Arkansas. March 1977. Accession Number 77-10, Tape Number T 58.

John P. Morrow Jr. interviewed by Melissa Jobe. Batesville, Arkansas. 21 November 1977; 24 November 1977; 29 November 1977; 11 December 1977. Accession Number 77-22, Tape Numbers T 115, 116, and 117.

Ed Trattner interviewed by Jim Hamilton. Batesville, Arkansas. April 1977. Accession Number 77-5, Tape Number T 51.

Adams, Walter M. *The White River Railway: Being a History of the White River Division of the Missouri Pacific Railroad Company, 1901–1951*. Branson, Mo.: Ozarks Mountaineer, 1991.

Allen, Barbara Lindsey. "The Death and Resurrection of Arkansas College." *Independence County Chronicle* 29 (October 1987–1988): 14–21.

American Historical Society. *Arkansas and Its People: A History, 1541–1930*, 3 Volumes. New York: American Historical Society, 1930.

Amsler, Mary Margaret. "The Changing Role of the Small, Private Liberal Arts College." Qualifying Paper. Harvard University, 1984.

Astin, Alexander W., and Calvin B. T. Lee. *The Invisible Colleges: A Profile of Small, Private Colleges with Limited Resources*. New York: McGraw-Hill, 1971.

Ball, Larry D., and William M. Clements. *Voices from State: An Oral History of Arkansas State University*. State University: Arkansas State University, 1984.

Banks, Wayne. *History of Yell County, Arkansas*. Van Buren, Ark.: Press-Argus, 1959.

Barringer, Paul B. *University of Virginia: Its History, Influence, Equipment and Characteristics, with Biographical Sketches and Portraits of Founders, Benefactors, Officers and Alumni*. New York: Lewis, 1904.

Barry, John M. *Rising Tide: The Great Mississippi Flood of 1927 and How It Changed America*. New York: Simon & Schuster, 1997.

Basham, Robert Harold. *A History of Cane Hill College in Arkansas*. Ed.D. diss., University of Arkansas, 1969; Ann Arbor: University of Michigan, 1970.

Bearden, Kenneth J., and Keith M. Alman. "The Ozark Scottish Festival and the Fluidity in Roles." *Mid-America Folklore* 25 (Fall 1997): 57–74.

Beimiller, Lawrence. "Innovation and Jean Brown's Generosity Help Tiny Arkansas College Prosper." *Chronicle of Higher Education* 29 (June 1984): 5–6.

Blethen, H. Tyler, and Curtis W. Wood Jr., eds. *Ulster and North America: Transatlantic Perspectives on the Scotch-Irish*. Tuscaloosa: University of Alabama Press, 1997.

Britton, Nancy, ed. *Independence Pioneers*, 2 volumes. Batesville, Ark.: Independence Pioneers Committee, 1986–1989.

Brubacher, John S., and Willis Rudy. *Higher Education in Transition: A History of American Colleges and Universities*, 4th edition. New Brunswick, N.J.: Transaction Publishers, 1997.

Burtchaell, James Tunstead. *The Dying of the Light: The Disengagement of Colleges and Universities from Their Christian Churches*. Grand Rapids, Mich.: William B. Eerdmans, 1998.

Chester, S. H. *Pioneer Days in Arkansas*. Richmond, Va.: Presbyterian Committee of Publication, 1927.

Coalter, Milton J., John M. Mulder, and Louis B. Weeks, eds. *The Pluralistic Vision: Presbyterian and Mainstream Protestant Education and Leadership*. Louisville, Ky.: Westminster/John Knox Press, 1992.

Counts, Michael L. "History of Harlequin Theatre." *The 75th Anniversary of Harlequin Theatre at Lyon College*. Batesville, Ark.: Lyon College, 2000.

Crider, Randall M. "G.I. Joe Goes to School: The World War II Veterans of Arkansas College." Unpublished senior thesis. Arkansas (Lyon) College, May 1994.

Cummins, Light Townsend. *Austin College: A Sesquicentennial History, 1849–1999*. Austin, Tex.: Eakin Press, 1999.

Cunningham, Rodger. *Apples on the Flood: The Southern Mountain Experience*. Knoxville: University of Tennessee Press, 1987.

Daniel, Pete. *Deep'n as It Come: The 1927 Mississippi River Flood*. 1977. Reprint, Fayetteville: University of Arkansas Press, 1996.

DeVane, William Clyde. *Higher Education in Twentieth-Century America*. Cambridge, Mass.: Harvard University Press, 1965.

Donovan, Timothy P., Willard B. Gatewood Jr., and Jeannie M. Whayne, eds. *The Governors of Arkansas: Essays in Political Biography*, 2nd edition. Fayetteville: University of Arkansas Press, 1995.

Dougan, Michael B. *Arkansas Odyssey: The Saga of Arkansas from Prehistoric Times to Present*. Little Rock, Ark.: Rose Publishing Co., 1994.

———. "Henry Gaston Bunn." *Dictionary of North Carolina Biography*. Vol. I. William S. Powell, ed. Chapel Hill: University of North Carolina Press, 1979. 270.

Executive Committee of Christian Education and Ministerial Relief of the Presbyterian Church in the United States. *Our Presbyterian Educational Institutions*. Louisville, Ky.: Presbyterian Church in the United States, 1914.

Frost, Dan R. *Thinking Confederates: Academia and the Idea of Progress in the New South*. Knoxville: University of Tennessee Press, 2000.

Gaston, Paul M. *The New South Creed: A Study in Southern Mythmaking*. New York: Knopf, 1970.

Goodchild, Lester F., and Harold S. Wechsler, eds. *The History of Higher Education*. ASHE Readers Series, 2nd edition. Needham Heights, Mass.: Simon & Schuster, 1997.

Griffith, Nancy S. "Aaron Woodruff Lyon: Pioneer Educator, Citizen and Christian Gentleman." *Independence County Chronicle* 35 (October 1993–January 1994): 52–67.

———. "Michael Shelby Kennard." *Independence County Chronicle* 38 (October 1996–January 1997): 33–52.

Hall, John Gladden. *Henderson State College: The Methodist Years, 1890–1929*. Arkadelphia, Ark.: Henderson State College Alumni Association, 1974.

Hawkins, Hugh. *Banding Together: The Rise of National Associations in American Higher Education, 1887–1950*. Baltimore, Md.: Johns Hopkins University Press, 1992.

Hempstead, Fay. *Historical Review of Arkansas*, 3 volumes. Chicago: Lewis, 1911.

———. *A Pictorial History of Arkansas*. St. Louis, Mo.: N. D. Thompson, 1890.

Herndon, Dallas T., ed. *Centennial History of Arkansas*, 3 volumes. Chicago: S. J. Clarke, 1922.

Hofstadter, Richard, and C. DeWitt Hardy. *The Development and Scope of Higher Education in the United States*. New York: Columbia University Press, 1952.

Jeffery, Mrs. Carter. "Lt. Coffin and the Confederate Silver." *Independence County Chronicle* 3 (July 1962): 35–39.

Jeffery, Virginia Fitzhugh, and Lucy Jeffery Yeager. *A Rich and Lasting Blessing: A 150 Year History of the First Presbyterian Church of Batesville, Arkansas*. Newport, Ark.: Craig Printing, 1992.

Lambda-Iota Chapter Alumni Association. "History of the Lambda-Iota Chapter of Kappa Sigma." *http://www.wlrcreative.com/LyonKappaSig/history.html*.

Lankford, George E. "Arkansas College: The Expansionist Years." *Independence County Chronicle* 29 (October 1987–January 1988): 3–13.

Leflar, Robert A. *The First 100 Years: Centennial History of the University of Arkansas*. Fayetteville: University of Arkansas Foundation, Inc., 1972.

Lester, James E., Jr. *Hendrix College: A Centennial History*. Conway, Ark.: River Road Press, 1984.

———. *The People's College: Little Rock Junior College and Little Rock University, 1927–1969*. Little Rock, Ark.: August House, 1987.

Levine, David O. *The American College and the Culture of Aspiration, 1915–1940*. Ithaca, N.Y.: Cornell University Press, 1986.

Leyburn, James G. *The Scotch-Irish: A Social History*. Chapel Hill: University of North Carolina Press, 1962.

Lindsey-Allen, Barbara. "The Death and Resurrection of Arkansas College." *Independence County Chronicle* 29 (October 1987–January 1988): 14–21.

Lynn, Robert Wood. "'The Survival of Recognizably Protestant Colleges': Reflections on Old-Line Protestantism, 1950–1990." George M. Marsden and Bradley J. Longfield, eds. *The Secularization of the Academy*. New York: Oxford University Press, 1992. 9–45.

Marsden, George M. "The Soul of the American University: An Historical Overview." George M.

Marsden and Bradley J. Longfield, eds. *The Secularization of the Academy*. New York: Oxford University Press, 1992. 170–94.

———. *The Soul of the American University: From Protestant Establishment to Established Nonbelief*. New York: Oxford University Press, 1994.

McCandless, Amy Thompson. *The Past in the Present: Women's Higher Education in the Twentieth-Century American South*. Tuscaloosa: University of Alabama Press, 1999.

McGinnis, A. C. "Arkansas College, 1872–1972." *Independence County Chronicle* 14 (October 1972): 3–61.

———. "A History of Independence County, Arkansas." *Independence County Chronicle* 17 (April 1976).

———. "Liquor Legislation and Independence County." *Independence County Chronicle* 18 (July 1977): 32–37.

McGinnis, Clyde. "Arkansas College." *Arkansas Historical Quarterly* 31 (Autumn 1972): 234–45.

McWhiney, Grady. *Cracker Culture: Celtic Ways in the Old South*. Tuscaloosa: University of Alabama Press, 1988.

Moneyhon, Carl H. *Arkansas and the New South, 1874–1929*. Histories of Arkansas Series. Fayetteville: University of Arkansas Press, 1997.

Morgan, Gordon D., and Izola Preston. *The Edge of Campus: A Journal of the Black Experience at the University of Arkansas*. Fayetteville: University of Arkansas Press, 1990.

Morrow, John P., Jr. "The Dr. Allen House: The Building and Its Owners." *Independence County Chronicle* 5 (April 1964): 52–58.

O'Connor, Frank. *An Only Child*. 1961. Reprint, Syracuse, N.Y.: Syracuse University Press, 1997.

Olson, Keith W. *The G.I. Bill, the Veterans, and the Colleges*. Lexington: University Press of Kentucky, 1974.

Paisley, H. L., ed. *Centennial History of Presbyterianism (U.S.) in Arkansas*. N.P.: 1954.

Potts, David B. "American Colleges in the Nineteenth Century: From Localism to Denominationalism." *History of Education Quarterly* 11 (1971): 363–80.

Ray, Celeste. *Highland Heritage: Scottish Americans in the American South*. Chapel Hill: University of North Carolina Press, 2001.

Reynolds, John Hugh, and David Yancey Thomas. *History of the University of Arkansas*. Fayetteville: University of Arkansas, 1910.

Reynolds, John Hugh, ed. *Publications of the Arkansas Historical Association*, 4 volumes. Little Rock, Fayetteville, and Conway, Ark.: Arkansas Historical Association, 1906–1917.

Roper, James E. "Southwestern at Memphis, 1848–1981." *Tennessee Historical Quarterly* 41 (Fall 1982).

Rudolph, Frederick. *Curriculum: A History of the American Undergraduate Course of Study since 1636*. San Francisco: Jossey-Bass, 1977.

———. *The American College and University: A History*. 1962. Reprint, Athens: University of Georgia Press, 1990.

Speight, Clarence Warren. *Brief History of the Campus and Buildings of Austin Peay State College and Southwestern Presbyterian University*. Clarksville, Tenn.: Austin Peay State College, 1962.

Synod of Arkansas, Presbyterian Church in the United States. *The History of Presbyterianism in Arkansas, 1828–1902*. Little Rock: Arkansas Democrat, 1902.

Tebbetts, Diane. *The West Years: 1972–1988*. Batesville: Arkansas College, 1990.

Tewksbury, Donald G. *The Founding of American Colleges and Universities before the Civil War*. 1932. Reprint, Hamden, Conn.: Archon Books, 1965.

Thompson, Ernest Trice. *Presbyterians in the South*. 3 volumes. Richmond, Va.: John Knox Press, 1973.

Wasson, Michele Roussel. "Gem of the Ozarks: A History of Mountain Home College, 1890–1934." M.A. thesis. University of Arkansas, 1982.

Winterer, Caroline. *The Culture of Classicism: Ancient Greece and Rome in American Intellectual Life, 1780–1910*. Baltimore, Md.: Johns Hopkins University Press, 2002.

Woodward, C. Vann. *Origins of the New South, 1877–1913*. Baton Rouge: Louisiana State University Press, 1951.

INDEX

Aberdeen Development Corporation, 295–96, 297, 312, 341, 354
Aberdeen Services Corporation, 296
Aberdeen University, 341
Abraham, Lucien, 111, 117, 150
Academic Search Consultation Service, 355
A. C. Crazies, 304
accreditation: efforts toward, 121–23, 129, 132, 195–96, 209–10, 213, 214–15, 216, 217, 218, 219
Adair, William, 302
Adams, Clarence, 322
Adamson, John, 64
Adler, Simon, 12, 38, 40
Agnes Scott College, 207, 222, 254, 255, 349, 355, 419n. 52
Alabama, 7, 8; University of, ix, 224, 237
Albright, Mac, 115
alcohol and dormitory visitation policies: liberalization of, 239, 264, 280, 330–31
Alexander, Bill, 272
Allen, John F., 8, 10, 12, 18, 20, 21, 37, 38, 50, 397n. 9, 398n. 36, 399n. 40
Alpha Chi, 245
Alpha Epsilon. *See* literary societies, L'Etoile Society
Alpha Epsilon Quartet, 104
Alpha Phi. *See* literary societies, L'Etoile Society
Alpha Psi Omega, 106
Alphin, Hazel, 225, 418n. 33
Alphin, Hendrick, 418n. 33
Alphin Building, 225, 239, 308–9
Alumni Association, 28
Alumni Council, 263, 339
Alumni Hall, 28, 35, 44, 53, 58, 62, 63, 65, 93, 100, 103, 104, 105, 140, 170, 172, 193, 206, 243, 353
Amateur Athletic Union (AAU), 160, 161, 162, 247, 420n. 82, 425n. 100
American Association of University Professors, 264, 327
American Association of University Women, 264
American Baptist Convention, 316
American Southern Trust Company, 141
Amherst College, 8
Amis, Lewis D., 71
ancient languages, 12, 23, 43, 49, 66, 67, 86, 120, 251, 402n. 19
Anderson, Rev. Frank, 138
Anderson, Wooten, 223, 230, 248
Anderson County, South Carolina, xiii, 45
Arkadelphia, Ark., 19, 38, 63, 73, 108, 113, 169, 175, 199, 200, 223, 283
Arkadelphia Methodist College, 46. *See also* Henderson-Brown College; Henderson College
Arkansas: higher education in, ix, 5, 6–7, 14, 121–22, 269, 274, 287, 343, 351, 359, 362; state of Presbyterianism in, xiii, 2–3, 14, 181; poverty in, 6; University of, 6, 84, 97, 105, 123, 129, 138, 148, 157, 195, 196, 213, 231, 237, 250, 252, 261, 291; state of education system in, 91, 120–21, 164, 181, 232, 292
Arkansas A & M, 237, 247.
Arkansas A, M & N, 237
Arkansas Association of Christian Colleges, 94
Arkansas Association of Teachers of Speech Festival, 106
Arkansas Baptist College, 360
Arkansas Best Corporation, 318
Arkansas Business Leaders Symposium, 325
Arkansas College (Fayetteville), 6
Arkansas College Athletic Association, 61, 64, 65
Arkansas College Bulletin, 267
Arkansas College Expansion Program, 131–32, 134
Arkansas College Magazine, 33, 44, 58–59, 60, 61, 63, 65
Arkansas College Monograph Series, 296, 424n. 75
Arkansas Collegiate Soccer League, 246
Arkansas Council of Independent Colleges and Universities, 282
Arkansas Cumberland College, 94, 107, 401n. 11. *See also* College (University) of the Ozarks
Arkansas Democrat, 297, 337
Arkansas Democrat-Gazette, 323, 342
Arkansas Eastman, 283
Arkansas Education Association, 91
Arkansas Experiment in Teacher Education (AETE), 213–14, 231

Arkansas Folklore Education Consortium, 296
Arkansas Forensic League, 94, 95
Arkansas Foundation of Associated Colleges (AFAC), 215–16, 217, 218, 219, 417n. 17
Arkansas Gazette, 24, 47, 201, 202, 296, 297, 425n. 90
Arkansas Governor's School, 311, 350
Arkansas Industrial University, 6, 7, 15. *See also* Arkansas, University of
Arkansas Intercollegiate Conference (AIC), 110, 191, 192, 239, 246, 247, 248, 306–7, 308; dissolution of, 334–35
Arkansas Literary and Debating Society, 30
Arkansas-Little Rock, University of, 307
Arkansas Little Theatre Tournament, 106
Arkansas Normal College, 46
Arkansas Power & Light, 295
Arkansas Presbytery, xviii, 5, 7, 8–9, 18, 19, 23, 26, 39, 182, 397n. 8
Arkansas School for Math and Sciences, 350
Arkansas Scottish Cultural Society, 298
Arkansas Scottish Festival, 298, 427n. 46
Arkansas State Athletic Association, 61, 62, 63
Arkansas State (College) University, 237, 267, 274, 307, 308, 338. *See also* First District A & M; First District State Agricultural School
Arkansas State Normal School, 62
Arkansas State Teachers College, 110, 113, 160, 162, 193, 237, 246. *See also* Arkansas State Normal School; Central Arkansas, University of
Arkansas Synod. *See* Synod of Arkansas (PCUS)
Arkansas Tech University, 110, 160, 193, 237, 247, 334
Arkansas Women's Extramural Sports Association, 308
Arkansas Women's Intercollegiate Sports Association, 308
Arnold, Fred, 216, 221, 225, 227
Arnold, Tom, 240
Arts and Sciences Club, 119
Ashley-Lewis Concert & Recital Series, 305
Ashmore, Harry, 296
athletics, 33, 59, 60–65, 106–17, 246–48, 306–8, 333–35; men's basketball, 35, 62–63, 113–14, 116, 159–62, 191–92, 246–48, 306–8, 333–34; football, 60, 63–65, 107–11, 116, 145, 149, 192–93; baseball, 61–62, 111–13, 191, 306, 333; track and field, 65, 114, 116, 306; tennis, 65, 114–15, 116, 191; cross country, 65, 246, 306; golf, 115, 246; women's basketball, 116, 308, 334, 425n. 100; intramural, 116–17, 190–91, 246; bowling, 246; soccer, 246, 306, 333, 420n. 80; swimming, 306; volleyball, 308
Augusta, Ark., 13, 21, 182
Aurora College, 196
Austin, Brad, 336
Austin College, 2, 69, 70, 78, 136, 222, 268, 271, 274, 276, 312, 314, 321, 360
Austin Presbyterian Theological Seminary, 89
Au-Young, Kenneth, 189

Balch, James Vernon, 250, 300, 421n. 86
Ball, Lois, 105–6, 117, 141, 149, 159, 179, 189
Ballard, H. Gerald, 414n. 71
Banker, Dennis, 245
Banks, A. B., 131, 136, 141
Baptists, 12, 23, 235; in Arkansas, 2, 67, 182, 231
Baptist Student Union, 179, 182, 242
Barker, Catherine, 119, 409n. 99
Barker, Lincoln, 102, 117, 118–19, 121, 145
Barnett, Catherine "Kitty" (Robertson), 93, 137, 138, 141, 404n. 86, 408n. 58
Barnett, Charles W., 142
Barnett, Ira Nelson "Nels," III, 137, 138, 139, 141, 143, 144, 145, 150, 151, 166, 170, 174, 177, 200, 201–2, 222, 255, 283, 404n. 86, 411n. 45, 411n. 49, 429n. 5
Barr, John T., Jr., 178
Barr, Rev. John T., Sr., 175, 180, 188, 203
Barr, Ruby, 188
Barron, Enid, 159
Barry, Capt. W. L., 83
Bartlett, Eugene, 159
Barton, Clark N., 273, 290, 301, 321
Barton, Mary (Perkins), 273, 290, 301, 321
Barton Apartments, 273
Bass, Beverly, 308
Bates, Robert, 215
Batesville, Ark., ix, 11, 15, 18, 19, 22, 26, 28, 34, 36, 47, 49, 60, 61, 63, 64, 65, 75, 126, 159, 177, 217, 243, 247, 259, 266, 274, 305, 343; Presbyterian Church in xv–xvi, 2–3, 5, 8, 9, 14, 20, 21, 23, 48, 69, 134, 252, 270, 342, 416n. 11; demographics of, xvi; geography of, xvii–xviii, 45, 180, 183, 230; education in, xviii, 6–7, 8, 94, 140, 141, 142, 293, 323; support for Arkansas/Lyon College in, 8, 9, 12, 20, 37–38, 48, 52, 53, 69, 71–72, 73, 81, 133–34, 138, 143, 151, 163, 166, 178, 200–201; Chamber of Commerce of, 83, 133–34, 150, 158, 200, 201, 277; support for athletics in, 111, 112, 113, 115, 145, 192; First National Bank of, 115; Citizens'

Committee of, 138, 139, 144, 145, 150, 411n. 49; Independence Federal Bank of, 295; Community Theater of, 305
Batesville Academy, xviii, 9
Batesville Academy for Young Ladies, xviii
Batesville Bee, 46
Batesville Business College, 71
Batesville Female Academy, xviii
Batesville Guard, 81, 143, 200, 407n. 38
Batesville Male Academy, xviii
Batesville Male and Female Academy, xviii, 8, 16
Baxter, Elisha, xviii
Baxter, Rev. Pat, 358
Bayless, Rev. Ed, 283
Beaver and Associates, 194, 195
Beck, Stafford, 198
Becknell Physical Education Building, James C., 228–29, 259, 265, 273, 296, 306, 307
Belhaven College, 233, 310
Bell, David, 289
Bellingrath, Ferd A., 283, 286
Bemis, Horace E., 143, 410n. 6
Benish, John, 102
Bentonville, Ark., ix, 9
Berea College, 50
Berry, Lloyd, 111
Berry College, 182
Bethel College, 112, 192, 193
Bevel, Harvey McKinley, 182–83
Bevens, Col. W. A., 20
Bevens, Joe, 61
Bible: academic study of, 12, 15, 43, 66, 144, 149, 187, 284, 289
Bizzell, Charles F., 42, 44, 45, 46, 50, 51, 62, 66, 68
Blackburn College, 217
Black River, 21
Black Rock, Ark., 114, 182
Black Student Association, 302
Blakely, Hunter, 200
Blandford, Eugene, 35, 45–46, 50, 55, 58, 60, 61, 62, 64, 65, 66, 70, 71, 118, 125, 155, 197, 270, 415n. 92, 418n. 38
Blandford Hall, 226, 418n. 38
Blevins, Kelvin, 307
Board, Veryl, 251, 301, 350
Boen, Don, 308
Boggs, David C., 7, 8, 9
Boggs, J. L., 80, 122, 126, 405n. 7
Boggs, Rev. Marion, 199
Bondurant, Barrie, 358
Bone, S. Marcus, 130, 166, 202, 222, 411n. 45
Boney, Rev. Bruce, 168, 195
Boone County, Ark., 22
Booth, Harvey, 102, 408n. 60
Boston University, 289
Bracy, Eugene, 35, 63
Bradley Manor, 342, 349, 350, 356
Bramlett, A. L., 118, 148, 409n. 95, 412n. 55
Brandywine Singers, 238
Braun, William H., 305
Bray, Kohn, 160, 162
Brenau College, 207
Brewer, Christene, 414n. 71
Bridewell, Capt. Charles A., 20, 32, 40–41
Bridewell, Charles P., 20, 108
Bridewell Medal, 32
Bridgers, Edward, 62
Brinkley, H. M., 223
Bristow, Bill, 264, 302
Broadwater, Peckham, 191
Brogdon, Ronnie, 248
Brooks, Katherine, 141
Brown, Adana, 405n. 10
Brown, Allan, 134–35, 137, 143, 145, 288, 405n. 10, 411n. 42, 418n. 38
Brown, Don K., 50, 55
Brown, Evander D. "Van," 23, 39, 73, 78, 80, 81, 405n. 9, 429n. 2
Brown, Jane Brookfield, 88, 118, 121
Brown, Jean, 216, 223, 257–58, 285, 286, 287, 290, 291, 301, 317, 405n. 10, 418n. 38
Brown, Josephine, 195, 301, 405n. 10, 418n. 38
Brown, J. Richard, 63, 65, 404n. 63
Brown, Max, 63, 404n. 63
Brown, Mitcheal, 237
Brown, Ray, 192, 193
Brown, Roberta (Dorr), 178, 188, 212, 250, 251, 261, 278, 286, 288, 292, 354, 421n. 86
Brown, Rosellen, 325
Brown, Thomas. R., 62, 65
Brown, W. C., Jr., 216, 223, 283, 286, 288, 290, 301, 347, 405n. 10, 418n. 38
Brown, W. C., Sr., 71, 82, 301, 405n. 10, 418n. 38
Brown Apartments, 273
Brown Chapel and Fine Arts Building, 216–17, 218, 222, 239, 241, 243, 259, 272, 304, 318, 341, 363, 418n. 38
Brown v. Board of Education of Topeka, Kansas, 237
Brubacher, John S., 14
Brunswick Foundation, 310
Bryan, R. C., 223, 301, 322, 418nn. 32, 38
Bryan, William Jennings, 77
Bryan, Willie, 223
Bryan Hall, 226
Bryan Lake, 273, 309, 418n. 32
Bryant, Ark., 247, 325

Bryant College, 356
Buchanan, Coach, 63
Budy, Andrea, 325
Bunch, Mrs. Leland, 87, 93
Bunn, Harry, 61, 400n. 62
Bunn, Judge Harry Gaston, 41, 50
Burns, Norman, 172
Burns, Robert, 298
Burns Nicht, 298
Burrow Cup, the Lawrence, 106
Burt, Dr. William J., 9, 397n. 9
Burton, Miss, 58
Bustin, Roberta, 251, 265, 290, 301, 328, 350, 358
Butler, Judge James W., 20, 22, 41, 197
Butler, Susie, 5, 20

Caddo Valley Academy, 180, 183, 188
Calaway, Robert Lee, 160, 161
Caldwell, Rev. J. L., 68
Cambridge, University of, 301
Camden, Ark., 19, 35, 83, 223, 224
Campbell, E. Fay, 200, 201, 202, 203
Campbell, W. W., 223
Campus Ministry Board, 283, 333
Cane Hill College, 6, 396n. 1
Cannon, Baxter B., 132
Career Development Center, 361
Carlton, Miriam, 106
Carnegie Foundation for the Advancement of Teaching, 360, 410n. 5; Council for Advancement and Support of Education (CASE), 328, 358
Carpenter, Roland, 302
Carpenter, Wesley, 114
Carroll College, 2, 312
Carter, Hodding, III, 296
Carter, Jimmy, 296
Carter, Minatree M., 25
Carvell, James "Slim," 114
Casey, Beulah, 404n. 74
Cash, Clarence, Jr., 238
Catt, Grace, 334
Cave City, Ark., 111, 160
Centenary College, 319, 360
Central Arkansas, University of, 274, 334
Central College (Iowa), 356
Central University (Indiana), 51
Central University (Kentucky), 14, 42, 45
Centre College, xiv, xv, 2, 14, 15, 17, 42, 310, 395n. 6
chapel attendance, 147; student protest against, 100, 241
Chicago, University of, 45, 72, 88, 119, 173, 184, 213, 409n. 95
Chlebak, George, 324, 358
Chow, Chun Wai, 190
Christian Brothers College, 64, 404n. 63
Christian Endeavor Society, 99, 138
Chunn, Dr. T. D., 20
Circle K, 245
Civilian Conservation Corps, 160
Civil Rights Movement, 237, 238
Claremont Graduate School, 301
classical curriculum, 14, 16–17, 24, 26, 43, 49, 66, 88, 251, 402n. 19
Cleland, John I., 42–47, 48, 60, 61, 63, 71, 73, 120, 402nn. 19, 29; post-presidential career of, 365–66
Clinton, Bill, 296, 311
Coccaro, John, 235
coeducation, 15–16, 67–68, 86
Coffin, Charles, 21, 56
Coffin, James P., 20, 21, 38, 41, 47, 50, 53, 56, 77, 96, 130, 165, 341, 406n. 15
Coffin, Maxwell, 21
Coffin Medal, 56–57, 137, 147, 248, 249
Coleman, Elijah, 238
Colgate College, 316
College Level Examination Program (CLEP), 266
College of William and Mary, 13, 23, 32, 45, 55, 61
College (University) of the Ozarks, 62, 94, 110, 113, 114, 115, 231, 233, 237, 246, 284, 334, 343, 417n. 17, 418n. 25, 420n. 80; discussions of merger with, 133, 136, 198–202, 206, 284–85. *See also* Arkansas Cumberland College
Collins, Rev. Ben, 283
Colorado, University of, 356
Colorado College, 279
Columbia Theological Seminary, xiv, 21, 395n. 6
Columbia University, 71, 88, 213, 301
Committee for Greater Access to Higher Education, 282
community college: establishment of in Batesville, 267, 275, 277, 293, 345
Compton, Van (Gore), 308
Conine, B. B., 65
Conine, Sonny, 191
Conner, Tillar, 114
Continuing Education, 267, 277–78, 287, 292–93, 299, 300, 311, 344, 345
Conway, Ark., 63, 95, 283
Cook, William Arthur, 50, 51
Coombs, Art, 35
Cooper, Gregory, 272
Cooper, Thomas E., 301, 358

Cooperative Education, 277
Cornell University, 17
Cort, Gen. Hugh, 215
Cossey, Bill, 248
Cotton Plant, Ark., 7, 9, 11
Couch, William T., 283, 286
Couch Gardens, 228, 239
Counts, Michael, 333
Covington, Dean, 329
Cox, LaVerne, 336
Cox, Martha Heasley, 325
Crane, Dr. J. B., 20, 22
Crawford, Chester, 95, 106
Creed, Travis "Pete," 114
Crockett, Rev. John, 151, 152, 157–59, 161, 163, 164, 165, 167, 170, 180, 181; post-presidential career of, 367
Crow, Darlene, 302
Cuff, Roger Penn, 148
Culver-Stockton College, 310
Cumberland Presbyterians, 51; in Arkansas, 2, 6
Cumberland University, 51
Cumnock Cup, 106
curriculum, 16–17, 24–25, 39–40, 43, 66–67, 72, 86–88, 117–21, 149–50, 171, 179, 187–88, 213–14, 251–52, 264–65, 274–77, 321–24, 426n. 16; secularization of, 43–44, 47, 277, 363, 398n. 27; role of music in, 68, 72, 85, 103–5, 149, 187, 322, 404n. 74; role of art in, 68, 214, 310, 404n. 74; role of home economics in, 87, 121, 187, 251; role of speech and expression in, 105–6; role of teacher education in, 121, 165, 188, 213–14, 289, 322–23, 361; role of business education in, 187, 214, 251, 322, 361; reorganization of, 210, 276, 321–24; role of general education (core) in, 213–14, 264, 276–77, 288–89, 323–24, 417n. 14; infusion of technical/professional courses/majors in, 264–65, 274, 275–76, 277, 289

Daffin, John B., 86, 88, 107, 115, 119, 167
Daffin Field, 107, 108, 110, 113, 114, 115, 191, 192, 252
Dagley and Associates, D. H., 287, 297
Dahlquist, John T., 288–89, 292, 294, 300, 311, 314, 317, 323, 324, 325, 328, 350, 429n. 6
Daniel Baker College, 78
Danville Theological Seminary, xiv, 7, 395n. 6
Dardanelle, Ark., 8
Davidson, Brownie, 171
Davidson College, 2, 14, 15, 21, 45, 80, 88, 128, 167, 172, 174, 176, 231, 316, 330, 342, 344
Davies, Samuel W., 7
Davis, Don, 284, 285
Davis, Fannie, 8, 12
Davis, Jefferson, 32
Davis, Rev. Roy L., 177, 199, 202, 203, 206, 207
Dawes, Thomas, 71
debate and oratory. *See* extracurriculum, role of debate and oratory in
Deener, Mrs. Samuel, 104
Derby, Larry, 283, 349, 359
Derby, Marilyn, 349, 359
Derby Center for Science and Mathematics, 359, 363
Des Arc, Ark., 5, 11, 218, 223
Dewey, John, 213
Dickinson College, 316
Dickison, Roland, 219, 416n. 8
Diehl, Charles, 206
Disciples of Christ (Church of Christ), 99, 235; in Arkansas, 2, 6, 182
Dixie Highway, 84
Dobson, Ella Myrl. *See* Shanks, Ella Myrl (Dobson)
Dobson, Iris, 106, 115
Dooley, Mrs. Otice C., 104
Dorr, R. C., 44, 72, 80
Downie, Blake, 101
Drake University, 356
Dramatic Club, 105, 106. *See also* Harlequin Little Theatre
Drew, Asa, 62
Drew County, Ark., 19, 23
Driftwood, Jimmy, 266, 409n. 99
DuBose, Mary, 297
Duke, Bernis, 415n. 78
Duke University, 207, 416n. 3
Dunklin, William H., 283, 291–92, 429n. 6
Durham, Carroll, 408n. 78

Earthlander Project, 424n. 75
East Arkansas Presbytery, 182, 203, 284
East Tennessee University. *See* Tennessee, University of
Ebersole, E. C., 8, 14
Edgar, Paul, 408n. 58
Edmondson, Charles, 185, 414n. 71
Edmondson, Rogers, 185
Edwards, John W., 222, 308
Edwards Dining Hall, 305, 308
Elcan, Harriet, 408n. 58
El Dorado, Ark., 80, 168, 177, 219, 225, 243, 273, 283, 290
Eliot, Charles W., 17

Emory University, 137
Emporia State University, 356
endowed faculty positions, 290, 300–301, 328
endowment: liquidation of, 135, 136, 137
Endrihs, Jim, 329
Engles, Jennifer, 420n. 76
enrollment, 26, 36, 39, 45, 46, 53, 72, 73, 74, 78, 84, 128, 131, 135, 144, 148, 156, 163, 171, 178, 184–85, 197, 208, 217, 225, 226, 230–31, 232, 233–34, 265, 270, 287, 299–300, 310, 314, 342–45, 350, 357, 359
Epworth League, 99, 407n. 52
Erskine College, 2, 207
Erwin, Maj. W. J., 72
Erwin Gymnasium, 63, 72, 85, 113
Ethridge, Lonnie, 113, 114, 408n. 78
Evans, Lester, 112
Evans, Malcolm, 138, 139
Evans, Pryor, 191
Evans, Rev. Henry C., 402n. 36
extracurriculum, 28–33, 54–56, 58–66, 159, 179, 189, 242–46, 304–5, 332–33; role of debate and oratory in, 94–95; role of music in, 103–5, 189, 243–45, 305; role of speech and theater in, 105–6, 149, 179, 189, 243, 305, 333. *See also* athletics; fraternities and sororities; literary societies; Young Men's Christian Association (YMCA)

faculty governance systems, 263, 279, 356, 358
Fagg, Dan, 251, 270, 301
Fagg, Jane, 251, 276, 294, 301
Fahl, B. Elwood, 186
Farina, Carl, 302
Fayetteville, Ark., 6, 7, 106, 177
Federal Emergency Relief Administration, 145, 149
Ferncliff, 284
Ferrill, Charles, 404n. 63
Ferrill, Irene, 122, 406n. 20
Ferrill, James, 97
financial struggles, 18, 19, 40, 41, 44, 47, 48, 52–53, 69, 73, 74, 81–82, 125–45, 147–52, 158, 165, 173, 178, 197–98, 203, 208, 218, 267, 269, 286, 314, 342, 346–48, 350, 360
First District A & M, 110, 112, 113, 114, 115. *See also* Arkansas State (College) University; First District State Agricultural School
First District State Agricultural School, 64, 404n. 63. *See also* Arkansas State (College) University; First District A & M
Fiser, Paul "Red," 110, 113
Fishback, William, 41
Fitzhugh, Fred, 404n. 63
Fitzhugh, Lucy, 71
Floyd, Sharon, 420n. 76
Flying Squadron, 141
Ford Foundation, 213, 214
Fordyce, Ark., 50, 52, 136
foreign students, 189–90, 358
Forensic Council, 94
Forrest City, Ark., 223, 308
Fort Smith, Ark., 283, 318
Forward Education Movement, 91
Fowler, Jack, 108
Frank, Robert, 271
fraternities and sororities, 95–98, 149, 174, 245–46, 303–4; B.E.L.L., 96; Beta Beta Beta, 96; Gamma Epsilon Theta, 96; H.B.K., 96; K.A.T., 96; Zeta Chi, 96; Alpha Mu Alpha, 96, 97; Eta Beta Kappa, 96, 97; Delta Kappa Sigma, 96, 97, 98, 407n. 49; Beta Sigma Omicron, 97, 98; Alpha Lambda Tau, 97, 98, 407n. 49; Delta Theta, 98; Kappa Kappa Alpha, 98, 149, 238, 242, 246, 303, 333; Delta Sigma Chi, 174; Sigma Alpha Sigma, 174, 242, 246, 303; Sigma Phi Omega, 245; Chi Beta Phi, 245, 246, 303; Gamma Delta Iota, 245, 246, 303; Kappa Sigma, 246, 303, 333; Tau Kappa Epsilon, 246, 303, 333; Omicron Eta Sigma, 303; Alpha Xi Delta, 303, 333; Zeta Omega, 303, 333; Delta Upsilon, 333; Phi Mu, 333; Phi Theta Gamma, 333
Frierson, Annie, 122
Frierson, Daniel M., 45–46, 50, 51, 60, 61, 67, 71, 74, 78, 80, 88, 118, 122, 155
Frost Foundation, 324
Fulbright, Deborah, 266
Fulbright, J. William, 296
Fulbright, Ruth, 420n. 79, 421n. 86
Fun and Profit Society, 33
fund-raising, 40, 41, 44, 46, 51–53, 81–82, 85, 127, 128, 134–35, 141, 145, 178, 215–17, 262–63; Expansion Campaign, 194–95, 197, 199, 202, 216; Loyalty Fund, 209, 218; ADVANCE Arkansas College Campaign, 216–17, 224, 229, 417n. 19; Progress Fund, 218–19, 223, 229, 235, 262, 269, 286; United for Christ Campaign, 224, 418n. 33; Forward Arkansas College Expansion Campaign, 227, 230; Challenge of the Decade Campaign, 286; Direction Toward Distinction Campaign, 300, 308; Universal Campaign, 311–12, 348; Past as Prologue Campaign, 348; Fulfilling the

Promise: The Campaign for Lyon College, 348–49, 357, 359

Galbraith, Russ, 325
Galloway College, 46, 133
Gamut Club, 58
Garner, Carl, 160
Garner, Terry, 307, 334
Garrett, William T., 118
Gateway Vocational-Technical School, 277, 345. *See also* University of Arkansas Community College-Batesville (UACCB)
Gatling, Randy, 334
General Education Board, 53, 79, 127, 209, 410n. 5
general education movement, 213–14
George, Absalom, 419n. 60
George Peabody College, 140, 198, 415n. 101
George Washington University, 88
German National Bank, 50
Gernert, M. L., 283
G.I. Bill, 156, 184–85, 186, 188–89
Giboney, W. A., 23
Gibson, George, 408n. 60
Gitz, Bradley, 328
Glaros, Glen, 297
Glasgow University, 297
Glass, Michael, 335
Glover, Arlis, 160
Gonser and Gerber, 226, 233
Goodlad, John, 322
Goodwin, Eugene R., 10
Governor's Scholar program, 311
Graham, Fred, 296
Graham, Lois (Patterson), 296
Graham, Otis, 296
Graham, Ralph M., 297, 298
Grammar, J. F., 411n. 45
Graves, Rev. Fred, 70
Gray, Clint, 408n. 76
Gray, Dorothy Hope (Landis), 189, 243, 251, 279, 301, 305, 420n. 76, 421n. 86
Gray, Laman, 102, 106
Gray, Mary, 408n. 60
Gray, Paul, 189
Greek. *See* ancient languages
Greater Arkansas College Program. *See* Arkansas College Expansion Program
Greek organizations. *See* fraternities and sororities
Greek Medal, 32
Green, Maj. John F., 23
Green, R. K., 23, 399n. 54
Greenberg, Paul, 323
Greeneville College. *See* Tusculum College
Greenfield, John, 404n. 63
Greers Ferry Lake, 263, 420n. 76
Gregerson, Robert, 358
Gregg, Eugene Stuart, 71
Gregorie, Anne King, 148, 412n. 55
Griffith, John V., 313, 354, 358; hiring and background of, 316–17; presidency of, 318–51; and Strategic Plan, 319–24, 328–30, 331–32, 336, 339, 342–44, 348, 349, 351; and the name change, 337–42; post-presidential career of, 368
Griffith, Nancy, 316, 317, 342
Grinnell College, 314
Grisham, Ewin, 108, 408n. 76

Haddock, Glen, 252, 416n. 10
Haden, Ernest F., 117
Hadley, O. A., 9
Haizlip, Beth, 308
Hall, June, 169, 173, 176
Hamilton, Luke, xiii
Hammerschmidt, Herman, 236
Hammett, Doris, 106, 189, 243, 250, 300, 421n. 86
Hampden-Sydney College, 7, 39, 78, 81, 88, 397n. 7
Handford, Charlie, 353
Haney, Jim, 248
Harding College (University), 110, 115, 417n. 17, 419n. 52
Hardy, Corinne McCombs, 416n. 11
Harington, Donald, 327
Harlequin Little Theatre, 106, 159, 179, 189, 243, 271, 305, 333
Harrin, Frank H., 186, 196, 250, 416n. 6
Harris, Jim, 247
Harrison, Galloway, 107
Hartford, University of, 356
Harvard University, 17, 21, 213, 289, 291, 295, 312, 335, 354; Business School of, 223; Law School of, 291, 302; Divinity School of, 316
Haverford College, 167, 201, 233, 253
Hawkins, Hugh, 121
hazing, 103, 158–59, 189
Heard, George, 408n. 78
Heasley, Therrill, 95
Heasley Lecture Series, Leila Lenore, 325, 327
Heather from the Hill, 250
Heat-Moon, William Least, 327
Helena, Ark., ix, xv, 62, 70, 91, 307
Helmke, Heidi, 294
Henderson, Robert, 11

Henderson, Vincent H., 9, 11
Henderson-Brown College, 64, 84, 94, 107, 114, 133. *See also* Arkadelphia Methodist College; Henderson College
Henderson College, 62. *See also* Arkadelphia Methodist College; Henderson-Brown College
Henderson State (College) University, 248, 307
Hendrix College, 46, 48, 84, 94, 122, 123, 127, 128, 129, 133, 231, 233, 237, 274, 285, 311, 314, 319, 337, 343, 350, 360, 361, 417n. 17; athletic competition with, 61, 62, 63, 108, 109, 111, 113, 114, 115, 116, 192, 334, 420nn. 80, 82
Henry, Rev. Alexander, 152, 162–63, 193
Herold, Amos, 416n. 6
Hersh, Seymour, 296
Hess, Herman, 251
Hicks, Elizabeth, 283
Hicks, Rev. Basil, 222
Hicks, Susan, 420n. 76
Higher Education Facilities Act, 227
Highland Cottage, 97, 159, 225
Highlander, 178, 183, 236, 238, 240, 241, 243, 272, 280, 297, 302, 303, 305
Highsmith, Sam, 283
Hill, Gen. Daniel H., 15
Hillerman, Ida M., 71, 84
Hillsdale Baptist College, 333
Hodge, Lois, 408n. 58
Hodges, Kaneaster, Jr., 283, 296
Hodges Lecture Series, Kaneaster, Sr., 296
Hoffman and Ryan, 38
Hofstadter, Richard, 23
Hogan, Pat, 111
Hoke, Charles J., 283, 348
Hoke-McCain Hall, 332, 335, 348
Holloway, Carolyn, 314
Holloway, Graham, 283, 286, 314, 325, 340, 349, 429n. 6
Holloway Theatre, 333, 350
Holmes, Bert E., 301, 311, 317, 319, 324, 358
Holmes, E. Fletcher, 419n. 41
Holmes, Mary Fuller, 419n. 41
Holmes, P. K., 283, 332
Holyer, Robert K., 301, 317, 328, 354, 358
Home Finance Administration, 224
Homesley, Johnny, 243, 251, 305
honorary degrees: granting of, 25–26, 36, 43
Honors International Studies Program, 294, 324, 325. *See also* Nichols Study-Travel Program
honor system, 72, 101–2, 149, 159, 174, 189, 329–30, 408n. 58
Hope, Ark., 20, 40, 52, 63, 104, 111, 175, 218
Horne, Rev. T. J., 25, 39, 42, 77, 396n. 1
Horton, Marie, 425n. 100
Hot Springs, Ark., 134, 140, 145, 195, 216, 257, 283
Houston, Le Roy D., 396n. 1
Howard, Charlie, 307
Howell, Rev. F. M., 19
Howell, Vann, 135, 136, 139
Hudson, Henry, 111
Hughes, Rev. Charles "Buddy," 283
Human Resources Center, 267, 275, 277
Husband, Robert, 288
Huser, J. Marshall, 283
Huser Track and Field, J. Marshall, 298, 306
Hutchins, Robert M., 184, 213
Hutchison, Jerry, 306, 308, 334

Illinois, University of, 356
Independence College. *See* School of Independent Living
Independence County, Ark., xvi, 7, 10, 26, 46, 53, 61, 74, 92, 97, 98, 149, 166, 173, 232, 239, 243, 267, 295, 330, 337, 402n. 28
Independence Hall, 85, 90, 97, 113, 126, 127, 129, 130, 144, 159, 163, 164, 171, 172, 178, 185, 186, 191, 196, 208, 212, 218, 222, 224, 225, 226–27, 246, 252, 264
Index, 58, 59–60, 62, 63, 92, 96, 101, 113, 115, 174, 179, 192, 242, 297, 403 nn. 44, 58, 407n. 38
Ingrum, William and Jonathan, 400n. 65
Interdenominational Council, 189
International Relations Club, 189
International Student Organization, 358
Irving, James, 115
Irving, William "Spider," 115
Izard County, Ark., ix, xviii, 39, 182, 191

Jackson, Charles, 307
Jackson, Cliff, 245, 249
Jackson, Elliott, 307
Jacksonport, Ark., xviii, 7, 8, 9, 11, 26, 30
Jacobe, Dennis, 271
Jamestown, Ark., ix, 46
Jamison, A. W., 138
January term, 265, 294, 324, 335
Jeffery, H. Carter, 222, 267, 283
Jenkins, Kevin, 334
Jennings, Clara M., 301, 302
Jinske, Henry, 173
Joblin, Miller, 61
Joblin, William J., 8
John Brown University, 231, 233, 308, 417n. 17, 419n. 52
Johns, A. Deane, 71

Johns Hopkins University, 42, 43, 45, 46, 48, 119
Johnson, Allen N., 50, 402n. 35
Johnson, James, Jr., 97
Johnson, Kevin, 307
Johnson, Raymond, 406n. 14
Johnson, Rev. J. V., 108
Johnson, Virginia Rose, 409n. 96
Johnston, Bruce, 331, 332, 358
Johnston, Ray, 404n. 63
Jones, Brenda, 306
Jones, H. G. M. "Gary," 189
Jones, Horace, 406n. 14
Jones, Orville, 416n. 10
Jones, Rev. Arthur G., 39, 69, 399n. 53
Jonesboro, Ark., 64, 65, 227, 283
Jordan, Nell, 68
Justus, Cecil "Red," 114

Kansas State Teachers College (Emporia State University), 261, 262, 266
Kansas State University, 301
Kansas Wesleyan College, 289, 294
Kappa Gamma, 95
Kasper, Bob, 245
Kaufman, Marcus, 192, 193
Keck Foundation, W. M., 324
Kelley, Kirk, 333
Kelley's Shamrock Room, 200
Kelley-Wyatt's, 353
Kelly, Alfred, 112, 408n. 58
Kelly, Tracy, 285
Kennard, Michael Shelby, ix, x, xviii
Kennedy, D. H., 11
Kennedy, Edward, 296
Kennedy, Joe, 61
Kennedy, Leland, 61
Kennedy, Rev. A. R., 19, 21–22, 53, 399n. 53
Kennedy, Rev. J. Leland, xiv
Kennedy, Sallie J., xviii
Kentucky, 21, 42, 45
Kerr, William W., 9, 397n. 9
Ketz, Wesley, 205
Key, Joe, 294
Kieffer, Ryland, 334
King, Harry, 186–87, 189, 210, 250, 416n. 6, 416n. 8
King College, 43, 172
Kinser, Dick, 237, 239, 241, 252, 421n. 86
Kinser, Mary, 252, 421n. 86
Kirk, Virginia, 212, 300, 421n. 86
Kirkin o' the Tartans, 298
K.K.K. Club, 95
Knott, Robert, 280, 288
Knox, Sam Y. T., 108
Knox College, 2, 226
Korean War, 193, 197, 208
Kresge Foundation, 308, 309
Kwok, Hing Yan, 190

Lacrosse Collegiate Institute, ix, x, 39
Lacy, Beverly Tucker, 80
Lacy, George, 405n. 6
Lacy, William S., 50, 52–53, 55, 74, 93, 95, 105, 111, 125, 127, 143, 157, 167, 169, 172, 354, 405n. 6, 407n. 51, 411n. 45, 412n. 66; efforts as president, 78–82, 83–84, 85–88, 122, 126, 144–45, 147–51, 156; resignation of, 89–90, 149, 151; post-presidential career of, 366
Lads, 305, 420n. 76
Lambuth College, 192
LaMotte, Louis C., 170
Lankford, George E., 296, 301, 317, 321, 323, 328
Lassies, 243–45, 298, 305, 420n. 76
Latham, Rev. James E., 43, 47, 49, 53, 429n. 1
Latin. *See* ancient languages
Lawrence, William Conway, 414n. 71
Lawrence County, Ark., 21, 39, 59, 182
Lawson, Don, 94
Lawson, Rev. John Franklin, 51, 134, 402n. 33
Learning Enrichment Acceleration Program, 292
Le Circle Français, 117
Lester, Margaret Berry (Pruden), 145, 251, 421n. 85, 421nn. 86, 88
Lewis, Bart L., 328, 335, 358
Lewisburg Seminary, 406n. 25
Li, Fook Kong, 190
Liberal Arts Teacher Education Program, 322–23
library, 32, 39, 44, 50, 71, 85, 122, 157, 169, 173, 188, 196, 209, 212, 215–16, 329, 406n. 20, 417n. 18; Mabee Learning Resources Center, 227–28, 272, 304, 329; Mabee-Simpson Library, 329
Life Service Band (Alliance), 99, 182
literary societies, 30, 44, 55, 92, 93–94, 325, 403n. 44; Philomathean Society, 30, 32, 33, 55, 60, 63, 93, 94, 95, 98, 400n. 76, 403n. 44, 407n. 51; L'Etoile Society, 30, 33, 55, 93, 95, 98, 403n. 44; Delta Sigma, 32; Erosophic Society, 32, 55, 63, 93, 94, 95, 98, 325, 333, 400n. 76, 403n. 44, 407nn. 50, 51; Delta Rho, 93, 98; Athaeneum Society, 400n. 76; Clionian Society, 403n. 44
Little Rock, Ark., xiii, xiv, xv, 6, 21, 26, 28, 35, 38, 41, 47, 50, 51, 53, 60, 62, 63, 65,

67–68, 79, 90, 104, 111, 131, 135, 145, 151, 155, 168, 191, 199, 200, 203, 215, 216, 218, 224, 227, 237, 243, 257, 283, 284–85, 295, 296, 319, 340, 341; Second Presbyterian Church of, 19, 22, 138, 288; Worthen Bank in, 130, 258; First Presbyterian Church of, 138, 142, 151, 163; University, 307
Little Rock College, 64, 107, 112
Lively, Rev. Bob, 283
Lockhart, Malcolm, 174
Logan, John, 347, 358
Long, Callie P. Kennedy, xiv, xviii, 155
Long, Eugene, 23, 26, 32, 33, 34, 36, 45, 47, 48, 52, 53, 60, 63, 67, 71, 74, 77, 78, 81, 88, 90, 94, 101, 102, 115, 117, 118, 125, 126, 141, 144, 155, 209, 290, 397n. 19, 409n. 96; efforts as president of, 38, 41, 49, 65–66, 69; resignations of, 39, 41–42, 50–51, 69–70; post-presidential career of, 365
Long, Irene, 397n. 19
Long, Isaac J., ix, x, xiii–xiv, xvi, xviii, 2, 5, 6, 11, 12, 15, 21, 22–23, 24, 25, 26, 32, 33–34, 35, 36, 37, 39, 40, 49, 60, 67, 77, 86, 100, 154, 155, 174, 206, 230, 260, 282, 341, 353, 362–63; and the founding of Arkansas College, 7–9; views on curriculum, 16, 17; duties as president, 17–18, 19; teaching duties of, 22, 23; and student discipline, 27–28
Long, Mack, 155, 156, 195
Long, Mary Louise (Jones), 155
Long, Ross Kennedy, 23, 32
Long, Sallie Meek, 70, 167
Long Memorial Building, Isaac J., 38–39, 40, 44, 45, 46, 53, 55, 80, 84, 119, 126, 129, 170, 186, 209, 212, 252, 271, 353
Lonoke County, Ark., 32, 42
Lost Chord Four, 93, 103
Lotridge, Bob, 191, 192
Louisiana and Arkansas Railway, 81
Louisiana State University, 243
Louisville Presbyterian Theological Seminary, 158, 176, 395n. 6. *See also* Danville Theological Seminary
Love, Brandi, 334
Love, Gordon, 223, 230, 418n. 38
Love Hall, 226, 418n. 38
Lowry, Margaret (Goodwin), 70, 167
Lowry, Thomas M., Jr., 161, 167–72, 177, 207, 270, 354; post-presidential career of, 367
Loyless, Darrell, 339, 340, 347, 348, 349, 358
Luther, William, 173
Lynch, E. C., 55
Lyon, Aaron W., xviii, 9–10, 20, 338
Lyon, Carra, xviii
Lyon, Frank, Jr., 348, 349, 356, 359
Lyon, Frank, Sr., 192, 194, 198, 199, 201, 202, 203, 207, 208, 216, 224, 227, 270, 282, 283, 285, 291, 292, 293, 311, 313, 317, 318, 338, 340–42, 357
Lyon, Jane, 359
Lyon, Marion (Bradley), 224, 282, 292, 309, 318, 341
Lyon Business and Economics Building, 318, 325, 350, 363
Lyon College: adoption of name, 337–42
Lyon Faculty Fellowships, 328
Lyon Fellowship Program, 348

Mabee Foundation, 272, 273, 314, 329, 348, 349, 350
MacDonough, H. T., 188, 195
Mackenzie, Donald M., 217, 219
Madrigal Dinner, 305
Magnolia A & M, 193. *See also* Southern State College
major-minor system: adoption of, 119–20
Makemie College, 2
Malone, Augusta, 44, 58
Malvern, Ark., 38, 106, 108
Manning, Lowell, 108, 110, 116
Marianna, Ark., 39, 70
Marion Hotel, 131, 135
Marsh, Claudia, 358
Marshall, Diane, 306
Martin, Allie Beth (Dent), 418n. 41
Mary Baldwin College, 119, 312, 419n. 52
Maryville College, 2, 180, 182, 198, 202, 414n. 52
Mask and Dagger Club, 106
Masonic Home buildings, 185, 196, 205, 212, 217, 222, 224, 241, 418nn. 38, 41; Long Memorial Building, 227, 228, 272, 418n. 38; destruction of, 259, 272; Education and Psychology Building, 259
Masonic Home campus: purchase of, 196–97, 201; move to, 200, 205, 212–13
Masonic Lodge, 6; orphans home of, 185
Massey, Marie, 425n. 100
Matheny, E. F., 61
Mathis, Cecil, 160
Maxfield, Bess, 103, 117
Maxfield, Charles, 77, 176, 396n. 1
Maxfield, Charles W., 411n. 45
Maxfield, Mary, 5, 77
Maxfield, Theodore, 20–21, 33, 38, 40, 47, 50, 54, 70, 77, 82, 129, 130, 165
Maxfield, Uriah, 176

Maxfield Bank and Trust Company, 54, 64
May, Evelyn, 414n. 71
Mays, John, 286
McAdam, Lorne Kerr, 210, 416n. 8
McCain, Charles, 206
McCain, Eleanor, 207, 254
McCain, James I., 207
McCain, James Ross, 207, 222
McCain, Paul M., 260, 262, 270, 312, 338, 350, 354, 416nn. 2, 3; hiring of, 206–7; background of, 207; presidency of, 207–55; post-presidential career of, 367
McCain, Rev. J. Herndon, 169, 170, 177, 203, 408n. 76, 416n. 2
McCain, W. S., 19
McColgan, Rev. W. L., 199, 222, 290, 301
McCombs, Charles A., 184
McCully, C. T., 127, 132
McDaniel, N. H., 191, 192
McDearmon, William W., 12
McFerran, Paul, 192, 193
McGuire, Catherine, 10
McGuire, Elam, 10
McGuire, William Lewis, 10, 20, 397n. 9
McKee, Charles, 50
McKee, George, 56, 60, 174
McKee, Mollie, 12
McKenzie, Ury, 94, 137, 138, 139–43, 144, 177; post-presidential career of, 366–67
McLain, Raymond, 200
McMath, Sid, 238
McMillan, H. W. "Bill," 198, 199–200, 201, 202, 203, 207, 208, 223, 253, 274, 283, 313, 317
McMillan, John E., 22–23
McMurray College, 94
McNutt, Walter Scott, 148
McRae, Carleton, 96, 318
McRae, Duncan L., 141, 142, 143
McRae, Thomas C., 90, 91, 96, 97, 127, 130, 131, 136, 175, 318, 410n. 6
McRae Hall, 332
Melton, Paula, 420n. 76
Memphis, Tenn., 105, 162, 167, 288, 331
Menard, W. B. "Chubby," 192, 404n. 63
Mentor Program, 288, 289
Mernone, John, 245
Merrick, Ruth, 87
Merrill, Henry, 19
Merrill Scholarship Fund, 48
Meserve, Judith, 420n. 76
Metcalf, Glenn, 105
Methodists, 15, 20, 99, 186, 235, 407n. 52; in Batesville, xviii, 138; in Arkansas, 2, 67, 133, 182, 231. *See also* Soulesbury Institute
Michigan, University of, 316
Mid-America Folklore, 296
Middleton, Lyle, 334
Millar, A. C., 48
Miller, Alva E., 35, 55
Miller, Violet, 283
Miller, William, xviii
Miller Creek, 197, 200, 205, 217, 259, 272, 345
Miller High School, E. O., 237, 238
Millsaps College, 314, 319, 360
Miniken, H. L., 40
Ministerial Association (Club), 99, 159
Mississippi, 7, 10, 33, 51, 238; Synod of, 143; University of, 237
Mississippi College for Women, 71
Missouri, University of, 122
Missouri, Synod of, 158
Mitchum, Jim, 226, 233, 235, 278, 311, 350, 354
Mitchum, Johnny, 295
Moncrief, J. William, 349, 354, 429n. 7
Montana State College, 162
Monticello, Ark., 181, 290
Moody, Dwight, 60
Moon, W. David, 416n. 10
Moore, Henry, 81
Moore, James Wilson, Chair of Biblical Instruction, 81, 144, 290
moral science, 12
Morrill Act, 6
Morrilton, Ark., 106, 110, 115
Morrison, Kent V., 108–10, 112, 113, 114, 116, 408n. 76
Morrison, Rev. James H., 73, 74
Morrow, John P., Jr., 111, 283, 403n. 58, 407nn. 49, 53, 409n. 96
Morrow, John P., Sr., 130, 135, 137, 143, 151, 152, 162–63, 166–67, 169, 170, 174, 176, 177, 193, 199, 202, 203, 208, 222, 224, 230, 338, 411n. 45, 418n. 38
Morrow, R. J., 55
Morrow Hall, 252, 270, 342
Morrow Quadrangle, 226, 227, 273, 335, 418n. 38
Morton, J. Ray, 39, 42
Morton, W. S., 42, 45
Moseley, John, 222, 271
Mosley, Ed, 270, 278, 301, 325, 335
Mosley, Ellis G., 187, 235, 300, 416n. 2, 421n. 86, 429n. 4
Mount, Elijah, 397n. 9, 398n. 34
Mount, Sophia, 93, 103, 116
Mountain View, Ark., 192, 247, 296, 325
Mountain Crest Academy, 183
Mountain Home Baptist College, ix, 46, 85, 108, 113, 114, 401n. 11

Muirhead, William, 358
Munn, W. C., 107
Murphy, Teresa, 358
Murphy, W. D. "Pete," Jr., 222, 283

name change. *See* Lyon College, adoption of name
Nashville, University of, 20
National Association of Intercollegiate Athletics (NAIA), 247, 248, 306, 307, 334, 335
National Collegiate Athletic Association (NCAA), 334–35
National Council for Accreditation of Teacher Education (NCATE), 265, 323
National Defense Education Act, 236
National Education Association, 245, 304
National Endowment for the Humanities, 296, 308
National Little Theatre Tournament, 106
National Science Foundation, 324
National Teaching Fellowships, 251
National Youth Administration (NYA), 149, 159, 163–65, 171, 172, 178, 412n. 59, 425n. 100
Neff, Harry, 192, 247
Nesbitt, Floy, 68, 404n. 74
New Albany Theological Seminary, xv
Newman Club, 235, 245
New Plan, the, 272, 273–79, 287, 288, 289, 304, 312, 319, 320
Newport, Ark., 26, 32, 58, 62, 104, 162, 219, 239, 242, 293, 305, 330
Nichols, Henry L., 348
Nichols, Laura, 294
Nichols, Shuford, 96, 102, 218, 223–24, 261, 267, 268, 270, 280, 282, 283, 285, 294, 318, 324, 328, 338, 408n. 60
Nichols (Administration) Building, 272
Nichols Study-Travel Program, 294, 311, 324–25, 358
Nisbet, John Samuel, 43, 45
Noel-Levitz, 357
nonsectarianism, 8, 14–15, 23
Norment, Sophia, 95
Norment, W. C., 55
Norris, Rev. Joseph I., 70
North Arkansas Community College, 293
North Arkansas Pilot, 22
North Carolina, University of, 21, 314, 409n. 95
North Central Association of Colleges and Secondary Schools, 122, 123, 132, 148, 195, 196, 199, 210, 213, 214, 216, 217, 219, 221, 232, 263, 335, 350, 360, 409n. 107
Northwestern State College (Oklahoma), 267
Northwestern University, 106, 226
Nott, Eliphalet, 9

Oaklawn Cemetery, 155
Oberlin College, 16
O'Brien, Louis, 408n. 76
O'Connor, Frank, 313
Oglesby, Stuart R., 136
Oglethorpe University, xiv, 2, 97
Ohlendorf, Harold, 283
Oklahoma: Synod of, 199, 201, 202, 203; University of, 250
Oklahoma Christian College, 295
Oliver, Charles, 251, 265, 301
Omer, Khursheed, 302
Omicron Delta Epsilon, 333
Orsi, Elizabeth, 235
Oscars and Oscarinas, 95
Ouachita Baptist College (University), 62, 71, 107, 108, 113, 114, 123, 127, 192, 199, 231, 233, 307, 337, 403n. 58, 417n. 17
Ouachita Mountains, the, 176, 180, 183
Ouachita Presbytery, 18–19
Owens, Lillian Elizabeth, 71
Ozark Folk Center, 266, 296
Ozark Folklore Workshop, 266
Ozarks, the, xvii, 6, 15, 22, 75, 158, 159, 167, 180, 181, 183, 198, 203, 234, 266, 296, 298
Ozarks Regional Commission, 267
Ozark Scottish Festival, 298

Padgett, Thomas B., 20
Paisley, Rev. H. L., 138, 151, 165
Pan-Hellenic Council, 189
Panther, 95, 101, 102, 108, 109, 112, 115, 142, 144, 174, 178, 409n. 96
Park College, 50
Parker, Earl R., 71
Parse, Irene, 239–40
Parsons, E. C., 82
Passmore, Corbett, 247
Patterson, Col. William K., 9, 12, 30, 397n. 9
Patterson, Hugh M., 110, 283, 298
Patterson, Rev. S. J., Sr., 145
Patterson, Samuel Jasper "Jap," Jr., 110–11, 113, 114, 115, 408n. 78
Patterson, W. K., Jr., 396n. 1
Patterson Lecture Series, Hugh B., Sr., 296
Patton, Hamilton, 65, 223, 404n. 63
Peace Institute, 78, 80

Peebles-Tucker School, 118
Pennsylvania, University of, 10
Penzel, Charles F., 48, 50
Peterson, Scott W., 301, 324, 328
Phi Alpha Theta, 333
Phi Beta Lambda, 304
Philander Smith College, 271, 420n. 80
Phillips, Harold, 108
Philo Syncopaters, 93, 104, 105
Phylogian Society, 30
Pickens, Sidney, 95, 121
Pickens, Thelma, 95, 250, 251, 300, 421n. 86
Pi Kappa Delta, 94, 95
Pilkinton, Judge James H., 218
Pine Bluff, Ark., 68, 70, 104, 108, 170, 176, 199, 223, 237, 248, 283, 291; Presbytery of, 19; Merchants and Planters Bank and Trust of, 132; Central Presbyterian Church of, 174; Second Presbyterian Church of, 182; First Presbyterian Church of, 290
Piper, 337, 344
Piper Club, 181, 184
Pollard, William G., 228
Ponder, Drew, 238
Ponder, Harry, 114, 118
Powell, Guy, 55
Powhatan, Ark., 8, 20, 21, 130
Prather, Augusta, 408n. 60
Pravada, 245
Preachers' Club. *See* Ministerial Association (Club)
preparatory school: Arkansas College, 292–93; dissolution of, 120, 121
Presbyterial High School, 8, 9, 11, 13
Presbyterian Church in the U.S. (PCUS), 395n. 2; in Arkansas, xiii, xv–xvi, 2–3, 41, 52, 81, 181, 195, 230, 284; and higher education, 7, 14, 79, 133, 172–73, 200, 207, 233, 284, 316, 417n. 22; and academic study of Bible, 15; financial support from, 40, 41, 51, 71, 76, 81, 89, 129, 132, 134–35, 139, 142, 147, 150, 163, 194–95, 197, 224, 251, 413n. 24, 417n. 16; Board of Christian Higher Education of, 212; Synod of Red River in, 284, 285
Presbyterian Church in the U.S.A. (PCUSA), 133, 200, 231, 284, 414n. 52; Synod of the Sun in, 284. *See also* United Presbyterian Church in the U.S.A.
Presbyterian College (South Carolina), 23, 42, 45, 231, 349, 402n. 29
Presbyterian Educational Movement, 89, 97, 123, 127, 128, 130, 131, 134, 137
Presbyterian Foundation of Arkansas, Inc., 229
Presbyterians, 28; and higher education, x, 1–3, 14, 96, 143, 154, 200, 262, 316, 396n. 2; strength of in Arkansas, xiii, 2, 14, 81, 96–97, 133, 139, 181, 195, 230–31, 343; number of on campus, 99, 180, 217, 231, 262, 344, 363
Presbytery of Arkansas (Union), 284
Presbytery of the Ozarks, 284
Prescott, Ark., 127; Bank of, 131, 132
President's Cup, 332–33
Princeton Theological Seminary, xv, 9
Princeton University, 50, 71, 118, 167, 291, 335; Westminster Choir College of, 189
Professional Food-Service Management Company, 240
Pryor, David, 282, 296
Purviance, Farris, 404n. 63

Qualls, R. L., 285
Quigley, L. J., 107

Radford, C. P., 58
Radford, T. E., 55
Railsback, Glen, 223
Rains, Phillip, 266
Ramsey, W. A., 33
recreation building, 227, 246, 310, 418n. 39
Red River, Synod of, 283
Reed, Stanley, 251, 261, 265, 266, 293
Reeder, Lyman, 408n. 60
Rhodes, Ann, 251, 301, 421n. 86
Rhodes, Joel, 404n. 63
Rhodes College, 314, 319, 321, 330, 338, 344, 360. *See also* Southwestern at Memphis; Southwestern Presbyterian University
Rice, Samuel, xiv
Rich, J., 411n. 45
Richardson, R. P., 222
Roanoke College, 342
Roark, Dwain, 307
Robbins, Helen, 358
Roberts, Leo B., 148
Robinson, Charley, 114, 200, 203
Robertson, Ethel, 408n. 60
Robertson, Jerome P., 64, 70–74, 78, 137, 404n. 86; post-presidential career of, 366
Robertson, Lavaughn, 248, 302, 307
Rockefeller, Winthrop, 215, 227
Rockefeller Brothers Fund, 215
Rockefeller Foundation, 296
Rockwood, Stanley Walker, 148, 186, 187, 250, 416n. 6
Rodgers, Frances (Burks), 292, 350
Roettger, Daniel, 356
Roettger, Peggy, 356

Roettger, Walter B., 356–61
Rogers, Bill, 95
Rogers, Edgar, 62
Rogers, Francis "Birdie," 247
Rogers, Larry, 306
Rogers, W. F., 63, 71, 72
Rose, U. M., 44
Rose Law Firm, 257
Rowton, Stephanie, 334
Royal Order of Sanguine Asininity (R.O.S.A.), 103
Rude Mechanicals, 32
Rudolph, Frederick, ix, 6, 14, 30
Rudy, Willis, 14
Rule, Herbert C., III, 283
Rulla, Jim, 358
Rush, Annie, 408n. 58
Rusk, Dean, 271
Russellville, Ark., 35, 106
Rutherford, Bobby, 191–92
Rutherford, Genevieve, 68, 71, 404n. 74
Rutherford, Joseph, 38
Rutherford, William, 408n. 58
Ryland, Rev. Xenophon, 51

Salmon, Stuart, 106
Sanderson, Henry W., 101
Sanderson, Kittie, 87
Satterfield, Mayola, 420n. 76
Scarborough, University College of, 325
Scherer, Cynthia, 5, 399n. 54
Scherubel, Edward H., 104
Schlater, Myron "Butch," 110, 111
Schmidt, Ruth, 346, 349, 354–55, 357, 361, 429n. 7
Schmutz, F. J., 135, 405n. 7
scholarships (merit): granting of, 232, 248, 288, 299; Anderson Scholarships, 248, 347; McCain Scholarships, 270, 299; Brown Scholarships, 288, 294, 299, 347; Alumni Council Scholarships, 336
School of Independent Living, 293
School of the Ozarks, 158, 180, 182, 198
Schwarz, Otto Henry, 303
Scot, 242, 297
Scotch-Irish, xiii, xiv, 1, 181, 207, 235, 298
Scott, Rev. J. Leighton, 198
Scott, Warren, 94
Scottish heritage, 183–84, 297–98, 427n. 46; Scottish Heritage Program, 297–98, 305, 325, 358, 427n. 46
Searcy, Ark., ix, 8, 20, 38, 41, 46, 91, 182
Seibert, Daniel, 421n. 86
Self-Help Division, 181, 182–83, 184, 196, 198, 199, 202, 204
Sensabaugh, Will A., 406n. 14, 408n. 58
Service Day, 333
Shakespearean Society, 189
Shanks, Ella Myrl (Dobson), 95, 106, 179, 189
Shaver, W. W. "Whit," 223
Shearer, Rev. J. B., 15
Shell, Frankie, 191
Shell, Hugh, 155
Shepperson, David, 62, 165, 168, 169
Shick, Hugh, 106
Shive, Ben, 32
Shive, R. W., 399n. 40
Simpson, J. D., III, 329, 348, 349
Sims, Elmer R., 72
Sloan, Frank, 283
Sloan, Horace, 59
Small Business Administration, 272
Smith, Archie, 93
Smith, Bobby, 247
Smith, Charles C., 212, 250
Smith, Mark, 240
Smith Science and Mathematics Building, J. Paul, 227, 424n. 75
Smylie, Nathaniel, 51, 66, 70
Snipes, Rev. J. P., 138
Snipes, Rev. Kenneth, 222, 408n. 60
Sommerville, R. C., 88, 94, 406n. 25
Soulesbury Institute, xviii, 12
South Carolina, xiii, xvi, 7, 20, 36, 42, 45, 46
South Carolina College, 20
Southeast Missouri State Teachers College (University), 111
Southern Baptist College, 215, 417n. 17
Southerland, Lowell, 184
Southern Presbyterian Church. *See* Presbyterian Church in the U.S. (PCUS)
Southern State College, 237. *See also* Magnolia A & M
Southwestern at Memphis, 110, 112, 119, 128, 133, 134, 136, 143, 148, 172, 177, 199, 206, 222, 253, 274. *See also* Rhodes College; Southwestern Presbyterian University
Southwestern Presbyterian University, 7, 15, 36, 41–42, 48, 51, 70, 404n. 86. *See also* Rhodes College; Southwestern at Memphis
Southwest Missouri Teachers College (State University), 110
Spaulding, Russ, 427n. 46
Speed, Maurice, 172
Spencer, Sylvia, 292
Spragins, Fitzhugh, 232, 238, 251, 265, 274, 278, 301, 325, 350
Spragins, Joel, 113

Spragins, John D., Jr., 101, 155, 167, 170, 174–76, 186, 193, 206, 233, 236, 250, 297, 338, 354, 421n. 85; duties as president, 176–84, 185, 187, 188, 191, 195–200; opposition to proposed merger of, 201–2; resignation of, 203–4; post-presidential career of, 367
Spragins, Mary (Fitzhugh), 176, 181
Spragins Hall, 208, 212, 218, 222, 226, 227
Staf-O-Life, 160
Stamps, Ark., 52, 63, 71
Stanford University, 356
Starr, John Robert, 337
State Scholarship Program, 282
Stayton, John, 32
Stayton Medal of Oratory, 32, 55
St. Edward's University, 94
Stein, Coach, 64
Stein, Floyd, 404n. 63
Stephens, Theodore, 196, 197
Stevens, Annie W., 88
Stewart, Anne, 283
Stewart, Vic, 162
Stewart College, 7, 15
Stillman Institute, 88
Stinson, Russell T., 358
Stirling Realty Corporation, 295
St. John's College, 6
St. Louis, Mo., 10, 197, 244, 288, 331
St. Louis, Iron Mountain and Southern Railway, 26
St. Mary's of the Barrens Seminary, 10
Stokes, Earl, 110, 408n. 76
Stone, George, 322, 358
Strategic Plan: of 1990, 319–24, 328–30, 331–32, 336, 339, 342–44, 348, 349, 351, 355, 356, 360–61; of 2000, 361–62
Street, Norwood, 404n. 63
Stricklin, David, 358
Stroud, Jonathan, 331
Stubbs, Thomas Jefferson, 5, 8, 12–14, 22, 23, 26, 32, 36, 45, 61, 100
Student Army Training Corps (SATC), 82–84, 87, 107, 177, 406n. 14
student body: demographic changes in, 226–27, 230, 233–37, 332; desegregation of, 236–37
Student Christian Association, 238, 241
student government: early form of, 72; Student Government Association (SGA), 100, 102–3, 149, 174, 236, 237, 239, 245, 280, 302, 408n. 60
Student Union Building (Edwards Commons), 273
Sullivan, Milton, 307
Sulphur Rock, Ark., 62, 111, 160
Summers, Anne, 289, 301, 305
Summers, L. J., 301, 305
Sunday, Billy, 60
Sunday School attendance, 147; student protests against, 100–101, 189
Sutherland, Paul, 414n. 71
Swarthmore College, 201, 253, 360
Sweets, Henry H., 89, 151
Swift, Duane, 404n. 63
Sydenstricker, Dorothy, 188, 216, 249, 416n. 2
Synod of Arkansas (PCUS), 7, 19, 36, 41, 42, 67–68, 111, 133–34, 180, 183, 231; discussion of moving college by, 37–38, 39, 73, 79; fund raising efforts by, 40, 41, 44, 46, 48, 51, 52, 69, 76, 85, 89, 127, 134–35, 144, 145, 155, 178, 194–95, 197, 216–17, 224, 230, 251–52, 417n. 16; efforts to merge Arkansas College by, 133, 134, 136, 151, 198–202, 284–85; attempts to retire debt of Arkansas College by, 134–35, 136, 138–39, 142, 143, 145, 150–52, 156, 162–63, 193; Educational Commission of, 136, 139, 145, 150, 411n. 52; discussion of closing Arkansas College by, 138, 142, 145, 168, 169, 177; Council for Christian Higher Education of, 218, 219
Syracuse University, 316

Tallman, Richard, 424n. 75
Tarkio College, 110
Tartan Troupers, 243
Taylor, Barbara E., 355–56
Taylor, Charles, 160
Teachers Insurance and Annuity Association College Retirement Equities Fund (TIAA-CREF), 212
Tebbetts, Terrell, 301, 321, 328, 341
Tennessee, xiii, 7, 9, 20, 21, 39, 41, 44, 108; University of, 21
Terry-Casey Drug Store, 98
Teter, Carl, 406n. 14
Texarkana, Ark., 52, 71, 81; National Bank of, 139
Texas, 7, 70, 88, 133, 167; University of, 268
Texas A & M University, 94
Texas Presbyterian College, 406n. 25
Thalian Academy, xiv
Thillen, Misty, 280
Thomas, Helen, 296
Thomas, Paxton, 72
Thomas, Richard, 292, 294, 295
Thompson, Charlotte, 420n. 76
Thompson, Kelly, 408n. 78

Thornwell, James Henley, xiv
Three Mile Act, 36, 40–41, 47, 73, 401n. 11, 402n. 28
Thuneman, Chris, 297
Timmons, R. K., 88
Tinker, Robert, 226, 233
Tornado of 1973, 259–60, 271, 272
Townsend, James H., 39, 42, 43
TranSouth Athletic Conference, 335
Transylvania University, 200
Trimble, John D., Sr., 301
Trimble, Mac, 110
Trinity (College) University, 51, 297
Tucker, E. B., 94, 105, 108, 110, 139, 210, 225, 354; background of, 90–91; role in student life, 96–98, 100, 102; role in curricular development, 104, 117–21; administrative changes of, 122; financial struggles of, 123, 125–37, 194; resignation of, 136–37; post-presidential career of, 366
Tucker, Ginni, 420n. 76
tuition: increases in, 129, 209, 232–33, 236, 314, 345; reductions in, 144, 173, 183
Turner, Emily, 420n. 76
Tusculum College, 2, 21
Twentieth Century Fund, 51, 52
250 Club, 178, 179, 181, 184. *See also* Piper Club

Union College (New York), 9
Union College (Tennessee), 110
Union County, Ark., 80, 175, 176
Union Theological Seminary (Virginia), xv, 52, 80, 88, 268, 395n. 7
Union Trust Company, 145
United Presbyterian Church in the U.S.A., 284
United Service Organizations (USO), 244–45, 305
University of Arkansas Community College-Batesville, 345, 361
University of the South, 329, 330
University Year in Action, 305
Upward Bound, 266
U.S. Naval Academy, 268
U.S. News and World Report: rankings of, 310, 314, 337, 342, 350

Vanderbilt University, 91, 108, 112, 118, 119, 268
Vanemburg, Bitha, 188
Van Lear, Rev. John, 138
VerBeck, C. A., 177
Vietnam War, 153, 225, 233, 234, 237, 238–39, 240, 245, 296
Vining, Bill, 307
Virginia, University of, 13, 71
Virginia Intermont College, 105
Visiting Writers Series, 325

Waddell, Rev. George R., 23
Wade, Victor, 71
Walnut Ridge, Ark., 114, 118, 182
Wann, Fred, 246, 251, 306, 358
War Assets Administration, 185
Ward, Wells, Dreshman & Reinhardt, 216
Warren, Ark., 51, 111, 149, 168, 283, 349
Washburn Presbytery, 19
Washington and Lee University, 223, 280, 317, 318, 329, 344
Watkins, Lyndell, 421n. 86
Weatherman, Donald V., 301, 317, 319, 321, 358
Weathersby, Van, 195, 223
Weber, William H., III, 301
Welch, John, xiv
Welch, Rev. Thomas R., xiv–xvi, 5, 7, 9, 12, 19–20, 21, 22, 24, 39, 51, 282, 354, 399nn. 41, 42, 402n. 35, 406n. 15
Welch Hall, 84, 144, 173, 185, 406n. 15
Welch Memorial Fund, 19–20, 40, 41, 44, 48, 399n. 40
Wesley Foundation, 179, 242
West, Dan C., 259–60, 313, 316, 338, 354; background of, 268; presidency of, 268–312; inauguration of, 271; and the New Plan, 272, 273–79, 287, 288, 289; sabbatical of, 291–92; financial innovations of, 294–96; resignation of, 312; post-presidential career of, 368
West, Sidney, 268, 282, 293, 309, 312, 317
West Endowed String Concert, 305
Westminster College (Missouri), 2, 50, 118, 157, 174, 199, 206, 210, 231, 253, 274, 356
Westminster Fellowship, 179, 182, 231, 242
West Point (U.S. Military Academy), 39, 207, 329
West Tennessee State Teachers College, 112
Whaley, Storm, 261
Wheeler, Debbie, 308
Whichard, Clarence, 236
White, Andrew, 17
White, J. Courtney, 108, 111
White River, the, xvii–xviii, 65, 75, 78, 181, 294, 400n. 65
White River Writers' Workshop, 325
Whitfield, A. L., 51, 68, 70
Whitmarsh, A. H., 71, 81

Wilber, V. A., 61, 62, 63, 64, 71, 72, 113
Wilkerson, Aleene, 425n. 100
Williams, Craig C., 400n. 62
Williams, Doc, 113
Williams, Edwin, 168, 169
Williams, Franklin, 148
Williams, Rev. J. C., 138
Williams, Samuel W., 118, 159, 172, 173, 186, 250–51, 252, 354, 416n. 6, 418n. 38, 421n. 85, 421nn. 86, 88, 429n. 3
Williams, W. H., 145, 152, 162–63, 169, 177, 411n. 52
Williams Baptist College. *See* Southern Baptist College
Williams Gymnasium, 191, 196, 222, 225, 247, 252, 294, 418n. 38
Williamson, Gaston, 257–58, 290
Williamson, James G. "Jim," Jr., 257, 283
Williamson, Octave, 61
Williamson Prize, Lamar, 290, 358
Willis, Dr. Lemuel Edwin, 84, 85
Willis, Rev. R. B., 41, 42, 44
Willis Hall, 84, 144, 145, 147, 173, 185, 186
Wilson, G. E., 219
Wilson, R. Sloan, 283
Wilson, Woodrow, 21, 53
Wilson, Yvonna, 217, 226, 233
Wilson and Rogers Hall, 332
Winningham, R. C. "Dick," 192, 246–48, 249, 302, 307
Winthrop Rockefeller Foundation, 285, 322
Wisconsin, University of, 148
Wisconsin State Teachers College, 94
Wisconsin-Stevens Point, University of, 307
Wittenberg, Delony & Davidson, 216, 221
Wolf, Bess (Millen), 141, 145, 266, 411n. 48
Wolf, John Quincy, Jr., 119, 200, 266, 409n. 99
Wood, J. Garnett, 45, 62
Wood, Mark, 266, 337, 358
Wood, Stanley, 205, 222, 283
Woodruff County, Ark., 8, 13
Woods, J. B., 93
Woodward, C. Vann, ix
World War I: effects of, 82–83, 92–93, 117, 407n. 38
World War II: effects of, 171–72, 177, 178, 179–80
Worthington, Cary, 236
Wright, Dennis, 292, 298
Wycough, M. A. R., 40
Wycough, Marion Adolphus, 10, 20, 21, 40, 397n. 9
Wycough, Ralph, 10
Wycough, William H., 30, 396n. 1
Wygle, Peggy Orine, 262
Wygle, Ralph William, 260, 268, 270, 275, 303, 421n. 5; hiring of, 261; presidency of, 262–67; post-presidential career of, 368
Wynne, Ark., 192, 193, 223
Wyoming, University of, 94

Yale Report of 1828, 24
Yale University, 46
Yancey, A. C., 40
Yeager, Lucy (Jeffery), 340, 420n. 76
Yellville, Ark., 83, 294
Youmans, Madeline, 408n. 60
Young, Mary (McRae), 318, 335
Young, Robert, III, 257, 258, 283, 286, 309, 311, 316, 318, 319, 329, 330, 335, 338, 340, 341, 348, 349
Young House, 335, 348, 350
Young Men's Christian Association (YMCA), 32–33, 35, 44, 47, 58, 60, 62, 63, 92, 99
Young Women's Christian Association (YWCA), 58, 99
youth culture: in 1920s, 91, 93, 95, 99–100, 147; student protests and activism, 100–103; in 1950s, 153; in 1960s, 154, 237–42; in 1970s, 302–3

Zilbergeld, George, 301